LUCKY POET

A Select List of Books by

HUGH MACDIARMID

POETRY

Sangschaw, 1925
Penny Wheep, 1926
A Drunk Man Looks at the Thistle, 1926
To Circumjack Cencrastus, 1930
First Hymn to Lenin and other poems, 1931
Scots Unbound and other poems, 1932
Stony Limits and other poems, 1934

Second Hymn to Lenin and other poems, 1935
A Kist of Whistles, 1947
In Memoriam James Joyce, 1955
Three Hymns to Lenin, 1957
The Battle Continues, 1957
The Kind of Poetry I Want, 1961
Collected Poems, 1962, revised edition, 1967
A Lap of Honour, 1967

PROSE

Annals of the Five Senses, 1923 (also verse)
Contemporary Scottish Studies, 1926
Albyn: or Scotland and the Future, 1927
At the Sign of the Thistle, 1934 (essays)
Scottish Scene, 1934 (with Lewis Grassic Gibbon)
Scottish Eccentrics, 1936
The Islands of Scotland, 1939
Lucky Poet, 1943

Cunninghame Graham: A Centenary Study, 1952
Francis George Scott, 1955
Burns Today and Tomorrow, 1959
David Hume: Scotland's Greatest Son, 1961
The Man of (almost) Independent Mind, 1962
The Ugly Birds Without Wings, 1962
The Company I've Kept, 1966 (autobiographical)
Selected Essays, 1969

EDITED

Northern Numbers, 1920, 1921, 1922
The Golden Treasury of Scottish Poetry, 1940, reissued 1946, etc.
William Soutar, Collected Poems, 1948

Robert Burns, 1949
Selections from the Poems of William Dunbar, 1952
Robert Burns, Love Poems, 1962

HUGH MACDIARMID

LUCKY POET

A Self-Study in
Literature and Political Ideas

———◆••••◆———

BEING THE AUTOBIOGRAPHY

of

HUGH MACDIARMID

(Christopher Murray Grieve)

UNIVERSITY OF CALIFORNIA PRESS

Berkeley and Los Angeles 1972

UNIVERSITY OF CALIFORNIA PRESS
BERKELEY AND LOS ANGELES, CALIFORNIA

ISBN: 0-520-01852-4
Library of Congress Catalog Card Number: 76-138287

FIRST PUBLISHED BY METHUEN & CO. LTD, 1943
REISSUED WITH A NEW AUTHOR'S NOTE, 1972
NEW AUTHOR'S NOTE © 1972 BY HUGH MACDIARMID

THE TEXT OF THIS BOOK HAS BEEN REPRODUCED, WITHOUT
ORIGINAL EDITION

PRINTED IN GREAT BRITAIN

ACKNOWLEDGMENT

I THANK all the friends (or the executors of those of them—a sadly increasing number—who are dead) who have allowed me to quote from letters, or from published writings about me, and also all the writers and publishers who have jointly permitted me to make too many quotations to acknowledge individually here from copyright material. I also thank my friend, Miss Helen B. Cruickshank, to whom I owe the frontispiece photograph.

This has been an extremely difficult book to 'handle', for many reasons, and my best thanks are due to the publishers and to my agents, Messrs. Gilbert Wright (London), Ltd., for their understanding sympathy and endless patience and help, and to my honorary private secretary, Mr. Henry Grant Taylor, M.A., for his most competent, careful, and painstaking labours.

C. M. GRIEVE

Whalsay
Shetland Islands

'Out of the fullness of the heart the mouth speaketh, as the Bishop of Bath and Wells said when listening to a speech of Mr. Balfour's, on the occasion of the introduction of the Compulsory Notification of Diseases of Poultry Bill.'—E. C. BENTLEY.—*Trent's Last Case.*

'As for writing poems and selling them at the door for twopence (or "what you care to give, lydy"), I simply haven't got the brains.'—AGATHA CHRISTIE.

'A nation which does not feed its best writers is a mere barbarian dung heap.'—EZRA POUND.

'The rule is that a tame goose never becomes a wild goose, but a wild goose on the other hand may well become a tame goose—therefore be on the watch!'
S. KIERKEGAARD.

'The situation here at home is becoming more and more confused. The question now is—in so far as it is true (as I am confident enough to sustain) that the literary and social and political situation requires an exceptional individual—the question is whether there is anyone in this realm who is fitted for this task except me.'
S. KIERKEGAARD.

'Such books are mirrors: when an ape peers into them, no apostle can be looking out.'—LICHTENBURG.

'Ups and downs there may be, and beneath them all there must be something inexorable, a moving onward. Without the inexorable something in him, a man is incapable of having a career.'—ROBERT HICHENS.

CONTENTS

The portrait of the author, reproduced as frontispiece, is from a photo by Helen Cruickshank

I DEDICATE THIS BOOK

TO

MY WIFE

VALDA TREVLYN GRIEVE

" Bugeilio's Gwenith Gwyn "
(Watching the Ripening Wheat)

First published in 1943

BOOK
PRODUCTION
WAR ECONOMY
STANDARD

THIS BOOK IS PRODUCED IN
COMPLETE CONFORMITY WITH THE
AUTHORISED ECONOMY STANDARDS

PRINTED IN GREAT BRITAIN

AUTHOR'S NOTE 1972

This book was published in 1943. Owing to wartime restrictions and shortage of paper, the publishers and I agreed that it should comprise only about a quarter of the typescript I submitted to them, and that the other three-quarters should subsequently be published in separate volumes. That has not happened, the material in question having been used instead in various other volumes of mine (*The Company I've Kept*, 1966; *Selected Essays of Hugh MacDiarmid*, 1969; etc.) and in contributions to various periodicals not yet collected in any of my books.

In the thirty years that have elapsed since I wrote this book in the little island of Whalsay in the north-east of the Shetland archipelago, a great deal has happened. I have for one thing published many other books in that period. My latest bibliographer says I have now published 135 books and pamphlets, including contributions to multiple-author books, but not including my contributions to scores of anthologies.

If I were asked are there important issues about which I have changed my opinion since 1943, I would have to reply, I spoke then as I speak now, but I do not speak now as I spoke then. I am accustomed to being accused of all sorts of contradictions, to which I have often merely answered, like Walt Whitman, 'I contradict myself. Very well! I contradict myself.' But I am interested to note that many of those who have written about me and my work now tend to agree that under the apparent inconsistencies and contradictions there is a basic unity, and they refer their readers to my first book, *Annals of the Five Senses* (1930), in which I express the main ideas of all my subsequent work. I have demonstrably pursued these undeviatingly through my whole career—not only in my writings (including, in addition to my books, the enormous mass of my journalistic outpourings), but in my speeches and broadcasts in Great Britain and in a score of other countries.

In an essay on my poem 'A Drunk Man Looks at The Thistle' (1926), Professor David Daiches says this gallimaufry broke 'on a startled and incredulous Scotland with all the shock of a childbirth in church'. I do not think Professor Daiches could have foreseen (and I certainly did not) that decades later many leading poets and critics in a dozen different countries would have come round to the conclusion that he was right when he called it 'the greatest long poem . . . in Scottish literature and one of the greatest in any literature'.

However that may be, if his obstetrical figure of the effect in Scotland of the publication of 'A Drunk Man' is correct, then my

next most important book, *Lucky Poet*, was still-born. It was hardly
reviewed anywhere, and, where it was, it was for the most part dismissed as a 'rag-bag'. H. V. Routh was a solitary voice when, in his
English Literature and Ideas in the Twentieth Century (1946), he said
it was 'the book by which MacDiarmid will be remembered'. Dr
Alex Comfort, the poet, was another who praised it highly. But apart
from these two, it was not till 1964 that Mr Duncan Glen could assert,
'it is certainly a book of ideas, and one of the few important autobiographies of the twentieth century.'

Despite this general neglect, *Lucky Poet* has continued to lead an
underground life throughout these three decades. All sorts of people
have come across it (heaven knows how!) and written to me most
enthusiastically about it. The number clamouring for its republica-
tion has increased notably in the last few years, in keeping with the
increased recognition now given to my work as a whole all over the
world.

The principal theme of *Lucky Poet*, and of all my other books, has
been my unqualified opposition to the English ethos. I do not claim
to have originated the growing belief that English literature is petering
out—but I certainly anticipated that it would. I agreed fully with my
friend the French poet and philosopher, the late Professor Denis
Saurat, when he wrote that unless the Second World War was to have
been fought in vain there must be a profound change in English
mentality (and he did not mean that availability of Yankee trash-
culture which has since developed apace). Saurat used his terms with
scrupulous care. (He also pointed out that he was not referring to
Scottish mentality but strictly to English mentality.)

Everything that has happened since—and is happening now—has
shown how right he was. He perfectly understood why I agreed with
Henry Miller's statement in *The Cosmological Eye*, namely, 'as for
English literature, it leaves me cold, as do the English themselves; it
is a sort of fish-world which is completely alien to me. I am thankful
to have made a humble acquaintance with French literature, which
on the whole is feeble and limited, but which, in comparison with
Anglo-Saxon literature today is an unlimited world of the imagination.' And he would have endorsed Cecil Gray's statement, which I
have said should be hung up in large print in the vestibule of every
library in Scotland, namely, 'Even today the whole hierarchy of the
English novelists from Fielding and Smollett, through Dickens and
Thackeray up to Hardy and Meredith means precisely nothing to me.
I simply cannot read them. I have tried hard. I have tried several
books of each. I have given them all a fair trial, but it is no use.'

Elsewhere I have quoted a dozen distinguished writers in various countries who are equally agreed now with what Cecil Gray said away back in 1936 in *Musical Occasions*: 'Present circumstances and conditions are uniformly propitious to creative activity in this country [Great Britain], save one which unfortunately also happens to be a very important one; namely, the attitude of mind and code of aesthetic values which largely dominate English life today, and are mainly responsible for all its worst features, and for our complete inability to induce other nations to take us seriously in literature and the arts— *the cult of the English gentleman*! It permeates every aspect of our national life. It may well be that our military triumphs have all been won on the playing fields of Eton; but it is very certain that most of our artistic failures have been sustained there. This spirit stunts or oppresses or forces into a pusillanimous compromise every potential native talent, and is the absolute antithesis of everything we call art, and *must be fought as one fights the devil, without rest and without quarter.*'

My attitude to the English ethos goes back to Hume, who wrote: 'I am only sorry to see that the great decline, if we ought not rather to say, the total extinction of literature in England, prognosticates a very short duration of all our other improvements, and threatens a new and sudden inroad of ignorance, superstition and barbarism.' 'I think', he wrote in another letter (which might be dated yesterday or today), 'you grow every day madder in England; there is a prospect that this worthless generation will soon bring themselves to ruin by their own folly.'

Since my own life-endeavour has been subsumed generally under the name of 'The Scottish Renaissance', it is of particular interest to turn to page 229 of Professor Mossner's huge biography of Hume, and read how 'Hume's efforts as literary patron to bring about a renaissance of Scottish letters were to form no inconsiderable part of his activities.'

What I have said again and again and again about the current stranglehold of mediocrity in Scotland, too—about the moronic character of most of our people—Hume anticipated (as did Burns despite his 'A Man's a Man for a' That') when he wrote: 'Think on the emptiness, the rashness, and futility of the common judgments of men; how little they are regulated by reason in any subject, much more in philosophical subjects, which so far exceed the comprehension of the vulgar. "Non si quid improba Roma, elevet, accedas examenque improbum in illa, perpendas frutina, nec te quaesiveris extra." A wise man's kingdom is his own breast; or, if he ever looks farther, it will only be to the judgment of a select few, who are free from prejudices, and capable of examining his work. Nothing indeed can be a

stronger presumption of falsehood than the approbation of the multitude; and Phocion, you know, always suspected himself of some
blunder, when he was attended with the applauses of the populace.'

Hume was at the beginning of what can now be seen to be 'the
general show-up of man's thought through the ages': 'the astonishing
and perturbing fact that almost all that has passed for social sciences,
political economy, politics, ethics, in the past may be brushed aside
as mainly rationalising. When we are offered a penny for our thoughts
we always find that we have recently had so many things in mind that
we easily make a selection which will not compromise us too nakedly.
On inspection we shall find that even if we are not downright ashamed
of a great part of our spontaneous thinking it is far too intimate,
personal, ignoble, or trivial to permit us to reveal more than a small
part of it. We find it hard to believe that other people's thoughts are as
silly as ours, but they probably are' (James Harvey Robinson, *Mind
in the Making*).

My principal concern has always been poetry, of course, and it is not
in Hume but in another great Scotsman, Lord Byron, that I find a
statement of the position that goes right to the root of the matter.
Byron continued throughout his life to have a dual concept of poetry.
On the one hand there were the romantic lyrics like 'Lackin Y Gair'
and 'So we'll go no more a roving'. On the other was the poetry of
serious moral purpose (as he conceived Pope's to be). This was a
poetry that would castigate the errors of the age with stringent wit,
would point out deviations from good sense and good taste in brilliant
balanced couplets, and would attack the corruptions and injustices in
society with Juvenalian fierceness, modified by Popean good temper.
In the middle of his career, after he had finished the fourth canto of
Childe Harold (which he thought his best), he wrote to Murray: 'With
regard to poetry in general, I am convinced, the more I think of it,
that *all* of us—Scott, Southey, Wordsworth, Moore, Campbell and I
—are all in the wrong, one as much as another; that we are upon a
wrong revolutionary poetical system, or systems, not worth a damn in
itself, and from which none but Rogers and Crabbe are free; and that
the present and next generations will finally be of this opinion. I am
the more confirmed in this by having lately gone over some of our
classics, particularly Pope, whom I tried in this way—I took Moore's
poems and my own and some others, and went over them side by side
with Pope's, and I was really astonished (I ought not to have been so)
and mortified at the ineffable distance in point of sense, harmony,
effect, and even imagination, passion, and *invention* between the little
Queen Anne's man and us of the Lower Empire. Depend upon it, it

is all Horace then and Claudian now among us; and if I had to begin
again, I would model myself accordingly' (*Letters and Journals*, IV,
169).

Claims are often made for what fiction, as opposed to poetry, can do
about our real lives, but Joseph Chiari is undoubtedly right when he
says (in another connection): 'If the speech of so-called characters
consists almost entirely of clichés and banalities tele-recorded from a
very small section of life, these characters will be no more than
mechanical parrots with very little human worth. Flaubert's obsession
with 'la bêtise bourgeoise et les idées reçues' had, one would have
thought, already explored the limits of the artistic value of this kind
of boredom.'

So the significance of this book in relation to my development as
a writer ever since is that it set me on the course of wide-ranging
references, and multiple allusions to out-of-the-way not only literary
but also scientific sources I defined when I said: 'It will be true of
any poetry I write in the future that in it, to quote Robert Musil's
Der Mann ohne Eigenschaften, one is likely "to meet Kenzinists and
Canisians, a Bo philologist doing partigen research, or a tokontologist
against a quantum physicist".'

The sort of thing I am increasingly interested in is, for example,
that it is wrong for a detective-story writer featuring a photographer
and his chemicals to make the chemical *potassium cyanide* an important
part of the plot, since this chemical is not in use in a photographer's
dark-room (though some process engravers still use it), and the
chemical which would be found with similar properties is *potassium
ferricyanide*, which could be difficult to administer since in its raw
state it consists of largish red crystals and when dissolved the liquid
is a greenish-yellow colour. Or, again, a speaker on botanical subjects
should not have said that the Chinese *Primula sinensis* causes a skin
rash. The primrose *obconica* is the one that causes the rash in some
people, though it is true that a few people may be sensitive enough to
be affected by almost any primrose including *P. sinensis*. This book
is full of such facts.

Yes. A great deal has happened since this book first appeared. A
dozen books about me and my work have been published, and scores
of theses and doctoral dissertations accepted by many European,
American, and Canadian Universities. There is a consensus of opinion
that I have achieved a miracle—inventing a new language out of the
dialects into which Scots has disintegrated; and, along with that,
reviving large elements of vocabulary obsolete since the sixteenth
century, and writing indisputably great poetry in this unlikely, if not
impossible, medium. It is claimed that I have written the only high

poetry attempted or achieved in Scots for over three hundred years, and won a place for myself as one of Scotland's three greatest poets along with Burns and Dunbar—and probably as the greatest of the three. It is claimed, too, that my work has had, and is increasingly having, political consequences—that I am largely responsible for the great escalation of the Scottish Nationalist movement of which I was one of the founders in 1928. Maybe! But I do not belong to the Scottish National Party. I am a Communist, a Scottish separatist, and republican—and I do not believe I have any idea in common with ninety-nine per cent of these so-called Scottish Nationalists, who seem to me simply sitting on their butts and giving an imitation of a respectable democratic bowel movement.

Lucky Poet saw me embarked on a course which I have pursued assiduously ever since, in the teeth of all the opposition of those who hate versatility, since it takes most men all their time to master one line of work or thought, and who in particular hate omnivorous readers (and especially readers of foreign literature not available to Tom, Dick, and Harry), since their own reading, when they have any, is so severely restricted as to be virtually non-existent for purposes of literary discussion. Two phrases from my long poem 'In Memoriam James Joyce' (1955) adequately describe my practice in this matter. They are: 'Jujitsu for the Educated' and 'Jerqueing every idioticon'.

HUGH MACDIARMID

Biggar, Lanarkshire
September 1971

AUTHOR'S NOTE: ON BEING A HIPPOPOTAMUS

'The main thing to remember in autobiography, I have always thought, is not to let any damned modesty creep in to spoil the story.'

MARGERY ALLINGHAM.

LORD DAVID CECIL in a recent essay in the *Times Literary Supplement* prophesied that the ' semi-imaginative autobiography ' is one of the coming literary forms which will play a great role in literature after this War. There are many indications that he is likely to prove right with regard to this. In launching this early example of the kind (I think in some ways this *is* the sort of thing Lord David has in mind), circumstances compel me to make some initial explanations.

At the instance of publishers both in this country and in America, my literary agents have been pressing me for several years to write my autobiography. Finally I consented, and was getting on with the job like a house on fire, when the World War was renewed in 1939. Finally my manuscript amounted to over half-a-million words. By that time paper shortage, emergency regulations, censorship, and other war-time conditions had rendered the publication of a work of such magnitude out of the question—if, indeed, it would have been a practicable proposition even in time of peace. As a way out, it was then agreed that I should evolve from that mass of writing three separate volumes of 150,000 words each. It was no easy task, this process of cutting up into separate books of a great mass of writing, the fruit of a lifetime of correlated thought, feeling, study, and action, written and re-written many times, not easily but from the depths, the record of a man whose mind has always been on the track of something which required an awareness that was integral and continuous, and, no matter how small the detail of life he was observing, always strove to relate it to something more inclusive, to make it part of a whole—the work of a poet who believes that the poet ' must be able to understand and communicate the complexities of the world that grows daily more complicated '. This remains the peculiar duty of the poet rather than of the statesman or philosopher, because ' poetry is the only branch of knowledge that can form a synthesis of our experiences so overwhelming, so obscure and para-lysing '. The effecting of such a synthesis will enable man to under-stand the soul (saving the word!) of man. My prose is hardly easier to break up than my poetry, of which it may be said that the sort of poems I have sought resemble the look at each other of the two lovers in a recent American novel, whose glances ' steadied, focussed, and then interlocked like parts of a gemel-ring '. And

A 2

what I have principally relied upon to secure my effect is a fury of
incontrovertible detail. A great deal of this effect is lost in such a
breaking-up as I am now discussing. Again, my interests are world-
wide and cover the entire field of all the arts and the sciences; and
the aim upon which I have always set my heart has been to achieve a
(to quote my friend Sorabji) ' combination in a quite unique degree of
a grand breadth and splendour of style with a Faberge-like jeweller's
precision and delicacy '. If then in this book there are many lacunæ
and loose ends of all kinds, it must be remembered that in prose, as
in poetry, my obvious, difficult job is to sum up my parts; and at this
I am but infrequently successful. The integers survive repeated
examination. The ' causes ' which engage me I feel to be one
cause, but, dialectician though I am and not prepared to concede
that I could not (granted space enough) synopsize them all right, I
must be content, when my work is broken up in this way, simply to
say that I believe that the *summa* of the future will properly adjust
their parts and demonstrate their compatibility. In the meantime
my only prayer is :

> Sharing Ovid's preoccupation with the thought
> That all things must be changed, let spiritual initiative not pass
> From us, and our qualities acquire fixity
> And like Hamlet's fall into Abraxas.

The first of these three volumes excavated from the whole was to
contain the parts dealing with myself as poet, my views on poetry,
my account of my poetic processes, and so on. This is that first
volume. The second volume is to be called *A Poet and His Friends*,
and to it have been relegated my reminiscences and assessments of
some of my better-known friends, a chapter each being given to A.E.
(George Russell), W. B. Yeats, A. R. Orage, Major C. H. Douglas,
Thomas Sturge Moore, R. B. Cunninghame-Graham, Compton
Mackenzie, John Buchan (Lord Tweedsmuir), William Archer, Sir
Ronald Ross (with whom I discussed the question of Science and
Poetry and years ago came to the conclusion which, as some of the
chapters of this book show, is now increasingly informing my work,
that, as Sir Charles Sherrington says in *Man on his Nature*, Man is
in conflict with nature, with men, and with himself, and that, while
the last two have been the subject of immortal verse, even as the others
the first is not unworthy of the epic and the lyric; only now
beginning fully to inform my work, I say, because although my
discussions with Ross took place nearly fifteen years ago, it is true
that just as the pursuit of science leaves little leisure for the writing of
verse, so it is no easy matter for a poet, busy not only with poetry but
with politics and many other things, to acquire a sufficient mastery of
science for such a purpose), the historian and biographer, Mother
Forbes of the Roman Catholic Training College at Craiglockhart, of

whom her biographer says truly that ' at the time of her death in 1936 she could have been called, without exaggeration, the best-loved woman in Scotland ', a worthy pupil, indeed, of that great personality, Mother Janet Erskine Stuart[1] of the Society of the Sacred Heart, Roehampton (whose favourite spiritual classic was *The Hunting of the Snark*), and that great character, Polar explorer, artist, and bagpipe-player, W. G. Burn-Murdoch, who, lecturing on pipe music, used to illustrate on the blackboard the kind of man who likes the pipes and the kind that likes brass bands, and all sorts of other delightful things.

Since I wrote the above paragraph, the increasing paper shortage has necessitated further ' cuts ', and I have been obliged to hold over also for the second volume of this trilogy a very long chapter I had to the last moment expected to include in the present book, dealing with four especial friends who have not only meant far more to me than the more celebrated men I have just named, but are, *à mon avis*, not only in relation to myself, but absolutely, far more important—namely, Francis George Scott, and Kaikhosru Sorabji, the composers ; Professor Denis Saurat, poet, philosopher, and critic ; and Dr. Oliver St. John Gogarty, the great Irish wit and lyric poet. An Indian, a Frenchman, an Irishman, and a fellow-Scot : all high intellectuals, wits, and great artists—a quartette, in short, who cover the whole field of my major interests (music, science, poetry, philosophy, and great fun !) artistically and intellectually, psycho-logically, geographically, and racially—East and West ; Scotland and the Gaelic Motherland, Eire ; Scotland and France, ' the Auld Alliance ' ; and Scotland and the Oriental cradle of our race. I question if any other four men in Europe to-day are equally rich in intellectual and artistic gifts, and, at the same time, such great and extremely diverse, yet not incompatible but mutually friendly, ' personalities '. To know them has indeed been like lighting upon a four-leafed clover.

The third volume will be entitled *Lament for the Children*, and will deal with my domestic life, marriage, divorce, remarriage, and my children by both mothers. The chapters in the original manuscript dealing with Scottish politics, and in particular the Scottish Republican and extreme Nationalist causes in which I have been so active during the past twenty years, have been held over to take their place in a book entitled *Scottish Politics, 1707–1940*, upon which I am now working. In like fashion the chapters dealing with the Scottish Vernacular Revival, the Future of Gaelic, and the Scottish Literary Movement of the last twenty years, with chapters on my friends Neil Gunn, William Soutar, William Power, ' Lewis Grassic Gibbon '

[1] For these two ladies, see *The Life and Letters of Janet Erskine Stuart* by Maud Monahan, and *Mother Forbes of Craiglockhart*, by Margaret T. Monro.

(James Leslie Mitchell), the Hon. Ruaraidh Erskine of Marr, and others will be published elsewhere in due course.

This explains why many matters which have bulked largely in my life, and with which my name is immediately connected in the minds of almost everybody who has heard of me at all, are not dealt with in the present book.

If, instead of spreading myself over half-a-million words (I do not apologize for that—I have never had any cause to regard myself as one of the minor spirits who cannot do anything *en gros*, and have always been blessedly exempt from that atrocious condition D. H. Lawrence described when he exclaimed in one of his letters to Edward Marsh : ' God help us, when a poet must hunt his muse like Tartarin de Tarascon the one remaining hare—his one eating, gnawing anxiety to write—as if he could sing when he's been straining his heart to make a sound of music for months ! It isn't as if he were a passionate writer, writing his *agon*. Oh, my God, he's like teaching a bull-finch to talk ! ' but sharing instead the feeling **Goethe** expresses :

> Was hilftes, viel von Stimmung reden ?
> Dem Zaudernden erscheint sie nie.
> Gebt ihr euch einmal für Poeten,
> So kommandiert die Poesie ! [1])

—if, I say, instead of all that is enclosed between these brackets, I had been constrained to compress the essence of my life-story into a single brief paragraph, I could not have done better, perhaps, than just adopt (from what source I do not remember—and have now no means of finding out) the following supposed Film Commentator's broadcast on the affair of Bruce and the Spider :—

' This is not a picture of night-starvation, but a dejected monarch, Robbie Bruce of Bonnie Scotland, in his famous cave. Hello ! Has Disney had a hand in this film ? No, this is just a brother of the insect that scared Miss Muffet. Up he goes ! A-a-ah ! What a fall was there, my countrymen ! But this Scottish spider, with true British pluck, tries again. That twig at the top of the tree is his goal. Will he make it ? Ho, Ho ! End of second round ! One, two, three, four !—No, Sir, not counted out this time ! Up again ! No short time in the weaving trade here ! Ah ! The third bid does it ! He makes it ! He makes it ! When did anything Scottish, even a spider, fail to make good ? And see, heartened once more, the great king rises from his rocky bed and the depression on his face clears up. A-and-no-ow, Buddy Bruce, it's up tew yew ! '

Politics, and even my concern with the Scots Vernacular and

---

[1] ' What is the use of talking so much about being in the mood ? The mood never comes to those who hesitate. If you pretend to be poets, command your poetry !

Gaelic languages, and my anglophobia having been virtually excluded from this book altogether, I must, so that no mistake may be made, just insist here that, if this is the autobiography of a Scottish poet, it is the autobiography of a Scottish poet who stands at the farthest possible remove from the feeling recently expressed by the *Evening Telegraph*, consoling air-raid victims of Dundee, Angus, and Fife : ' Every Scottish heart should beat high and proud to-day to know that the old country is taking its place in the front of the battle-line. Every bomb dropped on Scotland is one less for London.'

This attitude is, of course, no new one. Wolfe of Quebec, in one of his letters, expressed identical sentiments. It has underlain the British attitude to Scotland throughout. George Bernard Shaw in his preface to *On the Rocks* says : 'After Culloden, the defeated Highland chiefs and their clansmen were butchered like sheep in the field. Had they been merely prisoners this would have been murder. But as they were also Incompatibles with British Civilization—it was only liquidation!' I have no use for the British civilization in question. Happily, events in Scotland are at long last showing that there remains in our people a hard core of this incompatibility, not only unliquidated, but more intense than ever, and expanding and aggressive once more ; and it is on that fact that I base whatever hopes I entertain for the future of Scotland. Of those elements which are compatible with British civilization I have no hope whatever.

The bulk of the Scottish population (I refuse to call them Scots) to-day, however, are in precisely the same position as Mr. Alexander Maclehose, who, in his *The Scotland of Our Sons* (1938), arraigned England's studied neglect of Scotland's economic welfare—the dwindling population of the glens, the vicious concentration of over 50 per cent. of the inhabitants of Scotland in a handful of large towns, an infant mortality rate half as high again as that of England, a proportion of houses unfit for human habitation six times as great as that south of the Border, and so on—yet, after marshalling all these damning facts, after thanking the Scottish Nationalists too for having ' stirred up Scotland ', was not prepared to advocate the establishment of even limited Home Rule for Scotland, on the grounds that (1) good government *might* come from Whitehall yet, and (2) a Parliament in Edinburgh would very likely have a majority of Socialists (where else could the impulse towards reconstruction spring in Scotland save from Socialists ? (from the Clydeside capitalists, or the ' shootin' and fishin' gentry ?), and, finally, had nothing practical to propose at all except an ambition to see ' more craftsmen from Sutherland to Galloway engaged in the manufacture of small wooden replicas of Dunstaffnage and Dunolly Castles '.

No one has ever had any capacity for saying anything worth a docken about Scotland who has not felt about almost all that has been,

and is being, said of it, and about all the glib sayers, as Burns felt
when, on one occasion, a self-elected guide was pointing out the
capabilities of a scene for poetical treatment. Burns listened, and
looked on stolidly. A lady of the party ventured to ask him if he had
nothing to say about the scene. ' How can I, madam,' he exploded,
' while that ass is braying over it ? '

Goethe asked Heine on one occasion what he was thinking of
writing next. ' Oh,' replied Heine, with sublime impudence, ' I
thought of trying my hand at a Faust.' In the same way I have
always felt that if it were possible for me to encounter Sir Walter
Scott in the flesh and he were to ask me what I thought of writing, I
should reply, ' I think it's high time something was being written
about Scotland, for a change.'

In short, this book is the story of a hippopotamus. The hippopotamus is a big beast, and that explains why I should have difficulty
in getting it all on to a certain size of canvas, and even then cannot
present it ' in the round ', but only from one angle at a time, and far
from life-size.

' One might as easily shake a hippopotamus,' Margaret Irwin in
The Bride reports Clarendon reflecting with regard to the gross,
fanatical, cynical Lauderdale—in many respects one of the type of
Scot I most admire and seek to emulate, ' for the Earl of Lauderdale
had a reputation to keep up both as a wag and a scholar ; in compensation for his uncouth looks and messy habits, he felt that he resembled
his late Sovereign, King James VI of Scotland and I of England, who
had also been uncouth and messy . . . but was a glutton for learning
as well as dainties, could wield a pretty pen on any and every subject
from tobacco-smoking to witchcraft, and theology and classic fable,
and talked as much and with as shrewd and pawky a wit as Lauderdale
fancied in himself. He believed himself, not quite truly, to be as
much at his ease in a foreign Court as in the warm ale-breathing reek
of the " Black Bull " in his little town of Lauder, not far from
Edinburgh, where he liked to drop in from the seclusion of his
castle, cloistered in deep woods, for the casual company of the farmers
and travelling merchants who sat spellbound by the learned allusions,
the gusto and coarseness of the great lord's conversation.'

' They look upon me ', wrote Burns, half-amused, half-annoyed,
about his Nithsdale neighbours, ' as if I were a hippopotamus come
to Nithsdale.' I am similarly regarded by my Shetland neighbours
to-day ; but a poet is not only as incomprehensible a phenomenon to
most people as always in the past, but a more unwelcome one to-day
than ever, I think, and a target for the unconscionable brutalities of
organized mediocrity as never before. My own experiences in the
Shetlands since the present War started have certainly been far worse
than D. H. Lawrence's in Cornwall in the First Imperialist War.

There is more excuse for the indignation and incomprehension of the public in my case, perhaps, than in most. I have consistently ' asked for trouble ', and not merely in one, but in every connexion. Because of a profound interest in the actual structure of language, like Mallarmé's, like Mallarmé I have always believed in the possibility of '·une poésie qui fut comme deduite de l'ensemble des propriétés et des caractères du langage '—the act of poetry being the reverse of what it is usually thought to be ; not an idea gradually shaping itself in words, but deriving entirely from words—and it was in fact (as only my friend F. G. Scott divined) in this way that I wrote all the best of my Scots poems—a method in itself, of course, quite apart from my politics, enough to incur that ' fascinated bewilderment and sublime idiocies in the gutterpress ' which have been my continuous lot all these years at the hands of the Anglo-Scottish dailies in Aberdeen, Glasgow, and Edinburgh—' such vilification and such magisterial low comedy ' as no other Scottish writer has ever had to contend with.

How a poet who gives no such causes of offence as I do is apt to be regarded in Scotland to-day may be illustrated by what a lady correspondent in a recent letter says of my friend, William Soutar, who, as Mr. Herbert Palmer recently insisted, is a ' very good poet indeed ', and one who has not received anything like his due, as well as being one of the finest natures in the whole of Scotland to-day. Mr. Soutar lives in Perth, and has been a bed-fast invalid for many years, though he is considerably younger than myself. ' One thing more than another that has struck me since I came to reside in Perth ', writes my lady friend, ' is the average native's complete unawareness of William Soutar as a writer or a poet. They speak of him as a sort of " tragedy " because he cannot get about as *they* do ! When I question them about his work, they are completely ignorant of it ! Even the few to whom I have spoken who *do* know only know that he writes but they are not familiar with anything he has written. It fell to me one day to gift to his old schoolmaster—the man who taught Willie—Willie's latest book, and so introduce him to William Soutar, Poet, as apart from William Soutar, former pupil ! ' That's it, exactly ! No wonder I felt constrained to write in October, 1939 :—

TO NEARLY EVERYBODY IN EUROPE TO-DAY.

A war to save civilization ; you say ?
Then what have *you* to do with it, pray ?
Some attempt to acquire it would show truer love
Than fighting for something you know nothing of.

Since I have made scarcely any other reference to it, I may say here that my attitude to the War now proceeding is, in the first place, that indicated by the following quotation : ' Perhaps there wasn't anything to save. Perhaps men who have given up the right to think aren't really alive. They aren't really men. So it doesn't matter what happens to them,' and, in the second place, that indicated by the following ' Verses Written During the Second World War ' :—

> At last ! Now is the time with due intensity
> 　　To hew to what really matters—not
> ' Making the world safe for democracy ',
> 　　' Saving civilization ', or any such rot.
>
> But what there was about the Welsh handling, say,
> 　　Of Arthur and Merlin (as good an example as may be got)
> That conquered the imagination of Europe in a way
> 　　Conchobar and Cuchulainn did not.
>
> Let it at least be said of us when we die :
> 　　' Of all the slogans to which mass-man clings
> Only a Chinese could have thought more lightly than they
> 　　—They had so much love for real things.'

A soldier friend writes to me from a big training camp in England, of all the men with whom he is in contact there : ' Literary taste—interest even—is *completely* absent, and there isn't much attention paid to music on the wireless, beyond sentimental popular airs and a few operatic songs—apart from a unanimous move to switch off the set ! Painting and sculpture, architecture and design are quite outside the scope of the men I've met, but political thinking—or rather vague revolutionary feeling—abounds. There are immense resources of power waiting to be tapped.'

I think this is true of the vast majority of people in all so-called civilized countries.

Finally, with regard to the War, my view is perfectly expressed by an anonymous writer who says : ' This frightful idea that force decides is really no more wrong, though more nakedly evil, than the notion that " profit decides " which it is supplanting. We ought not, then, to enter the new epoch of militarism with less courage and faith than we took with us into the epoch now passing away in thunder—nor with a less consecrated determination to oppose its ruling fallacy. . . . Dictatorship and democracy, militarism and financialism, federation and imperialism—these are outworn and now really irrelevant categories of thought, if our thinking is to have any savour of salvation. Instead, we must begin to think of the Earth itself and its demand upon us ; of the real credit earned and unearned of human society, and of the needs and the inspiration of individual men.'

A forgotten poet of ancient Egypt wrote :—

> I have seen violence, I have seen violence—
> 　　Give thy heart after letters,

and all my diverse interests and activities can certainly be subsumed in the demand that a system which produces and enthrones the nonentity be wiped out.

If people will persist in regarding me as a hippopotamus, they must remember that ' I am a dangerous animal—I fight when I am attacked ' !—and I have a certain amount of zoological knowledge myself, and can retaliate in kind.

The majority of literary critics, especially London literary critics, recall to me that extraordinary chirruping conversation which sounds almost human but, on investigation with an electric torch, is found to be merely a couple of hedgehogs courting beneath one's window; but a few of the more impudent commentators—I would like to give their names here, but I suppose I mustn't—at their very best remind me instead of Mr. W. S. Berridge's authentic accounts of weasels killing hawks which had carried them into the air.

To mix my metaphors from the animal world, my function in Scotland during the past twenty to thirty years has been that of the cat-fish that vitalizes the other torpid denizens of the aquarium. And what a job ! Since the Union with England, Scotland's has been simply the role of caterpillar-grub stung into immobility by devouring wasp; a paralysis that will certainly last the lives of 99 per cent. of all Scots now over forty years of age, and was complete and lifelong in the lives of nearly 100 per cent. of their fathers, grandfathers, and great-grandfathers.

Nearly all the prominent people in Scottish public life today—and particularly in the nobility, the Church, the law, the Universities, journalism, and the teaching profession—remind me of the oxpeckers, an African genus of starlings. These birds are parasitic on the large mammals whose bodies they search for tick and other vermin. By the aid of the long, pointed tail and the prehensile claws they move at will over the body of an animal, like a nuthatch on a tree. So strikingly prehensile are their claws that Millais relates that when ' a dead bird that had grown stiff was thrown on the back and sides of an ox, so that the feet touched the animal's hide, the claws held fast at once, and could not be easily withdrawn '. That is precisely the relationship of most of these people (all dead—born dead, in fact) to Scottish life. Many writers credit these birds with warning their hosts of the approach of the hunter, and Dr. Stark describes the indignation and horror of oxbirds when a domestic ox refused to act on their warning. They became frantic in their endeavours to stampede the beast, flying wildly at his face and eyes while screaming their loudest. It would be difficult to find anything more closely analogous to the leading articles of the Anglo-Scottish dailies on, say, the ' Socialist menace '. But I had better say no more on this subject, lest I make my book too like the palace of the Nineteenth Dynasty at Kantir, in which the very steps leading up to the dais of Pharaoh's throne were adorned with glazed images of his fallen foes, meet to be spurned by the feet of their overlord ! I would only add that I myself, to continue this Rhodesian ornithological figure, resemble one of the weaver birds, whose hanging nests may be blown out horizontally by the wind and then, when the gust has passed, clash into each other as if every egg must be broken. Yet a fortnight later the same nests are alive with young clamouring for food !

Confined almost entirely to myself as poet, this book is accordingly an account of the development of my mind, ' absorbed in its own forked speculation ', or, more precisely, of what Jung would call my *persona*, defined as ' the private conception a man has of himself, his idea of what he wants to be and of how he wants other people to take him'.

In other words (if small things may be compared with great), a book somewhat similar in kind to the two volumes of Romain Rolland's *Le Chant de la Resurrection* (parts of a still uncompleted cycle, *Les Grandes Epoques Creatrices du Beethoven*), which deal with the seven years from 1816 to 1823, for ' in these years of crisis the drama of Beethoven opens up to us an access to those unknown regions of the Soul enveloped by the fluorescence of the Subconscious.   Here there unrolls itself the creative enigma and the Life, profound and mysterious, whose laws dictate his work and his existence. . . . Here the creations of Beethoven do not appear before us in a state of completion.   We see his work moving in the depths of his soul from its first uncertain steps.   The creator himself is sometimes uncertain of its significance and its direction on noting it down.   What we see is the whole secret labour of the creative Self, like the organized fever of beehives we can watch through a pane of glass.'   But, as an American critic says, ' Let no one think these books are light or easy reading. Let those avoid them who enjoy the sentimental or easy-going biographies annually flooding the market, flowery rehashings of ancient platitudes or superficial interpretations and analyses. Rolland's monumental, indeed epoch-making, work is neither biography, psychological nor spiritual analysis, but inevitably and inextricably, all of these.   It is not the business of such a book to furnish diversion or to propagate easily digested information.'

I have commented on the mindlessness—the increasing aversion to all arts and letters, the avoidance of thinking at all costs—of the vast majority of people.   These people—ninety-nine point nine per cent. of mankind—make me feel like Suvorov, when he asked the cuirassier :

- ' Tell me, now many cannon are there in your regiment ? '
- The cuirassier was taken aback.
- ' I do not know, your Excellency.'

At that instant Suvorov made a sudden bound away from him.

' Proshka, Mitka,' he shouted, ' open the windows, quickly ; there's a stench in here, the stench of ignorance !   Chase it out ! Hey ! '

A young boy ran in, opened wide the windows, and rushed about the room, going through the motions of sweeping.

'I'm afraid, I'm afraid,' Suvorov continued to shout, 'he's a dangerous man, an ignoramus. A pox upon him! Today he doesn't know this, tomorrow he won't know that. What has he got a head for? Do a better job of your sweeping, Mitka!'

When surprise is sometimes expressed that after these years of isolation on a little island, that has been described as a ' chuckie stone cast into the sea on the north-east of Shetland ', I should still be so well-informed and thoroughly *au courant* with political, philosophical, literary, artistic, and scientific developments of all kinds, and I am asked how I manage it, I say I am in this respect like Tom Mooney, and quote from a writer who saw him in San Francisco County Jail : 'After all, twenty years in prison is long enough to make any man concerned with himself alone. But Mooney was not only not pre-occupied with himself, he was not even concerned only with politics. The latest books (he read them only in review), the Russian theatre, changes in journalism, the death of Lincoln Steffens, the conversation swung round and round through the whole range of modern thought. And this was a prisoner! For twenty years he had lain in prison, cut off from the world, allowed only one newspaper per day, allowed no books on politics, sex, economic or social questions, permitted to read only cowboy and adventure tales. Then how had he kept informed? By reading his paper thoroughly, cover to cover, and by having a good enough background before he went inside!'

As the years of my exile on this little Shetland island stretch out, it becomes increasingly strange to have my rare interludes back in Edinburgh or Glasgow or Manchester among civilized people. They are to me like sparkling water in a thirsty land, these comings into relationship again with minds keen, alert, attuned to beauty. I realize that I had almost forgotten that there were people who had thoughts and could clothe them in words not only worthy of rational beings, but even make such words interesting, eloquent. (I do not want to be unfair to Shetland in the least. If there are no such people in Shetland, there are exceedingly few in Scotland or England either—not more than one per 100,000.) Except for these brief visits in Scotland and England, and the rare occasions in the summer-time when I have friends—authors, artists, and students—to stay with me in Shetland, I see nobody who has read widely enough to possess grounds on which to base, if not opinions, at least reasonable speculations. I hear nothing but the inane phrases of women. ' It's all in the Bible, you know. . . . Moore, you know, Old Moore. He knew, and they do say that the Queen had a dream. . . . And you remember what Churchill said. . . .?' And the men are as ignorant and incoherent as the women, even the young men, sailors who have been all over the world and soldiers in the present War and

the previous War, with their easy laughs and childish pronounce-
ments upon the development of the awful dramas in which they have
taken part. They have read nothing, seen nothing—never open a
newspaper, even. What in Heaven's name have I to do with such
people ? Why, how, have I made such an association possible ?

Apart from the working-class movement generally, and the
question of Scottish Independence, what is the enemy I have been
fighting in this life-long warfare—often with my heels backed to the
very edge of the bottomless cliffs of destitution (or, rather, clinging to
that verge by my eyebrows—to leave both my hands and feet free to
fight with !) ? The enemy is human stupidity in general, and in
particular that cant of literature and illusion of knowledge Mr.
George Sampson so well described in Volume XX of *Essays and
Studies by Members of the English Association* (1935), when he wrote :
' In the schools the teachers want to begin where the great scholars
ended. They . . . set forth generalities to pupils who have no
particulars. . . . Pupils who should be acquiring some standards of
value acquire instead an illusion of knowledge. . . . The peculiar
danger of a classroom course in literature is that pupils may be set up
for life with third-hand and fourth-hand generalities and with a stock
of details swept up by the industrious housemaids of literature, and
never learn the need of wrestling in solitude with a great work of
creative art. And then the students so taught will themselves become
teachers and pass on a cant of literature to the young, or divert
literature into a form of useful knowledge.'

I am, like my friend the American poet and critic, Horace Gregory,
with my back to the wall, pleading quietly for power ' to stay in no
retreat and not to die '—acknowledging chaos with a candour which
cannot evade fear, but seeking refuge neither in an irrecoverable way
of life nor in oblivion.

Since I wrote this book I have had the satisfaction of finding that
two entirely unrelated writers (one in America and one in Latvia)
have written books containing chapters about me which show that I
have in fact succeeded in large measure in putting across in its main
essentials that conception of myself which in greater detail I am here
concerned to present.

The first of these evidences of my success in this way is from
*Sowing the Spring : Studies in British Poets from Hopkins to
MacNeice*, by Professor James G. Southworth, of Toledo University,
Ohio, U.S.A., who concludes the chapter he devotes to my work as
follows : ' One thing is certain. To all classes with their increasing
awareness to social problems and their revision of their views of life
as science has pushed back the boundaries of the universe, Mr.
MacDairmid has much to say and he says it with force. One may
cavil at individual poems, one may disagree violently with specific
ideas ; but when one lays aside the volumes of his work and thinks

about his accomplishment one realizes he has been in the presence of a man of erudition steeped in the best thought of the past and the present, if not always in the presence of a great poet ; that he has been in the presence of a man who by sincerity of expression, by subtlety and keenness of intellect, and by indomitable energy has sought to fire his readers to an adequate perception of the universe, of our immediate world and its needs, and of their place therein.'

I think I establish the point I am making when I follow that with what Mr. John Spiers says in *The Scots Literary Tradition* (1940), in the section he devotes to me : ' He turns and turns like a caged tiger. But through all his inconsistencies there is a consistency of direction —a devotion, a concentration of all his powers to the end in view. In this he shows a quite extraordinary strength of character. . . . If Grieve finally succeeds in solving his own problem it will not be only his own problem he will have solved ; he will have helped towards solving the problem of any other Scotsman who may aspire to poetry (or, for that matter, prose).'

My internationalism is like that of the American artist, Richard Bishop, of whom, in his introduction to Bishop's *Etchings of Water Fowl and Upland Game-Birds*, Colonel Harold P. Sheldon of the United States Biological Survey says : 'And friends ! the man is abundantly blessed with them, as the Quakers say.   Artists, soldiers, authors, lawyers, business men, boat paddlers, camp cooks, guides, gillies, and Scottish lairds—a variegated lot, to be sure '—all men who have felt at one time and another the thrill of the wildfowler. It may be at Currituck or the Erie marshes, or on the Illinois, or in the pin-oak bottoms of Arkansas, or in the roseau cane of a bayou in Louisiana that Richard Bishop has known his friends to set up his decoys, but most of the ducks and the geese that he shot and sketched are known to our British gunners of the Solway or the Blackrock, and there is no difference at all in man or continent when a pair of mallard cross a twilight sky or a flock of geese come planing down to a waiting gun behind an English sea-wall or in a gunning pit of the ' Ole Miss '.   So it is with all literature and the other arts to me.   And in the same way the mystic is as cosmopolitan as the man of science, and his experience is not the monopoly of a particular religion nor the concern of particular individuals ; as Professor Radhakamal Mukerjee says, in his *Theory and Art of Mysticism*, ' The stages and degrees of mystical contemplation reached in different religions by different persons are as uniform as, for instance, the psychological laws of perception and feeling . . . as the mystic rises on a higher plane of consciousness he frees himself more and more from the traditional categories and symbols of his particular religion until his meta-physical statement becomes of universal import and acceptance.'

While my intimate friends and associates all belong to the most highly educated class, and I have never been afraid to surround myself with brains, I am, nevertheless, like the old Campden labourer who said, ' Well, I like eddicated people, but the wust o't is they be so doomed ignorant'. I agree with Mr. Edward Sackville-West when he says : ' The simpler people are the less easy it is to deceive them, for unspoilt instinct is a correct informer. Inarticulate persons see straighter, further, and more rapidly than those whose wisdom has been blurred by the habitual veil of glib phrases.' Or, as Thomas Carlyle put it in his review[1] of ' Corn-Law Rhymes ' in the *Edinburgh Review* of July, 1832 : 'An observer, not without experience of our time, has said : " Had I a man of clearly developed character (clear, sincere within its limits), of insight, courage, and real applicable force of head and of heart, to search for ; and not a man of luxuriously distorted character, with haughtiness for courage, and for insight and applicable force, speculation and plausible show of force—it were rather among the lower than among the higher classes that I should look for him." A hard saying—that he, whose other wants were all beforehand supplied, to whose capabilities no problem was presented except even this, how to cultivate them to the best advantage, should attain less real culture than he whose first grand problem and obligation was nowise spiritual culture, but hard labour for his daily bread. . . . He who wants everything, must know many things, do many things, to procure even a few ; different enough with him, whose indispensable knowledge is this only, that a finger will pull the bell ! '

If my attitude to the rich is not quite that of Leon Bloy (whose peculiar hatred of them is instanced by the following passage : ' In 1897, when there was a fire at a Charity Bazaar in Paris, and many rich people were burnt, he wrote to a friend : " I hope I will not scandalize you when I say that in reading the news of the terrible event I experienced the delicious sensation of a weight being lifted from my heart. It is true that the small number of victims limited my joy " . . .'), it is at least that of the Linton minister, William Faichney (1805–54), who (in these days Scots was still generally spoken in the pulpit as elsewhere) ended a sermon on the difficulties

---

[1] Carlyle was undoubtedly right in this same essay when he said that a society such as ours, where *kenning* and *can-ning*, the first principle of human culture, the foundation stone of all but false imaginary culture, have become two altogether different words, is in a bad way, and these two must become one again if humanity is to survive. He was right too when he said : ' My decided idea is that authors will associate and become the most stupendous body incorporate, but it will be, I think, when they cease to be *canaille*. Hunting merely for pudding or praise, we all have, like animals of prey, to do it in a solitary manner.' As matters stand, ' we are condemned ', wrote R. L. Stevenson, ' to avoid half the life that passes us by. . . . They give us a little box of toys and say to us, " You mustn't play with anything else." ' Stevenson continued nevertheless to play with the box of toys and avoid real life. So has every subsequent Scottish writer and nearly every writer of every other country too.

of the rich entering the Kingdom by saying : ' The truth is, my friends, you might as weel expect to see my red coo climb the muckle pear tree in the manse garden tail first and whistling like a laverock ' ! Like Bhartrihari, the Sanskrit poet (in whose poems great things are said and whose influence for two thousand years upon Indian thought should be known and shared by British men of culture), for ' beetle-minded men ' who amass wealth but make no sacrifice I have the greatest scorn. They are, to me as to him, ' lower brutes than brutes can be '.

My life has been all along, and will continue to be until the end, a desperate struggle. In what sense, then, is this book a paean of victory ? Is it in the sense Pilsudski had in mind when he said that to be defeated, and remain irreconcilable, is victory ? I think the nature of the battle I have fought—and claim to have won—is succinctly described by Mr. A. H. Fox-Strangways, when he says : ' Few things are sadder than to watch the numbers of young composers (substitute poets, painters, &c.) who leave the college year by year and are never heard of again. They explain their failure by lack of money, bad luck, scarcity of opportunity, few friends, little influence, by anything except the sempiternally true reason that they were and are not alert and alive—did not cut down their needs, make their own luck, meet opportunity half-way, scorn to wait for influential help. They were not really being artists, for the artist is a man who is vividly aware of his own power and never supposes for a moment that there is anything in his art that he cannot do, nor anyone who can do it better. In the work-a-day world this is called conceit, but that is not the artist's world. He ignores some standards, ideas, and conventions that hold the ordinary man prisoner. And then his work, his composition : that must " grow " too, from a seedling to a branching tree. Nothing must go into it that is not to be accounted for later. Commitments have to be redeemed, luxuries paid for with ill-health, good-will bought at a price, reticence rewarded by trust.'

I am a Communist, but *in excelsis* of the kind Lenin described when he said : ' Now, for the first time, we have the possibility of learning. I do not know how long this possibility will last. I do not know how long the Capitalist Powers will give us the opportunity of learning in peace and quietude. But we must utilize every moment in which we are free from war that we may learn, and *learn from the bottom up.* . . . It would be a very serious mistake to suppose that one can become a Communist without making one's own the treasures of human knowledge. It would be mistaken to imagine that it is enough to adopt the Communist formulas and conclusions of Communist science without mastering that sum-total of different branches of knowledge, the final outcome of which is Communism. . . . Communism becomes an empty phrase, a mere façade, and the Communist a mere bluffer, if he has not worked over in his consciousness the whole inheritance of human knowledge . . . made his own, and worked over anew, all that was of value in the more than two thousand years of development of human thought.'

I am continuously concerned with what Mr. T. S. Eliot has called ' the living whole of all the poetry that has ever been written ', and with the *sodaliciis adstricti consortus of* all the world's authors ; and my constant cry is :—

> Back to the eager appetites of the Renaissance ! Back
> To the ' best that has been thought and felt in the world ',
> Back to John Keats first looking into Chapman's Homer,
> Back to Karl Marx reading Aeschylus through every year !

In my insistence upon a poetry of fact—that nothing short of that is poetry, in fact—I have in mind, of course, two remarks of Plekhanov, with which I am in complete agreement : ' The quality of a work of art is, in the final analysis, determined by the " specific gravity ", as it were, of its content ', and ' when a work of art is based on a fallacious idea, inherent contradictions inevitably cause a degeneration of its aesthetic quality '. The programme for poetry I advocate is, in Walt Whitman's words : ' To conform with and build on the concrete realities and theories of the universe furnished by science, and henceforth the only irrefragable basis for anything, verse included ' ; and like Whitman, I cry : ' Think of the petty environage and limited area of the poets of the past, no matter how great their genius. Think of the absence and ignorance in all cases hitherto of the multitudinousness, vitality, and the unprecedented stimulants of today. It almost seems as if a poetry with cosmic and dynamic features of magnitude and limitlessness suitable to the human soul were never possible before. It is certain that a poetry of absolute faith and equality for the use of the democratic masses never was.'

- Last word ! As a Scottish poet I am frequently asked what I think of the virtual monopoly given to English language and literature in our Scottish schools and colleges and the almost complete exclusion of any attention to our Scottish languages and literature. I reply that it is as harmful and incompatible with the national genius as that inflow of romanticism which, as Maurice Baring showed, had distorted Russian literature and superimposed an immense falsification of imagination upon its essential practical spirit. The de-Anglification of Scottish poetry is as urgently necessary, and would undoubtedly be as rewarding, as the de-Frenchification of Russian poetry, and return to real native roots, has been. Again, I say that it is pretty much with Scotland as it has been with India in this respect, where, as Dr. K. S. Shelvankar in *The Problem of India* says, the educational system that took shape under British imperialism

' must surely be one of the most perverse and irrational in history. Its object was not intellectual development or character building or training for citizenship or any of the other " ideals " familiar to pedagogues, but solely to impress on middle-class Indian youths the glory and grandeur of Britain and to train them to be competent servants of a foreign bureaucracy. It was vocational education with a vengeance : vocational education of a vicious and stultifying kind which cramped the mental energies of a singularly gifted people, stifled free inquiry, discouraged criticism, and threw the weight of the curriculum on such matters as English syntax, Shakesperian prosody, and the dates of kings and queens, who had reigned over England.'

HUGH MACDIARMID

Island of Whalsay
Shetland Islands
March, 1941

Postscript :—Since this Author's Note was written, war circumstances have continued to delay publication for nearly two years. In February of this year I had to abandon my Shetland retreat, and since then I have been doing hard manual labour in big Clydeside engineering shops. Going from one extreme to the other like this is, of course, in keeping with my (and Gurdjieff's) philosophy of life, and, happily, at fifty, my constitution has been able to stand the long hours, foul conditions, and totally unaccustomed, heavy and filthy work perfectly well. Friends have suggested that surely I could have obtained instead employment of a more suitable kind— under the Ministry of Information, perhaps, or the British Council, or something of that sort. But I reply that I regard all such jobs with contempt, and vastly prefer to do what I am doing—and the company in which I am doing it ! For what I say repeatedly in this book of my Leontiev-like detestation of all the bourgeoisie, and, especially, teachers, ministers, lawyers, bankers, and journalists, and my preference for the barbarous and illiterate lower classes of workers, has been completely confirmed by my Clydeside experiences. Indeed, I feel I could not have seen the war through in the company of the former, but would have found association with them quite intolerable, and entirely lacking in the compensations I have found among these ' barbarian ' war-workers. It has been a great source of pride to me to have been able to ' keep my end up ' in this unfamiliar and most exacting milieu. Like Constantine Leontiev in the Crimean War, I am ' highly delighted and almost in love with my venal colleagues who do not give a damn for anything " refined " or " lofty " '.

As to my poetry, to obtain the maximum degree of aesthetic pleasure, a writer of my sort must not only take account of the *events*, but also of the *omni-psychic music* accompanying them ; he must estimate the *tendencies* of his age.

My insistence upon a poetry of fact and of thought in this book agrees with Ouspensky's contention that ' one of the main barriers preventing us from waking up is our imagination, which intrudes constantly into our thought. Imagination runs away with our thoughts and leads a thoroughly destructive life within us. We are only rarely able to think beyond a certain point, and this point is very soon reached. Our thoughts are then taken over by our imagination, which runs amuck with them, without direction, aim, or control. We can only stop the wasteful chase of our imagination by being attentive. The moment we are attentive the activities of our imagination cease, and thought can come into action. Imagination is a very violent destructor of energy ; mental effort on the other hand stores energy.'

The much lengthier delay than was anticipated in issuing this book has thrown out the tenses of many passages (e.g. my references to the late Lord Lothian), and an adjustment is needed in regard to these, and in respect of all statements about people's ages, the use of such terms as ' recently ', and so on. I must leave my readers to make these corrections for themselves ; all that is required is that they should bear in mind continuously that what they are reading was written in 1939 and has not been altered to accord with the lapse of time since then.

On reading the proofs of this straightforward record of my snake-and-ladder life so long—and in such changed circumstances—since the text was written, I must confess that it reminds me above all of a recent remark by Mr. George Hicks, M.P., viz., ' You get a good view of the Albert Memorial with the other railings down, do you not? '

Glasgow
  December, 1942

CHAPTER I

INTRODUCTORY

'For I am corn and not chaff. I will neither be blown away by the wind nor burst with the flail, but will abide them both.'—*Scots Worthies.*

' "No," Lup said simply, " I like folks or I can't abide them. I'm keen to clap eyes on them and have a crack, or else I want no dealings with them whatever. I'll not drink with them, nor sell them, nor pass the time o' day unless I'm put to it. I've no use for them at all."

' " That's simple, Lup, but it's blind—blind and narrow ! Folk are not all white or black ; they're different sides, different shades. You can pick out the one you want and leave the rest. Even Brack has his points."

' " Like enough," he answered carelessly. " He's welcome to them as long as he keeps out of my road." And she laughed a little and was silent. Brack's " points " did not interest her overmuch, either.'—CONSTANCE HOLME : *The Lonely Plough.*

' " Take what you want," said God. " Take what you want—and pay for it ! " '—SPANISH SAYING.

MY SURNAME—the name *Grieve*—does not figure much in Scottish history. It belongs to the Borders and has its home mainly about Selkirk, and it is known mostly in connexion with Border Rugby teams.

A' owre the Borders lie the unkent graves o' oor coontless hosts.
Only their ghosts might find them—and we're no' a folk that's gi'en to ghosts !

Representatives of my own family have been associated with the Hawick and Langholm teams for several generations, and I myself carried on this tradition in the Army and, prior to that, in my Edinburgh school team, and was a fleet wing three-quarter before I became overmuch ' sicklied o'er with the pale cast of thought ', or rather before the effects of malaria and, still more perhaps, the consequences of smoking an ounce of thick black tobacco a day (as I have done for the past twenty-five years) disqualified me for such exertion. One of my ancestors, however, was the Henry Grieve, the first name to appear (in 1399) in connexion with the office of Lord Lyon (though there were prior references to the *Leoni regi heraldoram*, but not to the names of the individuals who successively held that office). This Henry Grieve (a conjunction of Christian name and surname that has run through all the generations in our family and survives to the present day in an uncle and several cousins of mine), registered in the archives of the English Issue Rolls as ' King of Scottish Heralds ', was at the Tower of London about the time of the Coronation of Henry IV. Modern authorities are doubtful whether he actually held the office of Lyon or was merely Depute. Be this as it may, he is the first Lyon—depute or otherwise—to be mentioned by name. I have no intention of setting out here the genealogical tree of my descent from the gentleman in question, any more than I have of establishing that my friend William Power, the well-known Scottish journalist and literary critic, is lineally descended from the Hamish Power who made her banner for Joan of Arc (that banner of which she was more proud than she was even of her sword, though that was the very sword of Charles Martel and was given to her by St. Catherine herself).   I merely state the facts.

John Grieve (1781–1836), Hogg's friend and himself a poet, and William Laidlaw (1780–1845), Sir Walter Scott's amanuensis and steward at Abbotsford, were also ' connexions ' of mine.

For many generations, however, my forebears have belonged to the working class, and I would not have it otherwise if I could.   My grandfather, John Grieve, was a power-loom tuner in a Langholm tweed mill.   I only remember seeing him once—shortly before he died, when I was about four years old ; an alert, ' jokey ' little man.   I remember he wore a transparent, butter-coloured waistcoat or linen jacket ; and on the occasion I recall I caught him in the act of taking some medicine of a vivid red colour, and somehow or other got it into my childish head that he was drinking blood, and thought of him with horror—not unmixed with envy—for years afterwards.   I resemble him physically (in point of leanness and agility, though I am considerably taller) and facially (a big brow and all the features squeezed into the lower half of my face) ; but when I was a lad the older folk used to tell me I took after him in another respect—' juist like your grandfaither,' they used to say, ' aye amang the lassies.'

One of the few Grieves of any note to-day is Commander Mackenzie Grieve, the Atlantic flyer.   He is one of the Mackenzie Grieves of Bellfield, Cupar, Fife, and when I held a journalistic job in Cupar just prior to the 1914 War, my correspondence, addressed ' C. M. Grieve ', used to be delivered to their house at first.   But my middle initial, ' M ', did not stand for Mackenzie.   I took it, and my Christian name of Christopher, from my paternal grandmother, Christina Murray, and it is through her that I claim the right to wear the red Murray of Tullibardine tartan, which I have worn constantly in recent years, for it is a mistake to think that it is wrong for Lowlanders to-day to wear tartan—since many of the Highlanders settled in the Lowlands after the break-up of the clans, when, too, they often had to assume other names, whence it comes that now many Lowland Scots with names that are obviously not Highland are just as much entitled to the dress as any MacDonald, Fraser, or Cameron.

WHY I CHOOSE RED

I fight in red for the same reasons
That Garibaldi chose the red shirt
—Because a few men in a field wearing red
Look like many men—if there are ten you will think

There are a hundred ; if a hundred
You will believe them a thousand.
And the colour of red dances in the enemy's rifle sights
And his aim will be bad—But, best reason of all,
A man in a red shirt can neither hide nor retreat.

Murray is the oldest name in Scotland. My kinsmen on this side included Alexander Murray (1775–1813), the great linguist, student of the languages of Western Asia and North-East Africa and Lapland, and author of *History of European Languages*, and also Lindley Murray (1745–1826), styled ' the Father of English Grammar '. Thus—in so far from being mere affectation, one of my main prepossessions as a writer—my concern with linguistics—is hereditary.

As boys, my brother and I wore the Graham tartan. Our mother was Elizabeth Graham. If my father's people were mill-workers in the little Border burghs, my mother's people were agricultural workers. My alignment from as early as I can remember was almost wholly on the side of the industrial workers and not the rural folk, and it remains so to-day. I never had anything but hatred and opposition for deproletarianizing back-to-the-land schemes ; my faith has always been in the industrial workers and in the growth of the third factor between Man and Nature—the Machine. But even as a boy, from the steadings and cottages of my mother's folk and their neighbours in Wauchope and Eskdalemuir and Middlebie and Dalbeattie and Tundergarth, I drew an assurance that I felt and understood the spirit of Scotland and the Scottish country folk in no common measure, and that that made it at any rate possible that I would in due course become a great national poet of Scotland. To this day I have not lost the faculty of being able to go into cottar houses and secure immediate acceptance among the rural workers as one of themselves. This is far more than a question of being a ' good mixer '. I know the subtlest shibboleths, though I hardly know how. It acts (on a far wider section of the community) like a knowledge of the ' horseman's word '—a freemasonry. It acts not only in the cottages of the Border countryside, but equally well all over Scotland and in the Hebrides and the Orkney and Shetland Islands. It served me splendidly in my journalistic days in Berwickshire and Fife and Angus, and some of the most potent imponderables of my poetry derive from this secret source. For, as John Cowper Powys says : ' Deep within us is a secret fount, from whose channel, by a resolute habit of the will, we can clear away the litter that obstructs the water of life '.

There is an old saying—' Out of the world and into Langholm ', and throughout my life I have applied it in this way. It has been my touchstone in all creative matters : always I derive thence that ' intuitive perception of stillness of some sort, an idea or a quality '

which is the ' germ of composition '.   This—which explains how I
reconcile my use of a linguistic medium utterly unintelligible to ' the
mob ', and my highbrowism generally, with my Communism—the
extremes of High Tory and Communist meeting—is, of course, just
what Osbert Burdett was getting at in his book on Coventry Patmore
when he wrote : ' There is a force in a life removed '.   To say, then,
as Patmore does elsewhere : ' If you want to influence the world for
good, leave it, forget it, attend only to your own interests ', is merely
to affirm that to improve his own character is a man's surest means of
improving the world, a policy which would alarm the practical man
were his views long enough.   But he concerns himself only with the
immediate present.   Such influences and the virtues which they
breed are called ' passive ' only because their effect is reserved ; but
to be capable of reservation is almost a definition of capacity.   One
of my earliest interests was the genealogy of Border families, the
results of my researches into which I used to publish in the local
paper, the *Eskdale and Liddesdale Advertiser*, when I was in my early
teens.   (It was in that paper, too, that I remember defending—about
the same time—the claim of another Langholm poet, William Julius
Mickle, translator of Camoëns' *Lusiad*, to the authorship of ' There's
nae luck aboot the hoose '.)   I traced the distant connexion of my
mother's family with the Grahams of Netherby.   They had ' come
down in the world ', however.   Her great-great-grandfather had
been the Laird of Castlemilk, but had been a typical reckless, hard-
drinking, heavy-gambling laird of his time, and had gambled away
his estates on the turn of the card to, I think, one of the well-known
Border family of Bell-Irving, or to one of the Buchanan-Jardines, who
now own the property in question.   My mother's people lie in the
queer old churchyard of Crowdieknowe in the parish of Middlebie,
which is the subject of one of my best-known lyrics—' Crowdieknowe '—a wonderful name for a cemetery, even better, perhaps,
than the more sentimental one of Sleepy-hillock at Montrose, for
which for some time, years later in my life, I shared administrative
responsibility as a member of the local town council and of the parks
and gardens committee thereof.   These two names must, at all
events, be hard to beat for their aptness to such a purpose.   Long-
lived people they were, my mother's people—farm-labourers, game-
keepers, and the like.   Her father died in his ninety-sixth year
through accidentally slipping and falling down the stone steps from
the back-door of his cottage one dark night.   He was the first man I
saw die, and I remember to this day the ragged wounds on his forehead where he had hit the ground.   Some of her sisters are still alive,
in the neighbourhood of a hundred years old ; my mother's brothers
all died young, however, as a result, I think, of overstraining themselves by incessant wrestling.   Great strapping fellows they were.
One of them was, for a time, gamekeeper on an estate near Dingwall,

and I was fortunate in spending some of my earliest holidays there, and thus not only seeing a good deal of Scotland, while I was still a little boy, but being enabled to bridge, to some extent, the gulf between Highlands and Lowlands, and even to learn a little Gaelic from the Ross-shire woman who was my uncle's second wife. These early holidays were so many little unrealized rehearsals for what a score of years later was to become one of the main endeavours of my life—the effort to unite Scotland and to get rid of that false division of Highland and Lowland which has been so sedulously fostered under the English ascendancy.

There are two great divisions in Scotland, which may be illustrated by two stories, and I belong (exclusively of the other) to the first of these. Have I not always adjured my countrymen that they should be guided in their literary efforts—and practised according to that precept in my own writings all along the line—by Allan Cunningham's remark when writing to Sir Walter Scott about his *Songs of Scotland, Ancient and Modern* :

> ' I have not been very sensitive about our free songs. I have not excluded all that is over-free and glowing. I wished to preserve an image of the livelier moments of the lyric Muse when she sang without fear, without scruple, and without sin.'

Or by Joanna Baillie's when she wrote to the same correspondent that she wished to include a copy of Howieson's ' Polydore, the Robber ' in a collection :

> ' For it is good strong stuff such as School Boys and Country Lairds will like to read as well as fine Ladies, and I must not have my volume too much filled up with what is called *pretty* poetry ' ?

Or as D. H. Lawrence put it in a letter to my friend Donald Carswell :

> ' I read just now Lockhart's bit of life of Burns. Made me spit ! Those damned middle-class Lockharts grew lilies of the valley up their ——, to hear them talk. My word, you can't know Burns unless you can hate the Lockharts and all the estimable *bourgeois* and upper classes as he really did—the narrow-gutted pigeons. Don't for God's sake, be mealy-mouthed like them.—No, my boy, don't be on the side of the angels, it's too lowering.'

The first of the two stories to which I refer tells how a Border Scottish farmer, going out into his stackyard, found his young son engaged in sexual intercourse with one of the servant girls. He surveyed this scene for a little while, then shook his head and muttered : ' Yech, Jock, you're an awful lad. You'll be smokin' next.'

The other story is of a visitor to a hotel in a Highland district dominated by the Free Kirk. It was a lovely Sunday morning, so he thought he would go out for a little shooting. As he came downstairs carrying his gun, the hotel-keeper barred his way and told him that shooting was not allowed on the Sabbath day. He returned to his room, and then, at a loss to know what to do with himself to pass the time, it occurred to him that no exception could be taken to a little quiet angling. Once more he descended the stairs, carrying his rod and fishing-tackle ; but again the host met him and insisted that fishing, too, was quite out of the question on the Sabbath day. ' But ', he proceeded, seeing the visitor's crestfallen look, ' just go back to your room and I'll send you in a nice girl to keep you from wearying.' The visitor returned to his bedroom, and in a little while a tap came at his door and in walked a pretty girl, who, without more ado, began to undress. Not to embarrass the girl, the visitor strolled over to the window and stood looking out and whistling as he did so. Then his door banged and, turning around, he saw that the girl was gone. He caught her along the lobby and asked her what was wrong. ' Oh, I couldn't go to bed ', she said, ' with a man who whistles on the Lord's Day.'

There was certainly nothing ' lowering ', in Lawrence's sense of the word, in Border life when I was a boy. Langholm was full of genial ruffians like that employer to whom, Communist though I am, I look back with the utmost relish, who, after carefully instructing a work-man whom he was sending up Westerkirk way as to what he was to do, ended : ' And just call in when you come back and I'll gie you the sack ! ' Border life was raw, vigorous, rich, bawdy, and simply bursting with life and gusto. And the true test of my own work—since that is what I have sought to do—is the measure in which it has recaptured something of that unquenchable humour, biting satire, profound wisdom cloaked in bantering gaiety, and the wealth of mad humour, with not a trace of whimsy, in the general leaping, light-hearted, reckless assault upon all the conventions of dull respect-ability.

There is, however, a third division of Scotland, and it is with that that I have been mainly concerned of late, the world of Celtic legend and Celtic melody ; or, as Ezra Pound puts it :

> —the subtler music, the clear light
> Where time burns back about th' eternal embers.

Or, as Robert Frost says in ' West-running Brook ' :

> It is this backward motion towards the source,
> Against the stream, that most we see ourselves in,
> The tribute of the current to the source.
> It is from this in nature we are from.
> It is most us.

It was an immediate realization of this ultimate reach of the implica-tions of my experiment which made me adopt, when I began writing Scots poetry, the Gaelic pseudonym of Hugh MacDiarmid (Hugh has a traditional association and essential rightness in conjunction with MacDiarmid) ; and how deep this goes may be realized from the fact that I could never, by any possibility, have had anything to do with an English girl, but married first of all a Scots girl of old Highland descent, and as my second wife a Cornish girl, symbolizing the further development of my pro-Celtic ideas.

The appropriate story to companion, in respect of this part of Scotland and this Celtic element in the Scottish complex, the stories I have already told to illustrate two of the big elements in Scottish life, is that which tells how a traveller came late one evening to an isolated cottage on one of the Gaelic islands. The island cottages are small and have seldom any spare accommodation, but Highland hospitality is not to be defeated, and so it often happens in such cases that the only sleeping place available to a chance visitor is in a bed already occupied by a daughter of the house. It is customary in such emergencies for the mother, when the daughter goes to bed, to put both the girl's feet in a stocking and draw it up till the top is round the waist. Then in the morning she is all agog till she can assure herself that the stocking is still *in situ*. This course had been followed on one occasion, but the mother had had her doubts about the guest's worthiness, and was more than ordinarily anxious when she went to her daughter in the morning. ' Is it all right, Mairi ? ' she asked. ' He didn't try to interfere with you through the night ? ' ' Indeed he did, mother,' responded Mairi. ' He tried his hardest to get my legs out of the stocking.' ' Did he, the black-hearted devil ! ' said the mother. ' But he didn't manage ? ' ' No,' said the laughing girl, to her mother's great relief. ' He tried his hardest, but he only managed to get *one* of my legs out. So that was all right.'

So far as the vast majority of Anglicized Scots are concerned, however, they are always very much like the H.M. Inspector of Schools whom I heard, when M. Emile Legouis gave an address on Words-worth's love affair and his illegitimate daughter at a meeting of the English Association in Glasgow, missing the point by a million miles and solemnly assuring M. Legouis in the course of the subsequent discussion that despite all his (M. Legouis's) appalling revelations, they, in Scotland, would nevertheless continue to regard Wordsworth as a great poet !

To revert to the question of my pseudonym for a moment, the late Mrs. Grace Rhys (Mrs. Ernest Rhys) told me when I was helping her with her *Celtic Anthology* that—not knowing that my real name was Grieve—she looked up MacDiarmid in the British Museum Catalogue in order to consult my works, and only succeeded in getting a volume of sermons in Gaelic by a seventeenth-century Reverend Doctor Hugh MacDiarmid of Balquhidder or somewhere. Roy Campbell, the South African poet, libelled me in his book of reminiscences, *Broken Record* (1934), the publication of which I had held up until the offending page was removed, and *inter alia* he fell foul of me for using the name of ' Hugh MacDiarmid ' ' to conceal the fact that he has a mean, lachrymose little patronymic of his own '. MacDiarmid is, of course, the Campbell clan name, and perhaps Roy Campbell's resentment had some justification on that score.

A literary strain had been struggling to come to something on both my father's side and my mother's for several generations. I once saw poems (very bad !) my mother had written before she was married ; my father himself wrote nothing but a few sermons ; but two cousins of mine on his side of the house—John Laidlaw and Robert Laidlaw—had published poems and sketches and articles of various kinds. John, in particular, was a great newspaper controversialist in witty verse, and had a sardonic turn of expression and a faculty of biting invective which I greatly admired. They were, I fancy, largely instrumental in turning my aspirations towards literature and journalism, and my bent in that direction was so pronounced by the time I was about twelve, that Robert's services were enlisted to teach me shorthand. He taught me more than that : he gave a definite Scottish twist to my already well-developed tastes as a reader, and a modern twist as well, for he ' took out ' various literary papers and kept considerably more up to date than the local library.

It was that library, however, that was the great determining factor. My father was a rural postman, his beat running up the Ewes Road to Fiddleton Toll, and we lived in the post office buildings. The library, the nucleus of which had been left by Thomas Telford, the famous engineer, was upstairs. I had constant access to it, and used to fill a big washing-basket with books and bring it downstairs as often as I wanted to. My parents never interfered with or supervised my reading in any way, nor were they ever in the least inclined to deprecate my ' wasting all my time reading '. There were upwards of twelve thousand books in the library (though it was strangely deficient in Scottish books), and a fair number of new books, chiefly novels, was constantly bought. Before I left home (when I was fourteen) I could go up into that library in the dark and find any book I wanted. I could do so still if the arrangement of the shelves has not been altered, although I have not been in it for thirty years now ; and I can still remember not only where about on the shelves all sorts of books were, but whereabouts in the books themselves were favourite passages or portions that interested me specially for one reason or another, so that I could still go straight to them and open them—hundreds of them—at or about the very place in question. I was greatly interested the other year to see how closely my reading— albeit at an interval appropriate to the difference in our ages and to the facts that he had the facilities of London and Oxford, whereas I had only the facilities of a little Scottish burgh—in those years in my early teens had paralleled that of Mr. Compton Mackenzie as he details it chronologically in his book *Literature in my Time*. He does not mention a single book that I did not reach and read in almost the same sequence as he did ; but that applies only to the more recent two thousand or so volumes in the collection.   The other nine or ten thousand were much older books, and for the most part are much more solid reading.   I certainly read almost every one of them : had, *inter alia*, from the bound volumes of the *Century*, *Scribners*, and other magazines got an unusually thorough grounding in American history and in the beginnings of that American literature in which, as manifested in writers like William Carlos Williams, Gertrude Stein, Louis Untermeyer, George Sterling, Upton Sinclair, and scores of others, I was later so interested (and so active a *fugelman* of it) when I was literary critic of the London *New Age*.   Not only Emerson, Hawthorne, and the like were the familiars of my boyhood, but lesser-known (and then hardly known at all) writers like Ambrose Bierce, Sydney Lanier, Emma Lazarus, H.H. (Helen Jackson), and the humorous writer ' Squibob ', whom I still think by far the best of all the Yankee wise-crackers before ' Mark Twain '.

Hence, too, it came about, to my great profit—and I have always been very grateful for it—that as a Scottish boy in a Border town, nearly forty years ago, I was already familiar with Bret Harte (who was Consul in Glasgow for a time) protesting editorially against a massacre of Indian women and children about which the rest of the community thought it expedient to remain silent, and outgrowing his ' literary ' attitude and beginning to see the creative possibilities in the life about him ; Mark Twain writing for the *Territorial Enterprise* in Virginia City and along with the brilliant staff—Joseph T. Goodman, Denis McCarthy, Rollin M. Daggett, and Dan de Quille—having ' a good time in spite of alkali hell and high wind ' ; Ambrose Bierce, one of the first American writers to portray war realistically and one of the few satirists who refused to sell out during the Gilded Age ; Joaquin Miller, the poet of the sierras ; Prentice Mulford, ex sailor-cook-miner-pedagogue-politician, the Diogenes of the Tuloumne ; Charles Warren Stoddard, a maladjusted poet ; Alonzo Delano (' Old Block ') ; ' Dame Shirley ' writing from Rich Bar and Indian Bar letters which give the most detailed and vivid picture of mining life ; Ina Coolbrith, the poet daughter of Don Carlos Smith, brother of the Mormon prophet ; Charles King, first director of the Geological Survey, writing brilliantly of mountain-climbing ; and John Muir proving to the reluctant scientists his theory that the Yosemite Valley was formed through erosion.   The wonderful story of the Mormon enterprise of which Vardis Fisher has just written a splendid novel was known to me in great detail and has continued to thrill me ever since.   All these, and American politics and history and that completely indigenous humour which, as Bret Harte had the penetration to see, was ' the essence of that fun which overlies the surface of our national life ', enthralled my mind

B 2

and excited my imagination in a way that nothing English has ever done, just as American literature and American issues of all kinds greatly appeal to me to-day, while English literature and English issues leave me stone-cold. The early Roman features of Thomas Jefferson and the drawn, melancholy, ague-moulded face of Abraham Lincoln were among the early companions of my spirit—though many years had to elapse before I understood the neurotic Lincoln or the Mark Twain who was goaded to frenzy by the injustices of Heaven and earth alike ; and I was eagerly appreciative of all the energy and exuberance of life on the frontier, its gusto and games and gambling, and had no thought as yet that this frontier of high spirits and inextinguishable vivacity concealed the truth of the common man dying of malaria, malnutrition, overstrain, loneliness, exploitation, and just failure, the harrowing solitude and the terrors of the forest and of the prairie night, the energy that came to nothing, the high spirits that ended by proving unjustified and left the American character a legacy of neurosis and despair, or, as Bernard de Voto has said, the pervasive melancholy that was hardly a heartbeat away from the boisterous laughter in which I revelled so much. But even yet there are few things I enjoy better than to go again up the rivers and down the creeks, in the canebrakes, and prairies, the plantations, the bottoms, meeting-houses and doggeries, race-tracks, musters and court days the liveliness and boisterousness of which I enjoyed so much as a boy, and laugh once again at the traveller who tried to keep a tavern bed to himself by confession that he had the itch, but was trumped by an intruder who did not mind that because, he said, he was lousy ; or at the way a group of Millerites awaiting Judgement Day were dispersed when sceptics yanked one of them up a tree with a lasso. And one of the great stories always in my mind is that of the bitter encampment at Valley Forge, where the flame of revolt was mysteriously kept alive—kept alive by the resolution of Washington and by the genius common soldiers seem to have for enduring almost anything—that patient fortitude which, as Lafayette said, ' was a continual miracle that each moment renewed '. Something like 11,000 soldiers went into camp by the Schuylkill that December of 1777—a rabble of farmers and half-trained militia and boys who had gone to war for fun. Less than half of them remained in the spring, when cold and starvation, disease and desertion had taken their toll, but that gaunt and ragged remnant were a hard-bitten and purposeful army fit to turn the charge of the Royal Fusiliers at Monmouth court house. I remembered and used that great story with effect in my poem on the Spanish War.

It was certainly this early American reading that helped me to resist the refining influence of English education and has made me to this day like Mae West, ' not so much interested in the men in my life as in the life in my men ' and always avid of that kind of wit

which is typified in her order to her coloured maid, ' Beulah, peel me
a grape ! ' I look forward eagerly and confidently to the United
States supplanting England in the leadership of the English-speaking
world, and the speech and literature of ' the old country ' dwindling
in relation to the whole to a place of no greater importance or interest
than the quaint surviving traces of Elizabethan English in Dublin.

Perhaps Mae's best crack ever was her deathless utterance when she
had an interview with Dr. Frank Buchman, the American theologue
leading the Moral Rearmament Movement on the Pacific Coast.
' I owe all my success to the kind of thinking Moral Rearmament is,'
she remarked ambiguously, as soon as the doctor had finished explaining matters. Then, suddenly introducing the name of W. C. Fields,
her partner in a picture then in prospect, she was sorry to hear that
the doctor hadn't met him. ' Moral Rearmament ', said Miss West,
in her last great epigram of the day, ' is just what Bill needs.' (Why
is it, by the way, that not one of our Scottish ' coamics ', Sir Harry
Lauder and all the rest of them, has ever emitted a single memorable
crack at all ?)

Incidentally I must say here that a Scotland once again independent would assuredly send to America a type of representative who
would appeal to the better and more indigenous, instead of to the
worse and more imitative, however temporarily influential, elements
in the States in a way that Lord Lothian (who is one of my *bêtes
noires*) is at the furthest remove from doing. Let us have a Scotsman
with a good broad Scots tongue for a change. Lord Lothian walking
up and down, speaking easily and drawing upon a vast store of
experience in Africa, Asia, Europe, and America and upon a long
acquaintance with most of the leading figures in public life in Britain
and many in other countries, might seem the very embodiment of
that sort of ' world consciousness ' of which I write. He is in fact
the very opposite—he has known only all the wrong people—and
no one who reads this book will have the slightest difficulty in understanding how bitterly I necessarily hate him and all his type, and not
least when (with a very different content of purpose, however) I agree
with what his words actually say (as against what he really means by
them and proposes to do—or not do—on the basis of the avowal in
question), as when, for example, on his return from Russia, he said :
' Though we may reject the methods and institutions by which the
Communists have sought to realize their dream, the existence of the
Russian experiment has raised an issue which more and more will
have to be faced by Western civilization.' That issue, referred to
by this Anglo-Scottish nobleman holding six titles in Scotland and
the United Kingdom and owning some 28,000 acres, is ' the divine
right of property '. Before he succeeded his uncle, Lord Lothian
was Mr. Philip Kerr. Kerr means left-handed. There has been
far too much left-handedness in Scottish personality and politics.

Such a man in no way represents Scotland in America or anywhere else, and it is time to put an end to this supercilious farce
altogether. No such man would ever be chosen by the Scottish
people, and it is peculiarly unfortunate that such a man should
represent us in America of all places. Somebody a great deal more
like the late Will Rogers or Eddie Anderson would suit Scotland far
better. Lord Lothian's ' dubbing ' for the overwhelmingly working-
class and Socialist voice of Scotland resembles nothing so much in
its unfathomable falsity as Samuel Goldwyn, for instance, uttering
awesome sentences in his own voice while, thanks to the use of that
astonishing voice analysing and synthesizing robot, the Vocoder,
the pattern of articulation is provided by the Groton-Harvard trained
jaws of James Roosevelt, and is in its way a worse (since it lacks the
only possible excuse—of being amusing) miscasting than Charlie
Chaplin in the role of Napoleon.

Owing to this piece of good luck with Langholm Library, I am, I
fancy, one of the few Scots who learned anything at all in his boyhood about American history, a subject that has been almost entirely
neglected by Scottish and English education, although as long ago as
1898 Edward Dicey recalled how : ' Many years ago, when I first
visited the United States, I gave utterance in writing to the apparent
paradox that in order to understand England, it was necessary to
study America.' Yet, as the *Times* has said, ' The neglect of
American history in British universities hitherto has been almost
complete. From a purely intellectual standpoint that is a serious
loss,' and Sir Josiah Stamp in 1937 evoked a flood of correspondence
by stating in the same paper : ' It is significant that the study of
American history and literature since the Revolution plays no part
in British University courses.' Arthur Bryant believes that Englishmen have more to learn from American history than from that of
any other country. I agree with him, and disagree entirely with
H. G. Wells, who, preferring a ' more meaningful ' world history of
mankind, contends that any ' increased study of the events of the
separate history of America and Great Britain would only produce
irritation which would be accentuated by the common language so
long as British and American people could imagine no common goal
in the future ' (which they assuredly can't, until British Imperialism
is burst up and the English class system gives way to a genuine
democracy), and with Professor Hale Bellot, the English Professor
of American History at London, who holds that ' a demand merely
for the addition, because of its present impact upon us, of the history
of the United States . . . is as intellectually unsatisfactory as it is
educationally unsound ', and prefers to view American history as
the history of the Atlantic Ocean system, of which the European
system is a part. My own point of view is entirely different from
these typically English views, and I welcome the entrée American

history is at last securing here and there, and the vogue American literature is now enjoying ; and I count it as one of my fortunate chances that I learned a lot about both well over thirty years ago and have been able to keep my interests in them well up to date ever since, and am on terms of friendship and in constant correspondence with many American authors, though I have not yet been able to have, as I hope yet to have, an American lecture tour, nor to make an itinerary of the American Scottish societies and talk to them about the situation and requirements of Scotland to-day and the modern developments and prospects of Scottish literature. Both of these may come ere long ; in the meantime a good deal has been written about my work in the *New Republic*, *New Masses*, and other American periodicals, and lectures on it have been given in Cornell and other American universities.

In a room adjoining the library was housed the local museum, and the presence of preserved serpents and stuffed crocodiles and what not must have had a powerful, stimulating effect on a highly imaginative boy. I have maintained the same tremendous and omnivorous reading ever since (save while I was in the Army during the 1914–18 War). I have never met anyone who has read anything like as much as I have, though I have known most of our great bookmen ; and it is a common experience of mine to have professors and other specialists in this or that language or literature, or in subjects ranging from geology to cerebral localization or the physiological conditions of originality of thought, admit that I am far better read even in their own particular subject than they are themselves. The range of reference in all my books bears this out.

(I will give illustrations later on which will show the scope and nature of my interest in *welt-literatur*. But I remember in particular how surprised and amusingly indignant the late Dr. Laurie Magnus was when I reviewed his *Dictionary of European Literature* in the *New Age*. I simply listed scores of his errors of commission and omission and of his typically Eng. Lit. prejudices and grotesque freaks of disproportion in the space he allocated to many different writers, with the comment that his claim that his tome was intended to accompany English Studies was unnecessary—since a book which showed *in excelsis* all the traditional insularities and self-satisfied conceit and Imperial disregard for the literatures of the smaller nations and, in particular, for Gaelic literature, and which, in the level of its commentary, was so reminiscent of a Club Bore or the drearier type of don, and which involved also so much conventional cant and perfidious political propaganda and moral humbug, was fit for nothing else, and was certainly incompatible with any real interest in and understanding of international literature. Dr. Magnus was as mad as a hatter, wanted to know who on earth I was to cock such a snook at English Studies—but he did not attempt to controvert a single one of the specific points I made against him, though they were made in relation to issues arising in teens of different literatures and in as many different periods of history and on as many diverse planes of knowledge. Yet at that time I was no University professor— I was a local paper reporter in a small Scottish burgh, earning less per week than a London scavenger. And I did the job out of hand, out of my own immediate knowledge, in an odd half-hour one evening after my day's work. A. R. Orage told me he knew of no other man in Great Britain who could have equalled the feat. Neither did I know any such then, nor have I found any one since. But then I always believed in what my friend Oliver Gogarty calls *eutrephilia* and what goes with it—the power of instantly concentrating all one's relevant knowledge of any matter and having it immediately on tap, as it were. And I fancy Dr. Magnus would have been still more surprised to learn that, although there were few opinions he passed concerning them with which I agreed at all, there was not a single writer mentioned in the whole of his book of whom I had not more knowledge immediately available in my own mind than his pages gave. I could, indeed, have dictated extempore a volume at least as big as his and covered every single issue in literary history, aesthetics, and allied subjects and every author dealt with by him precisely as Professor Saintsbury is said to have put his *Short History of English Literature* straight on to the typewriter without any preliminary draft—and with practically no need for any corrections or amplifications or other alterations afterwards before it went to the printers.

I have, as was said of another Scot, a universal curiosity and did not need my journalistic experience to learn—indeed, I was drawn to journalism because I already knew the greatest lesson of journalism —that it is only ignorance which is boredom, and that everything is interesting and important if only you learn enough about it.

It is this intellectualist stand that differentiates me from all the other Scottish writers to-day and makes me so hated, as those who have taken this stand have always been hated right throughout history.

I have in recent years been greatly preoccupied with what I call the East–West synthesis, the bridging of the gulf between the East and the West, believing that the clue to the process lies in the Gaelic genius—that this indeed must be the world mission of the Gaelic refluence (and incidentally, in regard to India especially, the ' revenge ' of the Gaelic nations of the British Isles on English Imperialism)—and in this connexion, following upon what I have just said about my intellectual position, I may add here that I am of course in entire agreement with Dr. Ananda Coomaraswamy when he says : ' The true contrast is not . . . so much between Europe and Asia as such, as between mediaeval Europe and Asia on the one hand, and the modern world on the other. Europe and Asia can meet, and can only meet in complete accord, upon the common ground of the metaphysical and purely intellectual tradition, upon the basis of what is called in our terms *sanatana dharma*, though it is by no means to be understood that this " wisdom uncreate, the same now as it ever was, and the same to be for evermore " (St. Augustine) belongs to the Indian, European, or any other part of humanity exclusively.' I believe that this is what sent my friends Yeats and AE, via Scandinavian literature (the course I myself have taken) to the Upanishads (whither I have followed them—if indeed I did not precede them there) and accounted too for my friend Orage's concern with Indian philosophy and Indian literature, and is also the basis of the community of insight and resemblances in aesthetic outlook between my friend Kaikhosru Sorabji and myself—and constitutes indeed that necessary journey round the world which, just as Dicey said a knowledge of America was necessary to an understanding of Europe, and just as Doughty went to Holland and so to Arabia to discover the true English genius, is the only way of getting back fully to the essence of our own Gaelic genius, though (unlike the Irishmen, Yeats, AE, and others) I find the Near East—particularly Persia, Georgia, and Armenia—the key to this process of reunion ; the only way of seeing Scotland whole.

(I am reminded as I write this of a friend of mine for many years— the late Dr. Henri Leon. Much of my own out-of-the-way knowledge of Near-Eastern affairs was drawn from this curious little Manxman, the mystery of whose life has never been satisfactorily cleared up. He had had his finger in many extraordinary matters. He was a great linguist, and his published works cover an amazing range of subject-matter—literature, linguistics, medicine, politics. He was thoroughly *au fait* with the literature of Egypt, Persia, Turkey, Afghanistan, and many other Near-Eastern countries, and *au fond* a good Manxman, knew all the Gaelic languages, Scottish, Irish, Welsh, Manx, and Cornish. I was in constant correspondence with him on all sorts of subjects during the years I lived at Montrose, saw a good deal of him in London in 1929–30, where, amongst other things, he ran the Société des Beaux Arts in Gordon Square, and I think my last meeting with him was in Liverpool in 1930. He died either in that year or in 1931. He was certainly one of the strangest men I have known, and I would like to have had the full story of his career, but his secret service activities kept it ' wropt in mystery ' and he was of course extremely reticent himself.)

The library was astonishingly deficient in Scottish books, I say, but I was to learn, years after, that that was not astonishing at all, but an inevitable consequence of the relation of Scotland to England, and of a piece with the fact that little or no Scottish literature and a poor smattering of Scottish history are taught to Scottish schools or colleges. It was not, indeed, until after I was twenty-seven that I made this good in my case and did a thorough course of reading in

Burns, Dunbar, and the other Scots poets, and in Scottish history
(I have long been of the opinion that at least Scottish Members of
Parliament and Secretaries of State for Scotland and other high
officials should have to do likewise ; but public opinion seems dead
against me, and most of the people who have much to do with Scotland still know as little about it as the most active of the participants
in the great Ossian controversy knew of Gaelic—nothing !)   Prior
to that, I had only encountered a little of Burns—the best known
(which is to say, from my standpoint, the least Scots and least
valuable) items in his work, and, of course, the inevitable Sir Walter
Scott, whom I read in bulk and have never been able to look at again.
But, though I was unconscious of it, even thus early—in my early
teens—the way had been paved for what was to come later ;   there
was a strong local spirit in Langholm, and I had already, under the
influence of the Laidlaws and in answer to my own inborn propensities, developed a keen interest in the rich local psychology
(Langholm, like all the little Scottish burghs thirty years ago, was a
hotbed of pungent and peculiar ' characters ', and apart from that
there was the general recklessness and gusto and go of Border life)
and in local history and such like.   Still more important was the fact
that we did not speak English, but a racy Scots, with distinct
variations in places only a few miles away.   Hawick Scots was
strongly differentiated from Langholm Scots, though Hawick was
only twenty miles away.   Still more different was the speech of
Canonbie, only six miles south of Langholm, where the people always
used the Quakerish ' thee ' and ' thou '.   I early acquired an exact
knowledge of these differences, and discovered in myself in high degree
that passion for linguistics which is so distinctively Scottish (and so
republican *au fond*) and so utterly un-English—a passion which has
been an outstanding feature of all my subsequent work, and which is,
of course, though at first glance apparently in contradiction to that
impulse to use Scots in order to get back among the common people
and down to the roots of our national psychology, not only reconcil-
able with that save on a very short and superficial view, but indissolubly
connected with it.   Above all, there was the frontier spirit—the
sense of difference from, and not infrequently hatred of, the English,
which I certainly inherited to the full, and which later developed into
my· lifework.   It was in the phrases I have italicized that R. L.
Stevenson went so hopelessly wrong, making a mystery out of what
was perfectly natural and, indeed, inevitable, when he wrote :—

> ' There is nothing more puzzling . . . than the great gulf that is
> set between England and Scotland. . . . Here are two people *almost*
> *identical in blood* . . . *the same in language and religion* ; and yet a
> few years' quarrelsome isolation . . . in comparison with the great
> historical cycles . . . have so separated their thoughts and ways, that
> not unions nor mutual dangers, nor steamers, nor railways, nor all the

King's horses and all the King's men seem able to obliterate the broad distinction.'

There has been much debate in many quarters during the past decade as to the artificiality—the dictionary-dredged character—of the Scots in which most of my poetry is written ; but the fact is that Scots was my native tongue—I can still speak it as easily as I speak English, and with far greater psychological satisfaction ; while all my subsequent education and life in England and abroad have never robbed me of my strong Scots accent.   And, above all, it should be understood that my earliest literary efforts were all in Scots, for in those days many Scottish papers ran a ' Doric ' (i.e. Scots vernacular) column, and the influence of Sir J. M. Barrie (of whom my cousin Bob was a great devotee) and the other writers of the Kailyard school was in the land, and more people spoke Scots—or spoke more (i.e. richer) Scots than do so to-day, although after two centuries of English ascendancy, the surprising thing is not a certain decline of Scots, a general attenuation of the old vocabulary and a degeneration into mere ' gutter Scots ', but the amazing extent to which Scots still holds its own as the speech of our people, amply warranting alike my efforts to re-integrate it and Sir Herbert Grierson's[1] recognition that what lies behind my effort is an effort to ' come closer to the common people '.   This class antagonism has been strong in me from the very start : when I was a boy to speak English was to ' speak fine ', i.e. to ape the gentry, and the very thought of anything of the sort was intolerable.

In a portion of an unfinished autobiographical poem which appeared in *The Modern Scot* (July 1931), I wrote of my forebears and my relation to them as follows :—

> My clan is darkness 'yont a wee ring
> O' memory showin' catsiller here or there
> But nocht complete or lookin' twice the same.
> Graham, Murray, Carruthers, Frater, and faur mair
> Auld Border breeds than I can tell ha' been
> Woven in its skein.
>
> Great hooses keep their centuried lines complete.
> Better than I can mind my faither they
> Preserve their forbears painted on their wa's
> And can trace ilka tendency and trait
> O' bluid and spirit in their divers stages
> Doon the ages.
>
> To mind and body I ha' nae sic clue,
> A water flowin' frae an unkent source,
> Wellin' up in me to catch the licht at last
> At this late break in its hidden course,
> Yet my blind instincts nurtured in the dark
> Sing sunwards like the lark.

---

[1] See his essay on ' The Problem of the Scottish Poet ' in *Essays and Studies* (1936).

> I canna signal to a single soul
> In a' the centuries that led up to me
> In happy correspondence, yet to a'
> These nameless thanks for strength and cleanness gie',
> And mair, auld Border breeds, ken I inherit,
> And croun, your frontier spirit.
>
> Reivers to weavers and to me.   Weird way!
> Yet in the last analysis I've sprung
> Frae battles, mair than ballads, and it seems
> The thrawn auld water has at last upswung
> Through me, and 's mountin' like the vera devil
> To its richt level!

And in the same fragment of a poem I speculated in certain verses on the very different course my life might have taken if my father had not died when I was still a boy.[1]   A lean, hardy, weather-beaten man, he died at forty-seven after a few days' illness of pneumonia.   He had never been ill in his life before.   I wrote:

> . . . I ha'e his build,
> His energy, but no' his raven hair.
> Rude cheeks, clear een.   I am whey-faced.   My een
> Ha'e dark rings round them and my pow is fair.
> A laddie when he dee'd, I kent little o'm, and he
> Kent less o' me.
>
> Gin he had lived my life and wark micht weel
> Ha' been entirely different, better or waur,
> Or neither, comparison impossible.
> It wadna ha' been the same.   That's how things are.
> He had his differences frae some folks aroon'
> But never left the Muckle Toon.[2]
>
> He had his differences but a host o' friends
> At ane wi' him on maist things and at serious odds
> In name, a kindly, gin conscientious, man,
> Fearless but peaceful, and to man's and God's
> Service gi'en owre accordin' to his lichts,
> But fondest o' his ain fireside o' nichts.
>
> Afore he dee'd he turned and gie'd a lang
> Last look at pictures o' my brither and me
> Hung on the wa' aside the bed, I've heard
> My mither say.   I wonder than what he
> Foresaw or hoped and hoo—or gin—it squares
> Wi' subsequent affairs.

---

[1] Two well-known Scotsmen were great friends of my father, and he kept in touch with them until his death.   These were Rev. Dr. Adam Fergusson of Dundee (a native of Langholm—and a chum of my father's when they were in their teens together); and Sir James Leishman, a noted Edinburgh citizen, who rose from rural postman to a high position in the Civil Service in Scotland.

[2] Muckle Toon: synonym for Langholm.

I've led a vera different life frae ocht
He could conceive or share I ken fu' weel
Yet gin he understood—or understands
(His faith, no' mine)—I like to feel, and feel,
He wadna' wish his faitherhood undone
O' sic an unforeseen unlikely son.

I like to feel, and yet I ken that a'
I mind or think aboot him is nae mair
To what he was, or aiblins is, than yon
Picture o' me at fourteen can compare
Wi' what I look the day (or looked even then).
He looked in vain, and I again.

Gin he had lived at warst we'd ha' been freens
Juisst as my mither (puir old soul) and I
—as maist folk are, no' ga'en vera deep,
A maitter o' easy-ozie habit maistly, shy
O' fundamentals, as it seems to me,
—A minority o' ane, may be!

Maist bonds 'twixt man and man are weel ca'd bonds.
But I'll come back to this, since come I maun,
Fellow-fellin', common humanity, claptrap, (or has
In anither sense my comin'-back begun ?)
I've had as little use for to be terse
As maist folk hae for verse.

In the same poem I speculate as to what had kept me from going
back to Langholm (I have not been there for over twenty years, and
then it was only for one night ; and prior to that I had not seen it for
a good few years) and severed all the ties myself between myself and
my relative so completely.

> Guid kens it wasna snobbery or hate,
> Selfishness, ingratitude, or chance that reft
> Sae early, sae completely, ties that last
> Maist folk for life—or was't ?

Apart from the fact that I have always been extremely chary of
intimacy, making many acquaintances but very, very few real friends,
the reason was, of course, that by the time I had come to my early
teens I had outgrown them completely, lived in a different mental
world altogether, and felt that to retain relationships with them
would be to foster a kind of infantilism in myself. (No. That's not
the real reason, either. I have been friendly enough with any
number of people with whom I have no ' community of insight '. It
is just an accident that I've never been back to Langholm—it has
just never been convenient.) I wrote these verses at a time when I
realized, with terrible distress, that, against my will, the ties between
my wife and two children, Christine and Walter, were about to be
broken no less completely than I had allowed the ties between myself
and my relatives in Langholm and elsewhere to break. But so far as

Langholm itself was concerned, I wrote that ' if scenic beauty had
been all I sought I never need have left the Muckle Toon ', and added
that ' since then I've gone half round the world with faculties undulled
and not seen it equalled '.   The next verse, translated into English,
read : ' But scenic beauty's never mattered much to me before, since
poetry is not made of anything that's seen, touched, smelt, or heard,
and not till lately have the home scenes played—

> A part in my creative thought I've yet
> To faddom and permit.'

This was not strictly true.   In my earliest Scots lyrics—and in my
' Drunk Man Looks at the Thistle', written five years later—the
Muckle Toon was a good deal in evidence ; but it was true I was
beginning to think more and more about it, to draw upon it as a
secret reservoir, and that many of my best later poems are directly
concerned with it—poems like ' Tarras ' and ' Milkwort and
Bogcotten ' and ' The Seamless Garment ', which is about that
factory mill in Langholm in which my grandfather and several of my
uncles and my cousins were employed.

I will have more to say about the Scots language and its literary
future, since that is a central consideration in relation to my lifework ;
but it may be of interest to add here that in a recent pro-English
attack on the Scottish Renaissance Movement, a well-known
reviewer (Mr. Edwin Muir), whose prose has a marked resemblance
to Mr. Ramsay MacDonald's and the Reverend George Gilfillan's
(*vide Scott and Scotland*, 1936)—manifesting throughout a ludicrous
lack of that scholarship which, in the essay to which I have already
referred, drove Professor Sir Herbert Grierson to a very different
conclusion—observed with reference to the famous passage in
' Tam-o'-Shanter ' which begins : ' But pleasures are like poppies
spread ' :

> ' I had often wondered why Burns suddenly dropped into English
> at this point, and for a very long time I put down the whole passage as
> an unaccountable blemish, until I saw that it was the touch that made
> the poem perfect, the one serious reference that gave all the rest pro-
> portion.   The point to be noticed, however, is that when Burns applied
> thought to his theme he turned to English.   The reflection in this
> passage is neither deep nor original, but in the context it is quite
> adequate.   And it is clear that Burns felt he could not express it in
> Scots, which was to him a language for sentiment but not for thought.
> He had no language which could serve him equally for both.'

Mr. Muir's whole book, therefore, is based on a *non-sequitur* : he
assumes that because Burns felt he could not express thought in
Scots, which was to him a language for sentiment but not for thought,
the Scots language is itself limited in that way.   The contrary is the
case as—in relation to my own work—better poets and critics (like

'AE', A. R. Orage, Lascelles Abercrombie, and many others) than Mr. Muir (whom I have called ' a leader of the white-mouse faction of the Anglo-Scottish *literati* and a paladin in mental fight with the presence of a Larry the Lamb ', have generally recognized. Burns, in fact, betrayed the Scots movement.

(All this attitude of doubt to Scots is, of course, limited to English and Anglo-Scottish people. The sort of points a man like Muir raises would not trouble any Continental critic for a moment. Indeed, typical of the Continental attitude is what Professor Ants Oras, the Estonian critic, says when he writes :

> ' One of the phenomena that struck me most in Scotland is the extraordinary fact of one Scottish man of letters having managed to create what is practically a new language and of his having succeeded in writing poetry of genius in that medium. I am, of course, referring to Hugh MacDiarmid's *Synthetic Scots*, and have to confess to seeing no point in any objections to the " artificiality " of the experiment. What is the individual language of one writer at the present moment may conceivably develop into the literary medium of a whole com- munity, provided it is capable of reflecting the latter's consciousness with sufficient precision. My own mother-tongue, such as it is in this year of grace, would appear bewildering to anyone happening to return to Estonia after a total lack of contact with it during the last twenty years or so, this effect being due at least as much to " artificial " and rather sweeping innovations introduced by individual philologists and writers as to spontaneous developments in the Estonian language. What at first appeared artificial was presently adopted by writers because of its greater convenience and expressiveness as well as because it was in accordance with the genius of the language. Yet ours is a more negligible feat than Hugh MacDiarmid's unique achievement—a fact symbolic of what the Scottish litarary Renaissance is capable of per- forming, and indicative of a vitality comparable to that of the great generation of Queen Mary's and Queen Elizabeth's times.'

Vitality of that sort leaves Edwin Muir, like Queen Victoria, ' not amused ', and greatly preferring his own ' anaemic blah ! ' as the late Lewis Grassie Gibbon called it. It suits Muir to-day to declare that the whole Scots tradition is worthless and should be abandoned lock, stock and barrel, and that Scots has no potentialities capable of contributing to any literary future. But he used to know better, and will have to relearn whether he likes it or not, that he was right when he said away back in 1926 *apropos* a poem of mine :

> ' It is an almost fantastic economy, a crazy economy, which has the effect of humour and yet conveys a kind of horror, which makes this poem so original and so truly Scottish. It is a pure inspiration ; nothing could be better of its kind, and the kind is rare. This vision is pro- foundly alien to the spirit of English poetry ; the thing which resembles it most, outside other Scottish poetry, is, perhaps, the poetry of Villon. It is the product of a realistic, or, more exactly, a materialistic, imagina- tion, which seizing upon everyday reality shows not the strange beauty which that sometimes takes on, but rather the beauty which it possesses normally and in use. There is in this perception of beauty less magic

and less exaltation than in that of romantic poetry ; but, on the other hand, it has more toughness, vigour, and fulness.   The romantic note is of course often heard in Scottish poetry, and with supreme force in the Ballads, but it is this other note that is most essentially Scottish ; it is this that sets aside the Ballads, the poetry of the Makars and of Burns, the prose of Carlyle, and George Douglas Brown, from the litera- tures of all other peoples and gives these nationality and character. It is this note, too, that peculiarly characterizes Mr. MacDiarmid's poems.   How, then, does Mr. MacDiarmid compare with his English contemporaries ?   In curious speculation and half-fantastic thought he is certainly as original as Mr. Graves ; his descriptions are more economical and, I think, more vivid than Mr. Blunden's, and his mysticism more organic with his general mood than Mr. de la Mare's.'

But what I want to point out here is that (and most frequently when I am dealing with anything appertaining to Langholm or to my boyhood days) my own tendency is rather to deepen into quite untranslatable Scots than, like Burns, change into English.   Mr. Muir would have done better to perpend such entirely opposite instances to what happens linguistically in this passage of Burns, as may be found in the phrases I italicize in the following two brief passages from poems of mine, viz. :

> Ailie Bally's tongue's keepin' time
> To the vibration a' richt.
> Clear through the maze your een signal to Jean
> What's for naebody else's sicht.
> Short skirts, silk stockings—*fegs, hoo the auld*
> *Emmle-deugs o' the past are curjute and devauld.*

And again :

> We wha are poets and artists
> Move frae inklin' to inklin'
> And live for oor antrin lichtnin's
> In the haingles atween whiles,
>
> Laich as the feck o' mankind
> Whence we breenge in unkennable shapes
> *—Crockats up, hair kaimed to the lift,*
> *And no' to cree legs wi' !——*

In both these cases when I want to clinch the matter—when I rise to the height of my theme—I do not pass into English because Scots is inadequate, but I pass from dialect Scots little different from English into the real Mackay !—phrases of pure Scots a man cannot come by unless he is thinking in Scots and has recovered for himself, and achieved a mastery of, the full canon of that magnificent tongue. These two instances alone completely demolish Mr. Muir's case, and I would certainly be unable to express my profoundest ideas in English at all, for a variety of reasons which include the fact that, as a wiser critic than Mr. Muir put it—' all the important words (in

English) were killed in the war '. So far from agreeing with Mr.
Muir that thought cannot be expressed in Scots, another critic
(Mr.—now Professor—Ian Gordon, *vide Edinburgh Essays on Scots
Literature*) goes so far as to claim that it is precisely my great achievement that I have ' brought back thought to Scottish poetry, *though
occasionally one wishes he would take it away again* '. It is amusing,
in any case, to see this concern for thought—in other people—on the
part of Mr. Muir, who is himself so predominantly a mystic, and so
naïvely unconscious of the abysmal ignorance his lucubrations—at
least on Scottish themes—invariably disclose.

It is this unbridgeable gulf I have in mind in ' To Circumjack
Cencrastus ' when I say :

> I ken the stars that seem sae faur awa'
> Ha'e that appearance juist because my thocht
> Canna yet bridge the spiritual gulf atween's
> And the time when it will still seems remote
> As interstellar space itself.
> Yet no' sae faur as 'gainst my will I am
> Frae nearly a'body else in Scotland here,
> But *a less distance than I'll drive betwixt
> England and Scotland yet.*

That is my fixed and unalterable purpose, and the key to my whole
personality and life-story. Things have been made extremely
difficult for me, but they were bound to be for anyone with such a
purpose. The opinion has been expressed in various quarters in the
last year or two that having set my hand to the plough I have now
turned back. As will be seen from the narrative in this book, other
matters entirely are responsible for that unavoidable appearance of
defection, or at least of falling away in the quality, and especially in
the sheer Scotsness, of my work. For these reasons—from these
causes, rather—I have been unable to finish and publish certain
bigger works than any yet to my public credit, but the MS. of these
works is by me to attest that in so far from slacking from, or in any
way modifying my purpose, the contrary is the case. After all, I have
only been writing in Scots and conducting my anti-English propaganda for about a decade and a half. That is not a long time in
which to register definite results in trying to arrest and reverse what
has been the overwhelming course for a couple of centuries—' To
change a nation old into another mould '. Nevertheless, there is
ample testimony to the definiteness of the results I have already
registered, and if I have had so much success with relatively small and
tentative efforts, I have every reason to expect that the far biggar
works I have in hand will achieve at least proportionately greater
results—if, indeed, following upon what I have already done, they
do not acquire a cumulative force. *Who's Who* has long given my
hobby as 'Anglophobia '. But it is a great deal more than a mere

hobby. It is my very life. Mr. J. H. Whyte, in *Left Review*, was right when he said :

> ' Mr. MacDiarmid, it should be stressed, not merely denies that Scottish literature can gain from joining the mainstream of English literature (supposing it could—in fact, it never has), but in and out of season maintains that the present mainstream of English art is to-day a very small one indeed in the eyes of Europe, and is in imminent danger of drying up altogether. Where, he asks, in effect, is an English Rilke, a Kafka, a Pasternak, a Valery, even a Joyce ? And I am strengthened in my notion that there is much to be said for Mr. Mac-Diarmid's view of Scottish literature *vis-à-vis* English when I reflect that just as Welsh literature has flourished most during the periods when English literature flourished least, so Scottish literature reached its peak when English literature was at about its lowest level. No less than a revulsion to English literature and English thought generally is to be found to-day among many of the most alert spirits in Scotland.'

I do not fancy anyone will attempt to deny that I initiated, and have since fostered by every means in my power, that revulsion which, in any case, is only an insistence that what is sauce for the goose is sauce for the gander, since, as Babette Deutsch observes in her book, *This Modern Poetry*, of the Auden–Lewis school of English poets to-day—' they travel back some six centuries to take lessons from Langland and find in his homely Anglo-Saxon a suitable form '. The importance of Charles Doughty may not yet be generally conceded, but I am in no doubt of it whatever. The other English has developed along with, and is too bound up with the Empire, and will pass away with it—and that won't be long now. Besides, all sorts of English critics have stressed in respect of R. L. Stevenson, George MacDonald, and others the vast superiority of their Scots verse over their English.

' Doughty says ', writes my friend George Davie,[1] ' that in the course of his Bodleian reading he came to love Erasmus and Scaliger and to desire to work where they had worked. By comparison with Danish, Dutch, and its own earlier form, Doughty came to despise modern English. The lesson of Erasmus and Scaliger is to show how a language by reverting to its classical words and usages can be transformed out of a colourless jargon into language grand and precise, capable of being put to the highest literary uses. In Scotland it is necessary only to compare Hector Boyce with John Mair, his contemporary, to see how we too on similar lines transformed scholastic verbiage into a splendid literary vehicle. Doughty, then, learned from the Humanists that the artificial improvement of language (denied on all hands) is within human power. That is why he loved them. . . . The profoundest justification of Doughty's work is to be found in MacDiarmid's pamphlet, *Charles Doughty and*

---

[1] Unpublished. Delivered before the English Literature Society of Edinburgh University, February, 1937.

the Need for Heroic Poetry. MacDiarmid argues that the time is ripe for a complete change in the formal side of poetry, i.e. in genre and language, precisely because a completely new content—the interests of the coming communist era—demands expression. It is important to note that it was likewise the need to give utterance to popular demands that was at the root of the Humanists' formal innovations (even though the advocates of formally correct Latinity were not themselves partisans at first of Protestantism). . . . Doughty was an English Tory by upbringing and conviction, a member of the landed class. This class was very critical of the whole Industrial Revolution. I wish to call your attention to a well-known exponent of this standpoint (David Urquhart, a Scotsman) who produced a once well-known book (generally called *Familiar Words*) just a few years before Doughty was rejected from the Navy. It contained a burning indictment of contemporary conditions. In Section 10, Chapter XV of *Capital*, Marx gives an extract : " You divide the people into two hostile camps of clownish boors and emasculated dwarfs. Good heavens ! a nation divided into agricultural and commercial interests, calling itself sane ; nay, styling itself enlightened and civilized not only in spite of but in consequence of this monstrous and unnatural division." Marx's comments on this passage show at one and the same time the strength and the weakness of that kind of criticism which knows how to judge and condemn the present, but not how to comprehend. What the student of Marx may not see is the connexion of this subject-matter with the title, *Familiar Words*. But the title in full is *The Effect of the Misuse of Familiar Words on the Character of Men and the Fate of Nations*. What puzzled Urquhart was the purblindness on the part of the upper classes to the wretched state of affairs—class divisions, lowering of working-class conditions. His solution of this puzzle was ingenious and sensible in its way. This oppressive system reacts upon the oppressing, ruling classes themselves ; the material impoverishment of the people is accompanied by a cultural impoverishment of their rulers. Especially was he impressed with the evil effect the Industrial Revolution had on the language of the nation, and consequently on the language of the upper classes, which became a verbose jargon, concealing rather than revealing objective meaning. This decadence of language was not merely a symptom of the evil state of affairs, but was the chief reason why the ruling classes could not discern the national decline. The language was not a clear enough instrument for significant discussion about the situation. Urquhart compared *bourgeois* speech in England very unfavourably with the speech of Turkey and the Near East—this fact is a separate link with Doughty and had its influence, perhaps, in causing Doughty to learn Arabic. Further, Urquhart argued, a nation of dwarfs and boors is doomed. Clarity and distinctness of vision—the necessary preliminary of criticism and emendation—is impossible where the language is in such a state. The fate of such a nation must inevitably be to be conquered and subjugated—all its inhabitants are sure to be enslaved, and that means an end of even a chance of amelioration. Doughty certainly was deeply impressed with this position and made it his own, assimilating it completely. Marx in saying that Urquhart did not comprehend the present means that he was quite unaware of the function of the labour movement, of the possibility of the regeneration of society through the self-education of the working-class movement in its task of supplanting and absorbing the rulers. For Doughty and Urquhart improvement must come from above, from a regenerated ruling class.'

Mr. Davie also points out that Horace in discussing Virgil's work has some admirable remarks on the importance of the intimate knowledge of language which Doughty listed among a great poet's requirements, viz. : ' He will be resolute in displacing all words lacking in brightness, or weight, or nobility. He will dig out lovingly terms long forgotten by the populace but aptly describing things— terms used by the writers of centuries before, and now lying deserted and hairy-moulded. He will adopt new words sanctified by usage. . . .' (Ep. II. 2. iii).

This, then, is the ' determination ' of my nature which has led on since, by stages I will trace, not only via Milton and Blake and Doughty and Wilfrid Scawen Blunt to my (to quote from Blake's *Catalogue*)

Believing with Milton the ancient British history,

but via Marx and Lenin and Stalin to that concern to get rid of the English Ascendancy and work for the establishment of Workers' Republics in Scotland, Ireland, Wales and Cornwall, and, indeed, make a sort of Celtic Union of Socialist Soviet Republics in the British Isles which to-day engages most of my energies and has so greatly multiplied all my ties with these Celtic nations and keeps me in constant communication and mutual inter-activity with so many Irish, Welsh, and Cornish writers and political writers and language enthusiasts and history specialists. I have worked out all the interconnexions of these issues in my huge Cornish Heroic Song, and especially the essentially barbarian (i.e. outside European civilization) nature of the Celtic genius, and, via Cier Rige, Dr. L. Albert, L. A. Waddell, and others, the fact that the possibility of an East–West Synthesis lies here—a possibility that has been seized upon too by certain Far Eastern writers, since, as the *Times Literary Supplement* said in an article on contemporary Bengali literature four years ago :

' Parichaya marks the definite passing of Indian literary criticism into the modern world. Under the editorship of Mr. Datta, a clear and vigorous prose-writer, it has set itself ahead of anything else in Indian periodical literature, in catholicity, range, intelligence, and freedom from prejudice. The current number finds space for a long discussion of Fascism and for articles on the Chinese Renaissance and Hindu minor philosophical texts ; for detailed notice of such poets as . . . Mr. Hugh MacDiarmid.'

The findings I have come to are very similar to those expressed by Rudolf Bringmann in his *Geschichte Irlands* (1939), which led a *Times Literary Supplement* reviewer to exclaim : ' He makes the *remarkable statement* ' (sic !) ' that the Normans were culturally inferior to the Gaels ' (a statement, incidentally, which is happily paralleled by Vocadlo—*vide Studies in English, by Members of the English Seminar of the Charles University, Prague,* 4th Vol.—where he says, ' In literary culture the Normans were about as far behind the people whom they conquered as the Romans were when they made themselves masters of Greece,' and emphasizes the significance of Aelfric's Grammar as a test of the fitness of the West-Saxon literary language for the higher functions of science. Above all, I agree entirely with Herr Bringmann that ' Gaeldom was moving towards—and but for the English would have realized—a real People's State '. But I will come back to that.

I may add here, since the way in which I bespatter all my writings with innumerable quotations from the most heterogeneous writers of all times and countries is one of the most frequent points of complaint against me, that this habit springs from the omnivorous reading in which I have indulged ever since I learned to read, and that though I understand the prudential consideration which counsels against quoting other writers too much, since the effect of this on the minds of most readers is that the writer himself tends to be lost in the multitude of writers he is drawing upon, I have never been of those who are afraid of being ' too literary ' (deeming that to be as literary as possible is precisely the writer's job, just as it is a professional strong man's job to be as physically powerful as possible), and in this much-debated question of using quotations agree entirely with Havelock Ellis when he says : ' It is sometimes said that the great writer seldom quotes, and that in the main is true, for he finds it difficult to mix an alien music of thought with his own. Montaigne, it is also said, is an exception, but that is scarcely true. What Montaigne quoted he often translated and so moulded to the pattern of his mind. The same may be said of Robert Burton. If it had not been so, these writers (almost certainly Burton) could scarcely have attained to the rank of great writers. The significant fact to note, however, is not that the great writer rarely quotes, but that he knows how to quote. Schopenhauer was here a master. He possessed a marvellous flair for the fine sayings in remote books, and these he would now and then let fall like jewels on his page, with so happy a skill that they seem to be created for the spot in which they fell. It is the little writer rather than the great writer who seems never to quote, and the reason is that he is really never doing anything else.'

Mr. Muir, who is not a Scot, and whom I know sufficiently well to know he has never undertaken that arduous study by which alone even a Scot *pur sang* to-day can effectively re-Scoticize himself, in the book to which I have referred makes a great deal of the lack of Scots literature in the full range of literary forms and kinds. It has, he says, no bigger poetry, no prose, no drama, above all no poetic drama. Maybe not ; but his argument that we should therefore abandon the ' nonsensical trash ' of our old and outworn differences and assimilate ourselves completely to English culture with all the grace, and even gratitude, we can muster, is utterly absurd. It is a mere variant of that unprofitable old fallacy which, since the Union, had led to so many attempts to force Scottish history into the impossible mould of English Constitutionalism. This is something very similar to that Wellsian insensitivity which afflicts so much British Socialist, and even Communist, writing with an undialectical World State-ism, and to that dismissal of everything insusceptible of being generalized against which my favourite philosopher, Leo Chestov, inveighs so tirelessly, and which led one Scottish anthologist to exclude any poems of mine because my work was ' *sui generis* ', just as another excluded me because he said : ' It is claimed that Grieve's work is for the future—so we'll leave it at that.' It is as absurd as to contend that oranges should dispense with their distinctive qualities and covet the very different attributes of apples instead. This latest nonsense is in no way preferable to our old ' nonsensical trash '. What Muir does in this book—as in his work generally—is just the antithesis of an attempt to act as mediator between the man of genius (in Wyndham Lewis's special sense) and the parasite of the ape (ditto) in the belief that it is possible for the first to speak to the second in something like his own language of matters he rarely so much as guesses at. Barrie may ' achieve effects which are the prerogative of genius with an impossible apparatus of winkles, policemen with hairy legs, and walking statues ' : Edwin Muir signally fails to do anything of the sort with a hotch-potch of arguments in regard to a country overwhelmingly Radical and Socialistic based on a few equally impossible old Tories like Sir Walter Scott and Lord Tweedsmuir, which is like taking the present Queen (Queen Elizabeth) as a typical Scotswoman. (It is as wrong-headed—and politically dictated—as the opposition of Principal Sir Thomas Holland to the establishment of a Chair of Scottish Literature in Edinburgh University at the very moment when he is declaring that he thinks Africaans should be made a compulsory subject of the English curriculum ! No wonder, when I was standing for the Lord Rectorship of Edinburgh University, I said in a wise-crack, that achieved no little local celebrity, that the difference between Edwin Muir—who had just been a candidate for the Chair of English—and myself was that Muir was a man after Sir Thomas Holland's heart, whereas I was a man after Sir Thomas Holland's blood. Holland's attitude to Scots is certainly Dutch to me, unless one attributes the basest motives to him. We will have none of it. And when I say ' We ' I am conscious that by an extraordinary consensus of opinion, which I will detail in a later chapter, and against which Mr. Edwin Muir and all who think with him have no weight whatever, I am speaking for Scotland in a way which few men, if any, have ever been qualified to speak. And here I have no hesitation whatever in substituting my own name for Lenin's in those lines in my ' First Hymn to Lenin ' where I declare :

> Here lies your secret, O Lenin—
> No' in the majority will that accepts the result
> *But in the real will that bides its time and kens*
> *The benmaist resolves* is the po'er in which we exult.'

For I am assured beyond all assurance, with all the insupportability of the man who *knows* compared to those who only know what they learn and never really possess even that—never really ' make it their own '—that as another Scottish Border poet (Mr. Will Ogilvie) has sung in a poem which I was proud to include in the first anthology I ever edited, and of which F. G. Scott has made a magnificent song :

> The rough road runs by the Carter ;
> The white foam creams on the rein ;
> Ho ! for the blades of Harden !
> *There will be moonlight again !—*
>
> There are more than birds on the hill to-night
> And more than winds on the plain !
> The threat of the Scotts has filled the moss,
> *There will be moonlight again.*
>
> The ride must risk its fortune,
> The raid must count its slain,
> The March must feed her ravens,
> *There will be moonlight again.*

And my ardour is not in the least affected by the knowledge that many s sniggering fool will murmur on reading this : ' Not moonlight— moonshine, he means '.

Scotland is :

> A nation which has got
> A lie in her right hand and knows it not,

—and ' those who can best sing to such a nation are apt to sing in solitude. He would win their secret, so that armed by meditation, a habit of the mind, he might deal blows worthy of a cause the praises of which would be scorned and rejected. This is more than a counsel of despair.' When one takes into consideration the international literary-linguistic situation (the extent to which in all countries recent literary developments have been more and more concerned with dialects, archaic forms, technical vocabularies, and even personal peculiarities of pronunciation and word-selection, and less and less with any trend towards a common tongue) : when one considers that all the significant creative writers in English during the past century have been increasingly preoccupied with the ' exhaustion of English ' and with the utilization of out-of-the-way words : when one reflects, above all, on the fact that, as H. L. Mencken's book, *The American Language,* so conclusively demonstrates, in so big a part of the so-called English-speaking world as the United States, the English language has been completely smashed, and that, in Great Britain itself, as other specialists have shown, it has been increasingly adscripted to merely official purposes—or, again, when one finds the *Manchester Guardian* pointing out that in painting and the other arts in Scotland the principal influences at work no longer come from or *via* England, and suggesting that the same change must manifest itself in literature, too—Mr. Muir's advice to Scotland that to cling to the fragments of its old national languages and culture is no longer worth the candle, and that it should go over holus-bolus to English language and literature, becomes utterly inexplicable on any creditable grounds. In any case, English literature does not exercise in Scotland, and never has exercised, more than minimally the illuminating and enlivening functions that a true and indigenous literature exercises, and it is only necessary to consult Miss Anne MacAlister's *Studies in Speech Therapy* (1937), based on a personal study of scores of thousands of Scottish children, or to read Fr. Rolfe's diverting account of the constituents of Glasgow speech in *Hadrian the Seventh,* to realize that physiologically as well as psychologically the English language is incapable of meeting Scottish requirements save in a most rudimentary way far below the threshold of any availability for creative literary purposes. Mr. Muir admitted this himself in a striking passage a decade or so ago, in which he pointed out that no Scottish writer writing in English had done first-class or even second-class work, and that it seemed to him great work in the English language could only be done by someone born an Englishman and in some class in which the tradition of English ran pure. The historical fact is as Mr. Muir then stated it, and nothing has happened since to warrant his changed opinion.

A most infuriating kind of silliness which is constantly cropping up in public utterances in—and on—Scotland is exemplified by the recent description of ' Broad Glasgow ' as the most vicious of all dialects and a revolting garble by a well-known West of Scotland organist, an Englishman, Mr. Purcell J. Mansfield, who, speaking to Glasgow Rotarians, said the various accents in the country were fast becoming a menace to school-children in Britain and described the

Glasgow speech as ' one of Glasgow's biggest problems '. What rubbish ! What Glasgow should think of is the remarkable rise in Bronx-Brooklyn letters during the last few years ; the work of men like Irwin Shaw, Clifford Odets, Jerome Weidmann, Daniel Fuchs, Arthur Kober, and the writer who most frequently publishes under the name of Leonard Q. Ross. All these men are experts in rich, vivid local speech, that is right in thought and accent, the essence of bar-room and bath-house wit. Glasgow speech—precisely at its most vicious and revolting—is a medium which might well furnish writers of similar quality, and Glasgow would be well rid of all the nice B.B.C. English in the world (and the whole of contemporary English literature into the bargain) in exchange for a single racy manipulator like this of its most happily atrocious garble.

A most shameful example of England's attitude to Scotland— and the sorry pass to which toleration of it has reduced the Scottish people—was the refusal of the English Government to give any grant towards Dr. William Grant's *National Dictionary of the Scots Language*, and the failure of the Scottish people themselves to sub- scribe adequately for the carrying through of this great enterprise. Along with the latter goes the stupid feeling, so widespread in our midst, that such a dictionary at this time of day ' can serve no useful purpose '—that Scotland should forget her own old tongues and be content with English, ' the greatest language in the World '—and that, in particular, a stop should be put alike to any perpetuation of the local dialects of the country and to the infiltration of American slang—all this, of course, in the interests of ' good English '. On the contrary, this is simply a very stupid and typically English attitude to language, and, so far as its application to Scotland is concerned, a characteristic corollary of English Imperialism which ought to be resisted *à l'outrance* at every point. Instead of yapping about American slang in this ignorant way, it is high time to realize that, as Stephen Leacock puts it, ' the making of slang is a sort of living process of language like the scum on wine. Without it there is no wine, no life, no fermentation. A language that has ceased to throw off slang has ceased to live.' American English is simply the growing end of the English language—growing with an abundant wild vitality—and the objections to it on the part of our mentors spring from a hatred and fear of everything that is really alive. And Scotland would certainly be well advised to take an example from America, while there is yet time, and emulate in so far as its own dialects go what America has accomplished in the great *Linguistic Atlas of New England*—a three-volume work with 740 maps and a handbook, the fruit of ten years of field study in 220 communities in New England and the near-by parts of Canada, directed by Dr. Hans Kurath of Brown University, backed by the American Council of Learned Societies and aided by numerous colleges and foundations,

as well as hundreds of plain folks who have spoken dialect for the
recording instruments.   Prospects seemed hopeful for the Scottish
Vernacular some ten years ago, under the leadership of my friends
Mr. William Will and the late Dr. J. M. Bulloch, and with the
support of the World Federation of Burns Clubs and the formation of
Vernacular Circles in London, Edinburgh, and elsewhere ; but it was
speedily realized that, as with every other Scottish issue, no real
headway could be made under the existing political system—the
success of the Vernacular Movement depended upon the growth of a
strong political Nationalist movement.   That movement seemed
likely too at that time to develop speedily ; but it was astutely
derailed, and the line has not yet been repaired and traffic resumed.

Other Atlases are to follow the *Linguistic Atlas of New England*.
The next one will cover Maryland, Delaware, Virginia, and the
Carolinas, and so on, till all parts of the United States and Canada
have been language-mapped.   ' The project ', we are told, ' is a bit
of pure science, a research in the vagaries of speech and their
geographical distribution for the use and benefit of future students of
the American language, of the population, history, and the folk
culture of America.'   It is in all these ways that Scotland is stupidly
mutilating itself and destroying its own future by failing to initiate a
similar enterprise.   And from the scientific point of view Scottish
dialects are at least as well worth studying as the American ones, and
a language map of Scotland would show a variety no less than that
exemplified by the facts that ' between Coscob and Skowhegan there
are actually four " dialects " ' and ' talk in the New Haven region
differs widely from Boston talk, Rhode Island has a lingo of its own,
and the folk speech of Fairfield County in South-western Connecticut
is something else again '.   Much of Western Europe has been mapped
for dialect.   England, however, remains unmapped—the nigger in
this woodpile, as in most others—except that Dr. Guy S. Lowman of
the American atlas staff has made a beginning in Southern England.
The Scottish work too may yet be done by American researchers,
since the Brown University linguists feel that the work done in New
England and to be carried on throughout English-speaking America
can never be quite completed till the language forms and usages across
the Atlantic can be traced back to their sources on this side.   In the
meantime, while nothing is being done with regard to Scots, the
situation with regard to Scottish Gaelic is as Mr. John Lorne
Campbell, the proprietor of the Island of Canna, indicates : ' To-day
the Scottish Universities are sending expeditions every year to study
the flora and fauna of the Hebrides and the north-west coast.   Why ',
asks Mr. Campbell, ' are they not sending also students trained for
research in an area which is one of the richest storehouses of folk
song and tradition in Europe ?   Must the Scottish Universities
remain enslaved by eighteenth-century political prejudice and

nineteenth-century utilitarianism, leaving the work of collecting
Gaelic folklore and recording dialects to be carried on by Scandinavian scholars and local amateurs ? '

Mr. Muir's book is, he says, not designed as an attack on myself
and others who have been active in reverting to and reviving Scots
(though it amounts to that in point of fact), but as an *apologia pro
vita sua*. For the latter purpose, however, to be in keeping with his
literary significance, and his connexion with and knowledge of
Scottish matters, a volume argues an amazing conceit, where the back
of a postage-stamp would have provided ample scope. Apart from
such misinformed defeatism—peculiar to Anglo-Scotland itself and
not encountered by my own work, at all events at the hands of the
critics of any other country in the world from Iceland to India—the
most unfortunate (and, indeed, inexplicable—no matter how clearly
one realizes the ubiquity and tightness of the English Imperialist
strangehold on Scotland) thing is Scotland's utter inability in modern
times to launch and maintain literary organs devoted to Gaelic or
Scots literature, or indeed, from a progressive angle, to Scottish arts
and affairs generally. This is not due to the relatively small public
in Scotland for Scots or Gaelic reading. As H. L. Mencken points
out : the 52,000 Armenian fraction in the United States of America
to-day keeps going ten periodicals—including two dailies ; and in
France no cultural group or political minority fails to run its organs.
In Scotland, either the Scots or the Gaelic-reading public is
considerably greater than those which suffice in these, and other
countries, to equip themselves with and maintain the periodicals in
question ; while the present membership and adherence of the
Scottish Nationalist cause would be ample, like that of the Seventh
Day Adventists, either in France or the United States of America,
to run several dailies, and also an impressive complement of weeklies,
monthlies, and other vehicles of expression.

I have written not only poems, but plays and short stories and
descriptive essays in Scots, and I could have written this autobiography
in Scots as easily as in English, and the more effectively the more I
remembered Paul Valery's insistence that ' it is the thought which
makes the man. The ordinary biography affords no indication of
what a man is like. It recounts his ancestry, the outer facts of his
education and activities ; but the deeper part of him, the inner
functioning of the intellect, the mode in which, and the passages by
which, ideas flowed into his mind and stirred his will, this, which
is the true index of the human character, is omitted ; ' while Valery,
on the other hand, only cares for this essential and inner kernel of
history—' the functioning of beings and the generation of works '.

For such an essential and inner history of myself I would have had
to use Scots, and I might then have written a book not unworthy of
shelf-room alongside Rilke's *Notebook of Malte Laurids Brigge* or,

c

at least, Strindberg's *Black Flags* (for, indeed, there are in Scotland not a few upon whom I should—and perhaps yet will—revenge myself as—literally—killingly as Strindberg in *Black Flags* revenged himself on Geigerstam).   This book, however, is of a less ambitious kind : it is not designed (though, doubtless, I will ' give myself away ' in it completely enough) to afford a personal revelation so much as to serve certain practical purposes.   I have known many famous men and women of whom posterity will treasure every scrap of recollection. Many of these are now dead—W. B. Yeats, Lascelles Abercrombie, ' AE ', R. B. Cunninghame Graham, Arthur Lynch, A. R. Orage, Edward Garnett, and many others.   It is my duty not to withhold any such illuminating details as I may be able to vouchsafe, especially as—owing to my vicissitudes in recent years—the great bulk of my correspondence with them has been destroyed.   A certain interest, I am assured in the opinion of men whose judgement I value very highly in other connexions and see no reason to doubt altogether in this, will attach to my own work, and it calls for a good deal of explication and annotation I am myself best—if not solely—qualified to supply.   Again, a lot of biographies or autobiographies have recently been published of friends of mine, and I am able to stroke the *t*'s and dot the *i*'s of these to a considerable extent.   But above all, I have been Scotland's Public Enemy No. 1 for over a decade now, and I have certain accounts to settle while (a recent very grave illness prompts the phrase) there is yet time.   Above all, I owe it to my children to deal faithfully with certain libels which have been sedulously circulated to my detriment and are now widely accepted as the truth about me, and, in view of certain sensational and widely publicized happenings in my domestic life, I owe it to my children again, and to my friends generally, to break the silence I have so far maintained in the face of the utmost provocation and set down ' my side of the case ' once and for all.

As it says in the last lines of the ' Mountain Corn Song ' of West Virginia (that little-known sharply-individualized State, largely peopled by Scots-Irish, for which Louise McNeill is now doing what Caroline Miller once did for the piney woods cracker and Jesse Stuart is still doing for the Kentucky mountaineer),

> . . . This is the season to kneel in the muck
> And strip each ear from its withered shuck,
> With ' One for dodger and one to feed,
> One for likker and one for seed '.

All the same, this is not the book I should have written—and may yet write.   English, I must repeat, is not my native language, and the limitations of this autobiography, written in English, may, perhaps, be realized and allowed for when it is understood how impossible it is to transmit the quality of my consciousness, the tone of my being, in a language in which, for example, ' *Egypt* ' spells *ee, gee, wy, pee, tee*, whereas in the speech of my boyhood (and in which all my best poetry is written) the spelling of ' *Egypt* ' is (I know no English equivalent for the sound and therefore use the pronunciation of the French word ' *oeil* ', which gives it exactly) *oeil, joeil, woeil, poeil, toeil*. Or, again, I may suggest its character by telling how on the platform of the railway station at Hawick, twenty miles from my birthplace (Hawick, which, the story goes, got its name from the fact that in the days of the Flood the Ark foundered on a hill in the neighbourhood, and the first animal to emerge was the pig with its cry of ' oik! oik! '), two commercial travellers heard a couple of porters arguing which of them should pull a trolley of luggage, and heard them say to each other : ' Yow pow ' and ' Pow yow ' (*anglice*— ' You pull ' and ' Pull you '); whereupon one commercial traveller turned to the other and said : ' I never knew before that they speak Chinese here '.

Just as a glass can be shattered by striking a certain note on the fiddle or—if an alleged American case is authentic—a suspension bridge can be broken down in the same way, and just as (I have heard it said) during the 1914–18 War soldiers disintegrated without being touched if their ' number was up ' and a shell came over with a certain sound, so it is only in the Scots language I can achieve or maintain if not, in certain senses, integrity of expression, at least ' the terrible crystal '; its sounds affect me in the opposite way to the sounds of the above-mentioned shells and bring me fully alive. No one who has done much public speaking in Scotland can have failed to realize the far greater effect on the audience of a phrase of Scots to anything that can possibly be said in English ; and Sir Herbert Grierson tells of a striking case in point in the essay to which I have already referred. I believe that in every way it is true of the effect of the English on the Scots, that, as Mr. Tom Harrison says of the effect of Europeans on the Southern Melanesians—' apart from the difficulties of adaptation to our bacilli, there is a sort of spiritual despair or at least apathy that, in some obscure way, causes infecundity—very much as confinement in a zoo influences some of the higher animals '.

Certainly, even if English were all that Mr. Muir and others claim that it is, a Langholm man at least must refuse to avail himself of it, to ' break his lip on an English micky ', quoting, perhaps, Wordsworth's :

> The beetle loves his unpretending track,
> The snail the house he carries on his back ;
> The far-fetched worm with pleasure would disown
> The bed we give him, though of softest down ;

disdain to resemble the more sybaritic frogs in Cowley's ' The Plagues of Egypt ' :

Insatiate yet they mount up higher
Where never sun-born Frog durst to aspire,
And in the silken beds their slimy members place,
A luxury unknown before to all the watery race,

and remember how accurately a modern critic defines the inevitable consequence of the opposite practice in observing that when Burns unwisely discards the vernacular his efforts resemble ' nothing so much as a bather whose clothes have been stolen '.

I always like to feel—and generally succeed in securing an adequate basis for feeling—that my principal personal characteristics exhibit clearly the great historical directives of my people and dream, of course, always of such a moment in relation to Scotland as, when St. Paul wrote to the Galatians, ' universal ' history stood over him and dictated his words—a marvellous work of the spirit, to collect the possible in the present, the infinite in the intrinsic of the present, and this as a value, a principle-value, a motive-value. Take, for instance, my indifference to money-making and material comfort, and my constant readiness and ability to meet life on all sorts of different levels. Does not this betoken an attitude that is perfectly natural in a Scots Borderer ? To see that it does, one has only to remember the traditional circumstances of life in that Debatable Land—to recall such a passage as this, for example (from W. H. Maxwell's *Hillside and Border Sketches*) :

> ' When one remembers that life and prosperity were merely held . . . from day to day. A man went to bed in independent circumstances, and in the morning he rose in poverty that might have competed with Job's '.

That is what lies behind the fact that one of my poems begins ' To Hell with Happiness ' : and behind Eric Linklater's recollection of an occasion on which, expounding Douglas' Social Credit, I ' hotly denied any concern with the increase of wealth that might be expected to accrue from his policy. " I have no interest whatsoever in prosperity," he declared, and left the uncommon impression that here was a man who advanced an economic theory for purely aesthetic reasons.'

Or again, it would be difficult to give a better account of my methods and the results I have registered than simply by applying to myself the following description of the characteristics of my forefathers (from *Lesley to Camden*, pp. 56–57) :

> ' They go forth in the night by troops out of their own Borders through desart by-ways and many winding Crankies. All the day-time they refresh their Horses and recreat their own strength . . . until they be come thither at length, in the dark Night, where they would be. When they have laid hold of a Bootie, back again they return home, likewise by Night, through blind ways only and fetching many a compass about. The more skilful any leader or guide is, to pass through these wild Desarts, crooked turnings, and steep Down-

falls in the thickest Mists and deepest Darkness, he is held in greater reputation, as one of an excellent wit. And so crafty and wily these are that seldom or never they forego their Bootie, and suffer it to be taken out of their hands. . . . But say they be taken, so fair spoken they are and eloquent, so many sugared words they have at will, sweetly to plead for them, that they are able to move the Judges and Adversaries both, be they never so Austere and Severe, if not to Mercy, yet to Admiration and some Commiseration withal.'

And, indeed, Sir Alexander McEwen and other all-too-pedestrian-minded Scots, who deplored that the Scottish Nationalist Movement in its early stages was led by poets and novelists, instead of by business men like themselves, would have done well to remember (as their utter failure to maintain the Movement they wrested from us at the pitch to which we had lifted it has since given them ample and bitter cause to reflect) that (in the words of Francis Bacon) they would have done better to ' beware of being too material, when there is any impediment or obstruction in men's wills : for preoccupation of mind ever requireth preface of speech ; like a fomentation to make the unguent enter '.

Finally, there could be no better parable of my persuasion and purpose than what Lord Ernest Hamilton says of Hermitage Castle, so well known to me as a boy (see his *Old Days and New*, p. 316) :

> ' I know no ruin which is so impressive as Hermitage, impressive in its splendid isolation and in the curious suggestion of habitability which it carries in its massive substantial walls. . . . The place is, of course, technically a ruin, and internally it is literally a ruin, but it has neither the appearance nor the common characteristics of a ruin. There is no symptom of decay about its huge shell, which looks as if it might at any moment pour forth from the great doorway a troop of Border riders, with their leather jackets, their steel caps, and their faces set southward.'

That is only another way of phrasing what the *Times Literary Supplement* recognized when it said, *apropos* my first volume of Scots lyrics :

> ' He writes in the faith without which there can be no conquest ; the belief that Scotland still has something to say to the imagination of mankind, something that she alone among the nations can say, and can say only in her native tongue '.

For, as Vivante says, in poetry ' the words find by themselves a thousand avenues, the deepest and truest conceptional affinities ; " they reconnect forgotten kinships " '.

The Borders account in full measure for another element, for, as Lord Tweedsmuir, a fellow Borderer (who, in introducing my first volume of Scots lyrics, found in it ' a proof that a new spirit is to-day abroad in the North, which, as I have said, is both conservative and radical—a determination to keep Scotland in the main march of the world's interests, and at the same time to forgo no part of her ancient heritage '), says :

' Yet the centuries of guerilla warfare had produced something more than hardihood and independence. The Border was the home of harpers and violers, and from it came some of the loveliest of northern airs, and most of the great ballads in any literature. It had always had a tradition of rude minstrelsy, for during the peace of the winter season, at the Yule and Hogmanay revels, at the burgh fairs, at sheep-clippings and " kirns ",[1] and at the shieling doors in the long summer twilights, wandering minstrels would sing of old days, of the fairies in the green-wood and the kelpies in the loch, and of some deed of prowess the rumour of which had drifted across the hills. Out of this tradition, perhaps some time in the sixteenth century, the great ballads were made by singers whose names have been lost—maybe the dead poets chronicled in Dunbar's " Lament of the Makars ". The innominate balladists left behind them poetry which often reached the highest levels of art, and which at the same time woke an immediate response in those for whom it was composed. So the Borderer, however scanty his learning, fell heir to a body of great literature, passed by word of mouth from father to son.'

That's it. That's what's behind me and in me. But we are a queer lot, we Borderers. Mention of Lord Tweedsmuir reminds me how I once went to take tea with him while he was yet John Buchan, M.P., in the House of Commons. I had just been going for England head first—in other words, I had fallen from the top of a London double-decker motor-bus going at speed, and landed on my head on the pavement, sustaining severe concussion. I did not fracture, but it was a miracle I did not break my neck. We were speaking of this, and then Mr. Buchan told me he had fractured his skull twice and showed me the consequent grooves on his head. But some time later a friend told me that he had been speaking to Mr. Buchan and my name had cropped up, whereupon Mr. Buchan at once exclaimed : 'Ah, yes ! Poor Grieve. Most unfortunate fellow. Always fracturing his skull ! '

[1] I.e. Harvest Homes.

CHAPTER II

PORTRAIT OF A GUTTERSNIPE

' Without cudgelling our brains, we can all think of a dozen celebrities acclaimed by the crowd, flattered in the papers, made welcome by ministers, noblemen, and rich ladies, whose lives are poisoned none the less by a handful of uppish intellectuals who will not accept the verdict. Such gnats raise trifling lumps ; but they itch and the mighty scratch. One wonders why. Can it be that sometimes, between three and four of a morning, the celebrities suspect that the ragamuffins may be right ? Can it be that these highbrows and intellectuals, call them by what bad name you will, are the attendant skeletons at the feasts of the be-knighted painters and best-selling authors ? ' —CLIVE BELL.

' This is not genius, but the impudence of a gamin. It is not poetry. Here, most frequently, we have neither rhyme nor reason. We have the utterance of much that should never find expression in decent society, of the healthily sane. . . . It sounds like Homer after he had swallowed his false teeth.'—VERY REV. LAUCHLAN MACLEAN WATT, ex-Moderator of the Church of Scotland. (Reviewing ' To Circumjack Cencrastus '.)

' To hold the interest of a reader throughout a poem of such length—a poem, moreover, in which a man of remarkable calibre and audacity is throwing himself up against some of the most intricate and subtle problems in philosophy, aesthetics, and religion—is no ordinary feat. I cannot think of any living poet except MacDiarmid who could do it. . . . It gives us the rich fermentation, and much of the pure wine, of the most vital mind in present-day Scotland.'—WILLIAM POWER. (Reviewing ' To Circumjack Cencrastus '.)

' Mr. MacDiarmid's work is so immense in its range and in some respects so incomprehensible that it might well be termed a " pantheistic " poem, absorbing people, institutions, and things into an infinite but unknowable " One " (like the Brahma of the Hindus or the Absolute of Hegel)—the " One " in this case being the mind of Mr. MacDiarmid, so great in its power and all-embracing egotism. . . . He has given us a " MacDiarmid Universe ", and whatever our criticisms may be, they cannot alter the fact that the peculiar nail pointed genius of this modernist poet will overhang literary Scotland like a vast cupola, shutting out the sun we have been accustomed to, but glowing with an elusive light of its own.'—JOHN MCLENNAN BOYD.

I WAS born, as I have said, in the little Dumfriesshire town of Langholm, on the 11th of August, 1892. Being now in my 48th year, I am perhaps at that ' crown of the hill ' which is the best stance for surveying my life—old enough, and yet still near enough all the matters of which I must write to have the advantage of undimmed memories of them. I have travelled a long way intellectually and otherwise during these forty-eight years, yet, as I have hinted in the preceding chapter, I have in many respects all but physically come full circle. All the chief elements of my life to-day, however developed and enriched by subsequent experience, were quick in me by at least my early teens, and I am now, despite my long absence from the scenes of my boyhood, more of a Langholmite than ever .

39

I was, indeed, fully conscious of some of these elements not only before I came to my teens, but as far back as I can remember—and my very earliest recollections carry me back to the time I was four—I was no child prodigy ; any more than I have proved a world beater since ; indeed, my brother did much better at school than I did—I had an insuperable objection to medal and bursary competitions and the like, an objection which has since made me continuously contemptuous of the directions in which one competes with one's fellows, and more and more determined to plough a lonely furrow and concentrate upon matters in which there is no competition and in which to achieve effects which are *sui generis* is the very essence of the task, ' that frontier ', as Chestov says, ' beyond which the might of general ideas ceases '. My objection to the competitive system developed the widest applications ; my hatred of all forms of trade and commerce stems from that (Sir J. M. Barrie has declared that it ' is a gr-r-and sight to see a Scotchman on the make ' ; I have never been able to appreciate it in the least), and so does my indifference to money. (Let me interpolate a good story against myself here. A year or two ago I was travelling down to Manchester, and at Preston a commercial traveller, obviously a Jew, got in. He was determined to talk to me, and began grumbling about the state of business, averring that he might as well have stayed in London for all the orders he had booked. I was disinclined for conversation and gave him no encouragement. Observing this, he asked, after a while, what line I was in. Just for devilment, I said, ' Poet.' ' Oh,' he retorted. ' But surely there isn't any call for that sort of thing at this time of day ' !)

I was very early determined that I would not ' work for money ', and that whatever I might have to do to earn my living, I would never devote more of my time and my energies to remunerative work than I did to voluntary and gainless activities, and *actes gratuits*, in Gide's phrase. The notion of self-advancement—of so-called success—was utterly foreign to my nature from the very beginning. I have held to that determination throughout, giving infinitely more of my services free than for payment. I probably owed my inclination to go in for ' public work ' to my father ; I was certainly (to use the French word) very much *mouvementé* from the time I was fourteen onwards, with the exception of the years I was on active service (another form of the same thing, of course) during the War until recently. The way in which I have been debarred by circumstance from ' public work ' or, as I prefer to call it, ' active citizenship ' during the past few years has been one of the greatest hardship of an exceedingly trying phase of my life. And certainly, though my parents were very devout believers and very Churchy people, I must have been very young when I arrived at the position—which I have never abandoned since—which Professor Kemp Smith defines when he says : ' Hume's attitude to true religion can therefore be summed up in the threefold thesis : (1) that it consists exclusively in *intellectual* assent to the somewhat ambiguous, at least undefined proposition, " God exists " ; (2) that the " God " here affirmed is not God as ordinarily understood ; and (3) as a corollary from (1) and (2) that religion ought not to have, and when " true " and " genuine " does not have any influence on human conduct—beyond, that is to say, its intellectual effects, as rendering the mind immune to superstition and fanaticism.'

I have said I have come back to my starting point all but physically. Physically I am at the extreme other end of my country. I came to Whalsay, this little north Isle of the Shetland Group, in 1933. I was absolutely down-and-out at the time—with no money behind me at all, broken down in health, unable to secure remunerative employment of any kind, and wholly concentrated on projects in poetry and other literary fields which could bring me no monetary return whatever, involved continuous intense effort ridiculously out of proportion to my strength, and called for facilities, in the way of books, papers, and even intercourse—the friction of mind upon mind, since isolation and a too complete self-centredness were definitely dangerous, not only to the qualities of the work to be produced but to my own mental stability or, if scarcely that—for if I had been capable of developing any form of insanity, I would certainly have carried myself irrevocably over the border line long ago—at least to the generation and maintenance of the necessary, or at any rate the most helpful, moods.

We—that is to say, my wife, our son (now going on five, and so a baby then of little more than eighteen months), and I—have been ' marooned ' in Whalsay ever since, and are like to remain so. Things, indeed, have worsened. Four years ago there were still papers and periodicals in Scotland open to contributions from my pen. The principal newspapers had always rigidly excluded me ; but some of the few organs that used to be open to me have now ceased publication, and I had ceased to be *persona grata* to the others. After (as will be seen) one most unfortunate interlude in London, and a subsequent year in Liverpool (equally unfortunate, but for other and far more painful reasons, and owing perhaps to a considerable extent to my own blame), I have been desperately anxious not to leave Scotland again—though life in the Shetlands, albeit part of Scotland, involves a virtual expatriation all the more exasperating because it is a case of ' so near—and yet so far '. But if there is one thing abundantly clear, it is that I need never look for a suitable post in Scotland, or indeed for regular employment, a staff job of any kind. I am not complaining ; but this complete boycott is a fact to take into consideration alongside the following public testimonial presented to me in the Spring of 1936 and signed by Sir James Barrie, the late R. B. Cunninghame-Graham, Compton Mackenzie,

Lady Londonderry, Sir Herbert J. C. Grierson, Edward Garnett, Sean O'Casey, and several hundreds of other well-known people, including practically every contemporary Scottish writer of any consequence whatever :

> ' We, your fellow writers in Scotland and elsewhere, and other friends, whose signatures are appended hereto, desire to express our profound sense of the great services you have rendered to Scots letters and to literature in general.
>
> ' The place you have won as a poet is that of creative pioneer, inimitably bodying forth the form of things unknown, fusing passion and intellect, enlarging human and Scottish consciousness, and bringing your own country into vital touch with the main currents of world thought. Our appreciation of your genius is deepened by the fact that in your spontaneous self-expression you have expressed also the struggle of the Scots soul to regain a fuller and freer sense of the eternal universe of things. You are more than a " typical " Scot; you are the " different " Scot who, by the magic of a genius which is at the same time intimately Scottish and widely European, can raise native elements to a higher, a universal, synthesis. It was through this power, exercised with passionate and gallant disinterestedness, and always with Scotland as the background and inspiration of your achievements, that you became a major force in the cultural and national life of your own country, supplying the dynamic of many forward movements.
>
> ' Genius is beyond calculation and above appraisement, but at least we can express our thankfulness that your high powers have been so closely allied with the intellectual cause of Scotland; and we can express also our admiration and esteem for a distinguished writer who has never swerved from his central purpose or failed to give kindly encouragement to anyone who had the highest interests of Scotland or its literature sincerely at heart.
>
> ' We trust that you may be spared for many years to bring fresh honour and inspiration to Scotland.'

In any other country in the world, I venture to think, a testimonial of that kind, signed by all his leading literary compatriots and other distinguished public figures, as well as by many famous foreign writers, would have signified that the recipient had ' *arrived* ' in the fullest sense of the term—crowned as one of his country's famous men and representative writers by a consensus of the best-qualified opinion. But it is precisely of the very essence of the problem of Scotland to-day, to which my life has been dedicated, that such a testimonial is compatible with the outcast condition, the freezing-out process, I have described. It is not wise to look a gift horse in the mouth, but I cannot forebear a shrewd glance at the teeth of this testimonial. I do not agree (not through any undue modesty) with the wording of it. I have, as will appear, a much narrower and more exact sense of my achievement. The flattering phrases describe my aspirations, my ambitions, well enough. But this testimonial came at a time when the Scottish national and cultural movements with which I had been so actively concerned seemed to me to have become completely perverted and to have entirely forfeited my sympathy and support. I had founded the Scottish Centre of the International P.E.N. Club and taken an active part as Scottish delegate in the Annual Congresses in Austria and in Holland. I had ceased to be a member of it. Along with Cunninghame-Graham and Compton Mackenzie I had helped to form the National Party of Scotland. I had now been expelled from it, and not only had no sympathy at all with the way in which it had developed, but was wholly and implacably opposed to it and to almost all of its leading personnel. I had been personally friendly with many, perhaps most, of the writers who signed the Testimonial, but I had now ceased to have any contacts whatever with most of them, and certainly could not have reciprocated their flattery to even the smallest extent. On the contrary, I was disappointed in those few of them of whom I had ever had any hope ; most of the others I regarded as mere con-founders of counsel and cumberers of the ground, intellectually, artistically, and politically negligible where indeed they were not a positive nuisance. I had long known, if I had ever for a moment imagined otherwise, that I had nothing whatever in common with them. I realized too that the Testimonial was likely to do me more harm than good. I have always had far more enemies than friends in Scotland—I should be greatly perturbed were it otherwise—and the former were always far more active than the latter—if indeed for the most part the latter were not so indistinguishable from the former as always to give me ample cause to cry : ' Deliver me from my friends '. It was certainly not without good reason that my friend, Kaikhosru Shapurji Sorabji, dedicated his *Opus Clavicembalisticum* (Messrs. Curwen & Sons, Ltd., 1931) to me in these terms :

To my Two Friends (E DUOBUS UNUM) :

HUGH MACDIARMID

and

C. M. GRIEVE

LIKEWISE

TO THE EVERLASTING GLORY OF THOSE FEW MEN
BLESSED AND SANCTIFIED IN THE CURSES
AND EXECRATIONS OF THOSE MANY
WHOSE PRAISE IS ETERNAL DAMNATION

No modern Scot has been less likely to forget that, as Alexander Webster says : ' If we take the period of dogmatic dominance from 1649 till 1843, we find the manifestation of the native mind in Hume, Burns and Carlyle, rather than in any of the leaders in the orthodox field. The deeper sincerity and more vital thought came out in expressions which were treated as heretical. We trace the line of spontaneity and verity from one reprobated man to another—the daring thinkers who stood forth against dogmatic dictation and the shams of conformity.' And in fact the most atrocious jealousy was the first consequence of this unique presentation, and a very thorough campaign was at once launched to sabotage my reputation and undo my work—an attack that, cut off as I was from all the Scottish Press, I was in a much worse position to meet than ever before ; an attack moreover conducted for the most part in organs actually controlled by signatories of the Testimonial. In so far from crowning my work, then, this Testimonial largely represented a disposal of me—the signatories (or some of them) felt that they had done the gallant and generous thing and so for the future I could be safely ignored. And indeed whatever truth was in the phrases of the Testimonial was, I knew, not the truth to *them*—I knew most of them well enough not to credit them with any concern for or even understanding of either what I had attempted to do or actually done. It was, of course, very kind of them all, and I was duly grateful—though it meant little or nothing, and has certainly added to my difficulties instead of (as the prime movers in the matter meant it to do) decreasing them. All this, I think, is peculiarly Scottish. It must not be imagined that I think the signatories did not act in perfectly good faith—they thought they thought what the document said all right—but they are for the most part just hopelessly muddle-headed, anti-intellectual, and with a loose amiability which constantly leads them to sign this and that and the next thing and contribute mites here, there, and everywhere—and with no disinterested or serious concern with any intellectual cause whatever. They are entirely typical of the vast mass of the Scottish people to-day in their utter inability to accept or conceive the artist's doom—to live by absolutes, come what may, instead of being mere family providers driven to press for security, whatever the cost. They all live less by principles than by mutual tolerance, less by logic than by humour. (I have all the humourlessness in the world in such connexions, and am, of course, utterly unreasonable in the sense in which recently, when a member of the City Council was opposing the granting of the Freedom of Edinburgh to a Royal Duchess and remarked that it ought rather to be given to one of the city's heroic working-class mothers, the Lord Provost sharply called him to order and adjured him to be ' reasonable ' in his opposition.) My story, on the contrary, is the story of an absolutist whose absolutes came to grief in his private life (leading to a whole host of slanders responsible for the bad name he has now been given, as a dipsomaniac, wife-beater, and Heaven knows what else). Came to grief—for, of course, the ' lucky ' in my title embraces both good luck and bad—and I am not sure which has been the luckier for me ; I am certainly equally grateful for each, as the earth for summer and winter. But despite that tragedy (or, perhaps, because of it) I have pulled my world together again in such wise that, asserted more strongly than ever now, I am very unlikely to come to grief in it a second time. I may have paid in pain for my

insights into the universe, but the pain has gone—the insights
remain ; ' Richard is himself again '.   Faustus-like, I have tried to
encompass all experience, and find myself at last happy enough
marooned on this little island of Whalsay and only very slightly, I
think, in any relevant respect, a failure.   In my address to ' The
Kelpie in the Dorts ', I sang

> . . . Multiply new shades o' joy and pain
> Kittle and mony-shaped as licht or rain,
> Tak' nae fixed shape.   Nae suner kythe [1] in ane
> Than to anither 'yout belief you're gane
> Until you show in sicna sequence plain
> A' that we'd tine [2] if you s'ud halt and hain [3]
> This form or that, that silly folk are fain
> To fix. . . .

And went on to pray—banish our beliefs or glorify them, overturn
our sanctities or honour them,

> . . . shed on us bliss or bane ;
> But oot and aboot !   Nor in the *dorts* [4] be lain.

I could not have lived anywhere else that is known to me these last
four years without recourse to the poorhouse.   We were not only
penniless when we arrived in Whalsay—I was in exceedingly bad
state, psychologically and physically.   I am always least able to
to ' put my best foot forward ' and do anything that brings in money
when I am hardest up.   I do my best work when I have most irons
in the fire, and the fact that here I had all my time to myself and had
' nothing to do but write ' for a long time made it almost impossible
for me to do anything at all and is, recurrently, a drawback still.
Besides, I was ' out of touch with things '—I had not the advantage
of being ' on the spot ' where ' anything might be going '—and worst
of all I had no books.   Indeed, we had practically no furniture.   I
succeeded in getting a nice commodious four-roomed cottage standing on a hillside and looking out over a tangled pattern of complicated
tideways, *voes*, and islands with snaggled coasts to the North Shetland
mainland and the Atlantic—for 27s. *per annum* !   Houses are
practically impossible to get ;   I got mine because a little earlier a
child had died in it under tragic circumstances, and the islanders
were fighting shy of it.   I have forgotten what that first winter was
like ;   no doubt my wife remembers all too well—it must have been
one long nightmare of cold and damp and darkness and discomfort.
Comfort never mattered very much to me, and after all one of my
poems begins ' To Hell with Happiness ', and I have always been
accustomed to practise what I preach—I only write what I live.   I
am not a ' knacky ' person ;   what furniture we had at the beginning

---

[1] kythe = appear.   [2] tine = lose.
[3] hain = keep.   [4] dorts = sulks.

was made for the most part by my wife out of orange boxes, tea boxes, and the like.

Somehow or other—in the face of all likelihood—we have flourished (never sufficiently, of course, to be secure at any time for more than a week ahead). To-night as I sit writing, the cottage is amply and comfortably furnished, and though I have never succeeded in securing again many of the books which were the background of my own earliest books and which, many of them, were and remain so vital to my creative processes that in their absence I have subtly to reorient my writing in other directions than, if I could recover my old collections, I would be likely to take, many hundreds of books have accumulated about me again; all my principal intellectual interests are well represented and catered for—geology, biochemistry, plant ecology, physiology, psychology, and philosophy—and I have a fine array of the works of my favourite writers, Rainer Maria Rilke, Charles Doughty, Stefan George, Paul Valery in poetry, Leo Chestov in philosophy, Pavlov's *Lectures on Conditioned Reflexes*, and Lenin, Stalin, Marx, Engels, Adoratsky, and other dialectical materialist writers.

It is not a restful place in which to write. The cottage is rattling like a 'tin lizzie' in a 90-miles-per-hour wind, and every now and again there is a terrific rattling of hail. We have had well-nigh continuous gales, with heavy snow-storms and great downpours of rain, for the last two months—the worst winter the Shetlands have had within living memory.

It is, indeed, a curious turn of fortune's wheel that has pent me in this little cottage where I who used to be so active in public work of all kinds a few years ago, and who ' went everywhere and knew everybody ', can go for a week at a time and see no one to exchange a word with—nay, even so much as get a passing glimpse of anyone— except my wife and son ; and, indeed, except for the local doctor (a friend whose presence here brought me to this island rather than to any of the sixty other inhabited islands in this archipelago) and one or two others, I go in this case often, not for a week, but for a month at a time. Yet I do not allow myself to become rusty, and somehow or other I contrive to keep wonderfully *au courant* with all that is going on in most of the departments of arts and affairs all over the world, and despite my almost Trappist existence here can go down to Manchester and keep my end up, discussing Faroese literature with Professor E. V. Gordon, the authority on Gothic and Old Norse ; or ultra-modern developments in music—and the relationship of the great bag-pipe music—the *Ceol Mor*—to plainsong and the neuma with Professor H. B. Charlton ; or racial and archaeological questions with Professor H. J. Fleure ; or geology with Professor Lang ; or the poetry of Trakl and other little-known German poets I like for the sake of a certain Gothicity or the role of *grotesquerie* in revitalizing phases of literature with Professor Barker Fairley without feeling too much of an ignoramus, backwoodsman, or has been. Or go from the austerities of this prohibitionist area back to London for a spell in Soho again and the company of such Bohemians as Eileen Comtesse de Vismes, Nina Hamnett, the authoress of *Laughing Torso*, Betty May, the 'Tiger Woman', Aleister Crowley, and the rest of them. I feel equally at home in all the rooms of life. (Incidentally I may say that if I have been a collector of anything it has been Professors—only I did not collect them deliberately; it just happened. Charles Sarolea, Sir Herbert J. C. Grierson, the late J. S. Phillimore, Walter Starkie of Dublin, Denis Saurat of King's College, the late Sir Patrick Geddes, Janko Lavrin of Nottingham University, Professor William Rose, Professor Louis Cazamian of the Sorbonne—the list is endless, and I must have discussed almost everything under the sun with them. Geddes, indeed, latterly at any rate, did *that* himself every time he opened his mouth, and, alas! a great deal more!)

And, in America, there is, amongst others, Professor Herbert Faulkner West of Dartmouth College, Hanover, New Hampshire, the friend and biographer of Cunninghame-Graham, who writes me:

'I have always had a real interest in Scotland, not because some of my people came from there, but because what I have seen of the country has given me a lasting and most favourable impression. I've never been west, however, of Inverary, save by sea, and during the first World War I was close by on another transport when the *Otranto* went down off Islay. I wrote this up in a sea story two years ago but at that time could find no publisher interested in war transports, and up to date have not rewritten the first part, which I agree with them needs revising. However, I became interested in the National Party through Cunninghame-Graham, and under his auspices learned what little I know about Scotland. As a book collector, too, I have kept up fairly well with contemporary Scotsmen's writings. . . . Whether or not you are still living in the remote Shetlands I cannot know, but if you ever do get this letter please accept my thanks for the pleasure your poetry and prose have given me. There are a few kindred spirits writing in the world to-day, and with a certain amount of intellectual humility, I recognize one in yourself. I, too, have long admired Doughty and Blunt; my wife is a Robson, for three hundred years a Swedish family, but once from Scotland, and most of what you have written I should have liked to have written myself.'

My friends and acquaintances are indeed legion, and in the ups-and-downs of my life I have been accustomed to mix on all levels (and have never lost a friend once made—except once; and in that case, as I shall show, the one I happened to value most and for whom I would if need be have sacrificed all the others). Those I encountered (many of them old friends of mine) the last time I was in London included Augustus John, 'Michael Arlen', Lazarus Aaronson, the poet, Emily Coleman, authoress of that extraordinary book,

The Shutter of Snow, Oliver Simon, the printing expert, B. J. Boothroyd (' Gadfly ' of the *New Leader*), Will Dyson, Ethel Mannin, William and Beatrice Kean Seymour, Paul Selver, Edgell Rickwood, ' Stephen Hudson ', Ruth Pitter, Austin Clarke the Irish poet, Stephen Graham, Charles Duff, of the Press Department of the Foreign Office and author of the famous *Handbook to Hanging*, Olive Moore, Malachi Whitaker, John Brophy, H. E. Bates, John Rodker, Rhys Davies, L. A. Pavey, the short-story writer (who, during the War, was a co-N.C.O. of mine at the Sections Lahore Indian General Hospital, stationed at Marseilles, and who holidayed with me in the Pyrenees at Cirque de Gavarnie, Pau, Lourdes and elsewhere), Gerald Kersh, Philip Jordan, Anna Wickham, Mairin Mitchell, Frank Kenyon, Geoffrey Grigson of *New Verse*, George Malcolm Thomson, Alexander Werth (the brilliant analyst of modern French politics and Paris correspondent of the *Manchester Guardian*), Sydney R. Elliot, editor of *Reynolds*, Desmond Harmsworth, Kay Boyle, Robert Lynd, C. B. Purdom, Watson Thompson, editor of *New Britain*, and Donald and Catherine Carswell. Again I frequented ' Douglasite ' circles a good deal and associated with Major C. H. Douglas himself, Arthur Brenton, editor of the *New Age*, John Hargrave, the leader of the Green Shirts and later I think Economic Adviser to Mr. Aberhart's Government in Alberta, the Rev. V. A. Demant, Maurice B. Reckitt, W. T. Symons, editor of *Purpose*, R. McNair Wilson, the two (very different) veterans, Frederick J. Gould and the late A. J. Penty, Philip Mairet, editor of the *New English Weekly*, Michael Sayers, John Shand, the dramatic critic, and all the rest of them. Again I was in the company of young Esmond Romilly, Mr. Winston Churchill's nephew, and already a Communist, later to fight with the International Brigade for the Spanish Government, like two other friends of mine (Ralph Fox and Tom Wintringham), John Strachey, the Hon. Ivor Montague, the Hon. Nancy Cunard. My friends included, too, such extraordinary characters as Count Geoffrey Potocki de Montalk, editor of the *Right Review* (who went and still goes about London wearing a long red cloak—as did his brother, Count Cedric—and whose cottage at Thakeham in Sussex I ' took on ' while he was in gaol for publishing obscene literature), that amazing Serbian ' village Jesus ', Dimitri Metrinovic, and that Napoleon *manqué*, A. G. Pape, whose ancestors on either side embraced almost all the great diplomats of France and of Great Britain and with whom, for a time, I had a good deal to do in Edinburgh. There is no one else on the island who has any intellectual interests or who reads anything except a newspaper, a magazine, or a detective novel. The local teachers may occasionally—very occasionally—read something outside these narrow limits, but not much. Yet I get on well with the island people when I do meet them, and of this I am sure—that I know no group of my fellow writers, no group of intellectuals or politicians, with whom I would be happier to associate than I am with the entirely unlettered crews of the little sailing-boats on which I go to the herring fishing, thirty miles beyond the Ramna Stacks on the edge of the Main Deep. Nor indeed, though (in so far as I can afford the postage stamps) I have a world-wide correspondence and know many of the most distinguished writers, politicians, and other public figures in the world to-day, do I wish I was placed where (with one or two exceptions, and these by no means the best known) I could see more of these people because of any importance I attach to them as apart from my personal liking for them. How I got in touch with them all is, in fact, a mystery ; I have never been a collector of celebrities ; my considered opinion now is that almost all of them are very small beer indeed. Indeed, it is here in the Shetlands, where it seems that the end has already been reached to which the whole of the rest of the world is tending, that reduction to bare rock and water and light still hidden elsewhere in trees and the activities of industrial civilization—as in the wilds of Africa of which A. R. Orage wrote years ago : ' I shall be told that events like the rise of China, the Russian Revolution, the discovery of the North and South Poles, and the invention of the aeroplane, not to mention the great social movements of labour and capital, are as great as any that ever inspired a dramatist. And I shall reply that there is not a shadow of hopeful wonder, of awe, of grandeur, of beauty, of mystery, or even of intelligent human power, in one of them. Go into the wilds of Africa and be out of reach of newspapers for a month or two, and the whole cosmic show fades into trivial gossip.' One comes down to bedrock and, alive, one feels indeed ' this smoke of thought blow clean away, and leave the steadfast and enduring bone '—' the last of life, for which the first was made '. Or, as I have put it in one of my short stories, ' But now—this ! hard, intrinsic, whittled down to the last essentiality and directness, cruel yet so unswervingly sure in its concentration, so distinct in its surety. Does it not make you aware of another freer element in which each fate is detached and isolated ? Here is no confusion. Is not this our natural element ? ' I have written elsewhere : ' Just as the adventures, the dangers, the thrills of work in these dim Northern waters are best brought out, not by over-statement, but by a calm regard for fact and an intimate knowledge of the subject—just as the fishermen are engaged in a trade that still demands the qualities of individual judgement, courage, and hardihood that tend to disappear both from literature and life elsewhere—the Shetlands call alike in the arts and in affairs for the true creative spirit. Anything pettier would be sadly out of place in these little-known and lonely regions, encompassed about with the strange beauty of the North, the fluctuation of unearthly colours at different levels of the sun, the

luminous air, the gleam of distant ice, and the awful stillness of
Northern fog.   Or transfigured with such marvellous spectacles as
when ' the stars are almost dimmed by the shaking curtain of aurora,
at first a nebulous radiance but gradually changing to clear-cut
ribbons of light, quivering and wavering like seaweed fixed to a rock
in a strong tide'.   As I have put it in one of my Shetland poems
(' Raised Beach ' in *Stony Limits*, 1934) :

> It will be ever increasingly necessary to find
> In the interests of all mankind
> Men capable of rejecting all that all other men
>   Think as a stone remains
> Essential to the world, inseparable from it,
>   And rejects all other life yet.
> Great work cannot be combined with surrender to the crowd.
> —Nay, the truth we seek is as free
> From all yet thought as a stone from humanity.
> Here where there is neither haze nor hesitation
> Something at least of the necessary power has entered into me
> I have still to see any manifestation of the human spirit
> That is worthy of a moment's longer exemption than it gets
> From petrifaction again—to get out if it can.
> All is lithogenesis—or lochia ;
> And I can desire nothing better.
> An immense familiarity with other men's imaginings
> Convinces me they cannot either
> (If they could, it would instantly be granted
> —The present order must continue till then)
> Though, of course, I still keep an open mind,
> A mind as open as the grave.

How do I get on—in so far as I encounter them at all—with the
local crofters and fishermen ?

These men belong to an age when man's sense of the drama of
life was strong and undimmed by the physical ease and psychological difficulty of urban living.   It may be said of them, as Pierre
van Paassen says of the people of Bourg-en-Forêt : ' Those peasants
amongst whom we lived were poor in worldly goods ; they lacked
many of the modern amenities of life, but they did not envy those
who had them.   Thoughts of to-morrow did not torture them. . . .
Their rule was to " cultivate their own gardens ".   I think that the
serenity of their existence, which often evoked the envy of strangers
who watched them, resided in the fact that they insisted on being
men before social beings.   They were individualists.   They were
content to be human.   Thus they had retained something of that
fundamental dignity which is the sole condition of human happiness
because it is both our physiological norm and the law of nature.'
But while I recognize and value this for all it is worth—and find
concerning the Shetlands and still more the Hebrides and the Faroes,
compared with the cities of England and Scotland, and most European
cities, that, as Struthers Burt says of America, ' the small town and

city of the Far West is always a less provincial place than towns and
cities of equal size in the East and Middle West ' (though Lerwick,
the capital of the Shetlands—a place I avoid like the plague, seldom
leaving the lonely North Isles to go near it at all—is an exception,
and it would be difficult to find any place where the citizens are more
class conscious—though not in the Marxian sense—more purse-
proud, more snooty towards their supposed inferiors, more utterly
destitute of all intellectual and artistic interests—a place where, just
as Benjamin Franklin never succeeded in making himself quite
' socially acceptable ' to the Philadelphia gentry, no poet or painter
or composer could ever make himself socially acceptable to these
smug *bourgeois*, or Christ himself to these self-righteous Church-
goers !), it must not be imagined for a moment that I think that
dialectic after dialectic, in destroying the conception of man as a
person that it was the great glory of the mediaeval thinkers to have
formulated, has destroyed human individuality, or that André
Malraux is wrong when he calls Communism ' a great fertilizer of
individuality '. I do not value the mediaeval conception, or think
that its disintegration has been any human loss. Nor do I agree at
all that if Man can now be conceived as ' but a place of intersection
and conflict of a primarily sexual libido and a desire for death ' and
this depersonalized being is ready to abdicate in favour of the
collective man, and that with this abdication a socialist humanism
can arise, to that idea of a socialist humanism can reasonably be
opposed a ' true or integral ' humanism in Jacques Maritain's sense, a
humanism which would restore the Aquinean person defined as ' a
unity of a spiritual nature endowed with freedom of choice, and so
forming a whole which is independent of the world, for neither
nature nor the state may invade this unity without the permission
of God himself '. I have no belief whatever in a ' Christianly
secular conception of the temporal order ' in which true or integral
humanism with its idea of the person as a spiritual and inviolable
unity would be made more and more realizable, because I do not
believe in the validity of these categories, the sense of these terms, or
that mediaeval man was any better realized and complete a human.
being than modern man, and because I do not believe in God at all.
Like Etienne Gilson, ' I still want to know if my religious experience
is an experience of God, or an experience of myself. . . . In the first
case only can there be a religion. . . . I can follow Bergson in his
description of mystical intuition as a source of religious life, but I am
still left wondering what the nature of that intuition actually is.'
Only I do not ' still want to know ', I *know*—it is just ' an experience
of myself '. There is no religion. And there is a great deal more
to be said of irreligious socialism than Maritain says, when he
declares : ' It was a noble work to bring capitalist civilization to
trial and to waken against powers that know no pardon, the sense of

justice and the dignity of labour.' There is nothing I object to more than Christianity's appropriation of everything decent and upright in humanity as directly or indirectly a product of Christian teaching, and certainly if it can be said of me, as I think it can, as Pierre van Paassen says of himself, that ' the ashes of the martyrs beat against his heart, whenever or wherever in this world there is an injustice or a wrong committed ', the credit does not lie with the Church of Scotland, or Christianity at large, at all! I am all for the driving, restless movement of the critical intellect, and my withers are quite unwrung no matter who may stigmatize that as ' a defect of contemporary society which has split into segments that integration of life from which poetry and joy both flower '.

The first time I went out with the Shetland herring fishing fleet I was on a sailing vessel. It was—this was in 1933—one of the very few still left of a fleet that had used to number many hundreds. But the competition of motor boats and steam drifters and trawlers had been too much for them. They could not compete in the race to land their catches and secure a good market. Now they are all gone. I am glad to have had an experience of them before they disappeared. It was the most exhilarating and enjoyable of all my sea experiences, and to-day if I could take over any other man's job I think it would undoubtedly be that of the Finn, Captain Gustav Erikson, who from a two-roomed office in the tiny port of Marienhamn in the Aland Islands in the Baltic directs the coming and going of his fleet of great wind-jammers—the *Pamir*, *Archibald Russell*, *Olivebank*, *Lawhill*, and all the rest of them—upon the oceans of the world. Captain Erikson's job—or that of any of his officers! Lovely vessels! Sail—the finest training possible not only in seamanship, but also in all the qualities of character and resource that the sea demands.

I like these Shetland fishermen—at least when they are on the job—and I have dreamed of poetry that would do them justice ; poems so accurate both in their boat-handling and racing strategy that only one who knew all the intricacies of sailing and racing (which I have been steadily learning all these years) could do them ; poems that all who like small-boat sailing will delight in, full of thumb-nail sketches of local characters—like that

> Wistful child of whim,
> Whose boating skill held scarce a mental notion,
> 'Twas grounded all on love and sheer emotion. . . .
> His moustache settled to a careless droop,
> And, when the icicles began to loop
> Their bases round its fringes, he would look
> Like a walrus peering from an island nook.

And I would call the book *Haaf-Fishers' Lodge*, and have it hand-set and bound in sailcloth, and have illustrations by my friend Peter

Anson, the artist-author and great authority on fishing-boats and the fishing industry. Both for good and bad it is true of the Shet-lander's way of life as Marjorie Barstow Greenbie in her *American Saga* says of the New Englander's way of life : ' This was determined by his occupation, which was sea-faring. Careless people get drowned at sea. So he was careful. Untidy people die of disease at sea. So he learned to be neat and clean. On the other hand, those who learned how to live on the sea have great security. They can go long distances. They can invest their money in profitable ventures. They can bring back all sorts of luxuries and adornments. They feel that they need not bow the head to anybody, nor envy anybody : what they want they can go and get.'

It is amazing that the Shetlands should have given us no poetry—above all, no sea poetry. Desmond Holdridge in *Northern Lights*, that yarn of reckless voyaging, writes : ' There was the co-existence of the uttermost extreme of terror side by side with the wildest elation. We were completely pulled out of our bodies, wrenched away from our normal mentalities, and exposed, naked, to the wave on wave of sound and violence, the shrieking crescendos that were but the foundations on which were raised super-crescendos. . . . I write that the co-existence of abysmal terror and god-like elation is responsible for much seafaring, especially the small-boat kind, and so it is ; the survivor feels that, if he can design and build the perfect vessel, there will be no terror and only that tremendous thrill.' It was this co-existent terror and elation that found supreme expression in Alexander MacDonald's great sea-poem, ' The Birlinn of Clan-ranald ', of which I have published an English verse translation ; but unlike the Hebrides, the Shetlands have yielded nothing of this sort—no poem that is worth a minute's notice and nothing of any value at all in any of the arts. In this connexion—and in my whole attitude to the use of technical language—my point of view is borne out by Dryden, who said :

> ' In general I will only say I have never yet seen the description of any naval fight in the proper terms which are used at sea ; and if there be any such in another language, as that of Lucan in the third of his *Pharsalia*, yet I could not prevail myself of it in the English ; the terms of arts in every tongue bearing more of the idiom of it than any other words. We hear, indeed, among our poets of the thundering of guns, the smoke, the disorder, and the slaughter, but all these are common notions. And certainly, as those who in a logical dispute keep in general terms would hide a fallacy, so those who do it in any poetical description would veil their ignorance :—
>
> > Descriptas, servare vices, operumque colores,
> > Cur ego, si nequeo ignoroque, poeta salutor ? '

Much to my amusement, I have also found a letter of Sir Walter Scott's in which, replying to a correspondent who suggested that he (Sir Walter) should write a great sea poem, he confesses himself

unable to attempt anything of the sort, since he is the veriest land-
lubber, with no notion of nautical matters or of the proper terminology
for such a purpose.

What Scott said, replying to this correspondent who had conveyed to him a wish from Warren Hastings that he should celebrate
in verse the epic of Trafalgar and the naval war against Napoleon
(*vide The Letters of Sir Walter Scott*, edited by Sir Herbert Grierson,
Vol. XII), is as follows :

> ' In order to produce a picturesque effect in poetry, a very intimate
> knowledge of the subject described is an essential requisite. . . . It
> seems to me indispensably necessary that the poet should have enough
> of seafaring matters to select circumstances which, though individual
> and so trivial as to escape general observation, are precisely those which
> in poetry give life, spirit, and, above all, truth to the description. It is
> this which in painting constitutes the difference betwixt the work of
> one who has studied nature and a mere copyist of others' labours.
> Now, my total and absolute ignorance of everything of, and belonging
> to, the sea would lay me under the necessity of generalizing my descrip-
> tions so much as to render them absolutely tame, or of substituting some
> fantastic and, very probably, erroneous whims of my own for those
> natural touches of reality which ought to enliven and authenticate the
> poem.'

What Scott says there goes a long way towards what I mean in
this book when I insist upon a poetry of fact. What my ideal
amounts to is a poetical equivalent of one of Nature's annual miracles
—the flowering of *Daphne Mezereum*. Many people can never
quite get used to this sudden burgeoning of beauty from the bare
brown twigs, for it seems all against the natural run of things that
this wealth of blossom should come without the formality of green-
sprouting leaves.

Professor E. M. Butler in her study of Rilke compares one of
Rilke's Orpheus sonnets and the magnificent passage on biological
metamorphosis from Paul Valéry's *Le cimetière marin*, as showing ' the
power of a biological fact on one poet, and his statement of it on
another. They also show the difference between the powerful realistic
imagination of someone trained to face facts, and the fanciful play of
a less disciplined mind, sensationalizing and dramatizing them. For
Rilke could not allow the natural process to finish where Valéry so
magnificently left it.'

What I say about facts simply means that I take my stand with
Valéry rather than with Rilke in this matter. I can also say with
Anton Chekhov : ' Familiarity with the natural sciences and with
scientific methods has always kept me on my guard, and I have
always tried, where it was possible, to be consistent with the facts of
science. . . . I may observe in passing that the conditions of
artistic creation do not always admit of complete harmony with the
facts of science. It is impossible to represent upon the stage a death

from poisoning exactly as it takes place in reality. But harmony of the facts of science must be felt even under those conditions—i.e. it must be clear to the reader or spectator that this is only due to the conditions of art, and that he has to do with a writer who understands. I do not belong to the class of literary men who take up a sceptical attitude towards science ; and to the class of those who rush into anything with only their own imagination to go upon, I should not like to belong.'

I have said in one of my poems that there are few things I admire more than the alertness of the mate who, amid the hum of the breeze in the taut weather rigging, and the hiss and spurl of the sea as the forefoot clears a path through the watery waste, can detect a tiny unusual sound and suspect what may be causing it and shout gruffly, ' Get for'ard, boy, and see if the weather sheet of the inner jib is chafing on the forestay ! ' And like Scott I am always on the *qui vive* for those facts ' so trivial as to escape general observation which yet are precisely those which give life, spirit, and, above all, truth '. An excellent example of the kind of thing for which I value a wide range of interests so highly is what happened when Kurt Rockne, the legendary tactician who produced America's greatest football teams a decade and a half ago, took his team, to reward them for hard practice, to a Broadway musical. They were amazed to see how intently he watched the chorus dance. He took an envelope from his pocket and pencilled some notes. That night he cried : ' The girls gave me an idea for a new kind of backfield shift ! ' Using this new shift, Notre Dame's famed Four Horsemen rode to their great victories of 1922–24.

Again, as Mr. Wickham Steed has related : ' The news which enabled Lord Northcliffe to buy a controlling interest in the *Times*, came to him because his love of music and youthful skill as a pianist had enabled him to appreciate the genius of Paderewski.'

But while I am constantly on the look-out for the most unusual and surprising facts, I do not (or try not to) forget the limitations of material of this sort. I always bear in mind the discovery made at the performance of Antheil's *Ballet Mechanique* several years ago : eleven pianos do not make eleven times as much noise as one piano, or even nearly as much. In fact they make less than two pianos, *chose curieuse* but of a verity. Just so eleven successive chirps from the xylophone do not impress the listener eleven times as much as one chirp. The strange and fascinating Schönbergian school of orchestration, so well exemplified in *Der Glückliche Hand*, that consists of combining a small piece of celesta with a small piece of contrabass to make an odd sound containing an unknown quantity ($2\frac{1}{3} + \cdot02 = 4x$, as it were), reached a dead end in *Wozzeck*. Every bar there contains a crash on the tamtam, a flatterzunge, or a violin playing col legno—in other words, an abnormality, and a score filled

with abnormalities is no more effective, as it has been put, than a
novel describing a get together between M. de Charlus, Christine of
Sweden, the Marquis de Sade, and Sacher-Masoch. For a single act
the peculiar noises are valid, and rouse the emotions they are intended
to. But during the long second act they lose their power and clutch,
so that when the real climax is reached in the third act all Berg can
do is to pare down to the celebrated single B in one case, and revert
to a normal diatonic method in the other.

All the same, although scientific speculation has proceeded in the
direction of that *via media* of a modified Uniformitarianism which
Goethe seems to have anticipated, I never forget that, as Lord Kelvin
remarked, such middle path is not generally the safest in scientific
speculation any more than in anything else. And continue to go
myself under Montrose's banner of white damask, the device, a lion
about to leap across a rocky chasm and the motto ' *Nil Medium* ', as,
of course, befits a poet whose life is organized in keeping with Rilke's
words :

> Gesang wie du ihn lehrst, ist nicht Begehr,
> Nicht Werbung um ein endlich noch Erreichtes ;
> Gesang ist Dasein.

> (i.e. Song, as you teach, is not desire, not striving for something
> eventually attained ; song is Being.)

Making poems, however, is very like diamond-polishing—the
' dop ' in which the diamond or poem is held being the poet's
cortical understanding, and the ' schyf ' on which the ' dop ' is held
down to polish the diamond being reason in the fullest sense.

No matter how far-fetched or eccentric my illustrative material
may be, therefore, it is generally worth carefully considering to see
whether it does not disclose far more general bearings than may be
readily imagined. What I have said elsewhere in this book about
Sankara's Vedanta philosophy may seem to many readers just a
typical bit of my extremism and passion for the out-of-the-way, but
while I am undoubtedly attracted to a system which, as Max Muller
said, ' makes us feel giddy, as in mounting the last steps of the swaying
spire of an ancient Gothic cathedral ', it must be allowed that this
example is in keeping with the entire principle and purpose of this
book and of my life-work, since beyond the fact of the extreme
adventurousness of Advaita lies the fact that whereas in the West
Philosophical matters are known only to a select few, the fundamental ideas of the Vedanta, on the contrary, have pervaded the whole
literature of the Hindus and form to this day the common philosophy
of the people at large, or, as Dr. Burnett writes, ' As a purely
intellectual force it (Sankara's Vedanta) has had an incalculable
influence upon the minds and character of millions of Hindus in
nearly every station of life '. So also Paul Deussen says : ' Even
to this day, Sankara's system represents the common beliefs of nearly

all thoughtful Hindus—and deserves to be widely studied in the Occident '.

Reverting to Scott's difficulty with regard to nautical knowledge, I never forget the unfamiliar, almost incredible, truth Mr. Belloc states in his book *On the Place of Gilbert Chesterton in English Letters*, when he says : ' But in his omission of seafaring, he was more national than ever ; for though the English have a strong political and literary passion for the sea, they have as a people little personal familiarity with it, save on its shores '.

This is what Ezra Pound means when he says rightly (in that most admirable book, *How to Read*, which should be required reading for every youth, male and female) : ' After Chaucer we have Gavin Douglas's *Eneados*, better than the original, *as Douglas had heard the sea !* ' (Italics and exclamation mark mine.)

Most English poets apparently have never heard the sea—and consequently fail to make us hear it in their verse—no doubt because, amongst other causes, most of the great sea-passages in English poetry are written with images taken not from the sea, but, like the final paragraph of *Dover Beach*, from Thucydides' account of the battle of Epipolae, or like the magnificent coda about the Oxus in *Sohrab and Rustrum* from a passage in Alexander Burnes's *Travels in Bokhara*, which I remember reading—and discovering the source of Arnold's verse—when I was a boy of twelve in Langholm Academy.

This whole question of the necessity of first-hand nautical knowledge is, of course, the burden of the Spanish ballad of the noble Count Arnaldos and the sailors' mystic song :

> ' In the name of God, good sailor,
> Teach me, teach me, this your song.'
> Answered thus to him the sailor,
> ' No man teach I what I'm singing
> Save he sail with me along.'

Or, in Longfellow's version, *The Secret of the Sea*, the Count, strolling along the seashore, saw a wonderful boat approaching and heard its steersman singing a song which brought the birds to rest on the mast-head and the fish to swim on the crests of the waves. Deeply moved, the Count cried out :

> ' In the name of God, I pray you
> Teach me, shipman, what you sing.'

But the steersman would not :

> ' Wouldst thou,' so the helmsman answered,
> ' Learn the secret of the sea ?
> Only those who brave its dangers
> Comprehend its mystery.'

The answer, as Professor Entwistle says, was worthy of a New Englander with the hardy sailors of the clippers for his compatriots.

But the sea-traditions of Scotland, the Hebrides, Orkney, and Shetland have not yet produced an equally worthy poet. Most of the Scottish poets, on the contrary, have, like Sir Walter Scott, resembled the landsman in A. E. Housman's poem,

> . . . the mariner of Ocean
> He was calling as he came :
> From the highway of the sunset
> He was shouting on the sea,
> ' Landsman of the Land of Biscay,
> Have you help for grief and me ? '
> When I heard I did not answer,
> I stood mute and shook my head :
> Son of earth and son of ocean
> Much we thought and nothing said.

In contradistinction to all this, I would be like Homer, who, while composing Books IX–XII of the *Odyssey*, worked (according to the late M. Victor Berard, ' ce poète de la geographie ', as Albert Thibaudet called him in his *La Resurrection d'Homere : Au Temps des Heros* (1930), with a *periplous* or navigation guide for Phoenician sailors before him—a chart which M. Berard reconstructs, identifying Circe's island as Monte Circeo, between Rome and Naples, Calypso's isle as Perejil, outside the straits of Gibraltar, and so on.

And seek to achieve effects like those in Archibald Macleish's *Conquistador*, where Bernal records the names of towns—geography, the praise of nature, and the histories of men on the earth.

> How in their youth they stretched sail : how fared they
> Westward under the wind,

which are, by record, the subject-matter of great poetry—stiffly and precisely with the absolute precision of an old ship's chart, adorned but never merely decorated with the tiny details of his life and adventures, his dolphins and sea-serpents in its embellished border.

And never have need to cry like Robert Bridges (since I do not regard my seamen through a glass in the English fashion, but go to sea with them) :

> I hear the waves dash and the tackle strain,
> The canvas flap, the rattle of the chain
> That runs out through the hawse, the clank of the winch
> Winding the rusty cable inch by inch,
> Till half I wonder if they have no care,
> Those sailors, that my glass is brought to bear
> On all their doings, if I vex them not
> On every petty task of their rough lot
> Prying and spying, searching, every craft
> From painted truck to gunnel, fore and aft.

Yes, I want a poetry of fact and first-hand experience and scientific knowledge, but, on the other hand, I am of course aware that most of the matters perhaps with which as human beings we must be chiefly concerned can no more be effectively illuminated by any knowledge of their constituent facts than the apprehension or the sensation, if it be such, of a concord between two musical notes implies in any sense any apprehension of the vibrations which are its physical cause.

The essential weakness of the bad tradition of post-Burnsian Scottish poetry I set myself to destroy lay in its subjective rather than its objective character. The true poet never merely articulates a preconception of his tribe, but starts rather from an inner fact of his individual consciousness. When this is lacking (as it has been in the great bulk of modern Scottish verse), obviously poetry cannot be produced. My service to Scottish poetry has been mainly in the way in which I recalled all interested in it to this great central truth, as well as the way in which I have (almost alone—there are only two or three exceptions in the whole host of nineteenth- and twentieth-century Scottish versifiers, whether in Scots, English, or Gaelic) exemplified it in my own poems. It is this, not merely the fact of articulation, which constitutes the difference between the poet and the mere artificer.

My cry (which I have no difficulty here in the Shetlands at any time in making effective) is the cry of Antiphilos of Byzantium all those centuries ago : ' Oh ! Give me my berth in the worst corner of the boat. The joy to hear the leather panels sound under the pounding of the flying spray. Give ! Take ! Games and yarns of sailor-men—I had all this happiness—I who am of plain tastes.' And I would have poetry that is right about every technical detail, that is based formally on a thorough knowledge of seamanship and, like some of the Gaelic work songs and like MacDonald's *Birlinn*, goes through all the necessary operations and gives the illusion of actually handling the craft described in the required way—as some of the best of the sea-shanties do, a poetry of which it can never be said, as Verhaeran wrote,

> They did not understand the great dream
> That charmed the sea with its voyage ;
> For it was not the same lie
> That was taught in their village.

Mr. F. D. Ommanney in *North Cape* (1939) writes a splendid book about certain parts of the area with which in recent years I have been most concerned—the stern tumult of the waters round Iceland, and the life of the trawler-men who fish these waters, rough companions in whom he finds ample pathetic and amusing traits to reflect his view of life as a mystery both genial and tragic. And he makes one point which I have learned to appreciate very fully during the years I have lived in the Shetlands. If fish could be caught in city streets and stored in city factories, the trade would have lost its soul long ago, but since, as Mr. Ommanney experienced, it is a trade which exists both because of and in spite of the sea, ' a sturdy element prevails, some trace of individuality, a touch of adventure still '.

When, in my *Islands of Scotland* book and elsewhere, I first developed my view of the ancient Thulean continent, and coastal connexions between Scandinavia, Iceland, the Faroes, the Orkneys, Shetlands, Hebrides, Island of Man, Wales, Cornwall, and Ireland— a framework for all my chief enthusiasms and my sense of the inter-relationships, the underlying design, of all these—I seemed to many readers to be dealing with matters remote from reality ; establishing a poet's world. But this was not so. In that very year (1938) Scotland contributed towards a co-operative study of Gulf Stream waters, Germany, Denmark, and Norway each having a vessel operating simultaneously in neighbouring waters (*vide* the fifty-seventh annual report of the Fishery Board for Scotland). The F.R.S. *Explorer* carried out an extensive cruise westwards into the Atlantic from Skerryvore to Rockall, and thence northwards to latitude 63° N., within thirty miles of the south coast of Iceland. The sea-water conditions appeared in 1938 to have become more or less normal after a long-period cycle of abnormalities. Following on the early spring influx at the northern gateway to the North Sea, there was an invasion of the area by several typical Atlantic species, while boreal forms were conspicuously absent. There was no evidence of any unusual westerly expansion of surface water from the Baltic such as has been observed in recent years. The report shows that the sampling of the herring shoals in Scottish and adjacent waters was carried on throughout the year. About 15,000 herrings were examined, comprising samples from the Shetland and Forth and Clyde winter-spring fisheries, the Viking Bank in April, all herring-grounds between Shetland and Peterhead from May to August, and the Fladen Ground from September to November. The sampling of the West Coast shoals during summer was confined to the neigh-bourhood of Barra Head and Stornoway. I mention all this because it is one illustration of what I believe to be the fact—that I am so grounded in Scottish reality that even when my imagination seems to be leading me into remote directions which have no apparent connexion with my main concern, it will always be found, on sufficiently comprehensive and profound consideration, that the very opposite is the case, and that the matters in question, no matter how seemingly far-fetched and inapposite, have a very shrewd and practical bearing indeed. I have every reason to be confident that no matter where I allow my interests to carry me, it will be found that they remain related to Scotland in the deepest and most intimate way in pretty much the same fashion (or for pretty much the same reason) that the basis of Joyce's experiments with language is, a

Stephen Spender said recently, ' the fact that he is so deeply rooted in the Irish gab, that he can absorb any number of foreign words and influences without losing that fundamental rhythm '. This is, of course, just the ' other side of the medal ' to my assurance that, no matter how poverty-stricken I may be, and how isolated on this little Shetland island, there is nothing relevant to my main purposes appearing in any of the literatures of the world—and to a lesser extent in the other arts, and in the sciences too—of which I will not get to know as quickly as anybody in Great Britain, and that foreign languages, remoteness from intellectual centres, and all the other seeming barriers cannot prevail against—or even delay or impair— my reception of these subtle and searching communications from all over the world. And the same thing applies to the past as well as to the present ; there is nothing apt to my purposes in any past period of any literature in the world which will not come to my hand timeously somehow or other—and I fancy that the multitudinous references in this book give in themselves ample proof to my readers of the truth of these assertions.

What the sea itself means to me—the very intimate relationship I have had with it during these past six years on this little island (the first time in my life I have been so continuously pervaded by the sea over a long period—for, though Montrose is at the seaside, the sea there never entered into and affected my life in the same way during my ten years there)—goes a long way farther and deeper, of course, than the cry :

> Is not the sea the peacock of peacocks ?
> Even before the ugliest of all buffaloes doth it spread out its tail ;
> Never doth it tire of its lace-fan of silver and silk,

and is a little better indicated, perhaps (in so far as I feel inclined to indicate it at all here), in the closing lines of my poem, ' Diamond Body : In a Cave of the Sea ', which appeared in the *Welsh Review* of November, 1939 (not yet republished in any volume of mine) :

> And now I am in the cave. A moment ago
> I saw the broad leather-brown belts of the tangleweed,
> And the minute forms that fix themselves
> In soft carmine lace-stencils upon the shingle,
> The notched wrack gemmed with lime-white bead-shells
> Showing like pearls on the dark braid,
> And minute life in a million forms.
> And I saw the tide come crawling
> Through the rocky labyrinths of approach
> With flux and reflux—making inch upon inch
> In an almost imperceptible progress.
> But now I know it is the earth
> And not the water that is unstable,
> For at every rise and fall of the pellucid tide
> It seems as though it were the shingle

And the waving forest of sea-growth
That moves—and not the water !
And, after all, there is no illusion,
But seeming deception prefigures truth,
For it is a matter of physiographical knowledge
That in the long passages of time
The water remains—and the land ebbs and flows.
I have achieved the diamond body.[1]

I know a great deal about marine life, the movements of the shoals
of fishes, the traditions of fishing as they vary in different places, and
other matters bearing on the differences of various stretches of sea
with which I am most familiar, and I derive a great part of my pleasure
in sailing from the extent to which I am familiar with the different
treatment of the sea in different literatures.   There was an excellent
essay in the *Times Literary Supplement* in August, 1930, ' Sea
Thoughts of Two Races ', comparing the English and the Celtic sea-
poetry, and the matter of such a comparison not only between
English and Celtic, but also Scandinavian, and certain modern
American, sea-poetry is always in my mind, and the waters through
which I voyage are always complexly informed for me with such
considerations.

Of these seas surrounding and dividing and joining the Faroes, the
Shetlands and Orkneys, the Hebrides and Wales, Cornwall and
Ireland I can indeed say :

> My mind did at this spectacle turn round
> As with the weight of waters. . . .

and simultaneously

> How many days ! what desperate turmoil !
> Ere I can have explored its widenesses,

and yet

> Nor with aught else can our souls interknit
> So wingedly. . . .

---

[1] In *The Secret of the Golden Flower*, symbols having the form of mandalas
are reproduced.   Mandala means circle, specifically ' magic circle '.   (Jung
has published the mandala of a somnambulist in his *Collected Papers on
Analytical Psychology*.)   Magic, because the protecting figure of the enclos-
ing circle is supposed to prevent any ' outpouring ', that is, to prevent
consciousness being burst asunder by the unconscious, or by partial psychical
systems—complexes split off from the whole.   At the same time, the
mandala gives form to the transformation of inward feeling, such as Paul,
for instance, has in mind when he recognizes that ' it is not I who live, but
Christ who lives in me '—Christ being here the symbol of the mystical fact
of transformation.   This inner conversion, the assumption of a unique
individuality, is described by the Chinese as the production of the ' diamond
body ' or the ' sacred fruit '.

and

> Imagination ! lifting up itself
> Before the eye and progress of my Song
> Like an unfather'd vapour ; here that Power,
> In all the might of its endowments, came
> Athwart me ; I was lost as in a cloud.

Yet here where

> Mounted the roar of waters, torrents, streams
> Innumerable, roaring with one voice,

I have been vouchsafed the vision of my Muse, Audh the Deep-Minded :

> Surely I have traced
> The rustle of those ample skirts about
> These grassy solitudes. . . .
> Goddess ! I have beheld thine eyes before,
> And their eternal calm, and all that face,
> Or have I dream'd ? ' Yes,' said the supreme shape,
> ' Thou hast dream'd of me. . . .'

And anywhere in these scattered archipelagoes and Celtic coasts I love, I am continually compelled to cry :

> ' . . . She is alive ; behold
> Her eyelids, cases to those heavenly jewels
> Which Pericles hath lost, begin to part
> Their fringes of bright gold ; the diamonds
> Of a moat praised water do appear
> To make this world twice rich.'

As I have said, there is little Shetland or Orkney writing of any significance whatever, but, even as I write, Mr. F. S. Copeland sends me a copy of his charming fantasy of the North, *The Selkies* (Oxford, 1939), in which, as he says, he has drawn ' the curtain of the Grey World aside for a moment '—and apologizing to all lovers of Orkney and the North for the freedom with which he has sought to render and re-interpret their beautiful legends, observes that ' from the exile's perspective the outstanding moments of landscape and legend appear in a single plane, and discrepancies of time and place become immaterial '.

> How should I lose my way in the sea ?
> It carried my father, it cradled me :
> Bubbles of ocean, drifting wide
> *Roll, breakers, home !*

It is a far cry from here to Langholm.   Last year at Cunninghame-Graham's funeral a lady in a fur coat approached me and asked me if I recognized her.   I did not.   She had been a teacher of mine in Langholm thirty-five years earlier.   I had never seen or heard of her since.   ' We always expected great things of you, you know,' she said, ' even when you were just a little boy of seven or eight.'   I failed to elicit how that expectation had been come by, but I know, and she told me again, that it was widely shared in Langholm then. I have seen countless little children myself, but I could never discern the slightest indication of future distinction I have actually achieved. Indeed, I imagine it would be just about the last place on the earth to recognize anything of that sort. It was not only the other people who felt like this about me in my tender years, however : I was equally sure of it myself. And a little later, when I went to Edinburgh, I found confirmation in the way in which the great majority of people on Princes Street and elsewhere used to turn round and gaze and gape after me when I passed. It did not make me self-conscious in the least, though sometimes it was a nuisance. I got used to it, however, and took it as a matter of course. It was only lately, when I was on a visit to Manchester, I discovered that the same thing was still happening. I have been told that this is due to my eyes, but I cannot see that there is anything unusual about my eyes—no insane glitter or anything of that sort—or about my expression, gait, the impression of superabundant vitality I disengage, attire, or anything else. Certainly it is not my hair ; I used to have a head of towsy hair of the colour of teased rope, but it is not nearly so wild nowadays, and in any case it was never sufficiently unusual to explain the effect I am describing. (My only really unusual feature—too small, however, to be noticed except under close scrutiny—are two holes, like piercings for earrings, at the upper ends of the joinings of my ears to my head. These were the source of considerable interest to the examining doctors when I joined the Army and would, I was assured, serve to identify me anywhere. There was the usual sort of story current in our family, of course—that I owed them to the fact that my mother had her ears pierced not long before I was born. But that is just rubbish. They are, of course, vestigial bracts—deriving from the gills of the fish-stage of our evolution. They occur, I believe, in about one man per 100,000. In me they are exceptionally clearly defined. I happened to be saying something about them to some friends in London a few years ago, when one of them—a young Jew, a co-director of mine in a publishing firm—remarked that he had them too. As a matter of fact, he was only similarly holed at the side of one ear. But this is the only instance I have personally encountered of any one else with this very rare identification mark.) I undoubtedly felt I had the world at my feet in these early days. I have been told that I vowed I would be world-famous before I was thirty. I had not quite realized, perhaps, what slow ripeners we Scots are, thanks to the provincialization of our country ; nor had I counted on the War throwing my time-table out. Still I had established friendships all over the world—pamphlets appeared about me in France and Germany—an Icelandic review gave up the best part of one issue to a consideration of my work—Waldo Frank was writing to me from America—Carl Kjersmeier was translating some of my lyrics into Danish for inclusion in his world anthology *Liv Og Legende*—I had been a guest of the Irish Nation at the Tailtean Games and had enjoyed the kindness of W. B. Yeats, AE (G. W. Russell), Frank O'Connor, Esmonn de Valera, Seumas O'Sullivan, F. R. Higgins, and Oliver St. John Gogarty—John Buchan (later Lord Tweedsmuir) had prefaced my first book of lyrics and had found in it ' a proof that a new spirit is to-day abroad in the North—a determination to keep Scotland in the main march of the world's interests and at the same time to forgo no part of her ancient heritage '. The *Times Literary Supplement* held my claim to be regarded as an original poet established, agreeing that I could conjure in a certain type of lyric, and said : ' He writes in the faith without which there can be no conquest ; the belief that Scotland still has something to say to the imagination of mankind, something that she alone among the nations can say, and can say only in her native tongue '.

And the *Manchester Guardian* had hailed me ' a new lyric star in the North ', and Professor Denis Saurat had cried, in *Marsyas* :

> ' Il faut que MacDiarmid prenne la place de Burns. Je ne veux pas dire qu'il est un nouveau Burns. Ce serait une calamité. Mais, comme Burns a commencé quelque chose de nouveau, MacDiarmid commence quelque chose de nouveau ; par conséquent quelque chose qui n'est pas Burns. Et qui cependant est écossais, mais qui, en même temps, est européen. Burns n'etait européen que par ses platitudes.'

And I was in my early thirties—only a little behind my programme. Looking back, and recollecting my own conviction even as a mere boy that I was going to be a famous poet, it is surprising that I wrote little or nothing until after I was demobilized in 1919, and that then I ' found myself ' quite suddenly and quite conclusively in a medium —Scots—to which up to then I had never given a thought. If I was a little behind in securing a certain international reputation, I was certainly much longer in getting off my mark than I expected to be.

I have mentioned some of the disadvantages of my writing this book in English. There is another one—that to many English readers there will be an absurdity in the claim that I am a poet of any consequence whatever, or of any international repute, or in any way ' worth an autobiography ', an absurdity that would not be felt by French readers or German readers or American readers. It is, of course, inevitable that I have won little attention in the English literary Press (though I have always had enthusiastic English friends like Walter de la Mare and Gordon Bottomley and Lascelles Abercrombie and May Sinclair and the late Mary Webb). But my withers are not wrung because I am little if at all known to the English reading public—if the Testimonial I have produced ' cuts no ice '

D

with the English literary periodical criticasters—and though the *Morning Post* brushes aside the extraordinarily high praises given to my work by Compton Mackenzie and ex-Prince D. S. Mirsky and AE and A. R. Orage and Gordon Bottomley, and says that ' nevertheless we refuse to admit that he is anything more than a very well-informed doggerel-writer '.

But let me set out these discredited praises again, not only for my own comfort, but because, whether they are actually true or not, the fact that critics and fellow poets of their calibre, and so very different in kind one from the other, should concur in eulogizing me in this way, says something important about me surely, for reviewers' hyperbolical phrases are one thing, but tributes of this sort from men such as these fall into a very different category from those of the weekly trumpeters of new-found geniuses :

> ' A poet of genius with wide intellectual interests. . . . I find scarcely any contemporary poet so intellectually exciting as Mr. MacDiarmid.'—AE (G. W. Russell).
> ' Ever since I first encountered your poetry I have recognized you as one of the few living poets of the European world. Your translations from Blok and Hippius are the only real re-creations in English of modern Russian poetry.'—D. S. Mirsky.
> ' No one can send me anything I am so eager to see.'—Gordon Bottomley.
> ' I have no hesitation in saying that Mr. MacDiarmid is the most powerful intellectually and emotionally fertilizing force Scotland has known since the death of Burns.'—Compton Mackenzie.
> ' After all you are our only man's poet since Byron.'—A. R. Orage.
> ' You have done many lovely and passionate things.'—W. B. Yeats.
> ' By all odds the finest of the truly revolutionary poets.'—Eda Lou Walton.

It must surely be a somewhat unusual sort of doggerel that has won me, not only such remarkable tributes, but the personal friendship of all these men and of others of similar calibre all over the world.

It was the *Morning Post* too that dismissed me (in my Scottish Nationalist political aspect) as a ' self-appointed general without an army '. But, of course, that is no more than the wishful thinkings of an English Imperialist writer—one of the enemy's War lies. Despite all that I say elsewhere about the weaknesses of the Scottish Nationalist Movement and my complete dissociation from all the organizations now seeking to promote that cause, I am more confident than I have ever been of its conclusive victory at no very distant date, whether indeed I then take the head of the Army, or remain what I have been, ever since the end of the War, the power behind the scenes. In either case I shall not be associated in any way with any of those whose names are most frequently in the papers as the principal protagonists of so-called Scottish Nationalism to-day. I have had a certain sensitiveness to the currents running through the world (although it seldom serves me personally), and a very particular kind of luck—the journalist's luck—of being on the spot, of meeting the right person, of hearing the significant thing. So here !

Compton Mackenzie came to me when he returned to Scotland because as he said he realized that I was the *fons et origo* of the whole thing. ' You must ', he said, ' have a tremendous sense of responsibility.' I had, and have—too much to prefer rigidity to flexibility in the early stages of such a profound and far-reaching movement, though to most people I may have seemed, and still seem, utterly irresponsible—the *Scotsman*, for example, denounces me in a leader as ' one of the most extreme and unbalanced communists in the country ', in characteristic ignorance of the discipline of the Communist Party. But the trouble in my case is rather that I have always been (as I remember scrupulously warning Professor Charles Saroles, a quarter of a century ago, when I joined the Edinburgh University Fabian Society) ' an Anarchist of course ', and Freedom calls for an appalling discipline, just as any poet knows that *vers libre* is a far more difficult discipline than the traditional measures. (I must add, of course, that Communism is a stage on the way to Anarchism—a necessary and indispensable stage ; the only entrance to the promised land.)

It is this comprehensive discipline of the Anarchist which has led to what the *Modern Scot* calls one of the characteristics of my later poetry—the endeavour ' on so big a scale to bring into poems the social, moral, and other pre-occupations of modern man ' ; what, in other words, the well-known Scottish journalist, Mr. William Power, calls the secret of my influence :

> ' MacDiarmid's influence is due simply to the fact that his high poetic powers are organically identified with the whole history and life of his own country. He has an almost uncanny divination of the total human significance of apparently minor or prosaic happenings in Scotland. At every point he sees the universal in the particular. Therein he carries on the tradition of Dante and of Ibsen, for whom Florence and Norway were stages on which the whole drama of human life was to be enacted. If we rose to that conception of Scotland, we should put to shame the mass stupidities of " totalitarian States ".'

It is for this reason that I have had as my mottoes all along Thomas Hardy's declaration that ' Literature is the written expression of revolt against accepted things ', Rainer Maria Rilke's statement that ' the poet must know everything ', Chestov's ' To grasp and admit absolute freedom is infinitely hard for us, as it is hard for a man who has always lived in darkness to look into the light, but this is obviously no objection, the more so as in life there are difficulties which are far greater, simply inacceptable ; he who knows these difficulties will not shrink from trying his luck with the idea of chaos ', and, as Miss Babette Deutsch has said, I have in ' To Circumjack Cencrastus ', and elsewhere, taken as my theme ' the restless spirit of man ; the energy of thought which transforms the world '.

> A' man's institutions and maist men's thochts
> Are trying for aye to bring to an end
> The insatiable thocht, the beautiful violent will,
> The restless spirit of Man, the theme o' my sang.

Miss Deutsch concludes her excellent book *This Modern Poetry* (Faber and Faber, 1936) with the following paragraph :

> ' For MacDiarmid, and for not a few of his fellows, it is not the moral law which, as Kant had it, equals the stars in their glory, but that movement of the mind which expresses itself in poetry.   It is a claim for the art which only the greatest and most daring practitioners of it have made, and but a small fraction of the verse considered in these pages rises to that height.   Yet the progress of poetry from the harsh realism of Masefield, Masters, Sandburg, through the sardonic symbolism of Eliot and the cruel imagism of Pound to the ecstatic symbolism of Hart Crane, the revolutionary idealism of Stephen Spender and C. Day Lewis, is proof of Synge's affirmation that if verse learned to be brutal, it would become human again, and the tenderness and exaltation of the highest verse which is " not made by feeble blood ", might re-kindle English poetry.   With a new and deeper significance the contemporary, seeking no escape, repeats the words of a forgotten poet of ancient Egypt :
> > " I have seen violence, I have seen violence—
> > Give thy heart after letters."
>
> In the poem, sound and picture, emotion and idea, work together to satisfy a hunger which sets man apart from the other beasts.   The emotion is as old as his physical inheritance, but the music and the images and the ideas have altered with his changed circumstances, and poetry which takes account of these changes will speak most eloquently to the contemporary mind.   Philosophers have applied various terms to humanity in an attempt to distinguish it from the rest of creation, but if man is a talking animal, so is the parrot, and if he is a political animal, so, in a truer sense, is the ant.   Man is an imaginative animal. That is what gives meaning to his speech and may yet give meaning to his politics.'

This is, of course, the very theme of my ' Second Hymn to Lenin ' (1932) :

> Ah, Lenin, politics is bairns' play
> To what this maun be.

And I wrote in ' To Circumjack Cencrastus ' (1930) :

> Poetry's the movement that mind invents
> For its expression, even as the stars,
> And wins to a miraculously calm, assured,
> Awareness o' the hidden motives o' man's mind
> Nocht else daur seek.

And again I sang in the same book :

To hell wi' happiness !
I sing the terrifyin' discipline
O' the free mind that gars a man
Make his joys kill his joys,
The weakest by the strongest.
The temporal by the fundamental
(Or hope o' the fundamental)
And prolong wi' in himself
Threids o' thocht sae fragile
It needs the help and contrivance
O' a' his vital power
To hand them frae brakin'
As he pu's them owre the gulfs.
Oor humanity canna follow us
To lichts sae faur removed.
A man ceases to be himsel'
Under sicna constraint.
Will he find life or daith
At the end o' his will,
At thocht's deepest depth,
Or some frichtfu' sensation o' seein'
Nocht but the ghastly glimmer
O' his ain puir maitter ?
            What does it maitter ?
            It's the only road
The beaten track is *beaten* frae the stert.

Man's the reality that mak's
A' things possible, even himsel'.
Energy's his miracle,
But hoo little he's dune wi 't yet,
Denyin't at ilka turn.
Ilka change has Eternity's mandate.
But hoo little we've changed since Adam.

Talking of being more of a Langholmite than ever, and of all my travels having been to my starting-place, it was my friend, the late A. R. Orage, who pointed out, in regard to two of my poems (written, the one in English and the other in Scots, at a space of fifteen years) how, ' in spite of all their external differences, their spirit is one ' :

And if I pass the utmost bourne,
Why then, I shall be home again—
The quick step at the quiet door,
The gay eyes at the pane !

        .   .   .

Their queer stane faces and hoo green they got !
Just like Rebecca in her shawl o' sly.
I'd never faur to gang to see doon there
A wreathèd Triton blaw his horn or try,
While at his feet a clump o' mimulus shone
Like a dog's een wi' the world a bone.

But this chapter is out of order. I am away ahead of my story. Over thirty years elapsed between the matters I have discussed in this

chapter and those I discussed in the last.   Let us (after this most
exasperating exhibition of overwhelming self-conceit, extremism,
and impossibilism) get back to Langholm.

But before we do, suffice it to admit here (if it is not already clear)
that my right reverend enemy, Dr. Lauchlan MacLean Watt, who
affords the title to this chapter and whose strictures I quote in one
of the introductory quotations to it, was not wholly wrong.   There
are very questionable elements in my make-up—a yellow streak in
the very complicated sett of the tartan of my mentality (which,
however, would certainly not look nearly so well without it).   But
it is not these questionable elements—that streak—which is responsible for the extraordinarily equivocal nature of my position in
Scotland to-day.   That equivocality is due, alas, not to my weaknesses, but to my strength.

When I speak of this yellow streak in myself (it will be seen later
that my friend AE was not as antinomian as he professed to be in
this particular way), what I am at the same time remembering is, of
course, what Havelock Ellis wrote speaking of the dubious things
that Casanova had done, and of the ridiculous positions in which he
found himself now and again : ' But as he looks back he feels that the
like may have happened to any of us.   He views these things with
complete human tolerance as a necessary part of the whole picture,
which it would be idle to slur over or apologize for.   He records them
simply, not without a sense of humour, but with no undue sense of
shame.'   Or as Isaac Goldberg said :

> ' " There but for the grace of God go I," said a noted preacher, seeing
> a criminal led to execution.   A profound sentence which preachers may
> utter, but only Ellises feel, a sentence containing enough dynamite to
> blow up the world of the censors and their insensate " moral " judg-
> ments.'
> ' What offences against social codes he may have committed, Casanova
> can scarcely be said to have sinned against natural laws.   He was only
> abnormal because so natural a person within the gates of civilization is
> necessarily abnormal and at war with his environment. . . . The
> energy and ability which Casanova displayed in gratifying his instincts
> would have sufficed to make a reputation of the first importance in any
> department, as a popular statesman, as a great judge, a merchant
> prince, and enabled him to die worn out by the monotonous and feverish
> toil of the senate, the court, or the counting house.   Casanova chose to
> LIVE.   A crude and barbarous choice, it seems to us, with our hereditary
> instinct to spend our lives in wasting the reasons for living.'

And Ellis, too, stresses the language question, that dreadful
devitalized tendency which has culminated in the terrible menace of
the ninny-speech of the B.B.C.

> ' " Our (i.e. English) literature ", he says, " for two centuries has been
> hampered by the social tendency of life to slur expression and to para-
> phrase or suppress all forceful and poignant words.   If we go back to
> Chaucer or even to Shakespeare, we realize what power of expression

we have lost. It is enough, indeed, to turn to our English Bible. The literary power of the English Bible is largely due to the unconscious instinct for style which happened to be in the air when it was chiefly moulded, to the simple, direct, unashamed vigour of its speech. Certainly if the discovery of the Bible had been left for us to make, any English translation would have to be issued at a high price by some esoteric society, for fear lest it should fall into the hands of the British matron."'

This indeed was one of the principal factors in driving me back from English to Scots, and as to the moral issue, I put as epigraph on the title-page of my *Scottish Eccentrics* the saying : ' They do not love liberty who fear licence ' ; and my own life as a lover of liberty has been conducted in keeping with that.

However that may be, I think I have kept my head !

I can best end this chapter in which I have begun to promulgate my own view of myself by showing that it is also substantially the same as that entertained of me in very diverse quarters, however unlikely that may seem on the face of it to certain English reviewers who have never heard of me, know little of Scotland, and believe only in ' London reputation '. Here, for instance, is a graphic picture by the late ' Lewis Grassic Gibbon ' (J. Leslie Mitchell), whose untimely death robbed Scotland of one of the most powerful and prolific of its younger writers.

' Several years ago I sat at tea with a pleasant Scottish lady who had just written a pleasant book of Scottish verse. She was showing me a sheaf of reviews—laudatory reviews, patronizing reviews, deprecatory reviews. But only one had stirred her to any extent. " . . . the bloody little beast ! " she remarked succinctly.

' It was C. M. G. Where other reviewers shambled on broken-knee'd jades, here was one who galloped a war-horse. Dr. J. M. Bulloch had written a preface to the book, and had sneered at synthetic Scots in the process. But not unchallenged. Having demolished the verse and its author in a few brief sentences, dishonoured the corpse, and stamped on its face, Grieve had caught up a battle-axe and chased the unfortunate Bulloch (that decent couthy body, who never wrote an offensive or intelligent thing in his life) down half a column of such magnificent invective as made your toes tingle. Then, wiping the blood from the blade, he came back, glanced at the verse, saw a flicker of life in it, extinguished it, and departed—probably to teach revolutionary tactics to Trotski or confer with the leaders of the Pan-Negro Congress.

' He seems to have done, seen, and read everything. He launched the Scottish P.E.N. He launched the ship of Scottish Nationalism. Probably (if Mr. MacColla will forgive me) he invented the Celts, staged the rising of William Wallace, led a schiltroun at Falkirk, and wrote Dunbar's poetry for him. At the moment he is in the Faroe Islands ; the Faroes will probably declare their independence, cast off from Denmark, and elect him Archon for life.

' Between whiles of reforming the world and chastising the English (by some slight accident he was missing from the battle of Flodden, and has been making up for it ever since), he writes, in collaboration with his " distant cousin ", Hugh MacDiarmid, the only poetry Scotland has produced in the last three hundred years—stuff unexpected and beautiful, mellow and keen. The " Hymns to Lenin " are among the world's most magnificent hymns to the high verities of life. He has shown the Scottish speech capable of dealing, tremendously and vividly, with the utmost extremes of passion and pity.

' All good art is propaganda, and Grieve, *ex officio* or otherwise, is a splendid propagandist. Paradoxically, his weakness in prose is his delight in word-manipulation ; he might refer to an adversary as a negligible person ; instead, he refers to him as, say, a " negligible, nefarious, knock-knee'd nonentity ". Like bringing up the tumbrils and guillotine to execute a rat.

' Still, the rats of Scotland breed faster than ever, and God sent Grieve to exterminate them. If I were a very young man, with no direct creative talent, but a taste for letters, I would set about collecting all the Grieviana I could lay hands on—poems, essays, satires, journalistic fragments, political pronunciamentos, recorded conversations, denunciations, and disputes—everything written by or about the man. Then, when my subject had departed this planet (probably in a cloud-burst or in front of a firing squad), I would write up such a " Life " as has escaped biographical record since the days of the Florentines.

' In an era when literary criticism (confused with mere reviewing) has sunk to its lowest ebb, when the unauthentic Israelites of the Sunday press hand out " good notices " in return for intimate favours which would have made the average inhabitant of Sodom or Gomorrha blush a deep, vivid scarlet, Grieve is our Sea-green incorruptible. He is concerned only with the book and its contents, and is as likely to attack a friend as a foe. I (or rather, my own " distant cousin ", Lewis Grassic Gibbon) have earned some degree of commendation from him. But we are under no illusions. Next time it is as likely to be a bombardment with howitzers as a presentation of bouquets. So we keep our own powder dry.

' Some of his judgements have a breath-taking penetration ; some seem to me fantastically wrong. How he can approve of the anaemic Teutonic blah of the Muirs and yet find no admiration for a fine Scots writer like George Blake, is inexplicable.

' I have met him only once—in London, when we tried to form a section of the Revolutionary Writers of the World. He had just finished writing the " Second Hymn to Lenin ", founding a new English weekly, and (for all I know) retranslating the Analects of Confucius. Then, observing that poor old Scotland was taking an uneasy forty winks in his absence, he departed there with an alarm-clock.[1]

' When we have our Scots Republic, I hope they elect him First President. But also (in case he should insist on raising an expeditionary force to free the Maya Indians from the Mexicans or march to Westminster and reclaim the Scone stone), I hope they hand over the War Ministry to some such mild, pacific person as myself.'

Then William Power, the well-known Scottish journalist and literary critic, writes :

' You give me the impression, sometimes, of having the whole world under you—of having enacted the whole of history in your own person.

---

[1] We became intimate friends later and collaborated in a book, *Scottish Scene* (1934), and I had the pleasure of staying with him in his home in Welwyn Garden City.

You are one of the few people in whom I, at least, have never detected a really blind spot. Indeed, I might have faltered in my Scottish nationalism but for the fact that a man with a mind so universal and so penetrating as yours, considered Scotland the centre of this world.'

But these, it may be objected, are personal friends of my own. Consider then the following sentences from reviews of my *Scottish Eccentrics* in the *New Statesman* in 1935, and my *The Islands of Scotland* in the *New York Times Book Review* and the *Glasgow Herald* in 1939, which show at least that I was creating a like impression of myself in several quite unrelated quarters and at an interval of several years, thus evidencing a certain psychological consistency and capacity for running ' true to form ' in two very different kinds of books. Here is the *New York Times Book Review* :

> ' Mr. Hugh MacDiarmid is a national institution ; he is a radical, a Scottish Nationalist, a poet, and a fervent supporter of the Douglas Credit Scheme ; and whenever he leaves his island home in the Shetlands to speak or lecture in Aberdeen, Glasgow, or Edinburgh, he is pretty sure to start up a newspaper controversy and to disconcert some of his less mentally agile admirers who cannot keep up with his exuberant progress. . . . He has just produced a book on *The Islands of Scotland*, but Mr. MacDiarmid never says or writes the expected thing, and this book is quite unlike any orthodox history-and-beauty book. . . . This is no book for those who want to pick a nice island for a holiday, or to plan a cruise, or to fill their heads with local history and legend ; but for those who really are concerned to know how people live on the fringes of civilization, and who feel that perhaps the islander has something to teach the rest of us in the art of living, no more stimulating book can be recommended.'

And here is Mr. Donald Carswell, writing in the *New Statesman and Nation*, on an earlier book, my *Scottish Eccentrics* (about which the *Times Literary Supplement* said : ' But better company than any of his eccentrics is Mr. MacDiarmid himself, when he has a subject on which he can play his astonishing variations ').

> ' Now Mr. MacDiarmid is one of those aggravatingly gifted people, like D. H. Lawrence, with whom it is as easy as pie to find fault, but who leave you with the unpalatable suspicion that your pie is made of Dead Sea fruit—in other words, that in criticizing him you have missed the point and made rather an ass of yourself. Thus it is true that his style is often abominable ; that he is capable of saying on one page that Scotch professors always are, always have been, and probably always will be the smallest fry of academic poor fish, while on another page he extols them as the only lights that lighten the Gentiles ; that his notions of generalization are so accommodating that he can subsume in the same category a man of genius, a craftsman whose only eccentricity was his indifference to reputation, an unconscionable mountebank, a humorist in the new as well as the old sense of the word, a moron and a common lunatic. . . . All this may be granted, as also that Mr. Mac-Diarmid is himself by far the most impressive of his examples. His Caledonian pipings are characteristically ' wayward and wild, as wild as

D 2

the breeze, and wander about into several keys,' but they have the
saving grace of distinctly suggesting an air.

'Those who are tunefully inclined may object that the air would be
more distinguishable if in Mr. MacDiarmid's instrument the drones
were not so apt to drown the chanter ; but let that pass. The general
effect is a rousing pibroch. It proclaims the essential exuberance,
the disorderly profusion—the *praefervidum ingenium*, in fact—of the
Scottish race, and repudiates the convention which represents the Scot
as a spiritless compound of inhibitions and less amiable virtues. Mr.
MacDiarmid does not deny—on the contrary he most loudly laments—
that at the present day the convention is rapidly becoming the fact.
Scotland's only chance of saving her soul is forthwith to renounce the
copybook morals and genteel table-manners she has so painfully learned
during the past two centuries. Very true, if it can be done. Some of
us think that the call to repentance comes too late, that the corruption
is now past remedy. I myself, I note, come in for a gentle rebuke for
having once hinted so. "Be damned to all you defeatists", says Mr.
MacDiarmid in effect. "The outlook is black, but not hopeless. The
genius of Scotland still lives. Look at me!" And there is force in the
argument.'

And here is the *Glasgow Herald* :

'*The Islands of Scotland* is one of those difficult but lively books
which can now be expected from "Hugh MacDiarmid". Mr. Grieve
is a rebel against most of the accepted patterns, among them the convention that an author with something to say puts as few obstacles as
possible in the path of his audience. Here are truculences of manner
and headlong exuberances of style, large philosophical excursions and
magnificent irrelevancies, with an occasional scattering of curious
pieces of verse through the prose—a tumult of words which have the
effect sometimes of pushing the islands of Scotland into the background
and Mr. Grieve and his ideas into the foreground. About that there
perhaps need not be any complaint. His ideas are always vigorous,
and though he often gives exaggerated expression to them, they invariably have a core of soundness.'

But that capacity for entertaining many heterogeneous interests at
one and the same time, intermingling easily the most incompatible
moods, with a strong dash of what the Philistines deem pedantry, an
inability to respect professional compartmentalism rather than filter
out over the whole field of knowledge, with a quite un-English taste
for international cross-references of all kinds and in particular
linguistic proclivities of which our Southern neighbours are entirely
innocent, and all this mixed up with freaks of wild humour, no
respect of persons, and a leasing-maker's attitude to all established
authority, are—as I shall show later on—elements in the make-up
of every true Scot, and fairly frequently to be encountered even
to-day despite all the process of Anglicization and levelling down,
and properly understood afford the basis for an urgently desirable
psychological programme for the supersession of ninety per cent of
the types common in our midst to-day and the restoration to Scottish
life of many of its best and most challenging forms, which, up to the

last few years, have ever since the Union been steadily bred out in favour of vastly inferior types.

Certainly I have always stood—and stand to-day—in every connexion at the farthest possible remove any Scotsman can attain from the nature of the vast majority of my compatriots now and since the Union—in other words, I am quite singularly immune from that bleak and terrible disease of the modern Scottish spirit my friend Eric Linklater so accurately describes when he writes :

> . . . swordless Scotland, sadder than its psalms,
> Fosters its sober youth on national alms
> To breed a dull provincial discipline,
> Commerce its god, and golf its anodyne.

Whatever may be said—and I care little or nothing what is said—about my character, I am at least ' a character ', at a time when there is an appalling number of people of so-called ' good character ' and extremely few ' real characters ' of any kind.

This, I take it, is what A. R. Orage meant too, when, reviewing my *First Hymn to Lenin and Other Poems* in the *Modern Scot* in January, 1932, he wrote :

' Few at any time relatively to the number of imitative singers, the genuine first-hand " voices " of our day—of poets with themselves to sing—are possibly rarer than ever. It is not that ideas among them are fewer or are left neglected. The literacy, not to say the scholarship, of scores of our contemporary versifiers, are beyond even professorial reproach. But somehow or other the essential voice fails in so many instances to come through. Their utterance, as it were, derives from only a fragment of their being, not from their totality ; and they give us a piece of their mind or a piece of their emotional experience, but only seldom, if ever, the whole of themselves at once. Where is even the Swinburne of to-day, to say nothing of the Milton who should be living at this hour ? How little personal value is to be attached to the confessions and affirmations of our unofficial and official laureates in comparison with the significance of Milton's blood-signature against Tyranny or even Swinburne's lily-hand against Christianity ? For the most part they simply reflect their contemporaries. They represent, not themselves by the divine right of individuality, but some spirit of the age, and by mere election.

' Hugh MacDiarmid is a notable exception, and all the more so in the present silence. As a bird in the night or a friend's voice suddenly heard among strangers, the authenticity of MacDiarmid leaps immediately to the ear. " Hark ! That is a man singing ! " we instantly remark. There is no wonder " AE " recognized at once the voice that is MacDiarmid, since " AE " has such a voice himself, though he reserves its song-use for what may be called sacred occasions. MacDiarmid, on the other hand, though no less occasional—always having, that is, a particular reason for singing—finds more frequent occasion. His range of song is as wide as the range of interest of a man. There is no area set aside for poetry in his mind, but all is grist that comes to his mill. There will never be sections in MacDiarmid's collected works classified as Satirical, Narrative, Lyrical, &c. Each of his poems has the qualities

of all ; and though differing in mood, the moods are still subordinate
to the man.

' Though the present volume contains only a dozen or so poems, the
wide range is here too. The " First Hymn to Lenin " has the quiet
magnificence of homage rendered freely by one man to another ; it
approaches the spirit of the Pindaric odes. In the " Seamless Garment ", Lenin appears again, but as the subject of earnest conversation
between the poet and a " cousin " working in a mill. Here MacDiarmid
is affectionately " explaining " Lenin, much in the same way that
Ezra Pound wrote of Jesus in his " Ballade of the Goodly Fere ".
(Incidentally, Pound and MacDiarmid have many affinities.) The
" wisdom " that " AE " finds in MacDiarmid's poems—by which is to
be understood the *ancient* wisdom—is here also, and at its most intense
in the poem, " Charisma and My Relatives ".

' " We've focht in a' the sham-fechts o' the world," he says to his
relatives,

> " But I'm a Borderer and at last in me
> The spirit o' my people's no' content
> Wi' ony but the greatest enemy. . . .
> A fiercer struggle than joukin' it's involved.
> Oursels oor greatest foes."

' " Beyond Exile " is one of the few poems not written in Scots
Vernacular. In essential poetry, however, it compares with " Ex-
celsior ", written in vernacular. From this it is plain that MacDiarmid
is a poet in his own right and not merely by courtesy of language.
Compare the concluding stanzas of the two poems. In spite of all
their external differences, their spirit is one.

> And if I pass the utmost bourne
> Why then, I shall be home again—
> The quick step at the quiet door,
> The gay eyes at the pane !
>
> .   .   .   .   .
>
> Their queer stane faces and hoo green they got !
> Juist like Rebecca in her shawl o' sly.
> I'd never faur to gang to see doon there
> A wreathèd Triton blaw his horn or try,
> While at his feet a clump o' mimulus shone
> Like a dog's een wi' a' the world a bone.

' It would be absurd to talk of Mr. MacDiarmid's future as a poet.
His work may increase in quantity. His experience may ripen. But
the fruit from his tree will be always of the same kind, because he himself will always be the tree.'

In addition to imbuing me so profoundly, then, that I have never
been able to tolerate anything else, with the fact that, as Adam says of
God in Milton's poem,

> man over men
> He made not Lord ; such title to Himself
> Reserving, human left from human free,

and hence that any tyranny over man is a sacrilege, and endowing
me with my full share of the concise belligerent spirit of the Border
breed, Langholm did two other things for me. My parents being
quite exceptionally straightforward and serious-minded people, the

rest of the community who had easier standards—or none—were apt to jeer at them a little. And my parents too were singularly lacking in the indispensable faculty (indispensable for being 'a' Jock Tamson's bairns') of small pretences and insincerities, of conventional hypocrisies, which meant so much more to almost all the others than their genuine qualities, so much more that the latter were for the most part difficult to discern by anyone who did not know them intimately. This set my brother and I apart, gave us an unusual restraint, and, in my case at any rate, made me permanently incapable of any 'going with the herd', just as, while I was still a boy, I had no use for going about with any gang or group, but, if I was not to be alone—which I generally contrived to be—made me careful to go nowhere or do anything save with one friend, or at most two, at a time. And my parents' involvement in church work and the recourse to· our house of many ministers and fellow church officers of my father's, and the extent to which church affairs and theological matters were discussed in our house, together with my quickness to note the backbitings and intrigues and other features incompatible with their religious profession which characterized the 'walk and conversation' of all these people, soon led me to realize that it does not matter what most people profess to believe, most of them, while conventionally honest and law-abiding and respectable enough, are precious poor specimens, all things considered, and utterly destitute of any real integrity or worthy purpose in life. If I did not conceive such a contempt for them as led Mark Twain to wish to 'blow the gaff on the whole damned human race', I at least early realized that most people had no ideas or principles worth a moment's considera-tion, and that I had a drive in me that scarcely any of them shared in any degree at all. Yet these people were more to my liking in many ways than any I have met with since, and all my later wide experience has not modified, but only extended and emphasized, my sense of the worthlessness of the 'too many'—so much so that since I reached my majority I have understood clearly that only those few who are to some extent creative artists are really alive and capable of receiving and reciprocating true intellectual or spiritual communication at all, while all the others are consciously or unconsciously, but in the aggregate overwhelmingly and in a way that is responsible for all the major problems of mankind—on the merely practical as well as on every higher plane—traitors to the human process, to what I call in one of my poems

man's incredible variation,

a betrayal none the more excusable in any individual case, although it is common enough and seems right and natural and honest to all conventionalists everywhere. I felt that I had (or ever could have) no thought or principle in common with any of them in any connexion whatever. (What, it may be asked, of truth and duty and commonsense, &c., &c., &c. ? It is no use hurling these big words at me—I am concerned with their specific content in every particular case, and not to be fobbed off with any time-honoured windy abstractions of that sort.[1] These people might assure each other to their hearts' content that they were jointly and severally decent, patriotic, and civilized people. Their opinions in that or any other connexion would never worry me one iota. I knew I would never have anything but contempt for all the unction of general approval and orthodox opinion they might lay to themselves. The only way to get on in life, I realized, was to take people, if not at their own valuation, at least at the general valuation—as what they seemed to be to most other people—and to avoid any digging down to fundamentals. And I decided then—by my early teens—that I would do precisely the opposite, adopt a thorough antinomian attitude, abjure all ' conventional lies ', and carry my analysis deeper and deeper, thrusting incessantly at the fundamentals, and taking nothing whatever for granted—the process, indeed, as Kierkegaard points out, which is incompatible with any popularity and fatal to any possibility of worldly ' success '. I think I can claim to have done this unremittingly ever since—not, of course, as a moralist (I am rather an amoralist), nor out of priggishness, but simply with an implacable intellectual curiosity, an unscrupulous lust of analysis that bars nothing, and a violent detestation of every form of cant and humbug. And I have reaped my full reward of eye-popping hatred from all sorts of vibrantly commonplace people without ever finding my quiver too depleted or my energies unequal to maintaining the good fight, and volleying arrows of Ishmael in return at all such evincers of outraged sensibilities. I have no love for humanity—but only for the higher brain-centres, the human mind in which only a moiety of mankind has ever had, or has to-day, any part or parcel whatever. An intellectual snob of the worst description, in fact! One critic put it perfectly when he said : ' Scotland having had in Burns a great popular poet, Mr. MacDiarmid thinks it is high time it had—in himself—a great unpopular poet for a change ! ' And now I do not think it should have, I simply know it has ! A really insufferable snootiness !

So right at the outset I stood at the opposite pole from the prevalent type of freethinker to whom the freedom is more important than the thinking, and had nothing in common with such a man as E. M. Forster, for example—an individualist who values personal relation-

[1] Like Leontiev (of whom, as of Rilke, I was by a decade or so one of the first to write in English), ' when people talk of the *principle of love,* I have but the vaguest notion of what they mean until I recall some living manifestation of the emotion of love '. Like Leontiev, too, I am fully aware of the emptiness and insignificance of sentimental humanism, and share his whole aesthetic position.

ships as his sole anchor to reality, who hates all causes and movements, believes that of all qualities, ' tolerance, good temper, and sympathy ' are the most estimable and that people endowed with them can never be ' organized ', and yet pins his hope of progress on the emergence of a ' new technique ' whereby ' not by becoming better, but by ordering and distributing his native goodness, man will bring forth the harvest of his native virtue '. In other words, of course, he falls short, as I was incapable of doing from the beginning, of realizing a commonplace of sociology, that personality and behaviour are conditioned by institutions, and misses the conclusion that political and economic institutions must be made to encourage, instead of crippling, the more rational and more social outreachings of the spirit.

Incidentally English critics have always complained of my ' bad temper '. My habit of ' speaking right out in meeting ' (and my determination never to allow anyone else to decide when and how or whether or not I do so) does not exactly endear me to the majority of people to-day (when ' mum's the word ' and a paralysing fear of swimming against the tide in any way are as general in Scotland as in dictator-ridden countries like Germany and Italy) ; and in Edinburgh and Glasgow and elsewhere, either among the literati or in political circles, there's never anyone letting out whoops of welcome exactly when they see me looming into view again, large as life and twice as natural. Mr. Harold Nicholson, for instance, found my book on the Islands of Scotland ' an ill-tempered rather than an equable or contented book ', though he added, ' Obviously a man as gifted as Mr. MacDiarmid cannot write a book about his life-long passion without having much that is interesting to say ', and said that ' in comparison to Mr. MacDiarmid's highly intelligent work, Mr. Anderson's *To Introduce the Orkneys and Shetlands* is ridiculous '. But again and again he insists that I ' continue to be unnecessarily harsh ', that, unlike the Mr. Anderson (who, unlike me, writes exactly as almost all Scottish descriptive writers write), I fail to give the impression that I have ' derived immense personal pleasure ' from writing my book—but he never attempts to give any reason why I should be amiable, never attempts to suggest how on earth the kind of issues with which I am concerned could fail to make any intelligent and honest man other than indignant and rancorous, and only repeats *ad nauseam* his typically English plea for good humour, equable temper, smug complacency at all costs. He might have spared himself the trouble. These things have never been— and never can be—part of my make-up. I not only do not possess them myself, but I seldom like them in others, and fail to find them associated much, if at all, with any other kinds of writing I value.

I have, in fact, thought it part of my job to keep up perpetually a sort of Berserker rage, or *riastral*, in the way of the old heroes.

Nowadays, I might, indeed, write with Charles Morgan : ' I wish to
live in such a way that at last I may be able to say truly that there is
nothing except a pen and my own room that I cannot do without '.
I have long since counted the cost, knowing that only a man of
unusual ability with extraordinary strength of purpose can deliberately immure himself from distractions and apply himself week after
week and year after year to tasks so exacting and keep the standard so
remorseless and high—having reason to believe that (despite one or
two recalcitrant elements in my disposition) I am substantially such a
man.   It is in this connexion that my furious attacks on Sir Harry
Lauder, Will Fyffe, Tommy Morgan, and the other Scotch comedians
—and the ' chortling wut ', like the offscourings of the patter of these
clowns which is so large a constituent of Scottish life on every social
level—have been so generally misunderstood.   For, as Charles
Morgan says : ' It must be understood by whoever love singleness of
mind that " a sense of humour " is his enemy—an enemy in modern
England so adroit, so powerful, so artful in retreat, so brilliantly
subtle in the very stupidities of its attack, that it must be faced.'
Among those who had no sense of humour, and were therefore free
to apply their minds to serious work, he cites Jesus, Milton, Wordsworth, and Shakespeare—saying of the last named : ' Wit and mirth
he had, but not the sense of humour that is for ever blunting the edge
of spiritual truth '.   It is indeed necessary to eschew humour
altogether if a man is to make it possible for himself to pursue his
art with the almost inhuman tenacity and resolution which is
necessary.   Laughter has been called a ' vote of confidence in the
essential sanity of man's way of life '.   That is certainly a vote of
confidence in which for the past twenty years I have never been in
the slightest danger of acquiescing.   And to term the sense of humour
' fundamentally a sense of proportion that assigns practicable values
to different aspects of life ' seems to me just a very roundabout way
of smuggling in under disguise the same entirely undeserved vote of
confidence.

If through these disjointed remarks the reasons for the disposition,
the Ishmaelitish attitude, I have chosen to adopt do not clearly or
fully transpire, at least its nature may, the indeflectibility of my
determination and the resource with which I fuel it, and with that I
am content enough.

My immunity from the start from the E. M. Forster sort of thing
was, of course, intimately connected with my dislike and distrust of
everything English, which, for example, led me to read with no
surprise Winston Churchill's declaration that 'nothing has strengthened the Prime Minister's hold upon well-to-do society more remarkably
than the belief that he is friendly to General Franco '.   I had
understood clearly for over thirty years that that was just how it
would work out—and I had always loathed well-to-do society

accordingly. And, again, I well foresaw the attitude Churchill reports : 'All the " Heil Hitler " brigade in London society exploit and gloat over what they are pleased to call " the Parliamentary impotence of the French Democracy ". When a Churchill speaks of a Heil Hitler brigade in London, a Mr. G. T. Garratt I knew might speak of a Hitler's fifth column in the same place without fear of exaggeration—and in such connexions I have never had any fear of exaggeration at all ! It was, in fact, a horribly fascinating experience to me in the autumn of 1939 to see how slowly the most brilliant conservative mind in England faced the unpalatable truth, and gave the grudging admission : ' It would seem that to-day the British Empire would run far less risk from the victory of the Spanish Government than from that of Franco '. Which was as plain as a pikestaff from the day the rebellion broke out ! With Churchill so slowly and painfully seizing upon the obvious truth, it was no wonder that the overwhelming majority of the British electorate remained in an impenetrable fog. And it was Churchill too (in the same book—his *Step by Step*) who came round to express precisely what I had foreseen years earlier and sought to awaken Scotland in time against : ' No Prime Minister in modern times has had so much personal power to guide affairs. Everything that he has asked for has been granted ; and when he has not asked what many thought necessary, no steps have been taken to compel him. There has never been in England such a one-man government as that under which we have dwelt for the last year. He has taken the whole burden upon himself, and we can only trust that he will not be found unequal to it.'

I never had any such trust at all, and I guess that if the truth were known, Winston Churchill never had either. But whatever might be said of such a development in England, it was a negation of everything of value in the whole course of Scottish history, and in itself amply justified all the efforts my friends and I had made to persuade Scotland that disjunction from England was its only hope—that England was Scotland's worst and indeed only enemy—and that all Scottish efforts should be directed to salving what might still be salved from the imminent ruin of England and the Empire.

In such circumstances—if in any—I could have no special ambition to be regarded as a genial creature (while anything in the shape of ' Hail, fellow, well met ' would, of course, be anathema to me), and in any case I am well content that it should be said of me, as has been said of ' James Bridie ', that, ' like all good Scots, he has a fanged and clawed dislike of many things and persons, and none of them *eum impure lacessit* '. My ambition was to be the creator of a new people, a real bard who ' sang ' things till they ' became ', yet, as an individual, the incarnation of an immemorial culture. To live is to fight for life, as Heraclitus said. ' Bless,' as Blake maintains, relaxes, while ' Damn ' blesses. A few passionate prejudices in these

high matters are more effective than many tolerances. If it be
objected that my ill-conditioned attitude is incompatible with a true
regard for culture—as, indeed, it has often been objected—my reply
is like John Cowper Powys's :

> ' My feeling springs from a mania for the organic as contrasted with
> the aesthetic. The Scottish (I substitute " Scottish " for Powys's
> " Welsh ") spirit is as rich, and mysterious, and inexhaustible as the
> French or the Russian or the Spanish, and what I reluct at and rebel
> against in this word " culture " is the hint, the suggestion, the atmo-
> sphere it conveys of something not *absolutely inevitable*. As a Scotsman
> I am "too proud to fight" under the banner of *culture*. I don't hear
> Frenchmen talking of French culture, or Russians talking of Russian
> culture ; and why not ? Because such a thing is only one aspect of
> French and Russian life. And it is only one aspect of Scottish life. . . .
> The clue-word it seems to me is the word *cynneddf* or *kynnedyf*, which
> means a " magical peculiarity ". . . . And this notion that the way
> things go in our confused world depends on something in human nature
> as well as something in nature that refuses to be reduced to any law and
> insists on escaping all logical analysis has one admirable effect : without
> destroying psychology it puts it into its place. And may it not be that
> this poetical-whimsical tragical-arbitrary view of human character and
> human fate is one of the vital qualities that emerge from Scottish
> literature ? '

This old Scottish view of human character as dependent upon
pure *kynnedyf* rather than upon motives that can be logically analysed
is, of course, what underlies my insistence upon the vital importance of
the ' Caledonian Antisysygy ' with which I deal elsewhere in this book.
And it is certainly true (despite the protestations of the Scottish
National Party that it has no anti-English feeling), to substitute
Scots for Welsh again in a passage from another of the Powys
brothers, Llewellyn, that :

> ' The cat and dog antipathy of the Scots and the English has obstin-
> ately persisted to this day. Century after century it has remained
> unchanged. . . . It is clear that the " creeping Saxons ", have never
> loved the Scots, except maybe as pedlars love cats—would strip the
> skins off their backs, and they could catch them. From the English
> proverbs it is easy to learn from which door the draught comes. There
> is scarce one of these folk-saws that does not reveal either fear, hostility,
> or derision. . . . The difference between the English race and the
> Scottish race is a profound one.'

And that is one of the reasons why I have thought it desirable to
write this book, for I am the most *gegensudliche* being, and in my
poetry such a ' *Geist-und-Form-grubler* ' that such full explanations
as I am giving here of my purposes, methods, and results seem
necessary if I am not to have to continue to complain with reference
to all the efforts made to understand my work by my over-Anglicized
compatriots, as Rilke once wrote with reference to Jethro Bithell's
translations of his poems (my own first introduction to Rilke's work,
and to Stefan George's, Richard Dehmel's, and many another

German poet who has since meant so much to me, away back in 1909, when a young poet friend, John Bogue Nisbet, who was killed at Loos, and I used to go cycling and camping in Berwickshire and elsewhere with Bithell's little volumes in our jacket pockets) : ' Mir scheinen die Übersetzungsversuche nicht anfechtbar, aber kalt and schematisch '. Certainly all the best even that has yet been written about my work by Anglo-Scottish critics is full of most disputable (anfechtbare) interpretations, and the Anglo-Scottish consciousness using the English language is certainly not a medium through which I can expect a creatively successful Umwertung of my philosophy, imagery, rhythms, and sounds.

Nor in Scotland itself, let alone elsewhere, are there any longer even such means of educating the still-existing public for work in the Scots language that there were when I was a boy—the ' Doric columns ' in various newspapers to which my cousins John and Bob Laidlaw used to contribute poems and brief prose sketches. These have long since disappeared, and the kind of literary activity they exemplified is now, I think, peculiar to Wales. A good example is the work of D. Emrys James (Dewi Emrys), and in part collected in his Odl a Cynghanedd (London, 1938). As T. J. Morgan said in the Welsh Review :

> ' The poetry columns have always been popular in Welsh news-papers, but lest any reader misunderstand, let me say that in function and significance they bear closer relation to the competition pages of an English paper than to the pure-poetry sections of literary periodicals ; they provide a means for ordinary talent to get into print. And as most Welsh newspapers have been local in circulation and interest, the verses generally published have been " local " in content and ordinary in quality. The net of Dewi Emrys's page is much wider, as the paper itself is more national in appeal, and the contributions come from all parts of the country ; they are thus less local, less " newsy ", and as a result more " high-class " if I may use that slang phrase without a sneer ; in other words, the standards set by the editor and the con-tributors themselves are the standards of pure poetry. As editor and judge, Dewi Emrys writes short criticisms of the works submitted, and imparts instruction on points of grammar and prosody and the tricks of the trade of poetic composition.'

A too popular appeal, and consequent dilution and vulgarization, and the temptation to be old-fashioned, non-academic, and cheap is the danger of this sort of thing, and Dewi Emrys (who has won many of the principal competitions of the National Eisteddfodd in recent years, including two Chairs and one Crown) is far from free of these defects. Yet how excellent he is when he deals with concrete laws of language and rime and cynghanedd! There is nothing like the poetry columns of this Welsh weekly in the whole range of Scottish journalism to-day, and indeed the tendency during the past twenty years has been all the other way. The valuable literary features of the Glasgow Herald, including the so-called ' Ham-and-

Meat' feature on the leader page, which used to print a poem and a short prose sketch every day, in the years before the War, have all disappeared, and the Scots features that used to be run in the Dundee papers and elsewhere have vanished too. As I write, I notice that Mrs. N. A. Macdonald, the authoress of the popular Scottish song, ' We're a' Scottish Here ', has just died at the age of seventy-four. She was well known in the West of Scotland, and contributed verses to the *Glasgow Herald* and other journals. She would have found it impossible to secure any such outlet during the past twenty years, though prior to that such outlets abounded. Nor has this loss been at all made good by any facilities through the Scottish B.B.C., which does nothing whatever for specifically Scottish work, and of which it is even more true than of Broadcasting House in London that, as Rayner Heppenstall has well said :

> ' Broadcasting House is too full of individual ninnies. Once in a while an intelligent man works there as a producer, but sooner or later the ninnies prove too much for him, and he takes another job, so that the writer is compelled either to change his style and write ninny whimsies for ninny producers and contemptible actors or else get out too.'

Scotland, once so famous for its educational system, and the devotion of its people to learning, is to-day almost wholly without any means of educating—or any desire to educate—in any of the matters that most closely and specifically concern them, and its Press and publishing trade is mobilized to prevent any attempted recurrence of any kind to the *status quo ante*. There is a widespread spite against the idea of having (save as something appertaining to the remote past) any national culture—any concern with Scottish literature as such—any attention to the national languages. It is a state of affairs to which there has never been any equivalent in any country—a general determination to dispense with all the national roots.

Mention of Wales reminds me of Mary Webb. I have never been able to make friends of English authors. Those I have known and got on with best have all been half-Scots, like Gordon Bottomley, Lascelles Abercrombie, G. K. Chesterton, Bernard Shaw, Mrs Dawson Scott (the founder of the P.E.N.), and May Sinclair. I got to know Mary Webb so well, and liked her so much, because, I have no doubt, as Miss Gwendolyn Thomas reminded the readers of the *Welsh Review*, her maiden name was Mary Gwladys Meredith and she came of an old Welsh clan whose original home seems to have been the Aeron Valley. As Miss Thomas says, Mary Webb's tales ' are full of glimpses of living nature. If you have read the poetry of Dafydd ap Gwilym and Rhys Goch ap Rhiccert you will remember the beautiful pictures of primrose banks, green dingles, and above all of birds in those old Welsh poets. The same kind of little picture is found over and over again in Mary Webb and especially in her poetry. If Dafydd ap Gwilym had known her he would have loved her silvery water-ouzel who sits upon a water-kissing bough in the green light above the wrinkled stream. And both he and Rhys Goch would have delighted in her coloured catalogue of what she saw along the field path going to town—the pale green hazel hedge, the ivory honeysuckle horns, the blackbird with his cawl, the green caterpillar, and the crimson-sorrel grass.' This is well said. And these things belong to Scottish literature as they do to Welsh—an extreme sensibility to the whole of their conscious existence, but especially with what has to do with the physical world from star to leaf is the essence of the Celtic contribution, and I remember how delighted Mary Webb was with the examples of it she found in my own work.

Above all, I have always hated British Imperialism lock, stock, and barrel. Reading in an American magazine recently an article on Sir Henry Lawrence, I hit upon a passage, worthy of a leading place in any *sottisier*, which perfectly describes the Imperial achievement from my standpoint.

> ' If to-day,' the passage runs, ' in Lahore and Lucknow and Bombay you can find cocktail lounges in first-class hotels—excellent bridge partners in the Service Club—Anglo-Saxon ladies in revealing evening gowns, moving pictures, and all the pleasures of Western civilization— with no threats from Afghans and Sikhs and Sepoys, it is due to such men as Sir Henry Lawrence, who dedicated their lives to making the frontiers safe. England may continue to honour incompetents and muddle-headed bureaucrats with dukedoms and lordships—but such soldiers as Lawrence and Nicholson, Rhodes and Gordon and Burton have been the real bulwarks in the structure of Empire. They were never as concerned with recognition as they were with achievement— and their achievements will never be forgotten as long as men admire strength and courage.'

Their achievements!—cocktail lounges, Anglo-Saxon ladies in revealing evening gowns, bridge partners, films!

I set against that what Marx said in his letter to the Russian economist, Danielson, of February 11, 1881 :

> ' What the English take from them (the Indians) annually in the form of rent, dividends for railways, useless to the Hindus, pensions for military and civil service men, for Afghanistan and other wars, &c., &c.—what they take from them without *any equivalent* and *quite apart* from what they appropriate for themselves annually, *within* India— speaking only of the *value of the commodities*, the Indians have *gratuitously* and annually to send over to England, amounts to *more than the total sum of income of the 60 million of agricultural and industrial labourers of India !* This is a bleeding process, with a vengeance.'

And against all that can possibly be said in favour of any aspect of British Imperialism—drowning out all the rhodomontade of glory, and the ' white man's burden ', and the work of the Christian missions, and the white man's supremacy, and Western civilization

—I set the terrible story of the women's rising in Nigeria, which began in the Calabar and Owerri provinces of Nigeria in December 1929, among the peasant women. Ralph Fox in his great book *The Colonial Policy of British Imperialism* tells the story.

And I have always thoroughly agreed with what Mr. Fox says in the final paragraph of his book :

> ' A socialist Britain without a people's revolution in India and the other Colonies is unthinkable. All schemes for ending unemployment, for raising the standard of life in Britain, are mere Utopias or demagogy intended to deceive the workers and lower middle-class masses, unless they admit the essential fact that a prosperous Britain, prosperous in the sense of guaranteeing the work and well-being of the whole toiling people, is impossible while the Colonies are enslaved. The path outlined by the Labour Party, Empire Free Trade, Ottawa agreements, cannot raise the standard of life of the Colonial workers and peasants, but only depress them still further, preparing the way for another war for the redivision of the world between rival robber powers. The worker can see his way to freedom only in the maxim of Karl Marx, " no nation can be free which oppresses another ".'

This is the root of my utter and unqualified loathing and contempt for the ' officer class ', all ' officers' ladies ', all the ' huntin' and shootin' and fishin' crowd ', all ' big business men ', and all their supporters and associates. I regard the lot simply as gangsters.

But while my attitude is as I have described it—and I have been the object of relentless political victimization as a consequence—there have, of course, always been a few quarters in which the quality and bearings of my attitude have been more sympathetically understood, and an excellent example of that (in which I have happy reason to know that the writer was not only speaking for himself but for a substantial body of intelligent Scots who have always supported me through thick and thin, no matter how baffled they may have been at times to understand my work, yet always moved by a fundamental belief in me which remained unaffected by all the difficulties and misunderstandings in which I was involved, and in which any attempt to champion me involved them) is the following passage from William Power's Autobiography :

> ' Grieve came on the scene at a time when it was plain that Scotland would have to choose between national extinction and an enlargement of national consciousness. It is all very well to say that in identifying himself with this issue Grieve was departing from his proper business of lyrical self-expression ; the issue was part of his inspiration, and Grieve could not, any more than Burns, dissociate himself from Scotland. His impulse was to express that which was high, profound, searching, bold, and subtle ; he could not do this except as a poet and a Scot, and he wished to bring the Scottish heart and brain more closely together by making the Scots vernacular as comprehensive a medium as Danish or Swedish or, for that matter, French or German. Hence as I have noted, his use of " synthetic Scots "—that is, a Scots taking in words and phrases from all districts and periods. . . .

' Grieve is ever the boy David, ready to take a stone from the brook and sling it at the fat head of any Goliath who may be clumping about the Scottish scene. Like Heine, he is a good soldier of freedom. His nationalism arose out of anger at the domination of public life in Scotland by uncultured third-raters, ignorant of their own country's history and literature, and hanging on to the coat-tails of England. His fulminations have been directed against people who in some way were preventing Scotland's full expression of the best that was in her. He wants to see Scotland " respected like the lave ", not for her ships and engines, banks and investment companies, prize bulls and sporting estates, Empire-builders and " heids o' depairtments " ; not even for her kirks and her Sabbath ; but for her intellect and art, her developed national culture, her social justice and equity.

' Grieve has been a wild hitter at times. . . . From some of his writings one might picture him as a truculently arrogant person. He is the very reverse. Unmistakably the genius, with tensely thoughtful features and smouldering, deep-set eyes, like those of Burns in Mac-Gillivray's statue, he is simple, modest, and friendly, and almost rustically Scots.

' His one piece of *panache* is the admirable habit of wearing a kilt and a plaid, both of bright tartan. In debate he shows courtesy and dignity. The only thing that makes him really angry is anyone's failure to recognize the musical genius of his friend Francis George Scott, who had the honour of leathering him in the school at Langholm. He lacks that most disagreeable of literary affectations, the pretence of not being interested in literature. Like Chaucer's Clerk, " Gladly wolde he lerne and gladly teche ". To know Christopher well is to love him.'

And if I have been a wild hitter—what Power means by wild is just hard—I have seldom missed my mark. I may give a brief example of my endearing little ways in this connexion by quoting a letter I wrote to a Lerwick paper apropos a batch of appeals against increased assessments the County Assessor had levied on a number of poor Whalsay cottars. I had organized the cottars, and secured the services of Sir Alexander MacEwan of Inverness to represent them at the local Valuation Appeal Court, but war-time exigencies made it impossible for Sir Alexander to get there, and the appeals were dismissed. The Assessor then published in the Lerwick paper a long letter purporting to justify his impositions and, incidentally, jeering at the ' great Grieve ', and expressing the opinion that I was ' no gentleman '. I made the following characteristic reply :

Whalsay.
16.9.39.

To
    The Editor.
        The ' *Shetland News* '.

SIR :

' Kindly permit me to reply to Mr. Thomas Johnston's letter. I fancy Mr. Johnston—and all the yes-men of the County Council— would have sung to a very different tune if the exigencies of war-time in upsetting steamer services and delaying mails had not robbed the

Whalsay appellants of the services of Sir Alexander MacEwan as their legal representative.

'The cases having gone by default, Mr. Johnston is welcome to the cheap satisfaction of assuring your readers that these appeals were without substance and would have been dismissed anyhow. I am satisfied, on the contrary, that, even with the doughty assistance of Captain Campbell and the other worthies of a reactionary Council, he would not have succeeded in sustaining his increased assessments. All the gentlemen concerned may plume themselves on having made things appreciably more difficult—and that with no adequate reason but quite wantonly and out of class prejudice—for a number of very poor people ; but, as Mr. Johnston, to give him his due, recognizes, the matter will arise again next year. In the meantime therefore there is no need for me to enter into the merits of these particular cases.

'Mr. Johnston naturally enough takes umbrage at the tone of my criticisms. Officials like him are accustomed to being regarded as gentlemen and as men of honour and entitled to a certain measure of respect. They have an elaborate defence mechanism which represents what they do as "their duty" and issues in the common attitude of "attacking not the man, but the system". From my point of view the men are the system, which would be unworkable without them, and I attack that system and the men who work it in the most thorough-going and fundamental fashion. I repudiate all the "conventional lies" which are used to dignify Mr. Johnston's business—and mask his personal responsibility for what he does. I am simply and solely concerned with the ultimate fact that on no matter what specious pretexts in the home country of the wealthiest empire in the world, and at a time when national service is being appealed for on all hands or made compulsory, the administrative system finds it necessary to "put the screw" on the poorest of the poor and wring a few more shillings out of people below the subsistence level. That is what it all boils down to, and I have no hesitation in stigmatizing it as a shameful and intolerable state of affairs and condemning lock, stock, and barrel the system under which it takes place and the officials who work that system.

'The present Lord Chief Justice—Lord Hewart—wrote a sensational book in which he exposed and stigmatized as a terrible public danger the encroachments of *le droit administratif* ; i.e. of entrenched officialdom— and it is because I agree entirely with Lord Hewart's statement of the matter, and find in Mr. Johnston's actings a thoroughly typical local case of this evil process at work, that I permit myself to condemn his actings with all the bitterness and determination at my disposal.

'Mr. Johnston is, he says, only "administering the law" for which he is not responsible. This is the common plea of his kind, and as specious as it is common. The man who acts in this way betrays the whole human process—a betrayal none the more excusable in any individual case although it is common enough and seems right and natural and honest to all conventionalists everywhere. I have no thought or principle in common with Mr. Johnston or any of his kind in any connexion whatever. (What, it may be asked, of truth and duty and common sense, &c., &c., &c. ? It is no use hurling these big words at me—I am concerned with their specific content in every particular instance, and not to be fobbed off with any time-honoured wind abstractions of that sort.)

'Mr. Johnston has all this weight of general acquiescence in the system behind him and a "safe" County Council that he knows in advance will support him, yet he has to call my attacks "cowardly and

vicious ". How? I made them openly and saw that they were
publicly reported ; and they were not random shots but derived from
a complete and well-known political and social philosophy and a rich
and varied life-experience in which it has been amply tested and not
found wanting. I skulk behind no County Council or any other body,
and whereas Mr. Johnston makes his living by his work as County
Assessor, the matter means no personal gain to me whatever. I simply
agreed to do what little I could on behalf of the Whalsay cottars and I
did not thrust myself forward as their champion—I only agreed to do
what I could when several of them came to me and asked me to take
up the matter on their behalf. And since the Shetland workers are for
the most part entirely unorganized and have scarcely begun to awaken
to class-consciousness and Dialectical Materialism, I knew in advance
that I would be easy prey for unscrupulous persons (whose interests lie in
the maintenance of the existing system) to misrepresent and vilify. But
I am convinced that the cause of the workers is right and will ultimately
prevail, and I have no respect whatever for the existing political and
economic system and its auxiliary, our Civil Law—and not even for the
petty bureaucrats and all their Greek chorus of Lerwick *bourgeoisie*,
so—as Mr. Johnston says in other words—we live to fight another day,
and in the interval he and all who agree with him may assure each other
to their hearts' content that they are jointly and severally patriotic and
civilized people, only doing their duty without fear or favour, and that
I am a scurrilous dog. Their opinions in that or any other connexion
will never worry me one iota. I have nothing but contempt for all the
unction of orthodox opinion they may lay to themselves. I believe that
the bulk of the workers will see them and all their practices in their true
light yet, and as for their impartiality, respectability, dutifulness, and
all the rest of it—all that will come out in the wash.

' Yours sincerely,

' C. M. GRIEVE.'

My cry has always been Liam O'Flaherty's :

' Capitalist finance has completed its enslavement of mankind, turning
five-sixths of the earth into an internment camp, where poor slaves
starve in the midst of untold wealth. It is no longer possible for a
hungry slave to stow himself away in a ship bound for the Argentine
and eat a cow from among the countless herds that roam the pampas.
If he escapes imprisonment 'and reaches the cows, he will find that he
cannot eat the leanest steak from one of them. They are all in pawn to
some damned financier in Wall Street, or in the City of London ; to
fellows who would rather slaughter them and leave their bodies to the
vultures than allow a hungry man to fill his belly with their flesh.
There is no longer any haven of refuge on five-sixths of this mad earth,
for any poor creature who wishes to escape from the horrors of capitalist
civilization. He must stand his ground and fight it or go under. If he
is barred by the collapse of capitalist finance from being a 'wage slave,
he must become a brigand, or sell his talents in some whorish way, or
die of hunger where he stands. Men of my profession generally take
the choice of whoredom. While literature is still regarded as a noble
art, those who pursue it are in the main a spineless horde, grovelling
before some rump-fed boor, who has made millions by selling trashy
newspapers, or else they are mouthpieces of the fantastic creeds that the
mediocre mob has invented in its war against the human intellect. I
have never been able to stomach any of these creeds, to the degree of
becoming abject before it and writing to its bidding. On the other

hand, I would rather rely on my vomit for sustenance than attempt to
cater for the rump-fed boors. "Then I must run to earth," I cried,
"like a hard-pressed fox, until I have re-organized my strength, weave
cunning plots, throw by the board those vices that have placed me at the
mercy of my enemies, to appear once more with shining eyes, a weasel to
hypnotize the rabbits, who shall be forced to give me bread for my
dreams." I had at least established the identity of the devil. That was
half the battle. The other half lay in getting rid of the habits that had
placed me at the devil's mercy. You must understand that the devil
for a writer is a hankering after success and the fruits of success : luxury,
social respectability and fame.'

That is one side of me. What is the other ? In a long essay on
my poetry in the *Aberdeen University Review* of November, 1938, Nan
Shepherd, the novelist, said :

' It might seem comfortable to divide the man up, to say, There goes
Grieve the politician, here MacDiarmid the poet. But that would be
fatal, to the poet. The man is one. Yet his particular political creed is
hardly relevant. What is relevant—with a fierce relevancy that focuses
everything he has written in a point of light—is the vision behind his
creed. That never changes. Always he sees man " filled with lightness
and exaltation ", living to the full reach of his potentialities. In that
clear world, " all that has been born deserved birth ". Man " will
flash with the immortal fire ", will

> rise
> To the full height of the imaginative act
> That wins to the reality in the fact,

until all life flames in the vision of

> the light that breaks
> From the whole earth seen as a star again
> In the general life of man.

The actuality is different. Men are obtuse, dull, complacent, vulgar.
They love the third-rate, live on the cheapest terms with themselves,
" the engagement twixt man and being forsaken ", their " incredible
variation nipped in the bud ". Their reading is " novels and newspapers ", their preoccupations " fitba " and " weemen ", their thinking
" treadmills of rationalizing ",

> The concoction instead of the experience,
> A sketchy intellectual landscape, not the search for truth. . . .
> Out of the reach of perceptive understanding
> Forever taking place on the earth.

They have hardly yet issued

> Up frae the slime, that a' but a handfu' o' men
> Are grey wi' still.

They refuse to explore the largeness of life. This refusal he sees as
cowardice. If for the mass of men this picture is true, he believes that
human society must be wrongly ordered. Therefore the poet demand
a political change that will give men such living conditions as may mak
the finer potentialities actual :

And have one glimpse of my beloved Scotland yet
As the land I have dreamt of where the supreme values
Which the people recognize are states of mind,
Their ruling passion the attainment of higher consciousness.

If then he sees the Douglas Credit System as an economic rule of life that will set men free from the shabby and niggardly anxieties of poverty, and Dialectical Materialism (issuing in Scots Republicanism) as the true nurturing ground of a culture that keeps individuality and distinction of mind and spirit, whether or not one agrees with these ideals, it is plain that they are accidental to this moment in history, and his vision of humanity's need remains valid beyond them. He is therefore more than the poet of a particular movement, and for his political opponents to condemn his poetry *because* they condemn his politics is like refusing a cup of cold water because one dislikes the colour of the cup.'

Then, dealing with my strange vocabulary, Miss Shepherd goes on to say :

' In this strange philologist's underworld I personally have found most delight from the long opening paragraph of *On a Raised Beach*, where the poet is evoking one of those moments of recognition in which we see something familiar as though for the first time and know it with a sort of primordial knowledge. Stones : to have seen them as he sees them here is an astonishment. His sense of their utter strangeness, their stone-ness, their sharp hard identity, demands words that will rake aside all stock description. In *Water Music* and *Scots Unbound*, he is attempting the same effect for the movement and colour of water (this water poem is one of his most musical), and for the colours, scents, and textures of the world. Yet, for all his uncanny and subtle skill in expressing these infinite distinctions, I feel that I would give his whole phalanx of words for one of his swift illuminating metaphors. For, putting aside philosophy and philology, what matters in poetry is neither meaning nor vocabulary, but the fusion of both in utterance that is itself an experience. Such utterance MacDiarmid has, both in English and in Scots, in phrases, and in imagery. His metaphors, like Rilke's, become " autonomous imaginative realities ". He is, in fact, a *makar*, creating new life. . . . There is, indeed, in this man, in some quarters regarded as a mere unmannerly tub-thumper, a mystic apprehension so sensitive and aware that there is no mode of expression for it but metaphor—" the mad leap into the symbol ". . . . Bewildering changes of mood and metaphor, or image and intention, are inescapable in his work. They are part of the amazing fecundity of the man. " Gleids o' central fire " escape in a thousand forms. Men do well to fear him, since fire is formidable, and even those who scoff, " glowering " callously, may

Yet slow but surely heat until
You catch my flame against your will
And the mureburn taks the hill.'

Guttersnipe, genius—Scotland's Public Enemy No. 1, or ' the most vital of living Scotsman ', ' nobody has ever been so Scotch before—he makes even Burns seem like a Cockney by comparison ', —well, you pays your money and you takes your choice. But I do

not think it is a matter of choice, really; rather, that there is an
element of truth in each of these alternatives. And of those that are
conventionally less flattering I am certainly, in so far as they are true,
quite unashamed. For, like the late Havelock Ellis, writing on the
ulterior significance of psycho-analysis, I see in it a ' hand that is
pointed towards an approaching new horizon of the human spirit.
I am careful not to say that I see the new horizon itself. That only
exists in my own mind, for these books ' (i.e. the various volumes on
psycho-analysis that have prompted his remarks) ' are too pedestrian,
too prosaic, too (as they used to say before " matter " was recognized
as a poetic fiction) materialistic, for so large a gesture. Yet they really
point the way towards the direction in which poets and prophets will
raise the curtain that covers the new horizon. They are doing more,
they are actually laying the foundations of the structure on which the
poets and prophets will stand. . . . For they are like the Hans
Andersen child who saw that the Emperor had no clothes on. They
have demonstrated the fact that Man, who fancied he had dressed
himself in such fantastic disguising garments, has no clothes on, but
remains a mass of primitively fundamental, even unconscious, human
impulses, woven in and out of each other, as equals, no longer divided
into some that may be shown, being respectable, and others that must
be concealed, suppressed, or aspersed with contempt, as though they
had no right to existence. So the way is opened for a new vision.
. . . That is still some way ahead. The psychoanalysts are not
themselves the people who can bring it. But glimpses were caught
of it—as by Whitman—before they even existed.'

I made my irrevocable choice early, and have never gone back on it
—that rank and office and title, and all the solemn plausibilities of the
world would never mean anything to me ; that I would never take
any degree or in any other way secure and utilize any of the protective
devices of the freemasonries of mediocrity ; that I would never care
a brass farthing for what any man had, but only for what he *was*, and
preserve an absolute absence of the enthusiasm of the market-place ;
that I would never acquiesce in any sacrifice of what I deemed higher
values to lower, or in any of the means whereby place and power
can be achieved by inferior types of men at the expense of superior,
or culture and art relatively little esteemed in comparison with
physical attributes or money-getting or nepotism or class privilege ;
that I would never accord any of the conventional respect to law,
order, honour, duty, respectability, and all the rest of these attributes
as long as they were a superstructure resting on and co-existing with
the exploitation of man by man, preventible death, disease, and
hardships of all kinds and the maintenance of a social system which
accorded homage to classes deserving none, and under which it was
impossible to rise to position and power without a great sacrifice of
human values at every upward turn ; and that, so far as I was

personally concerned, all I wanted of society was the minimum necessaries of life and freedom to devote myself to my own work. I had no desire to ' rise in the social scale ' as it is called, nothing but contempt for all the forms of so-called ' success ', and a bitter hatred of the way in which most men adjust themselves to circumstance, and imagine that as bankers, lawyers, shopkeepers, and what not, they are doing ' man-size jobs ' (things to which men can devote their whole lives) and that these forms of ' work ' can possibly be regarded as ways of living in any way as worthy or as exacting as a creative artist's. My point of view—the point of view I have held continuously since I was a boy in Langholm—emerges clearly in what I wrote recently, when I wrote of ' John Maclean, John Murdoch, Thomas Muir, and John Swinton (who aided the negroes in South Carolina before the Civil War, became a friend of Walt Whitman, and knew Karl Marx personally), and other Scots who are relatively far too little known and yet, in our opinion, of far more consequence than most of those who figure prominently either in our history-books or in contemporary life. Towards most of the latter, indeed, as we will make very clear we feel precisely as Burns felt to-wards their equivalents in his life-time, of whom he wrote : ' Few of the sore evils under the sun give me more uneasiness. Conscious that men are born equal I meet with the self-sufficient stately stupidity of a Squire Something or a Sir Somebody. How it mortifies me to hear the fellow's shallow idiot attempts at wit applauded—a fellow whose abilities would scarcely have made an eightpenny tailor and whose heart is not worth three farthings ! . . . The Noble Lord Glencairn showed so much attention—engrossing attention—one day to a dunderpate that I was within half a point of throwing down my gage in contemptuous defiance.' It is an appalling commentary on the condition of Scotland to-day that the ' famous fatheads ' we have named should be held in high public esteem and exercise great influence, and that the ballyhoo of Royal publicity—all the disgusting publicization of our Scottish Queen (sic !) and her daughters—should be almost as rampant in our midst as in England, with no one apparently to re-echo what Burns said in his ' Lines on Fergusson the Poet ' :

> O why should truest Worth and Genius pine
> Beneath the iron grasp of Want and Woe,
> While titled knaves and idiot-greatness shine
> In all the splendour Fortune can bestow ?

And for this, if for no other reason, I was bound, as I have done, to be a Republican, with an utter hatred of all Royalty, and in particular of our present Royal Family. What lay behind this attitude was clearly recognized and described by certain critics from the outset.

One wrote as long ago as 1923 of my first book, *Annals of the Five Senses* :

> ' It could only have been written by a Scotsman, and one of a type quite unguessed at by other peoples. He is not interested in the mean, nor in that kind of violent and obvious exception which is so often the reversed reflection of the mean, but in the natural, involuntary aberration where life gives itself away without knowing it. The more imperceptible this aberration is the better it is for Scotsmen of Mr. Grieve's type, and if it should happen to have two faces, and in deviating from the 'rule appear at the same time to conform to it, then it is perfect, and satisfies completely the subtle Scots mind. For the source of this curious, and, as it appears, living and fruitful cast of thought, one has not to search far, though one must search much, in Scotland. *It is the intellectual complement,* infrequently present in fact, of Scots republicanism.'

And again, in the (American) *Saturday Review of Literature*, that

> ' This vision ' (in the poems in Hugh MacDiarmid's *Sangschaw*) ' *is profoundly alien to the spirit of English poetry* ; the thing which resembles it most, outside other Scottish poetry, is, perhaps, the poetry of Villon. It is the product of a realistic, or more exactly, a materialistic imagination, which seizing upon everyday reality shows not the strange beauty which that sometimes takes on, but rather the beauty which it possesses normally and in use. There is in this perception of beauty less magic and less exaltation than in that of romantic poetry ; but on the other hand it has more toughness, vigour and fullness. The romantic note is of course often heard in Scottish poetry, and with supreme force in the Ballads, *but it is this other note that is most essentially Scottish* ; it is this that sets aside the ballads, the poetry of the Makars and of Burns, the prose of Carlyle and George Douglas, from the literatures of all other peoples, and gives these nationality and character.'

The phrases I have italicised in these two quotations seem to me to express the key truths of my whole life and work.

Above all, it must be remembered that, while the nature of the stand I took inevitably brought me into conflict with powerful vested interests of all kinds, and made me hosts of enemies—as to which I have no complaint to make at all, since I never wished it otherwise and was all in favour in this connexion (as perhaps in all connexions) of a policy of no quarter given or received—I have also from the beginning and all along had many entirely staunch and loyal friends and the necessary handful of those who were not only staunch and loyal friends but who completely understand and agree with my purposes ; I won quite unexpectedly rapid national and international recognition ; in most quarters in Scotland itself where my work did not find favour, it was at least not ignored, and controversial criticism and even condemnation served me as well in most ways, if not better, than praise would have done, and I got plenty of both, and all along the line have been singular in modern Scottish life in being a regular subject of newspaper controversy and having columns of the daily papers devoted to double-barrelled reviews—one writer for, and another against—of each of my new books, and further columns given to readers' letters on the issues so raised. So on all these scores I have no complaint to make, and my extreme bitterness does not derive from personal disappointment or wounded vanity at all. I have, indeed, got off on the whole more lightly than a writer taking my particular line in such a country as Scotland had any right to expect—or than I ever in actual fact did expect. That has sometimes worried me as a possible reflection on the efficacy of my work for my chosen cause ; but then I have thought in turn that the surprising degree of tolerance and interest that has generally underlain the stupidity and stubborn denigration and personal vilification which have characterized ninety per cent of what has been written about me gave me, after all, good ground for believing that the battle was not lost, and that below the surface qualities capable of responding to the cause I was so eager to create were still there all right—and, despite all the surface confusion, that served to sustain me. All these things cut both ways, and *au fond* I was only concerned with watching just when and how—and seeking to increase the frequency with which—they cut *my* way.

I fully recognize, of course, that, not without a certain amount of reason, many people in Scotland feel about me pretty much as Napoleon felt about Chateaubriand, of whom he said to Metternich :

> ' There are men who think themselves apt for anything because they have a single quality or gift. Chateaubriand is of their number and has gone into opposition because I will not have him in my service. This man reasons *in vacuo*, but has great powers of argument. If only he could employ his talents in the direction indicated to him he might be useful. But he will not lend himself to it, and therefore is good for nothing. A man must know how to guide his own course or how to submit to orders. He knows neither the one nor the other, and so one cannot use him. He has offered me his services twenty times ; but since it was in order to bend me to his imagination, which always misleads him, and never to obey me, I refused his services.'

There is an element of truth also in the view which complains about my work for Scotland in general that ' it is not always easy to tell when you are summarizing your facts, and when you are trying, so to speak, to civilize your readers '. I have, as is always obvious, a strong working-class bias. My next most important bias, if it may be called such, arises from a keen perception of impending change, a complete impatience with what I consider to be outmoded institutions and beliefs, and a lack of reverence for those who cling to or profit by the same. This is a bias with which many will sympathize. To me it seems as logical as a prejudice against witch-doctors or tuberculosis or old-fashioned methods of sanitation. Whether or not I stretch a point when I compare the sins of Business with those of burglars, bank robbers, and confidence men, or the more or less unconscious and automatic pro-English agency work of most of

Scotland's public placemen with the activities of secret service agents, spies, and saboteurs (an indictment levelled at the practices of almost all Scotland's leading citizens) is a point for readers to decide, as also is the validity of my contention that (1) there is no necessary connexion between financial success and either intelligence or any other desirable quality, and (2) that nourishment, breeding, and education have not the slightest importance in the racial heritage. What alienates most people's sympathy or regard, however, is the very widespread and deep-seated suspicion of versatility and hatred of many-sidedness, and the feeling that no man can be master of so vast a field or so many fields as I have set for myself.

What I possess, these people appreciate, are tireless energy, an ability to see the relationships of subjects each to the other, an earnest awareness of the great crisis of our time, a certain sense of historical perspective, a generous sympathy for people who are having a hard time, and a kind of sturdy rationalism. I am pretty sure of things. All these qualities commend me to people who wish to take a large view of the world—though that they go with a passionate concern with Scotland in particular seems contradictory to many of them, and I am frequently accused at one and the same time (and often by the same people) of a narrow nationalism and an inordinate internationalism. My defects come partly from the nature of the tasks I set myself. I try to cover too much ground, repeat myself a lot, am often inconsistent, and not infrequently so dogmatic that one who really agrees with me feels nevertheless the temptation to ask, ' How do you know ? ' If, for example, I say, as I no doubt often have done and will do again, that ' all realistic historians recognize that life has not been worth while for a large majority of human beings from the dawn of history to our own day ', is not this an example of indulging in such large and flowing statements ? Have I polled the ' realistic historians ' ? If I have, on what evidence do they rely ? Where can the line be drawn between a life worth while and one not worth while ? I have no doubt that in many such connexions I have undertaken tasks that cannot be perfectly performed. I have no doubt, however, that what I have accomplished has been an eye-opener for many people and has proved suggestive and stimulating for others. One can easily pick flaws in it, but that does not worry me unduly if, whatever the fault-finding, there is also, as there generally is, the admission that I have written in a fine and courageous spirit and dealt with tough realities.

' But why indulge in these endless newspaper controversies with nearly illiterate people ? ' I have frequently been asked. ' You will never get anything into their heads. What does it matter if what they like is to any intelligent person sheer doggerel ? ' The answer, of course—the reason for my tireless indulgence in these humiliating and apparently useless controversies—is simply that the only thing

I do care about is what the masses of the people think and believe and like and dislike. I do not care a rap in comparison what the educated classes think, believe, like, &c. But if the great masses are bogged in ignorance and shocking bad tastes, that is precisely what I am vitally concerned about, and I cannot lie back, aloof among my intellectual peers, and in that way acquiesce in the degraded standards of the generality. I must get in amongst them—I must seek to interest them in better work, to give them better standards, by every means in my power, and next to face-to-face talking to them I find the best means to my hand just these endless controversies in newspapers, and particularly local newspapers. The plane of discussion may be deplorably low—the whole experience of participating in such discussions humiliating and tiresome in the extreme—yet it is the only way, here and there the seed of sounder knowledge and better ideas will take root and grow ; it is impossible just to shrug one's shoulders and let this stupendous stupidity continue, it is impossible to acquiesce in that way in the mental and aesthetic victimization of the masses and let the whole fight go by default. It is necessary to be vigilant all the time, never to spare oneself, never to allow anything inimical to the workers' cause to pass unchallenged ; all along the line the wheel of one's life must engage the hard facts—one must deal all the time with ' the minute particulars, the mutual forgivenesses '. Easy enough to say this is beneath one—that it derogates from one's dignity. To Hell with dignity ! I have no use for this top-lofty superiority—and know only too well that these ' superior persons ' have precious little to plume themselves on anyway. It is the condition and future of mankind that are at stake, and so it is necessary to join issue every time, to be in the thick of the fight, and never for an instant to say ' What does it matter what foul rubbish these people like ? We are intellectually all right ; devil take the hindmost ! ' As Thomas Hardy said,

> If Hope for the better there be
> It exacts a full look at the worst.

Nor am I unaware that all my desperate preoccupations may seem small beer indeed, since the Scottish Cause has not yet emerged into action, and it is natural enough that until it does, the *Daily Telegraph* and the rest of the world should doubt that it ever will, and continue to regard me, as one of its leaders, as a negligible fantast who thinks he is helping to lead a non-existent army in a purely imaginary cause. When the publisher's description of Fritz Cahen as ' chief of the anti-Hitler forces since 1932 ' can be termed ' the blurb's euphemistic description ', the organizer of an underground movement in Scotland against England and the Empire cannot expect to be taken seriously. And yet I know that if the Scottish Movement with which I am concerned can take effective shape, it must prove the most important

E

thing in the world—a mortal blow to the greatest Empire in the world at the very centre of its power. And it is to that, and nothing less, that I have devoted my life. It must always be remembered that I regard it as true of Scotland as of Ireland, that, as Sydney Smith said in 1825, ' the moment the name of Ireland is mentioned, the English bid adieu to common feeling, common prudence, and commonsense, and act with the barbarity of tyrants and the fatuity of idiots ' ; or as General Gough, of Curragh Mutiny fame, protesting in the English Press against the methods of violence adopted in Ireland, said (as it would require to be said of English action in Scotland too if Scotland was really set on independence) : ' Law and order have given place to a bloody and brutal anarchy, in which the armed forces of the Crown violate every law, in aimless and vindictive savagery '. It is useless to talk to me in such circumstances of good humour, tolerance, and the like. ' I die loving England and passionately praying that she may change completely and finally towards Ireland ' were words written in a last letter to his wife by Erskine Childers before his execution on November 24, 1922. He was not the first man who died for England as well as Ireland. For in the last analysis what is right and good for Ireland—and for Scotland—is also right and good for England. And as matters stand, it is true (thanks largely to the unceasing work of myself and my friends during the past twenty years) that a far larger section of the Scottish people to-day than anyone outside Scotland itself can possibly believe echoes what John Richard Green said—'All faith in English justice has been torn from the minds of the Irishry (i.e. of the Scottish people).' I am perfectly aware that all this must sound like so much ' hot air ' to those who are not in the know—and extremely few are. At the same time, it is no use taunting me with phrases about ' the brave music of a distant drum '—as I have been taunted by anti-Communists who have not hesitated to say it was easy enough professing Communism in Scotland, where it means little or nothing, but a very different matter doing so in, say, Germany or Italy. The fact of the matter is that the Class War is as intense in Scotland as anywhere else ; even if one does not run as much risk of prison and torture and beating-up and death, one can be—as I have been— sentenced to virtual death, denied the means of livelihood, systematically vilified, have one's private life invaded and poisoned in the most appalling fashion, and have to suffer all this without anything like the opportunities available elsewhere of getting one's own back— of the relief of real action—and with the ' zero hour ' drawing ever closer, little or nothing being done to really arm the left, and the constant prospect of passing from the kind of modified terror I have been describing to a real terror with all its concomitants of police brutality, prison horrors, and hideous death. It is the shadows of such coming and inevitable events that colour all my work and determine the tone and texture of my life. All this may seem the wildest pipe dream to most and perhaps all of my readers. That does not matter. I believe it, and my life has been shaped accordingly, and in this book I am not trying to justify my life to anyone, but merely to describe it. I have believed that, and acted as if, I was engaged in civil war—an invisible war, without any recourse to direct physical force, but none the less real and deadly for that—and my work has literally been a life and death matter all the time.

The finest pattern of the right attitude to adopt to Royalty and Society people and to all the intolerable nuisance of lionization and ' mobbing ' I know of was that of the Curies, the discoverers of radium.

> ' In the presence of her admirers, or the potentates of the day, who now treated her like a sovereign, Madame Curie—like her husband— showed only astonishment, lassitude, an impatience more or less covered over, and, above all, boredom: the crushing mortal boredom which dragged her down when people rattled on about her discovery and her genius. One anecdote out of a thousand sums up beautifully the response of the Curies to what Pierre called " the favours of Fortune ". The couple were dining at the Elysee Palace with President Loubet. In the course of the evening a lady came up to Marie and asked:
>
> ' " Would you like me to present you to the King of Greece ? "
>
> ' Marie, innocently and politely, replied in her gentle voice, all too sincere : " I don't see the utility of it."
>
> ' And in one of her letters Madame Curie cries : " . . . Always a hubbub ! People are keeping us from work as much as they can. Now I have decided to be brave and I receive no visitors—but they disturb me just the same. Our life has been altogether spoiled by honours and fame. . . . And, then, naturally, hundreds of requests for autographs and photographs. I hardly reply to these letters, but I lose time by reading them." And Pierre Curie said of it all : " On this regime I can feel myself being overwhelmed by brute stupidity. . . ." '

I remember when I was in Liverpool, AE wiring me he was arriving that night. I had a big Lord Mayor's Banquet on which I had to be at in connexion with my work. I did not want to miss AE, so I managed to get him invited to the banquet too. In due course I called at his hotel to tell him about this arrangement. I was already in ' glad rags ', and with miniature medals on my breast. But would AE go ? Not a bit of it ! He wouldn't be seen dead in such company. But we arranged I'd cut away from it as soon as I possibly could and get back to him. I did—about one in the morning. AE was waiting for me, and we talked till breakfast.

The real reason of my unpopularity, of the insensate fury I rouse in so many quarters, however, is something that lies much deeper than political and cultural differences. Kierkegaard in his *Journals* describes it when he says : ' One is not unpopular because one uses technical language, which is accidental and might become the fashion, as does in fact happen successively right down to the ordinary man.

One is unpopular if one thinks one's thoughts out to the bitter end. Socrates was unpopular, in spite of the fact that he used no technical language, for his ignorance, if it is to be thoroughly grasped and retained, is more strenuous to carry out than all Hegel's philosophy put together.'

And in literary circles I have been unpopular mainly because of my extremely comprehensive and thorough knowledge of world-literature, differentiating me completely from almost everybody else in the British literary world, for of these I have always believed it true—and taken no heed to disguise my belief, but expressed it again and again—that, as A. R. Orage once said to Denis Saurat : ' You, as a Frenchman, have no idea how ignorant present-day English literary critics are. They know present literary production very well ; and, within that boundary, can judge of the works, relatively to each other, fairly accurately. They know works that have been published during their own life-time also fairly well ; say, during the last ten or twenty years. Beyond that they know very little. When it comes to the great masterpieces of English literature they know nothing at all ; as a rule, have not even read them. And then, beyond that, there are the other literatures : French, Russian. How can you judge a novel if you do not know the Russian and the French novelists ? And then, beyond that again, there is antiquity ; and then the East. . . . This means that our critics can only judge of present-day works by comparing them to one another. They have no standards ; they cannot compare to-day's work with yesterday's, or with foreign work. They cannot be competent critics. They cannot even be competent journalists ; a journalist's business is to know what is happening in China as well as here. They know nothing. They are frauds, who thrive on ephemeral literature, and are doomed to disappear with it.'

I believe that is absolutely true of every living literary critic or book reviewer in Great Britain who is known to me personally or whose name I know. Certainly of all those I know personally I could add : ' And if I were to give them an idea, it would crowd their heads '. Literary critics in Scotland are like snakes in Iceland, and the method of what passes for literary criticism either in Scotland or (with hardly an exception) in England to-day seems to me precisely similar to that of the man who had an abnormal sense of taste and boasted that he could immediately identify anything he put into his mouth. He was given a small dull pellet. He popped it into his mouth, rolled it round a little, put his head on one side like a bird, and said, ' Um . . . Yes ! . . . Batshit ! ' That is exactly what the judgement of almost every writer of signed reviews in Great Britain amounts to. Just that !

The kind of misunderstanding that my work has encountered in many quarters, and the reasons for it, can be realized from the following passage in *The Modern Scot* dealing with the work of my great friend (and the composer of splendid settings to most of my lyrics—a collaboration so exceptionally close and complete that it is, I think, quite unique in European literary and musical history) Francis George Scott :

'When the Active Society of Glasgow gave a programme of Mr. Scott's part-songs and solo lyrics, the critic of the *Glasgow Herald*, for instance, complained the next day that Mr. Scott's songs are full of violent contrast, that they abound in " sudden outbursts " and cannot therefore be regarded as representatively Scottish ; that their mannerisms are monotonous ; and that Mr. Scott does violence to some of the texts he sets to music. There was no attempt on the part of this journalist to interpret the composer's aims ; no straightforward reporting, even ; only this sort of inanity : " The sudden outbursts that he indulges in are not characteristic of our nation ; but reflect rather the mercurial and almost volcanic natures that are to be found in Eastern Europe. The true Scot makes his meaning clear in more subtle ways, and can be, for that reason, more impressive because more controlled." Before anyone thus dismisses the idea that the Scot is capable of extremes of feeling, he surely ought to have paused to consider some of the landmarks in the history of the Scottish arts—the flytings of Dunbar, Burn's whirling clouds of words, the music of the pibrochs, Urquhart's Rabelais, and some of the modern poems Mr. Scott is accused of distorting. As conservative a writer as the late Professor Gregory Smith insisted on the violent contrasts of the national make-up, which he dubbed " the Caledonian anti-syzygy ". The *Glasgow Herald* writer's remarks are born of an ignorance of other musical idioms than nineteenth-century tunefulness ; or if not ignorance, then of apathy—equally inexcusable, in anyone with pretensions to being a critic—to such musical vocabularies as the Russian Nationalists ; of ignorance or a wilful misreading of the Scottish tradition ; of such a fear of anything with life in it as prompted Roy Campbell to write to a third-rate novelist :

" They praise the firm restraint with which you write ;
    I'm with them there, of course,
    You use the snaffle and the curb all right—
    But where's the bloody horse ? "

' Our Music Critic commits himself to asking for " control " from the composer of " Cupid and Venus ", and for more subtlety from the musical genius that has given us the superb setting of Hugh MacDiarmid's " Milkwort and Bogcotton ". There's a figure for a *Dunciad* ! But he sinks to still deeper depths of absurdity : " The music often suggests that he became too absorbed in the pleasant task of composition for its own sake, and had overlooked for the time being his responsibilities towards his chosen text. The result is sometimes a fragmentary quality in the music, and, especially in settings of a lively mood, a spasmodic utterance." Now apart from the suggestion that the composition of songs is a pastime like ping-pong—" the pleasant task of composition for its own sake "—how could a composer neglect his text, as the writer so wrongly suggests, and produce as a result of giving rein to his pure-musicanship " a fragmentary quality in the music " ? One of the most technically daring of Mr. Scott's songs is " Love " (a setting of Hugh MacDiarmid's lyric), to which the *Glasgow Herald* writer took exception, and it is at once a perfect rendering of the

poem and a closely knit composition of extraordinary skill. It is
characteristic of Mr. Scott's music ; and it is characteristic of people like
the Scottish pseudo-critics that they do not like it. Schonberg, say, is
not to their liking either ; but he comes with a foreign reputation, and
one has to be polite, whereas Mr. Scott is merely a fellow-countryman,
and, some say, a Nationalist to boot.'

It is pleasant, after considering the sort of booby that comes
between the Scottish artist and the Scottish public—and their
possibly pernicious influence is the only reason why a Percy Gordon
is worth a moment's consideration—to turn to what a foreigner has
to say about *Scottish Lyrics*. Mr. Kaikhosru Sorabji is a composer of
amazing gifts and a critic who, besides his splendid essays on Mahler,
Reger, Busoni, &c., in his *Around Music*, is acknowledged to be one
of the most authoritative of living judges of singers and songs.[1] In
the *New English Weekly*, he writes :

' I do not hesitate to say that no finer work than these songs has been
done in these islands in our time. One is first of all struck by the superb
shape and design of all the songs ; next, to treat of technical matters,
which are not nearly so technical as they are said to be, but inherent in
the very stuff of which the composer is made, there is the finely convincing vocal line, observing the exigencies and inflections of the verse
with exquisite and loving, but never exaggerated nor laboured, care.
Idiomatically one is struck at once by the marked independence, the
freedom from any sort of harmonic *parti-pris*, but also is to be marked
the sensitive and subtle way in which the composer modifies his
harmonic vocabulary to suit the needs of each poem. The freshness
and variety of treatment in these respects is remarkable and cannot be
too highly praised. Compare, for instance, the harmonic ambience of
" Moonstruck ", a poem by that extraordinary artist, Hugh MacDiarmid,
with that of " Rorate caeli desuper ", of Dunbar. The difference of
the five years between the composition of the two songs has plainly
nothing whatever to do with the case, as the superficial might be
tempted to think, for some of the other songs in the volume prior to
" Rorate Caeli " show, in the idiotic cant phrase, a much more " advanced " harmonic scheme. It is merely one more indication of the
composer's fine artistry. Unlike people of the Schonberg kidney, who
have one and one only very constricted vocabulary, which they apply
with impartiality, or would, to a poem of Edith Sitwell, or a Ghazal of
Hafiz, Mr. Scott does not *change* his idiom for different songs . . . all
is plainly Scott, but his idiom is sufficiently wide to allow within its
own extensive limits a diversity of expression without any idiomatic or
stylistic incoherence. In rhythmic flexibility and elasticity these songs
recall the finest specimens of Hugo Wolf. In fact, for highly organized
unity of shape, style, vocal line, and expression, I should not hesitate
to place them, worlds asunder though they are spiritually, in the same
rank.
' In the light of that, consider musical Scotland's neglect of its most
consummate artist.'

Since my best friends are all of the *haute volée* of intellectualism,
and, like the materials of my poetry, drawn from the four corners of

[1] *Vide* Dent's *Dictionary of Modern Music and Musicians*.

the world, since no one country, least of all Scotland, affords more than one or two such at any one time, and like Mr. Propter in Aldous Huxley's *After Many a Summer*, I despise ' all the innumerable interminable anecdotes and romances and character-studies ' and what not which have ' no general theory of anecdotes, no explanatory hypothesis of romance or character . . . no co-ordinating philosophy . . . and no principle of arrangement more rational than simple aesthetic expediency,' except in the rare cases which are so utterly removed from any of these things that objections on such a score would ' miss the point by a million miles ', my attitude to ' the vast majority of people '—' the too too many '—emerges clearly. I remember what the late Ford Madox Hueffer (whose former wife, Violet Hunt, was, with Mary Webb and May Sinclair and Rebecca West and Lady Gerald Wellesley and Ursula Greville, the singer, among the earliest friends I made when I first adventured into literary and artistic circles in London) said : ' The best writers of to-day can find only a handful of readers apiece in the United States ; and only one handful for all the lot of them in the British Empire— say 14,000. The populations of the British Empire and the United States are, say, three hundred millions ; thus, mathematically put, the fraction of readers for the best work of to-day in the English-speaking world is

$$\frac{14,000}{300,000,000}$$

It means that in each 100,000 souls, five are reasonably civilized.' Scientists contend that there have lived on this earth a total of thirty billion people, only five thousand of whom have achieved immortality. That is one in six millions. If I could believe in a life after death, I would be perfectly certain that those who realized themselves in this life so incompletely that they could not achieve what we call ' immortality ' would have no part or parcel in that other life after death either. Finally, to complete these statistical references, I say in my long poem on Glasgow (which takes its text from the *Listener's* comment that ' it is not every poet who has the inner authority for remarking that Glasgow contains a million slaves ') that

> Orage said that ' of the hundred million people in America
> Not more than a hundred are using their brains
> To the fullest capacity '.   Of Glasgow's population not one !
> Not one !   Even such poor brains as the best of them have.

And I go on :

> It's a far cry from the ' *Jolly Beggars* ' of Robert Burns
> To Marc Blitzstein's ' *The Cradle Will Rock* ',
> The measure of the leeway Scottish poets must make up.
> Mr. Blitzstein's unjolly proletarians are not beggars
> But demanders . . . and are much more interested
> In the steel strike than in warbling the delights of rolling in the hay.

Would Glasgow had a Blitzstein too ! We need
His remarkable ferocity of satire, his raffishly amusing lyrics,
And his savagely cumulative absurdity even in the smallest matters of life,
For above all we need artists who live
Somewhere near the human centre and know
Innumerable truths that cannot be taught,
And thus can be good-natured without being sentimental,
Ridiculous without being fatuous,
And with whom, as with any first-rate artist, we feel
We are in good hands . . . artists
We can trust with our hearts and our wits.
Scotland has scarcely had a hair of one since Burns.

In thinking of the ' great majority of people ', then, if I recall
Burns's hope for the day when ' man to man shall brithers be for a'
that ', my consciousness inevitably varies it to read in Lewis Carroll's
way :

> Say, whence is the voice that, when anger is burning,
>   Bids the whirl of the tempest to cease ?
> That stirs the vexed soul with an aching, a yearning,
>   For the brotherly hand-grip of peace? . . .
> 'Tis a secret ! None knows how it comes, how it goes.
>   But the name of the secret is Love.
>   For I think it is Love,
>   For I feel it is Love,
> For I'm sure it is nothing but Love.

Unexceptionable sentiment, no doubt, but hardly a reassuring
rhythm ! In other words, in all matters of æsthetic or intellectual
significance, or meaning of any kind, I find the General Public
exactly like the famous dachshund :

> There was a dachshund once so long
>   He hadn't any notion
> How long it took to notify
>   His tail of an emotion.
> And so it happened, while his eyes
>   Were full of woe and sadness,
> His little tail went wagging on
>   Because of previous gladness.

For I certainly think literally true of an appalling proportion of our
population what Fion MacColla (T. D. MacDonald), the novelist,
whose *Albannach* is by far the best and most radical novel of the
Hebrides, said to me in Edinburgh one day of our mutual friend,
William Power. Power was coming towards us along George IV
bridge. He had on a coat with a fur collar (which MacDonald
insisted on styling monkey skin), and, with stout boots and a walking-
stick, combined a countrified appearance with the Thespian effect the
coat gave him. ' Here comes Power,' said Tom. ' You know, if he
suddenly started barking instead of speaking, at least five minutes
would elapse before anyone realized that anything out of the way was
happening.'

Preferring darkness rather than light, I have likened these people in
my Glasgow poem to those insects which are repelled rather than
attracted if an electric light is substituted for an old-fashioned kero-
sene lamp, and speculated on consulting Helsmoortel as to what the
effect on their mentalities might be if irradiation methods were
applied to their genital organs. As matters stand, almost everything
they are so incessantly busy with merely reminds me of the picture
of a great hulking gorilla of a man about to enter a taxi and shouting
to the driver : ' Royal College of Needlework—and drive like Hell ! '
    It is even worse with Edinburgh than it is with Glasgow. No
Scottish writer has yet given us anything half so blistering as the
story (in Humphrey Pakington's novel, *Family Album*) of the
Duchess of Glencockle's sale of *objets d'art* in Edinburgh to help
' the dear wounded Tommies '—and prevent anybody but the
' right ' people from giving a hand—which is a veritable classic of
satirical pulverization. A city, in Garcia Lorca's phrase, peopled by
' a mob wearing clothes without heads '.
    I do not like Edinburgh (or any city very much), for I have never
been able to find one that was not full of reminders of the fact that
Cain, the murderer, was also the first city-builder. Yet I love
Dublin ; I greatly enjoyed Salonika, where (like Leontiev) I was
stationed for a couple of years ; I completely lost my heart to Faenza,
where I stayed for some time when passing through Italy on my way
home from Salonika, from which I had been invalided as a consequence of malaria ; I had a great nine months in Marseilles—helping
to run Sections Lahore Indian General Hospital from the Château
Mirabeau at Estaque—Marseilles with the Rue Cannebière, where, as
Phyllis Bottome says, there is always everything to be found, from
Algerian tumblers to pink-and-white English middies, and where men
of every profession, including murderers and even a saint or two, are
standing about ready to pick up a job ; I could write a pæan of praise
to Liverpool, where I spent a wild year as Publicity Officer of the
Liverpool Organization, the Merseyside civic publicity organization
supported by the Corporations of Liverpool, Birkenhead, and
Wallasey ; and I even had a most enjoyable time in Blackpool when,
in August 1918, as Sergeant-Caterer for our Depot Sergeants' Mess
(R.A.M.C.), with over 300 warrant officers and senior N.C.Os. in
average daily messing strength and a great influx of visiting sergeants
belonging to other units, I sold forty-five cases of whisky and ninety
barrels of beer in the month—and that at a time of strict rationing,
when Blackpool licence-holders had great difficulty in getting hold
of the stuff—particularly the ' hard stuff '—at all, and would have
given me two to three pounds a bottle if I would have diverted any
of it to them : a feat which brought me to loggerheads with the Army
Authorities and led to an investigation from which I emerged with
flying colours. But Edinburgh is the most interesting city in Scotland

E 2

by a long way, and it is the only city I know that I can at all bracket
along with the most beautiful and romantic and theatrical city I have
been to—pre-Hitler Vienna.   How I enjoyed my visit to Vienna as a
guest of honour of the Austrian P.E.N., staying in the Hotel Bristol
in the Opernring, motoring about with Barbara Ring and Jo Van
Ammers Kuller, talking with the Socialist Mayor, Seitz, seeing over
the great Karl Marx and other blocks of workers' flats, and having
the details explained to me by the officials, enjoying *slacht-obers* in
the cafés, endless cups of afternoon tea-with-rum, the new wine
festival at Semmering, the mighty beer-drinking with my old friend,
the German poet, Theodor Daubler, the magnificence of Schonbrünn,
and all the rest of it—the happiest of all my European experiences,
save perhaps my walking tour in 1919 along the Franco-Spanish
frontier and in the Pays Basque, or my trip round the Zuider Zee
reclamation scheme and my talk then with Karel Capek.

Vienna, full of memories of Johann Strauss and Offenbach, Freud,
Kraft-Ebing, Gustav Mahler, Hugo von Hoffmansthal—the spirit
that is celebrated in Berta Szeps's memoirs, a spirit neither of surface
gaiety and indolent acceptance, nor of rigid nationalism and partisan-
ship, but a civilized sense of values, free kinships of the mind,
tolerance, a patriotism not so much concerned with domination and
glory and aggrandisement, but mindful of man's individual worth
and liberty—the spirit that is to-day in eclipse over much of the
earth's surface, and has now been extinguished in Vienna itself,
where so many of the able and delightful people I met while I was
there have now been murdered or tortured or ruined and obscenely
put upon.

Vienna !—And I think of the one hundred per cent ' Wiener ',
who, with artillery fire roaring in the streets of his beloved city,
exclaimed : ' Wife, do you know what I would like above all things ?
I long like a child to hear a little good music again.'

Vienna !   As Henry Dwight Sedgwick says :

> ' And so the great city goes upon her untried way.   Cultivation,
> grace, delicacy, refinement, a fostered childhood of music and slow
> time give way to all that the swastika stands for.   There may be
> economic betterment ; the Treaty of Saint-German left the imperial
> city stripped of its resources, its markets, its ordinary means of liveli-
> hood, left it poverty-stricken. . . . The body will be taken care of, but
> how does the soul ? . . . Revenge, hate, cruelty.   How far they take
> us from the sweet city and its happy state, where Mozart, Schubert,
> Strauss had created a temporary earthly felicity, and sent the Danube
> waltzing and singing towards the sea ! '

But Edinburgh never had, of course, what made Vienna a city
unique among cities—its indescribable blend of depth and solidity
and substance happily wedded to light-heartedness and the ecstasy
of life for life's sake.

' Gone,' say the brothers David and Frederic Ewen, writing of

how, after the Nazi annexation, they found this Vienna, that had
been the queen city that drew to itself all that was greatest in music
and that ruled musical life for almost two hundred years, ' was every
vestige of a free culture and a free art. Gone the old charm and
Gemütlichkeit. Martial music replaced the waltz in the café-house.
Franz Lehar re-wrote " The Merry Widow " to conform to the edicts
of the Nazi Kulturkammer. The bust of Mahler was removed from
the vestibule of the Hofoper, and the Mahlerstrasse was renamed.
The last of the great creative spirits fled abroad.'

Nay, what I have said in a previous essay describes fully those
elements in its history which so fleetingly gave Edinburgh just a
soupçon of Vienna's quality in a single respect. Otherwise there is
practically no comparison. Vienna! One cannot think of Mozart,
Beethoven, Schubert, Brahms—four of the towering geniuses of
music—without recalling their failures and their triumphs, their
struggles and their personal crises in Vienna. But these were not
all. There were Gluck and Mahler and Bruckner and Johann Strauss
and Hugo Wolf and dozens of other creators and interpreters who
were drawn to Vienna's glory, added to it, and were rebuffed by the
city and its influential people—for there is no need to forget that the
record is, despite all its high lights, mainly one of the battle of
dreamers against want, enmity, and cabal, and if we become lyrical
about the works of genius and the performers of genius that were
nurtured in Vienna, we must not be indifferent to the shoddiness and
superficiality of most that attracted and succeeded in the city.

I have mentioned Karel Capek. I found that we had a great deal
in common, and enjoyed my talk with him immensely (H. W.
Nevinson and Arthur Lynch made it a ' four-handed crack ', as we
call it in Scotland). Our talk was mainly of matters which were the
themes of his last book—*Travels in the North*—a few years later.
When Karel Capek was a little boy he dreamed of discovering a
marvellous island above the Arctic Circle, where mangoes would be
growing on the slopes of a volcano, amid the eternal ice. Later there
was his mind's lifelong journey to the North, on the wings of the
great literature of Scandinavia. And always he cherished the thought
of an actual pilgrimage to ' just the North ' ; the North of birch trees
and forests, and sparkling water, and dewy mists and silvery coolness,
' and altogether a beauty that is more tender and severe than any
other '. So at last he made his Northern journey ; across the neat
fairy-tale landscapes of Denmark, among the lakes and islands and
granite boulders and red plank farmhouses of Sweden, up through
Norway and the great Northern forests, and beyond the Arctic Circle
into that unreal world where one may see ' midnight rainbows
hanging from one shore to the other, a mild and golden sunset
mirrored in the sea before a frosty morning dawn ' ; so to the ' end
of Europe ' at the North Cape. ' Oh, no, this is not the end of

Europe; it is her beginning. The end of Europe is down there below among men, where they are at their busiest.'

> ' This ', another writer has said, ' is the book that he has left behind at his death, a book of profound simplicity and moving beauty and sudden arresting thought. It is a rare and lovely book, " exemplified ", as the title-page puts it, with the author's own delightful drawings : a book to be treasured and gone back to again and again. It is also a book whose charm cannot be captured in a review ; for its quality cannot be conveyed by describing it, or by telling what Karel Čapek saw and did and thought. Only by reading *Travels in the North*—and, too, by looking at the pictures—can one understand and savour its pungency, its fragrance, its exquisiteness, and its whim.'

Karel Capek loved the trees and those forests that stand in their solid ranks across the Northern earth, as if they were still guarding earth's infancy. He had keen eyes to see lands and people, and he could see, too, what the people were like and how they lived and whether they trusted one another. He had a brisk humour in little things. And he was absolutely himself. Every page of this book is individual, whether it reflects simple enjoyment, wistfulness, fancy, or insight ; and every page is set to the book's own rhythm, in a haunting simplicity. There is a double-edged bit of sadness at the volume's end, the sadder because its symbolism was unintentional. The sturdy old boat on which he had voyaged to the North Cape will never carry passengers again ; ' my word, it was a good boat, and a good journey ', is the sentence which closes the last chapter. Then a footnote tells of the good old ship's passing, and her captain's sorrow, and the author adds : 'And be her memory honoured to the last full stop '. They are the final words in Karel Capek's last book ; they need only to be redirected in application, from a ship to a man.

Karel Capek died at forty-eight years of age, on December 25, 1938, from pneumonia, according to the physician, but his friends are unanimous in the opinion that he died of grief. His last written words were the prayer of October 5, 1938 : ' Dear Lord, Creator of this beloved land, You know our suffering and our despair. To You we need not express our thoughts, nor how our heads are bowed. Not bowed in shame ; we have no cause for shame, though fate has struck us with an iron hand.'

His works together with those of his brother Josef Capek mounted to forty-four volumes. Cosmopolitan, yet essentially Czech, his plays were played in twenty-six countries and translated into all the languages of the civilized world. I have never had the pleasure of meeting his wife, Olga Schienpflugova, though there is perhaps no woman in Europe I would like better to meet. She, too, the leading actress of the National Theatre in Prague, is the author of some thirty volumes, collections of poetry, novels, and plays.

Like Karel Toman, the greatest contemporary Czech poet, Karel Capek seems to have said at the end :

I shall not live with the new masters ;
I wish to be taken to your breast,
To lose myself in the ashes of my ancestors
Of the Czech country.

I must not leave this chapter in which I have written of Vienna without mentioning that I made there one of my most unexpectable literary contacts—just as I did when I happened to find myself the only foreign author present at the unveiling in the park at Thorshaven by Mrs. Carl Nillsen of the statue of Rasmus Effersoe, the Faroese national poet. This was my meeting with Chaim Nachman Bialik, a poet of the stature of Jehudah Halevi and Ibn Gabirol. As William A. Drake says ;

> ' It is at once Bialik's greatness and his limitation as a poet that his work cannot be considered separately from the social situation and aspirations of the Jewish people. His talent arose at the time of his people's greatest need, when the wave of anti-Semitism had reduced Jews to abjectness and the horrible succession of pogroms in Central Europe had left them cowed and helpless. . . . These bleak years, which have crushed many a stouter spirit than his—years which the Russian Jews call " Bezvremenye ", because they are the obliteration of time—only made his apprehension of life the more eager and poignant. . . . Bialik's true mission was to stir up his people out of the lethargy of their despair and ignominy. The voice of the prophet gradually rises, through *On Pisgah Height, Surely the People are Grass*, and *The Exile's Tear* to its first full utterance in *The Dead of the Wilderness*. This remarkable poem is based upon the Talmudic legend that the rebellious Jews who left Egypt for Canaan did not perish in the desert, as the Bible states, but were cast into a deep slumber from which, from time to time, they awaken to struggle onward through eternity toward the goal which they are destined never to reach. Filled with the rebellious grandeur of Lucifer and the stubborn courage of the Maccabees, to Bialik the example of these insurgent heroes indicated by contrast the abyss of enslavement into which the Russian Jews had fallen. *The Dead of the Wilderness* was written in 1902. In the next year occurred the massacre at Kishinev. Bialik emerged from the shock of that bestiality in his full stature as a prophet. In such flaming poems as *On the Butchery* and *The City of Slaughter* he flays his people for their submission to such infamies, for their cowardice in not fighting back as their homes were pillaged and their daughters ravished, for their abjectness in praying through the carnage for forgiveness of the sins that had brought these misfortunes upon them, when their manhood required that they should die defending their honour. " How could such creatures sin ? " he makes God exclaim, in scorn.'

I have been wonderfully fortunate in my contacts. There is no need for me to comment on the way in which I was drawn to this passionate spirit, nationalistic without bigotry, pious without austerity, and alert to every actual flavour of life, just as I was drawn to Capek—the leader of the younger Czech generation which, since the war, had superseded that of Vrchlicky, Brezina, Machar, and Sova, of all of whose work I knew a good deal ; but except Brezina, in refusing to be Austrian, they became international, whereas Capek

was more after my own heart; the first notable poet of Czech
nationalism, the nature of his genius was conspicuously Slavic. And
his work was peculiarly congenial to me in the extent to which what
Van Wyck Brooks wrote of Wells is exactly applicable to Capek—
' He is an intellectual, rather than an artist; that is to say, he naturally
describes and interprets life in the light of ideas, rather than in the
light of experience '—which, of course, is true of myself as well!
Yet, greatly as I admired Capek, and profoundly as I admired
(hating my own compatriots for not equalling it) that indomitable
patriotism by which their native language was kept alive through so
many proscribed years, to leap up like a released spring in a new
literature as soon as the Czechs were freed of the Hapsburg yoke and
of the dead weight of its compulsion, it was the older poet of a
brilliant and vilely persecuted people, Chaim Bialik, who made the
profoundest appeal to my sympathies and the nature of whose spirit
was most congenial to my own, so that I regard my meeting and
intercourse with him as one of the greatest privileges of my life.
' Filled with the rebellious grandeur of Lucifer and the stubborn
courage of the Maccabees '—were not these the very attributes a
Scottish poet to-day must covet most? And had I not a fair share
of them?

I was fortunate too a little later in another of my Jewish friendships
—with Jakob Wassermann (who lived for a time in Vienna and found
his wife there), of whom it has been well said : ' Like Heine, he was a
Jew and a German, the keenest spirit, yet the most remote, in the
mêlée of modernity; the type closest to the heart of our changing
culture, yet the least a part of it.' Wassermann's world conception,
as old as Nature itself, was peculiarly congenial to me—the idea of
the common identity of all things in Nature, of man's individual
responsibility for the whole of humanity. This idea colours and
directs all his thought, gradually taking form through the long
procession of his early novels and tales : in *Die Schwestern, Casper
Hauser, Die Masken Erwin Reiners, Der Goldene Spiegel,* and his first
great success, *Das Gansemännchen,* before it comes to its first complete
and mystical expression in *Christian Wahnschaffe.* That is one of
the few really fine novels of our time, and affected me more perhaps
than any fiction I have read save Dostoevsky, with whom Wassermann
had much in common, though he was, of course, a much smaller man,
with insights far less profound than the titanic Russian's. Yet what
Wassermann told Pierre Loving in 1914 appealed to me greatly. ' I
am interested primarily in life, in making a synthesis of life which is
based firmly upon my own visible contacts,' he said. ' I try not to
ignore the inner vision; the inner vision is of overwhelming
importance, but my objective observation is always at work correcting
that inner grasp of reality. My aim is to pack the whole complex
modern scene into my books . . .'

That, in a different way, is of course my aim too, as the verses I have given of ' The Kind of Poetry I Want ' show, and precisely this has been the conscious or unconscious aim of my people through the ages ; it is what lies behind their world-ranging propensities, the endless capacity for simultaneously entertaining the most diverse interests, the encyclopædic character (elsewhere dismissed as ' the Scotsman's pedantry—there is always a dominie at his elbow ') of their intellectual curiosity, the polymathic powers that manifest themselves so markedly in the field of Scottish biography, from the wandering scholars downwards to our own day, and, too—lest anything should escape them !— behind that Caledonian Antisysygy with which I deal in a later chapter.

It is this which makes Professor Gregory Smith single out as one of the chief characteristics of Scottish literature that piling up of details the completed effect of which ' is one of movement, suggesting the action of a concerted dance or the canter of a squadron.   We have gone astray if we call this art merely meticulous, a pedant's or cataloguer's vanity in words, as some foolish persons have inclined to make charge against the " antiquary " Scott.   The whole is not always lost in the parts ; it is not a compilation impressive only because it is greater than any of its contributing elements, but often single in result and above all things lively.   The verse forms of both popular and artificial Scots poetry aid this purpose of movement. In the older popular verse, partly cast in the mould of the alliterative romance, as well as in the seventeenth and eighteenth-century copies, the details catch each other up like dancers in a morris.'

It was in Holland too that I fraternized with another novelist who writes in Yiddish, Joseph Opatoshu, with whom politically and otherwise I found I had a great deal in common.   I agree with John Cournos (whom also I met in London fifteen years ago or so— introduced to him, I think, by Professor Allardyce Nicoll), who brackets him with Sholam Asch (whom I met in Vienna) and I. J. Singer, declaring that Opatoshu is by no means the least of the three, and in dealing with that world of Jewry known as the cult of Hassidism (in which I was keenly interested through the work of Martin Buber) —a strange cult so quintessentially Jewish and yet so close to the spirit of Christianity divested of dogma—Opatoshu goes deeper than Ansky in his play *The Dybbuk* or Sholam Asch in his superb novel *Salvation*.   Opatoshu in Amsterdam gave me the typescript of the English translation of his novel *In Polish Woods*—the first of his work to be translated into English—and I found it, as I expected from my intercourse with the man himself, the product of a distinguished and original creative mind, with strongly marked lyrical elements, and apocalyptic elements hard to define, but expressive of the very innermost soul of Jewry in the travail of eternal struggle and flux.

In a charming reminiscence Professor G. R. Elliott quotes Babbitt as saying : ' It seems that you and I agree that what America needs to-day is a new deal in ideas.' And on receiving an affirmative reply, Babbitt exclaimed loudly, shaking his fist at things in general : ' Well, then, why don't you get out and fight ? ' Substituting Scotland for America, that is just what I have done.

John Maclean heard his last terrible sentence unmoved. Turning to the comrades he cried : ' Keep it going, boys ; keep it going.' We will ! Maclean's slogan was ' Through Marxism to Revolution—the only way ! '

As to reasons for confidence in the great possibilities of literature in the future, it may be true that infinite sensitivity would be a self-contradiction and that nobody is perfectly integrative, but with the advance of science towards the supersession of any need for human drudgery, insensitivity is steadily ceasing to have any ' survival value '.

It was precisely the implacable and arrogant element in my nature to which I have referred in previous passages, clearly manifested at the very beginning of my work for Scotland after my demobilization in 1919 and my return to live in my own country, that that shrewd observer and experienced journalist, Neil Munro (for whose own writings either in prose or poetry I had little use, and whose character in relation to Scotland's requirements I condemned before and at the time of his death in flaying articles which gave great offence to his family and all his host of friends), seized upon. He pointed out in one of the first articles devoted to me that these attributes were precisely those which promised best for (and not, as most of my critics imagined, those most likely to prevent) my eventual leadership of the Scottish cause—and he illustrated his argument by pointing to Parnell's character and his treatment of and attitude to his colleagues, and to the case of Thaddeus Stevens in America, of whom his biographer, Alphonse Miller, well says :

> ' He rose to leadership in the House just when the crisis demanded men of his inflexible temper. Stevens's very shortcomings made him all the more exactly gifted for the task at hand. His unapproachability, his imperviousness to gentler influences, his fearsome reputation as one who never gave ground, were of the utmost help in bending Congress to his will, always and indomitably the will to win. When it came to war morale, the savage fighting spirit so vital just then, the North was ill-equipped. There were all too few leaders at Washington with the courage to sound the charge. Stevens's most signal service to his country was precisely that. Amid the secession sympathizers, the quaking money-changers, the legalistic martinets aquiver with constitutional misgivings, his voice and example were a perpetual call to arms.'

It is not for nothing, perhaps, that one of my favourite stories is that of Paderewski's playing through a whole series of concerts with an injured finger which left the keys actually red with blood at the end of every performance.

The kind of man I admire is a man like Nicholas Ostrovsky, whose *Born of the Storm* is one of the ' classics ' of Soviet fiction—full of undeniable merits despite certain shortcomings. Ostrovsky, a sincere hundred per cent Bolshevik who had fought, since the age of seventeen, in the Red ranks against the Whites and the Poles, spent the last years of his life as a bedridden invalid. Afflicted with some strange illness, undergoing one operation after another, he lay paralysed and blind, suffering from terrific headaches and neuralgic pains. It was *in this condition* that he dictated *The Makings of a Hero* and composed the first volume of *Born of the Storm*. For he was prevented by death, which put an end to his torments in 1935, from completing it. As a record of this human story lying behind them, these novels are impressive, irrespective of their qualities or defects. And it was this that prompted the Soviet Press to make of Ostrovsky a sort of saint—a glowing example of an ' iron Bolshevik ' whose creative will no sufferings could break.

It was this quality too that gave me such a tremendous feeling for the great Scottish Leninist, John Maclean. William Gallacher rightly writes of him as ' a living dynamo of energy, driving, always driving, towards his goal . . . certainly the greatest revolutionary figure Scotland had produced. . . . The work done by Maclean during the winter of 1917–18 has never been equalled by anyone. His educational work would have been sufficient for half a dozen ordinary men, but on the top of this he was carrying on a truly terrific propaganda and agitational campaign. Every minute of his time was devoted to the revolutionary struggle, every ounce of his extraordinary energy was thrown into the fight.' No wonder I say in one of my poems :

> Scotland has had few men whose names
> Matter—or should matter—to intelligent people,
> But of these Maclean, next to Burns, was the greatest
> And it should be of him, with every Scotsman and Scotswoman
> To the end of time, as it was of Lenin in Russia
> When you might talk to a woman who had been
> A young girl in 1917 and find
> That the name of Stalin lit no fires,
> But when you asked her if she had seen Lenin
> Her eyes lighted up and her reply
> Was the Russian word which means
> Both beautiful and red.
> Lenin, she said, was ' *krassivy, krassivy* '.
> John Maclean too was ' *krassivy, krassivy* ',
> A description no other Scot has ever deserved.

CHAPTER III

THE KIND OF POETRY I WANT

The East
—Ah, the East!
The Watch Tower at Mandalay,
The Dragon Pagoda at Amarapura,
Sagaing!
The pottery houses at Bandigarampudur,
The Yanesh Temple at Vijayanagar,
The Rock Temple at Kondane,
The Buddhist cave at Nasik,
Champaner, Dwarka, and Yirnar! . . .

A poetry with bells ringing everywhere,
Even on the thin white ponies
In from the hill country
With loads of tsai-birds' eggs and wild oranges.

' What I require is a voice as piercing as a lynx's eye, as terrible as the
sigh of a giant, as persistent as a note of nature, with a range extending from
the deepest bass to the highest and most melting chest-tone, with a modulation capable of the lightest sacred whisper, and the fire-spouting violence of
madness. That is what I need in order to get my breath, to deliver myself
of what lies in my mind, to thrill the bowels both of anger and of sympathy.'
—KIERKEGAARD (in a letter to Emil Boesen).

I HAVE written of my practice of omnivorous reading, my interest in
linguistics, and so forth, but the best way perhaps in which I can
illustrate the scope and direction of my intellectual interests and
manifest the æsthetic position I now take up as a result of the literary
experience and the developments of my mind with which this book is
mainly concerned is, I think, to devote the rest of this chapter to a
hitherto unprinted poem which is in the nature of a comprehensive
manifesto. Mr. T. S. Eliot in this country, and in America Mr.
George Dillon, the editor of *Poetry* (Chicago), both of whom read it
in manuscript, but were unable to use it in their respective periodicals
because of its length and the extent to which it depends on its
cumulative effect and does not lend itself to ' cutting ', wrote me very
enthusiastically about it, and about the immensely long poem of
which it forms a small part, and expressed their eagerness to see it in
print, while recognizing to the full the increasing practical difficulties
in the way of the ready publication of anything of the sort. It will
suffice to add that this poem exemplifies the aspiration to world-
consciousness which has been the guiding principle in all my more
recent work, agreeing as I do with the passage in which Count
Keyserling says :

' The real goal of progress is then on the one hand a total live
experience of the whole of the real, and on the other such a deeply

rooted fixation in spirit that, thanks to it, man can, by the function of
comprehension and by spiritual initiative acting through it, make the
entire universe his own.'

I˙dream of poems like the bread-knife
Which cuts three slices at once ;
Of poems concerned with technical matters
(Poems braced by Carducci's ' cold bath of erudition '
—As befits one of the new ' *Gli Amici pedanti* '—
Knowing Sotomayor's [1] essay on poetic erudition too
And all the other manifestations
Of *cultismo* and *conceptista* through the ages,
(Since of course everything depends on providing the divining power
With the preparatory bath of practised concentration
We roughly call ' an interest in the subject to hand '),
Which, as masterpieces of intricate lucidity
(The power to penetrate as with the lens of the X-ray
Into the interior and exterior of a solid
Free from the distortion of perspective)
Or in cut-gem clearness surpass even Huxley's
Prose account of the endophragmal system of the crayfish
And his Anatomy of the Vertebrata ;
Crystal clear as Joule's first full exposition
—Given to a popular audience, a church-reading-room audience,
Of no special knowledge—of the central doctrine
Of modern science, that of the Conservation of Energy ;
Or beautifully acute as Moritz Geiger's
Fragment uber den Begriff des Unbewussten und die psychische Realität ;
Or like the way in which the Pada text
Is converted by a process of euphonic combination into the Samhita,
Or like the more than six-score synonyms of gamati he gives
Which include all forms and varieties of motion ;
Or like Fred Astaire, who has combined
All forms of dancing into one perfect whole
—Endowed his work with all the intricacies,
Incorporated all the things that make dancing difficult,
But developed them to such a point that they seem simple
—So great an artist that he makes you feel
You could do the dance yourself—Is not that great art ?
A poetry in which the disorder and irrelevancies
Of the real world are seen
As evidence of the order, relevance, and authority
Of the law behind, so that what
Is misleading (private or untidy) becomes
By its very irrelevance significant of a reality
Beyond the bewilderment of external reality ;
And a brain and an imagination that takes
Every grade without changing gears.
Like glancing at the rev-counter, partially closing the throttle,
And gliding down to make a fine
Three-point landing into the wind.
For this is the poetry I seek
—The vividness of the orchestra in the cobbling song,
The unbelievable control of the crescendo of the fight in the street,

---

[1] Luis Carrillo y Sotomayor (1585–1620).

Then the decrescendo, the watchman's horn and call,
The lovely modulation to the lyrical,
The peaceful, and the miniature,
(The performance's shape and life-giving forms
Never forced before us after the opening
Concentration on clarity in the preliminary unfolding of the argument)
To the end—where the banner of song is opened
With a width and nobility which cause
Happiness and sadness, laughter and tears,
To express one and the same pride in life
—After the prelude,
The running waves of song to the finale,
The heart-wounding cry of adoration,
The reconciliation of all things gay and sad in the quintet,
The colour and Shakespearean love of all sorts and conditions of
    humanity
In the meadow scene, the swelling heart of the music
In the homage to Sachs—all brought
To a high noon of love of life.

Swift songs, in keeping with the ever-expanding
And accelerating consciousness Brezina has sung so nobly,
Sdrucciolo-swift and utterly un-English,
Songs like the transition from the *urlar* to the *crunluath*,[1]
Those variations which suggest hidden reserves
Of strength, of ingenuity, to follow,
Of undreamed-of gracenotes hidden in the fingers,
Then into the *crunluath breabach*,
Before the merciless variety, the ranting arrogance of which
Even the wonders of the *crunluath* pale to insignificance,
And finally into the fourth and greatest movement of the *piob mhor*,
The most fantastic music in all the range of the pipes,
The *crunluath math*—where miracles of improvization
Form themselves of their own volition under the fingers ;
The expert ear may trace the original melody
Of the *urlar* weaving its faint way
Through the maze of gracenotes,
But the very gracenotes are going mad
And making melodies of their own
As the player conceives new and ever louder diversions.

Ah, sweetheart, what a pool !   Broad, deep, strong, silent, and sedate !
The foam-patches spinning round in the eddies and then
Hurrying onwards betray the speed of the current.
A sturdy Norsk-Murdoch spinning-rod, a 4-inch Silex reel,
A steel trace, and a box of artificial minnows
—A selection essentially for a big water.
(Very unlike the dainty but deadly outfit
Used when the streams are at summer level.)
Indeed, the river is a gorgeous colour,
Golden in the shallows, black in the depths,
Foam-flecked all over the pools.
For the initial attempt I choose a 3-inch anti-kink minnow, brown and
    gold.

---

[1] These and the remaining italicized words in this verse are Scottish
Gaelic terms for different tempi in pipe music.

—First, one or two casts downstream, to make sure
The tension of the reel is correctly adjusted to the weight of the bait,
That the line is well and truly wound,
Then out goes the minnow at the correct angle,
To drop on a circle of foam possibly 50 yards away.
Minnow, line, and rod are in one straight line.
The rod-point, dipping low almost to the surface,
Is slowly moved around, the minnow is bravely spinning its way across,
When a vicious tug sets the reel screaming.
A salmon is on ; it makes no attempt
To increase the distance between us.
After I persuade it out of the full strength of the current
And get on terms with it,
I keep it moving to a speedy end,
A perfect picture of a fish of 17 lb.
With the silver of the sea undimmed.
Oh, surely, the due attendance of the lying-in Muse
Always calls for *scodelle da donna di parto*
Of at least nine single pieces so made
That placed on one another they form
A vessel with the outline of a fine vase ;
And all the world must visit her
Abrogating all restrictions like the 1537 Naples Senate's.
Then let the branch of pandanus be hung up,
My house be in the power of the Phong Tong,
And give me trumpeters whose trumpets are adorned
With wide hanging cloths bearing coats of arms.
Betokening most august rank.

A poetry—since I was born a Scottish Gael
Of earth's subtlest speech, born with a clever tongue,
Moving one's tongue and lips and throat
In bird-sounds, mocking the cheewink of the joree,
The belly-hoot of the great horned owl—
To put the skids under the whole of modern consciousness,
Not unaware of our great crisis of opportunity nor unfit fully to seize it,
Nor ignorant like those who prate of ' empty air ',
Unaware of its ceilings and vaults, the Heaviside Layer and the Apple-
    ton Layer,
Along which the sound-waves run as tho' along vaults of stone
And against which we can throw things and have them bounce back,
Our shelter also from the torrent pelting outside ;
A structure so strong and sound it throws back waves
Which, if they got through, would sweep away
All life from the surface of the earth ;
A structure sturdier than Earth's horrendous stone
And strong almost as this poem even.

A poetry like the hope of achieving ere very long
A tolerable idea of what happens from first to last
If we bend a piece of wire
Backwards and forwards until it breaks.
' Toute l'industrie de l'homme ', disait Bacon,
' Consiste à approcher les substances séparées
Les unes des autres, ou à les séparer ;
Le reste est une opération secrète de la Nature.'

Nor insensitive to any difference such as that between
The earlier Kajanus interpretation of Sibelius's Second Symphony
And that of the Boston Symphony under Kussevitsky,
The latter scrupulously faithful, though the glow and fire
And inner passion of the performance may make it doubted
Thanks to the common prepossession that a sound performance
Like a sound man inevitably predicates one
Utterly without imagination, insight, or sympathy.
—Poems of prodigious observation and alarming chic,
Couched in a language so adroit that at no matter how
Deep levels the introspective exploration
Of the inner essence of the self proceeds, the thought
Can never break through it and escape.
And with an exquisite finish that redeems them
From the appearance, if not from the reality,
Of obscurity—a language *serré*, quick with Ithuriel's spear,
With no thought *sine mucrone*,
And all its sword-play with a *ricasso* edge
To let my thumb rest on the blade,
A language like ' *mar leine-chneas aig a brathair* ',
—The true form, the ' garment next the skin '.
Such poems as might be written in eternal life if there
By such a steady vision of God as in the present life
Is altogether beyond our reach we are relieved
Of the intolerable burdens of temporality,
—Its rude interruptions, and tragic endings, but no less
Its *Langweiligkeit*, its ennui, the irksomeness of its petty pace,
Yet retain a certain form of successiveness.

A poetry that goes all the way
From Brahma to a stock,
A poetry like pronouncing the Shemporesh,
Unremitting, relentless,
Organized to the last degree.
Ah, Lenin, politics is child's play
To what this must be.
(If I have evolved myself out of something
Like an amphioxus, it is clear
I have become *better* by the change,
I have risen in the organic scale.
I have become more organic.
Of all the changes which I have undergone
The greater part must have been
Changes in the organic direction,
Some in the opposite direction,
Some perhaps neutral—but if
I could only find out which,
I should say that those changes which have tended
In the direction of greater organization
Were good—and those which tended
In the opposite direction bad.
The words good and bad belong
To the practical reason, and if
They are defined it is by pure choice.
I choose that definition of them which must,
On the whole, cause those people who act
Upon it to be selected for survival.

The good action, then, is a mode of action
Which distinguishes organic from inorganic things
And which makes organic thing more organic.)

A poetry with the power of assimilating foreign influences,
As in the wonderful flowering of the Golden Age in Spain
—The exceptional receptivity due to no poverty of inspiration,
No *Mangel eigener Begabung*, but rather
To the strength and fervour of the indigenous character and genius,
Der unerhörten formalen Begabung des eigenes Landes,
The absorbing power irresistible because collective ;
A poetry finding its universal material in the people,
And the people in turn giving life and continuity
To this poetry by its collective interest.
An extraordinary breadth of material that can only
Be coped with and confined within the limitations of art
By great subtlety, sense of proportion,
And delight in concrete expression.

Or, like that mile-long gallery, broken
By open bridges roofed with a flutter
Of thousands of municipal flags, the *Hohe Weg*,
In which, by means of relief maps, revolving globes,
Moving herds, and armies of Noah's Ark figures,
And occasional gigantic frescoes, the history,
Geography, industry, engineering,
Agriculture, and defiant Chauvinism of Switzerland
Are displayed to, by, and for the people,
With a Scotswoman (married to a Swiss architect)
Who acted as official interpreter during the Lord Mayor of London's
    visit
To Zurich in July as my guide, sometimes,
And sometimes a Nazi woman—a lady
Once as intelligent and well-mannered as she had been dark-haired,
But now a peroxide blonde (*vernordert* is the word for this)
With plucked eyebrows and a bright pink make-up
That only enhances the desperate artificiality of her hair.
—The vine-wreathed wine-bars, the attractive
Alkohol-frei restaurants, the teleferique cars
Swinging across a wire looped three hundred feet
Above the surface of a lake,
And all the rest of it.
And at night the Sechselauten again.

A poetry in short in which, as in Spain
With the Roman, Germanic, Catholic Church, and Jewish elements
As the unifying influences, and the Iberians,
Berbers, Greeks, Phoenicians, and Carthaginians
As the disintegrating elements, in the wavering balance
Between unity and great achievement on the one hand
And particularism and chaos on the other,
By the end of the fifteenth century the whole nation was a great group
The component parts of which remained individual and distinct
Like the blades of wheat in the sheaf
Which was the emblem of the Catholic Kings,
And the Nation could thus express itself
In a form at once genuine and universal.

A poetry like the character of Indian culture,
Which is and always has been its universal contacts.
Motifs flood in from Iran and Persia,
Nestorian monks colour the practice
Of Thibetan devotees, and in the Court
Of the rude Mahmud of Ghazni is a Moslem scholar
Acquainted with Plato.   A wonderful panorama
In which, though its strength is rather
In arts and thought and race
Than in social structure and growth,
Innumerable reflections and parallels
For European culture strike us,
In the types of wergeld and feudal fief,
Land custom, paternal justice, and the bards ;
A vast picture in which we see
The furious passage of Tamerlane or Zinghis Khan,
Or the great conquerors who have left hardly a wrack behind,
Taxila, with its memories of Alexander,
The Greek king who reigned in Sialkot,
And thousands more—with everywhere
The impression of universality,
Of the million grains of sand and gold
Which have rolled to the delta.

A poetry at the worst adept
In the artful tessellation of commonplaces
Expressed with so exact a magnificence
That they seem—and sometimes are—profound.

A poetry the quality of which
Is a stand made against intellectual apathy,
Its material founded, like Gray's, on difficult knowledge,
And its metres those of a poet
Who has studied Pindar and Welsh poetry,
But, more than that, its words coming from a mind
Which has experienced the sifted layers on layers
Of human lives—aware of the innumerable dead
And the innumerable to-be-born,
The voice of the centuries, of Shakespeare's history plays
Concentrated and deepened,
' The breath and finer spirit of all knowledge,
The impassioned expression
Which is in the countenance of all science '.

Finally, a poetry such that if someone asks,
As of the forest by the river Kundalini,
' Of what nature is the monk
Who adds glory to this forest ? '
The reply, like Dhammaasenapati's, must be,
' It is the monk who is of his own mind the ruler ;
His mind does not rule him !
At the opening of each day he considers,
In what state of mind shall I spend
Each hour until night falls ?
As a king with a box of many robes,
Of many and varying colours,
In the first watch of each day decides

What robe he will wear, and at noon
Changes to the robe which then he chooses,
And so also at night—so here ;
The ascetic, Moggallana, adds glory
To this forest by Kundalini.'
So here, in this poetry of one who knows
An ontological system behind physics
In which a past event has no finality
Of being absolute past,
And has a Philosophy of Art
That throws light on the unphysical question
As to whether there are other perspectives
In which the factual status of the past
Is transformed into an actual appearance ;
Nothing guaranteeing that event is an ultimate category
Which may not be expressed in terms of as yet unknown
But more basic entities—
Robes worn by the Master of my Art !

A language like the magnetic needle,
The most sensitive thing in the world, which responds alike
To Polar light in the north, electric currents
Flowing round the equator, the revolutions
Of the earth on its axis, the annual course
Of the earth round the sun, the revolution of the sun itself,
And the mysterious processes in sunspots,
And hence we shall have a poetry in which,
As after Schwabe's discovery that the number of sunspots
Occurring within a given time reaches a maximum
Every eleventh year, led to efforts
To see whether this eleven-year cycle appeared
In any other terrestrial phenomena until now
Schostakowitsch in *Gerland's Beiträge*
Examines the statistics of North Atlantic air temperatures,
Nile flood levels, wheat prices, winters in Europe,
Tree-rings, sedimentary layers and lake deposits,
The dates of the sprouting and bloom of hawthorn,
Of the first cuckoo, of the beginning of harvest,
Of cattle products, herring and salmon catches, diphtheria,
Typhus and measles epidemics, prices of Consols,
Workers' wages, coal production, discount at the Bank of England,
British export trade, American wheat productions,
Suicides and lynchings—and finds the eleven-year cycle in them all
And shows the connexions between them.
Or as through the influence of *buddhi*
The whole of the subtle body is affected by dispositions or conditions
In the same manner as a garment is perfumed
By contact with a fragrant *champa* [1] flower,
Or like the *akūta* by which organs
With defined and separate functions act upon each other,
Or like any *linga paramarsa*,
Or like the specific elements, the supports, without which,

---

[1] The *Bauhinia variegata* of Linnaeus, called *kovidara* in the *Asiat. Res.*
IV, 285) : a leguminous plant ; ' flowers chiefly purplish and rose-coloured,
fragrant '.

As a painting does not stand without a frame
Nor a shadow without a stake,
The *linga-sarira*, vehicle of the *linga*,
Whose substance is like light, does not exist
—The *linga* which enters into the womb and forms the inner frame
Over which the bodily form, derived from the mother,
Is gradually wrought.
A speech, a poetry, to bring to bear upon life
The concentrated strength of all our being
(Eloquent of victory in the stern struggle for self-conquest
—Real freedom ; life free, unhampered, unalloyed ;
A deep religious impulse moving us, not that
Interpreted by others through systems of belief and practice,
But the craving for the perfect synthesis of thought and action
Which alone can satisfy our test
Of ultimate truth, and conception of life's purpose.)
And not like only the 8 per cent of the fuel
That does useful work in the motor-car—the bare 2 per cent
The best incandescent lamp converts of the energy received
Into radiation visible to the human eye
—Against the glow-worm's 96 per cent efficiency.

Is not this what we require ?—
Coleridge's esemplasy and coadunation
Multeity in unity—not the Unity resulting
But the mode of the conspiration
(Schelling's *in-eins-bildung-kraft*)
Of the manifold to the one,
For, as Rilke says, the poet must know everything,
Be μινδεδνεος [1] (a phrase which I have borrowed
From a Greek monk, who applies it
To a Patriarch of Constantinople),
Or, as the *Bhagavad-Gita* puts it, *visvato-mukha*. [2]

Or as when the track of the excavator
Has been advanced about 26 feet
The first conveyor is slid sideways,
The second conveyor runs at right angles
To the first and finally rises
At 1 to 3 to enter the tower.
The structure is flexible in elevation and rigid in plan.
It is light to move and entirely protects the return belt.
The upward curve of the conveyor can be so sharp
Without the belt's lifting off the idlers
Because the idler friction is extremely small.
So we can rise to any height.

A poetry like Pushkin's in the morning sky of Russia,
Predestine, lumineux, et insolent de bonheur;
A poetry as when Pierrina Legnani
Walked into the middle of the stage
And took an undisguised preparation.
The conductor, his baton raised, waited.

---

[1] I.e. myriad-minded.
[2] *Visvato-mukha* = facing in all directions.

Then came a whole string of vertiginous pirouettes
Marvellous in their precision and brilliant as diamond facets.
Academically, such an exhibition of sheer acrobatics
Was inconsistent with purity of style,
But the feat as she performed it had something elemental and heroic
In its breathless daring.   It overwhelmed criticism.
Or like seeing Diaghileff at work
—I saw a Japanese performer once
Exhibiting feats of quadruple concentration.
I failed to be impressed by him.
I had seen Diaghileff at work.
And again, a poetry of which it may be said,
As of Plato's position in relation to the culture of the race,
That it is unique, and he owes it
Not to the closeness of his reasoning,
Not to the extent of his knowledge,
Not even to his great passion for truth
Or any specially firm grasp of it,
But to the unparalleled fecundity of his thought,
That is, to the breadth and length of his view.
A poetry full of *cynghanedd* [1] and hair-trigger relationships,
With something about it that is plasmic,
Resilient, and in a way alarming—to make cry
' I touched something—and it was *alive.*'
There is no such shock in touching what
Has never lived ; the mineral world is vast.
It is mighty, rigid, and brittle.   But the hand
That touches vital matter—though the man were blind—
Infallibly recognizes the feel of life, and recoils in excitement.
See how from all the points of the compass
My subject-matter races to me now,
A race magnificent beyond description,
With in it all the elements of greatness
—Wonderful speed, wonderful tactics, constant fluctuation,
And all the romance of the great race
These matters have been running in modern times
Through which they have been making history.
But this is X's day.   His mood is on him.
He is running in a rapture.   No rival
Can live with him to-day.   Y takes the lead,
But at the bell X and Z (X going so exquisitely
That we suspect the truth already)
Pass him unhurriedly.
And now at the top of the back straight,
With 300 yards to go, the smouldering fire
In X bursts into blinding flame—as though he cried
To the rest of the field, ' No cleverness or trickery to-day.
Here I am ; come and beat me if you can.'
And away he comes—one's memories
Of that delirious last lap are a little incoherent.
Climax remains in the mind—Z falling
And seeming to drift backwards, as letter after letter
Passes it, W tearing through the field with giant strides,
V coming from nowhere to pass the flagging W in the straight.

[1] A complicated metrical device in Welsh poetry.

U, steady as a rock, never gives up the chase,
Never won a victory so glorious as this defeat.
T's bitter spirit drives it round the last lap.
The two great runners fall greatly.   S fights its way
Into sixth place, like the grand old warrior it is,
And does the fastest time of its career.   But none of them
Could catch X—winning by five yards,
And the freshest of them all.
A poetry full of erudition, expertize, and ecstasy
—The acrobatics and the faceted fly-like vision,
The transparency choke-full of hair-pin bends,
' Jacinth work of subtlest jewellery ', poetry *à quatre épingles*—
(Till above every line we might imagine
A tensely flexible and complex curve
Representing the modulation,
Emphasis, and changing tone and tempo
Of the voice in reading ;
The curve varying from line to line
And the lines playing subtly against one another
—A fineness and profundity of organization
Which is the condition of a variety great enough
To express all the world's,
As subtle and complete and tight
As the integration of the thousands of brush strokes
In a Cézanne canvas),
Alive as a bout of all-in wrestling,
With countless illustrations like my photograph of a Mourning Dove
Taken at a speed of 1/75,000 of a second.
A poetry that speaks ' of trees,
From the cedar tree that is in Lebanon
Even unto the hyssop that springeth out of the wall ',
And speaks also ' of beasts and of fowl,
And of creeping things and of fishes ',
And needs, like Marya Sklodowska on her laboratory table,
For its open-eyed wonderment at the varied marvels of life,
Its insatiable curiosity about the mainspring,
Its appetite for the solution of problems,
Black fragments of pitch-blende from Saxony and Bohemia,
Greenish-blue chalcolite from Portugal and Tonkin,
Siskin-green uranium mica from France,
Canary-yellow veined carnotite from Utah,
Greenish-grey tjujamunite from Turkestan,
Pinkish-grey fergusonite from Norway,
Gold-tinted Australian monazite sand,
Greenish-black betafite from Madagascar,
And emerald-green tobernite from Indo-China.
And like my knowledge of, say, interlocking directorships,
Which goes far beyond such earlier landmarks
As the Pujo Committee's report
Or Louis Stanley's ' Spider Chart ' ;
And everywhere without fear of Chestov's ' suddenly ',
Never afraid to leap, and with the unanticipatedly
Limber florescence of fireworks as they expand
Into trees or bouquets with the abandon of ' unbroke horses '.
Or like a Beethovian semitonal modulation to a wildly remote key,
As in the Allegretto where that happens with a sudden jump of seve
     sharps,

And feels like the sunrise gilding the peak of the Dent Blanche
While the Arolla valley is still in cloud.
And constantly with the sort of grey-eyed gaity
So many people feel exalted by being allowed to hear
But are unable to laugh at—as in the case of the don
Who, lecturing on the first Epistle to the Corinthians,
In a note on the uses of αλλα mentioned αλλα *precantis*,
Which an undergraduate took down as *Allah precantis.*
In photographic language, ' wide-angle ' poems
Taking in the whole which explains the part,
Scientifically accurate, fully realized in all their details,
As Prudentius's picture of the gradually deputrifying Lazarus,
Or Baudelaire's of the naked mulatto woman,
Or Pope's most accurate particularities
In the Epistle to Lord Bathurst,
Or like a magic of grammar, a syntactical magic,
Of the relations of thought with thought whereby
By means of the syntax a whole world of ideas
Is miraculously concentrated into what is almost a point.
No mere passive hyperaesthesia to external impressions
Or exclusive absorption in a single sense,
But a many-sided active delight in the wholeness of things
And, therefore, paradoxically perhaps,
A poetry like an operating theatre,
Sparkling with a swift, deft energy,
Energy quiet and contained and fearfully alert,
In which the poet exists only as a nurse during an operation,
Who only exists to have a sponge ready when called for,
Wads of sterilized cotton wool—nothing else
Having the smallest meaning for her.

A poetry not for those who do not love a gaping pig,
Or those made mad if they behold a cat,
And least, those who, when the bagpipe sings i' the nose,
Cannot contain their urine.

The poetry of one the Russians call ' a broad nature '
And the Japanese call ' flower heart ',
And we, in Scottish Gaeldom, ' *ionraic* '.
The poetry of one who practises his art
Not like a man who works that he may live
But as one who is bent on doing nothing but work,
Confident that he who lives does not work,
That one must die to life in order to be
Utterly a creator—refusing to sanction
The irresponsible lyricism in which sense impressions
Are employed to substitute ecstasy for information,
Knowing that feeling, warm heart-felt feeling,
Is always banal and futile.
Only the irritations and icy ecstasies
Of the artist's corrupted nervous system
Are artistic—the very gift of style, of form and expression,
Is nothing else than this cool and fastidious attitude
Towards humanity.   The artist is happiest
With an idea which can become
All emotion, and an emotion all idea.

A poetry that takes its polish from a conflict
Between discipline at its most strenuous
And feeling at its highest—wherein abrasive surfaces
Are turned upon one another like millstones,
And instead of generating chaos
Refine the grist of experience between them.
The terrific and sustained impact
Of intellect upon passion and passion upon intellect,
Of art as a vital principle in the process
Of devising forms to contain itself,
Of germinal forces directed,
Not upon a void or an ego,
But upon living materials, in a way
That becomes physically oppressive
To almost everybody,
Recalling the figure of Aschenbach, ' whose greatest works
Were heaped up to greatness in layer after layer,
In long days of work, out of hundreds
And hundreds of single inspirations '.

And a poetry in which as in a film
Pure setting—the physical conditions
Under which action takes place—is extremely important,
So important, in fact, as to make us sometimes impatient
With a tale that is but crudely attached to it.
A poetry, in short, like that great Sheep Dog Film [1]
Whose setting is in my own native countryside ;
The landscape and the people match perfectly.
The slow roll of the border valleys,
The timeless fells and the ledges of tough rock,
The low dark sky and the hard going of the ground
Are an environment for no other human beings
Than those seen in this film.   The first sequence
Brings men and stones together in one meaning.
After that we would watch with fascination
Anything whatever that happened, and believe it.
Then, of course, there are the dogs which introduce
The ripple of movement into an otherwise rock world.
They are the spirit of the place, not only
When they streak after their sheep at the trial
—The high moment, naturally, of the film—
But at all times.
They have the freedom of the mountains,
And it is their movements,
Even when they are miles away,
That the minds of the people follow.
It is through the dogs that the men become alive,
And again it might not matter too much what the dogs did,
Or whether what they did was intrinsically interesting.
We are committed to them from the moment
We see them as part of this world
And understand their role in it.
The film has won us long before
We know it has a story to develop.

[1] ' To the Victor ' (Gaumont British).

This is something that can only happen
In the movie art.   I want a poetry
In which this happens too,
In a poetry that stands for production, use and life,
As opposed to property, profits, and death.

A poetry throwing light on the problems of value,
—Deriving its stimulating quality, its seminal efficacy,
Not from the discovery, as old as the Greeks,
That moral codes are relative to social factors,
But from the nice and detailed study of the mechanisms
Through which society
Determines attitudes in its members
By opening to them certain possibilities
By induction into objectively recognized statuses
While closing quite effectively other possibilities
—A poetry, not offering a compromise between naïve atomism,
Giving an utterly unrelated picture of social phenomena,
And the unrealistic conception of a mystical social *Gestalt*,
The defining quality of which is intuited by transcendental means
(That growing danger, as a reaction from the bankruptcy
Of the atomistic approach, of a mystical
Organismic approach instinct with anti-rationalistic obscurantism),
But seeking to do justice to the discrete
As well as to the organically integrated aspects of society,
To the disruptive as well as to the cohesive forces
—A poetry that men weary of the unscientific wrangling
Of contemporary social and political dogmatists
Will find a liberating experience
—Rich in its discoveries of new problems,
Important questions so far unsuspected,
For which field research does not yet apply
The data necessary to answer them.

A poetry that is—to use the terms of Red Dog [1]—
High, low, jack and the goddamn game.

In the light of that poem, the following short one may be welcomed
by my readers as a useful key to my poetic habit—and to my
personality :

THE PUFFIN

' *By which the whole . . . is governed and turned like fishes by the
tail.*'—SWIFT.
   Old lady, studying a balloon barrage—' They tell me there's nobody
in them.   Isn't it wonderful how they manage to get them all to turn
the same way ! '

> In my dealings with facts I resemble
> One of the puffins we see in the Shetlands here.
> The puffin flies in from the sea
> With as many as ten little fish
> Held sideways in its beak,
> And the fish are usually arranged
> With heads and tails alternating.

---

[1] Red Dog = American pastime.

How is it done ?   Even allowing for the fact
That the beak has serrations
Which slope back to the throat
It would seem a difficult task
For the bird to go to a fishmonger's shop
And pick ten dead fish off the slab
And arrange them in that fashion.

But to catch a live and presumably active fish
Under water, with nine others
Already held in the beak ?
How is it done ?   I have the knack
Of dealing with facts as the puffin with fish,
But I cannot tell how I do it
Any more than the puffin can.

Enough human seed can be housed
In a tooth-paste cap to father
The world's 2,000,000,000 population.
In the complicated process of reproduction
48 chromosomes are released.
These minute pieces of tissue form
The physical heritage of every human's life.
Soon after fertilization each member
Of the two packs of chromosomes splits in two.
Half range on one side of the egg-cell,
Half on the other.   A wall grows between,
The cell begins to divide, and soon
There are two cells in place of one.
After 48 complete divisions
There are enough cells to constitute
A fully developed baby—26 billion.
My poems will drill the whole world of fact
Precisely like that !

Such is the poetry I now conceive.

In my as-yet-unpublished ' Third Hymn to Lenin ', I define
again the kind of man I admire and the kind of poetry—and life—I
seek when I say :

On days of revolutionary turning points you literally flourished,
Became clairvoyant, foresaw the movement of classes,
And the probable zig-zags of the revolution,
As if on your palm ;
Not only an analytical mind but also
A great constructive, synthesizing mind,
Able to build up in thought the new reality,
As it must actually come
By force of definite laws presently
Taking into consideration, of course,
Conscious interference, the bitter struggle
For the tasks set before the Party and the class it leads
As well as possible diversions and inevitable actions
Of all other classes.—Such clairvoyance is the result
Of a profound and all-sided knowledge of life
With all its richness of colour, connexions and relations,
Economic, political, ideological, and so forth.

Hence the logic of your speeches—' Like some all-powerful feelers
Which grasp one from all sides as in a vice ',
And one has ' no strength left to tear away from their embrace ;
Either one yields or decides upon complete failure '.

And again, at the end of that poem :

Our concern is with human wholeness—the child-like spirit
New-born every day—not, indeed, as careless of tradition
Nor of the lessons of the past : these it must needs inherit,
But as capable of such complete assimilation and surrender,
So all-inclusive, unfenced-off, uncategoried, sensitive, and tender,
That growth is unconditional and unwarped—Ah, Lenin,
Life and that more abundantly, thou Fire of Freedom !
Multiplying talent and virtue without end,
Firelike in your purity and heaven-seeking vehemence,
Yet the adjective must not suggest merely meteoric,
Spectacular—not the flying sparks, but the intense
Glowing core of your character, your large and splendid stability,
Made you the man you were—the live heart of all humanity !
Spirit of Lenin, light on this city now !
          Light up this city now !

Again I say :

          Or like riding a squealing *oscuro*
          Whose back has never held saddle before

          Or a *grulla* with a coat
          Like a lady's blue-grey suede glove

          Or a bayo coyote in the red morning sun,
          His coat shining like something alive,

          A poetry wilder than a heifer
          You have to milk into a gourd.

          Charged with a power that only needs
          The throwing of a switch to let loose
          A devastating power.

          A force reaching out as an electric current
          Leaps a gap between two opposing nodes.

          The poetry of one like a wild goat on a rock.
          You may try to rope him on one crag.
          He leaps to a still more dangerous perch,
          Where, flirting with death, he waggles his beard
          And fires you an ironic ba-a-a.

And again :

Yea, and with, and because of all this, the poetry
For which the poet at any moment may be smashed to pulp
By a gang of educated chimpanzees
Beating out the scansion with a rubber truncheon

F

For metronome on the small of his back
Till his kidneys burst—the poetry,
Not in Germany and certain other countries only,
But everywhere, England, Scotland, America,
The poetry of War and Civil War everywhere,
The poetry of the world-wide Night of the Long Knives
In which 99 men in every 100 are Gestapo Guards,
The poetry that entails the Family Trial
Of the poet's wife and children too,
And makes hulking Black Guards seize the Muses,
Tie their clothing tightly above their heads,
Truss, blind, shamefully humiliate them.
The Black Guards are among the helpless Muses now,
Beating them with clubs, kicking them in the guts,
The Black Guards carry on their dastardly work
While splitting their sides with laughter,
The Black Guards—Finance, Religion, Law, Capitalist Culture.
Himmler never moves a muscle—shows no pity
When, on his departure, frightful screams from the parade-ground
Tell of the most shameful deeds of all. . . . Next day
Ladies he meets at State functions
Are charmed by his quiet courtesy.
The poetry that is scheduled as a Dangerous Occupation,
The most dangerous occupation in the world to-day.
. . . Locked in a cell with a Luger pistol
I make my poetry of World Consciousness.
But will any of it ever be smuggled out
From the Sondergericht to which all Consciousness is subject
All over the world to-day ?

Long poems.   The kind of poetry I want
Is poems *de longue haleine*—far too long
To be practicable for any existing medium,
For there is no editor or publisher in the world to-day
Who if he were suddenly presented with what was obviously
By far the greatest poem that had ever been written
Would give it a moment's consideration if its publication
Would take up a whole issue of his magazine
Or unbalance his publishing list,
Which, no matter how high the level taken,
Demands a certain variety, the sense
Not to put all one's eggs in the same basket,
The wise policy of having ' something for everybody '.
The sudden appearance of a stupendous masterpiece.[1]
Is the last thing any of these people want.
It would shock them tremendously.
They would hasten to hush it up.
There are no means they would not take
To deny its nature and prevent its appearance.
The poetry of one sane man left in a community
All the rest of whose inhabitants are seized by epidemic insanity ;

---

[1] John Davidson, the Scottish poet, points out that no great poet can
work at all except on the assumption that the next thing he writes may out
distance all previous composition completely—so completely that all other
poetry becomes negligible in comparison.

A poetry therefore that only its maker can hear,
Since all the channels of communication are blasted away,
And if the poet hopes or believes there may still
Be elements hidden away here or there
With which with a little luck he might yet get in touch
How can he do so ?—The Guards are infernally cunning—
His least move would be fatal.
A poetry nevertheless that will brook no restraint,
But insist upon moving freely. . . .
The poet a Tarzan among apes all
Suddenly murderously inimical.

And again :

A poetry that hates the à peu pres.
A poetry that sees all the pins on the floor.

A poetry that, like Mussolini, gives
Over 60,000 audiences and interests itself
In at least 1,887,112 individual ' affairs of citizens '.

And once more again I say :

A poetry taking unerring instantaneous account
Of all the angles in a complex manoeuvre
As one who in a tangled thicket
Of manzanita, cactus, chaparral, mesquite, and the like
Adjusts the sights of his Winchester,
Windage, trajectory, distance
All taken into consideration,
And nothing forgotten.
Or again as when the butts of a man's twin Colt guns
Seem fairly to leap into his palms
As the weapons flash out
In smooth, eye-defying movements.

A poetry like a bridge player
Applying method to the plan of the hand,
Asking himself the necessary series
Of definite questions before deciding
On a piece of play after the first card has been led
And then deciding on the necessary tactics to employ
In developing the extra winners in his hand,
These tactics including the finesse, throw-in play, the squeeze,
Ducking, elimination play, and all the rest.

And, above all, a poetry
Like a billiard player
Who knows how to screw
—The gripping or clinching of the cue
At the precise moment of the contact with the ball
That prevents or lessens the chance of a miscue.
Even though the cue-tip may have been properly chalked
A miscue is almost inevitable
When the cue-tip hits the ball as low down
As is necessary for a strong screw
If the cue-hold is not tightened just then.

(Imagine a heavy piece of machinery
Fixed to the floor and at a convenient distance
From the table, and from this machinery
A piston-rod with its end
Shaped and tipped like a cue.
Made to shoot out like a horizontally-held cue
And strike a cue-ball
Exactly where it must be struck
To play a screw-back stroke,
Also that it travelled two or three inches
Beyond the point where it made contact with the ball.
Clearly this steel piston-rod
Could not be deflected
Either to the right or the left
By its contact with the ball.
Nor could its point be raised or lowered.
Its rigidity would only allow it
To move backwards or forwards
In a straight line.
When you grip your cue in screw-strokes
You are really attempting to make your cue
Resemble the imaginary steel cue
Which cannot deviate
From the line on which it travels.)
There are cuemen who will tell you
That they never grip the cue
For any kind of stroke.
These players *do* grip it
For screws and for many other strokes,
But this clinching of the cue
Is an unconscious action with them.
To-day practically all professionals
And most of our great amateurs
Hold the cue in the palm of the hand.
Watch the cue hand of any first-class player
When a screw stroke of any kind
Has to be played,
And you cannot fail to notice
This gripping of the cue.
You can see this closing of the hand
Round the cue quite easily
Even if the stroke
Is quite a gentle stroke.
—This is the kind of poetry I want.

' But ', as Paul Claudel says, ' to develop the idea logically, to bring the conclusion pleasantly out of the premises like the joints of a telescope, is something I do not feel up to every day. My own mind is so geared that at times it works by leaps and bounds. The reader has to get on friendly terms with the stray rabbit that knocks up against the furniture, to watch the right moment to catch him by the paw or by the ears before restoring him to the conjurer's hat.'

Another section of this *ars poetica* strewn through my poem runs as follows :

Pinwheeling poetry.

Poetry giving a rapid premonitory perspective view
Of schemes of thought not yet articulate.

A poetry that can always turn on a dime
And leave a nickel for change.

On my muse's tea-table appear
Such delicacies as Austrian pfeffermuss, iced honey-cakes,
Round or oblong in shape, or those other honey-cakes
From Dijon, wrapped in green and gold, very gay,
And many varieties of the German lebkuchen,
And oblaten, thin biscuits from Salzburg,
And delicious French pain d'épice,
While to dine with her is to know
The truffle of Perigord, the brocarra of Tulle,
Auvergnian roast ham with chestnut sauce,
The thick cabbage soup of Thiers, the poulards of Bresse,
Algerian couscous, Spanish puchero,
Polish barszcz and kromeski, Italian gnocchi,
Calves' tongues cooked with almonds from Greece,
Goulash and sherbert au Tokay from Hungary,
Bamboo sprouts from the Far East,
Watarzoie de Poulet from Belgium,
Scotch grouse, Scandinavian hors d'oeuvre,
American lemon pie, and Viennese linzertart.

With here, incidentally, a cultural synthesis
Of thought, action, belief, and education which covers most
Of the important gradations of thought and human learning
From Greek and Roman times, to the times, say,
Of Ignatius Loyola and the Counter-Reformation.
Religion, the eternal borderline of inarticulate science,
Led to scientific and political concepts ; the Greeks
(With their philosophic contempt for things)
Began the process of anthropomorphizing
Which passed on to the Roman world.
The propulsive motivation of Christianity
Was derived from the supreme universalist, Alexander the Great.
Out of the universality of Christianity evolved
The idea of universality of education—the modern idea
That every man should be taught.   Gnostic philosophy
Gave to Christianity its survival value in the West,
And the Christian teaching that passed on to the mediaeval world
Was far from being a reformed Judaism,
For in its matrix there lay embedded
All the creeds, all the orthodoxies, all the heresies.
And so, passing on to Saracenic culture, we meet,
Among the hundreds, Al-Jahiz of Bazra
Admitting the debt of the ancients ;
And on, past hundreds more, to Petrarch
Writing in his ' Greetings to Posterity '
Of his insignificant and obscure activities,
And on, past the German humanists, and hither
To Loyola and the Jesuits. . . .

A poetry like a lance at rest,
Motionless but vibrant with hidden power.

Poetry in a land where the hills flow down
In long, irregular curves, flattened into tables
Scored deep by canyons and ravines, shadowy, mysterious,
Where even the searching fingers of the sunshine cannot wholly
    penetrate
The sinister gorges whose gloomy, overhanging walls
Baffle all but the heavier dregs of the light
—A land where the tawny sunshine shimmers
The drooping, lily-white blossoms of the yuccas,
And glints on the sky-rocket blooms
Of green-and-white mescal plants, and even
The weirdly deformed arms of the cholla cactus
Are a little de-devilled by the soft caress.
The canyon floors are littered with boulders and up-jutting fangs
Of stone, ground and scoured in the iron jaws
Of long-gone glaciers.   White water brawls amid the rocks
And spatters the straggly growth with a diamond-glitter of spray,
And the giant sounding-board of the hills flings back
Its growl and grumble magnified and distorted.
But over the outer vestibule of the hills is sunshine and peace,
The rumble of the canyon water dulled to a musical whisper,
Rich tints of brown and chocolate and purple
Mottle the cliffs.   Long ledges of soft grey
Marbled with black and reddish-yellow
Stripe the upper slopes.   Dry washes are green and gay
With gramma grass and flowering weeds.

Like a lonely ghost with fear for its pacemaker
The false dawn flees across the sky.
Follows a period of sullen darkness.
Then, so gradually as to be
Almost imperceptible, the true dawn
Drifts up over the edge of the world.
Little flecks of high clouds burn amber and gold.
The hills are formless loomings of tremulous jet.
A pale mist films the grasses with translucent grey.
All things are unreal, elusive.   There is a tense silence
As yet unbroken by song of bird
Or the silvery voices of the wind.

A poetry that has developed to a high degree
An uncanny sense of direction—unerringly following
A route of general direction that, after hours of wandering
Among the buttes and gorges, leads me
To a long, twisty canyon whose far mouth
Faces almost due east, and so
As the spears of the rising sun turn the blue wind-ripples
Of the prairie grasses to long curves of bronzed gold
I ride out of the canyon on to the rangeland.

This is the land in which my poetry goes
Like two great galloping horses—
The big black goes like the shadow of a star
Before a lightning flash, but the golden horse

Is like a ripple of sunlight racing across clear water.
Ahead looms the mouth of a canyon, a narrow fissure
Slicing through a shoulder of the hills.
Straight for its blue-shadow
The two horses hurtle.

And, again, delicate as the kiss of wind-shadows
On trembling drops of dew.

It is, in short, a poetry only comparable to that splendid undertaking, *One Day of the World*, initiated by Maxim Gorky, and issued, edited by him and Koltsov, after Gorky's death.   Gorky described his idea to the First All-Union Congress of Soviet Writers (stressing the ' method of collective creative work ' to be employed—a matter that does not concern me at the moment, but which should be borne in mind in connexion with what I say elsewhere about co-operative literary work—though even one man's work, in a poem such as this, demands too, as such a joint enterprise of numerous writers in many different lands would do, what Gorky called ' an audacious scope to which we are unaccustomed ') in the following sentences :

> ' I have in view any day—September 25, October 7, or December 15—
> it matters not which.   An ordinary day should be taken just as it is
> portrayed in the pages of the world press.   A complete picture should
> be given of the motley chaos of modern life in Paris and Grenoble, in
> London and Shanghai, in San Francisco, Geneva, Rome, Dublin, and
> so forth, in cities and villages, on the water and on land.   It should
> portray the carnival of the wealthy and the suicide of the poor ; the
> sessions of Academies and scientific societies and news items reflecting
> arrant illiteracy, superstition, crime ; facts on the subtleties of refined
> culture, and the strikes of workers ; anecdotes and everyday dramas,
> loud-mouthed arrogant luxury, the tricks of swindlers, the lies of
> political leaders—it should portray, I repeat, the artistic creative work
> of history during some one day, an ordinary day in all the insane
> fantastic diversity of its appearance.'

These sentences would, indeed, serve fairly well as a description of my enormous poem.   Gorky realized that only one of the most powerful publishing concerns would be capable of organizing a book like this, that it would need huge funds and a powerful promoting machine.   So some of our leading publishers have been tremendously enthusiastic about my vast poem, but, while commenting on the typescript in terms of the highest praise, have felt that its publication was beyond the scope of their firms—i.e., not ' a business proposition'.   One publisher—not in London, but in Paris—was ready to publish it, however.   This was Jack Kahane, of the Obelisk Press, in the Place Vendome.   My secretary (H. G. Taylor) went to Paris and saw him about the matter and the thing was *en train*.   Alas, Kahane's death in the autumn of 1939 put an end to the project.   This was only the latest of many misfortunes with publishers : Foulis, Stanley Nott, Leonard Parsons, and others either died or their businesses came to an end when they were about to publish books of mine ; I lost publication—or had it delayed—in several cases, in others I lost considerable sums of money in respect of books already published. Kahane's death was a particularly severe misfortune for me.[1] Few publishers could have contemplated the publication of so enormous a poem. Kahane was in a special position to undertake it. I may be long enough in finding another who will and can. In the interval many of the sections which would have made a great impact if they had been published in 1938 or 1939 will cease to be so opportune ; worst of all, I have the whole unwieldy thing lying about on my hands —and in my mind, whereas, if I could have got rid of it when it was finished, I would have been free to turn to other projects in a way that I am now unable to do.

Yes, *One Day of the World* is the nearest example of the sort of thing I am after in my recent poetry—of what I mean by world consciousness in my work—that I can think of. Consider—weather conditions in Colombo, Canada, and elsewhere ; the Italo-Ethiopian conflict—the resistance preparations of the Ethiopian people on the one hand, and *Italy in the Fire* showing life in the Fascist rear on the other. *England at the Cross-Roads*—economic data, a letter to a newspaper, an appeal to the magazine, the *Other World* (English spiritualist organ) calling on people to combat war by prayer, alarming items on the growth of unemployment. A certain Rev. Cooper's reports on a visit to a jail. ' Many of the prisoners are persons of great ability and some have finished high school and even the university. Why are these people in jail ? Chiefly because of unemployment.' Court trials. Plays and cinemas on that day in England (and elsewhere) reviewed, detective and sex dramas predominating. On to Hungary and Poland. Then to Germany. The *Koenigsberg Allgemeine Zeitung* recommends sparrow-hunts : ' Sparrow-hunting has begun everywhere. Gourmets already dream of boiled sparrows' breasts.' The same newspaper prints : ' The village population is urged to participate in harvesting beech cones. This will contribute to the improvement of the German butter market.' Following this are chapters on Latvia, Lithuania, Esthonia, Austria, and Czechoslovakia. Then come Rumania, Jugoslavia, Bulgaria, Greece, Belgium, Holland. Then France—*France at the Turning Point*. Louis Aragon's *One Day at Haphazard* ; Jean-Richard Bloch's *A Day in Poitou*. Then Spain, Portugal, Switzerland, Ireland, and the Scandinavian States. Then Japan. Then Indo-China, Indonesia, India, Syria, Tunis, Algiers, Morocco, Turkey, Iran, the young Tannu-Tuva and Mongolian republics, the United States of America, and so on to *A Day of Writers*—Heinrich Mann, Julien Benda, Bert Brecht, Oscar Maria Graf, Jean Cassou,

[1] His son, Maurice Kahane, later revived the project, but the Fall of France finally prevented him from carrying it through.

Emil Ludwig, Hans Marchwita, Karin Michaelis, Gustav Regler, Stefan Zweig, H. G. Wells, Karel Capek, and Romain Rolland saying : 'And before going to sleep in the anarchic and cruel world chaos where I hear the shock of colliding masses of diverse nations and differing spirit, I recall the wise and clear thought of Lenin, and I know that our freedom is secured, for we are right.'

My poetry is like that . . . and it has always known, and been alive and alight with the knowledge of the truth Thomas Mann voiced about Spain and the behaviour of men of letters in relation to Spain :

> ' The poet who has failed in the face of human problems posed in the form of political problems, becomes not only a traitor to reason for the sake of mercenary interests, but is lost also as a person. His ruin is inevitable. He loses his creative powers, his talent, and will never again create anything of lasting value.'

I have not failed and cannot fail, for I have never once betrayed the glorious traditions of the Scottish people by preaching any submission in the face of Fascism, or behaved shamefully by indulging in sickly-sweet idylls or (shameful above all for any man who lays claim to poetical vision) glorifying a life of servility, but played a true man's and true poet's part to the utmost of my power ' to-day when ', as Evguenia Galpernia has said, ' everything—thoughts, emotions, words, poetry—all must be mustered, clenched into a fist, and flung in the face of fascist aggression.'

' Traitors to reason for the sake of mercenary interests '—that is precisely how I have always seen almost all my fellow-writers and other artists and members of the educated classes in Scotland, and that is why I have treated them with the absolute intolerance—the uncompromising contempt and vitriolic invective—by which I am best known. It is impossible to have any intellectual intercourse with almost all of them. Surface amiabilities, conventional exchanges, a modicum of literary chit-chat—but no getting down to fundamentals. They are quite incapable of anything of the kind and regard it as ' bad form '—' talking shop '. There are only three or four out of all the dozens of Scottish writers I know with whom it has been possible to have any real conversation. The others are either afflicted with a most unnecessary fear of being too clever, or of taking anything (except their own petty vanity) ' too seriously '—as if creatures like they could have any conception in any case of what a really serious concern with anything means at all !

I agree with almost everything Ezra Pound says in his *How to Read* —and certainly with his general principles and classification of authors. And with Kierkegaard when he says in his Journals : ' One can divide authors into two classes, those who write for readers, and the real authors—those who write for authors. These latter are unintelligible to the reading public, are looked upon as mad, and are almost despised—and in the meanwhile authors of the second class plunder their works and have a tremendous success with what they have stolen and spoilt. And thus the authors of the second class become the worst enemies of the others—it is a matter of some importance to them that no one should discover the real position.'

This is what accounts for the fact that in several instances Scottish writers first of all enthusiastically praised my work, and then shortly afterwards attacked it just as venomously as they had before lavishly lauded it—the reason being that in the interval I had shown clearly that I was not going to ' play the game ', that I was not going to comply with the rule, ' Scratch my back and I'll scratch yours '. All these people were prepared to be pleasant enough as long as the assumption held—and was maintained so far as the public were concerned—that we were all authors together, much of a muchness ; but it was a very different matter if one showed any tendency to outgrow this mutual-admiration-circle business, and to manifest a stature which relegated these authors too obviously to their proper category as negligible scribblers.

Very close to my view too—and to the subject-matter of a great deal of my huge poem—is Maxim Gorky's essay on ' World Litera-ture ' (1919), published in *International Literature* in April, 1938, and setting forth the attitude towards literature advocated by the collective on the staff of Vsemirnaya Literatura (World Literature), that Moscow publishing house which aimed that its books taken together ' should constitute an extensive historical literary compendium enabling the reader to acquaint himself with the origin, course, and decline of literary schools, with the development of the technique of verse and prose, with interacting influences in literature among nations, and, in general, with the entire sweep of literary evolution in its historic sequence from Voltaire to Anatole France, from Richardson to H. G. Wells, and so on. Later Vsemirnaya Literatura plans to acquaint the Russian people with the literature of the Middle Ages, with the literature of Russia and other Slavic countries, as well as with examples of the thought and literature of the Orient, with the writings of India, Persia, China, Japan, and Arabis.' Gorky expresses his view—which is also mine—in these paragraphs :

> ' Besides the atmosphere and the photosphere our whole planet is encased in a sphere of spiritual creativeness, the manifold and joyous emanation of our energy, from which is woven, fashioned, and moulded all that is immortal and splendid, from which are created the great ideas and wondrous complexity of our machines, the temples and tun-nels, the books, the pictures, the poems, and the millions of tons of iron that span great rivers, hanging in the air with such marvellous lightness, the entire austere and charming, mighty and delicate poetry of our lives.
>
> ' As we strike ever brighter sparks from the iron walls of the un-known, sparks of hope in the triumph of reason, and victory over the elements of nature and the animal element in man, we may talk with

legitimate joy of the planetary significance of the great efforts of our spirit, efforts which find their clearest and most vivid expression in literary and scientific work.

' The great merit of literature is the fact that by deepening our consciousness, amplifying our sense of life, and shaping our feelings, it reveals to us that all ideas and actions, that the whole world of the spirit, is made of human nerves and blood.

' It tells us that the Chinese Hen-Toy is as torturingly unsatisfied by sexual love as the Spaniard Don Juan, that the Abyssinian songs of joy and sadness are like the Frenchman's, that a Japanese geisha in love is quite as touching as Manon Lescaut, that the quest of a soulmate in woman was and is shared with equal ardour by men of every land throughout the ages.

' A murderer is just as loathsome in Asia as in Europe, the miser Plyushkin is just as pitiful as the French Grandet; the Tartuffes of every country are alike; misanthropes everywhere make themselves equally miserable; and everywhere the same glamour attaches to the touching figure of Don Quixote, the knight of the spirit.

' In the last analysis, all people whatever their language have the same theme : themselves and their lot.

' These innumerable similarities and endless differences give us real literature, which is a living mirror of existence, sensing what it reflects ; with quiet sorrow or with anger, with the good-natured grin of a Dickens, or with the hideous smirk of a Dostoyevsky, the full complexity of our spiritual life, the world of our aspirations, the inexhaustible, murky pools of banality and stupidity, our heroism and cowardice before destiny, the courage of love and the drive of hatred, the full foulness of our hypocrisy, the shameful abundance of falsehood, our endless travails, trembling hopes, and cherished dreams—all that makes the world alive, all that throbs in the hearts of people. By observing a man with the eyes of a considerate friend or the stern gaze of a judge, sharing his suffering, laughing at him, admiring his courage, cursing his pettiness, literature rises above life and, together with science, shows people the way to attain their ends, to develop the good that is in them.

' Literature, that living history of the exploits, mistakes, merits, and misconceptions of our forbears, literature with its powerful faculty for influencing the organization of thought, softening the coarseness of instinct, and strengthening the will, must at last embark upon its epic role, the role of an inner force which firmly welds people in the knowledge of the community of their suffering and desires, the awareness of the unity of their striving to attain the happiness of a beautiful and free life.

' The sphere of literary creation is the International of the spirit ; and in our day, when the idea of brotherhood among peoples, the idea of a social International is being clothed with reality, in our day we are bound to make every effort to hasten the assimilation of the redeeming concept of all-human brotherhood by the mind and will of the masses.

' The broader his knowledge, the greater is man's perfection. The more eager a man's interest in his neighbour, the quicker the process of merging good creative impulses into a single force and the sooner we shall finish our journey to the world triumph of mutual understanding, respect, brotherhood, and emancipated labour for our own benefit.

' After the criminal and accursed slaughter, shamefully provoked by men besmirched by idolatry of the yellow devil gold, after the sanguinary storm of wrath and hatred, it is timely to present a broad picture of man's unity in his literary work.'

As Li-Shang-yin's aphorism has it :

> Literature endures like the universal spirit
> And its breath becomes a part of the vitals of all men.

My ideas on education are in keeping with my literary practice and aspirations. I have nothing but contempt for Scottish Education to-day, largely corrupted as it has been by the English connexion and by the absurd over-influences of English literature, history, politics, and the English language. It is a system which serves very other ends than its professed ends, does not result in the faintest approximation to an ' educated democracy ', and is run by a horde of teachers themselves extremely poorly educated and practically destitute of, and ignorantly contemptuous of intellectual interests. If the aims of education include the following—to put a child in touch with the inherited knowledge and culture of his race, so that he will know not merely how to read, to write, and to figure, but letters and the arts, the rudiments of science, and what great men have thought and said memorably about life ; to prepare the child for citizenship, i.e. impart an understanding of the workings of the world in which he lives and a care for the community of which he is a member, so that he will regard its concerns as his concerns, its welfare as his, and have not only the will to assume the responsibilities of a citizen by active participation in its affairs, but the knowledge to make his participation effective ; and to enable the child to develop his personality to the full and to realize all that he has it in him to be, or, in other words, education conceived as aiming at the creation of intelligence rather than at the provision of information, teaching not what to think but how—then the Scottish educational system to-day signally fails to achieve any of them. The only educational aim it does achieve in a very rough-and-ready way is to train the child specifically for a vocation, so that in the struggle for employment and a career he may start with an advantage over his untrained contemporaries. As against this horrible mess, I detail, with complete approval, the Grade System of Education set out in Mr. C. T. Smith's *Apsa*, which is based on the belief that human beings should have as full a life as possible ; therefore they must ' be in touch with the things that matter ', which are, broadly, those that ' cultured people think suitable for themselves ', and those which have had significance for the human race as a whole, so that it is necessary to know what the things that have ' mattered ' to human beings, what the things they have thought ' significant ' are ; therefore we must let the children learn how the world became what it is, why the human race values what it does, and this means that we must present to them ' in related panoramas of national achievement the story of the ups and downs of human progress '. And as to practice ? The work is divided into eight Stages. Each Stage consists of a cross-section

of the history of the world. During the Stage in question one
nation—it may be Egypt or it may be Greece—is dominant in culture
and in thought, setting, as it were, the tone of the Stage. The other
nations are graded by the degree of their approximation to the
achievements of the peak nation. In any Stage there are six such
graded nations, and the whole school at any given moment is engaged
in the study of a Stage. The top standard studies the peak nation ;
the other standards study the different nations graded according to
their various degrees of departure from the peak, the lowest standard
studying the most primitive people ; the next lowest that which is
one grade above the primitive, and so on to the peak nation studied
by the top standard. In the following year the whole school moves
on to the study of the next Stage. In this way each pupil reviews in
his progress through the school the whole pageant of history. The
peak nations chosen for the eight different stages are Egypt, Greece,
Rome, Islam, Spain, eighteenth-century France, the British Empire,
Britain, and the U.S.A. Having been through all the grades of all
the Stages, the boys in their last year become ' Overgradors ' and
take, as it were, a bird's-eye view of the whole process as it appears
from the standpoint of the detached spectator. ' He was once a
childish witness of an ever-changing world ; he is now an *experienced*
witness of an ever-changing world, for he himself has been through
all the changes.' The knowledge acquired in the course of the
journey must be immense. We hear of the literature of ancient
Egypt, the science of Greece, the art of Babylon, the achievements of
' odd nations not in the text-books ', the making of ancient modes and
mediaeval minstrelsy. Mr. Smith holds that nothing is too deep for
the understanding of the child (this is another form of what I express
elsewhere—everybody is ready for the highest ; there must be no
' talking down ' ; Lenin's refusal to give any Marxism-without-
tears, &c.), there is scarcely anything in existence beyond his powers
of comprehension, always providing he is *in competent hands*—and
nothing too high for his appreciating. We hear of performances of
Maritana, The Bohemian Girl, Orpheus, even *The Magic Flute.* Not
only is Cervantes read, but Mendoza, Aleman, Quevedo, and
Montalvan ! Theses are written by the Overgradors a hundred
pages long, complete with maps and diagrams, on the geography,
music, science, art, and literature of each stage.

It is poetry for these Overgradors I am writing, or, as one reviewer
of my work says, I am a modern Druid, and my conception of poetry
is one that allows at once for the functions of education, historical
guardianship, discussion of all manner of issues with all manner of
people at all manner of levels, reportage of all sorts, exercises in the
art of conversation, sheer entertainment, the fitting commemoration
of great occasions, due summoning to high tasks, and, in short, all
the forms of appeal and commentary compatible with intercourse

with people who are, in Apsa's sense, ' fully developed personalities possessing high-grade critical intelligences ' ; a kind of poetry through which blow the winds of a terrific energy and high faith, and a poetry not for an arbitrary One Day of the World (nor dependent upon any immense network of material drawn from newspapers and periodicals—but concerned above all just with the really important things which escape all that network), but for every day and any day ; the expression of the life of a man with boundless interests, eyes constantly open to the whole ' field of folk ' filled with an unqualifiable upward and onward.

How miserably far short of any such conception fall all the so-called educated people, the University professors and lecturers, the school-teachers, the literary people in Scotland to-day ! No matter in what direction one turns, one finds complacent ignorance, inertia, ineptitude. A friend writes me :

> ' I have been quite unable to touch the Scottish Philosophy question yet, and my Professors have rather wisely warned me from tackling prematurely this very promising line of study. It is better for me to make myself at home in the Scottish Philosophy of to-day before examining its nobler ideological ancestry. Even now, the directions of English and Scottish philosophy are quite different. English Philosophy strives to comprehend the universe. Scottish Philosophy strives to comprehend Kant. Indeed, since the decay of original speculation in Scotland, killed by the Disruption, the sole contribution of our country to philosophy has been four gigantic (in bulk) commentaries on Kant : Stirling's in 1880, Caird's in 1895, Kemp Smith's in 1918, and Paton's in 1935. Add to these the shorter works of Adamson and Watson on Kant, and that completes the list. England and America think for themselves and leave us to do the donkey-work. (Naturally, simultaneously with the interest in Kant, Campbell, Burnet, and now Ferguson have done good work commenting on Plato.) I don't think that the Englishmen and the Yankees have done well to neglect German thought, but it is surely up to us to make something of our philosophical erudition, which, especially in Smith's and Caird's work, is of a very high level. All this is merely to indicate that, in devoting myself solely to Kant and Plato, or, rather, our compatriots' conflicting interpretations thereof, I am brought face to face with fresh aspects of our perennial national question ! '

The same correspondent recurs to another aspect of this crucially important and little-ventilated matter in another letter, where he says :

> ' It is no matter for wonder to discover that J. F. Ferrier, the last original Scots thinker (d. 1866) and Professor Flint, the last with an European outlook (d. 1909), who receives a commendatory mention both in Plekhanov's 1896 exposition of Marxism and in M. V. Hay's Chain of Error in Scottish History, were excluded as dangerous men from attaining the plum of the Metaphysics Chair at Edinburgh. As a preliminary to dealing with recent European criticism of the Scots Philosophy I tried the experiment of handing in a class-essay on some aspects of the work of Thomas Reid, and was chagrined to find the lecturer, while admitting the soundness of my exposition, so far removed

from contact with the Scots Philosophers' work as to be unable to assess its value one way or the other. I next consulted the Professor on the subject—a Kantian scholar of deserved reputation, whose work on Hume is first-class—and received the reply that I was wasting my time on Hume's successors. Timidly pointing out that their work was valued in France, I learned that their disciple, V. Cousin, was nothing but a journalist, orator, charlatan. When I instanced, further, contemporary interest in their work in Scandinavia, that was, according to him, just the sort of aberration you'd expect of such an out-of-the-way corner of Europe. We sat there in his study regarding one another with suspiciousness natural to a meeting of two provincials, united by a common town of origin, in a capital. He spoke scornfully of a query put to him by Dr. Mary Ramsay as to the absence of a national school of philosophers in Scotland. " They'll be asking for a national geometry next." I suggested that an object of philosophy must be the problems set it by its country and its time, citing the concern of the Italians with Aesthetics. Without regard to my main point, " Croce ! " he said, " he's not of much importance. A revolt against a Catholic upbringing has led him to explain everything in terms of history, and " (with a superior air) " to pay no attention to the Supernatural ". Unwillingness to use a like " short way with " his own and our other Scots philosophers' devotion to the Supernatural made me hold my tongue. He dismissed the subject and proceeded to rhapsodize over the merits of John R. Allan's *Farmer's Boy !* '

' Why,' asks my friend A. S. Neill in his useful little *exposé* of our much-boosted Scottish education, *Is Scotland Educated?* (1936), ' is not a university like that of Glasgow leading the workers to a better civilization ? Why do students as a class become blacklegs in a strike ? The answer is that our university system is tolerated and supported by the powers that be only when it is an obedient servant to these powers. Scottish education is a bulwark of entrenched capitalism.'

While almost all our contemporary Scottish writers are the inevitable products of the educational machine just described, and most of the writers in question have been quite unable to outgrow the distortions to which they were subjected in their school days and at college, the residue of work that has shown real progress is quite sufficient to justify the Scottish Renaissance Movement. But it was necessary to break with it—to say good-bye to that Movement and go forward to Scottish Workers' Republicanism *à la* John Maclean, and that I did (carrying with me in so doing all the other Scottish writers of my own age or—in so far as I knew them—younger, of whose creative possibilities I still had any hope) in 1936 in a statement which included the following paragraphs :

' Having regard to the future of Civilization and the intensifying War and Fascism menace of this phase of the imminent collapse of Capitalist Society, and being passionately anxious to " pull our full weight " (as Scotland has hitherto failed to do in the work of world-revolution) in our native country where these issues come closest to us in an immediate practical sense, we are convinced that, just as Connolly

said that in Ireland the social revolution would be incomplete without
a national revolution too, so in Scotland here it is clear that the objectives
of the social revolution can only be fully realized if it is accompanied by
autonomy on a Communist basis.

' In this we are adverting to Keir Hardie's admonition that a much
greater impetus would have been given to Socialism if Scottish Socialists
had given priority in their programme to Scottish independence con-
currently with the Irish Independence issue, and taking up again the
great lead given by John Maclean which circumstances have so amply
vindicated since, viz. (from his Gorbals Election Address, 1923):
" Scotland's wisest policy is to declare for a Republic in Scotland, so
that the youths of Scotland will not be forced out to die for England's
markets.   I accordingly stand out as a Scottish Republican candidate,
feeling sure that if Scotland had to elect a Parliament to sit in Scotland
it would vote for a Working Class Parliament.   Such a Parliament
would have to use the might of the workers to force the land and the
means of production out of the grasp of the brutal few who control
them, and place them at the full disposal of the community.   The
Social Revolution is possible sooner in Scotland than in England.   The
working-class policy ought to be to break up the Empire to avert war
and enable the workers to triumph in every country and colony.
Scottish separation is part of the process of England's Imperial dis-
integration and is a help towards the ultimate triumph of the workers
of the world. . . . Had the Labour men stayed in Glasgow and started
a Scottish Parliament as did the genuine Irish in Dublin in 1918, England
would have sat up and made concessions to Scotland just to keep her
ramshackle Empire intact to bluff other countries. . . . Ireland will
only get her Republic when Scotland gets hers."

' Further evidence of the correctness and unescapeable necessity of
this line lies in the statistics of voting showing the persistent tremendous
Radicalism (leading more than once to all-over Socialist majorities)
of the Scottish electorate *vis-à-vis* the English, and the extent to which
the progressive will of the majority of the Scottish people has been
stultified by the English connexion.

' A return now to this separatist and anti-Imperialist line (about
which Scottish Socialism has always been so deplorably weak that these
considerations have constituted a disastrous blind spot in the entire
development of the working-class movement in Scotland) is in incontrovertible keeping with the present historical development in every
other country.

' Along with this anti-Imperialist line of Scottish separatist Socialist
Republicanism invaluable impetus can be given to the social revolution
in England, Ireland, Wales, and elsewhere.   As against the all-too-
simple cry that the interests of the workers in Scotland and England
are identical, we have no hesitation in stressing that far more exact
dialectical discrimination must be given to the alleged consequences of
the identity of the interests of Scottish workers and English workers,
since this in no wise conflicts with the question of Scottish independence
nor necessarily involves any incorporating Union of the two peoples,
whose relationships signally illustrate the fact that, as Marx (and subsequently Lenin) insisted : " No nation that enslaves another can itself
be free."   The freeing of Scotland should be a foremost plank in the
programme of the English workers themselves—in their own no less
than in Scotland's interests.

' The line we advocate—in addition to greatly strengthening anti-
Imperialism *vis-à-vis* the great weakness of our Socialist M.P.s in
this connexion—will put an end to the sinister association in the

Scottish cultural movement of abstract highbrowism and politics which
have no concern with the cause of the workers, and greatly speed up
the proletarianization of Scottish Arts and Letters, i.e. the beginnings
of self-education of the Scottish proletariat in their revolutionary tasks
with the aid of their own intelligentsia.   It is for this reason that we claim
that we have, along this Red Scotland line, the end of Scottish Nationalism and the beginning of Workers' Republicanism.   *Our line represents
a complete break with recent Scottish cultural developments, and the
realization that further such developments must of necessity be revolutionary.*   The Communist and Social Democratic neglect of and side-
tracking of the Scottish Cause up to now has been responsible for the
long confused and inefficient Scottish Nationalist groping, and the
extent to which the whole thing has now played into Fascist hands, and
incidentally—through failing to deal effectively with the anti-social
power of the Churches—bred the growing religious fascism of the
Scottish Protestant Party to-day.   *No Scottish Socialist can read this
exposition of the John Maclean line with any feeling other than shame at
not having been engaged in pushing it all along.*
    ' In this connexion, we must point particularly to the glaring danger-
signal of the fact that while Fascism everywhere else in the world claims
to be a unifying policy (e.g. phrases like *Hitler unifies Germany,* or, in
Croix de Feu proclamation, *France is one* ; there can be no question of
disintegration—the Breton and Provencal movements must simply be
disregarded—it is a question of maintaining the superiority of *L'Esprit
Latine* over *L'Esprit Celtique*), similarly British Finance Capitalism
forced back to its last line of defence will cry : " *Britain über alles* ",
though for the moment, Socialism having neglected Scottish Nationalism, Sir Oswald Mosley does not hesitate to use it and cries in Edinburgh
(1936) amid loud Socialist disapproval, " No Scotsman wishes to be an
Englishman ".   There is no gainsaying the sinister significance of
this—it is the nemesis of Communist and Social Democratic neglect of
the Scottish Question.   In contradistinction the Red Scotland line we
advocate is in perfect keeping with the dicta of Marx, Engels, Lenin, and
Stalin, and with the practice of the Soviet Union in regard to minority
elements.   We too in Scotland must have an autonomous republic and
equal freedom and facilitation for our Scots Gaelic and Scots Vernacular
languages.   Our minimal demand is to have Scotland on the same foot-
ing in all these respects as one of the autonomous republics of the
U.S.S.R.'

I agree entirely with a friend who writes me :

    ' The intellectual deterioration of Edinburgh University in the past
hundred and especially in the past fifty years is clearly brought out in
comparison, in respect of scientific and cultural achievement, of the
tercentenary history of Sir Alexander Grant, with its Sept-Jubilee con-
tinuation volume compiled by Sir Thomas Holland and others.   The
remarks of Mr. Donald Carswell in his contribution to *Towards a New
Scotland* exhibit, I regret to say, a lamentable ignorance of history.
He has mistaken the empty bustle of decadence, produced both by a
willing subordination to Oxford and Cambridge standards, and by the
exploitation of Edinburgh for Imperialist ends from 1860–70, for a
period of solid intellectual progress the reality of which apparently is a
child of Mr. Carswell's imagination and is certainly unrecognized in
Europe, and devoid of evidence.   It is even more impossible to pretend
with Holland and Co. that the results of fifty years progress—the

erection of Unions, the institutions of the S.R.C. and the admission of
women, however potentially fruitful, or the creation of Honours Schools
(demonstrably, cf. the case of Honours History, designed to meet the
needs of Home and Indian Civil Service aspirants rather than to promote learning, a thing which Germany did without reliance on the
purely English institution of honours examinations) and the elaboration
of a Science Faculty (productive as yet of nothing comparable to the
discoveries of Black, Hutton, and others in the eighteenth century),
are in any degree compensatory for the University's total loss of reputation as a centre of science and culture in Europe.   I do not by any means,
with Sarolea, regard the eighteenth century as an absolute Golden Age
by the way, for the reason that, as you pointed out in your Tercentenary
Ode, our Universities even then, owing to the Anglifying influence of
the Union, were incapable of becoming centres of culture ; but the debt
of Europe, especially France, to their work in the sciences, whether
philosophical, e.g. economics and philosophy, or natural, e.g. geology
and chemistry, or technical, e.g. medicine, between 1740–1830 is
undeniably considerable.   However, Sarolea alone understood what was
wrong and suffered for it.   Geddes, too, likewise despised, did what he
could to improve the situation.   It is just because the truth—and I
could go on all night citing examples to back up my case—is so hard
to put across in this, as in other connexions, that your intervention will
be so welcome.   Our academic institutions rejected the Applications
of Hume, Burns, Carlyle (also R. L. Stevenson) for Chairs, and can find
employment for F. G. Scott only in a subordinate capacity.'

It is in the face of an endless and almost unalleviated panorama of
this sort of thing that, in a symposium of well-known Scottish authors
and journalists published in 1938, we find the editor saying in his
preface : ' We have omitted the misery and degradation of which
Scotland has a full share, because these are common to all countries
in this day and age, and we wish to concentrate on things that seemed
essentially Scottish '.   And one of the contributors—dealing with
my own Borderland at that—says : ' In its overweening sense of
history and in its traditional hatreds, the Border almost resembles
Ireland.   Also, the most violent of its hatreds all have their roots in
the old wars with the English.   The fact that for hundreds of years
it was rammed hard against a ruthless and superior enemy hardened
the Border character, you might say, and isolation has done the rest.
So, bless my Sam, this affinity with Ireland is no fanciful invention ;
it sticks out a mile.   But there is this distinction to be noted : the
traditional hatreds of Ireland are still liable to find expression in a
rattle of pistol-shots or a bit of bomb-throwing, whereas the Border
hates have all been idealized, and seldom lead to violence, except or
the football field.'

All these inane symposiasts remind me of the Philistines Maxim
Gorky portrays : [1]

' What is the Philistine to do ?   He is no hero ; the heroic is incomprehensible to him.   He has no prescience of the future, and, havin,

---

[1] Published in *Novaya Zhizn* in 1905.

only the interests of the present moment at heart, he states his attitude towards life thus :

> Why fuss, why argue ? Quiet keep,
> Let madmen search and fools inquire.
> Heal your daily wounds with sleep,
> To-morrow'll put its own on fire,
> Learn to take all, bright or blue,
> Hope or menace as they're ranked.
> What is there to want or rue ?
> The day is done—and God be thanked !

The philistine is enamoured of living, but life leaves no deep impressions upon him. Social tragedy is beyond his feelings. He can feel deeply only the terror of the hour of his own death ; and he sometimes expresses this strongly and vividly. The philistine is always a lyricist. Deep pathos is quite beyond his powers ; here he is as if cursed with the curse of impotence. . . . What can he do in the battle of life ? Here we see how anxiously and pitifully the philistines hide from the battles of life, each wherever he can—in the dark corners of mysticism, in the prettified arbours of æsthetics, jerry-built of stolen materials. Sadly and hopelessly they wander through the labyrinths of metaphysics, and return again to the narrow paths of religion, soiled by the rubbish of age-old lies ; everywhere bringing into their sticky triviality the hysterical groaning of souls full of petty fear, their lack of talent and their impudence, they strew over everything they touch a hail of prettified but empty and cold words which sound false and plaintive. . . . Philistines, I repeat, want to live in peace with the whole world at any cost, quietly enjoying the fruit of other people's labour, and striving by all possible means to preserve that peace of mind which they term happiness. What can those who have such a psychology add to the " common welfare " except falsehood and hypocrisy ? . . . They float on mechanically, like drowned bodies, in a foul stream of senseless and disgusting inanity, wrapped in acrid smoke and the odour of human sweat, surrounded by the greedy clanking of iron and the groans of the people who work at the iron to increase the amount of gold in the philistines' pockets—of the gold which killed the soul of the philistine, of the gold which is the metal god of limited and pitiful people.'

Most of these writers about parts of Scotland are like the French Contadours. They are Nature-lovers ; they write about mountain landscapes, the whispering of forests in spring-time, and other poetic matters—a few of them with a little neo-Tolstoyan sugar coating. Incidentally, as Sadoul sarcastically remarks, the Contadours are naturally strangers to work, and none too interested in the peasantry who inhabit the rural landscapes they write about, or the complex practical problems of farming. Their ' ideal life ' is lived at the expense of the labour of others. Scotland has been rotten with their senseless lucubrations for over a century now. What do such small-minded philistines care about the destiny of mankind ? In all their shoddy arguments these Nature-lovers expose their mean little souls, and formulate the most shallow, backward, and egoistic ideas of those who are prepared to live in servility, and, what is more, to consider it the normal form of existence. Gorky wrote about such puny people with biting scorn in articles in which he described the ' love of ownership which has developed along such ugly lines ; a constant tense desire for peace both within oneself and in the outer world ; an obscure fear of everything which in one way or another may upset this peace '. The philosophy of such a philistine serves merely ' for self-justification, to justify his passive attitude in the battle of life '. The Contadour evangelists, in Scotland as in France, are the expression of philistinism, frightened by the oncoming events, of the cowardly anxiety to find a place somewhere apart from the struggle, of the simple egoistic wisdom : ' My house is on the outskirts. This does not concern me.' Their idylls are not even worthy of the name of neo-Rousseauism ; they besmirch the noble name of Rousseau, the forerunner of the fiery Jacobins. They offer the ' poetic ', ' philosophic ' justification for what in the language of contemporary politics is known as ' non-intervention '. The Scottish literary scene is choc-a-bloc with these shameful creatures. Scotland— Scotland of all countries !—offers us only John R. Allans, John Smellie Martins, Ian Macphersons, and the like at a time when other countries are yielding writers like Ludwig Renn, Gustav Regler, Mathe Zalka, Ralph Fox—real people, many of whom have given their lives in battle. Whereas all true art has its foundations deep in the principles of things, and seeks as its end the bettering of our nature, these Scottish authors write for ready-made publics, and their work has no foundation but in empirical rules and no object but the immediate gratification of the senses. It is long past time that the majority of younger Scottish writers had the courage to realize, as Alexander Vidakovic wrote after his visit to Scotland to attend the International P.E.N. Congress when it met in our country for the first time, that the chief impression any decent intelligent human being can possibly carry away from Scotland to-day is of ' a dour, stolid face against the background of a darkened room with brownish paper-patched panes '—for how can any one see a country unless one ' comes to see eye to eye with the greatest need of the masses ' ? But these precious Contadours eschew Scotland's misery and degradation because ' these are common to all countries and we wish to concentrate on things that seem essentially Scottish '—so they concentrate on mountains and forests and lochs and pretty writing and touches of humour, because these are essentially Scottish and not to be found in other countries !

The poetry I want turns its back contemptuously on all the cowardly and brainless staples of Anglo-Scottish literature—the whole base business of people who do not act but are merely acted upon—people whose ' unexamined lives ' are indeed ' not worth having ', though they include every irresponsible who occupies a ' responsible position ' in Scotland to-day, practically all our Professors, all our M.P.s, and certainly all our ' Divines ', all our

peers and great landlords and big business men, the teaching profession almost without exception, almost all our writers—'half
glow-worms and half newts'.

My work represents a complete break with all these people—with
all they have and are and believe and desire. My aim all along has
been (in Ezra Pound's term) the most drastic *desuetization* of
Scottish life and letters, and, in particular, the de-Tibetanization of
the Highlands and Islands, and getting rid of the whole gang of high
mucky-mucks, famous fatheads, old wives of both sexes, stuffed
shirts, hollow men with headpieces stuffed with straw, bird-wits,
lookers-under-beds, trained seals, creeping Jesuses, Scots Wha
Ha'evers, village idiots, policemen, leaders of white-mouse factions
and noted connoisseurs of bread and butter, glorified gangsters, and
what 'Billy' Phelps calls Medlar Novelists (the medlar being a fruit
that becomes rotten before it is ripe), Commercial Calvinists, makers
of 'noises like a turnip', and all the touts and toadies and lickspittles
of the English Ascendancy, and their infernal women-folk, and all
their skunkoil skulduggery. (I have said a good deal about the
submersion, under inferior types, of the true Scotsman. Having
mentioned womenfolk, I must say here that the race of true Scots-
women, iron women, hardy, indomitable, humorous, gay, shrewd
women with an amazing sense of values, seems to be facing extinction
too in to-day's Scotland.)

And, with all due deference to those who have likened me to
better-known or more impressive models, I will be content if, apart
from my reputation purely as a poet, I come to be regarded as a sort
of twentieth-century Scottish Orestes Bronson (whom I rather
resemble facially)—not an attractive man, but a realistic and direct
thinker, knowing that the working man was to be saved by thorough
practical organization, not prayer, penetrating to the pressure groups
that controlled American politics, and being revolted by what
Arthur Schlesinger calls 'the naivetes and extravagances of tran-
scendentalism'. He wrote with an iron pen, had to have his personal
organ, and had so much to say that there was no room for contributions
by others. Perhaps his *Boston Quarterly Review* was not, as W. H.
Channing thought, 'the best journal this country has ever produced',
but it was certainly one of the most vigorous. Perhaps the essay on
the labouring classes was not 'the best study of the workings of
society written by an American before the Civil War', as Mr.
Schlesinger thinks, but it was one of the few studies which accepted
the fact of class conflict and dispensed with the romantic fol-de-rol of
the moral approach. If something very similar can be said about
myself, I will not have done badly, and I know no contemporary in
Scotland to-day who has done, or seems likely to, any better—or,
indeed, half as well. In any case, I stand almost alone in Scotland
to-day in being able to say, with Oliver Wendell Holmes, that 'I wear

my gills erect and do not talk sentiment '. (Holmes is one of my
delights. The man who said of William IV, ' The King blew his
nose twice and wiped the royal perspiration from a face which is
probably the largest uncivilized spot in England ', and characterized
Thoreau as ' the nullifier of civilization, who insisted on nibbling his
asparagus at the wrong end ', is a man after my own heart.)

And here, since I have referred to an American character, I may
mention an American Scot, since I have conceived it one of my
duties to know about and call to remembrance a whole host of little-
known or forgotten Scots who exemplify the qualities I admire which
have been ' drowned out ' under the tide of Anglicization.   The man
I have in mind at the moment is Robert Gair, maker of paper bags
and cartons.   As my friend Lewis Mumford says in his introduction
to H. Allen Smith's biographical study of Gair, ' such men are now
almost as fabulous as the dinosaur '.

But, he adds, their ' single-minded energy still compels our
respect '.   If Robert Gair ' dominated the factory as the patriarchs
of old used to dominate family and flock ', he worked as hard as any
of his employees and with as severe a discipline.   If he refused to
have a union man about the place, he was none the less emphatic in
his condemnation of George Pullman's industrial ' monarchy ', as he
called it, and he was quick to realize—and say—that ' working people
will never be happy and content unless their lives belong to themselves when they leave the factory '.   Gair's was the first industrial
plant to instal a sprinkler system and the first industrial establishment
to take out group insurance for its employees.   Work was a religion
to Robert Gair from the time he was a poor boy snooping about in the
paper-mills of Edinburgh.   He was fascinated by mechanics.   He
rigged up—from what looked like a pile of junk—' the first inter-
departmental telephone system ever installed in a manufacturing
plant '.   He invented a machine to make folding cartons, with the
initiative of a workman's error, and the equipment of a second-hand
printing press.   But (this is what I find attractive and like myself in
Gair) he never completed the process of patenting it ; that would
have meant having truck with lawyers, and neither lawyer nor banker
was admitted to a place in Robert Gair's life or business.   It is an
infinite pity that the same cannot be said of every Scotsman.

And since under the tremendous spate of conformist dullards in
the world to-day Scotsmen of the kind I like best are far too easily
lost sight of and forgotten, I may digress a moment to signalize here
another of this splendid unaccountable breed whom I have just
remembered—Hector Hugh Munro, whose first book, a creditable
but unheralded history, *The Rise of the Russian Empire*, was
published in 1900, and was followed two years later by the *Westminster Alice*, a collection of amusing political satires that had
appeared serially in the *Westminster Gazette* (which also housed some

of my own earliest poems a few years later). ' They were written ', as Edward Larocque Tinker reminds us, ' with such leprechaun wit and devastating irony that the *London Daily Post* appointed him their foreign correspondent, first in Russia and then in the Balkans and Paris. All this time, under the pseudonym of " Saki ", he had been contributing clever short stories to various English newspapers. They had a cosmopolitan brilliance, a malicious gaiety, and a subtle understanding that pilloried the foibles and mental habits of the British upper classes with deadly felicity. In a priceless paragraph he impaled the socially ambitious Lady Beauwhistle by making " Reginald "—the inconsequential, *fin de siècle* fop who was the pivot of so many tales—remark that : " Her frocks are built in Paris, but she wears them with a strong English accent. So public-spirited of her. I think she must have been very strictly brought up, she's so desperately anxious to do the wrong thing correctly." One can't help but hear overtones of the ironic wit and crackle of Wilde, but " Saki " had other qualities, among them a sense of comedy akin to Mark Twain's and the same hilarious predilection for the practical joke.' *The Jumping Frog* and *The She Wolf* are cousin under the skin. There is a reminder too of Ambrose Bierce's *Devil's Dictionary* in such synthetic quips as ' Beauty is only sin deep ', but ' Saki's ' cut and thrust is lighter and gayer and lacks the other man's somewhat heavy and bitter ferocity. Bierce defines a Christian as ' one who follows the teachings of Christ in so far as they are not inconsistent with a life of sin '. ' Saki ' makes ' Reginald ' remark that ' People may say what they like about the decay of Christianity ; the religious system that produced green Chartreuse can never really die.' Even more typical was ' Reginald's ' insistence that : ' The fashion just now is a Roman Catholic frame of mind with an Agnostic conscience ; you get the mediaeval picturesqueness of the one with the modern convenience of the other.' ' Saki ' was not an embittered personality that struck out savagely, for even his sharpest shafts were flung with an accuracy of aim and a sly humour that mollified the sting. Who could hold a grudge against him for making ' Mrs. Mabberly ' remark : ' I love Americans, but not when they try to talk. What a blessing it is that they never try to talk English.' As Mr. Tinker says : ' The verse of the " Rubaiyat " from which Munro (who was killed early in the Great War, having enlisted as a private after refusing quixotically two offers of a commission) took his pseudonym of ' Saki ' might well serve as his requiem :

> And when like her, O Saki, you shall pass
> Among the Guests star-scattered on the grass,
> And in your joyous errand reach the spot
> Where I made One—turn down an empty glass.

It is very pleasant to think of men like Norman Douglas, Hector Munro, Compton Mackenzie, and a few others when one is oppressed by the terrible lack of wit in Scotland to-day (and particularly—save for the blessing of Eric Linklater—in Scottish authors to-day) and disgusted by the antics of Sir Harry Lauder and the other Scotch ' coamics ' ; but it is not so pleasant to think how the brainless buffoonery and ' chortling wut ' of the latter are to-day general and accepted as particularly Scottish, while the brilliant sallies of the few such as I have named go for nothing and entirely fail to leaven the sad dough of modern Scottish *mœurs*.

And, above all, my poetry is Marxist :

The greatest poets undergo a kind of crisis in their art,
A change proportionate to their previous achievement.
Others approach it and fail to fulfil it—like Wordsworth.
Some, like Keats, the crisis helps to kill.
Rimbaud underwent a normal, not an abnormal, poetic crisis.
What was abnormal was his extreme youth, his circumstances, his
    peasant stock.
It killed Keats, but Keats was not born of French peasants.
It kept Milton practically silent for twenty years.
Rimbaud died at the end of nineteen.   Yet he explored it seems
After his own manner an even more hidden way.
Claudel said that, after reading him, he felt
' L'impression vivante et presque physique de surnaturel . . .
Il n'était pas de monde '.   The priest who confessed him
Said to his sister : ' I have rarely met a faith
Of the quality of his '.   That was not to be taken
(As his sister took it) in any easy pious sense ;
He remained very much *de ce monde*.
But it seems that through these years
He walked in granite within and without,
And perhaps only his poetry had not found
—And he but thirty-seven—
A method of being which was, for him,
What he desired, perdurable as the granite.
—I am forty-six ; of tenacious, long-lived country folk.
Fools regret my poetic change—from my ' enchanting early lyrics '—
But I have found in Marxism all that I need—
(I on my mother's side of long-lived Scottish peasant stock
And on my father's of hardy keen-brained Border mill-workers).
It only remains to perfect myself in this new mode.
This is the poetry I want—all
I can regard now as poetry at all,
As poetry of to-day, not of the past,
A Communist poetry that bases itself
On the Resolution of the C.C. of the R.C.P.
In Spring 1925: ' The Party must vigorously oppose
Thoughtless and contemptuous treatment
Of the old cultural heritage
As well as of the literary specialists. . . .
It must likewise combat the tendency
Towards a purely hothouse proletarian literature.'

But when I speak of Communism, of course, what I have in min⟨d⟩ is nothing less than what Lenin said in November, 1922, at th⟨e⟩ Fourth Congress of the Communist International, in the last speec⟨h⟩

he was able to make to the world : ' Now for the first time we have the possibility of learning. I do not know how long this possibility will last. I do not know how long the capitalist powers will give us the opportunity of learning in peace and quietude. But we must utilize every moment in which we are free from war, that we may learn, and learn *from the bottom up*.' Again and again Lenin insisted : ' It would be a very serious mistake to suppose that one can become a Communist without making one's own the treasures of human knowledge. It would be mistaken to imagine that it is enough to adopt the Communist formulas and conclusions of Communist science, without mastering that sum-total of different branches of knowledge, the final outcome of which is Communism. . . . Communism becomes an empty phrase, a mere façade, and the Communist a mere bluffer, if he has not worked over in his consciousness the whole inheritance of human knowledge—made his own and worked over anew all that was of value in the more than two thousand years of development of human thought.'

Alongside that, as expressing my own deepest and most determining conviction, I would set the following passage from a letter of Thomas Davidson :

> ' What shall we say of people who devote their time to reading novels written by miserable, ignorant scribblers—many of them young, uneducated, and inexperienced—and who have hardly read a line of Homer or Sophocles or Dante or Shakespeare or Goethe, or even of Wordsworth or Tennyson, who would laugh at the notion of reading and studying Plato or Aristotle or Thomas Aquinas or Bruno or Kant or Rosmini ? Are they not worse than the merest idiots, feeding prodigally upon swinish garbage, when they might be in their father's house, enjoying their portion of humanity's spiritual birthright ? I know of few things more utterly sickening and contemptible than the self-satisfied smile of Philistine superiority with which many persons tell me, " I am not a philosopher ". It simply means this, " I am a stupid, low, grovelling fool, and I am proud of it ".'

It is from Thomas Davidson (to whom I devote a long essay in my *Scottish Eccentrics*) too that I would cull the best definitions of my own general attitude and purpose in life, viz. :

> ' I think the time has come for formulating into a religion and rule of life the results of the intellectual and moral attainments of the last two thousand years. I cannot content myself with this miserable blind life that the majority of mankind is at present leading and I do not see any reason for it. Moreover, I do not see anything really worth doing but to show men the way to a better life. If our philosophy, our science, and our art do not contribute to that, what are they worth ? '

and :

> ' What I want to do is to help people to think for themselves, and to *think round the circle*, not in scraps and bits.'

And to that (since literature is my main concern) I add something that my friend Orage once said :

'Literary criticism is as much of a science as mathematics; only it is more complicated. The elements that go to the making of a literary formula are infinitely more delicate and difficult to appreciate properly. People do not understand this simply because they are ignorant. They think you can have this or that opinion of a book; that the opinion legitimately varies from one judge to the other, according to the judge's temperament. That is nonsense. A book has a value which can be assessed scientifically if you have the necessary knowledge and power of judging. I feel, more than that, I *know* that I can place a book or a poem where it belongs to a hair's breadth, without any possibility of controversy. But the ignorant will not accept my judgement because they do not possess the necessary knowledge.'

It is Marxism, however, that all the other Scottish writers I know need most to study. In thinking of them, I would second the plea put forward by Professor J. B. S. Haldane, who, pleading for the average citizen's dispassionate examination of Marxism, says: 'It is perfectly possible, without being a Mohammedan, to admit that Mohammed was the greatest man of his time', and, in answer to the query why one should worry about Marxism, says: 'One reason is because it is a philosophy of very great practical importance, a philosophy which is not less important if one decides it is entirely false'. One remembers Tolstoy's persistent refusal to read Marx, whom he constantly attacked. When told that he was really siding with Marx at times, he would have none of it. Haldane refuses to be an ostrich-intellectual *à la* Tolstoy. It is a great pity that a few of our Scottish literati do not follow his example and see from his account of Milne's cosmology how the new conceptions of matter fit the requirements of dialectical materialism, and in the section on biology note the serious application of the Marxist approach by Professor Haldane himself. His book *The Marxist Philosophy and the Sciences* is almost the only political book by a Scotsman in the last century that is not beneath contempt.

I may end here by saying that what the Scottish people need above all to-day to realize is that (in keeping with all that is really valuable in their past) static adherence to any particular methodology marks the decline of civilization, for the temporal character of the universe decrees that the only alternative to advance is decay; and the function of philosophy, as Professor Whitehead says, is to uphold the zest of life by the provision of novel goals of achievement; stupefaction before any particular methodology is that failure in adequacy which is the self-negation of philosophy and the betrayal of the future. The aim of philosophy is 'the understanding of the interfusion of modes of existence'. Or again, as Dr. Robert H. Thouless, head of the Department of Psychology at Glasgow University, says: 'We must be ready continually to revise our thought habits. . . . If we allow ourselves merely to become creatures of habit, we become automata and mechanical like the lower animals. . . . It is only by increasing flexibility of mind that we can continue to adapt ourselves to our ever-changing environment. Inflexibility of mind will lead to the extermination of the human race.'

This quality of quick adjustment, however, is worthless unless it is accompanied by an ideal of straight thinking—' the application of the scientific method of thought to all our practical problems, and the replacement of blind forces controlling our destinies by our own intelligent and conscious control '.

> There is no language in the world
> That has not yielded me delight
> (Ranging lightly from Mackay on the various forms of the Gaelic story—
> Comh-abartachd eadar Cas-Shuibal-an-t-Sleibhe agus a'Chailleach Bheurr—
> To the 218 plots of Kotzebue
> And Somdeva's Katha Sarit Sagara (Ocean Streams of Story)
> And the way Stesichorus learned his method of handling
> Some of his stories from the Hesiodic epic
> And owed his form to Dorian choral poetry).
> With exact appreciation of
> Its poets' various sleight,
> Even as I rejoice in the virgins
> Advancing slowly for the parados,
> Sliding gently into the famous processional anapaests,
> Facing the rhythmic movement of the emmeleia,
> —The long choric ode to Venus Anadyomene,
> The trochaic hymn to Artemis,
> And on to the final kommos, gathering
> The harmonies and rhythms, which have crossed and recrossed each other
> In subtle interchange throughout the poem,
> In one vast symphonic summary,
> And the whole purport and beauty of the drama is disclosed,
> As those of all language in my vision now.

So that it should become with me (' co-conscious ', in Gerald Heard's phrase, with all other parts of the human race), as with Vincent Sheean's Rayna Prohme (vide *Personal History*) :

> ' Man's inhumanity to man seemed to her a great deal more than that; it was an inhumanity of one part of man's body to another. The Shanghai entrepreneurs who employed thousands of Chinese men, women, and children at starvation wages for twelve and fourteen hours a day were, to her, like the hands of a body cutting off its legs. Capitalism, Imperialism, Individualism, were more than cannibalism, but had the same inner character. They differed from cannibalism in being more universal and more difficult to correct. She had reached her centre and was sure.'

And in so far as the expression of this in the practice of poetry has been concerned, I have always borne in mind, and endeavoured (and, think, succeeded) to act upon, what Yeats once said to AE : ' We possess nothing but the will, and we must never let the children of vague desires breathe upon it. Let us have no emotions, however abstract, in which there is not an athletic joy.' It must not be imagined, however, that what I wanted was invariably compulsive and overriding (like playing ' Chiarina ', as the Chilean pianist, Claudio Arrau, does, with much too savage an accent, so that the dotted notes appear double-dotted and the whole effect is trivialized), and failing to accommodate movements like those dance rhythms which are broken up so fine as to be all but imperceptible, yet ready to gather again into strictness at a moment's notice, if the mood changes. The poetic effects I have had most in view have, indeed, been like what Edward Sackville West says of the Mazurkas: ' These small masterpieces contain the essence of Chopin's genius compressed into a form as perfect and as supple as a miracle of jewellery. Each one is in fact a kind of microcosm into which an incredible range of emotions is packed ; high spirits are articulated with nostalgia and sadness, like the hinges of a bracelet.'

My friend Professor Denis Saurat, in his very remarkable little book, *La Fin de la Peur*, tells how, on his father's death, he, the professor, the intellectual, the metaphysician, was faced with the problem of making his metaphysics serve the ends of life, i.e., supporting his mother in her bereavement. It was a most difficult situation, for his mother was an unlettered peasant woman of remarkable force of character and with all the tremendous tenacity and shrewdness of her kind. Twixt their minds there might well have been a dead wall, but in their intimate conversations Professor Saurat soon discovered that his metaphysical ideas were not really new to her. His metaphysical mind had developed them and given them their form, but in embryonic form they had been in her mind for many a year, and she in turn had inherited them from her folk. This, Professor Saurat says, was quite unknown to him until the shock of his father's death drove them to the surface in these trying and sorrowful days. Thus, risking a return to nature, and from a crisis of dissolution, he found himself with strengthened faith and reinforced resolution.

There is a profound lesson here for the Communist poet. How many Communist or near-Communist poets in Great Britain can go to unlettered working-class people, and through their poetry give them comfort and strength, find common ground with them, and themselves derive strengthened faith and reinforced resolution from the experience ? Can we imagine Auden or MacNeice or Spende doing anything of the sort ? Can we even imagine them thinking o trying to find anything of the sort ?

' Contemplating the upheaval in my mother's mind,' says Professo Saurat, ' I saw all the ancestral primitive beliefs and was astonished t recognize in them my own metaphysical ideas. I remembered m *rêves enfantins* and saw how even in childhood my metaphysical idea visited me constantly, but, since my childish waking consciousnes could make nothing of them, they had free play only during sleep and dreams. And the note constantly struck in them, as in my mother's experience, is that in all forms of expression—in birth, in sexual life, in artistic expression, and in death—a point is reached where success or catastrophe must be accepted impartially—one must throw precaution to the winds and jump. So far from the fact of sharing this feeling with unlettered peasants and primitives being a drawback, I found in it the final proof of the rightness of my metaphysics. La seule qualité, c'est le courage ; on n'arrivé jamais a la verité, comme a la vie, que par le courage ; voir tout le risque, et sauter.'

Saurat has one illustration of extraordinary force in this little book —one which, living in a remote island where there are no sanitary conveniences, I would have been quick to appreciate anyhow, but which also recalled my earliest experience with my mother's rural-worker kind (a state of affairs I used to great effect in a famous if malodorous attack on the *bourgeois* Burns Cult—and which I also remember some one using, with exact description of the location of the outside closet and the way the prevalent wind in winter bore across the space between Haworth Parsonage and it, to bring right home—right down to brass tacks—certain vital facts about the lives of the Brontë sisters).

' Reality ', says Saurat, ' is often found not so hostile as it appears. I recognized anew—a thought which led me to the towering super-structure of hope that no doubt in the last analysis this will always be so—that the Inactual Evil is after all most probably a harmless phantom and death as benevolent as birth. In the peasant mind the fear of death is linked inextricably with the fear of the dead and of darkness. The peasants avoid the dark except as a covering for excretory acts of which they are ashamed. Having no indoor closets, they go outside at nights to relieve themselves, and the dead, knowing this, are apt to come and seek them at such times, to the great terror of the peasants. But those whose love for the departed outstrips their terror deliberately seek such rendezvous. Their terror makes their belief in the possi-bility of the coming of the dead a solid reality—so it is their great terror which is their great hope.'

An example of how this touchstone of general experience can be used is afforded by my poem ' The Seamless Garment ', of which Mr. Cecil Day Lewis (who recognizes it as one of my best poems, as, of course, F. G. Scott did immediately he saw it ; it attracted nobody else's attention—no reviewer so much as mentioned it), in his *A Hope for Poetry*, says :

' The Poet is speaking to a cousin in a cloth-mill, comparing Lenin's work with the work of Rilke in a different sphere and both with a weaver's ; and first, of Lenin—

. . . His secret and the secret o' a'
That's worth ocht.
The shuttles fleein' owre quick for my een
Prompt the thocht,
And the co-ordination atween
Weaver and machine.

The haill shop's dumfounderin'
To a stranger like me.
Second nature to you ; you're perfectly able
To think, speak and see
Apairt frae the looms, tho' to some
That doesna sae easily come.

Lenin was like that wi' the workin'-class life.
At hame wi 't a'.
His fause movements couldna' been fewer,
The best weaver earth ever saw.
A' he'd to dae wi' moved intact,
Clean, clear and exact.

He goes on presently to express that feeling which is at the back of a
great deal of the poetry written in the last few years, the feeling that the
system under which we live deprives the majority of the chance of a
decent life.

. . . Are you equal to life as to the loom ?
Turnin' oot shoddy or what ?
Claith better than man ?   D'ye live to the full,
Your poo'ers a' dellverly taught ?
or scamp a'thing else ?   Border cloth's famous
Shall things o' mair consequence shame us ? . . .

. . . The womenfolk ken what I mean.
Things maun fit like a glove,
Come clean off the spoon—and syne
There's time for life and love.
The mair we mak' natural as breathin' the mair
Energy for ither things we'll can spare,
But as lang as we bide like this
Neist to naething we ha'e, or miss . . .

The " First Hymn to Lenin " was followed by a rush of poetry sympathetic to Communism or influenced by it.   " New Signatures " (1932)
showed the beginning of this trend ; " New Country " (1933) contained
definitely Communist forms by Auden, Charles Madge, R. E. Warner
and others, Spender's " Poems " and my own " Magnetic Mountain "
both published in 1933, continued the movement.'

How I am striving to utilize this profound way of approach—and
above all to reach the workers *through their work*—may be seen from
the following passage of a recent poem, which I quote in full because
it is fundamental to an understanding of my present position and the
tasks to which I am addressing myself :

A poetry full of such tremendous insights
As when Buber cries
' Rendez-vous compte de ce que cela signifie
Quand un ouvrier percoit dialogiquement
Son rapport avec sa machine,
Quand un typographe dit qu'il comprend
Le bourdonnement de la presse
Comme un témoignage joyeux de reconnaissance
Pour l'aide qu'il lui a apportée

A surmonter les obstacles qui arrêtaient sa marche,
L'alourdissaient, la paralysaient,
Lui donnant ainsi
La possibilité de fonctionner librement.

Buber nous parle du typographe qui,
A travers le bourdonnement de sa machine,
A perçu sa reconnaissance et sa joie,
Cela est parfaitement comprehensible pour nous
Et admissible.   Mais voici une légende hasside
Du XVIII siècle ; elle nous raconte
La joie qu'éprouva la fondateur de la doctrine,
Le grand saint Balshem,
Lorsqu'il vit soudain par les yeux de l'esprit que,
Dans une petite bourgade lointaine,
Dieu avait accompli une miracle uniquement
Pour qu'un pauvre relieur put dignement
Fêter le sabat, c'est-à-dire acheter
Des cierges, des pains, du vin. . . .
Cette histoire qui est parfaitement à sa place
Dans un receuil de légendes hassides
Ne pourrait se trouver ni dans *Moi et Toi*
Ni dans le *Dialogue*.   Cela veut dire :
La théophanie du langage moderne
Doit essentiellement différer
Non seulement de la théophanie biblique
Mais aussi de la théophanie des hassides
Qui, dans le temps, nous sont relativement proches.
Les hommes de la Bible, les hassides, et nous
Nous pouvons tous parler de l'existence quotidienne
Et des manifestations de Dieu
Dans le cours ordinaire de l'existence.

Mais à nous autres, hommes du XX siècle,
Il nous est sévèrement interdit
De penser que Dieu peut à tel point s'intéresser
A la vie de tous les jours d'un pauvre homme
Qu'il lui envoie les quelques sous dont cet homme a besoin
Pour s'acheter des cierges et du vin.
Qui ou qu'est ce qui nous l'interdit ?
Il n'y a qu'une réponse à cette question :
C'est notre " connaissance " qui nous l'interdit.
Mais n'est-ce pas " un excès de pouvoir,
Qu'une connaissance qui sent ses responsabilités
Ne peut se permettre ",
Ainsi qui parlait Buber lui-même ?
Je vais plus loin encore ; est-il en général permis
A la connaissance de se mêler de ces choses ? '

Martin Buber is one of the rare thinkers
Who introduce into their work that ' earnest ',
That extreme intensity of which
Kierkegaard and Nietzsche have spoken.
His thought is not for him an interesting pastime,
Nor even a means of doing useful service
For culture and society.   And it is the same
With his writings.   He lives in his thought ;

In his writings he incarnates that life.
If he ' serves ' it is a case always
Of a particular kind of service.

It is not in vain
That he set himself an overwhelming task,
A task almost unrealizable for the modern man :
The translation of the Bible into German.
It was necessary to have his ' boundless (unrestrainable) passion '
(' Boundless '—forcené—is the favourite expression of Dostoievsky,
' Passion ', the term Kierkegaard employs ;
And Kierkegaard and Dostoievsky are,
Next to Buber, the greatest spirits
Of the nineteenth century) in order to dare to recreate
At this time the researches and discoveries
Of those distant times when it was not
Men who discovered truth, but truth
Which revealed itself to men.

A task almost unrealizable ;
We are, in fact, convinced that truth can be found
Only in clear and distinct judgements,
And how then can we express in our language
Which has moulded itself in accordance with this conviction
So deeply-rooted, what the men saw and heard
Who still possessed the faculty
Of entering into contact with the mystery ?
' The sparks of light of the original being
Who found himself directly face to face with God,
Adam Kadmon, have fallen into the prison of *things*,
After the light has fallen from the higher spheres
Into the lower which it has burst asunder.
The Shekinah of God
Descended from one sphere to another,
Passed and repassed
From one universe to another,
From one ether to another
Till it had reached
The utmost limits of its prison,
Till it had reached us.
In our World God's destiny is accomplished.'

' Dans les autres doctrines, l'âme de Dieu
Envoyée du ciel sur la terre
Pouvait être de nouveau appelée au ciel et delivrée :
Le création et la rédemption
Ne s'effectuaient que dans une seule direction,
De haut en bas.   Mais c'est inadmissible
Pour une doctrine juive qui est fondée tout entière
Sur les rapports réciproques
Entre le ' Moi ' humain
Et le ' Toi ' divin,
Sur la réalité de cette réciprocité,
Sur la rencontre.
Dans cette doctrine l'homme,
L'homme infirme, misérable,
Est appelé de toute éternité
A être l'aide de Dieu.

C'est pour lui que le monde a été crée,
Pour lui qui choisit, qui choisit Dieu.
L'apparence extérieure du monde
Existe pour qu'à travers elle
L'homme recherche son noyau même.
Le sphères sont écartées les unes des autres,
Afin précisément qu'il les rapproche.
La création attend l'homme.
Dieu lui-même l'attend.
Et c'est de l'homme ' d'en bas '
' Que doit venir l'appel du salut.
La grâce sera la réponse de Dieu.'
Que l'homme soit pénétré tout entier d'ardeur !
Que cette ardeur le reveille de son assoupissement,
Car la sainteté lui a été communiquée
Et il est devenu autre qu'il n'était avant.
Il est devenu digne de créer,
Et semblable lui-même au Saint,
Que son nom soit béni !
Tel qu'il était lorsqu'il créait son monde ! . . .
Et alors, je saisais instantanément l'âme hasside.
L'antique conscience juive se réveilla en moi
Dans les ténèbres de l'exil elle s'épanouit
Pour ainsi dire en moi :
L'homme—image et ressemblance de Dieu—
Comme oeuvre, comme devenir, comme tâche.
Et cette conscience essentiellement juive,
Essentiellement humaine,
Etait le contenu de la religiosité humaine.
Si ' l'expérience quotidienne ' ne lui avait pas montré
Que les succès et les échecs se repartissent indifféremment
Entre les bons et les méchants,
Et si les *oculi mentis*
Ne lui avaient pas suggéré
La conviction qu'il est impossible
D'échapper a cette expérience,
Il ne serait jamais arrivé à la conclusion
Que la raison et la volonté de Dieu
Diffèrent *toto caelo* de la raison
Et de la volonté de l'homme,
Qu'elles n'ont de commun avec celles-ci
Que le mot qui les désigne ;
De même que l'on appelle chien
Un ' animal aboyant ' et l'une des constellations du ciel.
. . . Le typographe avec lequel causa Buber
N'est pas plus près de la vérité,
Pas même d'un cheveu, que le relieur hasside.

Buber a raison de dire
Que la machine souriait
Avec reconnaissance au typographe.
Mais nous ne devons en aucune façon
Oublier le relieur hasside.
Et Buber a également raison
Quand il écrit dans *Moi et Toi* :
' Je perçois quelque chose.
Je me représente quelque chose.

G

Je veux quelque chose.
Je pense à quelque chose.
De toutes ces choses et d'autres semblables
On ne peut còmposer
Toute la vie humaine.'

A poetry full of such realizations as :

Il n'eût pas été inutile
De confronter la durée bergsonienne—
Effort grandiose pour accorder le rhythme du Vorhanden
Au rhythme de l'Existence—avec la ' Zeitlichkeit ' de Heidegger
Qui est une durée finie, mortelle,
Dont le temps nivilé tel que l'utilisient les sens commun et la science
N'est qu'un dérivé.
(Quoi qu'en dise Heidegger lui-même,
Sa ' Zeitlichkeit ' succède à la durée de Bergson,
Ne fût-ce que pour s'opposer d'elle.)
Et qu'il serait tentant d'étudier,
A la lumière de cette temporalité
Le caractère particulier de la durée musicale.
Elle se révèlerait, probablement,
Comme *l'unité extatique par excellence*
Du passé, du présent, et du futur.
Le thème musical n'est-il pas tout d'abord
Un trésor virtuel presque illimité de ressources mélodique
Mais à mesure qu'il se déploi et se développe,
Des formales tonales ou atonales
L'engagent et le contraignent,
Des combinaisons harmoniques limitent sa libertié,
Des rhythmes l'asservissent.
Projetant dans le futur un universe sonore,
Il s'alourdit du passé.
Il faut qu'il cède une part,
Et non la moindre,
De ses virtualités pour que cet universe ébauché vive,
Recoive de fermes en definitifs contours.
La melodie incarne, et enquelque sort,
La transcendance elle-même ; comme celle-ci
Elle est essentialement ' *überschwingend-entziehend* '.
A chaque instant de sa durée,
Touten s'élançant vers l'avenir
Elle est incorruptiblement son propre passé,
Le premières notes d'un thème musical, déja,
Sont chargées du passé de silence dont elles émergent.
Parce qu'elle est connaissance, choix du possible,
La musique s'ouvre à l'extase du futur
Et parce qu'elle est expression de la ' Befindlinchkeit '
Elle se fonde sut l'extase du passé.
(*Das Verstehen grundet sich primar in der Zukunft,*
Die Befindlichkeit, dagegen, zeitigt
Sich primar in der Gewesenheit.)

Comme la Zeitlichkeit de Heidegger,
La temporalité est une durée finie.
La perfection melodique tient essentiellement
Au caractère fine de cette durée,

Aux limites que celle-ci impose à l'art musical
Et dont il faut
Qu'il triomphe en les transcendant.
Elle l'oblige à tirer d'une liberté,
Finie la libertié tout court.
Faisant violence à son intime nécessité,
A l'écoulement qui est sa loi,
La musique réussit,
Au sein du mouvement même,
A creér un équilibre sonore,
Une presence accomplie,
Ou tout ce qui a été
Vibre encore et résonne,
Ou tout ce qui va être
Se laisse pressentir :
Elle est l'instant parfait.
' In der . . . (mettons ici " musique "
A la place d' " *Entschlossenheit* ")
Ist die Gegenwart aus der Zerstreuung—
Nicht nur zuruckgeholt,
Sondern wird in der Zukunft
Und Gewesenheit gehalten.'
C'est ce présent authentique,
A la fois tenu dans le passé,
Et dans le futur, que Heidegger nomme ' *Augenblick* '.
C'est en lui que la musique atteint à l'unité
Des trois extases : ' die ekstatische Einheit '.

And above all, Chestov, my master,
Dead while I write these lines,
' Das Dasein muss wesenhaft das auch schon Entdeckte
Gegen den Schein zueignen.'
A poetry that never for a moment forgets
The crucial necessity—that Existence
Must always necessarily appropriate for itself
(In conflict with appearance) the already discovered.
To lay bare the ' existing ' is to dispute it with appearance,
To wring, to ravish, its secret from it.
Truth (the discovered) must always first be wrung
From the existing. The existing is torn from the hidden.
Discovery (laying bare) is always a rape, a theft.
For this the ' courageous decision ' is necessary
And that is what ' *Entschlossenheit* ' is.

And now I am impelled by your death
To realize afresh and far more keenly than ever
That *Entschlossenheit* is
The will-to-possess-knowledge of our nothingness :
' *Gewissen-gaben-wollen* '.
This will-to-possess-knowledge of nothingness
Of Existence is, just as much
As self-comprehension, an aspect
—And not the least serious or important—
Of the *Entschlossenheit des Daseins*.
The world is not ' Nature ', neither
Is it ' representation ' (the perceived) ; it is

An ontological characteristic of Existence.
In the appearance of the world
Is manifested transcendance.
' Transcendance means surpassing '
(*Transcendenz bedeutet Überstieg*).
How are we to translate *Überstieg* ?
By surpassing ?   That is inadequate,
Giving the idea of a precipice
To be compassed, an abyss to be bridged.
Transcendance achieves always
A *totality* which may not
Have been coherently apprehended
But which is in no wise
The sum of all that which exists.
It does not present the thing-in-itself,
It is the ' being in the world ' ;
' *Das In-der-Welt-sein* '.
What Existence transcends is not only
The existing which distinguishes it
In every respect, it is primarily
The existing which it itself is ;
In the Transcending, existence comes first
To such existing things as it itself is,
To itself as itself—with the same movement
That awakens, vivifies, and stirs a world.

Existence, transcendent, gives form to the *self*
' *Die Selbstheit* '.   Creating a world (' *Weltbildend* ')
And, simultaneously, creating itself (' *Selbstbildend* ')
It hurls itself in advance of itself
Into the world which it permeates.

To exist means to-be-in-the-world, to be caught,
Encompassed by the existing things
Which there discover (offer) themselves,
And in that world to tie bonds,
To clear a way for oneself,
To conquer distances (*ent-fernen*),
To find materials (*zeuge*)
Which one uses for a definite end.
This is what Heidegger calls
' Availability ' (*Zuhandenheit*).
The existing as it is in itself is
Primarily the ' available ',
That which is within my reach,
Which concerns me, which I
Interest myself in (*Besorgen*).
Moreover, I must share this world with ' others '.
I must come against other existences
Similar to my own.   I must adjust myself
To their rhythms, or impose my own on them.
I must lose or find myself in them.
' *Die Welt des Daseins ist Mitwelt* '.
The world of existence is a common world.
To-be-in-the-world implies
To-be-along-with-others : Co-existence (*Mitdasein*).

And, constantly, I seek

A poetry of facts.   Even as
The profound kinship of all living substance
Is made clear by the chemical route.
Without some chemistry one is bound to remain
Forever a dumbfounded savage
In the face of vital reactions.
The beautiful relations
Shown only by biochemistry
Replace a stupefied sense of wonder
With something more wonderful
Because natural and understandable.
Nature is more wonderful
When it is at least partly understood.
Such an understanding dawns
On the lay reader when he becomes
Acquainted with the biochemistry of the glands
In their relation to diseases such as goitre
And their effects on growth, sex, and reproduction.
He will begin to comprehend a little
The subtlety and beauty of the action
Of enzymes, viruses, and bacteriophages.

Those substances which are on the borderland
Between the living and the non-living.
He will understand why the biochemist
Can speculate on the possibility
Of the synthesis of life without feeling
That thereby he is shallow or blasphemous.
He will understand that, on the contrary,
He finds all the more
Because he seeks for the endless
—' Even our deepest emotions
May be conditioned by traces
Of a derivative of phenanthrene ! '

In a longish poem I contributed to Nigel Heseltine's *Wales*,
entitled ' On Reading Professor Ifor Williams's " Canu Aneurin " in
Difficult Days ', in August, 1939, what I said in one of the verses
further illustrates the kind of poetry I have come to want, viz. :

So I am delivered from the microcosmic human chaos
And given the perspective of a writer who can draw
The wild disorder of a ship in a gale
Against the vaster natural order of sea and sky.
If man does not bulk too big in his rendering
He does not lose the larger half of dignity either.

And the sequence of defining stanzas from which I have drawn the
long succession of verses earlier in this chapter—a sequence which
runs, appearing and reappearing at intervals, through the entire
immense bulk of my *Cornish Heroic Song*, includes also the following
verses, which are, I think, all I need to quote here by way of completing this little revelation of my auctorial aims and aspirations :

A poetry like the barrel of a gun
Weaving like a snake's head.

A poetry that can put all its chips on the table
And back it to the limit.

A poetry full of the crazy feeling
That everything that has ever gone into my life
Has pointed to each successive word
And I couldn't have failed to write it if I'd tried.
Since a man cannot duck away from the pattern
That life lays out for him.

Or like testing with group-reagents for every known poison
And also for ptomaine, but all the solvents
—Alcohol, benzol, naphtha, ammonia, and so forth—failing,
And testing for the alkaloids, such as
Strychnine, digitalin, and cantharidin,
And using hydrochloric acid to find
Either silver, mercury, or lead,
And also ammonia in an endeavour
To trace tin, cadmium, or arsenic
And being utterly unable to arrive
At any conclusion—though it would appear
Death was due to the virulence
Of some azotic substance, of which
There is only a secondary and most faint trace.
Briefly, like a game of roulette, wherein
We always play en plein—a game of hazard
Played by the individual against the multiform forces
To which we give the name of ' circumstance '.
With cards whose real strength is always either more or less
Than their face value, and which are ' packed ' and ' forced '
With an astuteness which would baffle the wiliest sharper.
There are times in the game when the cards
Held by the mortal player have no value at all,
When what seem to us kings and queens and aces
Change to mere blanks ; there are other moments
When ignoble twos or threes flush into trumps
And enable us to sweep the board.

While I want all this highly complicated poetry—and regard myself in this way as in others (although not in language) as a purely Celtic poet, carrying on (newly applied in vastly changed circumstances) the ancient bardic traditions of a very intricate and scholarly poetry, and with all the bardic powers of savage satire and invective as well as the bardic concern for the Celtic countries—Scotland, Ireland, Wales, and Cornwall—and for Celtic history and the continuity of Celtic civilization—I agree entirely with what Professor Adolph Mahr says (in his *Ancient Irish Handicraft*, published by the Archaeological Society and Field Club of Limerick) : ' That which generally excites the greatest admiration for the " opus hibernicum " is the combination of complication of design and delicacy of execution, though it is not this extrinsic aspect but rather some emotional quality which constitutes its innermost essence.'

Finally, a word about the kind of poetry I don't want. I extract the following passages from a frontal attack I made in an editorial in my quarterly, the *Voice of Scotland*, on the English Literary Left, and particularly the Auden–Spender–MacNeice school :

'Restatements of position, and more definite commitments, are in order just now, and so far as the *Voice of Scotland* is concerned ours can hardly be better expressed than in what Henry Treece says, viz. :

'We can hope for life in poetry wherever the Nationalist sign is hung out, whether the Nationalism be Welsh, Scottish, or American ; for it is only their magazines which, because they need not kow-tow to the swinging *bourgeois* politico-literary fashions of English Communism, Fascism, or Social Credit, can show us an art cut free from the objective-mechanistic tumour.'

And in the following passage from a letter from George Campbell Hay :

'The slash at the " general stream of European literature " might be shocking if misunderstood. I do not mean that Gaelic should not widen its contacts. It must. But " European literature " as understood by people like Quiller-Couch (whom I choose as a particularly horrible example [1]) and as embodied in tomes with that title, a selected list of countries and a selected list of names from each of these countries, starting of course with the Greeks, well-bowdlerized into " Christian gentlemen ", is a ramp that no longer impresses—like " Western Europe ". I am all for the " minor literatures " and the " backward races " whose literatures have not been " etherealized " out of life. Our contacts might as well be with the Islaendings or with those grand rascals the Serbs as with Bloomsbury or the Seine. The big countries share a common foreign-ness and repulsiveness to me, and like Blunt I sometimes wish they would destroy one another.'

But of all the big literatures the one which has gone most hopelessly astray is English literature, and it cannot be too clearly realized that the work of the English Literary Left is no corrective, but merely an accentuation of this, and represents a development of the English Ascendancy spirit which should render it impossible for Scottish, Irish, Welsh, and Cornish readers to continue to form parts of the reading public to which it is addressed. It is at the furthest remove from anything that represents a reasonable synthesis of the various racial elements in the British Isles ; it is utterly opposed to and incompatible with the traditional and—however modified by English education and literary influence—continuing national literary elements in Scotland, Ireland, Wales, and Cornwall ; it is not truly

---

[1] The worst example of all was probably the late Dr. Laurie Magnus, whose books on European literature, designed to accompany *English Studies*, were most atrociously Blimpish in this way.

Left at all.   The dangerous pass to which post-Union subjection to
English Ascendancy has reduced the Scottish and other minority
elements in the British Isles cannot be more startlingly exposed than
by the readiness with which sections of our reading publics—and
especially of our student bodies—in the non-English parts of Great
Britain have ' fallen for ' this disgusting ramp (largely because of the
high-powered publicity which has made the work of Auden, Spender,
and others a literary fashion and succeeded in equating it with the
genuine Left tendencies which are long overdue but less likely to
manifest themselves in the quarters in question than anywhere else in
the world, and, owing to the objective circumstances, almost entirely
incapable of appearing in England, where their apparent discovery
has been so loudly and insistently proclaimed, but certain, on the
contrary, to manifest themselves in Scotland, Ireland, Wales, where
in fact they have to some small extent actually appeared, and
displayed their inevitable complete dissimilarity to what has been
hailed as of this kind in England, only, thanks to the monstrous and
unnatural organization of the English Literary Left, to be thus far
ignored and more or less successfully sabotaged by these precious
English ' comrades ').   It is, indeed, almost an infallible test of a
Scots (or Irish or Welsh) Socialist that he should have not only no
use whatever for but a positive objection to Auden, Spender, and the
rest, and the English Literary Left, but that, if they succeed in
imposing themselves even on English Socialists, that can only be
thanks to the appallingly inadequate grasp of Socialist theory which
has always characterized the English movement, and to that con-
stitutional incapacity for dialectic which has always been, and seems
likely always to be, peculiarly characteristic of the English people.
Gaelic literature, though learned and in the hands of a highly-
organized Bardic class, was always popular in a way that English
literature has never been, and in a way that the stupendously-
overboosted work of Auden and his associates is at the extreme pole
from being.   Scotland, unlike England, has even in post-Gaelic
days had a great popular literature which has only been whittled
away under the influence of that progressive Anglification of which the
Auden–Spender stuff to-day is only the final expression—completely
anti-Scottish and anti-popular.

What but harm and corruption to the great body of Scottish
radicalism can be the effect of work accurately described by John
Lehmann in the following sentences ?

' For a generation determined to accept nothing easy or uncom
plex, nothing that yielded its meaning at first glance, his (i.e
Auden's) frequent obscurities, and his love of mystification, privat
jokes, invocations to names and symbols that could have little sens
to those " not in the know " were by no means an obstacle t
admiration.   Through his early work he seems to be speaking t

an elect few, salvaged from the general wreck of civilization, his friends. Another trait that makes of him a peculiarly " intimate " poet, a poet for a private circle of friends, is his love of charades and clowning. . . . In *The Orators* the paraphernalia of a school-master's life, and the tone of the games-master giving the boys a talk before the match, made a rather overwhelming appearance. Auden, Day Lewis, Warner, Upward, are, or have at one time been, schoolmasters, and this style now spreads very rapidly, even to their followers, which gives their work of this period an unfortunate cliquish, even semi-fascist, flavour. There are other prose pieces, more obscurely written, in which the religious note appears. . . . The remarkable psychological and historical intuition, one feels, is being wasted for lack of clear historical direction.'

No nation that enslaves another can itself be free.

These incongruous peculiarities of this English ' Left ' literature are the natural phenomena of a Leftism in an oppressor-country which, no matter under which pretence of liberalism or social democracy, is determined to hang on to its Ascendance and the Empire it exploits and battens upon all the more cunningly and determinedly the more the oppressed elements are forced by their objective conditions to try to liberate themselves from its grip, and the more it is itself obliged to pretend to progressive sentiments it is in fact far from really holding, or indeed genuinely entertaining at all, before profound changes have been wrought in its relative position. This pretence of Socialist belief—while the silent sabotage of its own nationalities' problems continues not only unchecked but relentlessly intensified—is an impudent bluff. It is the same England that finds it necessary at this juncture to give widespread publicity to Auden and his associates, and to pass infernally savage sentences on young Irish men and women at the instance of judges who do not hesitate (without in any way violating the complacency of English belief in their famous—and utterly unfounded—tradition of fair play) to display a hellish sadism and to vent their personal political prejudices in passing sentence on their hapless victims.

It is for this reason—not because I write in Scots dialect but simply because I am a Scot, and because, unlike these English Communist and near-Communist poets, I actually belong to, and have never ceased to be organically related to, the working class—that I have never been grouped along with them or asked to contribute to their group-publications.[1] As Mr. Lehmann says, I ' stand alone, completely outside the Auden–Spender–Day Lewis group and its particular pattern of ideas '.

' In 1931 ', Mr. Lehmann continues, ' MacDiarmid had published his " First Hymn to Lenin ", a poem much more directly and pro-

---

[1] Before the 1938 issue of *New Writing* (edited by John Lehmann) to which contributed a short story.

foundly Communist than anything that the others had written. In
a sense it was the prelude to the whole movement. Though Auden,
for instance, had established the corner-stone of his creed with the
publication of " Poems " in 1930, he does not show any open and
clear Communist leanings until after the " Hymn to Lenin " had
been published, nor do any of the others. But considering the
barrier that Scots vernacular forms for most Southern Englishmen,
it is unlikely that MacDiarmid's actual influence can have been
more than slight.'

The fact, on the contrary, is that many of these writers had
encountered and liked my work, and established personal relations
with me, as early as 1926 ; and my ' First Hymn to Lenin ' was
written for Professor Lascelles Abercrombie and first published in
New English Poems edited by him ; and if the Scots Vernacular is a
barrier to Southern Englishmen, it has certainly not been so to many
younger Irish and Welsh and American writers, nor has it precluded
my work from recognition in Russia, France, Germany, and elsewhere. These excuses for my exclusion are, in fact, spurious, and
simply mask a continuance even in these avowedly-Communistic
circles of the English Ascendancy attitude and hatred of Scotland,
while if my work is ' much more directly and profoundly Communist ',
this is due to the fact that I am the heir of the great Scottish Republican and Radical traditions and have never been affected by the social
stratification, the public-school system, and the other peculiar
traditions of England which Auden and his friends manifest so
markedly.

The editors of *This Generation* (1939) point out (*op. cit*, pp. 384–5)
that for the most part contemporary British novelists have continued
to write of the decaying middle-class. ' They came from this class
and they could not have understood another. Almost none of the
younger English novelists record radical thought in England or treat
thoroughly of the English working-man. English poets, although
as a group more radical than the English novelists, nevertheless
. . . represent the upper middle-class, as Auden points out in his
review of *Enemies of Promise* by Cyril Connolly, published in *The
New Republic* of April 26, 1939. Certainly the British revolutionary
poets come from that six per cent of the English people educated in
what in America would be called private schools.'

Right from Elizabethan times, English literature (developing in
keeping with English Imperialism) has been a monstrous epinasty—
that ' curvature of an organ caused by a more active growth on its
upper side—hollow inside '. Matthew Arnold wrote in the first
essay of his first *Essays in Criticism* that ' it has long seemed to me
that the burst of creative activity in our literature, through the first
quarter of this century, had about it in fact something premature ;
and that from this cause its productions are doomed, most of them,

in spite of the sanguine hopes which accompanied and still do accompany them, to prove hardly more lasting than the reproductions of far less splendid epochs. And this prematureness comes from its having proceeded without having its proper data, without sufficient material to work with. In other words, the English poetry of the first quarter of this century, with plenty of energy, plenty of creative force, did not know enough.'

That was true of the English poetry of the first quarter of the nineteenth century ; it is far truer of the English poetry of the first two-fifths of the present century. The school of poets we are concerned with here are characterized by an appalling parvanimity infinitely worse than that ' not knowing enough ' which made ' Byron so empty of matter, Shelley so incoherent, Wordsworth even, profound as he is, yet so wanting in completeness and variety '. And with that parvanimity goes a perverseness ; a parageusia unparalleled perhaps in any previous phase of the parthenogenous evolution of English literature, and certainly without trace of precedent in any previous phase of Scottish, Irish, or Welsh literature. This is what one would expect, of course, of a literature produced by plutocrats posing as Communists, of English poets few of whom are English at all, and of the beneficiaries of a literary racket of the real nature of which they are cynically conscious (as is shown by the rigour with which the ' game ' is being operated against better poets and truer voices of working-class sentiments and needs, and in despite of the general interests of British literature).

Auden and his associates are working off on the public a trick in the realm of literature not dissimilar to that which has been played in the political sphere by Neville Chamberlain, and which is described in the passage of Upton Sinclair's *The Money-Changers* where he asks : ' Could a more tragic piece of irony have been imagined than this—that the man, who of all men had been responsible for this terrible calamity, should have been heralded before the whole world as the one who averted it ? Could there have been a more appalling illustration of the way in which the masters of the Metropolis were wont to hoodwink its blind and helpless population ? '

Outstanding points in the present set-up are these—that the Capitalist Press, &c., has far less objection to Socialism than to Nationalism. It is a ghastly scandal to see difficulties multiplied for men like Rhys and Dylan Thomas, and the way being cleared for people like Tony Heinemann, Willy Goldman, Julius Lipton (Lipschitz), Abraham Fagan, and Simon Blumenfeld. We are making no specific accusations against any of these individuals —but simply describing the general atmosphere in which the London Literary Left lives and moves and has its being—when we quote with complete agreement what a correspondent says : ' It's disgusting—this b——g and making proletarians out of *petit-bourgeois* Jews, nearly as disgusting as the proletarian accent of Calder-Marshall and others who contributed to *The Old School*'.

It must be stressed that all this goes with a hatred of and opposition to all Welsh, Scottish, and Irish work. ' Heinemann ', writes a friend, ' was quite open and said there weren't any Scots, Irish, and Welsh writers nowadays. But when one of his friends tells me that Auden doesn't think much of MacDiarmid and says his stories are "lots of things lying on the ground ", it makes me sick. . . . Lehmann's attitude in itself is also harmful : his group, " The Yellow Book of the Thirties ", swamps the younger writers, the younger group since *New Signatures*, who naturally take up a Wyndham Lewis stance ; they are too Left for them.'

There has been some uneasiness in Wales over this lately. The miners are beginning to see through the book club racket, which, with the Penguins, has spoilt the chance of any younger writers ever getting a novel out. George Evart Evans, who has had stories in *Left Review*, *New Masses*, &c., can't find a publisher—three years now, though his work is very good. Efforts were made by some gallery-playing authors to smash up Keidrych Rhys's group. There seems to be a conspiracy. The capitalists in Wales have come to terms with the Communists, ask Arthur Horner to shoot grouse, and spend time and money attacking Nationalists. They foully vilified Saunders Lewis when he was in prison. They even give the Left publicity (only recently, though) and review Lawrence and Wishart books ; the Nationalists get neither. ' Still ', a correspondent feels in face of all this, ' I feel, however, that something on the lines advocated by the *Voice of Scotland* is bound to come pretty soon. The public (the middle class) won't always be satisfied with racketeering and lies and public schoolmen with large private incomes. Edgell Rickword is about the only person with some idea of Nationalism, but even he was in the Black-and-Tans. . . . The time will come when contributors to *Wales* will be allowed to write plays and scenarios for our Miners' May Day pageant instead of Montagu Slater.'

So far no one has dared to attack this set-up except perhaps Dupee in an article on ' The English Literary Left ' in the *Partisan Review* ; and Herbert Read and Keidrych Rhys, indirectly in *Time and Tide*, and Savage in his brilliant, ' Poetry Politics in London ' in *Poetry* (Chicago), June, 1939.

' Trotsky ', writes a friend, ' now seems to give more hope for nationalism than Georgia's Stalin ! I can't see how one can possibly hope to build any militant organ upon a public-school clique, all of whom are making a comfortable living out of it, and know nothing whatever of the lives of workers. It will be a difficult job. I think one of the first essentials is to create a new group in opposition and get them publicized. *New Writing* of course won't print George Barker or Dylan Thomas because they'd only show up Auden. It is no good looking for support in the weeklies. And there is no entry to *The Listener*. . . . Robert Herring is the only editor who prints the younger people ; he is also tied up with *New Writing* and the old *Left Review* clique though.'

' *Tir Newydd* has had a good article on the C.P.'s attitude to the Welsh language and culture (says the Welsh C.P. branches haven't shown any interest yet, even after promises in their Report), also on the difference between the Welsh " People " and England's proletariat—a really excellent piece of work ! It is along this line only that hope lies. London is rotten through and through. But if the elements that realize these truths in Wales, Ireland, and Scotland can only make common cause, we can force the C.P. to adopt a very different line ere long and get rid of these abominable groups who are monopolizing the limelight to the detriment of far better writers than themselves. Dylan Thomas alone is worth a dozen Audens or Spenders or Day Lewises any day ; and *Wales* was a far more wholesome and promising affair than all the organs of the London Literary Left together. It must be revived.' [1]

But after all I have nothing to complain of if England has shown no interest in or appreciation of my work and vastly prefers inferior poets of its own to any ' damned Irishman or Scotsman or Welshman '. When has it been otherwise, and how could it ever be otherwise ? It is agreed that Burns is a great lyric poet—but is there anything beyond that mere agreement ? Is Burns really read, really appreciated, by the English ? Of course not. Is Burns given to the children in English schools as Scottish schools are compelled to give English poets to their pupils ? Of course not. And what goes for Burns goes for all other Scottish poetry of any consequence whatever. Only a moiety of the English public ever hear anything of it. It means nothing whatever save to an isolated individual here and there —the English prefer even their own insipid ballads to the magnificent old Scottish ballads ; the English have practically no songs of their own—how could they appreciate Scotland's unique treasury of popular song ? When I say the English in these sentences, I mean even that small fraction of the English people which constitutes the intelligent reading public and more specifically the poetry-reading public ; the vast majority of the English people, like all other people, never read anything worth reading, either of English or any other literature, except the miserable smattering they get at school and promptly forget all about when they leave school. I have therefore no just cause for complaint on the score of English indifference to or ignorance of my work. That is just ' the nature of

---

[1] It was revived almost immediately afterwards, under the editorship of Nigel Heseltine.

the beast '. What I object to is the indoctrination of our Scottish children under our compulsory educational system with the literature of a people of utterly alien and incompatible traditions, tastes, and tendencies to the virtual exclusion of any teaching of Scottish literature.

In any case, if the claims that have been made on my behalf are pooh-pooh'd, and surprise and even indignation are expressed at the presumption in writing an autobiography of a mere nobody, a negligible scribbler destitute of the indispensable stamp of London approval, I am heartened by reflecting that Gerard Manley Hopkins was turned down and ignored for a long time and then had a tremendous vogue ; that William Blake was obscure and thought mad in his time, that after he died his own students destroyed a considerable part of his work for fear its boldness might shock the public and cloud his name ; while now each scrap of print, each sketch, each set of the illuminated engravings which are the bulk of his remaining work are all collector's treasures and worth huge sums of money—yet this is the man whose first biography, thirty-six years after his death, was published under the almost sarcastic title, *Pictor Ignotis*, and he has his pedestal now in every history of art, and every school-child learns some of his verse, the art and verse of a man not understood in his own day or liked, not only ' ahead of his time ' but also against it, in violent nonconformity with its art, its politics, its philosophy, its morals, all its prevailing ideas, an enthusiastic supporter of the American and the French Revolutions ; and that Altgeld, long occluded, has beat back eagle-wise into the light, since it is difficult, almost impossible to keep a good man down—and I am confident that my work has enough of this undefeatable time-resisting quality (since, as Lawrence of Arabia said, ' Sincerity is the only written thing which time improves ') to justify my immodesty in writing a book like this, no matter how insignificant the smart Alecs of London literary circles may rate me or their political counterparts turn up their noses at my pretensions. As Arnold Bennett once said, hardly anybody ever knows at any time who is going to be esteemed as a writer of significance a hundred years hence ; the contemporary chatter of great popularities and big circulations makes it almost impossible. I have never cared a fig for London opinions on literary matters or anything else.

In any case I cannot make it too clear that I have little or no interest in English writers at all, and that what I am interested in, in addition to certain Scottish and Irish writers and certain anti-Imperialist, autonomist, and revolutionary writers in various parts of the British Empire, is, in Wales, the sequence represented by names like these : Gwenallt, Alun Llywelyn-Williams, Keidrych Rhys, Dylan Thomas, T. J. Morgan, Gwyn Jones, Waldo Williams, Nigel Heseltine, Glyn H. Jones, R. L. Edwards, Huw Llewelyn Williams, Thomas Jones,

Emry Humphries, Vernon Watkins, Gerallt Jones, Ancirin ap Talfan,
John Gwynedd Griffiths, David Evans, Dai Marcs, Robert Herring,
D. R. Griffiths, Gwyndaf Evans, George Ewart Evans, T. E.
Nicholas, and W. H. Reese ; and, in Cornwall, Halwyn (Allin-Collins)
—a great linguist, a Cornish speaker, a Bard of the Breton Gorsedd,
a personal friend of Taldir (in a word, one of the most interesting
figures in the literature of the British Isles to-day), and founder of
Tyr ha Tavas ; Lorgh Vras ; Trefusis of Trefusis (Standard-bearer
for the Cornish Gorsedd), and the like (I have written elsewhere
in this book of John Maclean as deserving the Russian adjective,
krassivy, that means beautiful and red ; T. E. Nicholas is a man of
like quality. A young Cornishman wrote me the other day saying,
' Rolant Jones (a prizewinner at many Eisteddfoddau) remembers
having " Nicholas Glais " to lunch one day and discovering for the
first time someone " scarlet " ').

Who am I that I should write an autobiography ? I am the author
of about twenty books and enough uncollected essays to make twice
as many again ; I have written plays, poems, short stories, literary,
dramatic, and musical criticism, essays on politics, economics, agriculture, and volumes of biography and topography ; I have been
hailed in many quarters as the greatest Scottish poet since Burns
(even if Robert Graves sarcastically emphasizes the *since!*) or—the
way I prefer it put—as one of a trinity with Burns and Dunbar ; I
have provided what are generally acknowledged by competent
authorities to be the best translations of the two greatest Scottish
Gaelic poems—Alexander MacDonald's ' Birlinn of Clanranald '
and Duncan Ban MacIntyre's ' In Praise of Ben Dorain ' ; I have
translated a novel from the Spanish ; I have done what ex-Prince
Mirsky regards as the best translations of modern Russian poetry in
any dialect of English ; I have known (or know—many of my most
famous friends have died in the last few years—'AE ' (G. W. Russell),
W. B. Yeats, Professor Patrick Geddes, A. R. Orage), James Pitten-
driegh MacGillivray, Lascelles Abercrombie, R. B. Cunninghame-
Graham, Keir Hardie, William Archer, ' Lewis Grassic Gibbon ',
and many more) almost everybody I know of I would wish to have
known. I have represented Scotland as a guest of the Irish Nation,
and at international literary gatherings in Vienna and at the Hague.
And I claim to have been the inspirer and central figure (there are
others who deny my claim and prefer their own) in a political movement which is becoming increasingly important, but the real potentiality, and inevitability, of which is still little suspected in Scotland
itself and hardly at all outside Scotland. And I have travelled
widely, touched life at innumerable points and on many levels (the
unfamiliarity of many of which should make for good reading), live
in a remote archipelago, and am intimate with little-visited places
like the Faroe Islands. And I am better informed than anyone else,

I think I can prove, on many aspects of Scottish arts and affairs, and have a very individual point of view and dynamic way of expressing it.   And in age I have come to that plateau at which a man can best pause awhile and write such a book.   Moreover almost all my friends have already published theirs—Compton Mackenzie, William Power, Wendy Wood, ' James Bridie ', Oliver Gogarty, Sean O'Casey, and many others.

But my greatest achievement to date, perhaps, has been contriving, while giving a broadcast from Aberdeen, to overrun my time by twelve minutes (surely an unprecedented happening !   And the Scottish Regional Director, Melville Dinwiddie, was standing at my elbow when I did it, and could have switched me off, but took no action) and hang up the next item—an Edgar Wallace play—to the disgust of thousands of thriller fans (I am one myself !) who found my talk on ' The Future of Scottish Poetry ' unintelligible.   The newspapers were full of correspondence denouncing me and supporting me. But my supporters outnumbered my critics, and the B.B.C. itself justified letting me take the extra time on the score of my importance as a poet.   There's fame for you, surely.   And in that broadcast I was allowed to put across pure Communism without censorship !

And I am one of a very few perhaps among contemporary authors in this country, in that, at a time when huge numbers of men were unemployed and in receipt of the ' dole ', and a very big section of our population were under the subsistence level, I would have scorned to be otherwise than equally naked in the ' economic blizzard ' and indeed, not being eligible for the ' dole ', was even worse off. Certainly I could never have tolerated being one of those in whose favour the system operated which dealt with such inhuman harshness against such masses of the working-class.   It was not for me to smuggle myself into any privileged position in such circumstances, but to stay out in the cold, and perish there if need be, with my own class, instead of ' getting on in the world ' (which can only be done by betraying the working class) and joining the ' upper classes ' who,

> safely lie
> Within the shelter of the fold.

I am no shorn lamb to whom any wind requires to be tempered.

I have always said to my friends and to younger writers seeking my advice what Henry George (with whom I too had cause to cry : ' I am afloat at forty-two poorer than at twenty-one ') said when he upbraided an easy-going friend : ' Why, when the great struggle is on, and history is being made, will you go into the woods and play the flute ?   I would rather see you put your lips to the trumpet,' and, like Henry George, I have all along been primarily inspired by the vision of a world without poverty, a vision that will inspire mer as long as poverty is with us and is, in his own words, ' the open-mouthed, relentless hell that yawns beneath civilized society', although I also know there are many worse things than poverty, and I would never lift a finger to make poor people wealthy if I thought it would also make them as stupid as most wealthy people are.

I think I have given ' good and sufficient cause '.

My job in Scotland was to discredit and hustle off the stage a very different kind of poetry—of mawkish doggerel rather, into which the Burns tradition had degenerated. The best collection of it is in the teens of volumes of *Modern Scottish Poets* edited by Mr. Edwards of Brechin (whom I knew personally)—an anthology of rubbish without a single redeeming feature, by railwaymen poets, postmen poets, scavenger poets, butcher poets, policemen poets, and Heaven knows what else. This octopus had secured an incredible grip on the vast majority of the Scottish people; the newspapers and publishing houses concerned with its production had built up enormous fortunes on the strength of it, and it was not easy to loosen their grip and re-erect creditable literary standards in such a *milieu*. The poets fought back with endless venom and insolence. (I was attacked by a pack of them recently in the Shetlands here, where, the Shetlands being without imagination and poetless, they still flourish as they were wont to do in Scotland itself). Even now, though they have years ago been knocked off the literary stage, they lurk legion-strong in the wings, ready to rush back if ever they get a chance. Powerful interests are on their side, ready at any moment to ' get rid of the nonsense of a Scottish Literary Renaissance ' and debauch the public again with this dreadful stuff, ranging from sob stuff to chortling ' wut ', which, if it has been knocked for the time being out of the heads of an adequate minority of our educated class, still maintains its grip on the hearts of the vast majority of our people. Thanks to my omnivorous reading—and in particular to that early interest in American literature of which I have written, and my boyhood perusal of files of old American magazines—I came upon a priceless example of the thing at its worst, and perpetrated by no illiterate grocer's assistant bard or cattleman poet, but by none other than Sir James Matthew Barrie, O.M., and reproduced it in *The Scottish Chapbook*, which I was then running in Montrose. No wonder I got myself thoroughly hated. Who was safe from such a man? What I said about this undoubted masterpiece of Bad Poetry, and the quotations I gave from it, read as follows :

' Sir John Squire in his notes on " The Beauties of Badness " finally decided, with sufficient cause, that the best whole bad poem he had encountered was one by a parson named Whur or Whurr who flourished in Norfolk about a century ago. The best whole bad poem by a Scottish writer is much more easily found, and the perpetrator is no mere Whurr. He is, in fact, Sir James Matthew Barrie, O.M., and the " poem " is " Scotland's Lament ", apropos the death of Robert Louis

Stevenson, contributed by him to *McClure's Magazine* in February,
1895. It runs to no fewer than seventeen verses. The first is as
follows :—

> Her hands about her brows are pressed,
> She goes upon her knees to pray,
> Her head is bowed upon her breast,
> *And, oh ! she's sairly failed the day.*

That fourth line cannot be bettered for badness anywhere. Worse
in certain respects, however, are some of the subsequent verses in
alleged dialect in which Scotland is supposed to lament her loss.

> Ye sons wha do your little best,
> Ye writing Scots, put by the pen !
> He's deid, the ane abune the rest,
> I winna look at write again.

What fearful and wonderful memories of her darling boy flock to Auld
Scotia's brain on this aweful occasion !

> He egged me on wi' mirth and prank,
> We hangit gowans on a string,
> We made the doakens walk the plank,
> *We mairit snails without the ring.*

The italics are again mine. The parting of mother and son is depicted
thus :

> Ahint his face his pain was sair,
> Ahint hers grat his waefu' mither.
> We kent that we should meet nae mair,
> The ane saw easy thro' the ither.

Scotland confessed that she found Stevenson trying at times.

> I'm auld, I pant, sic ploys to mak'
> To games your mither shouldna stoup.

Barrie, of course, finds the perfect filial response.

> " You're gey an' auld," he cried me back,
> " That's for I like to gar you loup ! "

' Barrie's infinite subtlety is a household word. It would be difficult,
however, to find a finer example of it than occurs in that last line. Only
absolute genius could have so fused Cockney and Doric.
' Courage ? [1] Fiddlesticks ! '

My activity in bringing about this *kulturkampf* was not confined to
this level, of course. Edwin Muir has said that the greatest change
in Scotland during the past twenty-five years has been in poetry—
any anthology to-day would be extremely different from any that
could have been compiled at the beginning of the century—and for
this change he says that I am chiefly responsible. I began, when I
issued my Northern Numbers anthology, by displaying the best of
the work available by living Scottish poets ; and side by side with
it introduced work by other younger and then quite unknown poets,
including myself, who had very different ideas from those prevalent.
I was able to do this because I had a completely different background

[1] A reference to Barrie's St. Andrew's Rectorial Address on ' Courage '.

myself—I was not limited to or over-affected by English influences, but was thoroughly *au fait* with the work of *l'avant-garde* of several European countries—France, Germany, Belgium, Russia. The well-known poets represented alongside *les jeunes* in the earlier issues—Neil Munro, John Buchan, General Sir Ian Hamilton, Violet Jacob, Charles Murray, Lewis Spence, Donald A. Mackenzie —were speedily, and no doubt a trifle unceremoniously, ' dropped ', and the field was left to the rising school.   I have been accused of ill-faith in securing the association in this way of men who were relatively distinguished—and then dropping them.   I cannot see that any ill-faith was involved at all.   I simply took the position as it then was at its best—determined to proceed thence to a different position altogether.   Whatever use I had for the work of Neil Munro and others at the beginning, I speedily lost as I got ' further ben ' in my chosen task.   And as to these men of established reputation associating themselves with young and then unknown innovators, that, it seemed to me, was not an act of grace on their part, but simply their duty—and, as the process developed, it was simply up to them to make way as gracefully as possible.   Not all of them did it very gracefully ; they hated to be hustled off the stage in this way.   But they had had a fair chance ; if the necessary development of Scottish poetry necessitated their drastic demotion in critical esteem and popular appraisal—as events speedily proved it did—that was their lookout, and I was not on that account to be deemed an ingrate who had bit the hands that fed me and kicked away abruptly the ladder by which I had risen.

Another writer (alas, with hopeless exaggeration !) has likened me to Eliezer Ben Yahuda, of whom Sir Ronald Stoors says :

> ' I liked Ben Yahuda, and used to visit him and talk with him at length on his immortal and unique achievement (the restoration of the Hebrew language to human speech).   Ireland and Hungary have by means of Movements and Committees rekindled the flames, never dead but till recently flickering, of Erse and of Magyar.   Here was a man who by himself had summoned from a sleep of two thousand years—almost from the next world—a mystic antique utterance ; breathing into it the breath of new life, so that the word of the Prophets became also the word of the leader-writer (their modern counterpart), the man of science, and the boy on the football field.'

And—with far less exaggeration—what Mr. E. M. Forster says of William Barnes has been said of me too :

> ' If we start pulling him to pieces we discover that contrary to expectation he is a scholar.   Like A. E. Housman, he knew exactly what he was doing in verse and what others had done.   He sang Dorset because he had to, but not without premeditation—he was not the gifted rustic who smudged some of his effects in Burns.   *Woak Hill* is composed in an elaborate Persian metre, the Pearl, and even those who discount its pathos are obliged to admire its dexterity.   Other poems are written as Ghazels, others imitate or adapt recondite Bardic

metres, and all of them have their words in the right places. Right words—rose petals of words, withered leaves, red dowst o' the ridges ; but they fall into their places with the assurance of marble. . . . He believed that only Anglo-Saxon words should be employed in English. . . . To believe this, and yet to create touching poetry in which Anglo-Saxon words are mainly employed is a unique achievement . . . and when he was told that the offering would from its nature perish, he replied : " To write in what some may deem a fast out-wearing speech-form may seem as idle as the writing of one's name in snow on a spring day. I cannot help it. It is my mother tongue, and it is to my mind the only true speech of the life I draw." '

But however I may resemble poets like Yahuda and Barnes because of my work for the revival of the Scots Vernacular, it is other poets and politicians that I would fain resemble—men like Vladimir Jaborinsky and his friend Pinhas Rutenberg :

' No more gallant officer, no more charming and cultivated companion, could have been imagined than Vladimir Jaborinsky. Had he not translated into English verse the poems of Akhad Ha'am, and the Divine Comedy into Hebrew ? Was there ever discipline of troops more effective or magnetic than his ? . . . His drastic suggestions at least served the Cause to this extent, that they made the most forward official Zionism seem by comparison to be the essence of practicable moderation.'

And Rutenberg :

' The most remarkable Roman of them all. Thick-set, powerful, dressed always in black ; a head as strong as granite and an utterance low and menacing through clenched teeth. He is no politician, he explains ; all he wants is " wurrk ", and such is the grip of his r's that your hands seem to close over an imaginary pick—or pen. He is no politician ? He was with Kerensky in the last pre-Soviet days. . . . Now he has harnessed the Jordan to light, heat, and energized Palestine. His Power-Houses are like himself ; the rugged Sphinx-like contour of Government House, Jerusalem, is said to be Rutenberg rendered in stone. No politician ? If, in a time of trouble for Israel, he were to raise his hand, he would be followed by all the Jews of Palestine, and as an impartial employer of Arabs as well as Jews, possibly by some of the Arabs also. A faithful friend and I should think a particularly disagreeable enemy ! '

The language element, the Scottish national character, of my poetry is not the most important thing about it. It has been said that Pushkin is not regarded as of the same stature as Dante or Goethe—' it is not because his verse is more difficult to translate ; although in translation the music of his style and the brilliant word patterns are more or less lost. The reason is to be found in the nature of his poetry—and of most good Russian poetry. There is a quality in his work which makes us hesitate, which puzzles us and prevents us from making an immediate response. That quality is commonsense. Pushkin's life is drawn from the everyday matter-of-fact life around him. Dante, Goethe, Shakespeare : we often call them noble, but that is a word we cannot apply to Pushkin, except to the architecture of his words.'

That is true too of Burns, and that realistic practical quality—it is misleading to call it ' common-sense '—is the distinguished feature of the whole Scottish tradition of poetry, and is indeed an element which makes lovers of the ' poetical ', especially in the English sense of that term, hesitate, and puzzles and prevents them making an immediate response to work of this kind. I am wholly at one with my friend, Professor W. J. Entwistle, when, in his splendid book on *European Balladry*, discussing Professor Halliday's statement, ' I believe that the aesthetic value of popular poetry, if we are to measure by an absolute poetic standard, is habitually overrated, perhaps mainly from reasons of sentiment ', he says :

' If we are to measure by an absolute poetic standard—and if, per-chance, such a standard exists. The classic and the critic demand the application of such standards ; but the search for a poetry that shall be pure dissolves even the greatest works of art into unrecognizable frag-ments. . . . The poetry of the commonalty we neither produce nor admire. Those who seek to express what many men feel we the more likely esteemed for their art; while, on the other hand, the tribe of those who refine and polish and sublimate their art is left to prophesy to the void. It is not so that much of the world's greatest poetry has been composed, and it is not the way of the ballad. The greatest poets have written neither to extrovert their personalities nor to comply with the demands of taste, but to voice the common thought of masses of men. So Homer has been, in a sense, the voice of the Hellenes, and Virgil of imperial Rome ; Dante, Cervantes, and Shakespeare were each the fruition of an age ; Camoes unburdened the illustrious Lusitanian breast ; and Spenser and Milton gave utterance to a Puritanism, either sweetly reasonable or embattled and dogmatic. There have been great poems which can be assessed as " pure poetry ", such as the *Orlando Furioso* ; but to the men of the sixteenth century Ariosto's master-piece seemed wanting in substance or seriousness. We cannot be sure that it expressed something clamouring for utterance :—

Glory and generous shame,
The unconquerable mind, and Freedom's holy flame.

But these are the themes of a " God-gifted organ-voice ", and these, rather than absolute perfection, assure survival in literature. And common, fundamental, moving themes of this kind inspire the best of the ballads. . . . It has been worth while to recreate them time and again throughout the centuries, since on each single occasion they have signified something to their unlettered hearers, and have moved them more than with a trumpet. It is a glory not often achieved by the great artistic poets, and when achieved, it is through some partial endow-ment of the generous ballad simplicity. In Tasso's case, for instance (as Countess Martinengo Cesaresco says), " the fishermen's wives of the Lido . . . sat along the shore in the evenings while the men were out fishing, and sang stanzas from Tasso and other songs at the pitch of their voices, going on till each could distinguish the responses of her own husband in the distance ". But how much of the *Yerusalemme* could be recovered from their memories ? How faithfully modern ballad singers have preserved versions of Danish and Castilian ballads unknown to the collectors in the sixteenth century ? In praise of Burns's and Gil Vicente's gift of spontaneous song, it has been said that one cannot know where the received traditional matter ends and the new creation begins. The ballads have survived, fragile and imperfect as they may seem, so long as the society for which they were created has endured, and longer. The critic's business is not to apply " a priori " standards, but to look for the qualities which have justified their amazing survival.'

It is, indeed, looking back upon Scottish literature in particular from this angle that I can feel something of the exaltation Tennyson attributed to Ulysses :

> Though much is taken, much abides ; and though
> We are not now that strength which in old days
> Moved earth and heaven ; that which we are, we are ;
> One equal temper of heroic hearts,
> Made weak by time and fate, but strong in will
> To strive, to seek, to find, and not to yield.

—or, more frequently, make me echo the words of Byrhthold :

> Thought shall be harder, heart the bolder,
> Courage the greater, as our might faileth.

What I say elsewhere in this book about the ' poetry of fact ' is in keeping with what Professor Entwistle says :

' Ballads are to be accepted as true. Truth is, perhaps, not a quality demanded by the aesthete, but it is the necessary leaven of traditional narrative poetry, whether epic or ballad ; and whether in Plato's thought or that of Alfonso the Wise, the discovery that the poet has indulged in fabling causes a sharp feeling of exasperation. . . . A sturdy and ancient balladry generally springs from a stout historical trunk. When they travel from one land to another, which is but seldom, they go as simple adventurers, but at home theirs is a solid veracity, which educates the people.'

Another point upon which I have insisted elsewhere in this book with a wealth of examples from many lands and times is admirably brought out by Professor Entwistle when he says :

' Relatively uninterested in the matter of the song, the Icelandic people were, and are, acute critics of the form. In the long winter nights there is time to discuss art in the minutest detail ; in fact, prosodic study took the place of the general conversation which often follows a recita-tion in the American mountains, though the latter turns on the subject-matter of the ballad. Only by research could the elaborate, but quite conventional, kennings be understood, and to serve this research the records of older literature were carefully preserved. Scholarship is greatly indebted to the " rimur " for their by-products. If it is scarcely possible for a European taste to esteem these poems for their own merits, though we may coldly admire their intricacy, the " rimur " serve to remind us that there is no inevitability about the " popular " in poetry. A " people " can be a people of connoisseurs. Indeed, an aesthetically enlightened people would display connoisseurship in some respect of the ballad art. The case of Iceland goes further, however, since it shows an undoubted " people " interested in the niceties and subtleties of an advanced art, to the exclusion of those ready appeals to the understanding and senses which are normally supposed to be " popular ".'

While I dismiss the standards of *bourgeois* society in every connexion as contemptuously as I dismiss the superior or patronizing attitude of ' official literature ' to the people's balladry, I would add here that I do not go so far as to hold that poets should necessarily take what is called ' an active part in public affairs '. Bulgaria's leading writer, Elin Pelin, has been chastised by some of his more public-spirited and social-minded colleagues for his serene isolation and detachment from questions and problems that stir his people. ' He is a great artist,' say his critics, ' but not a public man.' I am at one with Stoyan Christowe, who replies :

> ' It is true, strictly speaking, that Elin Pelin is not a public man. He makes no speeches, delivers no lectures, does not read his stories in public, gives no statements or opinions on this or that, joins no committees. And that indeed may be a regret. And yet, looking at it in another way, all of the characters Elin Pelin has created are social beings, flesh and blood, people whose joys and sorrows he seems to share and with whom he identifies himself as their equal, so much so, in fact, that to him it seems presumptuous to step out from their midst and become their leader or their champion, and so while he may not be a public man, Elin Pelin is certainly a writer of the people. His enviable position as the greatest writer in his country he owes not to any fantastic stories he has imagined, or even to the efforts of a personal ambition, but to the re-creation of his people's soul, which, as one Bulgarian critic has put it, " can see its image in the works of Elin Pelin as in a limpid spring ".'

But while it is possible for a writer to hold aloof from public affairs and yet be ' a writer of the people ' in that way, what is impossible for any writer of consequence is to identify himself with the *bourgeoisie*—to be on the side of the ' upper classes ' against the masses. My ideal, indeed, is an artist like Mozart—' not at all ', as Ernest Newman says, ' like the simpering darling of the gods that the older biographers and critics and conductors tried to make of him— he was as hard as steel and as corrosive as acid ' : Mozart, ' a realist who understood men and women and had moved in the world since childhood, knew it as thoroughly as Beaumarchais or Molière and had no illusions about either the princes or the people '.

> ' Why, then, was he a complete worldly failure ? There is a simple answer. Mozart hated the world and had in him a vein of stark realism and independence that made him very unpopular. There is not a little resemblance between Mozart and Swift, who was fobbed off with a deanery by his patrons as Mozart was by the Emperor who gave him a beggarly pittance while other and inferior musicians were loaded with money and honours. If you ask me why neither Mozart nor Swift could be successful diplomatists, although men of such acute intelligence and profound understanding of human nature, I have a ready answer. Both had too much energy of mind. The coarseness which is common to both, the sexual vitality which Mr. Newman so much dislikes in Mozart, are bound up with that energy which made Mozart and Swift downright, scornful, and unpleasant society. It is quite clear that Mozart preferred low life to the surface gentility of society.

A man who loved life with the passionate intensity evident in Mozart's music, could never have conformed to the conventional humbug in those days ' (as to-day and always) ' when a musician was considered by the aristocracy ' (and our plutocracy to-day is worse) ' as little better than a lackey.

' The explanation probably is that there was something about him that made well-bred people drop him almost as soon as they had taken him up. His manners suggest what that something was—manners so bad that even the higher social world could not endow them with a temporary varnish, and not only a roughness but a coarseness of speech that made him " impossible ".'

But the fact is that it was Mozart who dropped the well-bred people. So must every artist. It is impossible to touch pitch and not be defiled ; and any assimilation to the standards—any compliance with the claims—of the monstrous confraternity of lawyers, ministers, school-teachers, bankers, shopkeepers, landed gentry, the officer class, the titled and the wealthy, and *bourgeois* society as a whole, involves intolerable detriment to any artist.

In writing poetry of this kind I follow Pope's precepts in the matter of garden design :

> Consult the genius of the place in all,
> That tells the waters, or to rise or fall. . . .
> Calls in the country, catches op'ning glades,
> Joins willing woods, and varies shades from shades.

And I do not care if it be said of me too (as Horace Walpole said of William Kent) :

> ' The great principles on which he worked were perspective, and light and shade. Groups of trees broke too uniform or too extensive a lawn ; evergreen and woods were opposed to the glare of the champain. . . . He followed Nature even in her faults.'

And above all, it can be claimed for me as Kierkegaard claimed for himself :

> ' His whole nature was passionately opposed to the temperate maxim, *ne quid nimis*, never too much, no excess. For I have always lived consciously on the verge of eternity—that is to say, lived eschatologically.'

I have always hated above all else the mean little minds that can never do anything *en gros*, knowing that ' genius is like a thunderstorm which comes up against the wind. Genius is not a penny-dip to be blown out by the wind, but a conflagration which the storm challenges ', and that ' the human spirit is not to be likened to a hen's egg ', and wishing that it could one day be said of me, as of Mistral :

> Singing not of particular deeds and persons,
> But of a whole land and a whole people,
> And beginning with his native region,
> Ended by embracing all nations
> In one amphictyoncia—a vision *in parvo*
> Of the labours of all mankind.

It is for this reason that Riccardo Bacchelli enriches his great historical novel *Il Mulino Del Po* with summaries of historical change, popular opinion, agricultural method, or economic process—protesting, for instance, after describing the efforts to drain the lowlands of the Po, that there is so much and so plentiful humanity in this economic history that, ' contrary to the custom of narrative fiction ', he does his best to illuminate the general lie of the land. And in the same way Jean Tousseul's great Belgian novel, *Jean Clarambaux*, embodies every aspect of the life of the countryside in such a way that the whole becomes an epic of Ardennes village life. Such a book about England, Judith Paris had in mind when, speaking from the memories of nearly a hundred years, she said :

> ' I would put in everything—men sowing in the fields, horses plough-ing, old ladies selling sweets in the village shop, Mr. Disraeli with his oily hair and Mr. Gladstone with his collar, Horace's Manchester chimneys, all the Herries thinking they've made England, my father riding up Borrowdale, the snow on Skiddaw, the apple pudding I had at dinner, sheep on a hill, the man lighting the lamps in Hill Street. . . .'

Modern Scottish novels and poems are all very slight and trivial compared with such works as these ; one feels that the Scottish writers are hopelessly small-minded and immature and quite irresponsible in comparison.

What I am concerned with here, and have been mainly and ever more intensively in all my writing and living, is, of course, what David Jones in *In Parenthesis* calls ' the Celtic cycle that lies, a subterranean influence as a deep water tumbling under every tump of this island, like Merlin complaining under his big rock ', while, in general, like David Jones's, my concern is with ' the genuine tradition of the Island of Britain, from Bendigeid Vran to Jingle and Marie Lloyd '—the children of Doll Tearsheet, and those before Caractacus was—that great company in which ' every man's speech and habit of mind were a perpetual showing, now of Napier's expedition, now of the Legions at the Wall, now of " train-band captain ", now of Jack Cade, of John Bull, of the commons in arms.   Now of *High Germany*, of *Dolly Grey*, of Bullcalf, Wart, and Poins ; of Jingo largenesses, of things as small as the Kingdom of Elmet ; of Wellington's raw shire recruits, of ancient border antipathies, of our contemporary, less intimate, larger unities, of *John Barleycorn*, of " sweet Sally Framp-ton ", of Coel Hen . . .'   But, above all, a ' kinship with the more venerable culture in that hotch-potch which is ourselves '.   That elder element is integral to our tradition.   From Layamon to Blake, ' Sabrina ' would call up spirits rather than ' Ypwines floet '.   As Mr. Christopher Dawson has written : 'And if Professor Collingwood is right, and it is the conservatism and loyalty to lost causes of Western Britain that has given our national tradition its distinctive character, then perhaps the middle ages were not far wrong in choosing Arthur rather than Alfred or Edmund or Harold, as the central figure of the national heroic legend.'

Like David Jones, I have always ' had in mind the persistent Celtic theme of armed sleepers under the mounds, whether they be the *fer sidhe* or the great Mac Og of Ireland, or Arthur sleeping in Craig-y-Ddinas or in Avalon or among the Eildons in Roxburghshire; or Owen of the Red Hand, or the Sleepers in Cumberland.' Plutarch says of our islands : ' An Island in which Cronus is imprisoned with Briareus keeping guard near him as he sleeps ; for, as they put it, sleep is the bond of Cronus. They add that around him are many deities, his henchmen and attendants ' (Plutatch's *De Defecta Oraculorum*). Compare also Blake's description of his picture, ' The Ancient Britons ' : ' In the last battle of King Arthur, only three Britons escaped ; these were the Strongest Man, the Beautifullest Man, and the Ugliest Man ; these three marched through the field unsubdued, as Gods, and the Sun of Britain set, but shall arise again with tenfold splendour when Arthur shall awake from sleep and resume his dominion over Earth and Ocean. . . . Arthur was the name for the Constellation of Arcturus, or Bootes, the Keeper of the North Pole. And all the fables of Arthur and his Round Table ; of the warlike naked Britons ; of Merlin ; of Arthur's Conquest of the whole world ; of his death or sleep, and promise to return again ; of the Druid monuments or temples ; of the pavement of Watling-street ; of London Stone ; of the Caverns in Cornwall, Wales, Derbyshire, and Scotland ; of the Giants of Ireland and Britain ; of the elemental beings called by us by the general name of Fairies ; of those three who escaped, namely Beauty, Strength, and Ugliness ; ' this is indeed the abiding myth of our people. (The beautifullest *and* the ugliest, i.e. the Caledonian Antisysygy. Many of the leading ideas in this book, as in my life and work generally, are announced in these paragraphs—e.g. the idea of a Celtic Front ; my love of the North ; the Synthesis of East and West. The reader is asked to remember the boast of Taliessin at the court of Maelgwn : ' I was with my lord in the highest sphere, on the fall of Lucifer into the depth of hell. I have borne a banner before Alexander. I know the names of the stars from north to south ', &c., and the boast of Glewlwyd, Arthur's porter, on every first day of May. ' I was heretofore in Caer Se and Asse, in Sach and Salach, in Lotur and Fotor, I have been hitherto in India the great and India the lesser and I was in the battle of Dau Ynyr ', &c., and the boast of the Englishman, Widsith : ' Widsith spoke, unlocked his store of words he who of all men had wandered through most tribes and most people throughout the earth. . . . He began then to speak many word . . . so are the singers of men destined to go wandering throughou many lands . . . till all departeth, life and light together ; h gaineth glory, and hath under the heavens an honour which passeth not away ' (translation from R. W. Chambers, *Widsith*).   Just as I show in the passage about King Arthur and the armed sleepers above, here again many of the leading ideas in this book, as in my life and work generally, are announced and seen to be part and parcel of the very care of the abiding myth of our people—e.g. the synthesis of East and West, multi-linguistic interests, internationalism, world-consciousness, &c.   My aims and achievements, my boasts, are simply repetitions, in the circumstances of the world of to-day, of those of Taliessin, Glewlwyd, and Widsith again.   The essence of my luck as a poet is simply that I ' chance ' to re-embody all these master ideas in a dynamic—an existential—way to-day.   If I advance a claim to any personal credit it is simply because I have succeeded, by long-sustained and desperately hard work, in becoming completely conscious of these matters and all their inter-relationships and ramifications—receiving them into my very blood and bone and re-living them—and applying them anew to the crucial issues of the present and the future.

We are involved to-day in a condition of affairs that, thinking in relation to it of the kind of poetry that I should be writing, has recalled Dante and moved me to cry :

> This is the kind of poetry I want
> In this world at war when I see
> On the Dark Plain (la buia campagna)
> ' A vast multitude of spirits
> Running behind a flag
> In great haste and confusion,
> Urged on by furious wasps and hornets.
> These are the unhappy people
> Who never were alive,
> Never awakened to take any part
> Either in good or evil '
> . . . ' che non furon ribelli
> Ne fur fedeli a Dio, ma per se foro '.
> (Nor rebels nor faithful to God,
> *But for themselves !*).

What I want is :

> A poetry like a glazier caught between the peaks
> —A landmark among the high ranges of poetry,
> Not hung upon the clouds,
> But steadfastly descending to the *Plain*
> Where all men walk and talk and gaze and can look upward and forward,
> Not downward and backward,
> On Nature and each other.

My aim is a poetry, like Walt Whitman's aim, ' to conform with and build on the concrete realities and theories of the universe furnished by science, and henceforth the only irrefragable basis for anything, verse included '.   I agree with Whitman when he cries :

' Think of the petty environage and limited area of the poets of past
or present Europe, no matter how great their genius. Think of the
absence and ignorance in all cases hitherto of the multitudinousness,
vitality, and the unprecedented stimulants of to-day and here. It
almost seems as if a poetry with cosmic and dynamic features of
magnitude and limitlessness suitable to the human soul were never
possible before. It is certain that a poetry of absolute faith and equality
for the use of the democratic masses never was.'

That is why I insist on the necessity of world consciousness, and in
my attitude to science—my denial that science is putting an end to
poetry—and my insistence on a poetry of facts, Whitman has
perfectly expressed my standpoint when he says :

' Whatever may have been the case in years gone by, the true use
for the imaginative faculty of modern times is to give ultimate vivification to facts, to science, and to common lives, endowing them with
glows and glories and final illustriousness which belong to every real
thing, and to real things only. Without that ultimate vivification—
which the poet or other artist alone can give—reality would seem incomplete, and science, democracy, and life itself, finally in vain.'

A poetry therefore which will constantly render
In all connexions such service
As the protest of the nature poetry of the great English poets
Of the Nineteenth Century on behalf of value,
On behalf of the organic view of nature,
A protest, invaluable to science itself,
Against the exclusion of value
From the essence of matter of fact.[1]

Thus a poetry which fully understands
That the era of technology is a necessary fact,
An inescapable phase in social activity,
Within which men are to rise
To ever greater mental and emotional heights,
And that only artists who build on all that men have created,
Who are infused with a sympathy and sensitive appreciation
Of the new technological order,
And all it may mean for their art,
Can play their role with any certainty
That their work will survive historically,
And in doing so they will also make
Their contribution to the New Order.

A poetry which sees all the pins on the floor. . . . The be
instance of the complementary and mutually corrective developme
of poetry and science is perhaps that cited in the following stanza

A poetry fully alive to all the implications
Of the fact that one of the great triumphs
Of poetic insight was the way in which
It prepared the minds of many
For the conception of evolution,

---

[1] Vide A. N. Whitehead's *Science and the Modern World.*

The degree to which the popular mind
Was sensitized by it to the appeal of Nature,
And thus how poetry has progressed
Until, for example, flowers
Can never be thought of again
In a generalized way.
Chaucer's ' floures white and rede '
Gave way in Spenser's April ecloque,
To pinks, columbines, gilly-flowers,
Carnations, sops-in-wine, cowslips,
Paunce, and chevisaunce.

Bacon's ' Of Gardens ' is as much a formal plan as a Loggan print of a Jacobean Great House ; conceived as a whole, that garden is thought of as a generalized form of beauty.

It is the whole that matters, not the parts,
And where they are considered separately
The parts still tended to be
Such lesser exercises in design
As a topiary.   But the flower regarded as symbol
Rescued our forefathers from these horticultural patterns
And brought man and flower
Into a new relation.   By poets like Herbert and Vaughan
Tree and plant were recognized as having a place
In the same economy of which man was a part.
They obey the inner law of their being
And it is for man to emulate them.
' In the beauty of poems ', as Whitman said,
' Are henceforth the tuft and final applause of science.
. . . Facts are showered over with light,
The daylight is lit with more volatile light,
The poets of the cosmos advance
Through all interpositions and coverings
And turmoils and stratagems
To first principles. . . . Beyond all precedent
Poetry will have to do with actual facts.'

So, at the present great turning point in world history, I conclude with the reflection that

Great art has inspired action.
Even poor Essex
Before his futile rising tried to give
Drive and tone to his endeavour
By having performed before him
And his fellow protestors *Richard II.*
When Liberty once again
Becomes a faith and enthusiasm,
When the books are opened
And tyranny's claim
That it might do any violence
Because it alone
Could be " efficient "
Is disproved—then

It is not improbable
That we shall see the new rally
Express itself in a culmination
Of the present dance-form,
As Aeschylus in his new drama
Gave form and voice
To the Greek liberation from Persia.
This is the poetry that I want.

CHAPTER IV

ROBERT BURNS, SIR WALTER SCOTT, AND OTHERS

'Such a country, such people, so backside!'
W. D. Edmonds in *Chad Hanna.*

BETTER perhaps as revelations of my disposition than such quotations as I have given in a previous chapter from the *Times Literary Supplement* and the *Glasgow Herald* and other sources, will be my own studies of the two greatest figures in Scottish literature—Robert Burns[1] and Sir Walter Scott. My attitude to Burns in particular has been sorely misunderstood, because of the necessity I have been under of attacking the *bourgeois* Burns Cult, a monstrous misappropriation of Burns, whitewashed and respectablized and made, like statistics, to prove anything and everything except the inadmissible things for which he essentially stood. My real attitude, however, to Burns (who, it must be remembered, was taboo in my father's house and quite unknown to me as a boy—not, as in my friend F. G. Scott's home, bulking at least as prominently as the Bible, and far better liked and more resorted to—a state of affairs I have since had ample cause to regret I did not share!) emerges clearly in the following paragraphs, written as a review for the *Criterion* of Keith Henderson's *Burns—By Himself* (a mosaic of extracts from Burns' letters):

> 'This book is a complete misnomer. Mr. Henderson should have paid more heed to Burns' own statement: " I am no dab at fine-drawn letter-writing. I sit down when necessitated to write as I would sit down to beat hemp." The veridical Burns is no more to be found in his letters, which he wrote in English, than in his verse in the same

---

[1] It is of course inevitable that a man should be *non persona grata* to the Burns Clubs, boycotted as a speaker at their Annual Suppers, and widely regarded as an anti-Burnsian of whom it can be said, as Professors G. K. Anderson and Eda Lou Walton say in *This Generation* (1939): ' Hugh MacDiarmid carries forward the criticism of society implicit in many of Robert Burns's poems. Using a modified Scottish dialect, he urges the Scotch working-men's rights as against those of the upper classes. . . . His subject-matter is such as to arouse the poorer Scottish people to a sense of their own human dignity and potential rights. Nor has he any false sentimentality about the poor. He knows their ignorance and lack of character, but he sees them as the people whose desire to live is strong enough to force them to fight for their existence.' In a footnote to my poem, ' To Your Immortal Memory, Burns ', which satirizes these *bourgeois* Burnsians, the same editors observe : ' MacDiarmid continues the Burns tradition in praising the humble folk and is critical of the early romantic poet only because Burns's love and drinking songs (poetry of the intestines) are popular and his songs about the poor not so seriously considered as they should be in the light of their social significance.'

language.   Apart from that, the selection and arrangement are of course
Mr. Henderson's, and his sixty-eight illustrations obtrusively irrelevant.
The Burns who emerges is Burns the man, not Burns the poet.   There
are books about him by the hundred, says Mr. Henderson—he ought to
have added that few of these are of the slightest value and that almost
all of them are concerned with Burns's loves and other excesses, and
scarcely any with his poetry or questions of his literary latitude and
longitude.   This book sheds no light whatever on the two most
important points about Burns—his reversion to Scots from English
(a course in which he has been singularly lacking in imitators amongst
his legions of eulogists) and that indeflectible core of purpose which
enabled him, despite all his ups and downs, to turn out such an amazing
body of work (considering his circumstances).   Alcoholic and sexual
debauchery did not restrict or weaken that output.   The only comparable case I can think of, where habitual alcoholism and lechery did
not abate a man's energies or prevent him from reaching his high goal,
is Kemal Ataturk!   Since Sir James Crichton Browne's book showed
that Burns did not literally drink himself to death,[1] but died of endo-
carditis in the origination of which alcoholism had no part, but
rheumatism in early life was responsible, there has been an abatement
of the long-held idea that his excesses were responsible for his early
demise, but it has been realized scarcely anywhere (nor can it be, without
a careful chronological and critical survey of his output) that, so far
from his regardless manner of life having spoiled or curtailed his
creative energies, his powers manifested a continuous development, a
more dynamic concentration, right to the end, and that his best work
was done in the last phase of his chequered career.   He exercised all
along a wonderful self-control and tenacity of purpose in regard to
what mattered most, and far too little attention has yet been directed to
this steel core of self-discipline in his otherwise disorderly life.   He
confesses in his letters that his poems mostly dealt with himself and
happenings in his own life, but unfortunately, like all but a small
percentage of what has been written about him, they dealt with the man
and not with the poet and are at the furthest remove from what Fritz
Kaufman, in his *Sprache als Schöpfung*, finds inevitable in ages like our
own, namely that all the ostensible themes and subjects of the poet will
tend to be in the first place simply allegories for the creative process
itself.   " Der Vorgang des Bildens ist selber zum Gegenstand des
Bildens geworden."   Something of this sort, it is implied, may lie
at the back of Rilke's Elegies and Sonnets.   Like Stefan George's
Vorspiel, they embody in the first place the thoughts of a poet on his
own artistic vocation.   There are no such reflections in any of Burns's
writings, and he nowhere has anything of value to say about any of his
predecessors, except Robert Ferguson, or, very inadequately, on the
language question and the differences of Scottish and English song.
Nor do these letters (or, rather, extracts from letters, chosen with an
arbitrariness that springs from entirely erroneous preconceptions as to
what is really significant and of value in Burns and what is not, throw
any light on how he came by his knowledge of previous Scottish poets
from whom he borrowed so greatly (as greatly improving what he
borrowed—" Let any poet if he chooses take up the idea of another "

---

[1] Professor De Lancy Ferguson dealt further blows to this old idea and
conclusively dismissed other old controversial issues with regard to Burns'
life in a series of articles which, as he says in his biography of Burns (1939)
met, despite the world-wide Burns Cult, with ' almost passionate apathy '

Burns wrote, " and work it into a piece of his own, but let him mend it as the Highlander mended his gun ; he gave it a new stock, a new lock, and a new barrel ") ; and Burns is not to be understood save in relation to a full view of the very complex and little understood distinctive tradition of Scots literature, nor save in the light of such a study as that can the real significance of Carlyle's comment that if Burns had been a better equipped literary workman he might have changed the whole course of European literature be understood. That is true—and the qualities nearest to Burns's own surviving in Scotland, mainly among the working class, to-day still demonstrably retain a like potentiality ; hopelessly disorganized and intellectually most ill-equipped as they are, they can nevertheless still be discerned as susceptible of changing, because essentially outside, as Eugenio d'Ors and Dr. Kendrick alike recognize, the whole course of European civilization. Burns would probably have come nearer to his full stature in this sense, just as Scotland would have exercised the great politico-cultural role in question, if it had not been in both cases for the progressive provincialization of Scotland (inducing a time-lag which kept the Scots from timely access to the European influences most likely to strengthen and guide such purposes) due to the Union with England, which Burns so vehemently deplored. Even in Burns's own day, the Scottish national tradition was in a state of fragmentation and had so many mutually exclusive elements that it was practically impossible to articulate its *disjecta membra* and see it as a whole. Burns was constantly trying to get hold of books but even when he could get them they were generally the wrong books, since, owing to his circumstances, he was largely subject to English literary over-influences incompatible with his essential genius. Even to-day almost any English reading to which a Scottish writer with the root of the matter in him can turn appears to me (unless he has first possessed himself fairly fully of all the best elements of Scottish literature, alike in Gaelic, Latin, the Scots Vernacular, and English) as appallingly unsuitable, as shockingly beside the point, as these hapless confessions from Burns's letters.

' This curse of fragmentary knowledge of what in all its fullness should have been their birthright, has afflicted all modern Scotsmen with any spark of genius.

' Writing to Donald Carswell about his wife, Catherine Carswell's coming book on Burns, D. H. Lawrence said : " Cath's idea of a Burns book I like very much. I always wanted to do one myself, but am not Scotchy enough. I read just now Lockhart's bit of a life of Burns. Made me spit ! Those damned middle-class Lockharts grew lilies of the valley up their —— to hear them talk. . . . My word, you can't know Burns unless you hate the Lockharts and all the estimable *bourgeois* and upper classes as he really did—the narrow-gutted pigeons. Don't, for God's sake, be mealy-mouthed like them. I'd like to write a Burns life. Oh, why doesn't Burns come to life and really salt them ! " It is a great pity Lawrence did not write that book ; he had in abundance just what Edwin Muir and most other contemporary writers lack and that is in particular indispensable to any useful writing about Burns. Elsewhere Lawrence remarked, apropos Donald Carswell's book, *Brother Scots* : " You admire a little overmuch English detachment. It is often a mere indifference and lack of life. And you are a bit contemptuous of your Scotch ; one feels they are miserable specimens all told by the time one winds up with Robertson Nicoll. It's because you underestimate the vital quality, and over-estimate the English detached efficiency which is not very vital." This brings us to the heart of the matter—the reason why Burns reverted

H

to Scots, and the basic defence of it, against all such arguments as Edwin Muir's. By the end of the eighteenth century, the period of Burns himself, the disastrous division in the national culture was already deeply developed, that division in the light of which, properly understood, Burns is seen as a symbol of the Scottish character unable to express itself, even to itself, except in an alien or a bastard tongue which is incapable of giving beauty and shape to the seemingly half-daft but actually only different emotions and ideas of the Celtic race. The whole process of alienation and devitalization and its upshot in contemporary Scotland calls in a very special degree for the verdict in which Dr. Trigant Burrow in *The Biology of Human Conflict : An Anatomy of Behaviour, Individual and Social* (1937) summarizes the findings of the Lifwynn Foundation of New York as a result of its researches into this problem in relation to modern life generally, viz. : " Because of the increasing extension throughout the community of a dissociative process that substitutes words for the physiological experience presumed to underlie them, man has increasingly lost touch with the hard and fast mileau of actual objects and correspondingly with the biological solidarity of his own organism." This leads to conflict between the culturally on-grafted reaction systems which are restricted to the cephalic segment, and the biologically original reaction systems of the whole organism. What orthodox psychiatry calls neurosis is only the extreme manifestation of such conflicts. These conflicts are common to the modern race, so that the whole phylum is neurotic. And so the modern crisis—war, depression, insanity, criminality—arises on the basis of these conflicts. Freud's *Civilization and its Discontents* develops this argument with great precision and force. My point here is that this dissociative process has been carried further in Scotland than almost anywhere else and that the Scottish medical profession as a whole have been utterly blind or indifferent to Scottish phylobiology and have not so much as begun any phylo-analysis, as Dr. Burrow terms his own modification of psychoanalytic procedure, where the analysis is concerned with the neuroses of man as phylum rather than the individual neurotic. As Dr. Burrow says : " The proprioceptive problems of man will not be adjusted through tariff revisions, higher income brackets, child-guidance clinics, or Geneva parleys. Man's problem is an internal, anatomical one having to do with the organism of man in its phyletic totality." Burns realized this, and was a " whole and seldom " man to a far greater degree than any other Scottish writer yet. It must be said of him as Stevenson said of D'Artagnan : " There is nothing of the copybook about his virtues . . . but the whole man rings true like a good sovereign ". A recent English writer protested that an end should be put to the annual laudation by gatherings in all parts of the world in whose midst appear some of the most eminent in the Church, the Law, literature, and politics, of " one of the lewdest, most drunken, and most dissolute libertines who ever stained human records. . . . To drink a toast to a man like Burns ought properly to be considered as an affront to every decent thing in life. . . . In all the long erratic history of hero-worship there is probably not such another example where a reprobate, a deliberate, boasting defaulter from ordinary human decency, has carried his excesses to such repulsive extremes. No excuse whatever can be made for Burns's calculated violation all through his life of human decency. He was a deliberate moral anarchist." The actual facts of Burns's life either in regard to lechery, drunkenness, or other delinquencies do not bear this writer out, but Burns was certainly a moral anarchist. He had nothing to learn from Heidegger about *Vorlaufen zum Tode* (or, rather, *Vorlaufe zum Leben*) or from Shestov about " Earth's fruits to the flesh—to the soul the Abyss ! " but the elevation (or lack of elevation) from which he launched himself out, crying :

A fig for those by law protected !
Liberty's a glorious feast !
Courts for cowards were erected,
Churches built to please the priest ;

is another matter, as also—once he had cast himself upon the void—the strength and speed of the wings he developed, and the scope of his flight. " A mind at ease ", he wrote, " would have been charmed with my reasonings, but I am like Judas Iscariot preaching the Gospel. He might melt and mould the hearts of those around him, but his own kept its native incorrigibility." The steel wire (he himself called it his " stalk of carle hemp ") held through all the vicissitudes of his life—he was able to pursue his indeflectible purpose under all the trials that beset him, just as the " jogging of the chaise and Willie Nicol's chat ", or the company of noisy children or what not, never conflicted with concentration on the composition of his poems and songs. Burns did not need like Rilke any image of Saltimbanques or Seiltänzer to symbolize " das Existenzproblem im Durchschnittsmenschen ". And so he was able to sing

Wantonness for evermair,
Wantonness has been my ruin,
Yet for a' my dool and care
It's wantonness for evermair.
I hae loved the Black, the Brown,
I hae loved the Fair, the Gowden,
A' the colours in the town. . . .
Wantonness has been my ruin.

' " The strange, shifting, doubling animal Man is generally a negative and often a worthless creature. Of the men called honest and the women called chaste half of them are not what they pretend to be and many are thought to have even worse faults. But then virtue, everyone knows, is an obsolete business. Some years ago when I was young, and by no means the saint I am now, I discovered that even a *godly* woman may be a . . . but this is scandal. However respectable *individuals* in all ages may have been, I look on mankind in the lump as nothing better than a foolish mob." Willie Nicol was right when he called him " Dear Christless Bobbie ! " " Heresy ? " he says, in one of the letters Mr. Henderson quotes. " I do not care three farthings for Authorities ! " '

Even in Burns's own day it was difficult to possess oneself, save in discrete bits and pieces, of the very complicated and many-sided body of Scottish history and literature. Burns's requests to his correspondents for books are as numerous as Lenin's, but, owing to his circumstances too, he was largely subject to English literary over-influences incompatible with his essential genius. His reading of the *History of Sir William Wallace* had ' poured a Scottish prejudice in me veins, which will boil along them till the flood-gates of life shut in eternal rest ', but he was almost completely alienated from his proper pabulum, and it is pitiful to read : ' My knowledge of ancient story was gathered from Salmon's and Guthrie's Geographical

Grammars ; my knowledge of modern manners and of literature and criticism I got from the *Spectator* ; these, with Pope's works, some plays of Shakespeare, Tull and Dickson on Agriculture, The Pantheon, Locke's Essay on the Human Understanding, Stackhouse's History of the Bible, Justice's British Gardener's Directory, Boyle's Lectures, Allan Ramsay's works, Taylor's Scripture Doctrine of Original Sin, a Select Collection of English Songs, and Hervey's Meditations, had been the extent of my reading.' ' I was so lucky lately as to pick up a copy of Oswald's Scots Music, and I think I shall make glorious work out of it. I also want Anderson's collection of Strathspeys.' How shocking that he should consider the former *lucky* and *want* the latter ! Both should have been easily accessible ; he—and all Scots since—should not have had to come at their natural heritage in this fragmentary and hit-and-miss fashion. But the *vorarbeiten* had not been done ; the way had not been prepared for Burns—nor has it been prepared for any successor of Burns. ' My reading at about this period was enlarged with the very important addition of Thomson's and Shenstone's Works and a collection of Letters of Queen Anne's reign. This last helped me much in composition. . . .' Even to-day almost any English reading to which a Scottish writer with the root of the matter in him can turn appears to me (unless he has first possessed himself fairly fully of all the best elements of Scottish literature, alike in Gaelic, Latin, the Scots Vernacular, and English) as appallingly unsuitable, as shockingly beside the point, as these hapless confessions from Burns's letters. This curse of fragmentary knowledge of what in all its fullness should have been their birthright has afflicted all modern Scotsmen with any spark of genius. The late Sir Donald MacAlister told in a remarkable passage how it had retarded and mutilated his mental development. Mr. Ivan Sanderson, the brilliant young scientist author of *Animal Treasure*, testifies to the same effect and wishes he had been able to escape an English education. This accounted alike for the intervention in the Ossian controversy of disputants who had no Gaelic and for most of the observations made to-day on almost any phase of Scottish literature. It accounts too for the antiquarianism which is one of the besetting sins of Scottish authors, and for such a typical misconception as that of the late Mrs. Marjorie Kennedy-Fraser, of *Songs of the Hebrides* fame, who (obscuring the extremely scrappy and unscientific methods of herself and her collaborator, Dr. Kenneth Macleod, in their tremendously over-praised work, and eluding the crucial question of their super-imposition of an alien and inappropriate technique on their Gaelic originals) says :

> ' To keep alive the traditionally preserved hoard of racial song, the national poet must be reborn every three or four generations at least, if not every couple of centuries. And like Robert Burns in Lowland

Scotland in the 18th century, he must use all that comes to hand, all that has survived of the finest lyrical output of the previous generations. Single lines, refrains, beautiful thoughts, heart-stirring imagery, rhythms, metres, &c., must all be garnered and refashioned into lyrics that will be new and yet old. . . . Of Burns's " My Love is like a red, red rose ", Edmund Gosse says somewhere that not a line of it is original —that it was all fashioned out of the wreck, the flotsam and jetsam of earlier Scots songs.'

And she quotes this parable from Dr. Macleod :

' The Isle of Eigg, as the sheep know but too well, has its own share of bramble bushes. A hundred years ago, a woman who had a name for thrift as well as for art, went wool-gathering in these same bramble bushes as regularly as others went dulse-pulling on the shore. And in due time there came out of her loom a web of blues and greens and crotals,[1] which a king might envy. Generally the web went to a neighbour of her own, Iain Og Morragh, who had an eye for art, if not for thrift, and who, like herself, was a weaver, but of song-threads blown about by the four winds of heaven. It was he who, standing one day by the tomb of St. Donnan, and looking across to the face of Corravine (a hill in Eigg), weaved old threads into new so cunningly that none could tell what of the web was his own and what the angels'. If, after a hundred years, the loosened threads have been put once more through the loom, it is still the same web that comes out of it—" Youth on age, on the face of Corravine ".'

Whatever Iain Og Morragh was able to achieve in this way, it is certainly not thus that the illusion of a ' seamless garment ' can often be obtained ; Burns's own work is sleazy enough in all conscience, and what Mrs. Kennedy-Fraser and Dr. Macleod achieved in this way is open to devastating criticism.

Of Sir Walter Scott I recently wrote as follows in *The Voice of Scotland* :

' " The eighteenth-century English novel ", Edwin Muir once wrote, " was a criticism of society, manners, and life. It set out to amuse, but it had a serious intention ; its criticism, however wittily expressed, was sincere, and being sincere, it made for more civilized manners and a more sensitive understanding of human life. Scott marks a definite degeneration of that tradition ; after him certain qualities are lost to the novel which are not recovered for a long time. The novel becomes the idlest of all forms of literary art, and by a natural consequence the most popular. Instead of providing an intelligent criticism of life, it is content to enunciate moral platitudes, and it does this all the more confidently because such platitudes are certain to be agreeable to the reader. It skims over every aspect of experience that could be obnoxious to the most tender or prudish feelings, and in fact renounces both freedom and responsibility. Scott, it seems to me, was largely instrumental in bringing the novel to that pass ; with his enormous prestige he helped to establish the mediocre and trivial. . . . All that Scott wrote is disfigured by the main vice of gentility ; its inveterate indifference to truth, its inability to recognize that truth is valuable in itself. . . .

---

[1] Yellow dye from lichens.

Scott was the first writer of really great powers to bow the knee unquestioningly to gentility and abrogate his responsibility. . . . When we turn to his influence on Scottish literature we find the same story. There were not many genteel Scottish writers before Scott; there have not been many ungenteel ones since.   His gentility can be seen in his *Border Minstrelsy*, which he loved and yet could not but Bowdlerize. But the difference he introduced into Scottish poetry can be seen most clearly by comparing his own poems in the ballad form with the old ballads themselves.   It is pretty nearly the difference between

> I lighted down my sword to draw,
> I hacked him in pieces sma',

and

> Charge, Chester, charge!   On, Stanley, on!
> Were the last words of Marmion,

the difference between a writer fully conscious that he is dealing with dreadful things and one who must make even carnage pleasing and picturesque.   Scott was a man of great native genius and of enormous inventive powers.   But has any other writer of equal rank ever misused his gifts and indefatigably lowered the standards of literature with quite such a clean conscience ? "   Since despite all this, in his book *Scott and Scotland*, Mr. Muir declares that the Scots Vernacular has no future as a literary medium and advises Scots writers to abandon all the " trash of nonsense " of the distinctive Scottish past and cleave to the English language and the English tradition as indistinguishably and gratefully as possible, it throws a diverting light on the ignominious expedients to which the defenders of Scott and of the Anglo-Scottish Union are driven to recall that in an earlier essay, with precisely the same air of infallibility, Mr. Muir wrote :

' " Since English became the literary language of Scotland there has been no Scots imaginative writer who has attained greatness in the first or even second rank through the medium of English. Scott achieved classical prose, prose with the classical qualities of solidity, force, and measure, only when he wrote in the Scottish dialect; his Scottish dialogue is great prose, and his one essay in Scottish imaginative literature, ' Wandering Willie's Tale ', is a masterpiece of prose, a prose which one must go back to the seventeenth century to parallel.   The style of Carlyle, on the other hand, was taken bodily from the Scots pulpit; he was a parish minister of genius, and his English was not great English, but great Scots English; the most hybrid of all styles, with some of the virtues of the English Bible and many of the vices of the Scottish version of the Psalms of David; a style whose real model may be seen in Scott's anticipatory parody of it in ' Old Mortality '. He took the most difficult qualities of the English language and the worst of the Scots, and through them attained a sort of absurd, patchwork greatness.   But—this can be said of him—his style expressed, in spite of its overstrain, and even through it, something real, the struggle of a Scots peasant, born to other habits of speech and of thought, with the English language.   Stevenson—and it was the sign of his inferiority, his lack of fundamental merit—never had this struggle, nor realized that it was necessary that he should have it. . . . The other two Scots-English writers of the last half-century, John Davidson and James Thomson (the author of ' The City of Dreadful Night '), were greater men than Stevenson, less affected and more fundamental; but fundamental as they were, they lacked something which in English prose is fundamental, and the oblivion into which they have fallen, undeserved as it seems when we consider that great talents, is yet, on some ground not easy to state, just. The thing I am examining here, superficial in appearance, goes deep. No writer can write great English who is not born an English writer and in England ; and born moreover in some class, in which the tradition of English is pure, and, it seems to me, therefore, in some other age than this. . . ." '

The state of affairs to which the English connexion, and the cultural and other positions Sir Herbert defends, have reduced Scotland gives fresh point to what Scott wrote to Maria Edgeworth :

> ' No man can commit the extremity of folly with so grave a counten-ance and under the influence of such admirable reasoning as a Scotsman. The whole nation indeed deserves the character given to the sapient Monarch of old, the wisest fool in Christendom.

Scott found in Ireland ' widespread manifestations of the wanton and reckless profligacy of human mismanagement, the withering curse of feuds and factions, and the tyrannous selfishness of absenteeism ' ; Scotland to-day has been reduced to a similar and even worse state as the direct result of the policies Scott and his eulogists, right up to the Unionist clique who in our own day have kept their eyes shut to the appalling facts, have enforced or at least defended. There are many in Scotland still perhaps not yet alive to the terrible truth about the state of Scotland, but they are in the position of a woman who knows there is something far wrong with her, more than suspects just what it is, but dare not go to the doctor, and so waits until the cancer that might have been extirpated at an earlier stage becomes inoperable and fatal. On the cover of Sir Herbert's book we read, ' Sir Walter Scott, Bart. . . . *A New Life* '. A new Life it is (though it only differs in detail from previous lives and is written—admirably written, of course—from essentially the same angle), but, if there is one thing absolutely certain, it is that it will give Sir Walter no new lease of life in popular interest nor (despite the sedulous efforts of our educational authorities) secure his work any new body of readers.

What accounts, then, not only for the pro-Scott activities of Unionists like Lord Tweedsmuir and Sir Herbert Grierson, but even of a professed Socialist like Mr. Edwin Muir, at this critical juncture in Scottish affairs ? What applies to Mr. Muir's *Scott and Scotland* applies also to Lord Tweedsmuir's and Sir Herbert Grierson's work in their several degrees. *Scott and Scotland* is a restatement of the literary case of Scottish Unionism—that hireling caste employed by English Imperialism to perpetuate the provincial status of Scotland, the better to facilitate its exploitation—written with the design of discrediting the programme of the Scottish Renaissance Movement, and, what is more important, of reconciling, in view of the dis-integration of that literary movement and the political movement it aroused, opposition and vocal elements produced by the Renaissance efforts but now left aimless, with the English Ascendancy. It professes to adopt the standpoint of the Renaissance Movement as expressed in the P.E.N. Manifesto of 1927—i.e. that Scotland as a nation ought to have an autonomous national literature—and then attempts to show that the creation of this literature is hindered by the very programme which the Renaissance undertook to fulfil, and that this great task had best proceed along lines suggested in Mr. Muir's last chapter—which lines, though masquerading in the guise of brilliant novelty, turn out on analysis to be nothing but the re-affirmation of the programme of the pro-English type of Scottish literature—of which Scott is the high priest and in which Lord Tweedsmuir, Sir Herbert Grierson, and even Mr. Muir are them-selves creditable figures—with this difference, that the literature, as a condition of gaining excellence, must shed all concern with the Scots Vernacular and occupy itself wholly with English—i.e. must conform to practice which Mr. Muir, in contradistinction to second-raters like R. L. Stevenson with his hankering (like Scott's and Lord Tweedsmuir's) alone exhibits in their purity. It is fortunate for Mr. Muir that his genius is so well equipped for the reconciliation of opposites which his mystical consciousness can accomplish. Were he like the present writer, doomed to reside on the plane of mere understanding, he might find that the thesis of the book involves a split as irreconcilably self-contradictory as the Scottish ' spirit '. For instance, he is confident that pursuit of the pro-English line of literature will yield great literature if its hampering half-concern for Scots is dropped ; yet nothing can be clearer than that in the century in which this line has had unhampered opportunity of developing itself the small amount it has produced redeeming it from the utterest insignificance has consisted entirely of these ' unfortunate ' lapses into Scots. Mr. Muir postulates as the condition of excellence the relegation to insignificance of the one significant feature, the one semi-fruitful field of Scottish literary activity. Is that logic ?—but then we are dealing with a man for whom mystical consciousness is the supreme thing.[1] Well, but it is an interesting, however misguided an ideal ! ' It is a mere commonplace of the practice of the St. Andrews' School of ' polite literature ' of the last three-quarters of a century, and has produced nothing good. But the crucial contradiction in Mr. Muir's work does not reveal itself until the last pages. He cites the example of Ireland in order to show how we Scots can build up a worthy literature in English ; but, viewed comprehensively, modern Anglo-Irish literature derives all its motivation from the movement for the repudiation both of England's Empire and language, and is intentionally cultivated as at once a sort of barrier against English culture and a preparation for the

---

[1] Perhaps this is why, referring to Mr. Muir's book, Sir Herbert says : ' I probably do not quite understand the thesis '.

creation of an Irish culture in Gaelic. Far from taking advantage of the English literary tradition, as Mr. Muir in advising Scotsmen to assimilate themselves to it avers the Irish have done, the Irish have rejected it, and their present Anglo-Irish work is completely influenced in technique and in matter by Irish–Gaelic traditions and by foreign non-English models. If Mr. Muir is serious in his advice, then the point is—the pre-condition of our creation of a literature must be—to oppose all forms of the dominant English culture in the name of Scotland's past ; and to produce a temporary fighting literature for the purpose of carrying on the struggle for the creation of a Scottish Scotland, and the destruction of English control and influence. Mr. Muir's assumption that the alternative to English is Gaelic is true ; a Scottish Scotland must be a Gaelic Scotland. But for the purposes of the creation of a stop-gap anti-English literature in Scotland, what other medium ought there to be but Scots, which lies ready to hand, and which is in its major achievements of to-day and Burns's time already intensely anti-English ? The driving force of Scots from its creation in the hands of Barbour and Blind Harry (to make up for a lost Gaelic) down to the Scots poets of to-day has always been hostility to English Imperialism. Of course, the object of Mr. Muir's edict is this : Scots was only tolerable to England as long as it was tame—now that it has become once more the language of independence and been recalled to its real purpose, its use must be discouraged, its significance belittled, since it has become a danger to the *status quo*. If, then, we take Mr. Muir in his superficial meaning —i.e., what he means to mean—we have nothing but a pompous rehash of the ' Edinburgh view of Scots literature '—mere servility to English Imperialism ; if we try to understand his argument in the light of what he grants about Ireland, cleared from his vagueness and distortion, the trend of the book becomes the advocacy of intense Anti-Imperialism, Anglophobia, and Nationalism. But, in fact, Mr. Muir is putting up an incoherent sort of case against the Scots Renaissance Movement, more concerned to attack it than to understand it. His failure to understand it, and to come to effective grips with it, arises from the fact that he repudiates without argument the essential premiss of the Scots Renaissance ; the reduction of Scotland to subject nationality by exploiting English Imperialism. Muir says (p. 160, *op. cit.*) :

> ' England was overcoming Scotland and dissolving its ancient traditions of life by the same means with which the English King overcame Red-gauntler's hopes ; by a magnanimous gesture to which there was no act of reply.'

This ' magnanimous gesture ' has, in fact, the same historical status as the ' act of faith ' by which (p. 182) Ireland's sense of unity is said to have been preserved and to which Scotland is now exhorted

—both are merely ' English lies '. That anything can be achieved by ' an act of faith ' except self-stultification is reactionary mysticism of the worst type. So far as Ireland is united in its action or its thought, that is due to the persistence of Irish Nationalism in the face of English domination ; we find not ' act of faith ', but faith in action. Muir by his refusal to meet the case of the Scots Renaissance *ipso facto* gives away the reactionary aim of his book—the continuance of the nineteenth-century traitor attitude to Scots Literature and of Scott's prestige (all of which is implicit and simply taken for granted as axiomatic to all right-thinking and, above all, well-bred people in Sir Herbert Grierson's biography, not explicit as in Muir's book). *Scott and Scotland* is an attempt to recall the literary public in Scotland to its allegiance to its former idols. The dangerous thing in it is not its confused theorizing, which is of the ' swindling catchword ' Fascist–Imperialist order and is not expected to be taken seriously, but its glorification of Scott. Scott's novels are the great source of the paralysing ideology of defeatism in Scotland, the spread of which is responsible at once for the acceptance of the Union and the low standard of nineteenth-century Scots literature except in the hands of men like the Gaelic poet, William Livingston (1808–70), who were consciously anti-English—a defeatism as profitable financially to its exponents (Scott, Stevenson, Tweedsmuir, &c.) as it is welcome to English interests. ' The cause is lost for ever ', the ' end of an auld sang ', and that sort of stuff is an actual distortion of history—and that is what Scott did (cf. *The Heart of Midlothian*, in which Scott described the Porteous Riots as if they were temporary accidental disturbances instead of events of an international significance that accompanied a national anger at the Union and led to the Rebellion of eight years after, when the Prince, seeing that the ground was ripe in Scotland, and England at war, came over. That is their historical significance, but Scott's work has obscured this, and Mr. Muir and Sir Herbert accept Scott's estimate of the Riots). That ' the cause was lost for ever ' was exactly what Scott's own circle spent their energies in providing, and what all these new Scott books are endeavouring to ensure in the face of the new Scottish literary and political movement and all the objective facts of Scotland's condition to-day. It was a wish, rather than a reflection, and was for the time being made good only by the suppression of the ' United Scotsmen ' of 1797, and of the radical patriotic rebels of 1820—men belonging not to Scott's class, but to Burns's, and influenced by his work. Muir's book and Sir Herbert's are attempts to exalt Scott, and are most dangerous. What makes them so dangerous is Scott's real bigness —although in actual achievement he is small beer indeed compared with Balzac or Tolstoi. Muir has, for all his clever analysis, missed the point of Scott's significance, which the part his work played in inspiring the resurgence of Flemish and Catalan shows. As can be gathered from Brandes, Scott's only value is his objective treatment of parts of Scottish history and the partial revivification by his influence of the two mentioned and other minority literatures. The whole direction of Scott's line was his regret for the quite needless passing of Scottish institutions, mannerisms, &c., into English, as exemplified in many of his famous sayings—e.g., about an un-Scotched Scotsman becoming a damned bad Englishman, &c. This leads on naturally to the separatist position, and Muir and Lord Tweedsmuir and Sir Herbert Grierson cannot do justice to these— the only important elements in Scott—save in contradiction to their own anti-Scottish-separatist line. Properly, Scott can only be used as a battering-ram to drive home the failure of nineteenth-century and subsequent Scottish writers to crystallize phases of Scotland's developing history in the way Scott, though only poorly, did for certain previous periods. That Sir Herbert Grierson and Mr. Muir deny this, or turn a blind eye to its contemporary implications and applications, is typical of the irremediable confusion and constant self-contradiction of their own pretendedly-objective but wholly subjective pseudo-critical position. Where Scott is strong is in the way in which his work reveals that for a subject nation the firm literary bulwark against the encroaching Imperialism is concentration on the national language and re-interpretation of the national history. Scott's work has real value where a stand is being made against Imperialism ; for example, in Doughty's letters, Scott is the only writer mentioned with real approbation, and Doughty heads a nationalist movement against Imperialism in a nation whose own Imperialism has destroyed its national life. Also worth mentioning, in view alike of Sir Herbert Grierson's prelatic prepossessions, Scott's own Episcopalianism, and Mr. Muir's anti-Calvinistic writings (e.g., his ' debunking ' life of Knox), is the religious issue. Such repudiations of Calvinism are thoroughly religious repudiations —i.e., culminating in a sort of milk-and-water mysticism, Calvinist in tone but not in logic. Mr. Muir's revolt against Calvinism, for example, is nothing but a reform of the religious ideology necessary to the hold of England over Scotland so as to make it meet the problems with which post-War development has represented the Ascendancy. His book is performing the function of *The Causes of the Lord's Wrath against Scotland* again. Mr. Muir's anti-Calvinism is as much a red herring as Hitler's anti-Semitism, besides being incompatible with his own religious standpoint. His aesthetic antagonism to Calvinism finds its refutation in the fact that of the poets he quotes no less than three—Alexander Scott, Mark Alexander Boyd, and Alexander Hume—were Calvinists. Calvinism is no worse or better than any other religion ; its excesses were due entirely to the fact that from the beginnings its spread was closely connected with English policy and that it became England's ideological damper for suffocating Scottish action. Finally it is necessary to insist that Scott is bigger than either Brandes or Croce holds ; but since his significance lies in his preoccupation with the National Question, it has been the policy of English Imperialism to have its hireling scribes praise Scott on all grounds but the one praiseworthy ground, which it was essential to keep concealed. Hence, foreign critics of standing, unable, in view of the native critics' silence, to see any significance in Scott, were bound to consider his work but children's stuff. Now that the Scottish Question has again become a living issue in Letters, it is thought fit to disclose Scott's interest in it, since his point of view amounted to a fatalistic pessimism about Scotland's future.

I may add to these paragraphs on the crucial case of Scott the following extract from a friend's letter apropos Muir's *Scott and Scotland* :

' That such a book could be written in 1936 is a nasty shock to my own complacency. You once described your *Contemporary Scottish Studies* (1926) as of merely historical interest, advocating ideas resisted at the time but now universally accepted. But here is Muir ten years later blandly denying its whole thesis, and likely to command tremendous respect. His book is the cultural companion volume to Rait and Pryde's historical work, and must be answered, as theirs must be, with irrefragible systematic exposition of Maclean–MacDiarmidism. It is true that a series of books is no substitute for the absence of a political movement, but it is equally certain that no political movement can come into being without a sound theory contained in books. Especially I welcome your promised biography of Maclean, which will be the most important thing in Scots political writing since Maclean's last address. It must be a militant biography. Maclean is one of the few that deserve comparison with Wallace, and provides a magnificent standpoint for a devastating analysis of the antics of our Scots Politicians. . . . When all is said we must give Muir credit for his actual achievements in this book (i.e. *Scott and Scotland*). It literally puts out of date all criticism of Scott. What he has done is to reinterpret Scott's work in terms of the categories which you have—along with F. G. Scott—discovered and put across. Though, I must say, that revaluation is easy for anyone who has studied your work. In 1932 I made notes for an essay on Scott which was designed to show his significance for the Scots Renaissance novel. They are still extant. In fact, where Scott is shown up in new, true, and creditable light by Muir, his work can only be hindered from confirming our line by gross distortions—subtle silences, &c. Take *Redgauntlet*—I had myself never read it till yesterday, and agree at once that it is Scott's best work—all credit to Muir. Consider the hero's character. Muir says : " In *Redgauntlet* Scott produced his one character of more than practical heroism ; he came out of what Lord Tweedsmuir calls ' Scott's secret world ' ; he was a hero in the Nietzschean sense." All this merely obscures what a reading of *Redgauntlet* at once conveys—Redgauntlet is a real, not a sham, character because for once Scott had the courage to create a character at one with his suppressed longings, i.e. a passionate Scottish nationalist. He is heroic because he is concerned not with trifling issues like the other " heroes ", but a real issue of transcendent importance—the life or death of Scots nationality. The issue is, however, as living as ever—only the initiative had already in Scott's time passed from the Royalist Right to the Republican Left.

' Scott's real problem was the betrayal of Scotland by his own class that had forgotten Jacobitism in the Dundas regime's design to maintain English supremacy when Burns's patriotic republicanism was a real force. Further, and in conclusion, the most striking thing in the book is Muir's refusal to take your work seriously. However, you are in good company ; Burns receives like treatment—vague panegyrics but implied belittlement. Muir seems to rank not merely Scott, but Ferguson above Burns—which is sheer nonsense. But even in his treatment of Ferguson, there is an astounding illogicality : his admissions —true enough—about Ferguson's mastery of language run quite counter to his thesis that Scots is since the Reformation no fit language for literature. But whatever it may be in Burns, who was careless, it is perfectly used by Ferguson. The moral is surely not to abandon Scots but to study it as Burns did not and as you and Ferguson did before using it ; that is the force of your old dictum in " *Albyn* " that " Burns betrayed the movement Ramsay and Ferguson began ".'

The term ' betrayal ' is not one to be used lightly about Burns in any connexion, but my whole attitude has been based on the realization that Burns's poem of which a ' parcel of rogues in a nation ' is the refrain was applied to this tiny class of England's lackeys who have oppressed Scotland in England's interests ever since the Union. Further, a study of Burns from the Marxist angle shows that the poem in question (1794) was, like ' Scots Wha Ha'e ' (1793), inspired by Thomas Muir's movement—which Burns himself lived to betray and attack (vide ' Does haughty Gaul invasion threaten ? ' 1795). I also think that Burns betrayed his own keenest realizations of the kind of poetry he should write, lapsing back on too easy models and compromising too much with English standards, since, as Mr. J. B. Caird has pointed out, ' Burns's remarks on the song " The Mill, Mill O " show that he had reached conclusions regarding poetic rhythm, without endeavouring to work them out systematically or to put them into practice, which in some respects anticipate those of Gerard Manley Hopkins.'

Reviewing Mr. W. Murison's book, *Sir David Lyndsay, Poet— and Satirist of the Old Church in Scotland* (1939) in *The Criterion* on its appearance, I said : that it is mainly devoted to a work of supererogation—the justification of Sir David Lyndsay's attacks on the Roman Catholic Church—and while praising the book for its thorough scholarship and excellent analysis of Lyndsay's writings, wish it had been devoted instead to answering the question of the cause of the sudden eclipse of the great popularity of a poet whose work was for long regarded in Scottish homes as little less important than the Bible, and still had ' charms ' for Sir Walter Scott. The vital thing about Lyndsay to-day is the fact that he opposed great established powers, spoke to (and for) the great mass of the working people, and in circumstances in many ways not dissimilar to those the latter are now facing, succeeded in discharging to tremendous effect and with great historical results something very like the task to which the satirical poets and poetic dramatists of the Left are to-day addressing themselves in this and other countries.

'Last year' (1938), I continued, 'was the tercentenary of the publication of the *Delitiae,* the group publication of the Scottish Latin poets, and 1941 is the tercentenary of the death of Arthur Johnston. The transition from George Buchanan's to Arthur Johnston's work is of exceptional interest. In Johnston the cultural effects of the 1603 Union are plainly visible. Going abroad in 1598 at the age of 18, and living, apart from periods at Padua and Heidelberg, mostly in France, he produced the bulk of his work after his return to his native Aberdeen in 1621, and became the leading figure in the intellectual life of the country, including such diverse groups as Drummond and the Earl of Stirling, the humanists of the *Delitiae,* and the Aberdeen Doctors, as well as Jameson the painter. At that time Scottish culture was still vigorously but hopelessly without direction and becoming increasingly divorced from the real national situation. Owing to the difficulty of initiating what ought to have been the task before the age in Scotland as it was elsewhere in Europe—namely, the evolution of renaissance literature in the vernacular incorporating the lessons learned from the Humanists—a difficulty created by the centrifugal stampede of pre-viously coalescing Scottish life which the sudden utter loss of self-government occasioned, far from carrying on the tendencies introduced by Buchanan and Lyndsay—namely, tackling the real problems of the time and addressing the people, not the court—the literature becomes royalist and episcopalian as well as circumscribed in outlook. When the political sympathies of our literature had become so opposed to national interests, the success of the anti-cultural movement of the next generation is readily explicable, taken in conjunction with the blind-alley tendency of the literature itself. During the succeeding years, Humanism dwindled into a production of Grahameids—about Claver-house—or Pitcairn's epigrams, and lingered long after it had died. At the same time the forcible attempts of England to repress the masses had the effect of confining their cultural interests to the often striking and pathetic sermons which sustained them in their struggle, and to the ballad-literature of the times. The technical obstacles to attempts at the creation or resumption of a national literature were above all the politically caused loss of a standard of Scots, the absence of a prose-writing tradition in Scots, a certain consciousness, strongly expressed in Buchanan for example, that the real language of the Scots was Gaelic, and the resultant prevailing Humanist idea of solving the national linguistic problems by making Scotland a Latin-speaking country together with the scheme arising out of this situation and pushed by Urquhart and others of inventing and using a synthetic language. The unshaken influence of England—its Bible and Puritan and literary and political stranglehold—were factors contributing to the prose-use of English by Scottish writers. In fact, literature, in prose at least, was not reborn until the tension of the fight for freedom in the Scots Parlia-ment evoked care of expression, especially in the case of the immortal Fletcher of Saltoun, who is regarded as the founder of the Scots eighteenth-century prose of criticism and thought.

'This hasty retrospect described certain crucial phases of our literary history, the great wheel of which has now come full circle. Once again there is an increasing realization of the need for tackling in our poetry

the real problems of our time and for addressing the people—and with
that a need to make the political sympathies of our literature identical
with our national interests. There is also a sharper apprehension of our
still unsettled linguistic problems; and together with all these re-mani-
festations of the ancient difficulties of a Scottish national literature,
there is the general crisis of civilization and the incommunicability to
the vast majority of people of the great new scientific ideas which have
recently so profoundly affected our entire intellectual background. The
future of Scottish poetry lies in the success or unsuccess of its address
to these great problems.'

It is this problem of undoing the monstrous misdirection of the
Scottish national spirit, and getting back, in Scottish literature and
politics, to ' the real problems of the time and addressing the people ',
with which I have all along been mainly concerned—back, in other
words, to that particular Scottish democratic spirit which Lyndsay
in his time exemplified, and concerning which a splendid historical
summary was given by Dr. Mary P. Ramsay in her address to the
1938 Calvinist Conference in Edinburgh—an address which, of
course, the *Scotsman* and other Anglo-Scottish newspapers took care
not to report. Dr. Ramsay's address was an extension of her very
able and timely pamphlet, *Calvin and Art*, which, however, like
Murison's book, is largely addressed to a very unnecessary task—to
prove that Calvin himself was more intelligent about the arts than
Scottish Calvinists have been, and that it is therefore unfair to blame
Scotland's cultural declension on Calvinism, since Calvin's *Institutes*
afford no basis for the anti-aesthetic spirit that has flourished so
stupidly in post-Reformation Scotland. Dr. Ramsay proves this
purely academic point, of course—but if Scottish Philistinism is
wrongly attributed to Calvinism, those who have attacked it are right
in recognizing the profound relationship of this anti-cultural spirit
to the Scottish Kirk, and the fact that it has no warrant in Calvin's
own writings (no less little known to the vast majority of so-called
Calvinists than to recent so-called anti-Calvinist critics) is a matter
of very minor—if of any—consequence. Dr. Ramsay's pamphlet,
however, is a very able and scholarly piece of work, full of much
useful information, the fruit of careful study (although she unfortunately fails, not only to avail herself of such valuable recent
works as Douglas Nobbs' *Theocracy and Toleration*, but ignores
entirely both the bearings on her subject-matter of all modern
psychological research and of such books as R. H. Tawney's *Religion
and the Rise of Capitalism*), and apart from its main subject-matter
altogether, should be read by everyone interested in the Scottish
literary movement for its excellent chapter on an all-too-little-known
poet, Sir William Mure of Rowallan, whose *True Crucifixe for True
Catholicks* appeared in 1629. The Scottish Text Society has
published Mure's Poetical Works, Tough, in his introduction,
remarking that ' he was not only widely read in the classical authors,

but also . . . deeply imbued with their spirit and beauty '. ' His
mother ', says Dr. Ramsay, ' was a sister of Alexander Montgomery,
author of *The Cherry and the Slae*, and Mure felt a family pride in
this connexion with poetry. Unfortunately for his reputation as a
poet, the works by which he has been chiefly known are the didactic
and political pamphlets in verse which give least impression of his
real poetic gifts, *The True Crucifixe*; *Caldeon's Complaint*, 1641;
and the *Cry of Blood and of a Broken Covenant*, 1650, in which he
voices his indignation at the execution of Charles I, and utters a
stirring call to arms to his fellow-countrymen on behalf of Charles
II, all poems which were evidently widely read and appreciated by
his generation and party, however. On the other hand, his verse
translation of two books of Virgil, under the title *Dido and Æneas*,
made when he was barely twenty, is the work of a good poet; while
in his songs and sonnets, love-songs in his youth, religious in later
years, he shows a metrical skill and grace that link him with Dunbar.
. . . Mure is of special interest to us at this moment, when the
talents of Mr. Ian White have so lately been applied to the orchestration of the lovely tunes collected by Mure in his *Lute Book*, till
recently lying unpublished in the University Library in Edinburgh.'
The fifteen pages or so Dr. Ramsay devotes to Mure are of absorbing
interest, and above all in her analysis of those portions of the *Crucifixe*
where, as she says, this ardent Calvinist ' refers to the painter's
methods and achievement, and deals with the psychological aspects of
the artist's work. . . . It is only by keeping the historical point of view
that any kind of justice can be done to such writing and thinking.'

Ere long Scottish history will present a very different picture from
that which has been the accepted view during the past century and
longer. At a score of important points within the past decade
researchers have not only succeeded in ' torpedoing ' the stories and
interpretations hitherto generally entertained, but have shown that
the whole succession of modern Scottish historians were necessarily
engaged only in prolonging what Major M. V. Hay, in an invaluable
study, calls ' the Chain of Error in Scottish History ', since their
qualifications for their task (they even made a virtue of their ignorance
of Gaelic, and their consequent confinement, in respect of great tracts
of Scottish History, to ' one side of the story ', and that the least
valuable, since it developed long after the events in question,
expresses a mentality undreamt of by and antipathetic to the spirit of
the times of which it treats, and is associated with the governing myth
of our own times in a fashion which puts an irresistible premium on
mere official propaganda) were only of the same kind as those of
' Christopher North ' (Professor John Wilson) for the Chair of Moral
Philosophy in Edinburgh University, which he held for thirty years
(a monstrous appointment which, incidentally, Sir Herbert Grierson
defends in the biography of Sir Walter Scott—surely a new high-

water mark of political prejudice !), during which, in his complete ignorance of his subject, he was wholly dependent for the bones of his discourses on a friend who ' ghosted up ' the necessary material for him in response to continual frantic S.O.S's ; or, perhaps their feats resemble rather those of the French writer, Jules Janin, who, according to Thackeray, translated Sterne and other English novelists ' without troubling to learn a word of English '. The latest work on the subject—*Scotland*, by Sir Robert Rait and Dr. George S. Pryde (1934)—denouncing certain contemporary nationalist writers as inaccurate, prejudiced, and ill-balanced, refers to the poetry of a man who has not written any, totally ignores the greatest achievement in Scottish Music, while writing of Burns as if he had been a musician, and treating Mrs. Marjorie Kennedy-Fraser as ' the chief approach to Gaelic letters for Scotland as a whole ', than which nothing could well be further off the mark, speaks of the diminishing number of their readers as having consigned Gaelic authors to secondary importance as though (for it cannot only apply to Gaelic, and good literature in any language only appeals to a minority) literary values were determined by popularity, rehashes the vicious sectarian propaganda based on repeatedly disproven statistics against the Irish in Scotland, whereas the latest census returns show that what is really taking place in Scotland is a great English invasion, treats a financial statement forced out of the Westminster Parliament as gospel truth without any examination of the realities that lie behind the figures given, and actually believes—and worse, welcomes —the pretence that England is letting Scotland off from paying an additional £23 millions annually which would be exigible if Scotland proportionately to population were assessed on the same basis as England, and regards Queen Mary and Prince Charlie as ' ambiguous historical reputations ' about which—as about the Kirk and questions of relative aesthetic value—there cannot be legitimate differences of opinion. It is, in a word, a deplorable and typically Anglo-Scottish performance, and as gross an exhibition of obstinate and anti-national prejudice as even its field affords. This, of course, is in keeping with a country which, in its University of Edinburgh, has no Chair of Scottish Literature, and, in its University of Glasgow, a Chair of Scottish History and Literature which has made no substantive contribution to its greatly neglected subjects, and is largely concerned with discouraging any attempts at research or reinterpretation antipathetic to the existing order, and with opposing any propaganda for a fuller teaching of these subjects in Scottish schools, where they are scarcely taught at all, and, to the small degree that they are, only in a fashion strictly subordinate to English history and literature and slavishly considerate of English interests. Scottish History should rather be called Anti-Scottish History. Despite strong official opposition, however, recent independent Scottish

research has not only put an end at long last to the period in which
such paraphrasers of the accepted story could flourish; it has
revealed the extraordinary amount of research that remains to be
done—the huge masses of evidence that have not yet been consulted
by any Scottish historians—and the almost incredible extent to
which the bolstering up of the official story has been dependent upon
the neglect or destruction of all manner of source-material.   The
reasons for the neglect of all this remaining material up to the present
time have a shrewd bearing on the matter; a blind eye has been
turned to it advisedly, and simultaneously with that manoeuvre there
has naturally been, on the part of those concerned in it, such a
protestation of impartiality that it is still impossible to devote any
attention to the neglected aspects of Scottish history, or to suggest
that this, that, or the other element is susceptible of a very different
interpretation from that which has hitherto been so assiduously
promulgated, without being accused of a propagandist purpose at
variance with a true attitude to history.   When any attempt is made
to probe still deeper into the matter, and to suggest that the whole of
Scottish history has hitherto been the work of men whose minds
have had certain easily definable limitations, which have only to be
exposed to dispose of the claims made for the integrity and finality of
their conceptions—when, in other words, it is realized that they all
belong to a particular mental climate—these accusations become
more violent still, and the opposition behind the scenes is so strong
that it is practically impossible to make any headway against it.   Yet
it appears that forces outside Scotland as well as inside it are to-day
combining to render all the orthodox positions untenable, and to
show that Scottish history as hitherto told has been the product of a
culture which is now on its last legs and about to be superseded by
one which is not only of a very different character, but derives much
of its strength from the very elements the nature of its predecessor
rendered subordinate or occluded altogether.   The stone the
builders rejected may well become the corner-stone of the future of
Scottish History too.   'After Culloden,' says George Bernard Shaw
in the preface to *On the Rocks*, ' the defeated Highland Chiefs and
their clansmen were butchered like sheep on the field.   Had they
been merely prisoners of war, this would have been murder.   But as
they were also Incompatible with British Civilization . . . it was
only liquidation.'   ' Incompatible with British civilization ' may well
mean vital to the new order about to supplant that civilization.   The
chief of these hitherto vanquished ideas perhaps is just the denial of
the present general assumption that ' History had to happen ', and,
with it, of the idea of Progress.

    There is no study available yet of Alexander Stewart, the ' Wolfe
of Badenoch ' (1342–   ), a great Scotsman, the salient figure at the
greatest turning-point in our history to date, of whom little or no

mention is ever made in Scottish Histories, although—and that is to say, because—he was the principal protagonist of the opposite ideas to those which prevailed and have ever since dominated, and still dominate, our country. This opposition should have thrown him up into high relief as a figure of altogether exceptional significance ; the alterative value of such a character should have offset all the other leading figures in Scottish history in an invaluable manner. Instead of that he has been completely neglected, and with him all that he stood for (a fact which argues a very serious conscious weakness at the very heart of the prevailing system !). The closest parallel to the Wolfe's case is perhaps that of Wang An Shih, a Chinese statesman of the Sung Dynasty (A.D. 1021–86) : ' For nearly a thousand years his writings have remained on the index of oblivion ; to-day, thanks chiefly to the high praise bestowed upon them by the foremost of China's modern scholars, the late Tiang Ch'ich'ao, they have been republished at Shanghai, and have evoked considerable interest, not to say enthusiasm, among the educationists of Young China, and students of political economy.' The Wolfe's name is scarcely known to the majority of Scots, and outside Scotland even his bare name is known to few but specialists. That his name (or rather his nickname) survives at all is due to its association with certain legends for which there is little, or no, foundation—although they are not on that account to be neglected. Baseless stories though they may be, or the mere propagandist productions of his enemies—his personal enemies, and, since his own day down to ours, the conscious or unconscious enemies of the ideas for which he stood—they have played their part, and must be reckoned with, for though historians may attempt to base their narrations on truth, history itself is made at least as much by falsehood and misconception as by truth and accuracy (even to the very small and questionable degree to which we may speak of these at all). What legend has made of the Wolfe of Badenoch in history's careful avoidance of him is therefore not only actually an aspect of the Wolfe himself, as he takes shape in a world of alien ideas, but, in so far as it can be compared with the facts of the man's life, a means of arriving at a better understanding of the nature of the history in question. In any case, the fact that almost all that is popularly known of the Wolfe of Badenoch is entirely legendary, and is not based on what he actually was or did, does not, in itself, deprive it of value. For, as Compton Mackenzie has said of a somewhat analogous case, ' I who knew D. H. Lawrence well can watch already the mythopoeic process at work on his personality ; but, though I may know it to be mythopoeic, I am not therefore in a position to impugn its truth.'

The portrait of the Wolfe of Badenoch hangs in the gallery of the great classical criminals of history. So far it has been left to the Churchmen of his own day, who were his sworn enemies, and to historians pledged to a pious confirmation of their verdict. A later presentation, in a historical novel, after the style of Scott, by Sir Thomas Dick Lauder, uses the Churchmen's story as a basis, and then proceeds to romanticize the picture by further blackening until it is of quite incredible pitchiness and becomes the horrific likeness of a mere monster of cruelty, greed, violence, lechery, and devilish wrath. The novel is worth reading for a certain gusto with which it is written, and for the oblique value in relation to the Wolfe referred to above, but its hero is obviously a creature of legend and not a man.

> ' It is a sign of the times that there is a new edition of Sir Thomas Dick Lauder's famous historical novel, *The Wolfe of Badenoch* ', Mr. Cunninghame Graham wrote in his preface to that new edition a year or two ago. ' For a century Scotsmen have been content to remain pale copies of our " ancient enemy " from beyond the Tweed. Some degenerate sons of Scotia, even to-day, attribute the economic progress of Scotland to the Act of Union, and forget their own share in the job. Mesopotamia is a blessed wood. When you have said Act of Union there are still sporadic Scots who put on the same kind of long face as they assume on reading aloud the genealogy of King David. Mercifully, they are becoming rare, as rare as those who think John Knox invented Scotland, almost without the assistance of the Deity. A new generation of race-conscious Scotsmen is arising, and to it the publication of a Scottish novel that has stood the test of time will be a boon.'

But Mr. Cunninghame Graham would have been the first to agree that the publication of the true story of the Wolfe, and the emergence into Scottish History of chapters of it hitherto ruthlessly suppressed, would be a still greater and timelier boon.

Alexander Stewart, Lord of Badenoch and Earl of Buchan, born 1343–44, was the fourth son of Robert II, first king of that house in Scotland. He is remembered for his constant feud with the Church, which culminated in open defiance and the burning of the Cathedral of Moray in 1390, when he rode his horse up the Cathedral steps and himself directed the plunder and the looting. And bound up with the story of the burning is his leadership of the wild Katerans of the hills and forests of the North, who lived mainly by raiding the fat lowlands.

His challenge to the Church came at a moment in the struggle between the feudal and ecclesiastical powers in Scotland when the scale was slowly turning in favour of the Church, and it was necessary in the interests of both Crown and nobles that a check should be given to that turning. In spite of the fact that subsequent history has branded him as a criminal and an outlaw, it is clear that in the beginning he had the support of the great northern Lords in his attempt to supersede the growing authority of the Bishop in secular matters, and it is more than probable that his appointment as King's Lieutenant in the ' Northern Parts ' carried with it an unspoken commission to curb and curtail that authority wherever possible

It was notoriously the policy of contemporary sovereigns to keep the enmity and the attention of those two great forces focussed on each other, in order to prevent them from combining against the Crown. But above and beyond this it must never be forgotten that the main and most lasting preoccupation of the Stewart monarchs was their country's independence, especially of England, and for this purpose a strong hold had to be maintained on the Highlands. For in spite of the fine record in the Bannockburn wars of the Bishop of Moray, who exhorted his people to fight for their country as they would for Heaven, the Chiefs and their clansmen were still the surest and largest reservoir of force in any threat of danger to that central aim.

Alexander was by temperament a soldier rather than a politician. His attacks were direct. He challenged the authority of the Bishop's Court, he defied excommunication, a rare defiance of his day, he led bands of resisters who refused to pay tithes, he raided Church lands and cattle to recover tithes seized by violence, and finally he burned the symbol of the power he hated, the ' Lantern of the North '.

All this successively and cumulatively. But he began with a sincere attempt to meet his opponent on the ground of law and order. In a case of dispute over some lands claimed both by himself as King's Lieutenant and by the Bishop, he summoned the Bishop, another Alexander (Bur of Moray), to appear at his Court of Chamberlaine Aire, to show proof of his title. That is to say he attempted legally to establish his own Court as the undisputed and supreme seat of the law north of the Waters of Forth. He failed, and secular power never returned to the Highlands. If he had succeeded he would have been a national hero, a kind of Celtic Garibaldi ; thwarted, he ended in wanton destruction and ravage, and his true name is forgotten ; he is remembered in Scottish history only by his nickname of the Wolfe of Badenoch.

Fifty years after his death, the supreme power coveted by these two champions had passed almost completely into the hands of the Church. The Bishops' Courts were supreme in the north. They were to remain supreme for yet another hundred years, and to yield then only to a power whose future predominance was unsuspected by King, Wolfe, and Bishop alike, the Third Estate. But by that time the centre of the battle had shifted ; it was no longer a struggle between Church and nobles, but between King and Commons.

It is more difficult to understand Alexander's curious effort to combine the establishment of Courts of law with the leadership of the lawless Katerans, but it is probable that this activity also began in the name and style of justice. There had been pretty constant rebellion, punished by confiscation of land and vassals, in the North, and in the confusion the Katerans had suffered. There was room to gather and guide them in the name of the Stewart King, and

'Alasdhair Mhor Makin Re '—' Big Alasdhair, the Son of the King '
—knew, as the Stewarts have always known, how to make men follow
him.   But the truth is that Alexander was driven into lawlessness.
It was just as much the business of the Churchmen to inculpate him
in violence as it was his to discredit and diminish them.   Men
remember that the Wolfe burned the Cathedral of Moray in 1390,
but they forget what it was that the Bishop burned at the Stannyng
Stanes of Easter Kyngucy, ten years before, when he put into a large
fyre made for the purpose, and in the presence of his peers, tenants,
freeholders, and vassals, assembled to hear justice declared, Alexander's writ and decree, on the same day that it had been
delivered at his Court as ' King's Lieutenant in the Northern Parts '.
Alexander's authority never recovered from that ' ordeal by fire ',
and it is hardly surprising to find that he was deprived of his
Lieutenancy at the instance of the friends of the Bishop's party, on
the ground of neglect and inefficiency, just before he took his final
revenge.

Unable to assert his power by law, he asserted it by violence ;
thwarted in his authority, he defied the authority that suppressed him.
And it is clear that in all this he allied himself with the enemies of the
Anglo-Norman, with the Jarls of Orkney and the last defenders of
Celtic nationality, the Lords of the Isles.   Indeed, Alexander Lord
of the Isles repeated in 1402 the Wolfe's exploit of burning the
Cathedral, and reaped the same failure.   It is doubtful if either of
them visualized more than a campaign against a local enemy.   They
can have had little or no idea of effecting a counter-offensive against
the long and strong reach of Papal power and influence.   For the
nature of the struggle was very far-reaching, and the issues far too
vital for the Church to risk defeat or check.   On the continent of
Europe the Crescent was momentarily in the ascendant ; the battle
of Kossovo was fought in 1389, and the standard of the Turk was to
wave there until the year 1912, an extraordinary example of modern
re-statement.   Wars of Cross and Crescent were still raging in
Spain, and the issue was not yet out of doubt.   It was essential for
Rome to hang on to every possible foothold, every pawn in the game,
and Scotland was such a pawn.   To be able to smooth the path of
France in her wars with England by flinging the Scots across the
Border and so ' creating a diversion ', or vice versa, was a proved
winning move ; the Church could not afford to lose her pawn.

How clearly Alexander was aware of this or kept it in view it is
impossible to say.   He could not in any case have acted effectually
on a scale so wide.   His hatred and rebellion were primarily
instinctive, but he must have had some inkling of the real significance
of the supremacy of Rome in his country.   The ding-dong battles of
Scottish Church and Sovereigns against the establishment of a Papal
legate in their country are matter of history, and even when his entry

was secured, the powers of the Legate were limited and his jurisdiction expressly bounded on the north by the Water of Forth. There were sound secular grounds for the fight for religious independence.

In considering the reasons why Alexander Stewart made of himself a ' vessel of wrath ', it is impossible to leave these considerations out of account. But it is clear that his impulses were largely personal and temperamental. It is improbable that they arose from religious motives at all. The Church and the Norman-feudal *milieu* in which it flourished stood for ' law and order ', imposed from above ; the Wolfe was a born individualist and rebel ; they had learned ways of circumlocution and peaceful persuasion, of subtlety and intrigue ; he was direct, aggressive, violent. They stood for officialdom, for a wide organization, and he for the personal relation, as between the Chief and his clansmen. Above all, they wished to use his country for their own ends, not as an end in itself. He felt the poison of that attitude for himself and his people ; the hemming-in, the strangle-hold. And he made himself a ' vessel of wrath '. ' Some men have to be bombs, to explode and make breaches in the walls that shut life in. Blind, havoc-working bombs. . . .'

The real relation of the Wolfe to contemporary Scotland is becoming clearer for a variety of reasons. The tide of the feudal-imperial idea, the Anglo-Norman idea that has dominated our island for nearly nine hundred years, and the world, of course, for much longer, is receding. As it recedes the map of conquest is laid bare, showing some obstructions swept away and others merely submerged and sticking there in the rocky bones of the land. The Grampians are such a rocky bone. The Highlands have never been assimilated. They remain ' incompatibles with British civilization ', just as the Scots remain colonially-minded rather than imperially-minded as a people. British civilization does not know what to do with the lonely places ; it evacuates St. Kilda. It does not know what to do with the men these places breed ; they become outlaws and emigrants. Karel Capek, writing in 1925, speaks over and over again of the desolation and ruin of Scotland and of the Highlands. The tide of British civilization has ebbed from them and left them derelict, a ' distressed area '. That tide was in its early flow in Scotland when it caught the Wolfe, and the story of his unavailing struggle with it is the story of the man. It is obvious that he saw it, that indeed it was, at that time, merely a succession of waves from the southern half of the kingdom, waves that continually increased in volume and power, of men who represented a different idea, another species of growth, in religion, in government, and in social life—a foreign civilization, in fact.

It was a little country that the Wolfe fought for, ' about the size of Palestine ', but it is permissible for a Scot, under present circum-stances, to speculate as to just what was lost by its liquidation. The

Wolfe was destined to go under, but the fight he fought is not finished.

The Wolfe was the champion in whom the psychology and principles of a disappearing and little-known period of Scottish history finally confronted and were overcome by new historical forces which—though they seem to-day to be finishing their course—have since conditioned Scottish life to such an extent that it is now difficult to think outside them at all, and realize in any vital fashion the very ' other way of life ' embodied in the Wolfe.

The ease with which official history's neglect of the Wolfe of Badenoch can be excused on the ground that he contributed nothing to subsequent development, and is therefore irrelevant to the course of Scottish history—and the difficulty lying in the way of entering into such a personality as his, and realizing the spirit that animated him—can be strikingly paralleled in another case : that of Rousseau, of whom a recent writer has said in terms that, with due allowance for the different period in which he lived, and the fact that he was a man of action and not a writer, are for the most part just as applicable to the Wolfe's case :

> ' Rousseau's thinking belongs entirely to the pre-industrial age . . . his whole effort was to avoid it. . . . Economic forces have swept Rousseau's ideal into seeming oblivion. But that is no argument against the ideal, least of all in the case of Rousseau, whose contention from the beginning was that unless men were prepared to make a moral effort to withstand the advance of a false " civilization ", they must face a future of continuous degeneration. . . . It was treated as a delightful paradox by his contemporaries. But there is nothing at all delightful in the paradox by which those who have belatedly become sensitive to some of the shortcomings of " civilization " against which Rousseau warned them two hundred years ago should denounce him as the author of their woes. He stands clean outside the epoch from which they suffer. On him, least of all men, can be justly fastened any moral responsibility for the disease of modern civilization, social or political. Thus it is, in one sense, Rousseau has been irrelevant to the social and political history of the epoch that followed him. The main deter-minants of that history have been precisely those which he deliberately ignored. For his position, consciously taken and bravely held, was that if these were to be determinants history could not be a moral process and he, for his part, would have nothing to do with it on such terms. Therefore, to charge him with having no guidance to give in the problems of practical government in the nineteenth century, as Morley did, is in fact merely to confirm his own prescience. He was not, and could not be, concerned with showing men the way out of the bog into the morass. His mission, as he understood it, had been to show them how to keep out of the treacherous country altogether ; to require of him that he should be the guide on the path to perdition was unreasonable. He would, moreover, have retorted that the effort necessary to get out of the slough was precisely the same effort that was necessary to avoid it altogether ; and that to postpone it would not alter the nature of the effort required, though it might increase the magnitude of the obstacles. As Mr. Cobham points out, " the idea

of Progress is certainly not one which we can attribute to Rousseau ". Nevertheless, it is precisely this idea of automatic progress which, in some of its protean forms, the hostile critics of Rousseau—with the conspicuous exception of Morley—seek to father on him. That is because the idea of progress is still an element in the intellectual climate of the modern age. Because we cannot think ourselves free of the idea of Progress, whether we are for or against Rousseau personally, we unconsciously insist on dragging him into this alien circle of ideas and making him speak the language.'

It is only another effect of this ubiquitous sense of Progress that makes it difficult for most people to conceive of the Wolfe as other than a mere barbarian, only instinctively opposed to the forces against which he contended and with no real understanding of what was toward. The fact is that he was a typical man of action, but as intelligent, as far-seeing, and as civilized as our contemporary men of action—as, for example, the late Earl Haig.

CHAPTER V

ON SEEING SCOTLAND WHOLE

' I am come of the seed of the people. . . .
And because I am of the people
I understand the people.'
PADRAIG PEARSE : *The Rebel.*

' A wild corner, neglected and unknown . . . a mountain-land which
remains as created, unaltered by the hand of man—the land " in God's own
holding "—bounded by the line where the shepherd's crook supplants the
plough ; where heather and bracken repel corn, cattle, and cultivation. A
region of lonely moorland, glorious in all its primeval beauty.'—ABEL CHAP-
MAN : *Bird Life of the Borders.*

' Ma la vita mortal poi che la bella
Giovinezza spari, non si colura
D'altra luce giammai, ne d'altra aurora.

(' But mortal life, after the beautiful day of youth has disappeared, is never
again coloured with another light nor with another dawn.')—LEOPARDI :
Il Tramonto della Luna.

MY FIRST bit of luck was, as I have said, to be born in the wonderful
little Border burgh of Langholm in Dumfriesshire, and, since the
' Lucky ' in my title, of course, embraces both good luck and bad
luck,[1] my first bit of bad luck coincided with my first introduction to
my native land, for my mother wrapped me well in a Shetland shawl
and took me to the door to see—but, alas ! my infant eyesight could
not carry so far, nor, if I could have seen, would my infant brain have
understood—the most unusual sight of the Esk frozen over so hard
that carts and horses could go upon it for twenty miles as upon a
road, and the whole adult population were out skating upon it all day
and, by the light of great bonfires, at night. That, I think, has not
happened since—nor anything approaching it ; and there was I,
poor little mite, so unfortunate as to be unable to see it, though I was
held outside for the purpose.

It was some fourteen months later that I was caught in the act of

[1] I am afraid I am rather of Goethe's view that ' everything on earth can
be endured, except a succession of happy days '.

Alles in der Welt lässt sich ertragen
Nur nicht eine Reiche von schönen Tagen.

The motto on one of Cunninghame-Graham's books is

El mas seguro don de la fortuna
Es no lo haber tenido vez alguna.

That is to say, ' The most sure gift of fortune is not to have had it not once '
In that sense the readers of this book may well feel that I have been ver
surely a darling of fortune.

trying to commit my first murder—attempting, in short, to smash in
the head of my newly-born brother with a poker, and, when I was
disarmed, continuing to insist that, despite that horrible red-faced
object, I ' was still Mummy's boy, too '.

My boyhood was an incredibly happy one. Langholm was,
indeed—and presumably still is—a wonderful place to be a boy in.

Scotland is not generally regarded as a land flowing with milk and
honey—and I have lived in diverse parts of it long enough now to
know that it is seldom, perhaps, that it presents itself in that
guise. Nevertheless, it can do so at times, and probably does so far
more frequently than is commonly understood. It certainly did so
in my boyhood—with a bountifulness so inexhaustible that it has
supplied all my subsequent poetry with a tremendous wealth of
sensuous satisfaction, a teeming gratitude of reminiscence, and that
I have still an immense reservoir to draw upon. My earliest
impressions are of an almost tropical luxuriance of Nature—of great
forests, of honey-scented heather hills, and moorlands infinitely rich
in little-appreciated beauties of flowering, of animal and insect life,
of strange and subtle relationships of water and light—

> The recurrent vividness of light and water
> Through every earthly change of mood and scene,

and of a multitude of rivers, each with its distinct music and each
catering in the most exciting way for hosts of the most stimulating
and wholesome pleasures a fellow can know in the heyday of his
youth—ducking, guddling,[1] girning,[2] angling, spearing eels, and
building islands in midstream and playing at Robinson Crusoe. As
I have said of the Esk in one of my poems :

> Cut water. Perfection of craft concealed
> In effects of pure improvisation.
> Delights of dazzle and dare revealed
> In instant inscapes of fresh variation.
>
> Exhilarating, effortless, divinely light
> In apparent freedom, yet reined by unseen
> And ubiquitous disciplines ; darting, lint-white,
> Fertile in impulse, in control—keen.
>
> Pride of play in a flourish of eddies,
> Bravura of blowballs, and silver digressions,
> Ringing and glittering she swirls and steadies,
> And moulds each ripple with secret suppressions.

These were, indeed, the champagne days—these long, enchanted
days on the Esk, the Wauchope, and the Ewes—

> Vivid and impulsive in crystalline splendour,
> Cold and seething champagne,

---

[1] Catching fish by hand.
[2] Catching fish by slipping a wire noose over them, and then jerking them
out of the water.

and the thought of them to-day remains as intoxicating as they must have been in actual fact all those years ago. I have been ' mad about Scotland ' ever since.

There were scores upon scores of animals and birds I knew far better then than I now know the domestic cat,[1] which is the only specimen of the ' lower animals ' of which I see much in the lean days upon which I have fallen—and not only I ; a wholesale alienation and reduction of mankind to familiarity only with their own ' miserable matter ', as if it were a second and far more drastic and irrevocable expulsion from the Garden of Eden. My eye may, perhaps, still seek out and recognize and appreciate a dozen or so wild flowers in the course of a year, but my memory recalls—with a freshness and a fullness of detail with which such living specimens cannot vie at all—hundreds I have not seen for over thirty years. My poetry is full of these memories—of a clump of mimulus ' shining like a dog's eyes with all the world a bone ' ; of the quick changes in the Esk that in a little stretch would far outrun all the divers thoughts of Man since Time began ; of the way in which, as boys, with bits of looking-glass we used to make the sun jump round and round about us ; of

> . . . the thunder-plump,
> The moss-boil on the moor, the white-topped tide,
> A tow-gun frae the boon-tree,

the orchid that smells like cherry-pie ; ' the common buds o' thrift ', the sun ' when its rays in the grey lift (sky) blinter like honesty ' ; an old land whose ' hillsides lirk like elephant skins as we gang by ! ' of the ' last dark reid crawberries under the firs ' ; of ' a great fish *contra nando incrementum* ' ; of ' the way a wild duck when she hears the thunder dances to her own Port a Beul ' ; of charms of goldfinches on the thistles and hardheads, a cock siskin singing in a spruce, crossbills busy with the rowans, a big crop of beechmast attracting countless bramblings we'll hear ' breezing ' before they leave for the North again, a group of hungry waxwings stripping a briar of its hips in less time than it takes to write these words ; a yellow-browed warbler ; four grey shrikes ; milk-wort and bog-cotton ; corbie oat and corcolet and doulie water ' that like sheepeik seeps through the duffie peats ' ; sundew and butterwort. Well might I sing

[1] It throws a curious light on modern Scotland to know that a census of Edinburgh school-children in 1938 revealed that a very high percentage had never seen a live cow or sheep. Glasgow children evacuated to country districts at first ' looked at their porridge and milk with suspicion, and one or two refused it. After a few days, all supped their porridge with obvious re'ish.' Most of the children fitted in quickly to the ways of rural life and soon showed a marked improvement in appearance and physique. We are in a different world altogether from that in which a pig attached itself to Sir Walter Scott and gambolled about him whenever it was able to.

remembering all these things and a million more from that marvellous
boyhood :

> A whistle frae the elm,
> A spout-gun frae the hemlock,
> And, back in this auld realm,
> Dry leafs of dishielogie [1]
> To smoke in a partan's tae [2]
> And you've me in your creel again
> Brim or shallow, bauch or bricht,
> Singin' in this mornin',
> Corrieneuchin' a' the nicht.

Above all, when I think of my boyhood, my chief impression is of the
amazing wealth of colour.   A love of colour has been one of the most
salient characteristics of Scots poetry from the earliest period in our
literary history down to the best work of our contemporary poets,
and I have celebrated it again and again in my own work, since, as I
say in one lyric :

> I had the fortune to live as a boy
> In a world a' columbe and colour-de-roy
> As gin I'd had Mars for the land o' my birth
> Instead o' the Earth.

> Nae maitter hoo faur I've travelled sinsyne
> The cast o' Dumfriesshire's aye in me like wine ;
> And my sangs are gleids [3] o' the candent spirit
> Its sons inherit.

I must end these paragraphs on a still less familiar note, perhaps,
for what I remember above all else of these boyhood days is the
wealth of wild fruit.   Many a great basket of blaeberries I gathered
on the hills round Langholm (hills, as Sir G. M. Trevelyan says,
' Like the procession of long primæval ages that is written in tribal
mounds, Roman roads, and Border towers ') ; then there were the
little hard black cranberries, and—less easy to gather since they
grow in swampy places—the speckled crane-berries, but above all,
in the Langfall and other woods in the extensive policies of the Duke
of Buccleuch, there were great stretches of wild raspberry bushes,
the fruit of which the public were allowed to pick, and many a splendid
boiling of jam ' I gathered there—gathering more than the raw
material of jam, too, for, as I cry in one of my poems :

> And hoo should I forget the Langfall
> On mornings when the hines [4] were ripe, but een [5]
> Ahint the glintin' leafs were brichter still
> Than sunned dew on them, lips reider than the fruit,
> And I filled baith my basket and my hert
> Mony and mony a time ?

---

[1] Tussilago.   [2] A cutty pipe.   [3] Gleids = sparks.
[4] Hines = rasps.   [5] Een = eyes.

Or I would come cycling back into Langholm down the Wauchope road with a pillowslipful of crab-apples (as at other times a basket of plovers' eggs) on my carrier; and again there was the Scrog Nut Wood, shaking its bunches of nuts like clenched fists in the windy sunlight.

I have travelled most of Europe since I left Langholm—been in Macedonia, Greece, Italy, France, Spain, Holland, Austria, Cornwall, the Faroe Islands—but I have nowhere seen loveliness so intense and so diverse crowded into so small a place. Langholm presents all the manifold and multiform grandeur and delight of Scotland in miniature—as if quickened and thrown into high relief by the proximity of England.

Another thing about Langholm. There is an annual Common-riding, and amongst the emblems that are carried in procession through the streets in which I used to play ' Joch Shine the Light ' in the blue twilight of so long ago are—in addition to the Crown of Roses—an eight-foot thistle and a barley bannock with a salt herring nailed to it, with a twelvepenny nail, and all the children carry heather besoms. In the same way I was always determined that in whatever work I might do, the emblems of my nationality would figure second to none.

Another poet—Thomas Scott Cairncross, who was, when I was a boy, minister of the church my parents attended, and to whom in my early days I owed a great deal, since he introduced me to the work of many poets (some of whom subsequently became great personal friends of my own), such as T. Sturge Moore, Bliss Carman, Thomas MacDonagh, Joseph Mary Plunkett, Padraic Pearse, Eithne Carberry, and many others, but who subsequently ceased to be friendly with me because he was of fastidious upper-class temper, while my work from the beginning was Socialistic and anti-Christian, so that any association with it was likely to compromise his chances of ministerial promotion and the degree of D.D., while the fact that from the very outset my work attracted far more attention, and in important quarters at that, than his had ever done, chagrined him sorely and, on the part of a working-man's son, affected him as a piece of intolerable presumption—wrote of Langholm as follows :

> It lies by the heather slopes
> Where God spilt the wine of the moorland
> Brimming the beaker of hills.   Lone it lies,
> A rude outpost : challenging stars and dawn,
> And down from remoteness
> And the Balladland of the Forest
> The Pictish Esk trails glory,
> Rippling the quiet eaves
> With the gold of the sun.
>
> Here casts the angler
> Half-hid in shadow ; his eyes

Veiled in rapt contemplation,
Where raider and reiver darted and harried.
Those mild terrible eyes
Came down from Flodden.

He hints and bends over the crystal waters
In large content,
The Roman road all empty
By Death's stern, sure outlawing,
With here in great spaces of the wind and sunshine
Life at the full.

O Border shadow!
A silhouette of silence and old years
Ever abide ; now the clang of the long day over,
The little town shall fold itself to rest
With through its dreams the chequered river gleaming
In luminous peace!

I thought that was great stuff when I was a boy of twelve to fourteen, not recognizing then that what really attracted me to Cairncross's work was his technical experimentation, with Henley's rhymeless rhythms, and that I was very soon to recognize in myself a spirit to which such backward-looking resignationism and sentimental dreaming were utterly false and foreign.

My parents, as I have indicated in what I say of my freedom to read anything and everything I cared to, never put any pressure on me, though they were themselves intensely religious people, and they knew before I left home that their beliefs were utterly unintelligible and antipathetic to me. We discussed the matter freely and frankly —though I had them at a complete disadvantage ; they only knew their own side of the case—while I knew that side (by argument if not by vital personal experience or revelation) as well as themselves and was more than their match in the arts of disputation (though I always ' respected ' their feelings and did not outrage them or start arguments unnecessarily) ; but, in addition, I had read thousands of times more than they had and was already a capable advocate of the materialist position. I was, indeed, already a thorough antinomian, and there was not a single principle or belief entertained by my parents, or generally entertained by the people of Langholm, to which I could give any subscription at all by the time I was fourteen, without the narrowest of definitions and the most careful of qualifications.

What I did take an unholy delight in, however, was the eternal petty squabbling and incredible malignity perpetually manifested in Church affairs ! That was a constant joy to me ! So were some of the ministers I remember—one (the one who baptized me) going through the streets with top hat and flying coat-tails, who kept a clay pipe in half the homes of his congregation, ready to smoke when he visited them ; another whose study bookshelves were solely occupied by

bound volumes of two very different publications—*The Expositors'*
Times and *Comic Cuts*; and a third who married a local mill-girl, sent
her to Atholl Crescent in Edinburgh to learn domestic economy, to
the vast amusement of the Langholm folk, and who took a church in
another part of Scotland, after such a time of salty gossip and
'personalities' of all kinds in Langholm that he retaliated by writing
a book about it and giving the townsfolk a terrible showing-up.

My mother, of course, could not argue. She and I were always
great friends and had a profound understanding of the ultimate worth
of each other's beliefs—the qualities of character involved—though
no attempted statement of her beliefs ever conveyed the slightest
meaning to me. She dealt exclusively in incredible *clichés*. 'Ah!
wait till you see the light,' she would say to me; or: 'You see, you
haven't been washed in the blood of the Lamb yet '—phrases that
were hardly likely to be very effective in dealing with a son whose
favourite anecdote was of a party of Cambridge undergraduates
discussing the ethics of suicide, who in due course came to the method
of committing suicide by hanging, in which connexion the classic
case of Judas Iscariot was cited, when one of the students shrugged
his shoulders and said : 'But what could you expect of a *nouveau
riche?*'

Though, in fact, it did little or nothing to spoil our personal
relations with each other, there was an incredible gulf fixed between
that humble, devout little mother and the son who was to write poems
like :

> Hunters were oot on a Scottish hill
> A'e day [1] when the sun stood suddenly still
> At noon, and turned the colour of the port
> —A perfect nuisance, spoilin' their sport,
> Syne it gaed pitch-black a' the gither.
> Isn't that just like our Scottish weather ?

and the passage in which I complain of my—

> Thrang o' ideas that like fairy gowd
> 'll leave me the 'Review' reporter still
> Waukening to my clung-kite faimley on a hill
> O' useless croftin' whaur naething's growd
> But Daith, since Christ for an idea died
> On a gey similar but less high hillside.
> Ech, weel for Christ !—for he was never wed
> And had nae weans clamourin' to be fed !

Or, surveying the glorious landscape I have described, she would
invariably shake her head and quote : 'Every prospect pleases, and
only Man is vile ': and I would cry : 'Thank God for that !' We
were, indeed, in Langholm *in excelsis* the 'hairy ones'. The best
Langholm story, perhaps, is that of a day when the Esk was in great

[1] The day of Christ's Crucifixion.

spate and threatening to carry away the Suspension Bridge. It was a Sunday, and in the afternoon, just as the children had come out of the parish church Sunday school and crowded on to the Bridge, it suddenly broke in two and precipitated all the bairns into the boiling torrent like, as an eye-witness put it, ' jawin' a wheen tea-leaves into a sink '. The news spread like lightning, and in a few seconds— almost before the children touched water—a crowd had collected, human chains of linked fathers and mothers were made, and soon the children were being rescued. One woman in her excitement, however, grabbed a little girl, gave her a look, saw it wasn't her own child, and—threw her in again ! That woman was a Langholmite of the first water. The story reminds me of one day when my brother and I were angling. He had hooked a trout and was greatly excited. My father nipped over to advise him in playing it, but by the time he reached my brother's side the trout had got off the hook. Instantly there was a tremendous splash ; my brother had plunged into the pool after it.

The old Radicalism was still strong all over the Borders, though already a great deal of it had been dissipated away into the channels of religious sectarianism and such moralitarian crusades as the Temperance Movement, the Anti-Gambling agitation, and so forth. But, on the whole, the quality of attention to affairs was still clean and clear, and at any political meeting the ' heckling ' was of a far higher order than is to be encountered almost anywhere to-day. Not only that ; but if an election was on, the local paper would be full of clever rhyming—all sorts of pungent and provocative lampoons, while local talent also blossomed forth on the hoardings in a wealth of caricatures and cartoons, quick with local point, and infinitely preferable to the mass-produced posters and other ' literature ' characteristic of elections to-day. There was a spontaneity, and a shrewd and often highly diverting (if extremely personal, not to say libellous) insistence on purely local points and local applications in the election materials of these days that are now completely gone. But what I personally owed to the Langholm of that time was an out-and-out Radicalism and Republicanism, combined with an extreme anti-English feeling. I hated the gentry—but not at all in the same spirit that my brother and I were jeered at by a lot of the boys about us because we were kept tidier than they were, and better dressed, and even togged out, on highdays and holidays, in Highland dress. All that was mainly due to my mother, who had genteel ideas ; hence we were jeered at as ' Mother's angels '. It was not for their difference of dress, or the different tone of their voices, I loathed the gentry, or, indeed, for anything they were, but for the way they treated other people, for what they, by their very existence, prevented other people from being and doing, and, above all, for the way in which they wasted their superior opportunities, and the very obvious

I

fact that in all important respects they were not only not superior to the poor people of the town and countryside, but utterly inferior. Their privileges seemed to me to have no social justification whatever. I saw them as so many intolerably rude, dissipated, and intrinsically worthless petty tyrants and parasites. Another Border man, Thomas Carlyle, called them a ' set of hyenas '—a description with which, even as a boy, I was in entire agreement, and which all I have subsequently learned has only reinforced a millionfold. Even then, however, if any titled person had been asked to distribute the prizes at the School presentation, for example, and I had been on the list as a prize-winner, I would have refused to accept my prize at such hands, and in this my father—and ultimately my mother, too—would have backed me up, as would the majority of opinion in the community. Nothing of the sort happened, however ; the headmaster of Langholm Academy was too cute, and such gentry were never invited to distribute the awards, while even if it was no better having a local mill-owner, or his wife, doing it, even that was only because the mill-owner in question happened to be also the Chairman of the School Board, so that, logically, his performing the duty—or getting his wife to do it—could not be objected to ; there would have been lively scenes, however, if one of the local shopkeepers had been Chairman of the School Board and—even with his consent—any attempt had been made to call in either one of the county gentry or one of the mill-owners or their wives to perform the ceremony. Prior to my father's death—by which time I was at a Junior Student Centre in Edinburgh and a very keen Socialist and active member of the Fabian Society and of the Independent Labour Party—he was coming steadily towards the Socialist position, and was doing a great deal locally for the Co-operative and Trade Union movements. In other connexions also he devoted the bulk of his spare time to public service, and I vowed then, not only that I would do likewise when I grew up, but that I would always do at least as much free, gratis, and for nothing, as I did for money ; and that if I could not make my living by work in which I delighted, and which involved all my faculties to the utmost—or, at least, by work which, if I could have afforded it, I would have been equally keen to make my lifework without pay—I would do as little of it as I possibly could in order to secure a living wage, and reserve the bulk of my time and energies for what I called *real* work. I have kept that vow.

How do people arrive at notions of the promise and potentialities of young children ? I can never form any opinion as to how a young boy or girl is likely to develop, and have certainly in all my dealings with children never found myself in the position of being able to declare : 'Ah ! here is a boy who has a great future before him. He is not like other children : I am certain that he has exceptional gifts,' and so on. Yet that was what many people averred of me while I was a young boy (and, just as mysteriously, I myself was thoroughly convinced of the same thing from as early as I can remember—and boasted I would be world-famous by the time I was thirty, forgetting that provincialization makes us Scots slow ripeners, not knowing that the War was coming to throw out my time-table, and, above all, not realizing that ' Scotland had nothing ready for me '—that, when I came to my lifework, I would find no *vorarbeiten* to my hand !) Some of the teachers at the Academy were equally certain of it (though others resented the fact that I belonged to a working-class family, and were exceedingly spiteful and ill-disposed to me—women teachers, these, for the most part ; women who were nearly at the stage of being classifiable as ' old maids ', and whose fathers were bankers or lawyers or something of that sort.

One, in particular, I remember hated me venomously. I remember how I rejoiced when she suddenly vanished from the School, and we heard she was seriously ill, and, later, how we all gloated over the news that the cause of her illness was that she had been ' carrying on ' up one of the hills with one of the men teachers, and had got ' a straw in her womb '. You should have heard us gloat over that like the boys in Kipling's *Stalky & Co.*

It was the men whose suffrages I won. With one exception—one of the women teachers to whom I had been particularly attached, but who left Langholm when I was about eleven, and of whom I had not heard anything for over thirty years until, at Cunninghame-Graham's funeral in 1936, a woman came up to me and said : ' You're Chris Grieve, aren't you ? I suppose you don't remember me ? ' It was my old teacher, now the lady of the nearby Manse, to which I went to have tea with her when the obsequies were over. And then she referred to the notoriety I had now achieved, and said : ' But we always expected great things of you—even when you were a very little boy '. Even the old Headmaster, an excellent specimen of his kind, saw the writing on my forehead, and prophesied accurately—my brother, he said, would do well, and far better than I in medal competitions and bursary examinations and the like, but I was ' the one that really mattered if . . .' It was a big IF. IF, he said, I did not spoil it all by sheer carelessness. So he told my father—told him of the terrible vein of recklessness in me, and the fact that life was likely to be very hard on one who was so utterly unamenable to discipline of any kind, not in any overt acts of challenge or defiance, but behind his deceptively quiet exterior, inside himself—in the innermost recesses of his nature. And, indeed, I knew myself. I was fully conscious of my unconquerable aversion from entering into competition with anyone—I was determined to operate only in directions in which there could be no competition, since the whole aim would be the production of work that was *sui generis*. The idea of being a teacher or a Civil Servant (the two principal options presented to me) or indeed anything else was something I could not tolerate. Two very different ideas occurred to myself : one was that, like so many of my mother's people, I should become a game-keeper or a farm-labourer or a working gardener ; anything that involved a simple open-air life and the routine of which could be discharged without involving my mental processes much, if at all, since these I wished to reserve for something entirely different which had nothing at all to do with earning my living. Or, again, I horrified my parents by proposing to take to the roads and be a tramp. Pressed, I admitted that what I really was going to be was a poet ; and that, I think, horrified them even more. Poetry did not pay, and they pleaded with me and counselled and advised me until we were all exhausted.

The thing to do was to get a trade at my finger-ends—a secure position—and then I could write all the poetry I felt inclined to, in my spare time ! It was a great school, Langholm Academy, in those days—I remember a teacher going to a table-drawer for his tawse only to find the whole black length of leather neatly diced ; I remember a friend of mine throwing a frameless slate at the head of one of the teachers and how, almost simultaneously, it split one of the panels of the door as Black Jock, the headmaster, entered the room— if he'd been a fraction of a second earlier (as we wished he had) he'd have been sliced in two. And I remember—when the teacher was temporarily out of the room—one of the country lads (we averaged about twelve years old in the class then) giving a very able object-lesson in sexual intercourse on the top of one of the desks with one of our class-mates, a sousy wench. We were, indeed, the sons and daughters of a gloriously ' hairy people ', with gall enough for anything.

The upshot of that discussion was that—although I had realized then just how indeflectibly opposed I was to any *bourgeois* form of life, how unalterably indifferent to ' getting on ' and ' making good ', and how profoundly suspicious of any settled mode of life—I agreed to go in for the teaching profession. So, in due course, I went to Edinburgh. I had determined from the outset that I would never be a teacher, which I knew must be an utterly soul-destroying job, but trusted to luck to ' get out of it ' without hurting or alarming my parents too much. My father died suddenly before I was finished at the Junior Student Centre. I took immediate advantage of the fact to abandon my plans for becoming a teacher. That is one thing which I have never, for one moment, regretted. I was singularly fortunate in some of my own teachers—my English master at the Junior Student Centre in Edinburgh was a man in ten thousand, who meant a very great deal to me and of whom I shall have more to say in due course. Two of the men who were teachers at Langholm

Academy when I was a boy remain among my best friends, and, in my opinion, among the strictly limited number of the best brains in Scotland to-day. But for the Scottish teaching profession as a whole I can have nothing good to say ; the vast majority of them are hopeless Safety-Firsters, continually bending the knee to Baal in this connexion or that, or grovelling altogether, obliged, in order to secure their jobs, to tout and belly-crawl, and pull all manner of dirty little strings in the most ignominious fashion, the conscienceless agents of the Powers-that-Be, destitute of any vocation for teaching, and themselves most indifferently educated and utterly destitute of culture, while, as a body, they deserve the contempt with which they are generally treated in the community—as a kind of half-men, destitute of guts or principle, unconscionable toadies and time-servers. The Scottish Educational System as a whole is rotten with Sir Charles Clellandism and has, of course, been utterly de-Scoticized and adapted in the most shocking fashion to suit the exigencies of English Imperialism and the Capitalist system, and those who run it have no other interest in the successive relays of children committed to their charge than a farmer has in his hatches of chickens.

If I had gone on and qualified and become a teacher, my sojourn in the profession would have been of short duration in any event, and I would have been dismissed as Thomas Davidson and John Maclean and my friend, A. S. Neill, were dismissed.

The instability—this quiet unamenability to discipline—this utter indifference to the ' main chance ' was certainly manifest enough in me from an early age. So was an unusual readiness of speech, and a fluency in the use of a very extensive vocabulary which came from my wide reading. But apart from these things—and the fact that I had a big head (almost like one of the characters in H. G. Wells' *Food of the Gods*) and a fine deep forehead (and it was probably on the strength of that most of the prophets made their predictions !), there was nothing unusual about me, I think. I had a fine head of hair, originally in silky curls of canary yellow, but developed later into a wild mass of stuff like teased tow and, for the most part, coloured like rope.

Apart from such little matters, there can have been little to distinguish me as a boy save the fact that I did not believe in team work, was utterly destitute of *esprit de corps*, and was never (except on the school playground at the interval, where I took my full share in all the games) to be found where there was a pack of boys. I hated ' gangs ' then as much as I do now. I preferred—save when I was actually playing Rugby—to be by myself, or to have only one or at most two companions. I was no good with my fists. I can only remember being forced into one stand-up fight, and then—by pure accident—my first thrusting out of my fist caught my adversary a smack on the nose and brought the blood gushing out. The fight was over. It seemed that his nose was his weak point. Otherwise he was one of the best boxers we had.

There is an early photograph of my brother and myself—how slight and shy I look ; how burly and self-assertive my brother looks in comparison ! And even to-day I look timid and modest—who have never known what it was to meet a situation I could not handle, who would be entirely equal to the occasion if I were summoned at a moment's notice to address the House of Commons or the House of Lords, or to lead a Scottish Sinn Fein rising ; or, indeed, to deal with any other situation I can imagine. If there was ever a man who was ready, intellectually or physically, to start from any point to any other at a moment's notice, that man am I. I am emancipated—free—to an extraordinary degree ; and have been so in most respects (save, perhaps, sexually and alcoholically) since my early teens. Eric Linklater and other writers, however, find my appearance more striking and unusual than it seems to me. Here is one of Linklater's descriptions of me :

> ' His suit was unremarkably grey, but he wore a purple collar and shirt and a yellow tie with red spots. Apart from his clothes, his appearance was sufficiently striking to suggest genius. He had a smooth white face, dwarfed by a great bush of hair, and in brisk, delicate, rather terrier-like features his eyes shone bright and steady. His hands were beautifully shaped and somewhat dirty. . . . As if it were a pistol he aimed his slender and rather dirty forefinger at Magnus and said, with cold and deliberate ferocity : " You're feeding on corpse meat. In all its traditional forms English literature is dead, and to depend on the past for inspiration is a necrophagous perversion. We've got to start again, and the great literary problem confronting us to-day is to discover how far we must retract the horizontal before erecting a perpendicular." '

That's me to a T. The dirty hands are, of course, due to my going with my hands constantly in pockets full of loose black tobacco.

I have said a good deal in this book and in my poems about the hills and woods and rivers—but relatively I was not an open-air boy. I did a great deal of walking and cycling and bathing and all the rest of it, and my memory is stored with matters of natural history and countryside lore of all kinds, but actually I was probably far more of a house-bird than any of my contemporaries. I preferred to read and write, and my mother was constantly at me for not going out more—like my brother, for example, who was always on our golf-course and earned a good few shillings a week caddying.

I never earned a penny that way or any other way, except once or twice I won prizes of a few shillings in literary competitions for the Christmas or Summer Special Numbers of a popular weekly. At the same time, though it was conceded that I was a queer bird, I never had the reputation of being a milksop, and I never lacked physical courage, though I did not manifest it much in the usual ways. I early won the reputation of being a dare-devil cyclist, plunging over bridges into rivers, &c.—my mother declared that I never went out but she expected to see me carried in badly injured—and frequently used to cycle fifty to a hundred miles in a day. I was a great walker, too, and to go sixteen miles there and sixteen miles back in a day and climb a fairish hill between the going and the returning was quite within my compass.

How my father and mother managed I cannot imagine. I think the highest weekly wage he reached was thirty-seven shillings, and out of that they not only managed to keep my brother and me in lodgings in Edinburgh for several years (of course, we both had bursaries, but these left a good deal for our parents to make up to cover our lodgings and our other expenses and give us a shilling or two pocket-money each), but they kept us, and themselves, always ' very well put on '; and they always ' spread an ample board '—much more ample than I have ever been able to spread myself, though I have had a good deal more than ten times that weekly wage. They were generous ; my brother and I drew a lot of friends about the house always, when we were from twelve to fourteen, and later when we were home on holidays, and they were all handsomely entertained. And, withal —profoundest of mysteries to me !—they kept up insurances and saved money into the bargain.

The main thing about these early days, however—because of its bearing on my subsequent literary work and my later life generally— is that they made me a man naturally fitted for Communism—a man, moreover, who found ready and waiting in himself by the time he came to write poetry a sound relationship between the political thinker in him and the artist. I had not to adjust myself in either connexion ; above all, I had not to scrap or transform any part of myself which by education was antagonistically *bourgeois*, because I had been on the alert from the very start and had never developed any such part. If I came in the end to Communism (that is, to membership of the Communist Party, instead of the Independent Labour Party, of which I had by then been over twenty years an active member), I also *grew* into it through a class-conscious up-bringing which conditioned but did not distort my view of life. My development owed a very great deal to my growing up in a working-class family and being fed on out-and-out Radicalism and Republican-ism when still a child. This was so intense that I was spared any outgrowing of it by virtue of a *bourgeois* education and conversion to *bourgeois* manners—and remained solid with the working-class throughout. Even if I had outgrown the early influence through education and so on, I would have recurred all right to the early standpoint ; it was potent enough to have re-claimed me. But in point of fact this was not necessary in my case at all—I had never allowed myself to be drawn away from it ; the working-class have

always stood, and will always stand, in the relation to me not of
' they ' but of ' we ',—and so instead of having it recur to mind after
the disillusioning lesson of the War, the War only confirmed what
from the beginning was my strongest tendency, and completed the
course I had been pursuing into actual Party membership—a
decision that had been implicit in most of my previous reactions to
experience.   This book, therefore, is not (like the autobiographies
of so many fellow-writers of my own generation or thereabouts) the
story of a man who came belatedly to Communism, or came rebelling
against his temperament, or came—in bitterness of spirit—to save his
precious soul.   My coming to Communist membership was not the
resolution of a conflict, but the completion, as it were, of a career ;
no conflict existed except on very minor points—the attitude of the
Communist Party to Scottish Nationalism, for example, in regard to
which, for a time, I was at variance, not with Communism, but with
the unfortunate limitations of certain leading members of the
Communist Party in Scotland, and with a deplorable ' twist ' given
in this connexion to the Communist Party of Great Britain by the
circumstances of its inception.   For it had never been my aim to rise
above the class into which I was born—it had, indeed, been my
vigilant determination to see that I allowed nothing to come between
me and my class—and my regression to Scots was, in fact, the counter-
process to the usual course ;   where others were concerned to rise, I,
on the contrary, was determined to strengthen and develop my
organic relationship to the Commons of Scotland by every means in
my power, not to get back to the people—for I had never allowed
myself to get away from them—but to get right under the skin, to
get deeper and deeper into their innermost promptings, their root-
motives.   The tremendous proletarian virtue of the Langholm I
knew as a boy saved me—despite the religiosity, the puritanism, of
both my parents, and the ambitious gentility of my mother, and despite
my own literary gifts—from the ordeal so many young writers and
artists are going through to-day, the extremely difficult ordeal of
getting back to the people, of rising again to proletarian integrity, of
becoming once more organically welded with the working-class.
From the beginning I took as my motto—and I have adhered to it
all through my literary work—Thomas Hardy's declaration :
' Literature is the written expression of revolt against accepted
things '.

It is for this reason that Mrs. Naomi Mitchison, for example, was
impelled to say of me some years ago in a Burns oration she gave in
Edinburgh :

> ' There are several young or young-minded and fierce Scottish writers
> who are well in the thick of the modern world, politically adult, and one
> of international repute—I mean, of course, Hugh MacDiarmid.   He is
> one of the few poets who have never, except in his very earliest poems,

fled from his proper place and taken refuge in an unreal or childish world. He has almost always lived and written completely in the grown-up world of politics and conflicts. Occasionally he has jumped right out of poetry into politics without, apparently, noticing, and this is a pity. But his best polemics are also his best poetry, and his polemics are significantly akin to Burns's polemics. We must allow for certain differences. Where Burns, in his time, could only whisper, we can shout. Hugh MacDiarmid shouts, sometimes rather deafeningly. The two Scots poets are both beautifully tactless, but where Burns— in deference to his age—apologized and even effaced, though not always convincingly, Hugh MacDiarmid sticks it out and plunges deeper. Yet, perhaps he is most truly a poet when he is comparatively gentle— as Burns could be gentle.'

It is this that leads a more recent commentator to write :

' No fresh idea has entered the nation's head since the Disruption— our Socialism is still Burnsite in spirit. MacDiarmid has splendidly pioneered here. His thought-poetry, besides its criticism of lingering opinions, is a veritable mine of the best European ideas expressed in their relation to our living problems at home. Heir of our Radicalism, he is always a left-wing man, possessed with the idea of Freedom. In thought, as in his attitude to language, it is for the masses of us that he is working. His poetry is *essentially* popular. Our inner longings, our inmost " resolves ", so long inarticulate and half conscious, find in MacDiarmid the voice they have lacked since the time of Burns and the great Highland poets. One day his work will be allowed to get across to Scotland.'

Finally, it was this that led Mr. Cecil Day Lewis to point out in his *A Hope for Poetry* that the influence of Communism on English poetry was first marked by the publication of my *First Hymn to Lenin and other Poems* in 1931, and that this was followed by a rush of poetry sympathetic to Communism.

But Scotland not only suffers from Capitalist exploitation as England does ; Scotland also suffers from Imperialist oppression in a way that England does not, and, just as I came naturally and inevitably to Communism, so in regard to the Empire I did not, like so many of the younger French novelists,[1] require to go to one of the Colonies and see the iniquity at first hand, before conceiving an implacable detestation of the whole thing. I had that—and the bitter realization that the subjugation of Scotland was the completest

[1] Celine had a few months' fighting at the beginning of the War and was lucky enough to be so severely wounded that he was invalided out of the Army. At some time or other, either during or after the War, he went to French Equatorial Africa, and got a quick bellyfull of Imperialism at short range. It is surprising how many contemporary French novelists have been startled into a sense of the realities by a peep behind the façade of Empire. Gide's political awareness dates from his trip to the Congo, and *Voyage au Congo* and *Retour du Tchad* (1927) are the literary points of departure for this phase of his career. Henry de Montherlant has not yet dared to publish his *Rose du Sable*, which deals with French North Africa. Leonard Woolf is, perhaps, the best English example of this curious modern by-product of Imperialism.'—Felix Walter, in *New Frontier* (Toronto), February 1937.

I 2

achievement of British Imperialism—as far back as I can remember, and I understood, too, that ere long the Empire would begin to disintegrate and what desperate steps—leading on irresistibly to the naked confrontation of Communism and Fascism—would be tried to hold it together, and that the rôle of the Scotsman and Communist in that great issue must be to oppose Imperialism in every possible way and hasten its downfall, while so far as Scotland was concerned the effort should be to regain a measure of Independence—or set afoot a militant anti-English and anti-Imperialist movement to that end—with the object of preventing Scotland being overwhelmed in England's imminent and inevitable and well-deserved ruin.

And yet I made one serious miscalculation. I knew that the programme I embraced made me a sort of Ishmael; I knew that at every turn I would be up against enormously powerful and utterly unscrupulous vested interests, but I did not foresee the coming of times like the present, when a newspaper can say one thing to-day and the opposite to-morrow without its lack of consistency losing it any support and influence, literary critics with a platform in English or Anglo-Scottish reviewing can say one thing to-day and the opposite to-morrow with equal impunity—everybody knows it is all just a game and doesn't really matter—woe betide the poor fool who won't join in the game but insists on maintaining an unfashionable—and unremunerative—integrity. The gangsters put him on the spot without more ado.

Another writer has said of me:

> 'The extraordinary misprisal and antagonism MacDiarmid has encountered in Scotland are due to a variety of causes—his complete break with the traditional Burnsian sentiment; the totally unfamiliar range to Scotland's denationalized and provincialized mentality of his linguistic and idealogical interests; a complex, highly intellectual, and mordaunt humour that is not everybody's meat; his contempt for all manner of established institutions; his satirical power; and, as it has been put, "his three O's—obscurity, obscenity, and omniscience". His work is full of personalities, and he does not hesitate to denounce his enemies by name—Ramsay MacDonald, Sir Robert Horne (now a Viscount), Sir Hugh Robertson, Dr. Lauchlan Maclean Watt, ex-Moderator of the Church of Scotland, Sir Harry Lauder, and a host of others. He is a dangerous person; he not only defends himself when he is attacked, but shows a deplorable disinclination to give his foes a monopoly of taking the offensive. That such a "difficult" poet should shut himself up in no "ivory tower" but frequent the market-place, the hustings, and the pub, with a cork-like incapacity for being put down and a most exasperating faculty of bobbing up in unexpected quarters, has given further offence. But all these factors, together with his inability to "suffer fools gladly or, indeed, at all", and the recondite allusions, multi-linguistic diction, modernist technique, and incorrigible anti-nomianism of much of his work, pale before the last enormity—the unforgivable sin of being not only a militant "highbrow", not only a Scottish Republican, Sinn Feiner, and Anglophobe, but a Communist For this he has been generally ostracized, debarred from the Scottish

Nationalist Party, of which, with R. B. Cunninghame-Graham, Compton Mackenzie, and the Honourable Ruaraidh Erskine of Marr, he was one of the founders ; cut off from his means of livelihood as a free-lance contributor to many papers ; and, *apropos* each successive publication, treated as a butt by the office-boys to whom most of the reviewing in Scottish papers is relegated. Even those who, with the slogans " one step enough for me " and " you in your small corner and I in mine ", profess most concern with the development of the Scottish Literary Movement—which again MacDiarmid initiated, and still, in so far as it is of more than local interest, practically constitutes—he has mortally offended by going too far ahead of the main body, and we find the cream of naive questions surely in these : Is it sensible to suppose that in a campaign for the revival of Scots Letters the introduction of Joycean methods is either profitable or timely ?

' Is it not the last thing that should be done just now, this straining of credulity both in the learning implied and technique attempted ? In other words, MacDiarmid should manifest the team spirit, temper the wind to the shorn lambs, and mark time till the Scottish Literary Movement emerges from the infant school ? '

Here is a picture of a Scot :

' Alan had a weird innate conviction that he was beyond ordinary judgement. Katherine could never quite see where it came in. Son of a Scottish baronet, and captain in a Highland regiment, did not seem to her stupendous. As for Alan himself, he was handsome in uniform, with his kilt swinging and his blue eyes glowing. Even stark naked and without any trimmings, he had a bony, dauntless, overbearing manliness of his own. The one thing Katherine could *not quite* appreciate was his silent, indomitable assumption that he was actually first-born, a born lord. He was a clever man, too, ready to assume that General This or Colonel That might really be his superior. Until he actually came into contact with General This or Colonel That ; whereupon his overweening blue eye arched in his bony face, and a faint tinge of contempt infused itself into his homage. Lordly or not, he wasn't much of a success in the worldly sense. . . . Sometimes he would stand and look at her in silent rage, wonder, and indignation. The wondering indignation had been *almost* too much for her. What did the man think he was ? '

That (the quotation is from one of D. H. Lawrence's short stories) is the sort of Scot who is sadly in a minority to-day, but every one of whom is worth thousands of the other sort, the canny, respectable, hard-working, humorous sort. The Katherine of the short story succumbed to one of the latter sort, and it was profound understanding of Lawrence's to write :

' Gradually a curious sense of degradation started in her spirit. It was almost like having a disease. Everything turned into mud. She realized the difference between being married to a soldier, a ceaseless born fighter, a sword not to be sheathed, and this cunning civilian, this subtle equivocator, this adjuster of the scales of truth.'

That is just what has happened to Scotland ; that is what the Union with England has resulted in—the general, almost the complete, substitution of that first sort of man by this second sort.

' What do they want to do ? ' one asks of all these hordes of Anglo-Scots, these connoisseurs of buttered bread, and reply with Lawrence : ' Undermine, undermine, undermine. Believe in nothing, care about nothing ; but keep the surface easy and have a good time. Let us undermine one another. There is nothing to believe in, so let us undermine everything. But look out ! No scenes, no spoiling the game ! Stick to the rules of the game. Be sporting, and don't do anything that would make a commotion ! Keep the game going smooth and jolly, and bear your bit like a sport. Never by any chance injure your fellow-man openly. But always injure him secretly. Make a fool of him and undermine his nature. Break him up by undermining him, if you can. It's a good sport.'

It is certainly all that ninety-nine per cent. of the Scottish *intelligentsia* and *literati* know anything about, and they devote all their time and energies to it.

Modern Scotland is a disease in which almost everything has turned into mud.

I know practically every writer and public man and woman in Scotland of any reputation or influence to-day, and I can think of only about four exceptions (including myself)—about four men out of four and a half million people—who, on the contrary, can possibly be regarded as ' ceaseless born fighters, swords not to be sheathed '.

And they are all on the same side—Communists and Scottish Republicans.

The trouble is that you cannot fight malaria with a sword.

What Scotland needs above all else is a stiff dose of what my friend Oliver St. John Gogarty [1] invokes to defeat the dirty little Firbolgs, the Clumsy Louts in Eire—*eütrephelia*, well-bred arrogance—the over-weening blue eye arched in the bony face. A strange sentiment for a Communist ? But I am not a Communist because of any humanitarianism ; with Gogarty I have always recognized that ' you will not find the warriors who loved to follow the inspiration and example of their breed's best, casting all to the winds for an increase of wages '.[2]

That is how I reconcile my highbrowism and my Communism—believing that all that seeks to evade the stereotyped and to prevent the short-circuiting of human consciousness is in the interests of the people, and safeguards their inheritance, while all that ' keeps people in their place ', that prophesies easy things for them, life without tears, all that simplifies for their dull wits, all that talks down to them,

[1] In *As I was Going Down Sackville Street* (1937).
[2] I am above all a Socialist of the sort Henri Barbusse had in mind when he wrote in his study of *Stalin :* ' The Revolutionary . . . is, above all, a scholar, who goes out into the highways and byways. Moreover, all the scholars in the world practise Marxism without being aware of it, in the same way as Monsieur Jourdain, in Molière's *Bourgeois Gentilhomme*, spoke in prose,' only I am fully aware of it !

all that assumes that the heights are not for them, but only for such-and-such, are the shibboleths of their enemies—and, above all, the belief that the Future lies with ordinariness, the ordinary man, as John Strachey recently put it, is the very nadir of contemptible demagoguery ; on the contrary, I believe with Professor H. J. Muller that scientific development and a better social order can tap genius in every human being and create a society in which men like the greatest philosophers, poets, and scientists in human history will no longer be, as they have always been hitherto, very rare exceptions, but the rule—most men will be of a stature like that of Plato or Homer or Shakespeare. And I believe that is coming, as the result of scientific discoveries, very speedily—the time when the earth will be occupied by ' a race of people all of whom come up to the level of what we now call " genius " '. Of course, I am influenced in this by what Professor Daniel Corkery says in *The Hidden Ireland*—that splendid little book about the Munster bards of the Penal Age—when he tells how men labouring in the fields all day entered again at night into full possession of the high Bardic tradition and rejoiced in complex literary allusiveness and intricate rules of versification. Or, as Mr. H. I. Bell in his *The Development of Welsh Poetry* says of Goronwy Owen : ' He won speedy recognition from his countrymen and soon became a classic. His popularity, remarkable even in Wales, where many a farm labourer or village postman or policeman has possessed a knowledge of the intricate native metres which scholars might envy, would have been inconceivable in England, whose folk culture is so incomparably poorer than that of Wales ; for he made no concessions to human weakness. He is one of the most academic of poets. He polished and planed his verse with the last refinements of art. His diction is archaic and difficult ; his poems are strewn with obsolete words and expressions. His themes are often remote from popular interest and his treatment of them is austere and even arid. His poetry has won its reputation purely on its merits as verse, which are great.' So it should be in Scotland ; so it was before our Anglification, and so it may be again.

As Professor J. B. S. Haldane says : ' Professor Muller is one of the world's leading biologists, and his proposals are entirely practicable —if they are adopted, the results will be as important as those of the industrial revolution.'[1] If Communism did not mean that—if it only meant doing away with a great deal of hardship and preventible pain and disease and death—if it only meant raising the economic level of everybody until it was as high as that of the wealthiest man in the world to-day, I would not move a little finger to assist the process. Communism, the one hope of humanity, can least of all afford to cast anything at all to the winds for a mere increase of wages or reduction

[1] See Professor Muller's *Out of the Night*, 1936, with introduction by Professor Haldane.

of hours or anything of that sort. And I do not agree with André Gide (in his *Retour de l'U.S.S.R.*, 1937) that it has happened—nor have I any fear that it will happen—in Russia or in any other country that achieves Socialism that there will be any depersonalization of the individual—minds ' less free, more servile, more fear-ridden, more vassalized ' than in Fascist-Capitalist countries. Gide, of course, declared that ' my conviction remains for the lord, and I think I can analyse the reason ; he stands for an established order of things, for an household of continuance with the obligations its traditions confer. . . . " The men who dare not be afraid ", for there is no spot that can hide a disgraced member of a noble English family. There is the knowledge that they, like kings, seldom have any selfish or personal interest in mundane matters. Their axes were ground long ago,' &c., &c., it is necessary to remember in Muller's words :

> ' As good a case could, if we wished, be made out for the genetic inferiority of the so-called " upper " classes as for their superiority. Whereas they have acquired traditions favouring greater " gentlemanliness " of manners and observance of legal forms (made by and for them), nevertheless it is also to be noted that there is not so much spirit of mutual self-sacrifice among them as is to be found lower on the ladder of prestige. Moreover, it may be inferred that a certain amount of selection has been continually occurring, tending to raise the less scrupulous, less humane, and more selfish individuals and families higher and higher in the ruthless financial battle and therefore in the social scale, and pushing the more scrupulous, more humane, and less selfish farther and farther down. . . . If this should be true, then a higher rate of multiplication on the part of the " upper " classes—the condition so desired by most eugenists—would be eugenically most unfortunate, as tending to the establishment of a predatory in place of a constructive type. This reasoning, however, is probably almost as over-simplified and ill-founded as the more usual belief in the righteousness and genetic validity of the social stratification ; and both alike neglect the preponderant role played, in our society, by the social environment in determining the differences in question.'

And again ;

> ' That which the " wisdom " of the past and the standards of the complacent elderly rulers of most of the world to-day regard as the most fixed and eternal verities : the class state, the Church, the old-fashioned family and home, private property, rich and poor, " human nature " (to-day meaning mainly the private-profit motive), their heaven and their " immortal soul "—all this is patently evanescent.'

Or again, in the words of Robert Briffault :

> ' The human world in all its aspects, political, social, ethical, spiritual, aesthetic, has been built upon fictitious conventions, even held sacred, held at the worst to be expedient and convenient. Those conventions are to-day no longer believed. . . . Belief in the foundation upon which the edifice of the human world has been built having now passed away, it is impossible for that world to carry on. . . . We are engaged upon the lunatic occupation of trying to run the world in terms of things and

values that no longer exist as a belief in any human soul. In politics we think in terms of strategic reasons of state that are echoes of a history that is *past*, a tale that is told ; socially we deal in terms of a configuration that is only prevented from flying asunder by brute force ; economically with wealth that only exists on paper ; ethically with moral values to which no human " conscience " any longer corresponds ; intellectually with a truth that has become " pragmatic " ; artistically with the self-expression of a soul that no longer believes in itself. . . . It is no use fancying that the deluge will be a pleasant thing to look upon ; the melting-pot is not exactly an emblem of Paradise. . . . Veracity and intellectual honesty being psychologically impossible in the quarters where they could avail, it seems of little use to allude to those virtues. But even in the melting-pot there will arise an aristocracy—there always does, even in social melting-pots of " equality ". And since an aristocracy ruling by divine right of wealth and of figmental unveracities will never again be permanently possible, the only aristocracy of the future must be an aristocracy of poverty and believable thought. To breed such an aristocracy is the highest task to which in this hour of Nemesis we can hopefully set our hands.'

But let me admit that I would like, say, Stalin a great deal better if, like Mustafa Kemal, he spent his long nights in drunken orgies with his boon companions, his ' Desperadoes ', and his women—night after night—and yet carrying on his immense work, relentless as steel—' playing poker, quarrelling, haggling, and drinking till the sun was well up the sky and it was time that he went to his office and to his work to modernize and make a great nation of his Turkey '. I totally lack—and detest—the Puritanism that goes with most so-called Communism or Socialism.

What I have in mind is what Gogarty says of the late Lord Birkenhead : ' He was an example of what happens only once in a century, the rake becoming a success. When a rake succeeds, why is it that most of us are secretly gladdened ? It does me good to think of its ingredients ; and why ? Because we feel that his humanity is not sacrificed to success.' But Gogarty's examples of this—Caius Julius Caesar and Pitt—give me pause. I am thinking rather of Burns and Villon. And Dafydd Ap Gwilym, of whom it has been written : ' There was a good deal of the *gamin* in his nature. . . . He could be tender with a lovely wistfulness of affection, and again could strike a note of such flippant humour as to evoke a doubt whether he ever knew real love. Now he is prostrate in devotion before the one and only fair ; now he declares, "A murrain on me if Dafydd say no to ten beauties in a day ! " His mistresses are as various as his moods ; the modest girl of gentle birth, the nun, the *bourgeois* wife of an English merchant, the peasant girl, and mere trulls of the tavern—all are welcome. . . . He is surprised by his mistress's husband, he is attacked by the watch-dog, he takes refuge in a hen-coop, he falls into a bog, loses himself in the mist, makes an assignation in an inn, but, mistaking the room, wakes three English clowns, who raise the alarm, goes, on a winter's night, a little drunk, from the tavern to his lady's house and has an encounter with the icicles hanging from the eaves. That's the type of man I like—Dafydd who anticipated so exactly that minor classic of Scots verse, Mrs. Violet Jacob's " Tam in the Kirk " when he wrote : " There was never a Sunday at Llanbadarn but I was there, the rest taking stock of me, with my face to some dainty maid, and only the nape of my neck turned to the dear God. . . ." '

Gogarty is a poet, too. The abyss is our element. Flung into it, as Chestov says, we sprout wings.

Or, to quote Lachelier :

> ' Ne craignons pas de suspendre en quelque sorte la pensée dans le vide ; car elle ne peut reposer que sur elle-même, et tout le rest ne peut reposer que sur elle ; le dernier point d'appui de toute verité et de toute existence, c'est la spontané ité absolue de l'esprit.'

The abyss ? The end of a whole stupendous cycle of human history ? The complete collapse of our entire civilization ?—Yes. But the terrible thing surely is that even our young men are obsessed with the idea that something dreadful is impending : they are shaking in their shoes and cursing their luck ; or, worst cowardice of all, taking other people's orders instead of acting on their own initiative ; few voices are raised to welcome the great adventure, few give thanks for being alive at the greatest turning-point in human history. That is the worst feature of it all.

Friends have often contrasted the endless ups and downs, the startling discontinuities of my career, the constant need I have been under (a need that—as I have pointed out—originated in the unsettled mode of life of the raiders and reivers who were my forefathers) to address myself to entirely new conditions, my resilience, my cork-like buoyancy, my (the phrase is from Dostoevski) ' cat-like vitality ' with the little rut in which most literary men get early lodged and continue to sit in so self-consciously to the end, meeting only their own kind and preaching only to the converted. And it has been so—I have met life on far more different levels than the vast majority of men ever experience ; I have contrived to remain the metaphysical man—and now, when the world we have known through the whole course of historical time is breaking up, it is natural that my recent poetry should have been largely concerned with so stupendous an occasion and with contemptuous observation of the general cowardly craving for safety, cover, immortality—for anything but the Abyss which should be to our spirits as the fruits of the Earth to our mouths.

Security ? Continuity ? ' I thanked the bozo for you and told him nerts.'

For it is a true enough picture of me that Eric Linklater conveys, writing of a by-election in East Fife in *Magnus Merriman*, when he says that when I ' spoke, and in an instant had his audience afire. A lamp behind him lit his flaming bush of hair, his thin and lovely hands beat the air. He was more than a little drunk, and he spoke of revolution as though man were made only to break through barricades and run with torches down a ruined street. Whether the revolution he advocated was Communist or Nationalist he was not very clear, but it was exciting, and the miners cheered him loudly.' [1]

In this chapter, before going on with the direct story of my own career, I wish to write an extended note on the search for Scottish unity as one of the main concerns of my life.

I resumed my effort to get a complete knowledge of Scotland—my effort to win that happiness of which Euripides speaks when he says : ' Happy is the man whose lot it is to know the secrets of the earth . . . and how and when her order came to be '—immediately I was demobilized in 1919, and have maintained it in the most intensive fashion through the subsequent close on twenty years. Perhaps I have succeeded. It is this, no doubt, that leads William Power to say of me in a recent essay :

> ' MacDiarmid's influence is due simply to the fact that his high poetic powers are organically identified with the whole history and life of his own country. He has an almost uncanny divination of the total human significance of apparently minor or prosaic happenings in Scotland. At every point he sees the universal in the particular. Therein he carries on the tradition of Dante and of Ibsen, for whom Florence and Norway were stages on which the whole drama of human life was to be enacted. If we rose to that conception of Scotland, we should put to shame the mass stupidities of " totalitarian " states.'

In whatever measure I have obtained it, that has certainly been my most passionate and patient life-long endeavour. I have cried to Scotland in terms like Goethe's ' O Nature, how I long for you, long to feel you truly ! For me you will be a merry fountain, playing from a thousand jets. You will make all your powers bright in my mind and extend my narrow existence into an eternity.'

The matter also had a shrewd bearing on that mercenary taking of the line of least resistance on the part of contemporary Scottish writers, which has been the principal impediment to the realization of the entire programme of the Scottish Renaissance Movement as initially set forth by myself and my associates about fifteen years ago, or, as I have phrased it elsewhere, ' the fact that though all of them conscious of it and most of them definitely sympathetic to it, the great majority of the writers involved have not succeeded in embodying the principle of the Renaissance Movement effectively in their work, the reasons being that to do so would not only involve difficulties in

[1] As a Socialist, of course, I am, it should be obvious, interested only in a very subordinate way in the politics of Socialism as a political theory ; my real concern with Socialism is as an artist's organized approach to the interdependencies of life.

the reorientation of their own spirits and interests, and an arduous concentration on the discovery of new technique of expression, but it would part them from any established (i.e. ready-made) public, and *demand an abandonment of that refusal of a higher order of perception which is second nature to most of them.*' In terms strikingly similar to those used by Oliver St. John Gogarty in invoking a lost eutrephelia (' well-bred arrogance ') against the dirty little Firbolgs in Ireland, and similar, too, to those used by D. H. Lawrence in that short story of his I have already summarized dealing with the Scots officer with the overweening blue eye arched in his bony head, George Buchanan, no dull archaicizer, but a great revolutionary (whose work, indeed, bore in it the seeds of every possible future revolution), away back in 1558, says, in the Latin of his great Epithalamium on the nuptials of Mary, Queen of Scots, and the Dauphin of France :

' Not here will I tell you (Francis) about the country's (Scotland's) acres of fertile land, about its glens rich in cattle, its waters fruitful in fish, its copper-and-lead-laden fields, its hills where is found bright gold and hard iron, its rivers flowing through metalliferous veins— enriching commodities which other nations besides ours possess.   These things let the numbskull mob admire, and those who despise everything but wealth—those in whom constantly the keen thirst for possessions is making thick-and-muddy-witted with deadly poison.   But the real glory of the quivered Scots (" quivered "—the poem was written to win French sympathy for the marriage ; he therefore uses this epithet for the Scots, which properly describes the Scots Archer Guard in France) is this, to encircle the glens in the hunting, to cross, by swimming, the rivers, to bear hunger, to despise the variations of cold and hot weather, not by moat and walls, but by fighting to defend their native land, and to hold life cheap when their good name has to be maintained unimpaired, once a promise has been made to keep faith, to revere the holy spirit of friendship, and to love not munificence but character.   It was due to these qualities that, when wars roared throughout all the world, and when there was no land but changed its ancestral laws, made subject to a foreign yoke, one solitary nation in its old home still bade on and still enjoyed its traditional freedom.   Here the fury of the Angles halted, here stuck fast the deadly onset of the Saxons, here the Danes stuck after defeating the Saxons, and, when the fierce Danes were subjugated, the Normans too.   If to turn the pages of history wearies not, here, too, Roman victoriousness halted its headlong march, that onrush which the unhealthy sirocco repelled not, and not Arabia's rough desert plains, nor the Sudan with its heat nor the Rhine and Elbe with their cold delayed—to Italy's onrush Scotland put a stop, and it is the only nation in the world along whose frontiers not without mountain summit, not with a rapid river's banks, not with the barrier of a forest, not with stretches of desert plain did the Roman power defend the marches of its empire, but with walls and a trench ; and, though the other nations it drove by force of arms from their homes, or else defeated and preserved for a disgraceful life of slavery, here, content to protect its own territories, Rome built a long wall as defence against the battle-axes of the Scots.   Here all hopes of advancing further were abandoned, and, by the Solway water, the boundary stone marks the limit of the Roman Empire.   And think not that, so accustomed as they are to cruel Mar's pursuits, their hearts have attained not to the refinement of the cultural arts.   Scotland too when barbarous invasions shook the Roman world, almost alone among nations gave hospitality to the banished muses.   From here the teachings of Greek culture and Latin culture, and teachers and shapers of unlearned youth, Charlemagne brought across to the Gauls ; Charlemagne too who to the French and Latin fasces and quirinus's robe (i.e. the symbols of European hegemony) have to bear, to the French joined by treaty the Scots ; a treaty which neither the War-God with iron, nor unruly sedition, can undo, nor the mad lust for power, nor the succession of years, nor any other force but a holier treaty binding with closer bonds. Tell over the list of your nation's triumphs since that age, and of the conspiracies of the world in all its airts for the destruction of the French name—without the help of Scottish soldiers never victory shone upon the French camp, disaster crushed the French without the shedding of Scottish blood ; it has shared the brunt of all the vicissitudes of French fortune has this one nation, and the swords that threatened the French it has often diverted against itself.   The bellicose English know this, the wild Netherlanders know this, to this the Po's waters are witness and Naples attacked again and again by unsuccessful invasion.   This is the dowry your wife offers you, a nation for so many centuries faithful to your subjects and conjoined with them by a treaty of alliance—happy omen of agreement between you in wedlock ; a people unsubjugated by arms throughout so many dangerous crises—happy omen for wars and presage that to you will come victory's palm.'

That is one of the great passages in Scottish poetry, and ought to be known by heart by every Scottish school-child ; but so shameful is the pass to which Scotland has been reduced, that it is questionable if it is known to half a dozen people in the whole length and breadth of the country.

I have sought, ever since I applied myself to Scottish Arts and Affairs, to secure an all-in view—to end that monstrous self-mutilation of our culture which leads most Scottish literary historians to begin their books by the unashamed remark that, of course, they have paid no attention to Scottish Gaelic Literature and to the Scottish Latin authors, but have confined themselves to the consideration of work in English or in the Scots Vernacular ; and I have sought to show—and shown in innumerable cases—that there is a continuity running through the work of Scottish authors, no matter what language they happened to use.

Going up and down over the whole length and breadth of Scotland to-day, I may not feel, as William Bartram did, ' less like an insect in those ever-growing enormities, and a thin Voice like a wind came weirdly questioning : " How ! thou dreamer of dreams ! . . . hast ever dreamed aught like unto this ?—This is the Architecture of God ",' but certainly, from one of my favourite vantage-spots, giving a great panorama of varied country, I can stand and watch how over a ridge of black fir trees the first light of morning creeps.   The water is grey and still but the ripples brighten steadily, and think of the beauties of earth, the courage of people : the earth more perfect than anything men have yet done to it, the people better than most of the leaders and bosses they have yet found.

From one of my favourite vantage-spots for a great scene ? But where are Scotland's finest views to be found ? I would not be a Borderer if I did not rank high among them the summit of Hart Fell in the Southern Uplands, whence nineteen counties are to be seen, extending from the blue distance of the Cheviots, the Cumberland hills, the Lowthers and Blacklarg ; and all around stretches the billowy sea of the green hills of Tweeddale and the Forest. Below lies Blackshope ravine, dark and awesome. Guarding the parent hill are Whirly Gill, Cold Grain, Arthur's Seat, Swatte Fell, and razor-shaped Saddle Yoke, fit companions all for Bodesbeck and its Brownie and other local tales of tragedy and romance. To the east lies ' dark Loch Skene ', the mountain lake, source of the Grey Mare's Tail cascade, and visions rise as we ponder the names of Chapelhope and Riskinhope, where Renwick, youngest and last of Scotland's martyr sons, ministered to the hunted remnant for the last time, his ' fair rapt countenance with spiritual fire transfigured ' ; of Birkhill, Dob's Linn, the ' Covenanters' Lookout ' ; and the old bridle-track by Penistone Knowe to Ettrick Kirk and Yarrow's story. Silent and lonely, it still remains, yet vibrant with the hidden pulse of history and personality. And to the westward is Tweed's Well, where in a meadow the first fountain of silvery Tweed rises from ' its own unseen unfailing spring ', still bubbling up through sand and pebbles, but altered in shape from what it was when as a lad Dr. John Brown peered into its depths and saw ' on a gentle swelling like a hill of pure white sand, a delicate column, rising and falling and shifting in graceful measures as if governed by a music of its own '. Or, again, that view when you gain the top of the Mam Ratagan Road and glimpse the Atlantic and the Coolins of Skye, while behind you lies Loch Duich with its guardians the Five Sisters of Kintail. Or that view with the golden sands of Arisaig in the foreground, the sun playing on the dancing waters, and the Isles of the Hebrides beyond ' dim unto very dreaminess '. Or from Elgol across Loch Scavaig to the Coolin Mountains, where every peak and shattered crag, and all the naked black rocks, stand out clearly. Or from the Cathkin Braes over Glasgow to the Arrochar and Crianlarich mountains forty miles away. Or from Middle Eildon Hill, near Melrose, Sir Walter Scott's best view-point, of which he said : ' I can stand on Eildon Hill and point out forty-three places famous in war and verse '. Or from the Summit of Tinto Hill, whence in good weather you can identify Skiddaw in England seventy miles away, Lochnager ninety miles to the north, and Knocklard in Ireland 100 miles distant. Or the majestic panorama of ' the roof of Scotland ' from the summit of Bideam Nam Bien, the highest peak of Argyll. Or from the Ranfurly Castle Golf Club, at Bridge of Weir, which affords, it is claimed, the best view in the west. From the indicator on the wall near the 16th tee, the eye travels round from the Cowal hills to the Luss and Arrochar Hills, Ben Lomond, the Crianlarich peaks, Ben Venue, and Ben Ledi and the nearer Campsies. Even the giant Ben Cruachan beyond Loch Awe can be seen ; and visitors may try to pronounce all the names on the chart—Cruach Bhuide, Sgarach Mor, Mullach Coir A'Choire and Creagan Leinibh, and the rest. Preponderantly concerned with materials directly experienced. Digging and delving in the Scottish environment with unflagging zeal and vitality. Not merely recording appearances with a skilful technique or photographing the various appearances of my country ; my aim always to get at meanings, to know Scotland, and to design compact structures communicating the poetry and magnificence, the irony, the humour, the shabbiness, the tragedy, and, not least, the social significance of my chosen materials.

And always correlating all this inexhaustible storied beauty of the Scottish scene with facts such as these :

In the Irish Pavilion at the World's Fair, the Queen asked the significance of the dominant monument, and was told it was to Padraic Pearse and the men of the 1916 Rebellion. She was also politely shown the Proclamation of the Republic in 1916, stones from the Dublin Post Office, from the prison where the leaders were executed, and from the cemetery where they were buried. No comment by the Queen was recorded. . . . But the incident was— in the American Press. . . . Also in the Irish Pavilion is a map illustrating Partition in Ireland, the wars waged in Ireland by England, and Irish culture in its Golden Age when it was the inspiration of all northern Europe, including England—travel does broaden one's knowledge. . . . The Royal Party also visited the United Kingdom exhibit, where Scotland is represented by a cottage in Merrie England village—but the whole exhibit is generally regarded as one of the poorest, least imaginative, and most ineffective of the Fair.

Or W. Oliver Brown's statement as the representative of Scotland at a great Welsh demonstration at Caernarfon against Conscription :

' The tie of blood between our peoples is to-day as never before reinforced by common interests, common dangers, and common oppressions. We are united also in our loathing for the immoral political system into which our peoples have been caught. No people setting any value on honour, honesty, and ideals can look upon the present condition of English politics without disgust. We live under a Government without any principle except that of self-interest, whose solemnest promises are broken and explained away without even a blush of shame, which was elected with a mandate to support and strengthen a system of international law and equity but has sabotaged it, whose military allies are the oppressors of the Jews and of racial minorities. Despite all their protestations, the English Opposition parties share the Imperialism, the hypocrisy, and the selfishness of the Government.

While they seek to make political capital out of the broken promises
and mistakes of the Government, they condone them and are in fundamental agreement with their policies.   For the Welsh and Scottish
peoples there can be no satisfaction in such company.   English morality
of the political type is alien to everything in *our* idealism, *our* standards
of public conduct and national honour.   We must cut loose.   To the
Welsh and Scottish peoples it must be made clear that Empire and
Peace are not compatible, that England's world dominion—created by
force, intrigue, and brutal exploitation—can only be maintained by our
blood and unending sacrifices, that the aggression, brutality, and deception, against which she now calls upon us to fight, are but her own
precepts, now employed against her Imperial interests.   Peace, honourable peace, is the passionate desire of the Welsh and Scottish peoples.
Neither of them can achieve it until they resume control over their
national affairs.'

Or again :

 ' Out of 30 chairmen of the War Agricultural Committees (to control
agriculture in event of war) for Scotland, 16 are military or naval officers
and five others are titled ; the balance are probably " gentry "—a
democratic country ! '

Or again, regarding the visit of the English King and Queen to the
United States :

 ' Although over a longer route, the Royal parade did *not* draw as
many spectators as Lindbergh's famous reception—3½ millions to 4
millions.   Bullet-proof cars were used in U.S.A. as well as in Canada.
. . . East Side New Yorkers showed little respect.   " Hello, King ! "
" Hello, Limey ! "   " Hey, Sourpuss ! " were typical shouts.   (" Limey "
is the contemptuous slang for Englishman). . . . A small negro asked
" Is he God ? "   " Well, almost," replied his mother.
 ' The true Scottish attitude was well expressed by one of a group of
women standing at a High Street close-mouth in Edinburgh.   " Weel,"
she said to the others, " did ye see the Royal procession ? "   And,
ascertaining that they had, she proceeded, " Weren't the *horses* fine ? " '

Or finally, what is happening at the moment I write :

 ' A Gaelic college has been opened in Nova Scotia . . . but there is
none in Scotland. . . . Glasgow's infant mortality rate is 109 per
1,000 live births.   This is higher than in such " backward " cities as
Tokio and Montevideo, 180% higher than in Chicago, 276% higher
than in Oslo, and 290% higher than in Stockholm.   The extremes
between poverty and wealth in Glasgow, measured in terms of malnutrition and ill-health, are widening still. . . . Between 1922 and 1938
" poor " Italy spent 12,500 million lire on land reclamation, 14,250,000
acres were reclaimed, 5,400 miles of roads built, 1,800 miles of aqueducts,
7,500 miles of canals, 32,000 buildings, 160 irrigation plants, and 2,500
miles of levees—a total of 150 million days of work to Italian unemployed.
The aqueduct at Agri was typical.   It is 200 miles long, cost 82 million
lire, took 2,500 workers five years to build, but redeemed a vast region
which now supports 200,000 people.   Meantime " rich " England
allowed millions of acres in Scotland to go back to bog for lack of drain-
age, to be overrun by bracken, or to be deserted and left derelict by
disheartened farmers. . . . " I admire him ", said Mark Twain of
Cecil Rhodes, the great Empire builder, " I frankly confess it, and when

his time comes, I shall buy a piece of the rope for a keepsake." . . .
Evacuation has brought Scotland's deplorable statistics into the very
homes of her complaisant middle-class. Poverty, disease, and degradation, formerly only figures which could be ignored, stalked into their
bedrooms and left lice, dirt, and bed bugs. The evacuees were as
uncomfortable as the receptionists—they didn't like " flash " houses or
tablecloths or bed sheets or " fancy " food or the lack of fish and
chips and cinemas. . . . Crois Tara, Scotland's Gaelic newspaper, has
suspended publication as a result of the outbreak of war. Culture and
truth are ever the first casualties of a war.'

And I have a feeling of bitter disgust that one of the loveliest of the
Hebrides, the Island of Eigg, is owned by Lord Runciman, the hero
of the Sudeten Nazi ditty :

> Now Santa Claus is an ' also ran '
> His job is done by our Runciman.

How are the Scottish people ever to get clear of the ' body of this
death ', which the baneful drug of over-Anglicization has imposed
upon them—this appalling substitution of an entirely false and
minimal animation for the abundant life they should naturally
inherit—a kind of suspended animation of which the outstanding
features are their inability to do anything for themselves, to take any
interest at all in their own affairs, to act instead of simply being acted
upon, to live their own life instead of this horrible substitute wished
upon them by an utterly alien and incompatible people, so that to-day,
confronted with the utterly unnecessary and appalling ruin of their
country, most of them display only an almost completely English
ability to enjoy the most damaging criticism, point out to one another
how very true it all is, and continue, unmoved, in their ways, or treat
the whole thing, as Eden treated his differences with Chamberlain,
in the manner of a slow-moving camera wherein a knock-out blow is
unfolded as a love-pat to which the pugilist rhythmically yields adagio.
I speak out of sufficient personal experience—and with a sense of
the profound fitness of this particular illustration in view of Scotland's
alcoholic reputation—when I say that the only possible conclusion is
one very similar to that advanced in a different connexion by a very
remarkable book with a profound psychological foundation, *Alcoholics
Anonymous* (New York, 1939), which teaches the great and indis-
putable lesson that the alcoholic addict cannot, by any effort of what
he calls his ' will ', abstain from his ruinous indulgence. There is
only one way—the utter suffusion of the mind by an idea which shall
exclude any idea of alcohol or of drugs, since volition, what we glibly
call the ' *will* ', is only the automatic and irrefutable working of a
dominating idea so that every act, every ' willed ' action, is the
unconscious result of, flows from, that idea. The thesis of *Alcoholics
Anonymous* is that this all-embracing and all-commanding idea must
be religious. I do not subscribe to this, although the writers are

talking of what William James called ' Varieties of Religious Experience ' rather than matters of individual faith.   The addict may fall back upon an ' absolute ' or ' a Power that makes for righteousness ', but the whole point of the book—and it is equally true of Scotland— is that he is unlikely to win through unless he flood his mind with the idea of a force outside himself.   So doing, his individual problem resolves itself into thin air.   In last analysis, it is the resigning word : Not my will, but *Thine*, be done ; said in full knowledge of the fact that the decision will be against further addiction—any compromise with the enemy, the retention in a Scotland, nominally independent again, of the English language, for example, being bound merely to resemble the contributor who thought he had ' got by ' on a diet of milk, and one day said to himself that he could safely add a little whisky to his lacteal nourishment.   He did.   And then a little more, and a little more.   In the end he went back to the sanitarium.   His ' will ' was operating one hundred per cent ; yet there was a fallacy somewhere.   It is to root out this fallacy and supplant it that *Alcoholics Anonymous* has been compiled ; and Scotland's plight to-day is an exact parallel to that.   Better perish in alcoholic stupor and be done with it, than prolong the agony by being milk-and-water Nationalists like the leaders of the so-called Scottish National Party. Dominated by the English connexion, almost everything anybody in Scotland to-day does and thinks and is merely exemplifies the fact that ' when the drink is in the wit is out ', and is as ruinous in effect as, and has no better sanction than, over-indulgence in strong drink to the point of bestiality.   Scotland is simply a big Inebriates' Home the deadly tipple responsible being the English Idea.

This will seem a monstrous suggestion, but, on reflection, it will be apparent that the most debased tribe of cannibal savages share one thing at least with the Scottish people—an unshakable conviction that their practices are, if not divinely ordained, at least justifiable and, for the most part, self-evidently right and proper and in th inescapable ' nature of things '.   This conviction is of course no mor warranted in the one case than in the other.   The two cases are indeed, exactly on all-fours.

The differences between the at-first-glance apparently ver similar English and Scottish people are such in every connexion indeed, as to remind me of nothing so much as Gilbert White' declaration : ' The copulation of frogs is notorious to everybody . . and yet I never saw, or read, of toads being observed in the sam situation '.   Theodore Drieser in *Hey-Rub-a-dub-dub !* said : ' On is hounded by the thought that as with individuals, so with nation some are born fools, live fools and die fools.   And may not Americ be one such ?   One hopes not.   But . . .'   Looking at Scotlan from this angle, it is difficult to avoid the conclusion that Scotlan has been idiotized through her connexion with England.

Most of the population of Scotland to-day remind me at once of Leon Bloy's great description of Poulot, former sheriff's officer, ' the whole man gave an impression of pusillanimous humility . . . so acclimatized to the background that he seemed to be casting his own shadow on himself ', and of the Danish novelist, Harold Tandrup, in his picture of Jonah, as ' an insignificant little man . . . his features obliterated, as though the Creator had wiped them out while the clay was still wet '.

I had little enough in common with Sir J. M. Barrie, little liking for his work, and never met him in the flesh, though he was one of the signatories to the testimonial presented to me in 1935 by my fellow-writers in Scotland and elsewhere, but I appreciate to the full the words he uttered at the Authors' Club dinner in December, 1932, when he said : 'As for myself, I leave to the Authors' Club the most precious possession I ever had—my joy in hard work. . . . She is not at all heavy jowled and weary. She is young and gay and lively. . . . She is the prettiest thing in literature.'

It is no easy matter to get to know Scotland.[1] ' Norman Douglas ', an American critic remarks, ' refrained from writing fiction until he had arrived at maturity, had acquired a deep knowledge of man's eccentricities, a broad and tolerant point of view, born of twelve years' service as a British diplomat, and a precision and clarity of expression that came from a scientific study of zoology, archaeology, and the geology of the island of Capri—studies that put an uncannily acute edge on his powers of observation. He was as interested in the inhabitants of Capri (which he rechristened Nepenthe) as he was in her rocks and fauna, and made notes of the queer characters who surrounded him, the Italian Padres, monsignors, and servants, the municipal officials, queer British expatriates, and travelling American ladies, " charming but rather metallic ", as well as the strange relations between them. He waited until he was forty-eight years old to re-polish these reminiscences and set them in a book *South Wind* which he sold outright to an English publisher for £75. His character portraits were exquisitely subtle, eloquent, and tolerant. The fantasy and subtle humour of the book made it a great success, but Norman Douglas never made a financial one, and, after publishing many more books, he once remarked sadly that he had not in all his life earned £500 from his writing. *South Wind* has won an ever-increasing army of readers, however, and during the last ten years

[1] Scotland badly needs the best of her younger writers to set to and produce a series of books like the ' Discovering Hungary ' series in which Lajos Kiss's *A Szegeny Ember Elete* (' The Poor Man's Life '), which deals with the fertility of the Magyar soil and the poverty of its tillers, and Joseph Darvas's *Egy Parasztcsaiad Tortenete* (' The History of a Peasant Family '), an epic of Hungary's Everyman, have already appeared—both the product of first-hand investigation in the villages, living with the peasants, studying them from the inside and recording the facts.

the American Modern Library edition has sold approximately 10,000 copies annually.'

Mature age, a wide experience, a scientific study of zoology, archaeology, and geology—most Scottish writers have none of these. ' We did not begin to-day to consider the Border geologically, or bathy-orographically, or agriculturally or even historically, although the history is important,' says a recent symposiast whose subject was ' The Border ' ; and that abject confession might stand for 99·9 per cent. of all writing about Scotland.

If I had the power I would have all Scottish school-children learn by heart and recite every morning (no ! that would be no use. But I would try to make them feel it as I do) :

> ' Scotland is a hopelessly uncivilized country. Compare any of our cities and towns with the little Czech town of Nachod, recently in the news because the Germans murdered a Czech policeman there. Nachod has only 12,000 inhabitants, yet its Society of Chamber Music regularly invited the greatest international artists as its guests. Marian Anderson, the Kolisch Quartet, Alexander Brailowsky, the Pasquier Trio, Germaine Leroux played there under the same conditions as in London or Berlin. And in Moravska Ostrava, a city of 125,000 inhabitants, there were 85 amateur string quartets. The elimination of modern Scotland would have been no loss to civilization. Czecho-Slovakia was a very different matter. The only way we can atone for our share in that hellish betrayal is to devote all our efforts henceforth to trying to reach a level of civilization comparable to that of the Czechs.'

An artist must trust life, and it is extremely difficult to do that in modern Scotland, where one can only regard the prevailing condition —the absence of all means and purpose for artistic expression—as the depth of human degradation. Scotland for the past century has been a country in which emptiness has sat enthroned in a way to which history offers few parallels. All our efforts must be directed towards rescuing it from the cadaver of the English Ascendancy.

> Half a millennium ago in adamantine verse
> Proudly utilizing a wealth of historical truth
> George Buchanan celebrated in the Scottish people
> A cat-like vitality, through many centuries forsooth
> Like that amazing vigour, vitality, strength
> Of the common people of Spain, which saw unexhausted
> Romans, Visigoths, Moors, Napoleon
> —That ' *Improvisación creadora ibérica* ',
> The indefinable quality which astounded Napoleon and Wellington.
>
> —It is gone, for ever, incredibly, gone.
> Fain would I cry again to-day,
> ' My faith is in the Commons of Scotland ',
> But alas ! it is gone, it is a' wede away.
> Scotland is in the last stages of the fell disease
> ἀβουλία ; and in its glens there is only peace . . . peace ?
>
> The peace indeed that passeth understanding !
> For Scotland—Scotland !—has thrown her hand in !

And Alba [1] produces a wretched alibi
At the bar of human history.

The people crawl about—decaying things,
Their clothes like damp mould on trees, their faces green,
Beyond all doctoring—ghosts, we gaze at each other
As though the River of Oblivion ran between ;
Vitality, mentality, spirituality, sociality
All sucked away. . . .

And in another poem I say :

But what have Scotsmen to fight for ?
All the ends they have fought for or are likely to fight for
Are greater foes than any they have ever thought they were fighting.
And the only thing worth fighting for
Is something they know nothing whatever about,
But, if they could conceive it, would regard
As the final horror, the ultimate outrage,
The inhuman unspeakable torture
Of their being forced to think !

In the most haunting single play yet written
About the last war, much of the dramatic action
Hung on the fact that two English officers
About to go over the top
Shared a fondness for ' Alice in Wonderland '.

It is not too much to say
That many Englishmen fought for Lewis Carroll
And the dear remembered things of English life,
Just as Frenchmen, loathing war,
With the intelligent distaste of that paradoxical nation,
Fought for Anatole France and the Louvre,
Germans for Bach, Beethoven, and Bierhalle,
Italians for Verdi and the Sistine Chapel.

We Scots have nothing to fight for like any of these.

The best way to keep out of war is to say,
Speaking of war, let's get busy on something else.
For it is psychologically true
That while we will never lose
Our traditions of heroism,
Of manliness and self-sacrifice,
Of all those things which were behind
The personalities which made us a nation
We can bring them down to where Santa Claus is
If we have a domestic ideal.

The Soviet writer derives his most important and most valuable
subject-matter from his own country and from the people. The
principal method of Soviet literature is Socialist realism. The
writer who works according to its methods must possess a comprehensive knowledge of the reality which he describes, otherwise he

[1] Ancient name for Scotland, pronounced ' alaba '.

will fall into mistakes and fail to grasp his subject in its entirety and
complexity. Scotland for many reasons is perhaps the most difficult
country in the whole of Europe to comprehend, and it certainly calls
for an infinite amount of hard work. T. E. Lawrence knew that he
had achieved what he had achieved by sheer hard work and careful
preparation, and Scottish writers might well take him as their model
in this respect. To Captain Liddell Hart he wrote :

> ' You talk of a summing up to come. Will you (if you agree with my
> feeling) in it strike a blow for hard work and thinking ? I was not an
> instinctive soldier, automatic with intuitions and happy ideas. When
> I took a decision, or adopted an alternative, it was after studying every
> relevant—and many an irrelevant—factor. Geography, tribal structure,
> religion, social customs, language, appetites, standards—all were at my
> finger-ends. The enemy I knew almost like my own side. I wished
> myself among them a hundred times to *learn*. The same with tactics.
> If I used a weapon well, it was because I could handle it. Rifles were
> easy. I put myself under instruction for Lewis, Vickers, and Hotchkiss
> (Vickers in my O.T.C. days, and rifles and pistols). If you look at my
> article in the Pickaxe you will see how much I learned about explosives
> from my R.E. teachers, and how far I developed their methods. To use
> aircraft, I learned to fly. To use armoured cars, I learned to drive and
> fight them. I became a gunner at need, and could doctor and judge a
> camel. The same with strategy. I have written only a few pages on
> the art of war—but in these I levy contribution from my predecessors
> of five languages. You are one of the few living Englishmen who can
> see the allusions and quotations, the conscious analogies, in all I say
> and do, militarily. Do make it clear that generalship, at least in my
> case, came of understanding, of hard study and brain work and con-
> centration. Had it come easy to me I should not have done it so well.

> A plover requires a ploughed field to set his flight off.
> It is a flight that needs a good staging.
> So the Scottish spirit must be seen
> In relation to Scotland,

I say in one of my poems : and what I mean by hard work—b
seeking everywhere for the necessary material and endeavouring t
grasp the subject in its entirety and complexity—may be gathere
from verses such as these dealing with a hypothetical character, th
kind of Scot I want :

> He was especially full
> Of this love of movement
> And zeal of observation.
> He manifested anew
> All the leading characteristics
> (The high spirits conspicuous as the valour)
> Of the Scot before the Union
> —Breaking anew
> ' An enchanting and amazing crystal fountain
> From the dark rocky caverns below '.

> All traceable of course
> To the quick contrasts and amazing variety
> Of Scotland's incomparable scenery.

Our minds should surely hold a synoptic view
Of all the stages of world culture
Like the ' geological staircase ' seen on our West coast,
Or like the Tongland fish pass, the highest in the British Isles,
Of 35 pools each connected by a submerged orifice
Through which the water descends and up which the fish have to swim ;
Or like a Babylonian Ziggurat, ' soul ladder ',
Dante's Celestial Ladder in *Paradiso*, Canto XXI,
The Icelandic earth-mazes called Volundar-husar,
And the connexion between Daidalos and Wayland (Volundr)
And the Indian *Mahavrata*, Festival of the Revolving Sun,
Indra the Sun-god, also Nrta, ' the Dancer '.
Or like a *mc'od rten* unissant le ciel et la terre,[1]
Corroborant, nous semble-t-il, l'hypothèse
De la derivation du *caitya* relativement
Au type ziggurat sumero-akkadien
De plusieurs millénaires anterieur.

' Believing from the beginning that, as Rev. Charles Graves (*vide* Gilbert : *History of the City of Dublin*, Vol. III, p. 243) said to the Irish, " the history of our own country and its language has especial claims on our consideration unless we choose to renounce the name of Irishmen [substitute, Scotsmen]. It is no morbid feeling which leads us to turn with longing and affectionate interest to the ancestral history and literature. It is no fond national conceit which inspires us with the desire to gather and preserve those of its scattered records which have escaped the tooth of Time, the ravages of barbarism, and the persecuting rigour of a miscalculating policy. It is indeed wise in us to soar as high as we may, seeking wide and clear views of the entire horizon of human knowledge and science ; but even to those elevated regions let us carry with us a loving remembrance of the spot of earth from which we took our flight—of our birthplace—and the home which is the sanctuary of the purest and strongest of our earthly affections."

' The sort of model I set myself when I began my work for Scotland was this picture of John O'Donovan in David Comyn's letter to J. J. Doyle of February 19th, 1878 : " The amount of work that man (John O'Donovan) got through is something awful—even if there were no more than his Letters on the Ordnance Survey—which are bound in 150 volumes in the Academy, and which contain what might be called the Biography of Ireland—the description and history of every parish and townland. . . . Nothing but sheer love for, and delight in, the subject could have made O'Donovan work as he did, since, if he had given his wonderful intellect to anything but Irish, and to any of the various studies more interesting to ordinary men, with one fifth of the labour, he could have secured wealth and position. . . . The *Four Masters* alone could be the work of a lifetime, but it did not pay, or, at least, the publishers said it didn't." Desmond Ryan in *The Sword of Light* adds : " Some years later, he (O'Donovan) and his brother-in-law, Eugene O'Curry, began and completed an even more amazing task than the translation of the *Four Masters* : the transcription and translation of all the manuscripts dealing with the ancient laws of

---

[1] *Vide* Guiseppe Tucci's Indo-Tibetica I ' Mc'od rten ' e ' Ts'a ts'a ' el Tiber indiano et occidentale. II Rin c'enbzan po e la rinascita del uddhismo nel Tibet intorno al mille (Roma, Accademia d'Italia, 1932 and 933).

Ireland in a language so obscure that for two hundred years the best
Irish scholars, from Roderick O'Flaherty in the late 17th century to
Edward O'Reilly in the early 19th, had been defeated in all attempts
to translate or understand them. The last clue to these ancient laws
and customs of ancient Ireland had died with Roderick O'Flaherty's
master, Dugald MacFirbis, in 1670, last of the hereditary historio-
graphers and scribes, but John O'Donovan and O'Curry through long
brooding over the old glosses and prolonged study of old manuscripts
had found new maps for this old and lost territory, including some
portions of MacFirbis's long-vanished *Law Dictionary*.'

My aim in regard to Scotland was to be like the sword with which
Sergeant Troy bedazzled Bathsheba, which seemed to be anywhere
and everywhere ! And I kept constantly in mind Rilke's dictum that
' the poet must know everything ', and Pushkin's dicta (1) that ' the
whole of his country's history belongs to the poet ', and (2) that ' only
barbarism, villainy, and ignorance do not respect the past, cringing
before the present alone '. So for twenty years I have read everything
about Scotland I could lay my hands on, developing as a consequence
a faculty which seems to attract to me instantaneously all the available
information on points no matter how obscure or technical from
sources no matter how far scattered, and at the same time ' gran-
gerizes ' any such issue that is in my mind with a simultaneous
recollection of all manner of connected (or, no matter how remotely,
connectable) matters drawn from the whole field of my tremendous
reading, and at once establishes a compenetrant complexity of
relationships and ideas for their literary and political utilization. I
have acquired the knowledge of many sciences in relation to Scotland
—particularly geology, botany, and ornithology—and use them freely
in my work ; I have lived in almost every part of Scotland, traversed
every foot of by far the greater part of the whole country and all its
islands ; and I have made and maintained a host of friendships from
Maidenkirk to John o' Groats, and am in constant correspondence
with friends all over the country, so that, always concerned for the
concrete case, the particular instance, the exact detail, I have always
unlimited material to draw upon, all of it dyed through and through
with lived experience and carrying a rich burden of specific memory
and of feelings that have not ceased to vibrate. Above all, I reject
entirely the feeling that Scotland is too small to occupy a man's whole
mind and constitute his life-work—the feeling that some members of
Parliament have not hesitated to express when they have said that no
man of great ambitions would content himself with a Parliament in
Edinburgh in lieu of the tremendous platform afforded by the Mother
of Parliaments in London and the whole Imperial connexion, and
our consequent British rôle as a great—perhaps the greatest—world
power. This seems to me utterly false and contemptible and all the
ambitious politicians in question very small potatoes indeed. ' What
Scotland small ? ' I retort. ' Scotland that was able to contain a Burns

and a Scott at one and the same time ! Why, that is more than all
our Imperial possessions, and the United States of America, and
half the countries of Europe have ever done. He must be a titanic
figure indeed for whom the country that could do this affords
insufficient scope.'

I have recently written three poems entitled ' Direadh ', a Gaelic
word meaning ' the act of surmounting ', and these poems attempt
to give birds'-eye views—or, rather, eagles'-eye views—of the whole
of Scotland, each from a different vantage point. Only ' Direadh I '
has been published before, but I cannot illustrate my theme in this
chapter better than by quoting from these three poems.

On the point I have just been discussing there is, for example, this
verse :

    Scotland small ? Our multiform, our infinite Scotland *small* ?
    Only as a patch of hillside may be a cliche corner
    To a fool who cries ' Nothing but heather ! ' where in September another
    Sitting there and resting and gazing round
    Sees not only the heather but blaeberries
    With bright green leaves and leaves already turned scarlet,
    Hiding ripe blue berries ; and amongst the sage-green leaves
    Of the bog-myrtle the golden flowers of the tormentil shining ;
    And on the small bare places, where the little Blackface sheep
    Found grazing, milkworts blue as summer skies ;
    And down in neglected peat-hags, not worked
    Within living memory, sphagnum moss in pastel shades
    Of yellow, green, and pink ; sundew and butterwort
    Waiting with wide-open sticky leaves for their tiny winged prey ;
    And nodding harebells vying in their colour
    With the blue butterflies that poise themselves delicately upon them,
    And stunted rowan with harsh dry leaves of glorious colour.
    ' Nothing but heather ! '—How marvellously descriptive ! And incomplete !

And in the same poem I say :

    A great inheritance ! The tale is scarce begun.
    The outer and the inner Hebrides,
    The Dungeon amid the dark Merricks,
    Cairnamuir and the Cruives of Cree,
    Lone St. Mary's silent lake,
    Broomy Bemersyde, Flodden Field,
    Lincluden, Ellisland, Penpont,
    Drumlanrig, Durisdeer, Enterkin Pass,
    The Bullers of Buchan, the Laich of Moray,
    The enchanted land of Drumalbain,
    Kintyre, Crinan, Lorne, Inverness, Scone,
    Dunfermline, Edinburgh, Perth, Stirling
    —The successive stages of the Scottish Kingdom ;
    I see them all, an innumerable host,
    As Mistral saw the ' lou regard pacifi de mis Aupiho bluio ',
    ' L'immense Crau, la Crau peirouso. . . .
    La mudo Crau, la Crau deserto. . . .'

Singing not of particular deeds and persons,
But of a whole land and a whole people,
And beginning with his native region
Ended by embracing all nations
In one *amphictyoneia*—a vision in *parvo*
Of the labours of all mankind.
Every form of work appears,
Be it for a second only,
In Mireio.   Up and down the Rhone
Pass all aspects of humanity,
Pope and Emperor, harlot and convict,
And the manifold elements are grouped together,
In one final hubbub,
At the fair of Beaucaire.
So I hold all Scotland
In my vision now
—A Falkirk Tryat of endless comprehension and love.
In the wonderful diversity and innumerable
Sharp transitions of the Scottish scene,
The source of our Scottish antisyzygy,
Grundvorstellung des mannigfaltigsten Umschlags,
I who used to deplore the incredible shallowness
Of all but all of my fellow-countrymen,
So out of keeping with the Scottish mountains
Far more of them surely should have resembled,
Each with a world in himself,
Each full of darkness like a mountain,
Each deep in his humbleness,
Without fear of abasing himself
And therefore pious.
People full of remoteness, uncertainty, and hope,
People who were still evolving,
Suddenly (my master Shestov's *suddenly* !)
See now the reconciliation of all opposites,
Das Offene, das Ganze, das Sein, der Weltinnenraum,
And understand how ' . . . der reine Widerspruch des kosmischen
   Seins,
—Die Tatsache, dass das, was dem Menschen nur im Umschlag
   zusammenkommt
Im Kosmischen immer schonzusammen ist.'

And claim to have reached a complete vision :

Scotland seen, as Socialists have hoped to see
(Denouncing all the incidentals of Capitalism,
The low knavery, the ferocious cruelty,
The plotting and the lying and the bribing,
The blustering and bragging, the screaming egotism,
The hurrying and worrying) at last
(All the sham reformers self-stultified and self-convicted)
The radical Democracy left without a lie
To cover its nakedness, the rush that will never be checked,
The tide that will never turn till it has reached its flood.
Die Kunst ist überflüssig.
Sheer Communism !

' Direadh II ' sees the country from the view-point of Berwickshire
The following passages, I think, show my method of relying upon

direct personal experience, backed by thorough original research,
and a comprehensive concern to take in all the elements in the
situation or scene, wherever possible ringing the theme down to
concrete cases, individual men and women, and giving the latitude
and longitude with reference to the world outside Scotland—placing
the Scottish instance in the widest international context—and always
interpreting Nature in terms of human activities, being alert to the
historical process, and careful to avoid the heresy of separateness
which, in such an agricultural setting for example, so often segregates
food supplies from natural, social, and spiritual conditions when it is
the harmony of these that would produce constant adequacy, and
which, while there is now abundant evidence to prove that much of
the land of this country and elsewhere is in poor heart and deterior-
ating—plenty of it indeed already dead and gone—makes us regard
these matters, and the questions of disease in livestock and crops,
which are becoming more and more complex, together with our own
health, and the fact that no people ever had a cultural renaissance
without a renaissance of cultivation, i.e. seeing to the physical basis
for the former, as separate and distinct problems, just to be patched
up as best we can.

> This is the full, the immarcesible flower
> I divined long ago in the bud
> When I first trod the rough track that runs
> Along the Allt na Bogair
> Up to the shoulder of Meall a Bhuic,
> And turning found myself looking
> Over the blue waters of Loch Rannoch
> To the whole snow-capped range
> Of the Grampians and Cairngorms
> —One of the most stupendous views
> In all Scotland, and only to be seen
> By the airman, rider, or walker,
> Being far beyond the reach
> Of car or tram.
>
> And there as I found myself,
> Topping the glen, in the presence
> Of scores of stags almost indistinguishable
> From the moorland on which they fed,
> And, overhead, black specks in the sky,
> Saw, wheeling, falling,
> Circling at tremendous heights,
> The golden eagles, safe
> In their empyrean liberty,
> And knew squadrons of bomber planes
> Would never fly there instead,
> I cried : Here is the real Scotland.
> The Scotland of the leaping salmon,
> The soaring eagle, the unstalked stag,
> And the leaping mountain hare.
> Here, above the tree line, where the track

K

Is the bed of an amethystine burn
In a bare world of shining quartz and purple heather,
Is the Scotland that is one of the sights of the earth
And once seen can never be forgotten.

This, not Edinburgh and Glasgow, which are rubbish,
The Scotland of the loathsome beasties climbing the wall
And the rats hunting in the corners
Which it is next to impossible to believe
Coexists with this, and men value—*Men* ?

And then, I use my method of world-ranging literary allusion as follows :

And now as I look at the whole of Scotland
I feel as though I had Furmanov with me
And am discussing it all with him
In an atmosphere very similar
To that crystal-like, serious, and thrilling attention
Which characterized the creation of *Chapayev*,
Furmanov [1] with that special quality he had
Of being able to see himself objectively,
To weigh himself in the scales of the Communist Cause,
As I here my devotion to Scotland
In the balance of the whole world's purpose
With a like amazing sincerity, pitilessly truthful criticism
Of my political and cultural activities,
And painstaking and critical analysis
Of my emotions.

Then my precise location in Berwickshire is defined in a full context of historical and literary reminiscence :

I have come to this height as of old
In Berwickshire I thridded the ' Pass of Peaths ',
' So steepe be these banks on either syde
And so depe to the bottom
That who goeth straight downe
Shall be in danger of tumbling
And the comer-up so sure
Of puffyng and payne ; for remedy whereof
The travellers that way have used to pass it
By paths and footways leading slopewise ' ;
And fortified against the English at the East Lothian end
By Scottish trenches, ' rather hindering than letting ',
It was a difficult passage to put into prose
For an invader sworn not to step one foot
Out of his predetermined course.
But the part of Scotland brimful with life at the full
Into which it gave was the only part
Of Scotland in the past that was ever fulfilled
Like the whole of Scotland in my vision now.

---

[1] D. A. Furmanov, first Secretary of the Moscow Association of Proletarian Writers, and, in reality, the creator of this fighting organization, which gathered under its wing the overwhelming majority of the growing proletarian cadres of Soviet literature.

Unlike any other part of Scotland
And more unlike, needless to say, any region of England ;
No lusk hedgerows, no flowery lanes,
No picturesque unkempt orchards, no crooked lines ;
A garden of twenty or thirty-acre fields
Geometrically laid out and divided
By well-built walls or low-clipped thorn fences
Upon either side of which no foot of space
Was given to the unprofitable or picturesque in nature.

This is the cream of the country—probably
The cream of the earth, the famous Dunbar red lands.
These red loams combine a maximum of fertility
With friable easy-working qualities of unequalled perfection.
Potatoes, a level sea of lusty shaws and flowery tops
From fence to fence in summer-time,
Then wheat, going to eight quarters an acre,
And then the swedes and turnips
Flickering strong and lusty
In the wind over the large fields
And much fitter to hold birds
Than many a southern rootfield in early September.

No waste ground here—nor open ditches,
Nor rambling fences, nor tousely corners,
Nor ragged headlands, nor hedgerow timber
To draw the land and obstruct the sunshine !
The crop pushes stiff and level
Up to the stone wall or trim thorn hedge
Which, in the growing and maturing season,
Subside—as all over Scotland
In my vision now—
Into thin faint lines hardly discernible
Amid the lush abundance.

I bring the matter back to the type of human being involved :

And with me men like Henderson of Chirnside
—Admirable people, so fashioned that their native district
Provides an inexhaustible mine
Of affectionate interest and study of its people,
Its customs, antiquities, scenery,
Birds, beasts, flowers.
Every countryside has happily a few
Who have eyes to see and ears to hear
In this sense, and ask for nothing better.
And what could be better than to use and enjoy
These too-rare faculties and this happy temperament
Upon the soil that bred them and for love of it ?

I am always concerned to stress important but generally forgotten,
and indeed very little known, historical considerations, as in the next
passage :

Nor can I forget that the material development
Of English life between the accession of George III
And the death of George IV, great as it was,

Becomes almost as nothing compared
To the transformation of Scotland in the same period.
It is curious how little this sensational chapter
In British history is known, which sets forth
How completely, within the span of a single long life,
The Northern Kingdom turned the tables
On her more favoured Southern neighbour
—How the once-accepted, nay, the eagerly sought
Teachers of agriculture became the taught,
And the once-jeered-at microscopic rent-rolls of the North
Swelled to figures that became the envy
Of Norfolk and Lincolnshire in their proudest days.
The majority of folk, Scots or English, care nothing at all
For the past, certainly not for a past
Of mere, unembellished fact, though
They may owe their present condition to it.
And, alas for the interest, this dramatic revolution
That had in great part its origin
In a timely enthusiasm for lime
And Swedish turnips and subsoil-draining,
Sounds like bathos beside the theological strife
Which prolonged poverty and misery,
And the gorgeous pageants which accompanied
The truculence of Whig and Jacobite and made
Things extremely unpleasant for everybody.

Personal reminiscence flows in :

Now I remember in particular an inn near Coldingham.
Mine host was a man after my own heart,
A veteran of character and long memory,
A sportsman, a farmer, and, among other things,
A master-hand at a ' crack ',
And when a Scotsman shines in this,
And he very often does, he is hard to beat.

So far as I have known both upon their native heath
Along the Border, he is more efficient in this particular
Than his ancient enemy, the Northumbrian.
His Doric is richer and even racier ; he has also
The undoubted advantage of his R's in emphasis,
When, that is to say,
There is life and character behind them.
And men with a twinkling eye have always seemed to me
More abundant upon the left than upon the right bank of Tweed
—Around the Lammermoors than along the Cheviots—
Dour as is the average hind
In the low country of either.

I recur to the complete view and the balance of elements constituting
it :

Now I see all my land and my people
As I saw Berwickshire and East Lothian then,
With every potentiality completely realized,
Brimming with prosperity and no waste anywhere,
And note once more as I cast my eyes this way and that

How the healthy well-fed flickering turnip breadths
Are more vivid in their green between the woods,
And even that homely article, the potato,
When clustering over a thirty-acre field
With the slanting sun upon it,
Contributes a characteristic note.
And how every one of the streams of the Merse
Brings the spirit of the mountains and the wild
Into the rich low ground, and retains the buoyancy
Of its clear amber waters until its voice
Is ultimately silenced in the wide swish of the Tweed.
With fine disregard for the well-ordered landscape,
Its pride of timber and its pride of crop,
See how the impetuous Whiteadder churns
In the deep twisting valley its chafing waters
Have cut in the course of ages
Through the sandstone !   Narrow breadths of green meadow
Serve to set off the glitter of its rapid currents
And take no great injury from its floods.
Chafing always upon a rocky bed
The river gathers round it
All that fine tangle of foliage
You see only upon impetuous streams. [1]

And so to the Berwick Bounds, these few thousand acres
Of cornland windswept from the North Sea,
—Surely ' but scant counterpoise
For sunny Aquitaine and Guienne,
Opulent Bordeaux and the Pas de Calais,
All lost to the Crown of England
In the Hundred Years' War
—Part of the price
Paid for the lesson
That Scotsmen may never be coerced.'

I delight in great panoramas with due sense of all the diverse factors
that go to their making :

And now I am where, upon Hardens Hill,
After trailing between fine avenues of beech and ash,
And mounting higher into wind-swept pine woods.
The road sweeps out at last
Into the glorious heaths of Lammermoor.
The drubbing wings and vocal plaints
Of restless peewits close overhead,
The song of rejoicing larks,
In the air far above them,
And the call of distant curlews
Mingle with the faint bleat of sheep.
These edges of great moorlands, which open wide
Upon the one hand into sweeps of solitude,
And on the other over vast distances
Where rural life is thickly humming,
Are seats for the gods indeed

---

[1] These last four lines are, I think, applicable to and give a picture of my own life.

And I am indeed of the Duine Sidhe [1] to-day.
The heather is just touching with its first faint flush
The folding hills that heave away
Towards a far horizon that looks down
Upon East Lothian. Below,
The Merse glimmers far and wide
With its red fields, its yellowing cornlands and mantling woods,
Its glint of village church spire or country seat,
Beyond the line of Tweed spread the fainter
But yet clear-cut hills and valleys of Northumberland.
I can follow up the windings of the Till
From Flodden and Ford Castle to Wooler,
And from Wooler to the woody spur
Beneath which the wild white cattle
Of Chillingham have their immemorial range.
The Cheviots roll their billowy crests
From the ' Mickle Cheevit '
Looming large and near upon the Border line
To fade remotely into the more rugged heights
That embosom Rothbury
And the upper waters of the Coquet.

And in fancy I drink once again
—A final toast to Scotland fulfilled,
Every promise redeemed—
With one of the many hundreds of splendid men
With whom I have so drunk in days gone by.
Not drinking whisky and soda
As an Englishman does, which is very dull,
But with all the splendid old ritual,
The urn, the rummers, the smaller glasses,
The silver ladles, and the main essentials.
The whisky toddy is mixed in a rummer,
A round-bottomed tumbler on a stem,
And transferred at intervals with a silver ladle
Into an accompanying wine-glass
By way of cooling it
Sufficiently for consumption.

Time which has brought such prodigious changes
In the world below and in the world at large
Has here at least stood absolutely still.
The same old cry of curlews and wail of peewits,
Whistling of golden plover, call of anxious grouse,
Plash of waters, and bleat of far-scattered sheep
Still sounds the same unchanging music of the wild.
Black peat-hags, glistening mosses of emerald green,
Tawny moor-grasses flecked white with the wild cotton-flower,
Scaurs of red sandstone, and vivid patches
Of sheep-nibbled turf.
All add their note.

This is the full, the immarcesible flower,
Scotland, known like the music of a moorland stream
To which poets and musicians pay conventional tribute,

---

[1] Gods of the Earth.

But which few can approach with an understanding
Of what it means to an old fisherman
Who knows its infinite varieties of chord and melody
With an intimacy of a thousand day-long recitations.

Known, as often old gardeners and farm-hands
Understand the personality, as it were,
Of individual fields and gardens
To which they have ministered since boyhood
And their fathers, perhaps, before them.
For the constitution of a piece of land
Is more than skin-deep and draws
Some of its peculiar characteristics
From geological depths.
Pedology may tell us *why* a soil
Behaves as it does,
But only the rustic knows exactly *when*,
And, familiar with a tract of land, can often say
Without going to it
When the day has come to find it
In a humour to respond
To the caress of a harrow
Or when it will be found
As obdurate as iron.
But this is a kind of knowledge
Scotland has lost almost altogether,
Blighted in the shadow of great institutions
Of learning designed
For the depotentization of free intelligence,
The Fascist barracks of our universities,
The murder machine of our whole educational system,
And far gone towards that Naziism
Which is at bottom
A revolution of black-coated workers,
Multiplied in number by social conditions,
Striving for jobs they feel suitable
To their training and dignity ;
Scotland drowned under a percentage of clerks
That is rising by leaps and bounds !
And it's O for the Berwickshire bondagers
And the country folk and fisher folk of old
And many a great day I had with them
Thirty years ago now !
—*Ah ! quam dulce est meminisse !*
—We have fallen upon lean days.
Would Burns have sparkled upon small ale
And how would the Ettrick Shepherd
Who took his whisky in a jug
Fare in a time like this ?

Miss Nan Shepherd, in her essay on my poetry, says : ' Persons start
up from the pages, complete in a phrase, their whole environment
implied ', and, just as Buber used his bookbinder and his printer as I
point out elsewhere in this book, and just as Denis Saurat realizes via
his peasant mother, so here I cry :

All the clerks in Scotland are not worth one glimpse
Of an East Lothian bailiff I knew then
With a voice that would carry nearly all over
The six hundred acres of his farm
And a whistle that would carry
Even further than his voice
And not a tree or a bush on the whole place
To break the force of either
(Just as there is no higher ground between us here
And the Ural Mountains in the East!)
When he appeared at the gate of a thirty-acre field
The subdued cackle of the bondagers ceased abruptly
And twenty poke bonnets, bent over their Dutch hoes,
Pushed with renewed zeal along the wheat drills,
And the ploughman halting for a moment on the headrigg
Started and swung his pair of horses round
And geehawed away for his life
When he heard that voice two fields away. . . .

Then back from the concrete individual and the specific instance to
the broad view again :

Across the heavy-laden grainfields ;
Over the great broad rectangles of potato land,
Thigh deep in their dark green covering of shaughs :
Beyond the flickering blue-green tops of the thickly-clustering swedes,
Or the paler pastures, where heavy Border Leicesters
Or their crosses are lazily grazing the rye grass and clover ley
And tramping it hard for the autumn ploughing,
And between the woods the indeterminate line of the shore
And the gleam of the sea beyond,
Fading into the far-spreading woods of Tynninghame
. . . The sudden unfolding of the greatest of agricultural counties,
Girt about with wide waters and shadowy mountains.

If a vista of plain and mountain appeals solely
To his artistic sense, a man is obviously incapable
Of reading any deeper into it, or of responding
To any other appeal, and there is nothing more to be said.
No undervaluing of the elevating influence of nature,
Unilluminated by anything but its own form and colouring,
On the senses is intended here ; yet this is not
To ' feel ' a country, but only its physical surface,
Which might be occupied by negroes
Without the least disturbance of the emotions engaged,
But the great thing is to be able to drop at once
Into terms of intimacy with the local *genii*,
Till, whether it be the Tees, the Greta, the Trossachs, or the Welsh
Border,
All the rivers for you sound their tales, the woods shake out their
secrets.

I go on to make an exact comparison with a very different countryside :

How different Berwickshire and Wales ! The comparison
Suggests itself, because just such tracts of moorish country
In the counties of Cardigan and Carmarthen,

Sloping away as these do from the hills,
Are more or less reclaimed.
But how different custom and tradition affect the landscape
Of a tract of country in the making !
Instead of these great fields geometrically traced
By the stone walls that here take the place of hedges,
And the large substantial homesteads with their hinds' cottages
Standing on ridges far apart, we should have
A patchwork of little white- or pink-washed homesteads
In clumps of trees, each surrounded
By a network of small fields ;
There would be
Irregular patches or straggling belts
Of moorgrass, heath, gorse, or rough pasture,
The small man's more diffident plough had flinched from,
Straggling everywhere in and about.
The little streams too would claim
Their ample margins of copse and bracken.
—But ah ! there are no half-measures here,
No little corners or odd patches of waste-land,
No inconsequent straggling thickets of birch or alder,
And broom and gorse.—The symmetry is tremendous,
The treatment thorough to the last degree.

And one of the essential principles of all my work is stressed in the
following lines :

The rarity and value of this (i.e. scientific knowledge)
Is little understood—even as people
Who are not botanists find it hard to believe
Special knowledge of the subject can add
Enormously to the aesthetic appreciation of flowers !
Partly because in order to identify a plant
You must study it very much more closely
Than you would otherwise have done, and in the process
Exquisite colours, proportions, and minute shapes spring to light
Too small to be ordinarily noted.
And more than this—it seems the botanist's knowledge
Of the complete structure of the plant
(Like a sculptor's of bone and muscle)
—Of the configuration of its roots stretching under the earth,
The branching of stems,
Enfolding of buds by bracts,
Spreading of veins on a leaf—
Enriches and makes three-dimensional
His awareness of its complex beauty.

Above all, as my constant evocations of particular men and women
I know, friends who are farmers or farm labourers or shepherds or
fishermen, and my interpretations of scenes through their work and
through a thorough knowledge of the processes involved in particular
arts and crafts show, it is true of me, as De Lancey Ferguson says of
Burns, Nature to Burns meant work, not scenery, though it is certainly
not the case (though one understands the sense in which it is said
and agrees in the main) that Burns ' was too busy trying to wring a

K 2

living from the soil to note the scenery. That had to wait for Sir Walter Scott, who had nothing to do but admire it.' But it has never been the case with me in Scotland as with Odell Shepard in Connecticut that ' along the many miles I have walked in this little land the people who lived here before me have more and more come *between* me and the contemporary scene '. I have always wished to go up and down over the whole of Scotland as an itinerant bard, living by selling penny broadsheets of my poems, speaking about them at street-corners, discussing them with the men at public-house bars, and so forth. This appealed to Burns too—he envisioned spending his ' old age as a sort of Edie Ochiltree ', a romantic throw-back to the medieval minstrel-beggar, adventuring through the land with nothing but his wits and his poetry to live on. But, like myself, Burns had too many immediate duties : to his mother and sisters and brother, to Jean his wife, to the children that other women had borne him. The principal difference between Burns and myself is perhaps in ' the difficult position he was in as a ploughman become famous. He had to keep up that position : he could not go back to being a ploughman : as he says of his brother, " he can with propriety do things that I *now* cannot do ".' I have never allowed myself to feel anything of the kind. My Canadian friend, Paul Potts, has been selling penny broadsheets of his poems in the streets of London and giving readings from them in London pubs. Just before the outbreak of the second World War (which has been several weeks in progress as I write this) I agreed to take over the editorship of these, to issue them monthly, and to publish in this way poems of my own and by Paul Potts, Philip O'Connor, and other Communist poets. The first of these, confined to poems by myself, was published just before the war was declared and (a point of interest to those who know the difficulties, owing to small sales, of publishing poetry to-day, of which such depressing figures supplied by Messrs. Sidgwick and Jackson are given in Dr. F. R. Leavis's *New Bearings in English Poetry*) over 2000 of them found a ready sale at once in the streets of London and other cities. Whether, owing to war-time conditions, it will be possible to issue such broadsheets monthly or not, now remains to be seen,[1] but in any case this is not quite the same thing as I had hoped for, and may still manage to do—go up and down the whole country, talk to people in the streets, public-houses, &c., discuss my poetry with them, and live by selling penny broadsheets.

An intensive and comprehensive concern with Scotland such as I have maintained for the past twenty years naturally means that I have acquired and have at command an enormous amount of out-of-the-way knowledge—though I cannot claim yet in this respect to be like Charles Fort of New York, of whom Orage used to tell me, who

---

[1] I speedily found that it was not possible. The project was abandoned.

had accumulated a tremendous library of cuttings, &c., recording happenings all over the world traversing accepted scientific laws of all kinds or completely setting at naught the most generally accepted ideas on the subjects in question, or like Albert Cook Church, who has amassed over 40,000 illustrations of every phase of whaling and whaling ships. Yet I can never fail aptly to my purpose at any moment to remember a host of details, like the tombstones inscribed in the German language in the Shetland island of Unst, which tell of Bremen merchants of an older time who trafficked there, verifying a passage in George Buchanan, or of the wool lace of Unst, ' surely the most delicately exquisite fabric fashioned by human hands ', any more than in conversation with my friend Sadie MacLellan (sister of Robert MacLellan, the playwright), who has specialized in the art of stained glass, or with Harry Clarke or Sarah Purser in Dublin, I can fail to think of such matters as the sixteenth-century ' Vitro di Trino ', glass vessels with coloured threads, which, as Wilfrid Buckley has written, ' provide examples of the greatest dexterity of which glass-makers have ever shown themselves capable '.

> Names, deeds, grey legends, dire events, rebellions,
> Majesties, sovran voices, agonies,
> Creations and destroyings, all at once
> Pour into the wide hollow of my brain.

Yet always

> . . . specially delightful unto me
> Was that clear synthesis built up aloft
> So gracefully . . .

As I look at some of my recent poems I find that there has been an enormous extension of the instrument of the knowledge of natural history and allied subjects upon which my poetry is played. I think it may be said of me, as of Dafyyd Ap Gwilym, the Welsh poet, that ' he employs birds, beasts, and the forces of Nature as his love-messengers (*llanteion*). We find in his works a striking range of wild life. The thrush-cock, the blackbird, the lark, the nightingale, the cuckoo, the swallow, the heathcock, the magpie, the titmouse, the eagle, the owl, the swan, the grouse, the sea-gull, the crane are among the birds which occur in his pages, whether as messengers or incidentally ; and besides them there are animals and fishes such as the fox, the hare, the deer, and the salmon. Some of these wild creatures are described with a particularity and accuracy which show that Dafyyd possesses a keen eye and a close acquaintance with natural sights and sounds.' But have I not written of catching a ' Little Stint '

> After long pursuit, and with excitement shaking,
> Like a cock's tail on a windy day ' ?

And even Dafyyd's acuity of hearing must have been marvellous if it could go beyond what I say (of myself) in the poem I have been quoting :

> He knew the pretty snapping-like noise
> Of the Death's Head Moth in its caterpillar state ;
> Like electric sparks the chrysalis squeaks,
> More especially about its changing date,
> And as for the perfect insect itself
> He knew all the range of its mournful tongue,
> While its muckle bright eyes were believed to reflect
> The flames of Hell from which it had sprung.

In place of the simple Langholm list I find in my verses now the Oak Egger Moth, the Green Silver-Line, the lovely China Moth, the craiking of the landrail, the birbeck of the muirfowl, the plover's wail, the ring-dotterel's pipe, the plech-plech of the oyster-catcher ; ' an anceus or ensirus in a dish ', ' an Equoreal Needle-Fish ',

> And knew by sight
> And call-note the Osprey and the Erne,
> The Blue-Hawk and the Merlin and the Kite,
> The Honey-Buzzard and the Snowy Owl,
> The Ring-Ouzel, the Black Cap, the Wood Wren,
> The Mealy Redpole, the Purple Heron, the Avocet,
> The Gadwell, the Shoveller, and the Raven.

Or, again, turning to fishes, I sing of

> The Sandsucker and the Blue-striped Wrasse,
> Six kinds of Gobies, the Saury Pike,
> Yarrell's Bleny and the Silvery Gade
> (Long lost to science), and scores of the like.
> The Bonito, the Tunny, the Sea-Perch, and the Ruffe,
> The Armed Bullhead, the Wolf-fish, and the Scad,
> The Power Cod and the Whiting Pout,
> The Twaite Shad and the Alice Shad,
> The Great Forked Beard, the Torsk, the Brill,
> The Glutinous Hag, the Starry Ray,
> Muller's Topknot, and the Unctuous Sucker.

So much for cataloguing ! But in regard to penetration I think readers of my poetry will not fail to recognize that there are few of the great mystical experiences I have not had, and I can certainly claim that in Scotland, like Jacob Boehme on a green before Neys Gate at Goerlitz in 1600, I have on occasion been able to sit down, and, viewing the herbs and grass in my inward light, see ' into their essences, use, and properties ', discovered to me ' by their lineaments, figures, and signatures ', and have also been constrained to cry in my own way, as Boehme in his, ' Suddenly . . . my spirit did break through . . . even into the innermost birth of Geniture of the Deity, and there I was embraced with love, as a bridegroom embraces his dearly beloved bride '. Nor have I ever been unmindful of St. Augustine's remark : ' He created Angels in Heaven and worms in

the Earth ; and he did not show himself superior in the one and not
inferior in the other. For if no other hand could have created
Angels, neither could any other have created worms ' ; while I have
certainly always been at the furthest possible remove from a man like
Dr. Thomas Arnold, who, so Lytton Strachey informs me, found
Wordsworth's susceptibility to the meanest flower that blows
' morbid ', saying, ' Life is not long enough to take such intense
interest in objects in themselves so little ', and even that ' the whole
subject of brute creation is to me one of such painful mystery that I
dare not approach it '. ' Presumably ', says Mr. Joseph Wood
Krutch, ' what shocked Dr. Arnold was the absence in brutes of that
" sense of moral evil " to which he attached so much importance.
They could sin without suffering even the pangs of conscience by
way of retribution. But is not that exactly the fact which moved
Whitman to such envious admiration for the animals, who did not
make him sick " discussing their duty to God " ? " Not one ", he
said, " is respectable or unhappy over the whole earth." ' My vote
certainly goes to Whitman, and to Augustine in respect of the worms,
if not of the Angels. I was delighted to find recently even in respect
of a fine poem of Ruth Pitter's entitled ' Humble Simile ', in which
she says of the snail's slimy trail,

> Lo how each bitter stone for her doth keep . . .
> Long rainbows, strings of pearl, records in light,

that over fifteen years ago, in my ' A Drunk Man Looks at the Thistle ',
I had anticipated my friend Ruth and used the same figure.

It is just in the same way, too, that I can never fail to establish such
parallelisms (my work is full of them) as the following, in a long poem
to Duncan Ban MacIntyre, the Gaelic poet :

> . . . tales of men
> Unlettered like you, yet wise in speech and practised like you
> (Aye, even to the mental grasp of a Rob Donn
> Whose *Oran a' Gheamhraidh* is an exact counterpart,
> Line by line and phrase by phrase,
> Of Alexander MacDonald's *Oran an t'Samhraidh*,
> Tho' he could not read the original on which he wrought !
> —Greater even than Su Tungp'o's feat of writing
> A complete set of poems on the rhymes used
> By the complete poems of T'ao).

Or perhaps a still more extraordinary example of the bringing together
of illustrative material from the most diverse quarters :

> A Hindu poet may proceed to any length he pleases
> Within the limits of a thousand syllables to the half-line.
> The Dandaka metre (of which a specimen occurs
> In the drama called *Malati-madhava*, Act V)
> Offers more than any other
> An almost incredible capacity of expression.

It will admit, indeed, of the stanza extending
27 × 4 to 999 × 4 syllables
(Even as in Gower's *Confessio Amantis* the stories vary
In length from a mere mention in a single line
To the romance of Apollonius of Tyre in about 2000 lines :
Even as, in modern angling, size D line
May vary from thirty-seven thousandths
To forty-five thousandths at the thickest part
—A matter of no moment to the average fisherman
Content to buy a tapered cast on the shopman's word
With no more than a glance at the thick end and the thin,
But of vital concern to those who bring
The application of intelligence and intense concentration
To my favourite sport—who look over the sections
When they buy a rod to make sure
That the leaf-marks in the bamboo are well staggered,
Calibrate a ' leader ' (cast) with a micrometer,
Know the importance of proper taper in line and cast,
And are thoroughly posted in the Solundar Theory,
Problems of conservation, niceties of fly-dressing, *et al* !)

And I cite two interesting, if out-of-the-way, precedents drawn from
two widely separated literatures, for the kind of learned poetry I am
concerned with in the final lines of the following passage :

     . . . Exclusion from all power be theirs
Who do not know at least
Mazumdar's Typical Selections from Oriya Literature.
Goswani's Asamiya Sahityar Chanski,[1]
Taraporewala's Selections from Classical Gujarati literature
And, traversing the great stages of Hindu literature,
The hymns of each of the Asht Chhap,
And Tulsi Das, brightest star of Indian medieval poetry,
Unapproached and unapproachable in his niche in the Temple of Fame.
The teachings of the great saints, including Swami Ramanand,
Kabir, Guru Nanak, Guru Teg Bahadur,
Guru Govind Singh, and Mira Bai,
The principal writings on the Science of Poetry,
Together with the fanciful classification of women,
Technically called the Nayika-bhed,
And the writings of Vidyapati,
Malik Mohammad Jaisi, Keswara Das,
Rahim, Raskhan, Ninbarak, Usman Senapati,
Bihari Lal, Bhupati, and Sabal Singh Chauhan.
Let them know too Krisnadasa Kaviraj,
Who begins his Shri Shri Chaityana Charitamrita
With a string of fifteen slokas in Sanskrit
And quotes freely, as I do, from all classes of books
(A poet as bookish as Silius Italicus). . . .

Duncan Ban MacIntyre, in the poem already mentioned, I refer to in
the following passage dealing with our *Entwickelung des Naturgefuhls* :

You who were writing superb descriptions
Of wild scenery for its own sake

---

[1] Typical selections from Assamese Literature.

When the English were still complaining
Of the ' frightful irregularity ' of Highland mountains,
' Most of all disagreeable when the heather is in bloom ',
And making pained contrast of them
With that truly ' poetical mountain ', Richmond Hill,
It was not until the success of Scott and Wordsworth
Your attitude could be conceived of by the South of England.
In an age of brilliant Gaelic poetry, Scottish Lowlanders even
Regarded the Highlanders as illiterate savages
And the sad history of Highland education
In the three centuries after 1560
Reveals they did their best to make them so !

The poem is in the form of a conversation with Duncan Ban, who
spent his life among the deer as a stalker, and asks the following
questions :

What questions do I not ask
Now I have been all over Beinn Dobhrain with you
—Seeing the very small extent of the territory
Normally occupied by a particular group of deer
Whether this observance of definite territories
Does not tend as among human tribes
To the evolution of different races ?
Certainly the heads from different forests
Seem to fall into distinctive types,
As they do among the elk of Norway.
And are there not reasons for believing
The small size of the Dundonnell deer a genetic
As well as an environment trait ?
And if as I think weather conditions and insect pests
Are more important causes of movement among deer
Than the direction of the wind, does this
Hold good for all parts of Scotland ?   Some places
Seem to depend very largely on a suitable wind
To draw deer into them.   Yet the correspondence
Between weather and movement is abundantly clear
And there can no longer be any doubt that deer
Are so sensitive to meteorological changes
As to be able to anticipate them by hours, and sometimes days.
Then, though the importance of antlers as offensive weapons
May rightly be questioned, is it not probable
Casualties would be far more numerous and severe
But for the way in which the branched points
Engage and parry one another ?   If so
Antlers as normally grown would have a survival value.
But is there not a closer relation between horns
And the sexual psychology than is involved
Merely in the fights of the rutting season ?
Are they not an ' erotic zone ' ?   Fascinating, too, is the thought
Of the effect of light in altering
The reproductive rhythm—a discovery
Which probably explains how the deer
Acclimatized in the Antipodes were able
Swiftly to change their rutting season from October to April.
The antlers grow again every year and clearly

The rate of growth during the year
Is far greater than that calculated
From the average size reached by the antler
Over several years. In taxonomy
The attempt is often made to distinguish
Supposed species and even genera
By the proportions of their parts.
The systematists must be warned
Percentage measurements have no value.
What *are* diagnostic are the values
Of the growth-ratio and the absolute body-sizes
At which heterogony (if not uniform)
Begins, ends, or alters. So long as the growth-mechanism persists
It must of itself result in changes of form,
And to explain these it is no longer necessary
To have recourse to some imaginary adaptation
Or to the mysterious principle called orthogenesis.
Which postulates a succession of gene
All, for no obvious reason, in the same direction.
But should the heterogony of particular organs
Come into play, this must tend
To limit the size attained by the race,
For the animal would otherwise become overweighted
By the exaggerated organ—the great Irish deer
With its huge antlers, we must suppose
Had reached this limit of bodily growth
And only a slight change in its surroundings
Was needed to cause its extinction.

But it is mainly with vital, however little-known, elements in our national make-up that I am concerned. I was interested to read the other day, for example, an appeal by the O.C. Lovat Scouts for telescopes. It brought to mind the part played in the Great War by the stalkers recruited from the Highland bens and glens. Groups of them were formed under the name Lovat Scouts (sharpshooters), and after training in map-reading they were sent to France, each group (there were about ten) being allotted to a different army corps. They became famous as super-snipers, but their greatest contribution was their work as observers of what went on behind the lines. And that extra value came from their lifelong practice in the use of the telescope. A deerstalker's telescope has a magnification up to 25 or 30 diameters (as compared with the 8, 10, or 12 diameters of the binoculars), but its field is extremely restricted, and because of that fact it is very difficult to keep a particular spot under observation for any length of time. The unpractised eye becomes strained after four or five minutes. Stalkers can continue using the glasses for hours at a stretch. When the various High Commands began to realize just what these specialists could do they were used mainly for observation purposes. And after that many a German plan went astray because the eagle eye of a stalker in khaki had spotted some unusual activity a long way behind the lines. That is one example of the kind of knowledge I mean, and which I am full of in relation to Scotland.

Just as Devon is celebrated, botanically, for certain extreme rarities—*Corrigiola* at Slapton, *Scirpus Holoschoenus*, *Teucrium Scordium*, and other plants at Brauton, *Aster Linosyris*, *Bupleurum opacum*, and *Ononis reclinata* near Brixham, and *Romulea* on Dawlish Warren, for example, so I am familiar with the Little White Rose of Scotland which grows in abundance on the Island of Eigg, the rare blue of the *Primula scotica* to be found in the Orkneys, and with the Prince's Flower (found nowhere else in the Hebrides) on Eriskay— many attempts to take away specimens of which and grow them elsewhere have all failed.[1] And so in Cornwall too, where I was luckier than W. H. Hudson, who in one of his letters to Morley Roberts had to say : ' I really wanted to get back to Cornwall in July —when the *Erica vagans* will be in bloom—the heath I've never seen'. And, as a Border man, I know, of course, about vendace fishing—probably the most restricted sport in the British Isles. The Scottish vendace, a delicate salmonoid herring said to have been introduced by Mary, Queen of Scots, is found only in Dumfriesshire, in the Castle Lock of Lochmaben—the ancient home of the Bruces— and in the Mill Loch, not far away. It is never caught by the angler, for no form of bait has yet been found to entice it, but is taken by net. At Lochmaben, the operation used to be undertaken by the Vendace Club, and Mill Loch was netted by the St. Magdalene's Vendace Club. Later the two clubs used to meet to dine and compare catches. But these two Vendace Clubs have long been dissolved, though this rare fish is still found in these two lochs, one specimen of the exquisitely flavoured vendace caught in the Mill Loch a year or two ago proving that the fish had held its own there against pike and other enemies for many centuries. The real habitat of the fish, however, is the Castle Loch, which, in the days when Lochmaben Castle was used by the Stuarts as a holiday home,

[1] In the same way I know where to find on Ben Lawers, the highest peak in Perthshire, *Gentiana Miralis* (confined in Britain to about two localities in the Highland mountains) ; *Myosotis alpestris* (*rupicola*) ; and the exquisite lilac daisies of *Erigeron alpinus*, another great British rarity ; the white-flowered *Draba rupestris* (*hirta*) ; and—perhaps the rarest of all British plants, being confined to a small patch of rocks on Ben Lawers (from the summit of which a magnificent view, embracing nearly half of Scotland, can be obtained on a clear day), where it seldom flowers and is almost extinct—*Saxifraga cernus*, in addition to such commoner things as *Silene acaulis*, the inconspicuous *Polygonum viviparum* with its heads of red bulbils and tiny white flowers, the white crucifer, the golden cinquefoil, the rare little *Veronica fruticans* (saxatilis), the minute silvery Highland Cudweed, *Gnaphalium supinum*, and in the clefts between boulders and in crevices of the cliffs ferns like *Polystichum lonchitis*, the handsome Holly Fern with its stiff, prickly fronds, the light green and delicate *Athyrium* (*Polypodium*) *alpestre*, the small green-ribbed Spleenwort, *Asplenium viride*, and, lastly, the most adorable of ferns, tiny *Woodsia alpina*.

was known as the Queen's Loch. The most notable feature of the
vendace, apart from its rarity, is the curious heart-shaped mark on
the head of the fish—the mark corresponding to the shape of the
Castle Loch. All attempts to transplant the fish have failed, and
there are only four authenticated cases of a vendace having been
caught with rod and line.

> ' All compounded as he seems to be of the granite and gentians of
> our Northern mountains,' Amy Lowell wrote in her *Tendencies in
> Modern American Poetry*, ' Robert Frost is only of New England stock
> on his father's side. His mother was born in Edinburgh, of Lowland
> Scotch descent. A curious fancy, however, might trace here a kinship
> shared with his native hills, for geologists tell us that the New Hamp-
> shire hills and the Scotch Highlands are cousin-german to each other ;
> I have heard, even, that a species of land-locked trout found in Scotland
> is caught nowhere else but in New Hampshire ponds.'

Mass Observation methods have not yet been applied to Scotland :
when they are, there will be a very rich crop of surprising facts and a
tremendous riddance of general assumptions of all kinds. A boxing
writer recently said there is no Tony Galento in Scotland, and
continued by going through the various types and saying that there
is no Jack Dempsey, no Gene Tunney, no Georges Carpentier, no
Phil Scott, no Tommy Farr, and no Jack Doyle. There never has
been, and there is no sign that there ever will be. It is also true that
at all boxing weights, from fly up to middle, Scotland has produced
men who were at least within measurable distance of the world's
best, and that at the kindred sport of wrestling she has managed to
produce outsizes at whom the most terrible of Turks would have
looked twice without sneezing. But in heavy-weight boxing there
is hardly a sporting country from Sweden to Spain and America to
Alaska that has not sent out men who could have taken on both Bell
and Scally at Dundee with the greatest of ease. All of which is well
known (in sporting circles)—but still unexplained. All the answers
have been heard—there are some fairly obvious ones connected with
the condition of the game in Scotland—and explanation is still defied.
The thesis might be launched, from what one has gathered in private,
non-fistic society, that the most pugnacious elements in our midst,
the most cocksure of their own success, have these qualities in inverse
ratio to their avoirdupois. But in the name of Benny Lynch or Hugh
Gallacher, why should this apply only to Scotland ? Why should
what turns out in America to be Tony Galento, turn out in Scotland
to be—well, ' Big Aggie's Man ' ? You can't explain that, any more
than you can explain why, when you see modern Scottish Rugby
forwards in their traditional appeasement act, you are able to make
unflattering contrasts with certain light but fiery elements in club
play. It remains—a mystery. Another mystery (Scotland abounds
in them, if you only knew—I may write a separate book one of these
days about the most interesting fifty or sixty of them) is the *per*

capita consumption of water in Scotland, which is several times greater than in England or, so far as figures are available, any other European country, or in U.S.A. The matter was referred to in his Annual Report the other day by the Edinburgh City Water Engineer, but he vouchsafed no explanation of the very curious fact, and the *Scotsman* only devoted a light facetious leader to the matter. I can think of no explanation.

Scotland is governed from London. So little is known of Scotland there—so little of Scotland as it really is, as apart from what it is conventionally understood to be—that all manner of mistakes are constantly being made. How this works is shown in one instance (and instances could be multiplied in relation to every branch of Scottish affairs)[1] by the following quotation from the *Scots Correspondent* of May 20, 1939, viz. :

'The " progress " of air-raid precautions for civilians has been in the news again, with the announcement of alternative type shelters

---

[1] Another example was to be found in the criticism some Northern farmers directed against the Food Control Board and Department of Agriculture in October 1939. There was something more than a mere local protest in this. The matter of the criticism was the price-grading of cattle, and it would appear that the Government's top figure for prime quality—based, probably, on a general ' best ' which was in accord with most ' British ' beef production—was too far below the figure deemed fair for prime Scottish-fed beef, which is acknowledged to be the finest in home production. There is an echo here of a grievance that is as old as the Government's regulation of meat marketing—the grievance of a specialized output against the standardization which tends to be one of the defects of regulation by the State. But it fits into another and wider context, that of the whole effect of war-time regulation on needs and interests which are not really British, but distinctively Scottish. It is inevitable, when an imperative demand has to be made for concerted national behaviour and endeavour, that the subtler or superficial distinctions between Scottish and British conditions and problems should go. But there are distinctions which, so far from being superficial, are deep enough to be differences of real and vital importance to Scotland. The Government has almost always neglected these in the past, and it could hardly be expected to remember them when united war effort was the ' great and necessary ' preoccupation. Scots themselves must do the reminding from time to time, like the Northern farmers when the need arises. The actual relationship of Scotland to England, and England's intolerance of separate Scottish requirements, is well illustrated just now (October 1939) by the fact that since the war started the B.B.C. studios in Edinburgh and Glasgow have been practically unused and no Scottish news broadcast. There can be no possible excuse for this sort of thing—or for the Scottish people tolerating it for a moment. ' Why is it that Scotland has practically been wiped out of the B.B.C. programmes since the war commenced ? ' asks a correspondent. ' We have a very real grievance in the fact that for seventeen hours a day the programmes, with the exception of the news, are entirely devoted to England. For the past month we have had no Scottish Church Sunday services, while the English Church has had two each Sunday. We want an immediate return to good Scottish items, including our beautiful service.'

for use where the so-called Anderson shelter is impracticable, and of details of the approved reinforcement of basements. Both of these novelties in the sphere of home defence have been the subject of artists' and architects' drawings in the daily press, and some more or less generous publicity has been at pains to suggest that Scotland's grievance at the inadequacy of existing shelter arrangements to meet Scottish conditions can now be forgotten. But that seems to be a decidedly optimistic claim. Certainly the new shelter (which is dearer than the Anderson type) looks both bigger and sturdier. But, like the " garden shelter", which it is apparently designed to replace, it obviously needs for its erection the space of a back garden or court of some sort— an amenity with which not all Scottish tenements by any means are equipped. For those who are so equipped, it may well be found that the new shelter is at once too small and too big ; too small to provide accommodation for all the inhabitants of a three- or four-storey tene- ment, and too big to be duplicated for that purpose, within the space of the back court or garden available. Duplication, moreover, might lead—as it has led already in some instances of the Anderson shelter's erection—to trouble over the filling up of back yards with air-raid shelters to the exclusion of the housewife's domestic concerns. There is a further point about this whole shelter business on which, I think, Scottish enquiries might legitimately demand to be satisfied. The idea with these shelters is that they should be placed close to the outer wall of a building, so that if it should collapse the shelter would both withstand the impact and gain added protection from a covering of debris. As an idea this is sound enough. But the " satisfactory " practical tests which have been carried out seem to have been made mostly with brick buildings, of no more than three storeys in height. That may be a convenient norm for English towns. But in Scotland tenement buildings are far oftener of stone than of brick, and of four storeys height than of three. The difference in " collapse weight " between brick and stone buildings must be considerable. It's a differ- ence of some importance for civilian protection in Scotland. Are these new shelters, tested for brick, also able to withstand the fall of stone ? The same question is not without pertinence in the matter of reinforcing basements. In Scotland, of course, more tenements lack basements than have them—a fact which the London Government's A.R.P. planning seems very ready to ignore—but where they do exist, rein- forcement is not going to be of much value if it is not designed to cope with a fall of stone, as well as of brick. Owners of businesses and factories on whom this sort of shelter devolves as a compulsory obliga- tion may presumably be relied on, in their own interests, not to minimize the importance of this point. The danger is that it may conveniently be forgotten by London as a remote Scottish exception too difficult to make special provision for, in handling " mass " defence arrangements for the large section of the public which only the State can take care of. That is probably why, as it seems, no inquiry has been made into the possibilities of the typical Scottish tenement *per se* for protection against air raids. There appears to be a good reason to think, for instance, that the sturdiest part of the average Scottish tenement is its stair, which in some cases is already a metal skeleton in structure. It seems not impossible that where tenements are deficient both in base- ments and in backyards, their stairways, suitably reinforced, might be as safe a place as any for the tenants to seek shelter. The possibility at least seems to deserve more than speculative consideration by local authorities with any enterprise.'

The rest of this book could easily be filled up with instances of inefficiency, muddle, and harm due to the assumption that what is applicable to England applies to Scotland too, or at any rate, the failure of Parliament and other authorities to fit their measures to the specific Scottish conditions. How the difference between the two countries works out in another connexion is shown by the next paragraph in the same issue of the *Scots Correspondent* :

> ' In Glasgow the other day an Irishman of 46 was sentenced to fifteen months' imprisonment for having in his possession two sporting guns (lent to him by friends for duck-shooting, according to the evidence), some sporting ammunition, and four sticks of gelignite which, in the words of the judge, had been " lying about in an unlocked drawer for two years ". There were also some documents which connected him with the Irish Citizen Army, an organization of the extreme Left I.R.A. I'm very much inclined to ask whether, in " making an example " of this sort and in some other recent actions, the Scottish " authorities " are not quite wantonly asking for trouble. Scotland has not suffered in the I.R.A. campaign that has alarmed English cities. Indeed, one Scots political organization claims to have definite assurance that the I.R.A. will leave this country alone unless it is forced to do otherwise. Though the bombers in England obviously plan their attacks on property in a way that will, so far as possible, avoid danger to the lives and persons of innocent bystanders, their doings seem to me not only criminal, but also, from their own national point of view, foolish.[1] But I wonder if it may not be almost equally foolish, from the patriotic Scots point of view, to do anything which might seem to challenge the I.R.A. leaders to push their campaign across the Border.'

The paper goes on, apropos Palestine, to say :

> ' The lesson for Scots is obvious : nothing is to be got out of England except by squeeze—or a prospect of profit. Any appeal to English pity or honour is quite useless.'

This is the point of view the present author has made it his principal task to publicize for the last twenty years. The growing recognition of it is Scotland's only hope.

In a recent issue of *Discussion* the Secretary of the Aberdeen Communist Party stated that while addresses, &c., on international questions attracted good audiences, great difficulty was found in tackling local questions and getting hold of the necessary data on which to base addresses on these matters. This is a difficulty which is encountered everywhere, but seldom so frankly admitted. It is pre-eminently necessary to improve the ready availability of data of

---

[1] The present author, of course, dissents from both of these adjectives— criminal and foolish. On the contrary, his sympathies were entirely with the I.R.A. But he agrees with the general argument of this quotation in regard to Scotland, and, indeed, regards England as Scotland's only real enemy—Scotland's connexion with England its only danger—and the fact that, despite the systematic violation of the safeguarding clauses of the Act of Union, Scotland entrusts the English Government with its defence, a characteristic piece of folly and stupidity.

this sort, to stimulate systematic and relentless infighting based upon it, and to drive home the fact that the ' eyes of the fool are in the ends of the earth ', and that this is a form of eye-trouble peculiarly prevalent and persistent in Scotland and most urgently in need of correction. ' I am afraid very few of us know much of our own country ' is a platitude of which the present writer, for reasons not inscrutable, is the humble and constant recipient, and ' there is nothing for it but an unreserved acceptance of the obvious ', wrote A. G. Bradley in his *Gateway of Scotland.* ' There is a familiar type of politician, known only in Britain, whose motto is " Every country but my own ". In the more venial sense of the phrase now under discussion, irreproachable patriotic persons by the thousand might as justly be branded by it.' It is this type of ignorance and alienation in all its forms, venial or otherwise, that must be conquered and corrected—but above all that form of it which is the subject-matter of the very frank confession Mr. William Power makes in his autobiography, *Should Auld Acquaintance,* when he says : ' The most serious gap in my knowledge concerns life itself. I am rootedly middle-class. I never was a labourer, a miner, a stoker, a deckhand, a mill operative, earning a poor pay by hard manual work in poor conditions. I never lived in a model, or in an overcrowded house in a working-class or slummy district ; I never stood in the queue at the Labour Exchange ; and I confess that the thought of these things makes me shudder.' Mr. Power is not alone in this utter and most disabling lack of knowledge of life as it presents itself to the vast majority of the Scottish people—the working class. It is a great disability that it is shared to the full by the great majority of contemporary Scottish writers of any little reputation, and it completely invalidates their work. They have left unknown the only thing worth knowing, and it would have been infinitely better for them if they had been able to say with Richard Carlile that they concerned themselves only with the working class and knew ' nothing of the so-called higher classes except that they are robbers '. But Mr. Power goes on, immediately on top of his appalling confession, to opine that the younger Scottish writers of the Left ' make too much of the class struggle '. I should like their names. I have failed to detect any such. The fact of the matter is that scarcely anything has been made of the class struggle yet in Scottish literature, for Mr. Power by no means stands alone—there is scarcely a single Scottish writer of to-day of any reputation who is not in precisely the same boat, and as ready as Mr. Power, despite complete ignorance of the matter, to deprecate any tendency to make much—or indeed anything —of the Class War, and it is certainly high time we had a new body of Scottish writers very different from those at present in evidence in the sense that they are fully familiar with working-class life, belong to the working class themselves, and are competent Marxists. It is high time that an end was put in Scotland to twaddle like Mr. Power's in the last-quoted remark, and his still more utterly ignorant and unforgivable opinion that ' the strikers (in the General Strike) were hopelessly in the wrong '. On the contrary! The workers are always right, when they are on the aggressive. One would have thought that the realities of the whole infernal business would have pierced Mr. Power's brain when, going home about two on a rainy May morning, ' I heard ', he says, ' a muffled trampling. There was not a soul about. Were ghostly armies on the march with audible boots? Round a corner on the other side of the river came the head of a battalion in full war array. As they passed I saw they were an *English regiment*.' Precisely! People like Power actually see these things, make a note of them, and remember and write about them, but somehow *they fail to penetrate*—they see with their eyes, but not with their brains, and they write but fail to appreciate the real significance of what they set on record even.

This is why I say in a poem addressed to the younger Scottish writers that

> Art must be related to the central issues of life,
> Not serve a sub-artistic purpose that could as well
> Be served by the possession of a new motor-car
> Or a holiday on the Continent perhaps.
> What do we Scottish writers most lack, most need?
> —An immediate experience of the concrete,
> A rich overflowing apprehension of the definite
> Day-by-day content of our people's lives,
> A burningly clear understanding of the factors at work,
> Of the actual correlation of the forces, in labour to-day;
> A Dundee jute mill, Singer's, Beardmore's,
> The ghost towns, ruined fishing villages, slave camps,
> And all the derelict areas of our countryside;
> The writer not first and foremost concerned with these
> Lacks the centrality that alone can give
> Value to his work—he is a trifler, a traitor,
> To his art and to mankind alike,
> A fool choosing flight and fantasy,
> Not to be pitied, but despised.
>
> It is a lying cry to say
> That human nature cannot be changed.
> It can be, and is being, completely.
> We are long past the time when doubt of an accepted system
> Liberates great minds while yet the system itself
> Has not fallen into such contempt as to be
> Incapable of their action within its limits.
> Long past the affectation of being above the battle,
> Of being socially agnostic, seeing all systems
> As subject to historic change, and the will
> Of great men, and accepting none.
>
> Yet what are all our intellectuals saying?
> All victimized by repetition-compulsion

They are denying these huge horizons opening out
And crying ' Fundamentally man cannot change '
And bleating ' After all there's but one kind of man.
Men's ways of thought can never become
So inconceivably different from ours ! '
Can't they ?   They have already.   Mine have
And every fit member's of the I.U.R.W.
And are speedily disposing of the bourgeois notions
That art must be ' neutral, equally indifferent
To good and evil, knowing no pity, no anger '.
And that ' neither in its high countenance
Nor looks can its secret thoughts be read ',
Any more than the masked wizard-of-History's can.
We have read them all right !
The overcoming by life of its own limitations
The calling out of the major images of the future,
What and as is—and as should and will be
Reality in motion, advancing and developing
Not for us ?   They can keep their decrepit
Terms, which belong to a past we've sloughed off
Of realism, romanticism, classicism,
Naturalism, and all the witless rest
Of isms, flourishing in the parent mire of scholasticism.

(The primary capitalistic neurosis is narcissism.)
It is a libel to say we need these infantilisms now
And always will—lest these precious little scribblers
Prove Rip Van Winkles on the edge of by far
The greatest Kulturkampf in human history,
These fools who have already become unreadable
Not because their actual craftsmanship has degenerated,
But simply because, in the most literal sense,
They do not know what they are talking about.
So with our Scottish writers ; they are forced
Either to distort the content of Scottish life
In order to make it conform
To some desperate personal wish-fulfilment
Or flee from it entirely—into the past,
Into fantasy, or some other reality-surrogate.
Outside the revolutionary movement there is no place
For any writer worth a moment's thought.
The ' culture class ' for which they think they write
Has ceased to exist either as a class
Or as a repository of culture ; as the strain
Of economic struggle tightens the so-called
Middle-class vanguard immediately reveals
Its essential moral weakness and above all
Its intellectual poverty thinly coated
By a veneer of artistic sophistication ;
No self-respecting man can have anything to say to them.
They have no longer any real reason for existing,
And therefore literature and art can be nothing
For them except day-dreams or ' shots ' in the arm,
While a few of them, the sentimental stoics,
May read such a poem as this (or bits of it)
With a wearily-approving nod of cynicism.

There is nothing whatever in contemporary biology
Either the science of heredity or of genetics,
Nothing we know of the mechanisms of inheritance,
Nothing in the nature of the genes or chromosomes
To stand in the way of the radicals' enthusiasm
For social transformation—the revolutionists'
Advocacy of profoundly-altered social systems.
On the other hand there is a vast accumulation
Of evidence from the sociological sciences,
Economy, anthropology, sociology,
Politics, the philosophy of history, to substantiate
The necessity, the sanity, and the wisdom
Of deep changes in all institutions, customs,
Habits, values—in short, civilizations.
Human nature is the last thing we need to worry about.
Let us attend to the circumstances that condition it.

We live in a world that has become
Intolerable as the subject of passive reflection.
What is our response to the unescapable reality?
Are we too like these miserable little cliques to turn
Because of theoretic inadequacy
From social causation, from the poetry of purgative action
And try to find form and significance
In pure feeling itself, transplanted and re-imagined,
Seeking the meaning of experience in the phenomena of experience,
Pure sensation becoming an ultimate value
In the neurotic and mystical attempt
To give physicality an intellectual content,
In the sensitizing of nerves already raw,
Meaningless emotion aroused automatically
Without satisfaction or education, as in melodrama,
Man can find his own dignity only in action now.

Scottish writers, the height and depth of your writings
Will be measured by the extent to which
The dialectics of our era find expression
In the artistic imagery—how widely, forcefully, clearly
(Sir Thomas Inskip permitting or not!)
The burning contemporary problems are expressed in it,
The class war, the struggles and ideals
Of the proletariat bent on changing the world,
And consequently on changing human nature.

' There is nothing perhaps more puzzling . . . than the great
gulf that is set between England and Scotland,' wrote R. L. Stevenson
in a passage which was not only a very considerable understatement,
but wrong in some of its points, especially the one I italicize. ' Here
are two peoples *almost identical in blood* . . . the same in language
and religion; and yet a few years of quarrelsome isolation (in
comparison with the great historical cycles) have so separated their
thoughts and ways, that not unions, nor mutual dangers, nor steamers,
nor railways, nor all the king's horses and all the king's men, seem
able to obliterate the broad distinction.'

Most older people of the upper classes in Scotland would still deny that, and when the hard facts are hammered home, and pierce the ' conspiracy of silence ' maintained by the English and Anglo-Scottish press and they can no longer deny them (as many of the Scottish peers and big business men did deny the irrefutable facts upon which the new Scottish Nationalist Movement based itself at its start, and which have long since been generally established and admitted on all hands), they simply continue to act as if they were not. Yet the facts are steadily ' seeping ' through, and more and more people are joining the Nationalist organizations, and appropriate action cannot be long delayed.   However that may be, years ago I sang (in ' To Circumjack Cencrastus ')

> I know the stars that seem so far away
> Have that appearance just because my thought
> Cannot yet bridge the spiritual gulf between us
> And the time when it will still seems remote
>   As interstellar space itself
> Yet not so far as against my will I am
> From nearly everybody else in Scotland here.
> But a less distance than I'll drive betwixt
>   England and Scotland yet.

This is still my central purpose, and it is slowly but surely succeeding, and the difference between the Englishman and the Scot is becoming more and more clear in many quarters—often in unexpected quarters. Take this quotation, for example : ' I can vividly recall to mind the astonished looks of my comrades when they found themselves personally face to face for the first time with the Tommies in Flanders. After a few days of fighting the consciousness slowly dawned on our soldiers that those Scotsmen were not like the ones we had seen described and caricatured in the comic papers.'

Guess who wrote that.   None other than *Hitler* himself in *Mein Kampf*.   The English will naturally be slower ; they think they know their Scotsmen all right.   Let us wait and see.

A writer in *The Modern Scot* a year or two ago remarked :

> ' There is not in Scotland that tradition of nature-writing that extends in England from before the time of Gervase Markham, Izaak Walton, and Richard Frank down to Richard Jefferies and Hudson and later ;   Gilbert White, writing of the birds at Selborne, is typical of the most satisfying workers in this tradition.'

It is, however, one of the things to the credit of the Scottish Renaissance Movement that there has been during the past few years a steadily increasing flow of better writing on Scottish topography and natural history.   Scots are beginning to try to see Scotland as a whole, and more and more of the younger Scottish writers are approaching different regions of the country equipped with a full historical and scientific knowledge, a power of first-hand observation, a concern to write well allied to immediate practical purposes, political, agricultural, architectural, &c., and, with, informing their particular studies, a broad national understanding and informed regenerative purpose which have been almost completely lacking heretofore.

As one reviewer warned readers concerning my *Islands of Scotland*, they ' must keep in mind that the author is working primarily with ideas. No doubt many would rather have some thing more objective, but . . .' ' His concern is indeed not so much with topography, as with the human element and its fashioning by island life. . . . This fundamentally differentiates this book from others of the class.' My philosophy interrogates ' immediate experience '. This I find to be a flux or ' stream of consciousness ', whose constant basis is sensation. Distinction, variety, individuality, and definiteness are all the work of thought, and not *given* to immediate experience as such. So far, I go with Bergson—and also with Kant. The clearly defined ' perceptual object ', which we see, transcends the vague mass of sense-data presented to our visual organs ; it is more than these sense-data, or any combination of them, because it is permanent and public to many observers, whereas the sense-data are shifting and private. The object, in short, is object of *thought* (i.e. of sensation *plus* memory and imagination *plus* conceptual interpretation), and not object of sensation alone. But I do not follow Bergson in his view that thought falsifies or distorts the object. Nor do I conclude with Kant that space, time, and the categories are necessary forms of *human* consciousness. Instead, I proceed to inquire into the nature and aims of the thinking process. It is necessary to ' think our way back to thought itself ' (Chesterton's phrase)—not in order to deny that anything besides thinking exists, but in order thoroughly to understand what it means to think—hence what it means for thought to have an object such as common sense assumes it to have, and such as its validity seems to demand. All thought is analytic, a ' breaking up ' of the immediate unity of experience ; and it has two principal phases—analysis of the concrete datum, and universalization of the elements thus analysed out. This latter phase yields judgements that are universal and necessary (and not mere tautologies) and gives rise to deductive inference. Thus the original unity of experience is reconstituted on a higher plane ; unity *given* has become unity *understood*. Along this path we reach the notion of substance. For substance is precisely an ' intelligible unity ', to which the mind penetrates by means of sense-data and the analysis of them. Thought's true and final object is an enduring ' thing ', ' more fundamental than sense-data and which embraces and dominates sense-data in a higher unity '. With such a philosophy I, of course, break completely with the mere impressionism of most writing about Scotland, and the general anti-intellectualism of Scottish writers.

I have said a good deal elsewhere in this book of the fog of ignorance which wraps all Scottish matters,[1] and of the difficulty of

[1] There is, as a matter of fact, scarcely a single Scottish historical figure, male or female, in whom the present writer is interested (and the present writer is to-day far from alone among his compatriots in that re-orientation of his intellectual curiosity which singles out these individuals instead of the stock figures of Scotland's past), whose very names are known to ninety-nine per cent. of the Scottish people or who figure in the *Dictionary of National Biography*, or about whom it is possible to come to any real knowledge and understanding except by most difficult original research. Every department of Scottish arts and affairs lies under a cloud of ignorance similar to that partially dispelled by the Scottish Art Exhibition at Burlington House in 1939, which caused Sir William Llewellyn, former president of the Royal Academy, to say : ' Scottish art hitherto has been practically unknown in the south, and, for that matter, in any country other than Scotland. No estimate of its actual worth, therefore, has ever been made. Now that the exhibition is in the Royal Academy, it is quite clear that Scottish art has been misrepresented. From now on it must take a higher place than has previously been supposed.' Where Sir William was wrong, however, was in supposing that Scottish art was any less ' practically unknown ' in Scotland itself than anywhere else. Mr. William Power puts the matter truly in his *Literature and Oatmeal* when he says : ' . . . Gaelic has had a far bigger and longer run in Scotland than Scots or English. Teutonic speech is still a comparative upstart, and its sweeping victory did not begin till well on in the seventeenth century. A conscientious Chinaman who contemplated a thesis on the literary history of Scotland would have no doubt as to his procedure. " I will learn a little Gaelic, and read all I can find about Gaelic literature from the oldest Irish poets down to Ban MacIntyre ; and nearly a third of my thesis will be on Gaelic literature." He would be rather mystified when he discovered that historians of Scotland and its literature had known and cared as much about Gaelic as Chinese, and that they had gone on the remarkable assumption that the majority of the Scots were Anglo-Saxons and that their literature began with Thomas the Rhymer, in the reign of Alexander III.

Or again :

' One of the finest of the interlinking stories in the Red Branch cycle, that of Deirdre, is largely of Scots location, and was well known in Scotland and Scotland had a full share in the Fenian circle, in Finn, Ossian, Oscar Grainne, and Diarmid ; in the Ossianic lays, many of which are in the Dean of Lismore's Book, compiled about 1515 ; in the beautiful religious poem ascribed to Patrick and Columba ; and in the lovely old hymns, prayers, an benedictions collected by Dr. Alexander Carmichael in his *Carmina Gadelica* If all this were as well known as it ought to be in modern Scotland, or would not risk apoplexy by attempting to give some idea of it in a few sentences. It meant much to Scotland before the cold alien shadow of Calvin fell athwart Gaeldom. The tragic tale of Deirdre and the Sons of Uisnach, one of the great stories of the world, is told in the Glenmasa MS. of 1238, in the Scottish National Library. An independent and singularly beautiful version of it was taken down by Dr. Carmichael in 1867 from an old man in Barra, and a neighbour of his supplied a fine old lay on the subject. The names of Deirdre and the three brothers spring like wi flowers all over the romantic country between Crinan and Inverness, and Lochetiveside ; and in her Farewell to Alba she recalls the happy days th had spent in their lodges in scenes like Glenetive, Glen Orchy, Glendaru and Glen Masan. The story is pre-Christian ; and these immortal refuge getting at the essential facts behind the incessant pro-English propaganda and the distortions that have been at work in our midst ever since the Union. But in a book in the title of which I apply the adjective lucky to myself I must also stress the other side of this—the fact that we found ourselves with so much to discover, a whole *terra incognita* to revel in—once (no easy matter) we found our way thither. Even yet the surface has only been scratched. Most of our Gaelic and Scottish Latin poetry is still untranslated ; work has scarcely begun on our great treasure of pipe music ; there is still a tremendous body of uncollected folksong in the Hebrides—work that requires to be done scientifically, since Mrs. Kennedy-Fraser's methods did little more than queer the pitch. An instance of the treasure-trove that lies in all directions for our recovery is Arthur Johnstone's poem in Latin, ' Fisher's Apology ', which, with the collaboration of my friend George Elder Davie, I have translated for the first time and turned into English verse. Pointing out that this entirely unknown poem is of a kind that has yielded many well-known and popular sets of verses by later Scottish poets writing in Scots and English, I have said of it :

> ' While akin in theme and angle of approach and humour to this old-established vein of Scottish poetry found in our national poets in Scots and in Gaelic and in English alike, Arthur Johnstone's poem has a high civilization behind it, as it is as full of a roguish humour as any of them, but it obviously derives from a far stronger and more mellow culture and it paints a comprehensive picture of the Scottish country-side and the pursuits and psychology of the people with a scope, an amplitude of spirit, a richness of detail, that establish it as a veritable masterpiece of its kind, while its light-running versification, its dexterity of allusion, its mischievous wit, and the fact that Sabbath observance and angling rights remain subjects of as keen debate in Scotland to-day as they were four centuries ago, keep it as fresh and lively and true to life to-day as it was on the far-off day when it was written. Much of this attractive quality and perennial freshness is retained, I think, even in an English prose translation ; and Scottish poetry must indeed be surprisingly rich—or abominably misprized—if it has so many poems of this quality that it can afford to ignore one of them. This " Fisher's

seem to have come to Alba about the first century A.D., long before the Dalriadic kingdom was heard of. At a very casual first glance, Deirdre looks like an avatar of Helen of Troy. But she is Helen's anti-thesis. She is not a passively sensual piece of white pulchritude, allowing herself to be carried off from an old husband who wearies her by an effeminate young Adonis she despises, and displaying a fatalistic indifference to the consequences of her wicked stupidity. Helen is redolent of the harem. Deirdre has the wild freshness of the hills. Her passion is absolute and imperious, but tender and true. The scene in which she selects Naisi as her mate anticiates the theories of Bernard Shaw, but it is elementally noble and thrillingly right. This is the new woman of the West, worshipping love with proud reverence, man's comrade, not his chattel.' Mr. Power is right in claiming that Scotland was far ahead of every other country in this, and in many other humane developments.

Apology " is included in no Scottish anthology. Indeed, it may be
said that most of the greatest poems by Scottish poets have never been
included in any Scottish anthology by the anthologists of Anglo-
Scottish provincialization. Scottish anthologies give a perpetual show
to which " Hamlet, omitting the Prince of Denmark " is a poor second.
MacDonald's " Birlinn of Clanranald " and MacIntyre's " Ben Dorain "
—two of the greatest poems in the whole range of Gaelic poetry—have,
for example, always been left out of account in favour of worthless
Anglo-Scottish pieces. In any new Scottish anthology that pretends
to any completeness, " Fisher's Apology "—like the other great poems
I have named—undoubtably should, and must, be given its due place
at last. In the whole range of Scottish poetry the only poem with
which it can effectively be coupled and compared is Alexander Hume's
" Of the Day Estivall ", which is to be found in Lord Tweedsmuir's
anthology, " The Northern Muse ", and several other recent Scottish
anthologies. The life-times of these two poets overlapped—Arthur
Johnstone's dates being 1587–1641, and Alexander Hume's 1557–
1609. But something far deeper and more important than contemporaneity accounts for the likeness of spirit and the mutual concern
for the beauty and detail of Scottish country life which animate both
these poems. That the Scottish people with their traditional concern
for the poetry of nature should have failed to esteem Arthur Johnstone's
poem at its true value, and simply because it was written in Latin remained blind to its liveliness and wit and the fact that it was a perfect
little masterpiece in the very department of poetry which Scotland had
always regarded as peculiarly its own, is one of the extraordinary facts
in the complex history of Scottish poetry.'

While I had hoped—in vain—that the tercentenary of Arthur
Johnstone's death in 1941 might see a measure of justice done to this
very interesting figure, and his place among the greatest of Scottish
poets properly recognized, a Communist-Nationalist like myself must
make his position in regard to Johnstone quite clear. A memorable
item in Johnstone's work is his remonstrance addressed to the Scots
people—the only thing of its kind in his poems—on the eve of their
starting the Bishops' Wars in 1638. The poem—as sincerely meant,
I think, as it was also sensibly prophetic of the political and cultural
chaos that did ensue (he warns the Scots of the effects of the still-
proceeding Thirty Years' War in Germany)—was deservedly
neglected. Johnstone had no genuine claim upon the attention of
the people as a whole, whose situation had until then been no concern
of his. Buchanan had translated the psalms to strengthen his
mind when imprisoned by the Portuguese Inquisition; Johnstone,
though a great admirer of his great predecessor, produced *his* version
of the Psalms at the bidding of Archbishop Laud, who wished to
reduce the prestige of the dangerous Buchanan.

This all-in view of Scottish literary production throughout the
ages, no matter in what language—instead of the undue concentration
on that portion of it merely which is in English or near-English Scots
—was from the outset one of the main objectives of the Scottish
Renaissance Movement, and much has been accomplished towards it

though, as I have said, many times what has been done still remains
to be done ; and above all the casual pro-English dismissal of our
Gaelic literature (simply taking it for granted that because it is in
Gaelic it is not worth looking into)—although Gaelic held sway in
Scotland for a period of time compared with which the period
during which English has been used in Scotland is a mere bagatelle—
requires to be countered at last with a full range of intensive Gaelic
studies of all kinds, and a rendering into good English versions of all
the best Gaelic poems. Even more important than that, however, is
the understanding of the great literary potentialities inherent in
Gaelic.

I have, of course, only skirted the very fringes here of that ignorance
—that impatient disregard—that invincible determination to let
' sleeping dogs lie ' and lead an ' unexamined life '—of the roots of
our national being which is one of the most appalling features of
Scottish life to-day. A recent writer, describing a visit to Borreraig
to see the site of Patrick MacCrimmon's College for Pipers, says :
' Perhaps it is a monument to a civilization and an art that have almost
vanished. I don't know, but I am inclined to think that it is. At its
best to-day, bagpipe playing is a sort of atrophied art, without much
meaning. Yet I am told by a man who has given deep study to the
art of the great bagpipe, that it once had a nobility now beyond our
comprehension. The *Piob mor* or Great Highland Bagpipe, he says,
is the one instrument extant whose manual is derived in enharmonic
concord with a fixed fundamental bass. The key of the *Piob mor*, he
says, is derived from the upper responses of the human heart to the
fundamental sequence of the elements. These responses are sea-
borne Nordic, and consist of three Pentatonic sequences, a primary
sequence about the fundamental A, then the inversion of this
sequence, and one primary about the fifth. I could carry you into
the higher realms of music by quoting my informant at greater length,
but I think I have said enough to indicate that the art of bagpipe
music is not understood to-day. I guess modern bagpipe players
bear about the same relationship to the lost art of the pibroch as the
members of a swing-time jazz band bear to the genius of Bach.' The
writer's guess is correct. My friend Francis George Scott, the
composer, has spent two years or so making an intensive study of the
whole matter, and has hit upon some remarkable discoveries. I hope
he will yet write a book on the subject. There can be no piece of
research work on any Scottish cultural matter of anything like
comparable importance.[1] The great pibroch music of Scotland is

[1] I do not go deeply into this question of the great pibroch music here,
because since I wrote this chapter I have had the good fortune to meet, and
discuss the matter fully in many a long *sederunt* with, the head of the great
MacCrimmon family (for over four centuries hereditary pipers to MacLeod
of MacLeod in Skye), Dr. Calum MacCrimmon. It is generally believed

one of the most marvellous achievements in the whole history of music. I have dealt with the matter in a long poem, 'Lament for the Great Music', in my volume, *Stony Limits and Other Poems* (1934), in the course of which I say :

> It is the supreme reality (not the Deity of personal theism)
> Standing free of all historical events in past or future,
> Knowable—but visible to the mind alone ;
> Wherefore the Church for its own purposes borrowed
> The method you carried to perfection, and in plainsong
> Found the musical voice of a dividuality
> Which has no communal link with mankind
> Though, having the mystic association of primitive music,
> It still has the power to work on human superstitition.
> Yet the neuma, the song which hangs on to the end of a word
> Without a word—*uaill-gluth an Aoibhnis*—
> Avails it little now—the parrot-like contrivance
> Of the jubilant sound signifying that the heart conceives
> What it is unable to express. It is not in the Church
> That men now find, when they must, some similar means
> Of indicating a rapt and mysterious
> Communion with the spiritual world.
> But the *Ceol Mor* is only yours in your own perfect form.
> (The gracing that brings the notes of the melody from the flat to the round
> Are only melisma between notes in India and Araby,
> To smooth the transitions between the notes like the movements
> Of the dancers who do not disclose the physical means
> Of their passing from pose to pose.)
> It is world-wide, ageless. It is the Sufi *Nida* and *Saut* ;
> It is the Indian *Ragas*, and melodies of the old *slokas* and *ghazals*
> Deliberately cast in a non-rhythmic mould because the composers knew
> That rhythm is an animal function, whereas poetry and music
> Involving no bodily activity of the artist in their making
> Can exist in purely psychological relation to society
> And would be equally ' true ' in a world of disembodied spirits ;
> And, as Plato knew, it is futile for artists

that the MacCrimmon family is extinct. This is not the case ; in addition to Dr. MacCrimmon there are two kinsmen of his, in Canada, both of whom are pibroch players. Dr. MacCrimmon himself is an enthusiast for the great traditions of his family, and embodies the bardic conception of pibroch playing, which is a very different matter from the ' smart fingering ' which is the main criterion in piping contests to-day. He is at complete variance with the Pibroch Society of Inverness and the ideas of almost all pipers to-day on this great subject. But the matter is too intricate to go into here ; Dr. MacCrimmon's doctrines—which corroborate the findings F. G. Scott has arrived at independently on this subject—cannot be outlined in brief form ; to be properly intelligible they must be fully developed and properly posed against the background of the historical development of music, and the relations or differences between Oriental and European music. Space is not available for that here, but I propose to write a separate book going into the whole question fully. I have said elsewhere that I have been extremely fortunate in meeting people. My foregathering with Dr. MacCrimmon is a striking example of this good luck which has attended so many of my personal relationships.

To discuss subtle distinctions, nuances of the scale,
And listen as though they sought to discover secrets,
While all of them in the practice of their art neglect
The theories of the mind and follow nothing but the law of their own ears.
The supreme reality is visible to the mind alone.

And again, sarcastically I sing :

It is . . . absurd to say that most of those
Keenest on pipe-music only know its degenerate forms,
And that these are the foes of the great music [1]
Not knowing the difference between studying you and knowing you.[2]
It is equally absurd to say that lovers of music
The world over have neglected you to their loss,
That you showed the way to far greater heights
Than all the other courses music has followed.

But the fact remains. It is on the basis of this I quote ' the decivilized have every grace as the antecedent of their vulgarities, every distinction as the precedent of their mediocrities, no silly tune but has the excuse that the feint was suggested, made easy, by some living sweetness. . . . A vulgar doggerel concocted plainly, without excess of involution, prospers best now ! ' Praise no man nor any satirize !

An mhaith do bhi na' bi dhi
An mhaith ata', tar tairse.[3]

Of this same subject, I wrote in my pamphlet on Charles Doughty :

' He (Wagner) knew (as Charles Doughty knew) that we were coming to another of the quantitive—as against accentual—periods in culture. It is that lack of historical knowledge which disables no Marxist that is wrong with our mere impressionist commentators on such a phenomenon. (It is this question of quantity as against accent that distorts to most Scots the nature of our pibrochs of the great period.[4] These knew no

---

[1] To Poetry : i.e. the great music.
Uaill-gluth an Aoibhnis=' The exultant note of Joy.'
[2] The ' you ' in this extract refers to the great pipers.
[3] ' The good that hath been meddle not with ; the good that now is dwell on that ' (writ sarcastic).
[4] Before consenting to discuss bagpipe music with anyone not a Scot with a knowledge of Gaelic and Gaelic history and literature and Scottish Highlands and Islands, I would require that they read at least Mr. Fox Strangways' *Music of Hindostan*, Dr. Marius Schneider's *Geschichte der Mehrstimmigkeit* (Berlin, 1935), and Canon Galpin's *The Music of the Sumerians and their Immediate Successors the Babylonians and Assyrians*—and understood thoroughly what the latter is writing about when, evolving an interpretation of the notation of a Sumerian Hymn on the Creation of Man with harp accompaniment of the second millennium B.C., he says : ' The singer, no doubt, ornamented his part with grace notes as in the ancient Indian chanting, and the intervals taken in ascent by skip were rendered in descent with a light slide. The crotchet notation has no definite time value ; it merely denotes melodic progressions. Rhythm and stress depend on the words '—an explanation that, if Canon Galpin's solution is correct—and it is the only one so far put forward—means that Sumerian Hymn may be recreated in sound by any singer sensitive to the quasi-extemporaneous methods of primitive chant.

L

" bar ".   They were *timeless* music—hence their affiliation with plain-song, with the neuma.   Barred music—accented music—finds its ultimate form in symphony.   Unbarred music—quantity music—expresses itself in pattern-repetition ;   hence the idea that the Celt has no architectonic power, that his art is confined to niggling involutions and intricacies—yet the ultimate form here is not symphony ;   it is epic.) It is epic—and no lesser form—that equates with the classless society. Everything else—no matter how expressly it repudiates these in the mere logical meaning of what it *says* as against what it *is*—belongs to the old order of *bourgeois* " values ", to the nebulous entities described by terms like " spiritual " and " soul "—in short, it stands for the old romantic virtues, which is to say, pragmatically, for nothing.   Doughty, as against Auden and Day Lewis, say, is the only English poet who belongs to the New Order—that is to say, to our own time.   His significance to-day dwarfs all the other English poets since Elizabethan times into utter insignificance, and the failure of contemporary English *literati* to recognize that is only another confirmation of the Communist diagnosis of the present phase of English literature (it is significant that D. S. Mirski had no difficulty in recognizing the overtowering quality of Doughty) as being thoroughly in keeping with the imminent fatal crisis of a degenerate Capitalist society.   To those of us who are concerned about a Scottish Renaissance, Doughty's unique preoccupation with—and marvellous imaginative penetration into—ancient British (Gaelic) consciousness, is as convincing a " pointer " as Wagner's devotion to the study of word-roots.   " *The Dawn in Britain* [1] is a great storehouse of the history, fact, legend, and romance of the Celtic peoples ", truly observed one of its earliest reviewers.   That sealed its fate.   How the English Ascendancy policy treated Irish Gaelic literature, Dr. Douglas Hyde shows us.   How then could it tolerate Doughty's attack from inside—from within the English language itself ?   Never ! '

It does not take any very great musical knowledge to devise a few simple questions which can throw almost any piper to-day into a ludicrous fix and expose the extent to which his knowledge of his instrument is a mere ' dull mechanic exercise ', with incredible lacunae on the most elementary practical matters connected with it. The thing is known only on a mere abecedarian level, and any understanding of the nature and significance of the pibrochs of the great period—and their amazing superiority to anything the mind of Scotland to-day is capable of conceiving—is a ' transition into another field ', a getting-outside our modern European mental climate altogether, of which exceedingly few are capable under the most favourable conditions, while only the most unfavourable conditions are anywhere obtainable except for one or two exceptional persons. Only these probably can to-day understand why in the poem from which I have just quoted I go on from a ' metaphysical picture ' of the surpassing altitudes of the *Ceol Mor*, to sing :

[1] A complete account and examination of Doughty's sources is now under way.   Until that is published we will not know in any detail the means whereby Doughty came to his extraordinary understanding of the ancient British element.

It is now the duty of the Scottish genius
Which has provided the economic freedom for it
To lead in the abandonment of creeds and moral compromises
Of every sort, and to commence to express the unity of life
By confounding the curse of short-circuited thought
Circumscribing consciousness, for that is the thought
Of compromise, the medium of the time-server.
This must be done to lead men to cosmic consciousness,
And as it cannot be quick, except on occasion,
And that the creative instant, the moment of divine realization
When the self is lit by its own inner light,
Caused in the self by its intensity of thought
Possibly over a long period, it must be thought of as a craft
In which the consummation of the idea, not in analysis but in synthesis,
Must be the subject of the object—life.

Not to go too far afield at the moment, however, while I am dealing
with this incredible ignorance of and indifference to the past of our
country and its culture in Scotland, and the incapacity of most people
to contemplate for a moment any reconsideration of the bases of our
national life, or even to display any curiosity or interest whatever,
no matter what proofs or probabilities are adduced of premature
formulation, masses of evidence at variance with the established
conclusions, and new interpretations of the unassailable data even, it
must suffice to say that in Scottish history it is precisely as I have said
it is in regard to the great pipe-music. I have mentioned Charles
Doughty, but all that Charles Doughty did in regard to the ancient
British requires to be supplemented by a thorough assimilation of
Dr. L. A. Waddell's *The British Edda* (1930).[1] Dr. Waddell says :

'Strange to say, an immeasurably older, grander, and more important
epic of pre-Christian North-Western Europe than the Finnish *Kalevala*,

---

[1] Laurence Austine Waddell, born 1854, graduated M.B. at Glasgow in
1878, and had a long service on the north-west frontier of India. He
devoted himself to ethnographical studies, upon which he published several
important books, including *The Buddhism of Thibet* (1895), *The Tribes of the
Brahmaputra Valley* (1900), *Excavations at Pataliputra* (1903), &c.

See also *Civilization in Britain 2,000 B.C.*, by the late Dr. T. F. G. Dexter
(New Knowledge Press, Perranporth, Cornwall). 'Leaving out of consideration sundry lacunae of darkness, doubt, and uncertainty, we have a
fairly continuous history of Britain for nearly 2,000 years—from the first
invasion of Caesar to the present day. But there is another history of 2,000
years' duration from the end of the Stone Age to the first Roman invasion,
in other words, *there is as much history of Britain to learn as we already know.*
Here and there we get a fact or two, a glimpse or two of light. But we are
like little children who try to put together a jig-saw puzzle of which most of
the pieces are missing. But more and more pieces are being discovered
every day, and although we can never expect to find them all, yet we may
dare to hope to find so many as to be in a position to make a reasonable
inference regarding the nature of the whole picture. Perchance before the
next century is advanced, the history of Britain will be commenced, not at
55 B.C., the date of the Invasion of Julius Caesar, but at about 2000 B.C.,
the approximate date of the erection of Avebury.'

and now disclosed to be essentially of British heritage, and containing the earlier and hitherto unknown historical versions of the King Arthur and Grail legend, the *Faerie Queene, Paradise Lost*, and the real *Golden Bough* legends, has for centuries been lying mutilated, and all unrecognized as an epic, and one great consistent epic. This great heritage is now, after a sleep of many centuries, recovered, reconstructed, and resurrected in these pages in its original form from the jumbled and disjointed manuscripts of its score or so of ancient lays, as current in " The Dark Ages ", about the ninth century A.D. or earlier, and hitherto collectively known as *The Edda* or *The Poetical Edda*. It is now disclosed to be the glorious epic of hoary tradition of our British ancestors of the pre-Christian period, that had been sung adown the ages to the gathered crowds of Briton kinsmen on festival days, firing their imagination, inspiring them with hope, and thrilling their souls with the mighty deeds performed by their first ancestral king in procuring them and the modern world at large the blessings of civilized life. And based as it is upon the genuine historical tradition of the Rise of Civilization, uniquely handed down in writing through the centuries, it is of world-wide as well as British interest and historical importance.'

Dr. Waddell's book was of course virtually stillborn; English historians and *litterateurs* are not open to fundamental revaluations or any displacement of the upstart English tradition in favour of the far more important elements that tradition has so far wholly occluded and is all intent to keep in occlusion. In precisely the same way the discoveries of the archaeologists at Maiden Castle—virtually disclosing a false bottom to our accepted history—have not been acted upon nor effect given to the necessary changed perspectives, though these discoveries call for great modifications of our basic historical and cultural assumptions. But even with this we have by no means touched bottom—or got behind that inveterate tendency of English Ascendancy policy, which not only draws a veil over all these matters, but for like reasons did its utmost to stamp out Irish Welsh, and Scottish Gaelic literature, and even—but for Elizabeth Elstob's great fight—to ignore or deny Anglo-Saxon Studies.

It is to another book, which goes far deeper than Waddell's, touches the tap root of our national being far more shrewdly, and raises the most determined and ruthless opposition in the English, that I must direct Irish, Welsh, Scottish, and Cornish Gaels who want to call the whole bluff and get hold of all the essential links of the most important and deliberately contrived chain of error in our joint history. I refer to L. Albert's *Six Thousand Years of Gaelic Grandeur Unearthed*. Showing by an acute and wholly convincing consideration of the Ossian Macpherson and Chatterton cases that the ' most elementary laws of reason, logic, and commonsense, and the like, do not count with a certain class of forgery-mongers and arch-enemies of historic truth—especially when this truth is likely to enhance the national pride of the Gael,' the author expresses just indignation, but no surprise, at the persistent conspiracy maintained throughout the centuries to deny the validity of that ' continuous and consecutive history of the Gaelic branch of the Sumero-Caucasian (wrongly called Indo-European) race, covering the space of time from 5357 B.C. down to 7 B.C. and literally translated from the Old-Irish original, suppressed and hidden away these two thousand years.'[1] Finally published so recently as 1929, after stupendous difficulties, 'Alas ', says our author, in the volume cited, which gives in full the Writings of Eolus (5357 to 1335 B.C.), the Chronicles of Gael-Ag (Gallice) (1335 to 1006 B.C.), and the Chronicles of Eri (1006 to 7 B.C.),

' it was possible (despite a German critic who said that the author " produced weighty indirect proofs of authenticity, the chronicles offer us so many surprisingly novel facts in nearly every branch of historical knowledge, that henceforth it will be impossible for science to pass by in silence disclosures which are bound to create a revolution, the far-reaching consequences of which cannot yet be foreseen ") for science, or rather, the unworthy monopolizers of science, to prolong for a few years more the life of the stubbornly defended world-deceit. All efforts to obtain an official recognition of the revelation met with the adamant objection, or rather pretext : " Show us first the original Gaelic skins or parchments ; till then we refuse positively to take the slightest notice of the whole thing ". Note well that no such demand has ever been made with regard to other illustrious memorials of the past, such as the Bible, the Iliad, the Histories of Herodot, the works of the great Greek philosophers, &c. Nobody asks for the hand-writing of Moses, Homer, Herodot, Plato, Aristotle, &c. Their works are accepted on the strength of tradition and on their face value, the contents judged on their merits. Why is the oldest and most truthful document of Sumerian Caucasian humanity excluded from this self-evident procedure ? Why is it refused the favour of impartial examina-tion, leading to either final condemnation or solemn recognition, on the strength of evidence freely submitted for or against ? Why is this minute, sometimes even too minute and circumstantial, account of thousands of years of Gael–Scot–Iberian history, with all its irrefutable and unshatterable contemporary details, brutally condemned to remain buried and submerged for ever, solely because the Gaelic original which undoubtedly existed at the beginning of the nineteenth century, is at

---

[1] It is perhaps symbolical of my concern with the East—of the importance I attach in relation to Gaelic culture of this East–West synthesis, that the Thulean continent 60,000,000 years ago (when the Hebrides were tropical, the Alps, Carpathians, and Himalayas did not exist, and a great sea, the Tethys Sea, connected the Atlantic and Indian Oceans) had vines of which we have found the fossils that have their counterpart, flourish and fruit to-day only in the Far East, or, as Sir Albert Seward has said, ' The riddle of evolution remains a challenge, but from the ancient flora of the Western Isles we learn that in this immense interval of time there has been little difference in the nature of trees, shrubs, and ferns. For the most part a Western home has been exchanged for a home in the Far East.' If our forests have been ' wanderers ' resting in a temporary home until, as conditions changed, they moved on in stages until they reached their present refuge in Asia, that is perhaps a pointer to us that intellectually and spiritually we ought to follow their example. Our poets—Morris, Yeats, Æ, Doughty, and others—have increasingly tended to do so.

present unfindable or more probably hidden in some Irish archive or
library, if not altogether feloniously destroyed ? '

In the light of what the English have admittedly and undeniably
done to Scotland, Ireland, Cornwall, and Wales, it is easy to answer
these questions, and plenty other examples of the operation of
precisely the same sort of distorting and denying influence occur at
once to any well-informed student of the methods and effects of
English Ascendancy policy in our Gaelic countries, as Mr. Albert
alleges when he says :

> ' The exceptionally high level of civilization, organized government,
> and legislation in Ireland, at a time when the rest of Northern Europe
> resembled a swampy African jungle, peopled by half-savage cave-
> dwellers, wolves, vipers, boars and bears and the like, is inconceivable
> without the millennial educational works of the Olams of Spain and of
> Ulster, without the far-seeing initiative of the noble Iberian prince
> Eolus, who nearly 33,000 years ago, in an epoch of Europe often
> treated as " pre-historic ", laid the foundations to the work of national
> education. The light that for so many centuries radiated from the
> Isle of Destiny and the neighbouring British Isle to all parts of Europe,
> was kindled by Eolus the Wise and Good, and faithfully kept alight by
> his worthy successors ! Yet none of our history books, overflowing
> with the glorification of all the celebrated gangsters of antiquity, con-
> tains a single line about that great historic figure of Europe, one of the
> first who helped to build up British Imperial grandeur, ancestor of an
> endless line of Irish and Scottish kings, ancestors even of Fingal and
> Ossian. . . . All trace of his earthly existence, of his immortal bequest
> to humanity, of the millennial achievements of his worthy disciples, the
> Olams of Gallice and of Ulster, has been crushed and obliterated, not
> by hostile conquerors and foreign invaders only, but by the very de-
> scendants of the great benefactor ! Learned men whose sacred duty
> it ought to be to give due honour to the founder of Gaelic greatness
> and to the faithful instructors of generations, earliest creators of the
> intellectual and moral supremacy of the Nordic and North-Western
> World, vie with each other in their efforts to suppress their memory,
> in concealing or denouncing their priceless legacy.'

That sort of thing is nothing new to us in relation to Scottish
matters. And if we are to get behind it all—and encompass that
' revolution, the far-reaching consequences of which cannot yet be
foreseen '—we must not only follow the example of Charles Doughty
and avail ourselves of the work of L. A. Waddell, but we must broad-
base our movement on Cier-Rige's (i.e. Roger O'Connor's) records,
instead of on the faked and distorted versions of the Leinster or Tara
records, which were the only ones allowed to be circulated in Ireland,
and permitted to serve as a basis for the conquest of Ireland by the
propagators of Christianity when all further open activity of the
Olams was stopped, their free-thinking tenets being deemed to be
opposed to the tenets of the new Faith. Major Hay of Seaton's
Chain of Error in Scottish History (1926) was an important book in
the initiation of the Scottish Renaissance Movement, but it is only

in the light of these Chronicles that the utmost ramifications of the English Lie can be appreciated and its eradication and supplanting by the truth begun. But no one who has sought to oppose the English Ascendancy in these islands in howsoever trifling a particular will fail to recognize the gigantic nature of the task I am now indicating. As Mr. Albert says :

> ' The similarity, if not analogy, between the fate of the two revivers of Gaelic memorials (*Cier-Rige* and Ossian Macpherson) is indeed remarkable. The revelation of the Annals of the Olams, however, did not create in its time such a sensation as did the publication of Ossian's poetic legacy. Thus it was easier to stifle the disinterred historic monument by a conspiracy of silence, efficiently aided by the wholesale destruction of almost all the copies of the edition of 1821. Fortunately two or three copies, one of which is in the hands of the author, survived the renewed war of destruction. To denounce poetically embellished history, as the product of imagination of a modern poet, as was done in the case of Ossian, is of course easier than to make even the most credulous believe that a continuous historical record, extending over thousands of years and filling more than 500 folio pages, with an almost uninterrupted organically and logically connected sequence of chronological and genealogical data, the whole entirely free of all legendary distortions, adornments, anachronisms, contradictions, or inconsistencies, could be invented or compiled by a single man, however astute or endowed with semi-divine powers of dissimulation.'

But, as the dissertation of this volume conclusively shows, the internal linguistic evidence alone is ample proof of the authenticity of these Chronicles, which also respond convincingly to all kinds of cross-checking.

> ' In 1866 a Viennese savant tried to call the attention of the scientific world to the hidden document. The honest efforts of this Austrian professor were also in vain. He committed the fateful error of appealing to those who were most interested in ignoring or rejecting his appeal. A so-called " Geographical Congress " held in Laibach, Austria, duly denounced the annals as a " forgery ", without producing, of course, the least substantiation of this preposterous and scientifically insupportable charge. Another half-century passed, till an edition in two volumes appeared in Germany, the country known to be the birthplace of some of the most eminent " Celtic " (i.e. Gaelic) scholars. Many thousands of copies of this popular scientific Continental edition were sold and the reviewers of leading Continental dailies and magazines published highly eulogistic notices (though others, again without any proof, repeated the insinuation of forgery).'

Cier-Rige made several attempts to put together for publication his translation of these Chronicles—first in Dublin, then at Fort George in Scotland in 1799–1801, and succeeded, after extraordinary hazards, in 1821, only to have almost the whole edition destroyed in the manner mentioned. In producing the edition from the preface to which, and long dissertation in which, I have quoted, Mr. Albert had to surmount twelve years of such difficulties as amply attest the determination of certain interests to prevent further publicity being given to these records if they could possibly prevent it. That such difficulties exist—that there are extremely powerful interests which regard the matter as so important as to call for suppression at all costs—goes a long way in itself to attest the authenticity of the Chronicles. These books—Doughty's poems, Waddell's *British Edda*, and the *Chronicles*—preserved and transmitted through *Cier-Rige*, afford a basis for indeed doing, what Carlyle said Burns might have done on a much less fundamental and thorough-going basis, if he had been a ' better-equipped intellectual workman ', viz. changing the whole course of our literary history, and torpedoing the culture associated with the English Ascendancy policy. And that is the aim of the Scottish Renaissance Movement launched some twenty years ago, but then lacking—not the appropriate intuitions susceptible of this complete reach, but knowledge of the availability of the precise materials I have just listed, the indispensable *vorarbeiten* for this stupendous task—and, incidentally, a far more profound and effective basis than that which Doughty utilized.

It need not be imagined that I am over-sanguine. On the contrary, my feeling about Scotland to-day is best expressed by the word Aeschylus uses in *The Seven Against Thebes* for the hair-raising thrill of horror, μέφρικα τὰν ὠλεσίοικον θεόν, οὐ θεοῖς ὁμοίαν. I have set G. M. Cookson's translation of these lines at the top of a poem of mine, ' The Glen of Silence ', in which I express this feeling :

By this cold shuddering fit of fear
My heart divines a presence here,
Goddess or ghost yclept;
Wrecker of homes. . . .

Where have I heard a silence before
Like this that only a lone bird's cries
And the sound of a brawling burn to-day
Serve in this wide empty glen but to emphasize ?

Every doctor knows it—the stillness of foetal death,
The indescribable silence over the abdomen then !
A silence literally ' heard ' because of the way
It stands out in the auscultation of the abdomen.

Here is an identical silence, picked out
By a bickering burn and a lone bird's wheeple
—The foetal death in this great ' cleared ' glen
Where the *fear-tholladh nan tighem* [1] has done his foul work
—The tragedy of an unevolved people.

The feeling about Scotland I express in ' The Glen of Silence ' is of course, frequently to be found in modern Scottish poets. In hi

---

[1] Destroyer of homes.

' Fios thun a'Bhaird ' (Message to the Bard) Uilleam MacDhunleibhe complains :

> The inherited houses of those who have left us [1]
> Are throughout the land cold cairns.
> Gone are the Gaels, and they shall not return.
> The cultivation has ceased, sowing and reaping.
> The foundations of the melancholy larochs
> Bear witness. . . .
>
> There will not be heard the maiden's ditty,
> The chorus of songs at the waulking-board,
> Nor stalwart fellows as was wont
> Playing the game on an even field.
> The unjust violence of exile took them from us
> And gave the strangers victory as they desired.
> . . . The speckled serpent lies in folds
> On the floors where there grew
> The great ones I have seen. . . .
>
> The land of Oa has been made desolate,[2]
> Beautiful Lanndaidh and Roinn Mhic Aoidh,
> And sunny valleyed Learga
> Has a woeful remnant on her side.
> The glen is a green lea land
> Held by men who hate, without tenantry or crop. . . .

And Donald Sinclair (the Barra poet and dramatist who was a personal friend of my own) cries in one of his finest lyrics :

Is it a wonder that the western firmament is to-night in splendour
And that your abodes in the far distance are lit with an everlasting light ?
Is it a wonder that the bareness of every floor speaks of the fullness of your story ?
Is it a wonder that hills have the words of the twilight in their mouths ?
Is it a wonder that the harp of the songs is silent under the veiling of this cloud
And that the song-voice of the bards is without spell, without excellence of art ?
It is no wonder that the breast of the tombs is swollen *with the worth of what is gone.*
Oh world, it is a woe that there will not return one hour that has withered
And that my desire, however lasting, will not light on one message from the sleep of the dead.

The phrase I have italicized is terribly poignant in the original ; the words I have given by the adjective ' swollen ' are *an toic*—' in swelling abundance '. Much of Sinclair's work is quite untranslatable.

---

[1] In the last seventy years Scotland has sent about one and a half millions of her sons overseas—a proportion equal to the present combined populations of Edinburgh and Glasgow.
[2] Places in the Island of Islay.

L 2

Finally, here is the *Oran Eile* (i.e. Another Song) of Uilleam Ros. As a song it is one of the greatest of Gaelic songs, but the air, so far as I know, has never been published. The most notable thing about this poem is a marvellous vowel music. The emotionalism is controlled by a really classical purity of diction and technique. There are a great brevity and pregnancy about the language which I am afraid are not even suggested by my rough literal translation (which also I hope later to cast into English verses, giving some idea of the metre of the original).

It is I that am under sorrow at this time.
Dram will not be drunk by me with cheer.
A worm is brooding in my vitals
That has told the world my secret desire.
I may not see passing
The maiden of softest eye.
That is what cast down my spirit to the ground
Like foliage from the tops of trees.

O maiden, most ringleted of hair,
I am in great desire of you ;
Though if you have chosen a good place for yourself
My blessing every morn with you !
I am sighing after you
Like a warrior who has been wounded,
Lying on the field without use,
Who will go to the strife no more.

And I am left like a fugitive from the herd,
Like a man who gives no esteem to woman,
Through your journey oversea under a kerchief.[1]
That took an impetuous shedding of tears from my eyes.
Better were it that I did not observe
Your beauty, your sense, and your fame
Or the sweet courtesy of your mouth
That is more melodious than the tune of any music.
Each evil man who hears of my state,
The state that puts on my nature fear,
Says that I am not a bard
And that I will give birth to no poem of worth ;
That my grandfather was a payer of rent
And my father always a pedlar.
They would put geldings in the plough [2]
But I would cut a verse before a hundred !

Long is my spirit in gloom,
My apprehension will not waken to music,
In bewildered dream like a distressed wanderer of the ocean
On the tops of the waves in mist.
It is the knowledge that your gaiety is far away
That has changed the hue of my complexion,

---

[1] I.e. symbolizing the fact that she was married.
[2] There is really a pun here between geldings and cutting (or carving) a verse. Geldings = *gearrain* (from verb *gearv* = cut).

Without love-talk, without mirth, without pride,
Without music, without grace, without strength.

I shall not awaken the lay at will,
I shall not put a poem in order,
I shall not waken music on the harp,
I shall not hear the laughter of the young,
I shall not ascend the pass of the high hills
With joyful strength as was my wont.
But I shall depart to sleep forever
In the hall of the dead bards.

Whatever my hopes or fears may be, I have never been in two minds about the condition of the vast majority of the people in Scotland to-day. It is best described perhaps in these phrases of D. H. Lawrence's :

' I realized with amazement how rapidly the human psyche can strip itself of its awareness and its emotional contacts, and reduce itself to a sub-brutal condition of simple gross persistence. It is not animality —far from it. These people are much less than animals. They are cold wills functioning with a minimum of consciousness. The amount that they are *not* aware of is perhaps the most amazing aspect of their character. They are brutally and deliberately *unaware*. They have no hopes, no desires even. They have even no will-to-exist, for existence even is too high a term. They have a strange, stony will-to-persist, that is all. And they persist by reaction, because they still feel the repulsiveness of each other, of everything, even of themselves. . . . So we have the stark reduction to a persistent minimum of the human consciousness. It is a minimum lower than the savage, lower than the African Bushman. Because it is a willed minimum, sustained from inside by resistance, brute resistance against any flow of consciousness except that of the barest, most brutal egoistic self-interest.'

That is an exact description of about 95 per cent. of the population of Scotland to-day.

What about the glamorous Hebrides, you ask ? You think you will find a wonderful sensitiveness to nature—and to the super-natural—there ? Not a bit of it. That is the bunkum of the Celtic Twilight. There is nothing more detestable, perhaps, than this Tibetization of the Hebrides—this myth that represents the Islanders as all some sort of spiritual sportsmen, specializing in weird and wonderful soul states. The whole business is such an utter vulgari-zation and trivialization of spiritual matters. Man, from China to Peru, has learned to train himself in the great act of acceptance and union—disciplined himself to achieve what is called in Pali *Jhana*—a dynamic realization of complete integration ; disciplined himself by careful training in concentration. *Jhana* combines that alert passivity (which Roger Fry used to say was the attitude most needed by the art-lover) with the naturalist's intense but uninterfering attention and the great humanist's realization of his kinship with all life. But there is no training in concentration in the Hebrides.

Very much the other way about.   They are nit-wits—scatter-brains.
And their soul-states are all just infuriatingly silly. . . . And above
all there, as practically everywhere else in Scotland, there is no least
vestige of a science of the growing edge of the human mind, of how
that process can be consciously advanced, and so social life is utterly
destitute of any inherent sanction.

The third of my *Direadh* poems, which has not hitherto appeared
in print, reads as follows :

' *So, in the sudden sight of the sun, has man stopped, blinded, paralysed
and afraid ?* '

I am reft to the innermost heart
Of my country now,
History's final verdict upon it,
The changeless element in all its change,
Reified like the woman I love.

Here in this simple place of clean rock and crystal water,
With something of the cold purity of ice in its appearance,
Inhuman and yet friendly,
Undecorated by nature or by man
And yet with a subtle and unchanging beauty
Which seems the antithesis of every form of art,

Here near the summit of Sgurr Alasdair
The air is very still and warm.

The Outer Isles look as though
They were cut out of black paper
And stuck on a brilliant silver background,
(Even as I have seen the snow-capped ridges of Hayes Peninsula
Stand out stark and clear in the pellucid Arctic atmosphere
Or, after a wild and foggy night, in the dawn
Seen the jagged line of the Tierra del Fuego cliffs
Looking for all the world as if they were cut out of tin,
Extending gaunt and desolate),
The western sea and sky undivided by horizon,
So dazzling is the sun
And its glass image in the sea.
The Cuillin peaks seem miniature
And nearer than is natural
And they move like liquid ripples
In the molten breath
Of the corries which divide them.
I light my pipe and the match burns steadily
Without the shielding of my hands,
The flame hardly visible in the intensity of light
Which drenches the mountain top.

I lie here like the cool and gracious greenery
Of the water-crowfoot leafage, streaming
In the roping crystalline currents,
And set all about on its upper surface
With flecks of snow blossom that, on closer looking,
Shows a dust of gold.

The blossoms are fragile to the touch
And yet possess such strength and elasticity
That they issue from the submergence of a long spate
Without appreciable hurt—indeed, the whole plant
Displays marvellous endurance in maintaining
A rooting during the raging winter torrents.
Our rivers would lose much if the snowy blossom
And green waving leafage of the water-crowfoot
Were absent—aye, and be barer of trout too!
And so it is with the treasures of the Gaelic genius
So little regarded in Scotland to-day.
Yet emerging unscathed from their long submergence,
Impregnably rooted in the most monstrous torrents [1]
—The cataracting centuries cannot rive them away—
And productive of endless practical good,
Even to people unaware of their existence,
In the most seemingly-unlikely connections.

I am possessed by this purity here
As in a welling of stainless water
Trembling and pure like a body of light
Are the webs of feathery weeds all waving,
Which it traverses with its deep threads of clearness
Like the chalcedony in moss agate
Starred here and there with grenouillette.

It is easy here to accept the fact
That that which the 'wisdom' of the past
And the standards of the complacent elderly rulers
Of most of the world to-day regard
As the most fixed and eternal verities—
The class state, the church,
The old-fashioned family and home,
Private property, rich and poor,
'Human nature' (to-day meaning mainly
The private-profit motive), their own race,
Their Heaven and their 'immortal soul',
Is all patently evanescent,
Even as we know our fossil chemical accumulations
Of energy in coal, peat, oil, lignite and the rest
Are but ephemeral, a transitory blaze
Even on the small time-scale of civilized man,
And that running water, though eminently convenient and practicable
For the present, will give us a mere trickle
Of the energy we shall demand in the future.

And suddenly the flight of a bird reminds me
Of how I once went out towards sunset in a boat
Off the rocky coast of Wigtownshire
And of my glimpse of the first rock-pigeon I saw.
It darted across one of the steep gullies
At the bottom of which our boat lay rocking
On the dark green water—and vanished into safety
In a coign of the opposite wall
Before a shot could be fired.

---

[1] See John Ruskin's description of the spring at Carshalton.

It swerved in the air,
As though doubtful of its way,
Then with a glad swoop of certainty
It sped forward, turned upward,
And disappeared into some invisible cranny
Below the overhanging brow of the cliff.

There was such speed, such grace, such happy confidence of refuge in
    that swoop
That it struck me with the vividness of a personal experience.
For an instant I seemed to see into the bird's mind
And to thrill with its own exhilaration of assured safety.
Why should this be?   It was as though
I had seen the same occurrence,
Or some part of it, before.

Then I knew.   Into the back of my mind had come
The first line of the loveliest chorus in *Hippolytus*,
That in which the Troezenian women,
Sympathizing with the unhappy Phaedra,
Who is so soon to die by her own hand,
Sing of their yearning to fly away from the palace
Whose sunny terraces are haunted by misery and impending doom.
They long to escape with the flight of the sea-birds
To the distant Adriatic and the cypress-fringed waters of Eridanus
Or to the fabulous Hesperides,
Where beside the dark-blue ocean
Grow the celestial apple-trees.
It is the same emotion as filled the Hebrew poet
Who cried : ' O for the wings of a dove,
That I might flee away and be at rest.'
' ἠλιβάτοις ὑπὸ χενθμῶσι γενοίμαν.'
The untranslatable word in that line
Is the ὑπό.   It includes more
Than a single word of English can contain.
Up-in-under : so had the pigeon
Flown to its refuge in ' the steep hiding-places ',
So must Euripides have seen a sea-bird
Dart to its nest in the cliffs of Attica.
For an instant, sitting in that swaying boat
Under the red rocks, while the sunset ebbed down the sky
And the water lapped quietly at my side,
I again felt the mind of the poet reaching out
Across the centuries to touch mine.
Scotland and China and Greece !
Here where the colours—
Red standing for heat,
Solar, sensual, spiritual ;
Blue for cold—polar, bodily, intellectual ;
Yellow luminous and embodied
In the most enduring and the brightest form in gold—
Remind me how about this
Pindar and Confucius agreed.
Confucius who was Pindar's contemporary
For nearly half a century !
And it was Pindar's ' golden snow '

My love and I climbed in that day.
I in Scotland as Pindar in Greece
Have stood and marvelled at the trees
And been seized with honey-sweet yearning for them ;
And seen too mist condensing on an eagle,
His wings ' streamlined ' for a swoop on a leveret,
As he ruffled up the brown feathers on his neck
In a quiver of excitement ;
Pindar, greatest master of metaphor the world has seen,
His spirit so deeply in tune
With the many-sidedness of both Man and Nature
That he could see automatically all the basal resemblances
His metaphors imply and suggest.
Scotland and China and Greece !

So every loveliness Scotland has ever known,
Or will know, flies into me now,
Out of the perilous night of English stupidity,
As I lie brooding on the fact
That ' perchance the best chance
Of reproducing the ancient Greek temperament
Would be to " cross " the Scots with the Chinese '.[1]
The glory of Greece is imminent again to me here
With the complete justification his sense of it
In Germany—his participation in that great awakening
Taking the form of an imaginative reliving,
On behalf of his people, of the glory of Athens—
Lacked in Holderlin.   I see all things
In a cosmic or historical perspective too.
Love of country, in me, is love of a new order.
In Greece I also find the clue
To the mission of the poet
Who reveals to the people
The nature of their gods,
The instrument whereby his countrymen
Become conscious of the powers on whom they depend
And of whom they are the children,
Knowing, in himself, the urgency of the divine creativeness of Nature
And most responsive to its workings in the general world.
' Wer das Tiefste gedacht, liebt das Lebendigste.'

And remembering my earlier poems in Scots
Full of my awareness ' that language is one
Of the most cohesive or insulating of world forces
And that dialect is always a bond of union,[2]
I covet the mystery of our Gaelic speech
In which *rughadh* was at once a blush,
A promontory, a headland, a cape,
Leadan, musical notes, litany, hair of the head,
And *fonn*, land, earth, delight, and a tune in music,[3]
And think of the Oriental provenance of the Scottish Gael,

---

[1] Sir Richard Livingstone.
[2] Sir James Crichton-Browne.
[3] Macfarlane's *English and Gaelic Vocabulary* (Constable, Edinburgh, 1815).

The Eastern affiliations of his poetry and his music,
'. . . the subtler music, the clear light
Where time burns back about th' eternal embers ',
And the fact that he initiated the idea of civilization
That to-day needs renewal at its native source
Where, indeed, it is finding it, since Georgia,
Stalin's native country, was also the first home of the Scots.

The Gaelic genius that is in this modern world
As sprays of quake grass are in a meadow,
Or light in the world, which notwithstanding
The *Fiat Lux* scores of thousands of years ago,
Is always scanty and dubious enough
And at best never shares the empery of the skies
On more than equal terms with the dark,
Or like sensitive spirits among the hordes of men,
Or seldom and shining as poetry itself.
Quake grass, the ' silver shakers ', with their glumes shaped and corded
Like miniature cowrie shells, and wrapped
In bands of soft green and purple, and strung
(Now glittering like diamonds,
Now chocolate brown like partridge plumage)
On slender stems and branchlets, quick
To the slightest touch of air !

So Scotland darts into the towering wall of my heart
And finds refuge now.   I give
My beloved peace, and her swoop has recalled
That first day when my human love and I,
Warmed and exhilarated by the sunny air,
Put on our skis and began
A zigzag track up the steep ascent.
There was no sound but the faint hiss and crush
Of the close-packed snow, shifting under our weight.
The cloudless bowl of the sky
Burned a deep gentian.   In the hushed, empty world,
Where nothing moved but ourselves,
Our bodies grew more consciously alive.
I felt each steady beat of my heart.
The drawing and holding of my breath
Took on a strange significance.
Nor was I merely conscious of myself.
I began to be equally aware of my love ;
Her little physical habits
Sinking into my mind
Held the same importance as my own.

How fragrant, how infinitely refreshing and recreating
Is the mere thought of Deirdre !
How much more exhilarating to see her, as now !

' She said that she at eve for me would wait ;
Yet here I see bright sunrise in the sky.' [1]

---

[1] From a Chinese eight-lines lyric, twenty-seven centuries old.

Farewell all else! I may not look upon the dead,
Nor with the breath of dying be defiled,
And thou, I see, art close upon that end.

I am with Alba—with Deirdre—now
As a lover is with his sweetheart when they know
That personal love has never been a willing and efficient slave
To the needs of reproduction, that to make
Considerations of reproduction dictate the expression of personal
  love
Not infrequently destroys the individual at his spiritual core,
Thus ' eugenic marriages ' cannot as a whole
Be successful so far as the parents are concerned,
While to make personal love master over reproduction
Under conditions of civilization is to degrade
The germ plasm of the future generations,
And to compromise between these two policies
Is to cripple both spirit and germ,
And accept the only solution—unyoke the two,
Sunder the fetters that from time immemorial
Have made them so nearly inseparable,
And let each go its own best way,
Fulfilling its already distinct function,
An emancipation the physical means for which
Are now known for the first time in history!

Let what can be shaken, be shaken,
And the unshakeable remain.
The Inaccessible Pinnacle [1] is not inaccessible.

So does Alba surpass the warriors
As a graceful ash surpasses a thorn,
Or the deer who moves sprinkled with the dewfall
Is far above all other beasts
—Its horns glittering to Heaven itself. [2]

The controversy a few months ago in regard to the Food Ministry's
scale of fat-stock prices, which ended, after a long and hard fight on
the part of the Scottish feeders for a recognition that was no more
than their due, in a new scale awarding a special graded price to the
light-weight quality cattle which are a distinctively Scottish product,
and also in provision for a fairer return on the hill-bred ewe mutton
for which Scotland is famous, is only one other example of a host
of differences between England and Scotland which amount in the
aggregate to a different *ethos* altogether, and show that despite all the
surface assimilation Scotland is profoundly and permanently different
from England in the whole tradition, tone, texture, and tendency of
its national life.

Another striking example of the same sort of thing is the fact that

---

[1] Of Sgurr Dearg, in Skye.
[2] See *Volsungakvida en forna*, 41 (*Saemundar Edda*, Jonsson).

it is the custom of the Scottish trade to sell practically all bacon without the skin, but the rationing in the present war has been arranged on the English practice of selling with the skin on. In the 1914–18 War, the Scottish Control schedule for bacon and ham was 2d. per lb. higher than the control schedule for England to cover these points. The main complaint of the provision trade is that the control scheme has been moulded largely on English practice, although one or two concessions have been made to Scotland (not without a stiff fight on the part of the Scottish interests, however !). Most notable of the concessions is the inclusion in the control schedule of Ayrshire bacon, but the trade asserts that the specifications governing the processing of Ayrshire bacon in the scheme will mean that this article will be identifiable only by name. Under the scheme it is specified that Ayrshire bacon must be processed for fourteen days. This does not mean that the bacon must be kept in the brine for that period, but it will produce a much stronger cure, and probably an article that will shock Scottish consumers' palates. Normally Ayrshire bacon is processed for forty-eight to sixty hours, and is usually consumed within the next seventy-two hours. As the trade describe it, Ayrshire bacon is a quick job, serving the taste of consumers who appreciate a mild cure. As regards ham, the trade also fear the arrangement under which all hams, no matter what their source—whether it be Ireland, Denmark, or America—are priced at the same rate retail. In actual practice, they assert, this will mean that the working classes in Glasgow who appreciate the relative cheapness of American hams will have to pay 4d. to 6d. per lb. more under this flat-rate basis.

These and scores of other examples of the deep underlying or detail differences between Scottish and English practice in all sorts of connexions are, of course, quite unknown to most people. Most of the Scottish population are, indeed, in pretty much the same position with regard to Scotland as the woman who a few years ago, although she had never been in a jungle in her life, wrote so excellent a thriller about a jungle adventure that even experts paid tribute to the authenticity of the background. This reminds me of that famous Scotsman, Sir James Frazer, who, although he wrote so knowledgeably of savages and their ways in *The Golden Bough* (twelve volumes plus supplement), never saw a live savage in his native habitat. With this ignorance of all sorts of factors of vital practical importance in the nation's life there goes also, while the newspapers are swamped with matters of no real interest or account, a strange obliviousness to the really interesting and significant things that are going on in our own midst. Perhaps the strangest matter of the kind recently has been the employment of some 200 Newfoundland lumberjacks felling trees in the spruce and pine woods of remote Liddesdale which I knew so well as a boy. The Newfoundlanders were somewhat handicapped in their work because their billets were ten miles away from the woods, and in England at that !

I have, of course, a great collection of ' howlers ' with regard to Scottish geography. An English writer, discussing the possibility of Unity Mitford going for a holiday to Inchkenneth, her father's Scottish residence, placed that island in the Outer Hebrides, while another, writing in a Sunday paper, located it at Oban. One would have thought that Inchkenneth's proper position off the west coast of Mull would be known to most writers, for it was there that Dr. Johnson spent the most agreeable Sunday of his life during his tour of the Hebrides, and confessed himself charmed with the hospitality shown by Sir Allan MacLean. But Sassenachs are notoriously weak in Hebridean geography. Not so long ago a columnist asserted that Mr. Hugh Ruttledge, the Everest climber, was holidaying in Gometra, ' a hilly island in the Firth of Lorne ' ! And, of course, there is the classic story of the English tourist who thought the Sound of Mull was a quaint echo !

I have written about seeing Scotland whole, but it is one of the seeming paradoxes of my work that in my own practice I am mainly concerned with the odd fact, the exceptional instance, the elusive and out-of-the-way information. Thus I make a point of knowing where in its season may be found the small deep-yellow cow-wheat, *Melampyram sylvaticum*, a plant found only in the very oldest woodland, and I am less concerned with the sweet-william, the peony roses, the southernwood, the marigolds smelling like menstrual blood, of the Dumfriesshire cottage gardens I knew so intimately as a boy, than with where I may find the rare shrubby Potentilla (*Fruticosa*), or the neat white spikes of *Neotinea intacta* or the red helleborine, or *Pyrola media* (the wintergreen), or the Pyramid bugle. It is true that the matters with which I am most concerned are for the most part like snipe chicks. ' One moment they are in evidence, piping in subdued tones, or contentedly pecking about. Then, as one's advance under cover of boulders or ling can no longer be disguised, the parents resort to clamorous flight and in the same instant the spot where the family has been becomes to all appearance as destitute of life as though the grass had never bent beneath any weight more perceptible than that of a dragon-fly. Over it the bog-cotton waves, the clouds cast their reflections, but the tiny chicks have melted into the friendly heath, which so kindly lends its colours, like a screen, to shelter the young life which through the long course of the centuries it has produced and fostered.'

Then there is my predilection for the exotic. That puzzles people too, and seems inconsistent with my declared main purpose. I am like a poor cottage gardener who has been taken to a great International Flower Show. He has seen the amazing orchids ; his hand has touched the orange spadix of the brilliant scarlet *Anthurim*

Scherzerianium. He has no use afterwards for the dahlias and other ordinary flowers in his own little plot upon which previously he had lavished so much time and trouble, and ceases to grow flowers at all, giving over all his garden to vegetables. So I am concerned with the hibiscus hedges of Ceylon, the lurid poincarias of Panama, the jacaranda trees of Australia and the Cape—perhaps, seen against a blue sky, the loveliest sight of all creation—the bougainvillaeas of many countries.

How are these apparent inconsistencies reconciled? I have long realized that it is true with regard to everything as an American investigator found it with regard to the judging of pedigree bulls. ' How does a bull score points? ' he asked. ' The scale of points we judge on has 22 headings,' he was told, ' with a total of 100 points for perfection, which of course no bull ever got. Style and symmetry is 10 points, head 6, horns 1, neck 3, withers 3, shoulders 2, chest 4, back 8, loin 3, hips 2, rump 6, thurls 2, barrel 10, and so on. The biggest number of points for any heading is 20 points for Secretions Indicating Colour of Product. That's judged by the pigment secretions of the skin, which should be deep yellow·inclining towards orange in colour, especially discernible in the ear, at the end of the tailbone, around the eyes and nose, on the scrotum, and at the base of horns. Hoofs and horns should be yellow. There is a very close relationship between the colour of the skin, the colour of the internal fat, and the milk and butter. Now, that heading alone is 20 points out of the 100, and you can judge it only by a close-up inspection. . . .' The investigator nodded : ' I see. The subtleties rule, as usual.'

What I attach so much importance to, what I have always so much in view—the explanation of my seeming illogicalities—is very similar to what Sir Arthur Eddington in *The Philosophy of Physical Science* calls ' the special facts '. ' It is the essence of our conception of the special fact that it might quite well have been otherwise, that there is not a *priori* reason why it should be what it is.' He gives the impression of a world of diverse particularity which has quality other than obedience to physical law. This quality, he suggests, may be intrinsic and not imposed by the framework of scientific inspection. Finally, I would add that my point of view (stated in the first article on aesthetics I contributed to the *New Age* about thirty years ago) has always been that succinctly expressed by Professor Harold Laski when he says :

' It is good to find the " Departments of Language and Literature " moving into that hinterland where life and literature meet. One day its outcome may be the breakdown of the artificial boundaries which exist in our university curricula. For only as specialism understands how to relate its particularity to the structure of the universe can it cease to be a danger to understanding. Universities have reformed too many minds by confining them within a space too narrow for a vision of the horizon to be possible. The discoveries are made at the boundaries of subjects and not at their centres.'

It is for this reason that I am so vitally interested in every local *chauvinisme*,[1] why I am very dubious, for example, about proposals like Hatry's for transferring populations to more favourable economic conditions—knowing that better economic prospects will tempt few Durham men to move to the next county even.

' So it is with the whole story of biology—the suitability of the environment for the living structure, the cultivation of that environment by the living thing, the ecological pattern of correlation and interdependence—these are all special facts to the physicist. To the philosopher they are something more than this. They are glimpses of an architecture which is the condition precedent of life. They are indications of an organization of Nature where the true wealth of life resides ! In them is to be found the order against which destructive inroads have been made by the careless and irresponsible manipulations of applied science. . . . Now that physicists themselves proclaim the limits of their own methods, the opportunity is presented to the biologist of formulating his own understanding, not of the manipulation of life but of the order which makes free living possible and of the balance of that order and the requirements which it has for man. Under such knowledge, man could again turn his hand from destruction and death to the cultivation of life. The only hope which exists for the future of industrial man lies in understanding and recognition of the architectures of life and in co-operation with, and cultivation of, these. Out of such cultivation peace can be born ; the present organization of industry can never breed anything other than war and crisis.'

My seeming inconsistencies !—seeming inconsistencies many of which are very much of the same sort, of course, as Engels finding what he wanted in the work of Balzac, a Catholic and a royalist, rather than in that of Zola, the liberal republican !

Just as with plants, so with places. When I think of Scotland I do not think of Edinburgh or Glasgow or the Forth Bridge and other well-known places so much as of out-of-the-way and little-known places : ' The North face of Liathach lives in the mind like a vision. From the deeps of Coire na Caime, which is the Crooked Corrie, sheer cliffs rise up to spurs and pinnacles and jagged teeth. Its grandeur draws back the heart.' Scotland is full of such places ; few (few Scots even) know them. That is why, of all the pictures of Scottish landscape I know, I immensely prefer the wood-engraving of Coire Mhic Fhearchair by Brenda Chamberlain and R. John Petts, which glorified the *Welsh Review* of November 1939. Few pictures

[1] ' If you think that certain things do not show from what district they come, yea, even to an *arrondissement*, then, you are not out gunning for particular game, but simply any catch, and I'll have nothing to do with you ! I do not discuss weighty matters with water wits.' Djuna Barnes in *Nightwood*.

have ever affected me so profoundly and, I am sure, permanently. It is a marvellous picture of that stupendous cliff of Torridon Sandstone rising, on Beinn Eighe, above the deep loch-side in three bold buttresses capped with grey quartzite. It is a pity a big reproduction of it does not occupy one of the walls of every Scottish school-room. That would involve a tremendous revolution in Scottish education and life—precisely the revolution that is needed ; that picture would take such a tremendous living up to !—shallowness, meanness, stupidity would, I feel sure, soon be eliminated in those who had to face up to it daily in their most impressionable years.

I may add that I find it necessary in my poetry and other writings to draw so largely upon the Scottish landscape, not only because modern ecology has destroyed the delusion which encouraged people to jeer at any suggestion of geographic ' control ' and human ' response ' to such control and to-day physiology and psychology are agreed that there is a relation, a functional relation, between an organism and its environment, but because I am mainly concerned with the working class, who save in landscape have never known beauty in any form. But I fall foul of most Scottish enthusing and writing about Nature because I share the Chinese belief in the essential function of geography as a training of the mind in visualization, in the making of mental pictures of forms and forces—landforms and climatic forces—that are beyond the horizon, a belief the importance of which lies in the fact that Chinese painting developed as an art based on visualization and not on vision, on a mental picture and not on a Nature study, even when the subject was a landscape. The Scottish writing and enthusing in question has, on the contrary, no mind in it at all and is hopelessly anti-aesthetic and anti-intellectual.

And beyond that, I am constantly on the *qui vive* for every trace of that peculiar individuality which Duns Scotus called *haecceitas* and the *distinctiv formalis a parte rei*, agreeable to his love of objects between which minute distinctions can be made—and, further, the concrete individuality of each object known in at least a confused way intuitively ; every body having not merely a material form but also a vital form ; a special element of its being in its activity and movement. I cannot get rid of a certain participation in—or interest in and sympathy with—such Scotist ideas, since I myself am always so intent on ' the slightest integrity ', and inclined to find, too—among the lower strata of society—traces of the old common collective psychology, ' not a collective newspaper thought (a man could not then afford to have his life lived for him) but an acute common sense, lost to us ' ; the universal defensive observation each man, having to do his own summing-up, developed in these pre-specialist days ; swamped now by the second-hand knowledge of reading and writing.

And in Scotland, more and more (among a bigger and bigger proportion of our people, that is), it seems to me we also encounter the
opposite case, when all those activities which ordinarily do (or used
to) reach consciousness are suddenly no longer capable of doing so, a
far more alarming state of affairs than when those activities which
ordinarily do not reach consciousness, such as the beating of the
heart and the movements of the viscera, suddenly do so.

CHAPTER VI

THE IDEAS BEHIND MY WORK

' It was the hair-breadth accuracy of freedom which enchanted him. . . .
To build the new world he coveted he wanted only a single-mindedness of
aim and an urgency of desire, and without them he was lost. . . . Urgency
followed him, single-mindedness side-tracked him ; one had to harness
them both and drive the team to the furthermost limits of the spirit.'—
ROBERT YOUNG.

> And so the poetry of a poet
> Who is as much at home
> In Chinese or Indian thought
> As in Greek—nay, being a Gael,
> Knows well how the old dark crimson rose
> And the wistful tea-roses
> Brought their perfume out of the East
> But never exhale it so sweetly
> As when washed by the rains of the West.

TO TURN to my own poetry, the central passion that animates it is
expressed in the following passage from my ' Third Hymn to
Lenin '.

> Our concern is human wholeness—the child-like spirit
> Newborn every day—not, indeed, as careless of tradition
> Nor of the lessons of the past : these it must needs inherit ;
> But as capable of such complete assimilation and surrender,
> So all-inclusive, unfenced-off, uncategoried, sensitive, and tender,
> That growth is unconditional and unwarped—Ah, Lenin,
> Life and that more abundantly, thou Fire of Freedom !
> Firelike in your purity and heaven-seeking vehemence,
> Yet the adjective must not suggest merely meteoric,
> Spectacular—not the flying sparks, but the intense
> Glowing core of your character, your large and splendid stability,
> Made you the man you were—the live heart of all humanity—
> Spirit of Lenin, light on this city now !
> Light up this city now !

A fuller statement of this vision which informs all my work is in
the following lines :

> Poverty is nothing but an outlived fettering
> In the depths of the material regions
> —In the mechanical, dead, inanimate
> Or animal life of Nature.
>
> This life we have now outgrown.
> It lays the veil of the body over the spirit
> And drags everything down to the level
> Of a narrow materiality.
>
> It is nothing but meanness and ugliness,
> Stench, corruption, vice, decomposition, and dumbness.

The call is to intoxicated, burning lavishness.
Nothing now can bring poverty
Creatively to the front.
Poverty merely hinders the coming
Of the new Necessity
Which leads us to the End and Aim
Of our spirit and of the world,
Will make us steep and electric
And produce by force a new race
Of mariners on new and dangerous seas.

Poverty to-day desires nothing
But a material well-being.
But the entire hopeless comfortlessness
Of a satisfied well-being
Must first be lived through,
Not merely described
Or held out to the poor
From afar.
The lower paradises
Must be outlived through satiety.
This is the call of the Seraphim.

Only he who hopes nothing more
From well-being and philistinism ;
Only he who is no longer fettered
In the coarse material depths ;
Only he who yearns for new needs
—The needs of the Heights,
Not the needs of the Depths,
Immense and seraphic needs—
He only perceives
The impalpable and primordial life,
The Supreme—a life
Fuller, more real, and warmer
Than the chaotic deception
Of the palpable and objective
Which is apparently only effective
For everyday lower life.

To-day we are ripe to put an end
To poverty—to make an end
Of this necessity
For richness and abundance
In this world period
Become mankind.
But there is without doubt
Also a holy poverty,
A super-richness which falls to piece
In its own splendour,
A glowing love
That presses all fullness to itself,
Allows all small possessions to fall
More and more away from it,
All narrowness in relation
To things and to self—
Not from any ascetic discomfort,

But because of the poorness
Of these things in themselves.
Such is the glory
Of holy riches
And supreme prodigality.
The purpose of the old needs, therefore,
Cannot be ' well-being '
But only a new need.
Does the mighty proletarian assault
Of the poorest to-day desire nothing
But ' satiety ', nothing but ' well-being '
With a smattering of art and education
Built philistine-wise upon it ?

Does it not want as it asserts
To overcome the bourgeoisie,
But only to establish it forever
—Bourgeoisie itself in everything,
Not a step higher ?
And that disgusts the few spiritual men,
But how can it disgust
Those poorest ones ?
The deliverance of the proletariat cannot be
The affair of the proletariat itself,
As demagogic teaching declares.
It is in truth more than a sectional affair,
More than a class affair.

To-day something is beginning, as if the seed
Were losing itself in the bud.
Creation wants to-day to blossom
And raise itself to its topmost heights.
And if we wish to survive and not to suffocate,
Then in this day we must mount
An entirely new step higher, a greater step
Than that from the animal world
To the world of man.

That, however, is not technique,
Science, economics, organization, learning,
Or any kind of reform or ' cleverness '.
It is a *necessity* called for
By the eternal primordial life.
The new level of life does not depend
Upon a thing, nor upon
An individual.
It is an act of the never-ending creation,
Lying far beyond all individualist action.
Nevertheless we cannot mount
On to another plane of life
Until all the old possibilities,
Unto the very last,
Have been worn out and lived through.
For the way to the Supreme
Is in no way
The quickest and shortest.

It is a way most deeply sunk
And does not pass by
The smallest possibility of life.
For every part of the way
Is of equal value
In the Supreme.   Every part
Is an aim in itself,
For the Supreme knows no ' Evolution '.

' Evolution ' has only an entirely
' Inner-finite ' significance.
It is a barbarous adoption,
As if somewhere, quite positive,
There were a Process—if possible, quite temporal—
Which in its issue, in its *sum*, determines the
' Essence ' of the real ;
Is itself absolute reality,
Universalness, the Supreme.
All our ideas about such a world process
Are nothing but a human and temporal view
And entirely adapted
To a temporal standard.

Every ' World Process ' that we describe
Has only a world reality,
A reality of manifestation and technique.
We comprehend in it only
That which is objective and dead,
Never its life—for all life
Is incomprehensible.
Life is greater than all that can enter
Into the comprehensible.
Though I know all the limbs,
Entrails, organs, and functions of mankind,
Still am I as far as ever
From knowing ' man '
Who is more than the sum of his organs,
Which indeed only find
Their meaning and their life
When man's action precedes them.
We do not know a mosaic
By adding up the stones.
On the contrary,
The picture comes before the stones,
Without which the picture means nothing.

Whoever regards a ' World Process '
As a final reality
Is merely pursuing the anatomy
Of the corpse of all life.
This string of pearls, which in themselves
Are single and loose,
Is not the final form.
The world reality of such a process
In Thing, Individual, and Word
Is only its lowest form.

What we call *being* is only
The functioning of our consciousness,
Not the ' final Universal of All ',
But the lowest.
It is the feeling, groping, consuming spirit ;
Objective, matter-bound, but not living spirit.
That higher and stronger quickening life
We seek eternally and to-day
Must discover anew
Eternally transcends the objective spirit
Because it has nothing objective,
Only life.

But we draw the supreme Source of Life
Into the kingdom of Touch and Taste and Speech
If we signify it as something
' Behind ' or ' Over ' or ' Near ',
Conformably to some spacious picture ;
Or as the ' One ', the ' Without Shape ',
The ' Thing in Itself '.   These are all
Materialistic, mediate things,
But ' the Supreme' and ' life ' are immediate.
Pleroma is immediate, and is far away
Only from the gropers who seek
To muffle the infinite
In limitations and terms.
But to the high, crushing nearness
Of my exploding primordial life
The Supreme is ' that which is quite Nigh ',
That which is without distance,
Immediateness itself, love-embrace,
The paradisiacal awareness
In which all fullness immediate and unredeemed,
Since all time, is posited timelessly,
Over ' Being ', blessed in ' One '.
No empty abstraction, but the Life
Which can never be grasped,
That is transcendent.
And no bridge carries us
From ' Word ' to ' trans ',
Even as no bridge, but a leap,
Carries us from the plane to the cube,
From shallows to the bodily likeness.

No matter where it ranges, all my work comes home to Scotland,
as in this poem on Edinburgh :

' Most of the denizens wheeze, sniffle, and exude a sort of snozzling whnoff
whnoff, apparently through a hydrophile sponge.'—EZRA POUND.

' The capital of Scotland is called Auld Reekie
Signifying a monstrous acquiescence
In the domination of the ends
By the evidences of effort.
—Not the mastery of matter
By the spirit of man
But, at best, a damnable draw,

A division of the honours
And, far more, the dishonours!
—Dark symbol of a society
Of ' dog eat dog '.
Under which the people reveal themselves to the world
Completely naked in their own skin,
Like toads!
Yes, see, the dead snatch at the living here.
So the social corpse, the dead class,
The dead mode of life, the dead religion,
Have an after life as vampires.
They are not still in their graves
But return among us.
They rise with the fumes
From the chimney of the crematorium
And again settle down on the earth
And cover it with black filth.

To repossess ourselves of the primal power
' Let there be light ' and apply it
In our new, however more complex, setting
Is all.   And let us not cry
' Too difficult !   Impossible ! ' forgetting
That the stupendous problems that obsess us to-day
Are as nothing to the problems overcome
By the miraculous achievements of men in the past
—Yes, the first problems in the very dawn of human history
Were infinitely greater, and our troubles are due
To the fact that we have largely lost
The earliest, the most essential,
The *distinctively human* power
Our early ancestors hand in abundance measure
Whatever else they lacked that we possess.
Possess thanks to them !—and thanks to the primal indispensable
    power
They had and we have lost progressively
And affect to despise—
Fools who have lost the substance
And cling to the shadow.
Auld Reekie indeed !
Preferring darkness rather than light
Because our deeds are evil !

I see the dark face of an early mother of men
By a primitive campfire of history.
Her appearance is rendered all the more remarkable
Because of the peculiar performance of the smoke.
By some process, natural no doubt but mysterious to us,
She exercises a strange control over the smoke
As she shuffles round—with vast protruding lips
And with wide rings hanging from her ears,
Weaving her hands.   And it is
As if the billows of thick white vapour
Are forced to follow her will
And make a magical dancing cloud
Behind her as she moves.

Learn again to consume your own smoke like this,
Edinburgh, to free your life from the monstrous pall,
To subdue it and be no longer subdued by it,
Like the hand of the dyer in his vat.
So all the darkness of industrialism yet
Must be relegated like a moth that pursues
The onward dance of humanity.

So the mighty impetus of creative force
That seeks liberation, that shows even through
The scum of swinish filth of bourgeois society,
The healthy creative force will break through
—Even in Edinburgh—and good, human things grow,
Protecting and justifying faith
In regeneration to a free and noble life
When labour shall be a thing
Of honour, valour, and heroism
And ' civilization ' no longer like Edinburgh
On a Sabbath morning,
Stagnant and foul with the rigid peace
Of an all-tolerating frigid soul !

This is the great skill that mankind has lost,
The distinctively human power.
Lo !   A poor negress teaches this rich university city
Something more important than all it knows,
More valuable than all it has !
But Edinburgh—Edinburgh—is too stupid yet
To learn how not to stand in her own light.

And then I remember Dante's perfect description of the Edinburgh
people :

In Edinburgh—in Auld Reekie—to-day
Where 99 per cent. of the people might say
In Dante's words . . . ' Tristi fummo
Nell' aer dolce che del sol d'allegra '
                    (Sullen were we,
In the sweet air that is gladdened by the sun,
Carrying lazy smoke in our hearts).

Or turning from Edinburgh to Glasgow I cry in my Glasgow poem :

Only once in a lifetime a few of these hoodlums,
Embarrassed by some proffer of genuine affection
Or witnessing a personal friend die, may feel
Ashamed at being so poor and hard, so incapable
Of finding any place in their lives for the former, so lacking
In everything that might be of use in helping anyone to die,
And see, for an instant, that they have nothing inside them
Save things that serve the purposes of everyday life,
A life of comfort, one's own life, a damned insensibility.

              .   .   .

They spend their lives doing anything rather
Than what if they examined their lives for a moment
Even the stupidest of them would recognize
As the chief end of man—the one thing untouched,

Their specific aboulia.   They believe in everything
Except anything credible and creditable.
All they need is a Blake—George Blake, not William!—
To tell them, to keep on telling them, to be forever
Telling them, their lack of culture, their horrible devitalization,
Their putrid superstitions, their terror of ideas,
Their hatred of intellectual distinction, do not matter
—Their ' replacement of intelligence by sentimentality
Is yet a lovely virtue, and a country like Scotland is happy
With so many of its people resolutely devoted to that '.

' There are to be found among them degrees of plain worth,
Of warm hospitality and unaffected decency,
Few nations of the earth can rival, and all
The understandable squeals of the young intellectuals
Of the new age against a colourless bourgeoisie
Cannot deprive that fact of its value.'
Besides, as Power says, ' Glasgow to-day
Is becoming quite a literary centre '.—Quite!

Half glow-worms and half newts!
     .   .   .

All classes in the city are alike in this,
Running the whole gamut of life from A to B.
University professors, lecturers, school-teachers,
Ministers, and all that awful gang of mammalia,
The high mucky-mucks.   Bogged in servile and illiberal studies,
They have all the same pettifogging spirit,
So narrow it shows little but its limits,
The same incapacity for culture and creative work.
(Glasgow, *arida nutrix* of hundreds of thousands of callous Scots,
Incapable of any process of spiritual growth and conquest.
Destitute of all rich and lively experience,
Without responsibility or honour.
Completely insensible to any of the qualities
That make for a life worth having,
Pusillanimous and frigid time-servers,
Cold with a *pietrosita* deeper than the masonry accounts for
Though that would satisfy a theorist *a la Taine !*) [1]

And of Scotland at large :

       The Scots are a frustrated people,
       Victims of arrested development,
       Withered into cynics
       And spiritual valetudinarians, their
       Frustration due
       To a social environment

---

[1] Compare this, and many other passages ' attacking ' my fellow-Scots in
this book with Hölderlin's famous ' Strafrede ' against the Germans in his
Hyperion and, again, towards the end of *Der Archipelagus*—attacks so
uncompromising, as Mr. Roger Peacock says in his fine critical study of
Hölderlin (Methuen, London, 1938), as to seem (as no doubt mine do too
to my more superficial readers) ' irreconcilable with the poet's national
beliefs '.

Which has given them no general sense
Of the facts of life,
And no sense whatever
Of its possibilities ;

Their English culture a mere simulacrum,
Too partial and provincial
To fulfil the true function of culture,
To illumination of the particular
In terms of the universal ;
Beside the strong vigour of daily life
It is but an empty shadow.
Anywhere you go in Scotland to-day
You can hear the people
Struggling to think and feel as little as possible
Just as you can hear a countryside in winter
Crepitating in the grip of an increasing frost.

And of the British Empire :

The English play the waiting game the longest,
The best, and win most often.   In this angry world
They will be the last to relinquish
Their hereditary and imperial property rights.
They have an experienced technique for elastic decisions
Which may end in eventual war and dismemberment,
But not until every humanly conceivable policy
Or possibility of avoiding the latter
Has been consciously employed and exploited.
Their modest and resilient stupidity,
Inexorable acquisitiveness and stubborn ownership
Are their God-given armour ; and we have cause
To know how fierce a God they get their gifts from.
The tragedy of Lord Dufferin's declining days,
His involvement in just the sort
Of hideous and criminal scandal which would most
Hurt and destroy such a charming man,
Was not mitigated by his innocence
Or by his almost accidental connexion with the fraud.
Dufferin's tragedy is in miniature
The present drama of the British Empire.

And constantly I state my specific mission :

For I am not an Englishman, but utterly different,
And I throw Scotland's challenge at the English again :
Mine is the antipathy of the internationalist to the nationalist,
The cosmopolitan to the Englishman,
The doctrinaire to the opportunist,
The potential fanatic to the ' practical man '.

And I insist all along the line that

All men are ripe for the highest any man knows.
That is a present fact, as the mind of every man stript
Of all its accretions and pushed back to its foundations shows.

And since the question of the Gaelic genius lies at the very heart of all my work, I say, in a long poem entitled ' The Fingers of Baal Contract in the Communist Salute ', dealing with the origin of the Scots in Georgia (vide Cier Rige's *Chronicles of Eri* and L. H. Waddell's *The British Edda*):

> ' Stalin the Georgian,' I have said.   We are Georgians all,
> We Gaels.
> The name *Karthweli* by which the Georgians themselves call
> Their race and their country is none other
> Than our Scottish Argyll—the Georgian equivalent
> Of '*Ard-Gael* ' (High Gael).
>
> ' Og pierced ', we read, ' towards the fingers of Baal
> Even unto Gabacasan.'   Now let the fingers clench back
> To come to rest in the palm of the sun's hand again,
> The reconcentrated power of the human race.
> So let the first conceivers and builders of civilization give now
> (Since the others have poisoned the wells and perverted
> The noble impulse that originated with our fathers)
> The sign of the Clenched Fist—the Communist salute,
> For the Gaelic refluence, and the re-emergence
> Of the Gaelic spirit at the Future's strongest and deepest root !

I proclaim my faith in passages like this :

> All that is needed
> If the sum of human knowledge and expression,
> The sustaining consciousness,
> The reasonable will of our race.
> To produce this super-individuality, Man,
> In whom we all even now participate,
> Is the immediate purpose of the human race.
> The only alternatives we can envisage
> Are intolerable prospects of biological disaster,
> Chronic war, social deterioration, diseases,
> Specific differentiation, generation after generation
> Of distressed existences with extinction looming at the end.
> Either we take hold of our destiny, or, failing that,
> We are driven towards our fate.
> Cyclopean prejudices, innate misconceptions,
> Oceans, mountain barriers, limitless space,
> The protean blind obstructions of nature
> Within us and without, will not prevail
> Against the crystallizing will ; the ordered, solvent knowledge,
> The achieved clear-headedness of an illuminated race.
> Amidst the fear and lassitude and ugly darkness
> Of our world to-day I can believe *that*,
> Believe that the specific man in us
> Has the power to assimilate, utilize, override, and fuse
> All our individual divergences.

And the kind of poetry I am attempting to arrive at is defined as follows :

> A poetry that never for a moment forgets
> That if we study the position of the foetus

M

As it appears in about the ninth month
Of its development, we see the tiny body
Curled up with its head bowed over,
The hands crossed, and the knees drawn up
To permit the whole structure
Of bones, muscles, nerves,
And arteries to fit comfortably
Into the cage of matrix.
As it was in the beginning,
So it is again at the end of life.
Think of the decrepit old human being,
Bent over, head bowed,
Seated in a weary, curled-up position
Exactly similar to the unborn babe's.
The cycle of life begins and ends
In the same design.   Only the proportion,
Size, and shape of the human being
Change as he passes through the stages
Of babyhood, youth, maturity, and old age.
The eternal oval, the egg itself.
A poetry therefore to approach with two instruments
—Which, being mutually destructive,
Like fire and water one can use
Only one at a time
—Even as one may attempt to describe
The relative positions of the Imperial Palace,
Hagia Sophia and the Circus in Constantinople.
' On the one side the Palace was connected,
By open arcades and paradoxical gardens,
With the Golden Egg of Hagia Sophia ;
On the other side an intestinal system
Of passages and winding stairs
Led to the Circus.   But as regards
Byzantium in especial, these things are merely
The elements which combine to form
A stupendous life pregnant with symbolism.
Because the theme of that life
Was the world-embracing mystery
Of God and man,
It stands supreme
Above its ingredients.
The ingredients resemble the things
For which a woman with child longs.
Like the juice of the oyster,
The aroma of the wild strawberry,
The most subtle and diversified elements
Are here intermingled to form
A higher organism.

I take the whole world of knowledge for my province then, and sing :

So here I hail all the fellow-artists I know
And all the singers and narrators everywhere,
' *A rum lot they are, as the Devil said when he looked over the ten
Commandments.*'

Ashugi, akyni, zhirshi, bakhshi, and other folk singers,

Minstrels, histriones, jongleurs, juglares,
Skomorohi, guslari, forsangere, recitadoras,
Kalêki, ciegos, Sidney's ' blind crowder ',
And all the descendants to this day everywhere
Of Teiresias and blind Maeonides
(Fili, ollamhs, cainte, vates, and ιε ροποίοι,
And the ' poluphloisboisterous ' music
Of every anruth, cli, cano, and all the rest
From the ri-bhárd down to the bóbhárd and the bhárd-loirge,
And shanachie after shanachie
Down to the shanachie of the chimney-corner,
Wandering scholars, clerics of the Marbhán type,
And all the Cliar Sheanachain,[1]
The children of Manannán, *lá binn, lá searbh*,[2]
'. . . the patron saint
Of merry rogues and fiddlers, trick o' the loop men,
Thimblemen and balladmen that gild the fair.'
Ah, fain would I follow if I could
The *Imtheacht na Tromdháimhe* [3]
Of the whole round world !)
Ashugi, akyni, zhirshi, bakhshi, and other folk singers,
Creators of the new heroic epodes of to-day.
The Turkic poems of Hussein Bozalgonly of Tauz,
Uzbek and Darginian songs,
The songs of Suleiman Stalsky,[4] the singer of the Daghestan people,
The blind old *kobyar*, Ostap Vyeryesai,
And Timofei Ivanitch, the old *skazitel*,
Who knew all the songs of all Russia.
The songs of the *akyn* Kenen of Kazakhstan
(Kazakhstan in renaissance, strengthened by its new ' iron roads ') ;
Tajiks from a *kishlyak* in Obi-Garma
Singing of the flaming Stalin ;
The lyrics of the Mordovian minstrel Krivosbeyeva ; [5]
The Armenian legend *Lenin-Pasha* ;
The song of Jambul. . . .
      Run as a herald through our Kazakh auls,
      Make the whole steppe attend
' You, song of *Akyn* Jambul.
      Listen, Kaskelen, Karakol, Kastek,
      Glorious is the great Soviet Law,
      It enacts joy to the peoples ;
      It waters the steppe and brings fruit ;
      It lifts up our hearts to sing ;
      It commands all Nature to live
      In service and praise of the people ;
      The song of the old Kazakh *Akyn* Jambul
      To Hassem Lakhuti, the Persian Communist poet.

---

[1] Strolling satirists.   [2] One day sweet, another sour.
[3] The Proceedings of the Great Bardic Assembly.
[4] Died November 23, 1937.
[5] I have elsewhere written my appreciations of such poets as the Kirghiz poet, Toktogul Satylganov (born 1871), Ivan Franko (born 1860), the Western Ukrainian poet, the Bashkir poet, Mazhit Gafur (born 1880), and many others.

The ripened song swells in our hearts.
Let us strike up together, *Akyn* Lakhuti. . . .
The centuries will reverberate with our song,
And all the world's tongues will repeat it.
But . . . on the steppe, barren and waste,
A huge thousand-handed man moves in great circles
Ever wider girthing the earth,
And in his path the dead steppe comes to life,
Quivering, juicy grass shoots forth,
And everywhere towns and villages emerge ;
And he strides ever on,
Further towards the edge,
Sowing what is live and human.
Then one feels towards people
A new tenderness and respect ;
Feels in them an unquenchable vitality
That can vanquish death,
That eternally transforms what is dead into life,
Moving towards immortality by mortal roads.
—Death overshadows people,
But it cannot engulf them.

As I have said, I almost always bring the matter of my poetry home
to Scotland, and one of the principal elements in my view of life is
expressed in these lines :

It requires great love of it deeply to read
The configuration of a land,
Gradually grow conscious of fine shadings,
Of great meanings in slight symbols,
Hear at last the great voice that speaks softly,
See the swell and fall upon the flank
Of a statue carved out in a whole country's marble,
Be like Spring, like a hand in a window
Moving New and Old things carefully to and fro,
Moving a fraction of flower here,
Placing an inch of air there,
And without breaking anything.

So I have gathered unto myself
All the loose ends of Scotland,
And by naming them and accepting them,
Loving them and identifying myself with them,
Attempt to express the whole.

And what I mean by learned poetry is perhaps adequately represented
by this passage :

Come, follow me into the realm of music.   Here is the gate
Which separates the earthly from the eternal.
Have you loosened and cast off your chains ?   Then come.
It is not like stepping into a strange country
As we once did.   We soon learn to know everything there
And nothing surprises us any more.   Here
Our wonderment will have no end, and yet
From the very beginning we feel at home.

As yet you hear nothing, because everything sounds.
But now you begin to distinguish between them. Listen.
Each star has its rhythm and each world its beat.
The heart of each separate living thing
Beats differently, according to its needs,
And all the beats are in harmony.

Your inner ear grows sharper. Do you hear
The deep notes and the high notes ?
They are immeasurable in space and infinite as to number.
Like ribbons, undreamt-of scales lead from one world to another,
Steadfast and eternally moved.
(More wonderful than those miraculous isles of Greece
' Lily on lily, that o'erlace the sea '.
Than the marvellous detailed intensity of Chinese life,
Than such a glimpse as once delighted me of the masterly and exhaus-
tive
Classification of psychical penetrations and enlacements
On which Von Hartmann relied, giving here some slight dissection
Of the antinomies underlying ethical thought, discussing there the
gradations
Of the virtues, the stratifications of axiology, with an elaborate power
And beauty—but here !—Oh, Aodhagan O'Rahaille meets again
The Brightness of Brightness in a lonely glen [1]
And sees the hair that's plaited
Like the generations of men !)

Each sound is the centre of endless circles,
And now the harmony opens out before you.
Innumerable are its voices, compared with which
The boom of the harp is a screeching,
The clash of a thousand trumpets a twitter.

All, all the melodies hitherto heard and unheard
Ring out in full number together, bear you along,
Crowd over you, sweep past you—melodies of love and passion,
Of the Spring and the Winter, of melancholy and abandon—
And they themselves are the spirits
Of a million beings in a million ages
Revealed as Krishna revealed his form
In the Udyoga-parva of the Maha-bharata
Or like the Vision of the Universal Form (Visva-rupa-darsanam)
Before which Arjuna bowed with every hair on his body bristling with
awe [2]
(Or like the tremendous vision
Which came to Buddha under the Bo-Tree
Or to Socrates when he heard, or dreamt he heard,
The Sibyl of Mantinaea
Discoursing on mortal and immortal love,
Or like Descartes' dream of November 10, 1619,[3]
Near the environs of Ulm
When there were presented to him,

[1] Aodhagan O'Rathaille, 1670–1726. The reference is to O'Rahilly's great *aisling* (i.e. vision poem), ' *Gile na gile* '.
[2] In the Bhagavad-Gita. Compare also Matthew xvii, 6, and Luke v, 8.
[3] Chevalier : *Vie de Descartes*, pp. 40–7.

Coming as an enquirer after truth,
A Dictionary, representing knowledge,
And the volume of the Corpus Poetarum,
Which he took to be the symbol of inspiration,
Or like the ' sudden illumination ' that came
To Benchara Branford one night in his fortieth year :
' At once was born in vivid and enchanting consciousness
A new metaphysical calculus of sixty-four
Inter-related cardinal categories, of which thirty-six
Were the transmuted forms of the Geddesian concepts.'
Or like the moment (not like it—it !)
By which as Kierkegaard says in ' *Begrebet Angest* '
The individual is related to eternity,
The moment St. Paul refers to when he describes
Our all being changed ' in the twinkling of an eye '.
Because in the moment the individual chooses himself
And thereby all may be changed
The moment partakes of eternity :
It is then eternity penetrating time.
How the moment can be made eternity
For the individual Kierkegaard shows
In ' *Gjentagelsen* '—it depends on repetition
(Kierkegaard's substitute for Plato's theory of reminiscence).

If you examine one of them more closely you will see
How it clings together with the others, is conjoined with them,
Coloured by all the shades of sound, accompanied
By all the harmonies to the foundation of foundations
And to the dome of all domes in the heights.

Now you understand how stars and hearts are one with another
And how there can nowhere be an end, nowhere a hindrance ;
How the boundless dwells perfect and undivided in the spirit,
How each part can be at once infinitely great and infinitely small,
How the utmost extension is but a point, and how
Light, harmony, movement, power
All identical, all separate, and all united are life.

Svayam aham samharami.[1]

Or like the moment in which Kassner [2] assembles
The scattered fragments of his personality
By identifying a strain of music
Heard through the walls of his cell
With the struggle of his comrades throughout the world
In the same cause.

I am always stressing the vital importance of fact—of thorough
documentation :

I am with the New Writers who waste no words
On manifestoes but are getting down
To the grim business of documentation,

---

[1] I myself will again bind the braid together. (See Bhattanarayana's well-known drama, ' Veni-samhara,' i.e. ' braid-binding '.)
[2] Vide ' Days of Wrath ' by André Malraux.

Not seeking a short cut to the universal
But with all their energies concentrated
On gaining access to the particular.
I rejoice in André Chamson's description
Of the upsurge of his native *langue d'oc*
Against the pressure to ' talk French '.
This renewed impetus
Towards the local and the vernacular
Implies a changing conception of culture,
No longer a hothouse growth but rooted.
If all the world went native
There would be a confusion of tongues,
A multiplication of regionalisms.
Partikularismus, however,
Is hostile to nationalism
And friendly to internationalism.

I remember how Thoreau wrote :
' I have a commonplace book for facts
And another for poetry,
But I find it difficult always
To preserve the vague distinctions
I had in mind—for the most interesting and beautiful facts
Are so much the more poetry,
And that is their success.
—I see that if my facts
Were sufficiently vital and significant,
Perhaps transmuted more
Into the substance of the human mind,
I should need but one book of poetry
To contain them all ! '

That is the point I have reached.
And writing of an imaginary poet who will succeed in being all
I would fain have been, I say of him :

> . . . A lover of facts,
> Not such, however, as might cry,
> ' We are all conscious of facts
> And we are conscious of values,
> But a fact which has no value is not a fact,
> And a value which is not a fact has no value,'
> And make no more of it than a weak argument
> For the collaboration of church and science,
> Not seeing the real significance of it
> —*A fact that has no value is not a fact.*
> It means that when the scientist has discovered a fact
> Which is a fact, he has therefore discovered a value
> That is sufficient to gainsay all the nonsense
> That is being talked about ' blind forces ' !
> If a force is real it is also important.
> If it is blind its blindness has value.
> Why are so many people clamouring for free will ?
> Because they cannot see that fact has value,
> They cannot see that will as a fact
> Has any significance.   To give it value
> They must divorce it from fact,

Remove it from causation.   Why are there so many people
Rejoicing to-day in the supposed overthrow of the atom ?
Because they value fact ?   No.   Because they are afraid of it !
And because they hope to find
That what they feared was fact
Is just a bubble floating on the surface of Mystery.

We do not belong to the family—that is our trouble—
This is the analogy perhaps that comes as near as
Any, the family a group of sense-data actual and obtainable,
Consisting of a standard solid and infinite number of distortion series.
That he had in full and these he ranged at ease
With the genuine simplicity of immediate awareness while we
Had only the pseudo-simplicity of perceptual acceptance at best,
And little if any power of coping with obstacularity,
But if awareness of new existents is, *pro tanto*, a boon,
Many quarters condemned him too wholly and too soon.

And in an autobiographical passage I call ' In My Early Teens ', I
describe my own early factual equipment :

I can't remember anything before I was six.
Aren't I backward ?—But, later, in my early teens
I had a friend who taught me to remember everything.
(I mean everything about Scotland, of course.
Thanks largely to him I have lived my life
Fully and happily—finding fact
Not only delightful but sufficient
And needing no escapes into fantasy.)
Many a happy day I spent with him
Discussing the natural determinants of routes
In Lower Nithsdale ; white quartz pebbles
And their archaeological significance ;
Cumberland, Scottish, and Norwegian words ;
Logan of Restalrig as a letter-writer ;
Yevering, the place and the name ;
The Scalacronica of Gray of Heton ;
The Great Storm of 1785 ;
A Banffshire leader of Zouaves ;
Icelandic sagas and their bearing
On the population of the Moray Firth ;
Ptolemy's geography of Albion ;
The crannogs in Carlingwark Lock ;
Relics of the Norse language in Lewis speech ;
Oriental elements in Scottish mythology ;
Gaelic elements in South-west Lowland Scots English ;
Vernacular Gaelic in the Book of the Dean of Lismore ;
The story of Scottish dictionary-making ;
The dialect of upper Teviotdale ;
Gipsy loan-words in the Roxburghshire vernacular ;
Kossuth in the Borderland ;
The status of the Gaelic bard ;
The speech of Stirling in the sixteenth and seventeenth centuries ;
Points of resemblance between *Beowulf* and the Grettla or *Grettis Saga* ;
William Herbert and his Scandinavian poetry ;
Weather words in the Orkney dialect.
—Beetle-heads from a little owl's nest,

Which contained 705 of them
By the time I was fifteen.
And now, of course, I agree with H. G. Wells
That all the facts which are known should be collated
And available for immediate practical use,
Knowing that, about a great number of things,
Upon which men differ, there is exact knowledge,
So that they should not differ on these things.
That is true not merely about small matters in dispute
But about vitally important things,
Our business, our money, our political outlook,
Our health, the general conduct of our lives.
We are guessing when we might know.

In another poem I write of the nature of will :

It is hard to rid ourselves of the phantasy
That will is an independent compartment of our nature.
We have trained ourselves so long to think of it
As a reservoir of magical fluid—as a force
That can be increased or diminished—shall I say at will ?
But will is merely the interior side of our actions.
It is as strong and constant whatever we do.
For it is nothing but the deed considered in its origin.
What we do, we will.   The *doing* is the will.
The *deed* once accomplished is the exact definition of the will.
There is no will which does not issue in a deed.
—If you flog yourselves to will harder,
To make stronger efforts, you will turn everything to phantasy ;
Nothing is needed but clarity of feeling and objectivity of thought.

In my ' Third Hymn to Lenin ' I stress that necessity for many-sidedness, for really comprehensive knowledge, insistence upon which is one of the main elements in all my later work :

On days of revolutionary turning-points you literally flourished,
Became clairvoyant, foresaw the movement of classes
And the probable zig-zags of the revolution
As if on your palm ;
Not only an analytical mind but also
A great constructive synthesizing mind,
Able to build up the new reality
As it must actually come,
By force of definite laws eventually.
Taking into consideration, of course,
Conscious interference, the bitter struggle
For the tasks set before the Party and the class it leads,
As well as possible diversions and inevitable actions
Of all other classes.—Such clairvoyance is the result
Of a profound and all-sided knowledge of life
With all its richness of colour, connexions, and relations,
Economic, political, ideological, and so forth.

And, as a counterpart to this, I am constantly emphasizing the truth that

. . . most insidious and stultifying of all
The anti-human forces have instilled the thought
M 2

That knowledge has outrun the individual brain
Till trifling details only can be brought
Within the scope of any one man ; and so have turned
Humanity's vast achievements against the human mind
Until a sense of general impotence compels
Most men in petty grooves to stay confined.
(Just as in Scotland with a Haldane even
Rendering great service to biological theory
In persistently calling attention to the special form of organization
Existing in living things—yet failing greatly
Through his defeatist wish to accept
This principle of organization as axiomatic
Instead of tracing its relation to the lower principle of organization
Seen in paracrystals, colloids, and so forth
From the realistic ' moment ' to the abstraction of essential form,
And threading with great skill the intricate shuttling path
From ' spontaneity ' to preoccupation with design,
And ending with a fusion of all these elements
At once realistic and abstract !)
Consequently we have a Jeans accommodating the stars
To traditional superstitions ; and a Barnes who thrids
Divers geometries—Euclidean, Lobatchewskyan, Riemannian—
And Cepheid variables, white dwarfs, yet stubbornly heads
(Though he admits his futile journey fails to reach
Any solution of the problem of God's relation to Time)
Back to his starting point—to a like betrayal
Of the scientific spirit to a dud sublime.

This is the lie of lies—the High Treason to Mankind.
No one but fritters half his time away.
It is the human instinct—the will to use it—that's destroyed,
Till only one or two in every million men to-day
Know that thought is reality—and thought alone—
And must absorb *all* the materials—their goal
The mastery by the spirit of all the facts that can be known.
(Leaving only that irreducible minimum of alogicality
To which scientific explanation is always asymptotically tending.)

Aye, but the fact *and* the vision of the fact !
The basic classicality of what has been found,
Not what is being looked for !

The illiteracy of the literate !   But Glasgow's hordes
Are not even literate save a man or two ;
All bogged in words that communicate no thought,
Only mumbo-jumbo, fraudulent clap-trap, ballyhoo.
The idiom of which constructive thought avails itself
Is unintelligible save to a small minority
And all the rest wallow in exploded fallacies
And cherish for immortal souls their gross stupidity,
While in the deeper layers of their ignorance who delves
Finds in this order—Scotland, other men, themselves.

Of the vast majority of the people I say :

They have no strength of resistance.   They are weak
At the very core of personality—the power to choose.

Freedom of choice may be an illusion
But if so it is an inescapable one.
When the mainspring of choice is weakened or left out
The conflicts and contradictions of character
Lose their virtue and significance
And personality almost disappears.
They are hardly persons enough to sustain
Real relations with one another
Any more than billiard balls do.

With regard to literature I say :

It is possible that a change may come.
In the general revaluation that is taking place
All the commercial considerations, the moral greasinesses,
The Professors of Literature, *Vorschungen*, university curricula,
Honours examinations, all these phenomena commercial at base
Which stand in the way of the taste for
And honouring of literature
May be estimated at their true price.
To seek to abolish them is not much good,
For they are parts of the essential imbecilities
Of pompous men—of the highly refined imaginations
Of the More Select Classes.
They should be left isolated in little towns,
But their existence should not be forgotten,
Or they will come creeping in again.

And of Scotland :

Scotland ! Everything he saw in it
Was a polyhedron he held in his brain
Every side of it visible at once
Of knowledge drawn from every field of life !
—Polyhedrons everywhere ! He knew
There was a way of combining them he must find yet
(Like the movement, almost too quick for the eye to catch,
The no-meeting—but only change upon the instant—
Of spirit and sense ; the agile leaping
From the sensual plane to the spiritual,
This straddling of two universes,
This rapidity of movement and back again.
The change is instantaneous, it is dizzying.
Will it stop-stand out like a star,
This gale of crystalline mockery ?)
Into one huge incomparable jewel,
Like knowing the sunlight as a living thing
(For no man can see anything, save in proportion
As he sees everything, clear and complete),
An ultimate brooch of Lorne
To hold his plaid on his shoulder.
(Though when that happened, of course,
Everybody would say it was just one-sided !)
Scotland ! How he hated all those
Who said ' Scotland ' when they only meant,
When all they knew was only,
In their rich slug-like carneying voices,

Some little gimcrack abstraction,
Some Pisgah-vision down a city cul-de-sac
Of that made-in-England specialty, the Proletariat,
Some owl-blink of an anthropocentric routineer,
Some cheap glass bead of a single-track mentality,
Some wretched little worm-cast of their own casting,
Babes feeding a lion with spoonmeat!
Scotland—like a copy of Greek prose without any accents! . . .

And my use of *welt-literatur* is well illustrated in this brief description of the Propaganda Age :

. . . These days of ballyhoo, rubber-stamp minds, diabolical clichés,
When universal lies have mankind in their death-grip
And endless impotent and disloyal vility of speech
And the effect of the misuse of familiar words
On the character of men and the fate of nations,
' Verbomania, The Pathology of Language ',
(' eine Art Jardin d'Acclimatation fur die grosseren Arten von Lugen,
die man bei uns noch nie gesehen hatte, und ein Palmenhaus
von Uebertreibungen und eine kleine, gepflegte Figuerie falscher
    Geheimnisse.'
Or, as the *Atma-bodha* calls them, *avidya-vikshepan*) ; [1]
Everywhere the Diktatur der Luge,
In a world of which indeed the sightseer can only say,
' Is tric a bha na loingis mhor a' crionadh
'S na h-amair-mhuin a' seoladh,' [2]
Threatens to destroy the whole of the civilization
—In these days nevertheless of the revival and extension
Of Taal, Frisian, Faroese, Irish Gaelic, and a thousand more,
When the *diganta* lifts in Bengali poetry
Though MacAulay, the Englishman, would have prevented it for ever,
And of the heightened *lasciveté parfumée* of the best of the *motêng*
    Chinese poets,
I praise you then.

And with regard to manual labour :

Above all—though primarily a poet myself—
I know I need as large an area of brain
To control my hands as my vocal organs
And I am fully alive to the danger
Of only grasping so much of the scientific outlook
As is expressed in words or symbols
Rather than actions
—The common mistake of regarding
The skilful manipulation of symbols
As an activity altogether more respectable
Than the skilful manipulation
Of material objects.
I am organically welded with the manual workers
As with no other class in the social system,

---

[1] I.e. the projections of ignorance.
[2] Scots Gaelic saying, literally, 'Tis often that were the big ships a-rotting and the pots of piss a-sailing ' . . .

Though superficially my interests may seem to be rather
With the so-called educated classes.

And again by way of advice to younger writers :

Some of our younger writers ask me to give them a maxim.
I reply, the most useful perchance
Is ' Remember, the best snow for ski-ing on
Is also the most likely to avalanche '.

Or, again, ' A writer is a universe whose moments
Cannot be measured by equations, whose forces will ever give the slip
To the quadrants of science. Only the earth can be spelled by its
  seasons.
Watertight compartments are useful only to a sinking ship.'

Or, again, ' Remember how, detached from the forest,
Trees are apt to become deciduous
That would otherwise have remained evergreen '.
Such facts are pointers to us.

To conclude this quick selection of a few of the main themes in
my recent work, I will quote from another poem, ' To the Young
Poets of the World To-day ', and then give a few extracts from a
preface to a big unpublished poem.

The ground on which the world has stood is cracking and sagging
  beneath it ;
It was built in all its aspects on conventions once held true
Or at worst expedient, convenient ; but these to-day
Are no longer believed—they have all been seen through.
No human action can proceed except on a belief,
A human organism must needs have sure ground for its feet.
It is impossible for that old world to continue then.
Its whole foundation is gone, its fall is complete.
In politics we think in terms of strategic reasons of State
That are echoes of a history that is *past*, a tale that is told ;
Socially in terms of conditions only brute force holds together ;
Economically with fictitious money no eye can behold ;
Ethically with ' moral values ' to which no human ' conscience '
Any longer corresponds ; intellectually with a truth
Turned ' pragmatic ' ; and artistically with the self-expression
Of souls that no longer believe in themselves—and rightly forsooth !
No psychological legerdemain can save such a world.
It is no use saying : ' Unless you bring yourselves to believe
In these expedient conventions the social fabric will crash '.
That ballyhoo is running like water through a sieve.
Belief can be produced neither by promise nor menace.
It depends on the quality of its foundations.

No manipulation of old formulas, no glib phrasing,
No amount of tied-Press eloquence and mendacity,
No amount of *professed* belief shouting itself hoarse,
Can substitute itself for the motive power of humanity.
Our religious, political, historical, social, and ethical
Traditions are wholly disbelieved ; and being discredited

Can neither move mountains nor the smallest cogwheel
Of the world's machinery any more than the dead.

It is no longer just matters of polite argument
Among well-bred people, but the very substance and status
Of our life and death issues, our most crucial concerns,
That have become shams and unveracities.　That is
The appalling task that confronts us ; not to find truth,
That monstrous and shocking opposite of the foundations of society,
Scandalous in its gross unfamiliarity, only to be faced
With girded loins and hearts of trebled brass—vainly.
We live in a world that has become
Intolerable as the subject of passive reflection.
What is our response to the unescapable reality ?
Are we too like these miserable little cliques to turn
Because of theoretic inadequacy
From social causation, from the poetry of purgative action
And try to find form and significance
In pure feeling itself, transplanted and reimagined ;
Seeking the meaning of experience in the phenomena of experience,
Pure sensation becoming an ultimate value
In the neurotic and mystical attempt
To give physicality an intellectual content,
In the sensitizing of nerves already raw,
—Meaningless emotion aroused automatically
Without satisfaction or education, as in melodrama ?
Man can find his own dignity only in action now.

Most people live by a social discipline become intolerably artificial,
A construction whose only merit is its security ;
They feel that ; they feel the pettiness and emptiness of a social form
Repeated beyond the day of its absolute necessity ;
But they fear the possible chaos that always threatens those who break
　　through a form ;
They are right to fear it—for every creation risks being a destruction
　　only ;
Yet as long as there is strength for creation creation must be risked.

The deathly obliterating breaths of wingless civilizationism
And frigid metropolitan snobbery are intolerable to a forward art,
Time is confronting to-day with such majestic and responsible tasks
That no writer deserves the name save as his works impart
The motion of tremendous strata in history, the rough
Flaming beautiful language of popular spectacles, no
Superficial apologetics but deep artistic cognition of contemporaneity
—Young poets, these are the sign-manuals that your poems must show.

The working class is the noblest of all classes judged alike
By its historic mission and the everyday relations that exist within it ;
Its tremendous stores of good nature, solidarity, and comradeship.
The trouble is not with material want, life's maladjustments, and yet
These *are* primary factors, and one cannot rely
On spontaneity here—but art is a powerful means
Of communication, contact, drawing together ; it must
Expel the poison, the contagion, of the old society and transform these
　　scenes.

Wipe out the false word ' humanism ' ; our art is not to be
Misericordious, toothless, pacifist, but the art of full-blooded men,
Each in command of a full arsenal of feeling, including the feeling of
  social hatred.
No inertia, cowardice, quietism, weariness, apathy then.
(Even as sailors never want fair weather all the time
And have no savage exultation in the storm—no lust
Of life in their powers of endurance, their fighting strength, their
  desperate skill,
As all true sailors must.)
No hating by request but by oneself—vital images thrown in our way
  by life,
Grim selection of ideas and feelings, harsh opinions, intolerance, frank-
  ness—all
The red roaring life of Burns, Fergusson, old Scotland generally,
Hypocrites have whitewashed, emasculating us under their thrall.

The unpublished preface mentioned above contains the following
paragraphs :

  ' With regard to the formal character of my poems—or the informal
character ; the formless or chaotic character, or lack of architectonic power,
as it may appear to many readers—I am also not only quite impenitent,
but venture to suggest that it bears out one of my main themes by its
resemblance in this respect to what most Occidentals perhaps find most
disconcerting and unlikeable in Oriental art and music—as in Scottish
pipe music.   A Gael is only scornfully amused when, for example, a
Times Literary Supplement reviewer, quoting Dr. Nikolaus Pevsner's
statement that " the majority of the best 'examples [of South German
Baroque] are art of the people for the people ", enters the inevitable
English demurrer and opines that " a folk spirit may have survived and
given a peculiarly German character to the Baroque artists ; they may
themselves have been simple and pious craftsmen in the old anonymous
tradition ; but surely the Baroque idiom remains, what most of us have
always considered it, an aristocratic and sophisticated one ".   It is
precisely here that the great gulf yawns between the English middle
class and the Gaelic (like the Chinese) attitude to art, scholarship,
and literature.   Professor Daniel Corkery has pointed out in Hidden
Ireland, that fascinating study of the Munster bards of the Penal Age,
how the field labourers were adept and keenly interested in prosodical
niceties and the other intricacies of the literary craft ; H. I. Bell in
The Development of Welsh Poetry testifies to the same effect with regard
to the working class in relation to Welsh literature.   There must have
been something of the same sort in England in Elizabethan times, but
it is a phenomenon strikingly absent in England since then—and
crushed out of the Celtic countries by the English Ascendancy.   As I
have said in my pamphlet on Charles Doughty and the Need for Heroic
Poetry : " The great enterprise of Charles Doughty has gone unrecognized or obstinately opposed.   It is dismissed (in The Times
Literary Supplement) as a ' reversal of language '—which is on all fours
with the fact that Wagner's words are generally dismissed as of no
consequence.   Yet Wagner was right, not wrong, when he spent years
studying word-roots.   He knew (as Charles Doughty knew) that we
were coming to another of the quantitive—as against accentual—
periods in culture.   It is that lack of historical knowledge which disables no Marxist that is wrong with our mere impressionist com-

mentators on such a phenomenon. (It is this question of quantity as against accent that distorts to most Scots the nature of our pibrochs of the great period. These knew no ' bar '. They were *timeless* music— hence their affiliation with plainsong, with the neuma. Barred music— accented music—finds its ultimate form in symphony. Unbarred music—quantity music—expresses itself in pattern-repetition." That is why I use the term schlabone as one of the terms descriptive of what I do in my poems. " Hence the idea that the Celt has no archi- tectonic power, that his art is confined to niggling involutions and intricacies—yet the ultimate form here is not symphony ; it is epic.) It is epic—and no lesser form—that equates with the classless society. Everything else—no matter how expressly it repudiates these in the mere logical meaning of what it *says* as against what it is—belongs to the old order of bourgeois ' values ', to the nebulous entities described by terms like ' spiritual ' and ' soul ' ; in short, it stands for the old romantic virtues, which is to say, pragmatically, for nothing. Doughty, as against Auden and Day Lewis, say, is the only English poet who belongs to the New Order, that is to say, to our own time." In other words, my poem exemplifies my complete agreement with Professor Closs (vide *The Genius of the German Lyric*, London 1938) when he says : " The subordination of the atom to the whole and the simultane- ous recognition of the atom constitute the formative principle of baroque ". Or, as I say in the poem itself with regard to the Golden Age in Spanish literature—

A poetry finding its universal material in the people,
(For the English middle class *fehlt charakteristischerweise hier*).

' I also join issue with the typically English Communist reviewer who condemns David Jones's *In Parenthesis* as a flagrant example of " private literature ", because it requires a pre-knowledge of the work of many Welsh and other writers. In this connexion, all my work is designed to insist upon the fact that, as Lionel Trilling has recently observed in *Partisan Review*, " If there is one thing the dialectic of history teaches it is an attitude on cultural matters the very opposite of this splenetic one. But that attitude is difficult and complex, while the attitude of spleen and vulgarity is simple and easy. And danger- ous : because it is indiscriminate, irresponsible, and ignorant of the humanity it seeks to control ; because rejecting all history, it believes that all good was born with itself. It wants not so much a liberated humanity as a sterilized humanity, and it would gladly make a waste- land if it could call the silence peace."
' As against this, my whole teaching recalls *Ionmolta malairt bhisigh*— Eochy O'Hosey's satire on the simpler poetry in time of bardic decay. He has abandoned, he affirms, intricate carven ornament and adopted " a common sort of easy art that will bring him more praise ". Of old composition almost broke his heart, but this new verse is " a great cause of health " ! Or, as I have put it elsewhere, the interests of the real highbrow and the working class are identical—resistance to any intellectual short-circuiting or stereotyping. We are no " prophets of easy things ". One of the few English writers who have realized this is Mrs. Virginia Woolf. It is for this reason that she pleads (in *Three Guineas*) for the breaking of the " vicious circle "—appeals to writers to do this by writing only to please themselves and finding new methods (even street-hawking) of distributing the results, and to readers by neither subscribing to " papers that encourage intellectual slavery " nor attending " lectures that prostitute culture " ; rightly emphasizing

as she does that both the literature of fact and the literature of opinion
are adulterated : " in other words you have to strip each statement of
its money motive, of its power motive, of its advertisement motive, of
its publicity motive, of its vanity motive . . . before you make up
your mind which fact to believe, or even which opinion about art ".
And as a Communist, in this period of transition, agreeing almost completely with Mrs. Woolf's arguments in that book and bitterly diverted
to find that it is a rabidly anti-Socialist English paper which, in reviewing
it, suggests that " it might be said that Mrs. Woolf cannot solve the
whole problem if she only states it for educated women of a civilized
bourgeoisie ", I am, of course, gravely concerned over the blatant
Philistinism of the vast majority of my Communist comrades, and echo
what André Gide has said : " I was prepared to admire a new world,
and they offered me, *as seductions, mind you*, all the prerogatives I
abominated in the old. But, you don't understand, an excellent Marxist
told me. Communism is opposed only to the exploitation of man by
man ; how many times must I tell you that ? Once exploitation is
ended you can be as rich as Alexis Tolstoy or a great opera singer if
only you acquire your fortune by your personal work. In your scorn
and hatred for wealth and possessions I detect a very regrettable trace
of your early Christian ideas.—That may well be.—Which, let me tell
you, have nothing in common with Marxism. Alas ! . . ."
   ' As to the subject-matter of much of my recent poetry—*welt-
literatur* and the creative processes themselves—I agree with Fritz
Kaufmann, who in his *Sprache als Schopfung* contends that in the
modern world " der Ruckhalt der Kunst am ausserkunstlerischen
Gemeinleben Dahinschwindet " and that in consequence such artists
as Mallarmé or Rilke, finding no real ground under their feet, are driven
to strange expedients. " Im Entgleiten allen vorgegebenen Haltes
Bleibt dem Kunstler dock—das Selbstgefuhl des ihm geschenkten
Vermogens. So muss der Poietes das Poietische in sich selbst verabso-
lutieren." Thus in ages like our own all the ostensible themes and
subjects of the poet will tend to be in the first place simply allegories for
the creative process itself. " Der Vorang des Bildens ist selber zum
Gegenstand des Bildens geworden." Something of this sort, it is
implied, may lie at the back of Rilke's Elegies and Sonnets. Like
Stefan George's *Vorspiel*, they embody in the first place the thoughts of
a poet on his own artistic vocation.
   ' In addition to that, of course, I have remembered how Rilke wrote
to his wife from Sweden in 1904 a description of the poet-philosopher,
Larsson, who, he says, would never be in danger of choosing any easy
solution, because he was wise enough to know that when we accept the
difficulty of life, it becomes easy (since we have enormous resources of
strength within us), whereas to choose what is easy is an act of infidelity,
an evasion of life, a withdrawal from the scene of action. " Er weiss,
dass das Schwere, indem wir es tragen, das Leichte ist (weil wir im
Grunde Riesenkrafte haben), dass aber das Leichte tragen zu wollen
eine Veruntreuung ist, ein Sich-dem-Leban-Entziehen, ein Ausweichen
vor ihm." And in a letter to a young poet he declares epigram-
matically that our concern is essentially with what is difficult. " Aber
es ist Schweres, was uns aufgetragen wurde, fast alles Ernste ist schwer
und alles ist ernst." And we must adhere to what is difficult, if we
would make any claim to having a part in life. " Es ist aber klar, dass
wir uus an das Schwere halten mussen ; alles Lebendige halt sich
daran." What we are to understand by courage is a valiant attitude
in facing the strangest and most inexplicable things that can happen to

us. " Das ist im Grunde der einzige Mut, den man von uns verlangt : mutig zu sein zu dem Seltsamsten, Wunderlichsten und Unaufklarbarsten, das uns begegnen kann." Irreparable wrong has been done to life because men have been cowardly in this sense. " Dass due Menschen in diesem Sinne feige waren, hat dem Leben unendlichen Schaden getan." Readers should remember alongside these quotations the notes to " To Circumjack Centrastus " with regard to the sarcastic protests of O'Heffernan and other bards of the Penal Age in Ireland, who lamented the decay of the bardic traditions and deplored the " new kind of easy art " which had come into vogue.

' In my *Second Hymn to Lenin* also I stress that he is no poet who has chosen any but the hardest task ; and for this, too, scientific data are available—the act of artistic creation actually entails a far greater expenditure of foot-pounds of nervous energy in a given interval of time than the work of a buck-navvy doing his job for all he is worth.

' Again, with regard to another feature of my work, which has puzzled and annoyed some friends of mine and led them to protest that the effect of this characteristic, introduced every now and again in such a context, can only be to make readers exclaim : " But this man is not serious. At the height of his elaborate arguments he nose-dives into a stupid anti-climax or rides away on some silly bit of American slang," I have only to say that I regard this hint of the frivolous in my work with no little equanimity, recalling, for example (without, however, agreeing that he has interpreted rightly the phenomenon he has observed), that Dr. Rudolf Metz in his *A Hundred Years of British Philosophy* finds something very similar in certain aspects of Mr. Bertrand Russell, of whom he observes that " just as he can surprise us by depth and originality of thought, so he can by superficiality . . . true to his convictions but untrue to himself, the type of the cosmo-politan litterateur and journalist ". And certainly so far as languages—one of the main themes of all my recent work—are concerned, I could not be content with less than what Mr. Sinclair Lewis in *Dodsworth* calls " German and French and Italian and Woof-woof and all known languages " !

' To the dedicatees of these poems I would also add the name of Professor Friedrich Brie, of the University of Freiburg, in token of my appreciation of his excellent book, *Die Nazionale Literatur Schottlands Von Den Anfaengen Bis Zur Renaissance* (1937), in which, seeing the history of Scotland from the death of Alexander III in 1286 till the Reformation as " ruled by a single national idea, that of independence and resistance to England ", he observes : " We can best attain a proper idea of the quality and strength of the patriotic elements in Barbour by comparing them with those in contemporary works dealing with national themes from the French and English standpoint. At once we shall see that we are confronted with two different kinds of patriotism, an *offensive* kind, which we find among the English and in part among the French, and a *defensive*, which we find in Scotland struggling for its freedom. In the nature of things the defensive, by its closer con-nexion with ethical ideas, contains the greater potentialities, while the offensive too easily squanders itself in boasts about its own virtues and insults to its opponents."

' I would add the following extract from a letter I received (February 1938) from the friend in Freiburg who first put me in touch with Pro-fessor Dr. Brie, viz. : " Brie told me that for the Continent Scotland has supplanted Ireland as the centre of cultural importance in the wide realms dominated and thwarted by England. He too, as the others,

was well enough aware of the political issues at stake. . . . If I understand rightly, the Scottish Literature Society at Edinburgh University
seems to be in grave difficulties ; there were far too many opportunist
' revolutionary simpletons ' mixed up in it, ready enough to welcome
your work, but much more at home in the Auden-Spender racket,
which commended itself not merely because it looked forward to a
Utopia such as made the aims of the Scottish movement, artistic and
political, seem both petty and also too toilsome, but especially because
it involved a comforting reaffirmation of the indispensability of English
predominance. People of that sort, whether among the students or
outside, so far as they want anything for Scotland at all, want to see a
Scotland that is merely distinct but not really different from the existing
Scotland ; in short, they are obsessed by the fear of a revolution in
Scotland. Often depressed by the spread of Communism as escapism
in my milieu, I am at this distance disinclined to exaggerate the importance of worthless people occupying a position hopelessly unstable and
untenable, and recognize all the more clearly that an irreconcilable
negation of all that present-day Scotland is has established itself as a
living force that nothing can destroy. What the next advance will be,
I do not know yet—but it will certainly take place. At the time of
John Maclean's sudden death, it might have been thought that the
Scottish cause was betrayed for a generation. Then quite independently
of him and of one another, F. G. Scott and yourself appeared. The
objective necessities favouring further developments are more influential to-day than ever. All that can be positively done, however,
is to prevent the same conspiracy of silence that almost blotted out
Maclean's real work, from succeeding in its efforts to destroy awareness
of the achievement of Scott and yourself. . . . An occasional read of
The Times or *Morning Post* yields little of interest. But one thing I saw
was important—a first leader in *The Times* on the Scottish question
(about 8th–10th February). Its purport was to admit candidly the
bankruptcy in regard to Scotland of their National Government—even
on its own standards, to confess some of the outstanding evils of our
plight, to sneer at Scottish Nationalism, and to express finally the hope
and the importance of getting something done by the Government.
In fact it is clear that the English junta has been scared by the contradiction between the actual state of Scotland, which the Glasgow
Exhibition is bound to bring to general notice, and the complacent myth
circulated about its participation in the Southern prosperity. This is
all to the good. What is less good is that *The Times* is in a position to
be semi-candid only because of the hopeless failure of the Scottish
Nationalist movement. If Nationalism were proclaiming to our people
and to Europe our unfortunate lot as it really is, *The Times* would resort
to other tactics. In fact, *The Times* leader seems to me to mark the
complete degradation of the Scottish National Movement in English
eyes. They see that it has failed. With their usual perspicacity in
politics, they also see that the objective factors that found expression
in the movement are more living than ever ; but, for the time being,
they know the initiative is theirs. If this *Times* business does not rouse
the party which has still, I hope, the honour of your membership, i.e.,
the Communist Party, to treat the Scottish situation more seriously,
God knows what will . . .''

' As to the form my poems take, I agree with what Professor Barker
Fairley said in his article on '' Charles Doughty and Modern Poetry ''
in *The London Mercury* (June 1935), viz. : '' Poetry, he [Doughty]
reminds us, is made of words first and last—words which we may

blend or separate, flood with rhythm or lift high and dry out of rhythm.
Nothing matters for poetry, as distinct from prose of the utilitarian sort,
save to release the virtue, the lost or unsuspected power, the rare, the
added qualities that reside in words, in words joined or separated. To
make words rhythmical is one way of poetry, to make them unrhythmical
may be another ; it all depends on the sensibility of the author, and the
virtue in words which he proposes to release. Poetry is not rhythm,
it is ' making words do things '. Rhythm is one of the resources, a
chief resource, a necessary resource, of poetry, but it is not the basis
of it. Poetry is words, it is built of words."

' Indeed, my attitude to rhythm is now very similar to that of
Frederick Delius, the composer, of whom Mr. Eric Fenby, in *Delius
As I Knew Him* (1936), tells us that he thought primarily in chords.
The disposition of a chord and its passage to the next was the all-
important matter to him. " For him the power to stir or be stirred
was always measured by the harmonic intensity of the work." That
accounts for what many musicians feel to be the weakness of his music,
the absence of any compelling, forward-driving rhythm. By the time
that Mr. Fenby reached him he seems to have grown to hate rhythm
as much as he hated the Christian religion.

' Besides, I am a Scotsman who, his withers quite unwrung, agrees
with Coleridge : " To read Dryden, Pope, &c., you need only count
syllables ; but to read Donne you must measure *time* and discover the
time of each word by the sense of passion. I would ask no surer test
of a Scotchman's *substratum* (for the turf-cover of pretension they all
have !) than to make him read Donne's satires aloud. If he made
manly metre of them and yet strict metres, then—why, then he wasn't a
Scotchman, or his soul was geographically slandered by his body's first
appearing there."

' Nor am I greatly distressed if much of my work appears tentative
and clumsy, remembering that what has been written of Cézanne is
largely applicable to my work here : " The exclusion of all outside aid
suggests itself as a plausible explanation of Cézanne's clumsiness. . . .
Certainly Cézanne's work shows a refusal to use even legitimate clichés.
The analogy of writing may make this clearer. Even the best of writers
uses clichés. As he writes, a number of these occur to his mind. The
good writer painstakingly considers which exactly fit his purpose, and
his integrity lies in that. Cézanne is like a writer who never allows two
words to be joined together permanently in his mind. In using such a
method no artist, however technically gifted, could hope to appear
anything but tentative and clumsy." (And in this connexion, of course,
I remember—and my purpose is thereby encouraged—that William
Nelson, in his book on John Skelton, rejects J. M. Berdan's theory
linking Skelton to Accentual Latin Verse, and traces " Skeltonics " not
to any verse—for this would mean ignoring many prosodic irregulari-
ties—but to rhymed Latin prose ; a brilliant and original theory, which,
thanks to the recent discovery of a short treatise by Skelton in Latin
prose, Mr. Nelson succeeds in proving conclusively. Incidentally, I
think I can claim with Skelton, in respect of all I have written,

> Though my rhyme be ragged,
> Tattered and jagged,
> It hath some pith.)

' It will also be apparent enough that, as an old Rugby player myself
and member of a family associated for generations with Border Rugby
teams, I am not at all in the position of the Soccer fan attending his first

Rugby International at Murrayfield who, puzzled and indignant at the constant kicking to touch, at last bellowed to one of the full-backs who had just found touch with a magnificent long kick—" Hi, keep the ba' in the park, youse ! " '

A man does not devote several years to the writing of a poem which is bigger, in number of words, than two average-sized novels (say of 70,000 words each) if he despairs of the future of poetry : and how little I do despair of that is shown in the following quatrain :

> Is poetry done for ? Wars, the Robot Age, the collapse of civilization,
> These things are distracting and annoying, it is true
> —But merely as to an angler a moorhen's splashing flight
> That only puts down a rising fish for a minute or two !

I have devoted a great deal of my life to Scottish education, and have stood on divers occasions (unsuccessfully, of course, since I was standing *inter-alia* as a Scottish republican and revolutionary Socialist) as students' candidate for the Lord Rectorships of Aberdeen and Edinburgh Universities, been nominated for St. Andrews University too, and been closely associated with nationalist movements in Glasgow University, and with the unsuccessful candidature of Cunninghame Graham and the successful candidature of Compton Mackenzie for the Lord Rectorship there, and I would like to have devoted a great deal more space than I have been able to afford to Scottish educational problems and in particular to the degeneration of the Scottish Universities. Here, however, I would just amplify what little I have said in this book on these subjects, by saying that I agree entirely with the following remarks of Dr. Tudor Jones :

' University Teachers—except for a very few specialists—are not education-theorists or indeed educationists at all ; but observation of many recent generations of university students (medical) convinces me that they behave increasingly as though they have been deprived of at least one of the standard mental instruments—not just that the scholarship-holders or the " self-taught " or the foreigners have been deprived of it ; but as though all of them had been forced on instinct a particular and necessary instrument for full intellectual development. There are now *some* of the characteristic operations of the mind which *none of them* can perform, which, indeed, they do not know to exist ; but which, nevertheless, their fathers performed easily and habitually. Years before I read the Protocols of the Learned Elders of Zion (who, Lord Sydenham said, had " knowledge of a rare kind ; embracing a wide field "), I had formed the opinion that, nowadays, something was *done to* the child at school, which, by accident or design, produced this result. For this reason Protocol Number 16 seems to me an even more sinister document than it may appear to others with less minute knowledge of the innumerable details which it covers unseen. It begins : " In order to effect the destruction of all collective forces without exceptions we shall emasculate the first stage of collectivism—the universities—by re-educating them in a new direction. Their officials and professors will be prepared for their business by detailed secret programmes of action from which they will not with immunity diverge, not by one iota. They will be appointed with especial precaution, and will be so placed as to be wholly dependent upon the Government." I should say that has been done. The mechanism whereby it has been done is sufficiently intricate and ' long-term ' in character as largely to hide the fact of its existence from curious eyes, while at the same time ensuring that the curious eyes shall not be many or often. One university principal in England, when it was suggested to him that the real *policy* of the universities was the debasement of the intellectual currency, remarked dryly that " we must strive to retain those liberties we still possess ".'

I have mentioned in this book one of the great places on my spiritual map—the place ' where the unknowable ends '! I may mention another here—the place where reality, properly speaking, begins.

> ' The imagination ', says Kierkegaard, ' is what providence uses in order to get men into reality, into existence, to get them far enough out, or in, or down in existence. And when imagination has helped them as far out as they are meant to go—that is where reality, properly speaking, begins. Johannes *v.* Muller says that these are two great powers, around which everything revolves : ideas and women. That is quite true, and is intimately connected with what I have just said about the importance of the imagination : women, or ideas, are what tempt a man out into existence. Naturally there is this great difference, that among thousands who run after a skirt there is not **always** one who is moved by ideas.'

To what I have said about education, and medical education and the pageant of Scottish doctors in particular, and about the *terra incognita* of Scottish biography and the way in which under present conditions the emphasis is thrown on the wrong people, I would add here that among the scores of Scottish doctors I know well to-day, careful conversational testing has revealed only one to me with any knowledge of the non-Aristotelian biology of Professor C. M. Child, the non-Aristotelian neurology of Professor C. J. Herrick, based on that biology, or of such necessities to accompany such a biology and neurology, as Boole's ' laws of thought ' and the ' many-valued logic ' of Lukasiewiez and Tarski. The name and work of Thomas Graham are little known in Scotland, and in the articles devoted to chemistry in the little book summarizing Edinburgh's contributions to the different sciences, issued on the occasion of the British Association meeting there in 1921, his name was not so much as mentioned, yet his ' colloid chemistry ' *is one of Scotland's greatest contributions to the world*. As Wolfgang Pauli says : ' In fact, to-day, colloids may be regarded as an important, perhaps the most important, connecting link between the organic and the inorganic world '.

> ' Although physicians in their university days ', says Count Alfred Korzybski in *Science and Sanity : An Introduction to Non-Aristotelian Systems and General Semantics* (1933), ' are well acquainted with colloidal chemistry, yet somehow, in practice they have great difficulty

in " thinking " in colloidal terms. With the newest discoveries of
physics of high pressure and piezochemistry, with their bewildering
variety of physical manifestations, which, under different pressure,
change with every individual material, a modern physician will have to
" think " not only in terms of colloids, but of colloids in combination
with the data of high-pressure physics and piezochemistry. No such
" thinking " is humanly impossible under the traditional two-or-three-
valued Aristotelian disciplines, and becomes only possible with infinite-
valued non-Aristotelian general semantics. One of the immediate
results of the use of non-Aristotelian disciplines is the elimination of the
elementalism of " body " *and* " mind ", " intellect " *and* emotions, and
the introduction of the *non-elementalistic* point of view. This requires
every physician to be acquainted with psychiatry, which acquaintance
would eliminate many harmful cults. It should be fully realized that
the older chemistry, which dealt with different " substances ", having
different " properties ", could have been treated by Aristotelian subject-
predicate and two-, or three-, valued means. But not so to-day ; the
older chemistry is gone, and to-day we deal only with a special branch
of physics based on structure ; the newer physics of high pressure show
clearly that many of the older characteristics of " substances " are only
accidental functions of pressures, temperature, and what not, requiring new semantic principles, new epistemologies ; in short, a new non-
elementalistic and infinite-valued non-Aristotelian system. In other
words, whoever retains the Aristotelian semantic reactions is entirely
unable to " think " scientifically in the modern sense.

I have no hesitation in saying that those who possess any understanding of these matters and are able to ' think ' scientifically in the
modern sense in Scotland to-day could be counted on my fingers.

What is of most consequence for this book, however, is the remarkable way in which all the principal positions advanced in such chapters
as this on the ideas behind my work, and throughout this book
generally, are borne out in Count Korzybski's book in the fullest
context of modern scientific knowledge.

' If it is objected that science is so complicated that it would be
impossible to impart such knowledge to the masses, the answer is that,
as this enquiry shows, science involves some structural metaphysics
and semantic components which, once discovered, *are childishly simple
and can be given in elementary education.* Since the lower centres
produce the raw materials from which the higher abstractions are made,
and these higher abstractions again influence the working of the lower
centres, obviously *some means can be devised to put back into the nervous
circuits the beneficial effects of those highest abstractions.* The above
statement may appear visionary, and many are likely to say, " It cannot
be done ! " Now, the main contention of the present theory, verified
empirically, is that it *can* be done in an extremely simple way, provided
we study the neglected non-elementalistic aspects of mathematics and
science ; namely, their structural and semantic aspects. Such education allows us to give very simply to children the " cultural results ",
or to impart the semantic reactions, which are the aim of university
training, in a relatively short period and instruct any technicalities.
These benefits, under an Aristotelian education, are too rarely acquired
even by university graduates, and impossible to impart to the masses,
who are left, helpless with archaic, delusional structural assumptions.'

And again in the same book we read that the formulation of General Semantics, *inter-alia* ' discovers the multiordinality of the most important terms we have, thus removing the psychological blockage of semantic origin and helping the average man or scientist to become a " genius ", &c.' And in this connexion I may add three of my own favourite quotations.

From Cassius J. Keyser :

> ' Pitiless indeed are the processes of Time and Creative Thought and Logic ; they respect the convenience of none nor the love of things held sacred ; agony attends their course.   Yet their work is the increasing glory of a world—the production of psychic light—the growth of knowledge—the advancement of understanding—the enlargement of human life—the advancement of Man.'

From Martin H. Fischer :

> ' If a distinction is to be made between men and monkeys, it is largely measurable by the quantity of the subconscious which a higher order of being makes conscious.   That man really lives who brings the greatest fraction of his daily experience into the realm of the conscious.'

And from Henri Poincaré :

> ' One need only open the eyes to see that the conquests of industry which have enriched so many practical men would never have seen the light, if these practical men alone had existed, and if they had not been preceded by unselfish devotees who died poor, who never thought of utility, and yet had a guide far other than caprice. . . . The men most disdainful of theory get from it, without suspecting it, their daily bread ; deprived of this food, progress would quickly cease, and we should soon congeal into the immobility of old China.

The realization that forced me in the first instance to embark upon my intellectualist campaign in Scotland is admirably expressed by Dr. Oscar Levy in his *Idiocy of Idealism*, when, dealing with the results of the Reformation, he says of the Puritans :

> ' Yet if they had been really and truly religious their own faith might have shown them the way out of the wilderness.   For the religious conscience begot the scientific conscience, and the scientific conscience ought to produce the intellectual conscience.   Of the latter, Puritanism knew nothing ; it has stopped at the religious and, in few cases, at the scientific conscience.   It fought shy of the last step ; it did not allow truth to enlighten the intellect : it was not honest enough to criticize moral values, and has thus allowed the world to tumble into chaos which it tries in vain to organize now by mere reaction, by still more religion, by still more morality—that is to say, by still more alcohol for a world of dipsomaniacs.'

And I agree with Dr. Levy when he says—as indeed I foresaw when I was still in my teens, and as my chequered and ' difficult ' life has amply attested :

> ' In short, Christ and Christianity can be beaten by its own weapons : the weapons which they have forged and to which they owe their success

over what was better, deeper, nobler, and higher than themselves. To the general desire of " feeling elbows ", to the German *Tuchfuehlung* and " worship in fours ", to the victorious clamour of millions in every land, the higher man will reply with a stern S.O.S. or, as he will most certainly be alone and without friends, with a grim, but determined, S.M.S.—save *my* soul ! Only it will not be easy. That way, too, lies crucifixion. But Christ's was a crucifixion in public, lasting a few hours, sweetened by weeping women, comforted by a sponge of vinegar, or, if desired, by a narcotic, and brightened by the certain hope of being in Paradise " this very night " (Luke xxiii. 43). Ours will be a dry crucifixion, lasting for years and decades, without any consolation from man and woman, without conversation with God Almighty, without any refreshment from tender hands, without a drop of water in the desert of silence, calumny, and false applause. And when the final breakdown has come, there is sure to turn up a good Christian, or a candid friend, or, worst of all, the victim's own conscience, grown sick with misery, and telling him : " It was your pride, that deadly sin, which led you off the path of your ancestors into this hell of isolation, where you now give up, away from man, beast, and God, your supercilious and, alas, superfluous soul ! " No, it is dangerous to save one's soul nowadays ; but it is honourable, and in the best religious tradition. And if one escapes, it is also highly satisfactory—if one can convince by word and example that there is a way, even to-day, to save one's soul ; if one can persuade some men of our time to strive after a kingdom other than that of Heaven, to wit, that one " within you ", that which Christ never preached to his slaves, but which will finally conquer for the masters, de-Christianized, de-nationalized, and de-vulgarized : The Kingdom of this Earth.'

My attitude to the existing state of affairs could hardly be better expressed than by the passage in which Count Korzybski says :

' Our rulers, politicians, diplomats, bankers, priests of every description, economists, lawyers, &c., and the majority of teachers, remain at present largely or entirely ignorant of modern science, scientific methods, structural linguistic and semantic issues of to-day, and they also lack an essential historical and anthropological background, without which a sane orientation is impossible. Their ignorance is often wilful, as they mostly refuse, with various excuses, to read modern works dealing with such problems. As a result a conflict is created and maintained between the advance of science affecting conditions of actual life, and the orientations of our rulers, which often remain antiquated by centuries, or one or two thousand years. The present world conditions are in chaos ; psychologically there exists a state of helplessness—hopelessness, often resulting in the feelings of insecurity, bitterness, &c., and we have recently witnessed psychopathological mass outbursts, similar to those of the dark ages. Few òf us at present realize that, as long as such ignorance among our rulers prevails, *no solution of our human problems is possible.* . . . If the ignorance and identifications of our rulers could be eliminated a variety of delusional factors through home and school educational and other powerful agencies would cease to be imposed and enforced upon us, and the revision of our systems would be encouraged, rather than hampered. Effective solutions of our problems would then appear spontaneously and in simple forms.'

This connects up in my mind, of course, with what Pasternak says, in a poem which echoes Tyutchev's famous masterpiece, *Silentium* :

'There are in the experience of great poets the features of such naturalness that it is impossible, having tasted of them, having ascertained one's relationship with all that is, and being familiar in life with the future—it is impossible not to fall ultimately, as into an heresy, into an unheard-of simplicity.'

The extraordinary close correspondence between ' the ideas behind my work ', as stated in this chapter, or expressed elsewhere throughout this book, and Count Korzybski's findings (read since all the preceding part of this chapter was written) can be illustrated by a few examples. With regard to what I say about the manual workers, for example, Count Korzybski insists that it is necessary to emphasize that, while it is impossible to insist too strongly on the fact that all ' material ' progress among humans is due uniquely to the *brain-work* of a few mostly underpaid and overworked workers, who exercise properly their higher nervous systems, and that the mentality of the public men in every country is practically at a standstill because of a deliberate minimizing of the value of brain-work, it is far too seldom realized anywhere that *any* ' manual worker ', no matter how lowly, is hired *exclusively* for his human brain, his semantic reactions, and *not* primarily for his hands !

' The most lowly manual worker is useful *only* because of his human nervous system, which produced all science, and which differentiates him from an animal, and not primarily for his hands alone ; otherwise we would breed apes to do the world's work.'

Count Korzybski points out later in his book—this corresponding to the internationalism or world-thought I have adumbrated elsewhere in these chapters as one of the prime-factors of my poetry—that a non-Aristotelian revision ' will have an international and inter-racial application, requiring a very thorough revision of all doctrines, a better acquaintance of specialists in one field with the accomplishments in other fields, and an up-to-date epistemology.— Modern conditions of *life* are, to a large extent, affected by non-Aristotelian science, but exploited by the thoroughly Aristotelian doctrines of the commercialists, militarists, politicians, priests, and lawyers—which results in a bewildering chaos, resulting in needless, great, and imposed suffering for the great masses of mankind, as exemplified by such cataclysms as wars, unemployment, different economic crises. . . . Non-Aristotelian disciplines, or science *as such*, are thoroughly beneficial to mankind at large ; but an Aristotelian exploitation and use of these non-Aristotelian products are, and must be, a source of endless sufferings to the enormous majority of mankind, leading automatically to every kind of breakdown.'

I have stressed again and again the need to trespass across all boundaries (such over-spilling proclivities have, indeed, been an extraordinarily marked feature of Scottish personalities all through the ages), and to burst up all the professional rackets, and here again Korzybski says :

> ' The researches of the present writer have shown that the problems involved are very complicated and cannot be solved except by a *joint study* of mathematics, mathematical foundations, history of mathematics, " logic ", " psychology ", anthropology, psychiatry, linguistics, epistemology, physics and its history, colloidal chemistry, physiology, and neurology ; this study resulting in the discovery of a general semantic mechanism underlying human behaviour, many new interrelations and formulations, culminating in a non-Aristotelian system. This semantic mechanism appears as a general psychophysical mechanism based in four-dimensional order, present and abused in all of us, the primitive man, the infant, the " mentality " ill, and the genius not excepted. It gives us an extremely simple means of training our semantic reactions, which can be applied even in elementary education.'

While I thoroughly agree with the need for what Burns called ' intermingledons '—the switching through of all manner of subjects and interests—there are perhaps limits, and I am not sure that I agree with the reviewer of Dr. C. J. Shebbeare's *The Problem of the Future Life* who wrote :

> ' Among the long list of honours that follows his name on the title-page there stands " Master of the Wear Valley Beagles ", and the hint is enough to advise the reader that the author will write with his eyes constantly being lifted from his books to the lives of the real men and women outside his study.'

I have, however, fully in mind that unique characteristic of the structure of human knowledge by which, as Korzybski says :

> ' If we pass to higher orders of abstractions, situations seemingly " insoluble ", " matters of fact ", quite often become problems of *preference*, so that one question can sometimes be answered " yes " or " no ", " true " or " false ", depending on the order of abstractions the answerer is considering. The above facts alter considerably the former supposedly sharply defined fields of " yes " and " no ", " true " and " false ", and, in general, of all multiordinal terms. Many problems of " fact " on one level of abstraction become problems of " preference " on another.'

Korzybski illustrates this by a remarkable instance, among other examples, in the mathematical work of Lobatchewski, and, as Korzybski says, ' the psychological fact is of the utmost generality (as all psychological facts are), therefore . . . applies to all human endeavours and not merely to what a certain mathematician did under certain circumstances.'

Again, in relation to all these matters :

> ' Inversely, the layman, the " practical " man, the man in the street, says, what is that to me ? The answer is positive and weighty. Our life is entirely dependent on the established doctrines of ethics, sociology, political economy, government, law, medical science, &c. This

affects everyone consciously or unconsciously, the man in the street in the first place, because he is the most defenceless.'

Korzybski's *Introduction to Non-Aristotelian Systems and General Semantics* shows why a theory of *universal agreement*, in the broadest sense—namely, agreement with one's self, eliminating internal 'conflict', and with others, eliminating family, social, and international conflicts—is neurologically not only possible, but also a necessary semantic consequence of using the human nervous system in its structurally appropriate way. He himself points out that

> 'The greatest men of science have always had wide human aims and interests. From the point of view of psychiatry, it is well known that "mental" ills involve usually anti-social affective attitudes. When we see men with distinctly anti-social tendencies, no matter how they rationalize them, they are invariably ill in some way. A fully healthy individual is never anti-social.'

I have quoted elsewhere in this book what Mr. Edwin Muir said about the intellectual complement of Scottish republicanism as manifested in my work in the drawing of subtle distinctions, and especially between matters that were apparently as nearly similar as possible. If Mr. Muir had been scientifically informed he might have realized the key significance of just this 'intellectual complement of Scottish Republicanism' (which, as he says, is 'so entirely un-English'!) for the future of the *human* development of mankind, the achievement of general sanity in place of the present almost universal unsanity, since 'in the traditional systems we did not recognize the complete semantic interdependence of differences and similarities, the empirical world exhibiting differences, the nervous system manufacturing primarily similarities, and our "knowledge" if worth anything at all being the *joint product* of both'. Was it not Sylvester who said that 'in mathematics we look for similarities in differences and differences in similarities'? This applies to our whole abstracting process. It is for this reason that if I were asked to frame a test paper for literary aspirants, I would ask: (1) A poem on the fact that what is known as the 'Lorentz transformation' *looks like* the 'Einstein transformation'. When manipulated numerically both give equal numerical results, yet the meanings, and the semantic aspects, are different. Although Lorentz produced the 'Lorentz transformation', he did not, and *could not*, have produced the revolutionary Einstein theory. (2) A short paper discussing the fact that the semantic aspects of practically all important mathematical works by different authors often involve *individual semantic presuppositions* concerning fundamentals.

Elsewhere on the basis of a vast research into Scottish national biography from the earliest times to the present, I have dealt not only with the evidences right throughout history of the racial rivalry or mutual incomprehension and distaste of the Scots and the English, but adduced a stupendous body of evidence with regard to Scottish versatility, linguistic ability, freedom from English red-tapeism and social stratification and snobbery. Since these qualities must have a very great deal to do in determining the nature of the poetry with which I am concerned, a few paragraphs here may set this matter in its proper perspective relative to my present subject. My own especial exemplar, however, has been my own kinsman (on my paternal grandmother's side), Alexander Murray, the Galloway shepherd lad, born at Minniegaff in 1775, who could read Caesar, Ovid, and Homer when he was ten ; then acquired French, German, and Hebrew, and began on Abyssinian ; and before he was sixteen was studying Anglo-Saxon and Welsh. He tramped to Edinburgh, astonished the professors there, and won a bursary. In the short time that remained to him the poor Galloway shepherd boy won a European reputation. He became one of the greatest linguists of his time. He mastered Chinese, Sanskrit, Hindustani, Persian, and Icelandic. He specialized in the Abyssinian dialects. When Dr. Moodie, Professor of Oriental Languages in Edinburgh University, died, Murray succeeded him, but, alas, he broke down in health, and died of tuberculosis in his thirty-seventh year.

This is the blood that is in my veins, and this is the kind of man I admire, and in whose footsteps I have followed, delighting very keenly too in this passion for linguistics, that has been so marked an element in so many distinguished Scotsmen right down the centuries and is so completely absent in Englishmen, and making it one of my happiest hobbies to trace out all its workings—and which, like Alexander Murray and many other erudite Scots, I have developed by my own initiative and in my own way, not only, as Professor Eda Lou Walton has said of me, ' without benefit of Oxford or Cambridge ', but wholly by the side of, and apart from, any set education I have had—to which latter, indeed, like these others I have in mind, I owe little or nothing, and am glad to have escaped its stereotyping effects, knowing that, if I had had more of it, it could only have done me far more harm than good, and that I learned both infinitely more and better without it than I could with it. If I had my way, indeed, I would end all compulsory education straightaway. To close all the schools and universities could not have any ill—and in many ways would almost certainly have a stimulating—effect on the general level of intelligence and intellectual inquiry.

The truth that ' a little knowledge is a dangerous thing ' is fully borne out by any consideration of our ' educated classes ' from the point of view of their capacity and readiness to entertain new ideas. These people have reached their ' saturation level '. The planned indoctrination to which they have been subjected has practically insulated them from any mental activity altogether—and that appalling condition is accentuated by their conceit as ' educated persons '

and by their professional jealousy, &c. On any cultural subject—
' modern poetry ', for example—I would far sooner address an un-
educated audience than an educated one ; it would be easier to enlist
the interest of the former, they would follow the exposition far more
patiently and with a genuine desire to learn and without the inter-
position of intractable prejudices of all kinds. From this point of
view the professional classes in Scotland to-day are utterly hopeless
compared with the working class ; and the teaching profession is
the worst of all. These people have no real interest in intellectual
matters at all and simply kill out any intellectual aptitude in their
pupils, while of course, the creative faculty in any shape or form is
their *bête noir*. But in regard to art it is not only teachers and other
educated—which almost always means miseducated—persons who
must be rigorously eschewed. For, as Walter Pach says, ' it is
always, always, the artists who get deepest into questions of art'. Nor
is this to be deemed strange, since ' they think of it morning, noon
and night, waking or sleeping (literally), while other people consider
it only once in a while. So that if we want to get light on this
enigma of art, and our evolving conception of its value and meaning,
the men to talk to about it are the artists.'

There is only one man I know to-day who might stand beside
Murray—the veteran John Dyneley Prince of Columbia University,
who as a boy acquired not only a working knowledge of the Romany
dialect, but also a smattering of Shelta—the wandering tinker's talk
that is Gaelic spoken backward. Then he learned Welsh and
Turkish, and ere long could make a witty after-dinner speech in
Russian, Serbian, Danish, Swedish, French, Italian, Hungarian,
Gypsy, or Turkish. He has, besides, a working facility with Czech,
Polish, Bulgarian, Slovene, Slovak, Spanish, Portuguese, and once
he broadcast to Iceland in the Icelandic tongue. His scholar's
knowledge of obscure languages covers a huge field. Among my
personal friends the greatest linguists perhaps have been—or are, for
most of them are alive—Professor W. J. Entwistle, Sir Herbert
Grierson, the late Sir Donald MacAlister, Professor Janko Lavrin,
ex-Prince D. S. Mirski, and the late Professor E. V. Gordon, the
authority on Gothic, Old Norse, Icelandic, and Scandinavian matters
generally, and, like myself, a great lover of the Faroe Islands.
Though he is a friend of many friends of mine, I have never met
Professor John Orr, of the chair of French in Edinburgh University,
though he is a great authority on the French dialects, in which I too
have long had a special interest, fostered by my sojourn in Marseilles
and in the Pays Basque, and by my delight in the writings of Carco
and other prose-writers and poets who have used French dialect, and
slang, or thieves' argot. And my long unpublished poem—really
an epic of the developments of literature and the arts—which, because
it is concerned with world-consciousness, necessarily treats a great

deal of languages, celebrates my interest in all manner of languages and linguistic problems, among them the Shan dialect of Burma ; the Valiente *baragouin* of Panama ; the Cakchiquel of Venezuela, Efik, Volule ; the Lach dialect of Silesia ; and makes it clear that if I had to choose a small library for a Robinson Crusoe life it would consist mainly of dictionaries, especially early dictionaries, like Dr. Hepburn's Japanese, Cary's Sanskrit and Bengalese, Jaeschke's Tibetan, Krapf's Kaffir, Morrison's Chinese, and others.

It is true, of course, of all these many-sided Scotsmen, whose interests moved in such diverse channels, as of Matthew Arnold, that this versatility cuts both ways. One takes from Arnold as one pleases long poems or fragile lyrics ; phrases about society and Christianity, or haunting sentences on Celtic literatures ; Arminius von Thunderten-Tronckh, Marcus Aurelius, or the shy children of the forgotten merman. It is a varied feast, and its diversity has been Arnold's fortune. It has also done him harm. For he has been taken fragmentarily, and, therefore, at a discount. Yet it is also true of these Scotsmen as has been said of Arnold that, despite Arnold's own dislike of system, there are logic and architecture, ' none the less strict for being organic and not mechanical, which give his wide endeavours unity and show the true modulation of his thought. A central current in his own life flows in his poetry to his prose, from his youth to his age, from his restless and divided temper to that hard-won union of mind and heart which he called the " imaginative reason ".'

It is not, however, only practically all that is really valuable and of interest to intelligent people in the field of Scottish biography that is completely unknown to ninety-nine per cent. of Scots to-day ; it is practically all that is really valuable and of interest to intelligent people in regard to the subjects most Scots imagine they know a great deal about—like Edinburgh, for example. What is generally known about Edinburgh is a few so-called historical details drawn from that relatively most dull and unimportant fraction of the story of the past to which alone the term history has been quite wrongly generally adscripted, and so, in Edinburgh and elsewhere, we find people pluming themselves upon their knowledge of a number of kings, and queens, and hereditary nobles and military leaders of no human consequence whatever, and lacking even the haziest notion of the city's cultural and scientific and political records. Edinburgh in the eighteenth and early nineteenth centuries was the ' Modern Athens ' of Europe. Allan Ramsay the poet set up the first circulation library, and one of the first browsers was Gay of the *Beggar's Opera*. Benjamin Franklin received the freedom of the city. He spent six weeks in Scotland, ' the dearest happiness I have met with in any part of my life ' ! Raeburn was portraying the Scottish types of Highland chieftain and Lowland lawyer. Adam was designing

classical public buildings and elegant residential squares. Burns
came to town, and Scott followed. The Ossian poems were published, condemned by Johnson, read by Goethe and Napoleon,
whose pocket reading, indeed, it was during campaigns. Sir Henry
Mackenzie continued the peculiarly Scottish liaison between law and
literature. Haydn harmonized Scottish airs, Beethoven and Chopin
wrote schottisches, Mendelssohn wrote his Scotch symphony and
Hebrides overture, Berlioz his Rob Roy overture and his Waverley
overture, Rossini adapted Scott's ' Lady of the Lake ' and ' Ivanhoe ',
and wrote ' Robert Bruce ', Donizetti composed ' Lucia di Lammermoor ' from Scott's libretto, Verdi went back to the earliest history
of Scotland for his ' Macbeth '. The ballet flourished in Edinburgh,
and typical Scots dances and costumes became the rage of Europe.
Even that very brief list, covering only a single aspect, is enough to
show anyone who knows Edinburgh to-day the extent of our national
degradation in the interval.

I rank as one of the greatest Scottish writers, and personalities,
to-day, the young scientist and artist, Mr. Ivan T. Sanderson, author
of those fine books, *Animal Treasure* and *Caribbean Treasure*, but
though the latter deals with a scientific expedition to Trinidad, Haiti,
Surinam, and Curacoa, I feel that he is really writing all the time
about his native Edinburgh, and that when he describes a grison (a
kind of weasel) as ' circumambulating an obstacle by pouring round
it, like a train ', whence he mistook it at first for a snake, or writes of
a cave in which he flashed his torch on a circle of land-crabs who
' dropped their tall periscopic eyes, and waved their huge pincers in
front of them—a few blew bubbles that hissed and squeaked in the
silence ', or tells us of the three-fingered sloth, the absurdity of its
subhuman face only less absurd than its three blunt, stumpy, insensitive paws, or of the pigmy ant-eater whose eyes on capture filled
with tears, though if you were sentimental enough to be taken in by
that, it produced its highly effective armament, ' claws as dense,
tough, and sharp as a gaff ', he is not describing the strange fauna he
found round the Saramaca, Coppename, Surinam, and Parva rivers,
but giving masterly word-pictures of many of the types of citizens
of his native Edinburgh to-day, and wish that he would come back to
Scotland here and continue his work, on lines not unlike the ' Mass
Observation ' activities of Tom Harrison and Charles Madge and
their colleagues.

I have said in one of my poems :

> Mine is the antipathy of the internationalist to the nationalist,
> The cosmopolitan to the Englishman,
> The doctrinaire to the opportunist,
> The potential fanatic to the practical man,

and that might serve, I think, as a credo in brief of each of the younger

Scottish poets in whose work I have any interest, and as a key to all the recent Scottish poetry of any significance or promise.

Unlike Lenin himself, British Left-Wing critics (notoriously anti-intellectual and most incompetent theoreticians ; professed dialectical materialists destitute of dialectic) are prone to protest against learned poetry and literary allusiveness as being only for the few, and insusceptible of appealing to the big public.   This was never the case in the Celtic countries—nor even in England in Elizabethan times, as the complex word-play and high allusiveness in the plays show. But as Henri Hubert says in *The Greatness and Decline of the Celts* (English translation, London, 1934) (and Aodh de Blaeam, Professor Daniel Corkery, Dr. H. Idris Bell, and other critic historians of Irish and Welsh literature testify to the same effect) :

> ' Celtic literature was essentially a poetic literature. . . . We must not think of Celtic poetry as lyrical outpourings, but as elaborately ingenious exercises on the part of rather pedantic literary men.   Yet Celtic literature was popular as no other was.'

As Professor W. J. Entwistle points out in his *European Balladry* (1940), the same thing is true of the ' rimur ' in Iceland :

> ' The " rimur " are subject to very complex conventions of alliteration and rhyme, and they are grouped together under rules which forbid the repetition of the same devices. . . . Relatively uninterested in the matter of the song, the Icelandic people were, and are, acute critics of the form.   In the long winter nights there is time to discuss art in the minutest detail ; in fact, prosodic study took the place of the general conversation which often follows a recitation in the American mountains, though the latter turns on the subject-matter of the ballad. . . . If it is scarcely possible for a European taste to esteem these poems for their own merits, though we may coldly admire their intricacy, the " rimur " serve to remind us that there is no inevitability about the " popular " in poetry.   A " people " can be a people of connoisseurs.   Indeed, an aesthetically enlightened people would display connoisseurship in some respect of the ballad art.   The case of Iceland goes further, however, since it shows an undoubted " people " interested in the niceties and subtleties of an advanced art, to the exclusion of those ready appeals to the understanding and senses which are normally supposed to be " popular ".'

The significance of recent developments in Scottish poetry has been the abandonment of the dreadful post-Burnsian practice of ' lyrical outpourings ' (the abyss of Grobianism and Eulenspiegel into which we fell after the Reformation, and the bottom of which we have not yet touched perhaps, since that initial declension has been followed by the long disastrous sway of the Common Sense Philosophy, which, in turn, has led to the terrible tyranny to-day of that ' omnitude '—to use Chestov's word [1]—to which apparently no term can be set and which indeed may destroy civilization altogether), the long-overdue coming-together and intensified Anglophobia of the

---

[1] Léon Chestov died in Paris on November 20, 1938, at the age of 82.

N

younger and more radical Irish, Welsh, Cornish, and Scottish poets, and a return to ' elaborately ingenious exercises ' on the part of these rather pedantic literary men, most of them intensely concerned with the social question and the desperate necessity of bridging the gulfs that have been allowed to develop between poetry and the people.

Nothing is more marked in recent Scottish poetry than the keen concern of the writers involved with the whole range of *welt-literatur* and their many-sided knowledge of it. They have translated into Scots a great body of poetry from German, French, Russian, and other European languages. Translations from the Russian of Boris Pasternak by William Soutar, from the Russian of Alexander Blok and the German of Rainer Maria Rilke by myself, from the German of Heine and others by Professor Alexander Gray, from the Dutch of P. C. Boutens and others by Emeritus-Professor Sir H. J. C. Grierson, and from a great array of French poets from Ronsard to Baudelaire by Miss Winefride Margaret Simpson, are included in this tale of recent renderings into Scots, and healthy intromissions with the whole range of European literature, which have been a notable feature of our recent literary history, like a veritable return to the Good Europeanism of our mediaeval ancestors. The younger poets have carried the work of their immediate predecessors still further in this way. George Campbell Hay has made a great many translations from the Irish and the Welsh, and Douglas Young effects translation into Latin, French, Attic Greek, Romaic Greek, German, and other tongues, and translates from the Greek, the Russian, and the Lithuanian into Scots or English.

Writing to me about his brilliant essay, ' Gaelic and Literary Form ', which was published in *The Voice of Scotland*, June–August 1939, George Campbell Hay said :

> ' The slash at the " general stream of European literature " might be shocking if misunderstood. I do not mean that Gaelic should not widen its contacts. It must. But " European literature " as understood by people like Quiller-Couch (whom I choose as a particularly horrible example) and as embodied in tomes with that title, a selected list of countries and a selected list of names from each of these countries, starting of course with the Greeks, well-bowdlerized into " Christian gentlemen ", is a ramp that no longer impresses—like " Western Europe ". I am all for the " minor literatures " and the " backward races " whose literatures have not been " etherealized " out of life. Our contacts might as well be with the Islaendings or with those grand rascals the Serbs as with Bloomsbury or the Seine. The big countries share a common foreign-ness and repulsiveness to me, and like Blunt I sometimes wish they would destroy one another.'

And in the essay itself, he said :

> ' In three European languages at least lyrical technique has been highly developed, and intricate systems of ornamentation have been evolved. They are Gaelic, Welsh, and Icelandic. These are three

languages which stand outside the system which its rather parochial devotees chose to call European Literature. Curiously a tradition of democracy in literature and poesy now accompanies this technical skill in all three cases ; but in lyric poetry at least the people are generally the masters.   One would think that such traditions were too precious to be exchanged for anything, even for the pleasure of drifting down " the general stream of European literature " which gives signs at present of disappearing among its own silt.'

Increasingly, then, the attitude of all the significant younger Scottish poets is that which was expressed by such Irish bards as Eochy O'Hosey when he cried satirically, *Ionmolta malairt bhisigh*, with a bardic pungency that is lost when we feebly translate, ' a change for the better deserves praise ', and says he has abandoned intricate, carven ornament and adopted ' a common sort of easy art ' that will bring him more praise—of old, composition almost broke the heart, but this new verse is ' a great cause of health ' ; or Mahon O'Heffernan, warning his son not to study poetry.

> ' The profession of thy ancestors before thee forsake utterly ; though to her first of all honour be rightly due, Poetry henceforth is a portent of misery.   To the worst of all trades cleave not, nor fashion any more thine Irish lay. . . . A vulgar doggerel—" soft " vocables with which 'tis all-sufficiency that they but barely be of even length—concoct such plainly, without excess of incolution, and from that poor literary form shall thy promotion be the greater.   Praise no man, nor any satirize.'

They cry instead with Soren Kierkegaard : ' For when all combine in every way to make all things easier, there is only one possible danger, namely, that the easiness may become so great that it becomes altogether too great, and there remains only one want, though it is not yet a felt want, when men will want difficulty.   Out of love for mankind . . . I conceived it to be my task to create difficulties everywhere.'   And they understand and proclaim with Lenin himself that to be a Communist one must first master all that is of value in the whole cultural heritage of mankind.   Those who have not done this are, as Lenin says, ' not Communists, but mere bluffers '.

' Water-tight compartments are useful only to a sinking ship,' I have said in one of my poems ; and the essential principle of the intellectualism of these younger poets is admirably expressed by another Celt, Mr. John Cowper Powys, who, to all the critics of his refusal to talk down to his readers, to all who dub him an ' impossible idealist ' if he expects the common man to follow him in his adventures in international literature, replies :

> ' When they cry " Charlatan ! " what they really mean is : " How dare this fellow talk about Dostoievsky's Christ, and about Plato's Eros, and about Goethe's ' Mothers ', and about Wordsworth's *Intimations of Immortality*, and about the ' art ' of Henry James, and about the ' critical values ' of Walter Pater, and about the ' cosmic emotion ' of Walt Whitman, as if these recondite subjects, complicated enough to

fill the whole span of several real scholars' life-work, could possibly
be lugged into an address to working-men and tradesmen's assistants! ''
These natural enemies of mine, these " Philistines " of Culture, as
Nietzsche calls them, *dare not*, for the life of them, bring Christ and the
Mothers and the Grail and the Over-Soul and the secret of Jesus and
eternal recurrence and being-and-not-being and the monochronous
hedone of Aristippus and the pleasure-which-there-is-in-life-itself of
Wordsworth, and the absolute of Spinoza and the mystery of the Tao,
and Fechner's planetary spirits and the mythical elements of Empedocles
and the natural magic of Shakespeare's poetry into an interpretation of
the Sleeping Beauty or of the Castle of Carbonek.   These are very
special products of evolutionary thought, they would argue ; they are
questions for the erudition of scholars. . . . To parade such topics
before an unacademic audience is to give yourself away as no better
than a vulgar conjurer. . . . Personally I have always been prepared to
arise fiercely in defence of this sort of popular culture.   You will, I
believe, find on its side such great imaginative spirits as Pythagoras,
Socrates, Plotinus, the Gnostic Heretics, the Scholastic Heretics,
Montaigne, Goethe, Ruskin, Matthew Arnold, Walter Pater, William
James.'

The insistence upon this of these younger poets—their tendency
to regard it as the very crux of the literary position to-day—is readily
understandable in the light of the great tradition of Scottish education
and the sorry state to which it has been reduced to-day, and, above
all, the complete demoralization of the Scottish University system,
prostituted to the purposes of Finance Imperialism.   They have
been forced to recognize very clearly indeed that, as Anna Gammadion
has said :

   ' It is as though a kind of " anti-self-preservation " instinct were
   being developed which ensures that in whatever circumstances of
   difficulty the individual human being may find himself, he will more
   and more certainly turn the blind-spot of his mind towards it and
   unerringly select the most effective means for rendering himself incapable of coping with it.   That is, of course, exactly what thorough
   students of Douglas would expect as the outcome of the continuous
   operation of the reign of finance, and it may account for the small
   proportion of young persons in the Social Credit movement.   Douglas
   was only just in time.   Another decade or two, and collapse or no
   collapse of the debt-structure and the political order which it imposes,
   there could have been no *movement* and nothing but " free ", charming
   and highly intelligent young persons walking about with fully developed
   blind-spots where, among us, there *are* one or two sense-sensitive
   retinas. . . . University " teachers "—except for a very few specialists
   —are not education-theorists or indeed educationists at all ; but
   observation of many recent generations of university students (medical)
   convinces me that they behave increasingly as though they have been
   deprived of at least one of the standard mental instruments—not just
   that the scholarship-holders or the " self-taught " or the foreigners
   have been deprived of it ; but as though *all* of them had been forced on
   without a particular and necessary instrument for full intellectual
   development.   There are now *some* of the characteristic operations of
   the mind which *none of them* can perform, which, indeed, they do not
   know to exist ; but which, nevertheless, their fathers performed easily

and habitually. . . . The mechanism *whereby* it has been done is sufficiently intricate and " long-term " in character as largely to hide the fact of its existence from curious eyes, while at the same time ensuring that the curious eyes shall not be many or open. One university principal, when it was suggested to him that the real *policy* of the universities was the debasement of the intellectual currency, remarked dryly that " we must strive to retain those liberties we still possess ".'

It is against this situation in all its aspects, applications, and effects that the younger Scottish poets to-day have gone out like David against Goliath.

I may add here to what I have said in my programmatic poem, *The Kind of Poetry I Want,* that the ideal envisaged is that expressed by my friend, the late Mr. W. B. Yeats, in the preface to his *Oxford Book of Modern Verse,* viz., the ' poet to read a mathematical equation, a musical score, a book of verse, with equal understanding ' ; and to these qualifications I would add the practical activities—the capacity for using poetry as a weapon in the day-to-day struggle of the workers, with no scruples in using extra-literary means, in organizing rows and literary scenes, in doing everything *pour epater les bourgeois*—of a Vladimir Mayakovsky.

The younger Scottish poets are therefore all of a highly intellectual cast—very different from the pious or moralistic, or facetious, morons of local rhymesters who dominated the Scottish Parnassus (as it were 'Ampstead 'Eath on Bank Holiday) between the death of Burns and the early 1920's. They have worked over the whole Scottish tradition critically and creatively, renewing in themselves and effectively reflecting in their writing such traditional and very un-English attributes of the Scot as his aptitude for foreign languages, his internationalism, his tendency to ignore all manner of artificial and arbitrary barriers and overspill into the so thought most-widely unrelated fields of thought and feeling, his republicanism as opposed to England's snobbery and social stratification. Most of them are Marxian Socialists and all of them Scottish Nationalists (not *bourgeois* nationalist, but Workers' Republicans), dynamically preoccupied with Scotland's pressing social, economic, and political problems. While it was necessary to explore the possibilities of a Scottish Vernacular Revival first of all, those who initiated this new literature in Scots twenty years ago fully recognized and proclaimed that before major work could be looked for it would be necessary to carry this new creative process right back into Gaelic itself. This is now being done.

Complementary to the creative work of these poets (and often by the same hands) there has been a wealth of long-overdue activity in the fields of biography, criticism, and the re-editing of texts. Dunbar, Fergusson, and other Scots poets have been brilliantly re-edited and made accessible to the Scottish reading public, to whom they had long not been available. So have many of the Gaelic poets. The Saltire Society and the Scottish Gaelic Texts Society have done splendid work in this connexion and have had the services of scholars like Dr. Mackay Mackenzie, Mr. John Lorne Campbell, Dr. H. Harvey Wood, Dr. John Oliver, Professor James Carmichael Watson, and many others. And in this general recovery and revaluation the Scottish Latin poets like Arthur Johnstone and George Buchanan have not lacked their translators and biographer-critics. And historians, philologists, and lexicographers have accompanied these developments with supporting activities of various kinds.

Scottish Socialism has now found something like an adequate counterpart in Scottish literature, particularly in poetry. The prevailing anti-intellectualism of modern Scotland has been progressively challenged by a sequence of young writers *au fait* with the languages and literatures of many countries and a great range of contemporary knowledge in economics, psychology, philosophy, and science. Much of the poetry in which this *kulturkampf* is expressed is, of course, ' difficult poetry '—and advisedly so. As Somhairle Mac Gill'Eathain says in one of his short Gaelic poems, *Tri Slighean* (i.e. *Three Ways*) :

> . . . if I chose
> I could with comfort follow
> That paltry, dry, low way
> Of Eliot, Pound, Auden,
> Macneice and Herbert Read and their gang ;
> I could—were it not for the twist
> Put in my spirit for two years
> By my own country, the fate of Spain,
> An angry heart and a glorious woman,

and again, the same poet in another poem which pays tribute to his golden lady, says in a lovely Gaelic verse which may be Englished as follows :

> ' The shadow from her beauty lay over poverty and a woeful hardship, and the world of Lenin's intellect and his power of patience and his wrath.'

What beautiful lady is this ? She is the Scottish Muse, of whom, in a poem welcoming the first of Mac Gill'Eathain's and Hay's poems to reach me, I have said :

> At last, at last, I see her again
>   In our long-lifeless glen,
> Eidolon of our fallen race,
> Shining in full renascent grace,
> She whose hair is plaited
> Like the generations of men,
> And for whom my heart has waited
>   Time out of ken.

Hark! hark! the *fead chruinn chruaïdh Chaoilte,*
Hark! hark! 'tis the true, the joyful sound,
Caoilte's shrill round whistle over the brae,
The freeing once more of the winter-locked ground,
The new springing of flowers, another rig turned over,
Dearg-lasrach bho'n talamh dubh na h-Alba,
Another voice, and another, stirring, rippling, throbbing with life,
Scotland's long-starved ears have found.

Deirdre, Audh [1]—she has many names,
But only one function. Phaneromene,
Hodegetria, Chryseleusa,
Chrysopantanasa—Golden-universal Queen—
Pantiglykofilusa, Zoodotospygi,
Like the sun once more in these verses seen,
The light *angelicae summeque sanctae Brigidae,*[2]
Goddess of poets, of whom Ultan[3] sang;
The golden, delightful flame; the branch with blossoms,
The actual Air-Maiden once more we see,
Incorporated tangibility and reality,
Whose electric glance has thrilled the Gaels
Since time beyond memory.
Twelve centuries ago Scotland with her praises rang.
Mary of the Gael! Brigit born at sunrise!
Her breath revives the dead.
Your songs, my friends, are songs of dawn, of renaissance too.
Twigs of the tree, of which it is said
Uno avulso non deficit alter
Aureus.[4] Worthy heirs and successors you
Of *Ceile De,*[5] of Ultan, of Broccan Cloen.[6]
Let your voices ring
And be unafraid.

Muscail do mhisneach a Alba ![7]

---

[1] Audh = the Deep-Minded.
Phaneromene = made manifest.
Hodegetria = leading on the way.
Chryseleusa = golden-pitiful.
Chrysopantanasa = golden-universal queen.
Zoodotospygi = the life-giving fountain.
Pantiglykofilusa = all-tenderly-embracing.
Agniotisa = pure.
[2] ' Of the most angel-like and most saintly Brigit ' (vide *Leabhar Imuinn,* Dublin, 1855–69).
[3] Ultan of Ard Breccain, died in A.D. 656. Composed a great ' Hymn in praise of Brigit '.
[4] From Virgil, *Aen.* VI, of the Golden Bough: ' Though one be torn away, there fails not another, golden '.
[5] *Ceile De,* Gaelic bard of ' the time of Aengus ', whose poem (sometimes ascribed to Brigit herself) is preserved in the Burgundian Library.
[6] Broccan Cloen, flourished about A.D. 500, author of chief poetic tribute to Brigit's name.
[7] *Muscail,* &c. = ' Waken thy courage, O Scotland ! ' (after Padraigin Haicead's [? 1600–1656] similar cry to Banba, i.e. Eire).

Set up your *Cuirt na h'eigse* [1]
With a resounding Barrántas,[2] my friends !

Ah, Scotland, her footsteps, her voice, her eyes,
Agniotisa here, entire in our skies !

Too long the Bible-black gloom has spread.
Now let your red
Radiance and melody wed
Over all Scotland be shed
Till the Giants in the cave awake
And with a snap of their fingers break
Forever dull England's chains of lead
And every Scot turns from Britannia of the sugar-bowl jaws
To our own long-lost Queen of Queens instead.
You have sounded the rallying cry.
It cannot be long
Till the hosts of our people hie
On the heels of your song,
And we all make a colour to your red [3]
And flush redly to your Muse's fair bright cheek.
Ho ro [4] *togaibh an aird !*
' *Mi eadar an talamh 's an t-athar a' seoladh*
Air iteig le h-aighear, misg-chath', agus sholais,
Us caismeachd phiob-mora bras-shroiceadh am puirt.' [5]

She is our Scottish *Gile na Gile* [6]—the strange pulchritude
That is the secret Scotland of the Gael,
The personification of Alba as the discrowned,
Wandering heart of beauty, our Shiela-ny-Gara,
Our Cathleen-ny-Houlihan, our *Druimfhionn Donn,*
Our *pe'n Eirinn i,* ' whoe'er she be ', [7]
Sean O Tuama's [8] Moirin-ny-Cullenan,
—And she leads us all over Scotland and the Isles
As the faery queen in Eire led Sean Clarach [9]

---

[1] *Cuirt na h'eigse* = Court of Poetry.

[2] Barrántas = poetic summons.

[3] ' Make a colour to your red,' Gaelic idiom, meaning ' match you in colour '.

[4] *Ho ro,* make ready to go.

[5] Alexander MacDonald's lines beginning ' Mi eadar . . .' mean ' Between earth and heaven in the air I am sailing, on the wings of exultance, battle-drunken, enraptured, while the notes of the great pipes shrilly sound out their tunes '.

[6] *Gile na Gile,* brightness of brightness, the best of the Irish *aislingi,* or vision poems, telling of encounters with fair phantoms. By Aodhagan O Rathaille, 1670–1726.

[7] Uilliam Dall O'Heffernan's *Pe'n-Eirinn I,* ' Whoe'er She Be ', is ' a song of rare finish . . . the poet communicates the thrill that startled him on Fionn's Hill, where he had gone to seek despairing solitude, when she, that lovelier than Deirdre, came to him—whoe'er she be. The wonder of that secret love lives across two centuries.'

[8] Sean O Tuama, 1708–75.

[9] Sean Clarach MacDomhnaill, 1691–1754.

To view the faery strongholds—Cruachain, Brugh-na-Boinne,
Creeveroe, Tara, Knockfeerin, and the rest
—The knot of white ribbon on the hair
Of the image of fine-tressed Gaelic womanhood!

Here only is there no makeshift
Of seeking intimacy with other human beings
And never really finding it.
—Ah, my Queen, slender and supple
In a delightful posture
As free from self-conscious art
As the snowcap on a mountain!
—An absorbing attachment of the spirit,
Not a sexual relationship as that is generally understood,
But an all-controlling emotion
That has no physical basis,
Love resolved into the largest terms
Of which such emotions are capable,
The power of the spirit beneath that exquisite tremulous envelope
Possessing moral courage to a rare degree
Which can keep her steadfast in the gravest peril,
And a dignity so natural and certain
That it deserves the name of stateliness.
Death cannot intimidate her.
Poverty and exile, the fury of her own family
And the calumnies of the world
Are unable to bend her will
Towards courses she feels to be wrong
—Imparting with every movement, every look,
Some idea of what the process of literature could be,
Something far more closely related
To the whole life of mankind
Than the science of stringing words together
In desirable sequences.

(What is the love of one human being
For another compared to this?
—Yet I do not underestimate
What such love can be!
On vit plus ou moins à travers des mots
As a rule, but sometimes these moments do come
When words and thoughts are one,
And one with the receptive understanding;
And in such moments
The individual reality of two lives
—For reality is subjective, personal
To each one of us, held in
By the crystal walls of our experience—
Can be fully understood:
The crystals are broken down for a space,
And two realities mingle and become one.
There is little better.
The physical falls away,
Almost irrelevant,
When naked spirits meet in kindness.)

N 2

Alas ! The thought of ninety-nine per cent of our people
Is still ruled by Plato and Aristotle
Read in an historical vacuum by the few
From whom the masses receive
A minimum of it but along with that
A maximum incapacity for anything else.
The Greek, being a Southerner, was (and still is)
By temperament excitable and easily roused
To excessive display of feeling. Greek troops, we know—unlike
     Scots—
Were peculiarly liable to sudden panic,
And the keen intelligence of the race
Was no more rapid in its working
Than was their susceptibility to passion.
Wisely, therefore, the Greek moralists preached restraint ;
Wisely they gave their impressionable countrymen advice
The very opposite of that
The more steady Northerner requires,
And we in modern Scotland most of all !

CHAPTER VII

ROUND THE WORLD FOR SCOTLAND

' It seems to me that I must circumnavigate the whole world in order to find that region which I lack and which yet is indicated by the deepest source of my whole ego—the next instant you are so near to me, so present, mightily replenishing my mind, that I am transfigured for myself and feel that it is good to be here.'—KIERKEGAARD.

' Lo ! what a mariner love hath made me.'—SURREY.

' I went far with thee in a land that I knew and a good part of the adventure in a land where I was not acquainted.'—ALASDAIR MACMAIGHSTIR ALASDAIR in ' Angus ho, Mhorag '.

' WHEN WE think of the origin of English,' says Dr. Walt Taylor in his pamphlet on *Doughty's English* (1939), ' we at once realize that English is not entirely Germanic. It contains other important elements—French, Italian, Spanish, Roman, Greek, Hebrew. And we see Doughty leaving Holland, wandering in France, Italy, Spain, Greece, and finally to the Bible Lands, making a literary and linguistic pilgrimage, tracing back his literary and linguistic heritage to its origins. And study of the origins of the religious heritage led him, as all Semitic studies must lead, into Arabia. He left England in 1870 to study the Low German sources of English. Five years later he was in Sinai seeing Arabia in little ; and next year he entered the Desert itself. In this wilderness he found his ideal language. Arabic seemed to him a language " rich in spirit ", and " dropping with the sap of human life ". Here was a nation of word-lovers, enunciating their language with great care, and speaking with " perspicuous propriety ", emulating each other, as they talked round the coffee-hearth in " election of words ".'

As Dr. Taylor says :

' For a writer to write one language in the manner of another language would seem at first sight to be a strange and dangerous thing to do ; but we must remember that throughout the history of English there have been many writers who have written English prose as though they were writing Latin prose, some who have deliberately thought in Latin and then translated their thought into English, many who have used Latin grammar and vocabulary and method of expression as a touchstone for the correct usage of English. If it seems natural to us that Gibbon's *Decline and Fall of the Roman Empire* (partly because of its subject) should be written in a highly Latinized style, it should not be strange that Doughty's *Arabia Deserta* (if only because of its subject) is written in a highly Arabicized style ; the strangeness will not be in the fact of the Arabicized style but in the effect of that style ; for Gibbon is only one of many who have based their English style on Latin, whereas Doughty has been unique among English writers in basing his style on Arabic. . . . Living abroad enables an Englishman to see English objectively, as he sees a foreign language; and living in the countries where Germanic languages are spoken will bring him into contact with elements from which modern English has developed.'

Where are we to get a similarly objective view of Scotland? Certainly English will not serve us. We must have Gaelic and Old Norse and Latin and much else. But just as Dicey said that a knowledge of America was necessary for a knowledge of Europe, we must peregrinate just as Doughty did—but not in the same countries —if we are to get down to our national sources and secure a like all-inclusive view of our national process. Miss Dorothy Hoare's book, *The Works of Morris and Yeats in Relation to Early Saga Literature* (1937) describes not dissimilar explorations on the part of these two poets, and Yeats—and several other recent Irish poets— found cause to supplement the results of these by having recourse to India. We can get no adequate view of Scotland without following the examples of these men; but since the Scottish story is far more complex than the matters with which they were concerned, we find that, like the Scottish people themselves, who have been mankind's greatest travellers perhaps and have scattered themselves all over the globe, it is necessary to go all round the world to find the true Scotland of which we are in search, and that, whereas Iceland and the Low Countries and even the Bible Lands are sufficiently obvious sources for England, our analogous Scottish quest leads us into and compels us to linger longest in unexpected places, and particularly among the Red Indians and among the Chinese and the Georgians. For lack of this knowledge almost all Scots to-day are hopelessly confused; they, and their country, are posed against a wrong historical and cultural background altogether.

But how very difficult it is to get our background into proper focus and distribute the emphasis.

' If we view our knowledge of the many strata and many bearings of our very complex nature,' says Keyserling, ' in combination with the two facts that man can lay the accent on himself in one way or in another, and that reality, according to the position of this accent, not merely appears but *becomes* different—we shall reach the following con-clusion. If a man puts the accent on his mineral nature, he will become a stone : if he insists upon his reptilian being, he will become a serpent or a toad. If he lays stress on his Gana, then in doing so he subjects himself unreservedly to its laws, renounces his freedom, and the law of blind inertia will end in mastering him altogether.'

Yet man is free to lay the accent on the highest value—that is Keyserling's message. We know it to be true; but we dare not face this truth, so much more important than any other known to man— because it calls for private action and private courage, because it calls for nothing less than the rediscovery of virtue to best advantage among the different elements. How widely one must range in

Scottish matters may be illustrated by remarking that it is significant of the scattered state of Scottish source material that Miss Annie I. Cameron in writing her *The Apostolic Camera and Scottish Benefices 1418–88* had to pursue her researches for this work of remarkable erudition, the product of immense industry and original research, in the Vatican Archives at Rome, with auxiliary study in the Prussian Historical Institute, the Ecole Française, the Belgian Historical Institute, and other continental centres of erudition, while Miss I. F. Grant in her big and important volume on *The Lordship of the Isles* says of her subject that

> ' the idea of this shadowy Lordship has fascinated me for a long time. Authentic records of its history are very scrappy, and one best realizes its importance and its potentialities from the story of the utter confusion that reigned in the Highlands and Islands after its dismemberment, and from the fact that the old arts and legends of the Gael are most closely associated with districts that once formed part of its territories. It is when one thinks of its lovely setting ; of the arts, the music, and the literature that it fostered ; and of the wonderful " might have been " if this last political nucleus of the Gael had survived, that the old Lordship gains the appealing fascination of a " faerie land forlorn ".'

It is to be remarked how frequently, thinking of the Scottish Islands, one is driven for the only possible parallels and analogies to the case of the Red Indians. So, in an as-yet-unpublished book on the ' Wolfe of Badenoch ', that neglected champion of the Celtic order at a great turning point in history at which the cause he represented was overborne and lost, it has been remarked that :

> ' The Wolfe was the champion in whom the psychology and prin-ciples of a disappearing and little-known period of Scottish history finally confronted, and were overcome by, new historical forces which—though they seem to-day to be finishing their course—have since con-ditioned Scottish life to such an extent that it is now difficult to think outside them at all, and realize in any vital fashion the very " other way of life " embodied in the Wolfe. It was curious to read a couple of years ago the reviews of Miss Audrey Cunningham's *The Loyal Clans*, a pregnant revaluation of a great element of Scottish history, for the bulk of the reviewers, including distinguished Scottish writers, had to confess " the mystery of the clan system " and to show that in relation to it the great majority of modern Scots, including the descendants of the clans in question, are confronted with as superb a gift of evasion as are American writers on the Redskin Tragedy. . . . The names of King Philip, Pontiac, Tecumseh, Red Jacket, Osceola, and Black Hawk offer no conclusion because they left no chronicle. . . . Sitting Bull is a touchstone by which the Indian shown in the long pageant of literature and history is left in considerable disarray. . . . But it is only just over a hundred years ago since Sitting Bull was born (1831), and if this reconstruction is difficult in the Red Indian case, what must it be (behind no smaller wall of violent extirpation and wholesale clearances of territory for alien purposes) in this Scottish case, where we have to deal with a touchstone, a great irreconcilable, born six hundred years ago, and with opposing beliefs that have had all the intervening centuries in which to harden. The circumstances of the Wolfe of Badenoch and

Sitting Bull were very similar ; the forces that overcame them both were substantially the same forces ; the methods by which they, and the manner of life for which they fought, have since been misrepresented, have much in common ; and it need surprise no one who knows anything of post-Union Scotland that whereas a great literature has sprung up within recent years in America to undo the earlier misrepresentation and arrive at just conclusions in regard to the Red Indians, any similar effort in Scotland to do justice to such "lost causes" of our history as that for which the Wolfe stood has scarcely yet begun to be made.'

Can all this be made good yet? At a gathering held in Glasgow under the auspices of the Saltire Society to honour Dr. Frederick Lamond, the great exponent of Beethoven, Mr. Pat Sandeman, in proposing the toast of ' Music in Scotland ', drew attention to the possibilities of the old Gaelic melodies and thought that one day a genius would arise and combine them into a great musical work. A lot of lip-service to Gaelic music is paid in this way in Scotland to-day—but what does it really amount to? Despite all the ' success ' of the *Songs of the Hebrides*, the fact remains that the fringe of Hebridean song has scarcely been touched yet and there exist in the Islands awaiting a competent collector far greater stores than have yet been tapped, and the same thing applies to orally-transmitted Gaelic poetry, several important collections of which have been made but cannot be published owing to the lack of financial facilitation. Mr. J. H. Whyte, referring to our pipe music, ' a classical music more akin to Byzantine music than any contemporary European music, marvellously rich within certain narrow limits ', says that our greatest living Scottish composer—and the only one who has attempted to create a national music—Francis George Scott, ' has mastered this old music, and subsumed it in a markedly modern idiom, in which he has set some of the finest of Scottish lyrics, old and new '. That is true, but it is with F. G. Scott as it was with Edward Grieg (himself with Scottish blood in his veins), whose life-work is irrefutable evidence of the fissure in Norwegian cultural life and in whose art that battle was fought out. As his latest biographer says, Grieg throws light on the problem as much through what he *did not* as through what he *did* achieve. ' Looked at from this point of view Edward Grieg is still a living fighting and suffering personality, and above all a man who counts to-day.' In Grieg's album Ibsen wrote the following warning words (and like words of warning might be inscribed to F. G. Scott in Scotland to-day) to the composer, who, in spite of all, meant to settle in the homeland and dedicate his powers to the service of Norwegian culture :

Orpheus woke with crystal bones
Souls in brutes ; struck fire from stones.

Stones there are in Norway plenty :
Brutes far more than ten or twenty.

> Play, so stones spark far and wide !
> Play, to pierce the brutes' thick hide.

And it is true of Scott as it was true of Grieg that after his return home he had to suffer ' malice, venom, intrigues, pettiness, the instinctive attempt of the whole pack to pull down a great personality '. It is true of Scott, too, as of Grieg, that ' his work involves great obligations, since it waits upon a posterity that will complete what he began. And for this reason the banner of the future waves over his life's work.' And if it is true that ' if we are to follow Grieg's real development as an artist—and he never ceased to develop—we must follow him on the narrow path which leads always deeper and deeper into the forest, always farther and farther into the wonderland of romance, the path which he finds and points out to us every time comes into relation with Norwegian folk-music ', certainly the analogous path in Scotland will lead by most complex and difficult ways to regions far more remote from the prevailing *ethos* in the British Isles. This is the path of our speleological adventure here. The word ' lightning ' has cropped up several times in these pages already. Audh's coming again will be like lightning-break in the dark smoke-filled atmosphere—the dull chaotic life—of Scotland to-day.

> Out of this cloud, O see : so wildly hiding
> the star which just has been—(and out of me),
> out of yon mountain-country which has now
> for long had night, nightwinds—(and out of me),
> out of the river in the valley-basin, river catching
> the glitter of the torn sky-glade—(and out of me) ;
> out of me and all these things to make a single
> thing, O Lord . out of me, me and the feeling
> with which the herd, pent up within the pen,
> and breathing out, takes in the mighty darkened
> no-more-being of the earth—out of me
> and every light within the darkness of
> the many houses, Lord, to make one thing :
> out of strangers, for I know not one, O Lord,
> and out of me and me to make one thing ;
> out of sleepers, out of strange unknown old men
> in hospices who cough importantly within
> the beds, and out of sleep-dazed children on
> so strange a breast, and out of many unprecise
> vague people, always out of me and out
> of naught but me and things unknown to me
> to make one thing, O Lord Lord Lord, the thing
> which cosmic-earthly like a meteor
> assembles in its heaviness naught but
> the sum of flight : naught knowing but the arrival.

But it will be a tremendous struggle ! For in Scotland the cleavage goes far deeper than it did in Norway, and far deeper than anything I have yet said indicates. Since, as Mr. James H. Whyte has said :

> ' There are important respects in which the Gaelic culture of Scotland has not been reborn in the modern world, whereas the culture of Lowland Scotland has : Celtic art and thought in their various branches clearly demonstrate this. The reason lies to a large extent in the imperviousness of Celtic art to the classical influences, emanating chiefly from Graeco-Roman sources, that made, say, a Shakespeare possible in England and an Adams possible in eighteenth-century Edinburgh. Much has been made by a certain type of writer of the classical influences on Celtic culture, of the Gael's knowledge of ancient Greece, and so on, but although one can recall at random the use Irish writers have made of, say, the *Odyssey*, the *Aeneid*, Lucan Heliodorus, etc., the fact remains that there are stronger affinities between Celtic art and the art of the East than between Celtic art and modern European art. For the commonly-drawn comparisons between Celtic art and eastern art boil down to an insistence on the non-participation of those arts in the major developments of modern European art. Mr. T. D. Kendrick emphasized this when he wrote : " The art of the Celtic lands and of Scandinavia . . . were . . . both of them *barbarian*, although this may well sound a rather irreverent description of the lovely works produced by early monastic Ireland ; but the meaning is clear—they were both on the edge of the world wherein classical art progressed through Carolingian, Ottonian, Italian, and Byzantine phases, and neither of them was strong enough to stand aside from this main stream of European art. They aped it, and whenever they did, they fell from grace, as is the way with barbarian art." By comparison with this " barbarian " art, European art is a humanist art. The organizing, ordering, centripetal quality in European art and thought, first exploited by the Greeks, is opposed to the spirit of the Celt and the oriental. The art of classical Europe was an art of selection, an ordering and organizing of experience ; it has an aerated quality deriving from its humanism ; it is not so much organic as architectural in form. It is easy in the light of Mr. Kendrick's and similar remarks to see how the cultural inbreeding of the Celt came about, to appreciate its rich fruits and yet recognize, whilst bemoaning, the virtual death of Celtic culture in the modern world. Of all the people talking so glibly about a Celtic Revival, we can think of only one who sees the consequences of what a Gaelic Revival would be (supposing it possible). He would welcome it, not because he is ignorant of the European tradition, but because, with that tremendous romantic fervour that makes him hate Goethe, for example, he has no use for it.'

And, as that one, Mr. Whyte names the author of the present book.

Indeed, we think the fissure or conflict between Scotland and England is as deep as that which Professor H. F. MacNair discusses in his book, *The Real Conflict Between China and Japan: An Analysis of Opposing Ideologies*, and not dissimilar in kind. (If this seems intolerably far-fetched, readers may set beside it and reflect upon Sir Richard Livingstone's recent statement : ' Perhaps the best chance of reproducing the ancient Greek temperament would be to " cross " the Scots with the Chinese.') The clue to the matter lies in realizing that in direct contrast to the deification of their sovereign by the Japanese, in China, according to Mencius, a ' monarch whose rule is injurious to the people should be dethroned ', the people being the most important element in a nation.   George Buchanan and many others in Scotland have echoed Mencius, and therein too lies the principal difference between Scotland and England.   The characteristics of the Japanese and Chinese differ as greatly as their respective concepts of the significance of the head of the State, and here the attributes of the Japanese are very like those of the English, while the attributes of the Chinese resemble those of the Scots.   As Professor MacNair lists them, on the one side (Japanese) some of the outstanding features are will-to-power, tenacity of purpose, and decisiveness of action, ' direct or devious, the latter at times to the point of what the Westerner is inclined to term treachery ';   on the other side (Chinese)—passive resistance, tendency to compromise and procrastination, and in addition, having been pacifically inclined for ages, the Chinese, in contrast to what their aggressive neighbour was doing, tended to ignore ' realities '.   The parallel is very close.

It is not easy to enter into the soul of Chinese music,
Which is a mere ting-jang monotony to most Westerners.
Yet Laloy thinks the union of the music of China and Europe possible
Because the scales are constructed upon exactly the same notes.
' Music imparts the same emotion to all those who listen to it :
It encourages humanity.'
' The points of contact do exist.   To discover them
It would be necessary to know the history of music
Not only in Germany but in Europe
From the Middle Ages down to the present.'
He is right.   And that is true not only of music
But of everything else in regard to the union
Of the East and the West.   As Laloy says :
   ' The silence is only broken by a stream,
   Falling in a series of waterfalls,
   But invisible beneath the dark moss.
   We are like those initiated into the mysteries,
   Who hunt for the cloven mushroom,
   Shining among dark undergrowth,
   Which is said to prolong human life.'

' The third and most interesting of the party was a young man whose Scottish father had married an Indian squaw, and as a guide to this expedition he proved his worth time and again.   " He grew ", Mr. Scott says, " with the Indian's grace of movement and the intelligent Scotsmen's way of thought, which can make anybody feel a fool." ' — J. M. Scott in *Unknown River*.

' Civilization (to the tremendous contemporary betrayal and complete endangering of which England has all along been tending ever since the English language outgrew its native basis) needs to renew itself at its original sources (see Waddell's *The British Edda*, and Cier Rige's— i.e. Roger O'Connor's—*Chronicles of Eri* in L. Albert's *Six Thousand Years of Gaelic Grandeur Unearthed* and *The Buried-Alive Chronicles of Ireland,* for proof that the original impetus to civilization was an

Ur-Gaelic initiative, *nota bene* in the very region, Georgia, the original home of the Scots, which has given Stalin to the world!'—*The Voice of Scotland*.

On account of all these complex and ill-documented considerations, arising in spheres of history and culture utterly foreign to the vast majority of British people, for the veritable scientist of race, culture, mind—the scientist who derives his generalizations from fixed data instead of running fluid data through a funnel of generalization—the pertinent attitude in relation to the life of our area would seem to be that of the dying Goethe's unfulfillable demand, 'More light'. Certainly the average visitor who endeavours to get close to these Hebridean islanders—especially to those who are still completely un-Anglicized—must feel as Professor Edward Sapir of Yale did in contact with the Navaho Indians. We are in constant rapport with an intelligence in which all experiences, remote and proximate, 'trivial' and 'important', are held like waving reeds in the sensitive transparency of a brook—an intelligence in which the ingredients resemble the things for which a woman with child longs. Like the juice of the oyster, the aroma of the wild strawberry, the most subtle and diversified elements are here intermingled to form a higher organism. It is easy enough to see vividly this composite life of clan and people—the basic Navaho culture. What remains hopelessly baffling and obscure is the individual quality of this man of them, and that. Consider just one of the veils interposed between us, and the 'sensitive transparency' of that intelligence. The narrator knew Navaho but not English. The narrative reaches us across the desk of an ethnological field worker who knew English but not Navaho. Between the two stands an interpreter whom we are required to trust, not only for the denotative sense of every term of both tongues but also for the essentials of that style which is the man. Left Handed, when he recounts, for instance, his early adventures in sex, does so with a blunt physiological particularity, reproduced for us by a liberal use of the ancient four-letter colloquialisms. Maybe they are the best possible renderings. Maybe they come nearer than anything else English affords, in the sense of combining fidelity to precisely what the Navaho words said with avoidance of everything they did not suggest. But is this inherently a very likely possibility? The terms in question are conventionally unprintable in English and have to be sketched by typographic hints. Are we, then, to presume that Left Handed resorted to a vocabulary conventionally inadmissible in Navaho and invested with the same sniggering associations? Did he, perhaps, have correspondingly to sketch in unsayable words by gestures? It is a not very plausible presumption; the chances are that the Navaho words raised no issue of admissibility whatever. If that is true, the narrator is, *ipso facto*, belied; the occurrences may be translated, but the man is not.

Ethnologists and social psychologists are always taking us to task
for our proneness to ' value judgements ', moralistic and other; but
what is language itself but a set of implicit value judgements : a man,
Navaho or Nordic—or Gaelic—does not go into unreserved detail
about a sexual experience without disclosing in the very words he
uses what he thinks of the experience and of himself in connexion
with it.   ' Son of Old Man Hat ', as we have him in Professor Sapir's
English words, discloses next to nothing.

We might be in Gaeldom, too, rather than with the last of the Seri
Indians on the Sonora Coast when we read : ' In the four ceremonies
where a man dances on a plank the medicine man sings 350 songs—
different songs every night.   They ended their night chants with
one song in which their ancestral island was personified, in much the
same way as Americans to-day sing "America " :

> ' Watch me dance !
> I am heavy, but I can dance !
> See the edge of my skirt
> Wave back and forth.
> It is the waves of the sea
> On my beach.'

The Seris have a great deal in common with the Hebridean Gaels,
living on their island of Tiburon not far off the coast of Sonora, an
island that ' rises like the tip of a lost continent, saving from extinction
a people from an earlier world, these Seri Indians.   They are savages
now, but in the old days they had poets who sang songs to every fish
in the sea, and to every bird and animal.   Strange white men, with
blue eyes and yellow hair, they say, landed on their shores and taught
them how to live.   Priests came, bringing a religion not unlike that
of the ancient Greeks, but that was long ago, and now they have
relapsed into barbarism '—verminous, half-starved, dressed in rags,
and living miserably on the fringes of a white man's civilization.   In
my chapter on ' The Ideas Behind My Work ', I have not gone into
the question of the Caledonian Antisysygy, my writings elsewhere
upon which have fluttered the dovecots of the Scottish literati to no
small extent and evoked from Mr. Edwin Muir the blunt dictum that
' the concept is not intellectually defensible '.   Mr. Muir ought to
recognize, however, that it is a mental counterpart not only of the
Chinese Tin-Tang dichotomy (the peculiar beauty of which is that
both parts are regarded as equally necessary, valid and to be accepted
—there is no question of *triumphing* over the dark element and
altogether wiping it out as though it were an arbitrary evil—whereas
the Christian doctrine insists more on the *conflict* between opposites
than their sustained relationship, this conflict is supposed to be
waged to an end, until evil no more remains and Saint George has
killed his complementary dragon, at which point the morality play
leaves off and we do not know what becomes of the victorious saint,

or how he fares in the anomalous situation in which he finds himself now, with no dragon left to do battle with, and, consequently, no reason left for living, whereas the more civilized Chinese have an affection for dragons of all kinds—the profound relationship fraught with beauty and terror, which must nevertheless be entered into. It is not an easy relationship. It entails unceasing conflict, a conflict not of extermination, but rather akin to that state in biology known as hostile symbiosis, and a counterpart also of the fact that in higher animals we usually find a well-developed symmetry and muscles of which the activities oppose the results of the activity of other muscles. Such muscles are called *antagonists*. If two *antagonists* of equal strength are stimulated equally, no macroscopic effect of the stimulation of both muscles results. If one of the antagonists is stronger than the other, the macroscopic effects of the stimulation of both muscles results not in some general convulsion, but in one-sided action of the stronger muscle. Obviously these results are the necessary consequence of *structure on different levels*. Professor Henrick's terms, *differential dynamogenic cortical influence* and *differential activation*, cover all the known facts a selection of which, in their particular Scottish form, I call the Caledonian Antisysygy. How far the matter may go is well indicated by Count Korzybski when he says :

'Instead of " fixation " we should have means and methods to preserve and foster *semantic flexibility*.—Flexibility is an important semantic characteristic of healthy youth. Fixation is a semantic characteristic of old age. With the colloidal background (which modern science owes to the Scottish chemist, Thomas Graham), the imparting of permanent semantic flexibility, which every one acquires who becomes conscious of abstracting, might prove to be a crucial neuro-physico-chemical colloidal factor of, at present, unrealized power. The colloidal behaviour of our bodies is dependent on electro-magnetic manifestations, which, in their turn, are connected with " mental " states of every description. If the colloidal ageing, which brings on old age, " physical " and " mental " symptoms, and ultimately death, is connected with such " mental " fixity, we may expect some rather startling results if we impart a permanent semantic flexibility. The " ageing " involves electrical changes in the colloidal background, which must be connected with the older semantic states. The new fluid semantic states should have different electrical influences, which, in their turn, would bring about a difference in the colloidal behaviour on which our physical states depend.'

Mr. Muir ought at the very least to recognize that what he calls ' intellectually indefensible ' is simply equivalent in the context to which ' Caledonian antisysygy ' refers to what Pavlov described when he wrote :

' It is highly probable that excitation and inhibition, the two functions of the nerve cell which are so intimately interwoven and which so constantly supersede each other, may, fundamentally, represent only different phases of one and the same physico-chemical process.'

But the real trouble with my ideas on this matter (and many other matters) is that they arise out of and in connexion with our Gaelic background, thus involving factors of which Mr. Muir and all his kind know nothing and with which as a consequence they have no patience, just as Professor Joad, despite the reputation he has in certain quarters for a ' generous revulsion against every avatar of the demon of tyranny ', nevertheless has had the appalling hardihood to complain that the students at Coleg Harlech ' for three parts of the time were taught the Welsh literature. . . . It is difficult not to be infuriated by the imbecile waste of time which this involves.' It is true of Scottish and Irish Gaelic too in such connexions as H. D. Lewis in his spirited reply to Professor Joad in this Welsh case pointed out :

> ' My purpose is not to expose a particular writer. Nor do I wish to heap abuse upon him. The matter is far too perplexing for retaliation of that kind. What I wish to do is simply to raise the problem of how it is that educated Englishmen, who would be ashamed to mispronounce a French or German name, can be so completely uninformed about the richness and extent of a culture which is flourishing in their midst, and will continue to flourish if it is not overwhelmed by economic conditions which are, in great measure, within our control. Direct acquaintance with Welsh literature is not expected, except in the case of a few. But, surely, educated Englishmen ought to be aware of the independent life of Wales and the disadvantages under which it is now labouring. If, however, the passages here quoted represent the attitude of Dr. Joad, who holds a responsible academic post and is deemed to have read somewhat widely, what does the ordinary Englishman think ? '

Aspects of this Gaelic background of ours emerge in the following passages from one of my poems :

> To-day the spiritual values of Gaelic civilization have not dissolved.
> They have, however, shifted. They no longer form one
> With the flesh of human substance. We can still
> Attain to every one of the subtlest goods in Gaelic culture,
> But only mentally, analytically, or rationally. We must return
> To the ancient classical Gaelic poets. For in them
> The inestimable treasure is wholly in contact
> With the immense surface of the unconscious. That is how
> They can be of service to us now—that is how
> They were never more important than they are to-day.
>
> Our Gaelic forbears possessed their great literature
> As nothing is possessed by peoples to-day,
> And in Scotland and Ireland and Wales
> There was a popular understanding and delight
> In literary allusions, technical niceties, and dexterities of expression
> Of which the English even in Elizabethan times
> Had only the poorest counterpart,
> And have since had none whatever
> And have destroyed it in the Gaelic countries too.
>
> Le moment semble venu d'une resurrection de l'humain.

The counterpoint of incompatible societies
A characteristic and actual phenomenon of Scottish life.

Writing on ' Highlands and Lowlands ' a few years ago, Mr. J. H. Whyte said, amongst other things :

' Much has been made by a certain type of writer of the classical influences on Celtic culture, of the Gael's knowledge of ancient Greece, and so on, but although one can recall at random the use Irish writers have made of, say, the *Odyssey*, the *Æneid*, Lucan, Heliodorus, &c., the fact remains that there are stronger affinities between Celtic art and the art of the east than between Celtic art and English. But that overlooks the fact that English was at one time more like Gaelic than it is now. One has to go further back in English to get the phrase " he was a-hitting the tree " than one has to in Gaelic to find the still more primitive "he was at the hitting of the tree ". But are the older forms more alien, not to say " poetic ", than " he was hitting the tree " ? Only if you take a " Tudor Tea-Shop " attitude to the poetic. The translation difficulty is not caused primarily by some strange elemental opposition between Gaelic and English ; it arises out of the time-lag observable between what Mr. Kendrick calls the barbaric arts and the arts of modern Europe. Actually, the concreteness of Gaelic poetry makes much of it easier to render into English than some Continental poetry. In consideration of the Highland-Lowland antithesis, anthropologists like Sir J. G. Frazer and historians of culture generally are more helpful than almost all the Scottish writings dealing directly with the matter. So many prejudices mar Scottish discussion of the matter that a point has been reached where the question can be more profitably discussed in the light of the impartial history of almost any other culture. The trouble is that there has been a modern European culture, but not a modern Celtic one. Is the latter possible, supposing it to be desirable ? '

It is no doubt for the same reason that Lenin made such an immediate and stupendous appeal to me. For, as Christopher Hollis points out in his study of *Lenin* (1938), he was neither a Jew nor, strictly speaking, a European ; but was a man from the banks of the Volga, from Simbirsk, which is eight hundred miles east of Moscow and in the heart of the old Khanate of Kazan. He was, in other words, a man from the wilderness frontiers of Christendom, and the movement he led (to quote from an unsympathetic writer—I would express the matter rather differently myself) :

' was precisely the kind of revolution, compounded of religious corruption and apostasy, raw barbarism and the passion for justice and revenge, that arises occasionally on these frontiers, and never, we may admit, without historical justice and a moral superiority, in some measure at least, over that which it destroys. Mr. Hollis sees this and writes with admirable fairness and sympathy, recognizing the virtues that were in Lenin, but never losing sight of the fact that this man came from a land where half-mad sects dream of the reign of the saints upon earth, and that all his moving about in the international revolutionary underworld of Western Europe never formed him into a man of our civilization. Measured by the standards of that spiritual culture, Lenin was simply a barbarian and an enemy. For all his voracious reading and copious writing, he " knew but two schools of European thought—the conventional nineteenth-century liberalism and the conventional communist reaction to it " ; he read " only that small corner of the great corpus of European literature which is concerned with the economic explanation of history ". Of non-Russian writers his favourites indeed appear to have been Zola and Jack London ! Mr. Hollis repeatedly insists that he was Russian through and through, and that he understood Russians as did no other man of his time. " But his years of foreign residence and international conferences brought him into but little contact with foreign minds. To them he was extraordinarily insensitive. . . . These are the reasons, of course, why he could create a new state conforming to the social realities of Russia. . . . He could not speak to Europe because he was not of it. . . ." Reading Mr. Hollis on Lenin, one is led to reflect on how little all this has been realized by European and American Leftist admirers of the Red chief and the work which he did. They have not seen him for what he was because that is hardly possible in their foreshortened perspective of history. But in a larger view of the past Lenin's position in the line of Mithradates and Othman —not of Cromwell and Robespierre—is by now sufficiently clear.'

I do not agree with all this, of course, but with the fact that Lenin, like myself—the Slav and the Celt—lies outside Europe as Eugenio d'Ors also insisted, and this, not only going further than the earlier idea of Aodh de Blacam and myself and other Gaelic writers of the necessity of ' getting back behind the Renaissance '—behind that Greek national whitewashing of all other European countries which had prevented them getting down to their own Ur-motives and realizing themselves in turn as Greece itself had done—but also because here too the oriental element in Celticism emerges into higher significance, has been one of the principal considerations in all my work, literary and political, in recent years, is one of the chief themes in the huge unpublished poem with which I have dealt in another chapter, and seems to be by far the most important of the lines along which the Scottish Movement must develop henceforward.

The ideas of the East-West synthesis and the Caledonian antisysygy merge into one and lie at the root of any understanding of, for example, that greatest Scottish musical achievement, the *probaireachd* or great pipe music, and it is impossible to communicate any idea of pibroch to people who are not effectively seized of this joint-idea. Mr. Harold Picton's *Early German Art and Its Origins, from the beginning to about 1050* (1939) emerges from a grasp of related factors in the same field. This important book is the first in English—and probably in any language—to give a general account of what may be termed the non-classical standpoint of the origins of German art and thus of Northern European art generally. In an appreciative Foreword, Professor Josef Strzygowski, the leading authority on early European art, confirms the validity of the orientation adopted by Mr. Picton in this work. Tracing the characteristics of Germanic art from the earliest beginnings, the author makes clear the large part played by Syria, Armenia, and the East in general in the development of the arts of Building, Ornament, Painting, Carving, Goldsmith's Work, Enamel and Sculpture. He shows how the influence of the South often perverted into naturalism the talent of the German for pattern, fantasy, and abstraction, while the effect of the East often confirmed and stimulated that talent. One of the most important features of the book is the wealth of well-reproduced illustration with which the wave of Eastern influence, and the backwash of this influence from Ireland, is brought out.

It is all this that my friend John Tonge has in mind when he says, in his admirable little book, *The Arts of Scotland* (1938) :

> ' Scottish art as a whole—one must not forget the smooth façades and ordered simplicity of the New Town of Edinburgh—is much more involved and restless and dynamic than English art, and these characteristics we find in the asymmetrical, intricate, organic Celtic art. This, I think, is what Hugh MacDiarmid has in mind when he speaks of the Scottish genius as " in general brilliantly improvisatory ". Scottish architecture—and architecture is the mother of the arts in Scotland no less than elsewhere—at its most characteristic evolves from a cellular structure, not from the tectonic piecing together of elements in classical fashion. It should not be forgotten, too, when the filigree technique of Celtic brooches, or the patterning of the Crosses, is under consideration, that precisely the same technique characterizes the consummate and intricate atonal art-music of the composers of pibroch, some of the greatest of whose works date from as recently as the seventeenth century.'

Mr. Tonge carries the discussion a stage further when he says :

> ' The New Town that Edinburgh built when, after centuries of turmoil, she turned her back on Prince Charles and Celtic Scotland, is so different (from the Old Town of Edinburgh—" the High Street of which was called in the seventeenth century the loveliest street in Europe ") as to raise the question of whether such a classicism is in Scotland part of the artistic cycle into which Adama van Schetema resolves all artistic movements, or a departure from a racial norm, or both. For Celtic art comes within Worringer's category of Nordic arts, and from his viewpoint Scotland, in the neo-Greek movement, could be regarded as indulging something like the German *Sachlichkeit*, a merely temporary reaction from the characteristic Nordic *Expressionismus*.'

It is this profound Celtic pattern of my mentality—this Scotist spirit—that leads me at this great crisis in our history to advocate the following way-out ; *inter alia*, the way of Scottish separatism against British Imperialism, English Ascendancy and centralization in London.

It is deeply symbolic that humanity has now for several centuries been concerned with the bridging of distance ; for man has in the same period been confronted with an inner void—that spiritual fissure which Christianity introduced between his self and his soul, or between the conscious subject and the ultimate object of consciousness. When European man came out of the school of the medieval church, it was to exchange the universalities of Faith for the particularities of Life, and to seek in geography, in politics, and in art for that Journey's End whose type theology had abstracted and placed in the Nowhere. To alter the metaphor, the human creature finds himself on the edge of a chasm, and his continued existence depends upon his bridging it with a rope; but only if his eye be mathematically exact will he throw the rope so as to make it catch upon a jutting spike of rock. And just as man the Pagan concentrated upon the truth or sureness of his foothold and man the Christian upon the virtue or strength of his arm, so it has been left for modern man to develop that beautiful precision of the eye, that instinct for the right thing which is the property of artistic genius rather than of thought or moral character. It is evident that this is the stage of greatest peril, corresponding to our present perilous situation in history; for if the eye does not achieve the perfect ' tact ' needed for a successful throw, the whole body may be dragged down in the wake of the rope. It is therefore natural enough that many should declaim against the long-sightedness of our modern athletes of the Will, and declare that the new world to which they point is an egotistical mirage; the more so as we witness to-day a truly terrifying exhibition of the anarchic and demonic—which may be defined as long-sightedness without aim. The freedom of intellect unattached to instinct has led, in many writers of the last century and popular leaders of the present one, to diabolism, or energy beating in the void; when Mephistopheles mockingly described himself as ' a genius—perhaps the very devil ', his remark was prophetic of that modern liberated subconsciousness which is not the primal instinct but a bastard mental changeling for it. If genius to-day in art and, following art, in politics appears to be the Great Anarch, it is none the less the one hope and dynamic of men; and our salvation lies not in a timid *bourgeois* return to Law but in an aristocratizing of the Will, its purifying from its low-bred obsession of inferiority— not in the closing but in the cleansing of the bridge-thrower's eye. This must now be considered in relation to that people which has more and more come to represent the struggles of frustrated and poisoned genius against the negative rule of Classical reason and Christian morality. Our horror at the venom-spewing dragon of Nazism must not make us forget that the creative genius is, as Blake said, ' of the Devil's party in reality ', and that the monster's challenge to the St. Georges of negative order can be answered only by their appropriating to themselves something of his demonic positive force. And this means that that decentralization which, as applied to Germany, is becoming more and more imperative as a measure of self-defence for the Western nations, will, as applied to themselves, become more and more indicated as a means of self-expression; as the world was created in mythology by the cutting up of a giant. For that productive ferment which is the nature of the Germanies, and the nature of genius, is made sterile and explosive by being compressed within the fixed concept of the nation; and as villainous action is generally nothing but artistic instinct blocked in its proper channel, the nations to-day are evil in character in proportion as they subconsciously desire to be fruitful. And this desire can be granted to them, not as they vainly hope by an expansion which must meet with justified resistance, but by inward division, like the division of a diseased personal 'psyche' under analysis; a decentralization permitting of a creative rivalry between units too small and inter-dependent for any solipsistic nationalism. We shall show the needed French realism in imposing this regionalism on the enemy, and shattering his sickly idolatries of race and mass; we shall give proof of English progressiveness by adopting it for ourselves.

I have not been able to discuss the great questions of bagpipe music in this volume, though I have given a great deal of thought and study to them in recent years and have written a great deal about them elsewhere both in verse and prose, so—since I do not like to have a book of mine going out, which does not have something to add to all I have already said on this high matter, let me give here a short poem on bagpipe music:

Let me play to you tunes without measure or end,
Tunes that are born and die without a herald,
As a flight of storks rises from a marsh, circles,
And alights on the spot from which it rose.

Flowers. A flower-bed like hearing the bagpipes.
The fine black earth has clotted into sharp masses
As if the frost and not the sun had come.
It holds many lines of flowers.
First faint rose peonies, then peonies blushing,
Then again red peonies, and behind them,
Massive, apoplectic peonies, some of which are so red
And so violent as to seem almost black; behind these
Stands a low hedge of larkspur, whose tender apologetic blossoms
Appear by contrast pale, though some, vivid as the sky above them,
Stand out from their fellows, iridescent and slaty as a pigeon's breast,
The bagpipes—they are screaming and they are sorrowful.
There is a wail in their merriment and cruelty in their triumph.
They rise and they fall like a weight swung in the air at the end of a string.
They are like the red blood of those peonies
And like the melancholy of those blue flowers.
They are like the human voice—no! for the human voice lies!
They are like human life that flows under the words.
That flower-bed is like the true life that wants to express itself
And does . . . while we human beings lie cramped and fearful.

CHAPTER VIII

A RIDE ON A NEUGLE

' I saw these times I represent,
Watched, gauged them, as they came and went,
Being ageless, deathless.'
THOMAS HARDY : *Famous Tragedy of the Queen of Cornwall.*

' Are you sure that a world given
Is always more than a world forsaken ? '
Isolt's question in EDWIN ARLINGTON ROBINSON'S *Tristram.*

IF I were asked by someone, who was finding it difficult, to describe
in a single sentence—or express in a brief parable—just what the
sort of life I have had, as described in or implied by the foregoing
chapters, amounts to, I would probably reply : ' It's all just a matter
of a Hjok-finnie body having a ride on a neugle '. The trouble is
that that sentence in itself calls for a good deal of explication ;
' riding a hobby-horse ' is no equivalent for the latter part of it.

Men and boys astride
An wyvern, lion, dragon, griffin, swan,
At all the corners named us each by name,

as Tennyson says in ' Holy Grail '. My mount, which I here call
a *neugle*, is of course kin to the *Nri-sinha* or the man lion, as one of
Budd'ha's manifestations is called in the Paur'an'ics and in the
Baud'has ; the Assyrian Steer-god, *Kirubu* (of which *Xeref* is the
Egyptian equivalent), the idea of which some of the Ishmaelites,
whom King Saul drove out from Havillah unto Shur, took eastwards
with them via Persia and Afghanistan to India, where they arrived
about 750 B.C. *Kirubu* or *Keruv* (from the Hebrew *Korauv* =
near ; root : *korav* and *koreiv* = ' to come near ') became the Indian
Garud or *Garoda*, the Eagle. This root-word leads later to the Irish
garv = rough, coarse, and the Scottish *garvacht* = roughness, gives
its name to the river Garonne, and produced also the Welsh Christian
name Goronwy. One romani (gypsy) word for a ' turkey ' (which
Franklin desired to substitute for the American eagle) is *gaudra*,
metathetized *garuda* = the noise-maker, related to the Zendavestan
Garodemana, the Vedic *Garuda dhama* = the abode of the
singer. The noise itself is *gauder*. The Tyrolese readily took up
the romani word *gauder*, applying it to the bird, having already their
Jodel or voice-twisting from the Hebrew *godal* = to twist together.
English ' jabber ' is the equivalent of the Romani *gauder*, but from
Hebrew *gorav* by another immigration. The nearest English
expression to *Kauder* is Cornish *codgar* (lying stranger ?), from which

emanated codger and cadger. *Keruv, Garodman, garuda, gaudra, garuba,* the mythical Persian lion eagle *griffin, Cerberus* (metathet of *Cereb'rus* or *Keruv'rus*), Latin *Drako* (metathet of *gorad*) = the ' Dragon ', English drake ; Irish *guardal*—transposed *garudal* = the ' stormy petrel ', the German Grief stalking the Greifswald, the short-winged tailless *grebe,* and a host of others, many of which will easily occur to the reader, all give forth discordant notes, thus deriving their name from three roots all meaning to be rough, to scrape. And, of course, I need not point out that my own name, Grieve, is from the same source and has all these connexions. The Eagle Clan, once settled in its Capitol City of *Gorod* in Arabia, moved on to *Novgorod* (Russia) and so on. And in *Punch, or the London Charivari,* Charivari means ' Hubbub '. The metathetic of Chari-vari is *chavirer,* French for ' to turn inside out ', ' to upset ', ' to rough and tumble '. And *chari* comes from Hebrew *shorov* = heat of the sun, red or ruddy : and in Dicky Doyle's drawing at the bottom of the cover of *Punch* you see many of these interconnected ideas portrayed—the rough music of the dram, next the cherub, then Punch riding on a donkey (romani, *chari*), as Vishnu on his Garuda, and in the rear the sprite that eats the Baal fruit of the Ægle plant (note : the Hebrew, *Varekav gnal Keruv* = ' and he rode upon a cherub '),

> And the cherub like the bird does chirrup
> Cheer up !

Pardon the paronyme. *Cheer, cheerus,* and *chairus* are Anglo-Romani for ' time '. German-Romani, *Tscherus* = Heaven ; derived from the Greek word *kalpos,* pronounced *toalpos—tsairos* in Crete and Cyprus, Icelandic *Skirr,* clear and bright, and Gothic *Skeirs,* clear, from the prime Hebrew *charas* ; a poetic rarity = ' sun '. I may add that a philological relative of mine in the botanical world, therefore, is the *Garob* tree—the *garoba* or locust tree, so called because of the fibrous sounds of numerous insects settled therein to devour its leaves and pods ; French *courbaril* (metathet for a possible *courab'ril*), i.e. a buzzing, twittering, or humming. *De facto,* the humming-bird of Australia is (by metathesis) ' Kolabris '.

My very name is therefore a living reminder of the danger of over-refinement ; in language of the necessity of continual recourse to vernacular and slang ; in literature of Yeats' remark to Synge of the hope in poetry through becoming violent again ; in politics of the rôle of the common people ; in knowledge of the need of not con-fining oneself to books and papers and omitting contact with living human beings ; in philosophy and ethics, as in all else, of the need to preserve Burns's ' stalk of carle hempe ' ; in the organization of life to leave room for the gipsy, the nomad, the foreign, the intractable—to beware of any ' closed order ', any premature formulation, an exclusive principle. And whatever may have been disclosed in the lost *Cratylus*, certainly all my ideas, interests, and tastes are in keeping with the root of my name, and that carries me through all the dimensions of the world and establishes its appropriate connexions in every quarter of the world, and in all the languages of mankind.

My life has been an adventure, or series of adventures, in the exploration of the mystery of Scotland's self-suppression. It is an essay in Scottish speleology, travelling *in the flesh* where Dante or Jules Verne (although his *Twenty Thousand Leagues Under the Sea* did give one reader a full measure of the sensation of being snug and safe and secluded and unapproachable, since where, he reflected, could anyone be better hidden than at the bottom of the deep sea ?) had but ventured in the spirit, and penetrating in the *terra incognita* of ancient Scotland into deeper pot-holes and caves than the Gaping Ghyll Hole in England, the Spluga della Preta or Corchia in Italy, or the Gouffre Martel in France, and concerned with the finding of rarer trophies than helictites, cave-pearls and moon-milk, or the bisons of Tud d'Audoubert, or anything within the ken of medicine-men of the type of the imposing ' Sorcerer ' who appears on the walls of Les Trois Frères, or anything found in the Trou du Toro, the Grotte Casteret, or the cave of Montespan, and, while British speleologists will delight in the accounts of these and similar places in M. E. A. Martel's *Les Abimes* and M. Norbert Casteret's *Ten Years Under the Earth*, and even the mere surface-crawlers will be tempted to peep fearfully over the edge into such infinities as these yawning beneath their feet, and expression like that of Kubla Khan, when between ' sunny dome ' and ' caves of ice ', he heard the ' ancestral voices ', is attractive to-day, I fancy, to infinitely fewer—still less the voice of one who prophesies a crack in the System of Things, and the emergence of new dragon-slayers as well as of new sea-serpents—and how few and far between are they who do not flee what (worse than the Gulf of Corryvreckan which lies between Jura and Scarba—that conflux dreadful and spurning all description, a scene the horror of which even the genius of Milton could not paint) gives almost everybody to-day (having no deeps within them to speak to such deeps) a vertiginous and ghastly sense of a yawning gulf—' the planetary law of Nature that all human action is only a means to contemplation '. They find it like that strange river—

> ' Its dark waters were bursting out most bright
> From a great mountain's heart into the light.
> They ran a short course under the sun, then back
> Into a pit they plunged, once more as black
> As at their birth.'

It is of such abysses, and worse, with their ' roar and hiss, and mighty motion ',[1] that my life is composed—like Dr. Johnson's definition of a net as ' a number of holes tied together with string '. And to make matters worse, if possible, my sense of the fitness of things would compel me if I could (and perhaps I can !) to make the prose with which I bind together these appalling gulfs sound as though in very fact the Old Man of Storr (the Storr of Sutherland, sea-wet as Manannan himself, from the edge of whose rocks wandering sheep peer timidly down upon him in his foam-girdled dwelling) held converse with his kinsman Storr of northern Skye.

> I should use . . .
> A language not to be betrayed ;
> And what was hid should still be hid
> Excepting from those like me made
> Who answer when such whispers bid.

Nay, worse, the sound would need to be mostly (though occasionally enchanting as the song of sirens, or rather tiny and elusive as a ' scrae o' henkies ', a *henk* being applied to the movements of trolls, particularly in a fairy dance, and a ' scrae of henkies ' to numbers of puny beings dancing round a fairy knowe) like that of a *Hjokfinnie body*—i.e. a buried Finn up again, one of those Finns who could render themselves visible or invisible at pleasure, metamorphose themselves into the likeness of beast, bird, or fish, who could even assume the appearance of a beetle [2] (whence we have to this day in the Shetlands the *witchie-clock* and the *tur-diel*, two kinds of beetles), understand the language of the *corbies* or ravens, cross from Norwick in Unst to Bergen in Norway and return between the hours of sunset and sunrise, the traditional speed being nine miles to the *warp* (stroke of the oar), who were adepts at recovering things lost in the sea which to ordinary mortals were irrecoverable, and who above all were said to be the only beings who could safely ride the *neugle* or *nicker*, the water deity that appears in the form of a sleek horse,

---

[1] And not merely of the caverns dealt with in T. W. Baillie's old volume, *Cave Legends*, which deals with practically every Celtic cave of note, Scots examples dominating the work, especially those along the shore of Colonsay, that romantic honeycomb including the Kilchattan Cave, said to have literally swallowed a piper, and which has never yet been fully explored. One day the venturesome piper entered the cave, determined to solve the puzzle of the passage—which grows narrower and narrower as it advances. The strains of the pipes, says the legend, were heard for a long time, but they faded at last. And the musician never reappeared. Some one has estimated that Scotland has more than a thousand such stories on tap for the folk-lore fancier. Baillie's book, written eighty years ago, is out of print now.

[2] ' In discussing these things with intelligent Frenchmen I often have the impression of talking to human ants ; creatures marvellously intelligent . . . but who have lost their sense of light . . . the termite lives totally secluded from the sun, and . . . the faintest ray of light kills it.'—Count Hermann Keyserling in *From Suffering to Fulfilment*.

having an erect mane, and tail like the ' rim o' a muckle wheel ',
whereas, if any luckless nocturnal wanderer, mistaking the *neugle*
for a real horse, should get astride the uncanny beast, he was at once
borne with the swiftness of an arrow into the middle of the nearest
lake or dam, and there left struggling in the water, while he beheld
the creature rushing towards the opposite shore like a streak of
mareel. It is not said that anyone was ever actually drowned by the
neugle. Returning to dry land from such an adventure, a man will
at least have cause to realize that even the ferns and foliage of a
country lane appear rough and coarse after the eye has been accustomed to the polish of underwater vegetation. (But anything human?
The effect of long immersion on some woman's pride—a once
shining glory of auburn—is to rob it of every vestige of life.) Moreover, in the Shetland and Hebridean waters with which my life is
concerned, the usual form of the ocean surface is that imparted by
crossing waves, a condition arising from the changing direction of the
wind consequent upon the progression of the cyclonic systems.
Two sets of waves, crossing squarely, parcel out the surface in domes
and basins. So swift is the motion of the meeting waves that no
sooner is the eye attracted by some notable mound than the mound
subsides ; no sooner does the eye note some cup-like cavity than the
water here swells up in a dome. Though it is a common—indeed,
the general—experience in every sphere of life to-day, that

> Many a road and track
> That, since the dawn's first crack,
> Up to the forest brink
> Deceived the travellers,
> Suddenly now blurs,
> And in they sink,

and few people—only an isolated individual here and there—have
the resilience to ride the waves like the stormy petrel, and enjoy it ;
very few really like going to sea in a leaky sieve like the Jumblies ;
and very few indeed can cry—to quote one of my poems—

> So an ardent spirit
> Should submerge all it has learned.
> And enjoy to the full
> The leisure it has earned.
>
> For what is the end
> Of all labour but this ?
> —As Earth's fruits to the flesh,
> To the soul the Abyss ;

and fewer still welcome the opposite process when, instead of the
familiar road blurring, an unsuspected forgotten road or track
suddenly clears and heaves them up till they seem exposed in their
totality and *risen to the surface*. But the Finns, emerging from their
hadds—for the object is indeed to ' draw the badger ', ' the noblest

Old Briton of them all '—holes in the ground (their burrows or
hiding-places; places, too, like the Hellyer o' Fivlagord, the Den o'
Pettasmog, the Hole o' Henkie, and the Ha' o' Doon Hellyer or the
remains of that great earthwork called the Virkie across the narrow
neck of land between Infraneb and Fraeklesgeo on the Gibraltar-like
formation of the Outer Mull—and indeed a far more desperate
battle than that which took place on the Virkie centuries ago between
the small Picts and the great Vikings is being waged to-day on every
such outrunning dyke of rock and spit of sand, and is one of the chief
themes of this book—the mortal struggles to-day between the little
people, the lambs of God, and the ' big business men ' (Will Dyson's
' Fat Men ', the hard-faced men of the world), the militarists, the
scientists, the Colonel Blimps, the fascist realists) could ride the
water-horse, and were supposed to utilize him in some of their rapid
movements. In Shetland folk-lore the Finns, both men and women,
were supposed to possess a skin or garment like the covering of a
selkie (seal). Enrobed in this magic coat, they could take to the
water as readily and as safely as an amphibious animal. But if by
any mischance they lost or were deprived of it, then the rest of their
days must be spent on *terra firma* like other ordinary mortals.

The theatre of my story, then—the West Highlands and Islands of
Scotland and the Hebridean waters and all the weltering waste of the
Pentland Firth and that which lies about and unites and divides the
Orkneys and the Shetlands and on to the Faroes on the East, and
between these and Heimaey on the West—can best be described in
the first instance as resembling what Buddha said in the story that
tells

> ' that a Brahmin spoke to the Buddha that everything was produced,
> and the Buddha replied that this was a popular view. The Brahmin
> then said that nothing is produced, and the Buddha replied that this is
> the second popular view. Then when the Brahmin said that everything
> is eternal or everything is non-eternal or everything can be produced
> or nothing can be produced, the Buddha replied that these are all
> popular views. The Buddha further said that the notion of oneness,
> otherness, togetherness, and the notion of neither the one nor the other,
> the notion that everything depends on causes, that everything is a
> modification, that there is something which is not a modification, but
> there is a self and that there is not a self, that there is this world or there
> is not the other world, that there is emancipation or that there is no
> emancipation, that everything is momentary or that nothing is
> momentary, all these views are mere popular views. The Buddha said
> that he did not believe in the doctrine of causes nor in the doctrine
> that there are no causes.'

A bird's-eye view of the psychology of distinguished Scotsmen
throughout the whole of our history shows how the ' extraordinary
contradictions of character, most dangerous antinomies and anti-
thetical impulses ' all of them, without exception, manifested, make
the incredible psychological background (as wild and little-known

and avoided except in fair weather even by the few who ever visit it at all as the Hebrides–Orkney–Shetland–Faroe area accepted as the theatre of this volume) to the almost uniformly dull and common-sensible collection of appalling buddies that constitutes our Anglicized Scottish nation to-day. There can be no doubt that that most unfortunate psychological revolution in the wrong direction has been the inevitable (and intended) result of our Union with England, and that the vast majority of contemporary Scots are as destitute of any element of our true national spirit—any piety, any allegiance to or vision of Audh—instead of this extremely inferior Anglicized substitute as most of our modern poets are of any element of that distinctive Scottish note in poetry which is so clearly traceable all the way from Barbour to Burns ; the course indicated in the pregnant passages of Daniel Corkery's *Hidden Ireland*—that wonderful monograph on the Gaelic poets of Munster in the Penal Age—in which he stresses the human element of the Scottish Jacobite poems, with their intimate insistence on the ' golden-haired laddie ' and ' Bonnie Prince Charlie ' as against the formalism of their Irish counterparts, where no such endearing term, but ' Caesar ' is used instead. And then there is Thomas Davis's *Essay on Irish Songs*, which says :

' War, wine, and women were said to be the only subjects for song, and England has not a dozen good songs on any of them. One verse of the *British Grenadiers* and a couple of tolerable ballads are no stock of war songs. *Rule Britannia* is a Scottish song, and *God Save The King* a parody on another Scottish song. Bishop Stiff's *Jolly Old Ale* is almost the only hearty drinking song of England, and that is an antique. As to the English love poems—they are very clever, very learned, full of excellent similes, but quite empty of love. There is a cold glitter and a dull exaggeration through the whole set, from Marlow and Johnson to Waller and Turnbull, that would make an Irish or a Scots girl despise the man who sang them to her. Contrast such English songs with any of the hundreds of good Scottish songs. Or rather let us take an example from the early tunes of Scotland :

THE EWE BUCHTS, MARION

Will ye gae to the ewe-buchts, Marion,
    And wear the sheep wi' me ?
The sun shines sweet, my Marion,
    But nae half sae sweet as thee. . . .

Sae put on your pearline, Marion,
    And kirtle o' cramasie,
And soon as my chin has hair on
    I shall come west, and see ye.

And then, skipping over such names as Ramsay, Burns, Scott, Campbell, and Hogg, and the often nameless and obscure authors of the Jacobite minstrelsy, to come on such songs as Cunningham's ' Nannie O ', ' My Ain Countree ', ' Phemie Irvine ', or the fine ballad song of ' My Gentle Hugh Hereies '. Oh, *that* Scotland is worth a hundred Englands ! The
o

Scots songs evidently are full of heart and reality. They are not written
for the stage. They were the slow growth of intense passion, simple
tastes, and a heroic state of society. Love, mirth, patriotism are not
ornaments, but the inspiration of these songs. They are full of personal
narrative, streaming hopes and fears, bounding joy in music, absolute
disregard of prettiness, and, then, they are absolutely Scottish.'

Recovery of that previous widely antinomian and extremely non-
common-sensible character of the vast majority of our distinguished
forefathers—the true sons of Audh—is a sine-qua-non if Scottish
poetry is to be lifted from the sordid little rut in which it has been so
long confined ; the perhaps seemingly bottomless Abyss of Grobianism and Eulenspiegel into which the high culture of that fallen
race of whom Audh is the eidolon has collapsed and dissolved away.¹

' In the field of metaphysics,' says the Russian philosopher, Leo
Shestov (one of the exceedingly few who have seen Audh entire),
' rules the daimon of whom we are not even entitled to assume that
he is interested in any " norm " at all. Norms arose among the
cooks and were created for the cooks. What need is there then to
transfer all this *empiria* thither whither we flee to escape *empiria*?
The whole art of philosophy should be directed towards freeing us
from the " good and evil " of cooks and carpenters, to find that
frontier beyond which the might of general ideas ceases.' It is
certainly there, on that frontier, that Scottish genius has throughout
our history most abundantly manifested itself, though not in poetry—
but if we are ever to write great poetry in the future it can only be
on that frontier, and certainly for every reason, poetical and otherwise, the sooner we abandon commonsense and re-acquire the habit
of living exclusively along that ultimate border-line the better.

Although the Scottish renaissance movement has made a certain
amount of headway, Scotland—Scottish genius—has scarcely begun
to recover yet from the fact that Scotland accepted Dugald Stewart
and rejected David Hume, and has been dominated by the ideology
of ' common-sense ' ever since—even in our philosophic chairs.
Burns's favourite tenets were drawn from

> Smith wi' his sympathetic feelin'
> And Reid to commonsense appealin'.

For instance, the famous ' to see oorsels as ithers see us ' is an
unmistakable reminiscence of a phrase in Adam Smith's *Theory of
Moral Sentiments*. The Burnsian philosophy of life is in fact nothing
but a poeticized version of the Scots philosophy of his time. Any
effort to grasp the nature of the live elements in the Scottish

¹ The new development in our age cannot be political, for politics is a
dialectical relation between the individual and the community in the
representative individual ; but in our time the individual is in the process of
becoming far too reflective to be able to be satisfied with merely being
represented.'—S. Kierkegaard (*Journals*).

renaissance movement brings whoever makes it into conflict with the lingering commonsense outlook of Reid, Stewart, and Hamilton, whose disciples did not lose control in Scottish Philosophy until about 1900, and who have even yet several influential Scottish professors and lecturers among their numbers. Scotland's most pressing problem is undoubtedly the continued sway (in the head, if not on the lips) of the Common Sense Philosophy. The revolution which will rid us of the persistent and most pernicious ballyhoo which has so long ruled over our arts and affairs will involve commensurate technical changes, and since Scots and Gaelic—and not English—are at the roots of our national life, a reversion to these.[1]

This is the point at which perhaps to give full-length portraits of Audh, the heroine of this book, and of her opposite, her enemy, the villainess of the piece. Rilke, the German poet, affords perhaps the finest glimpse of the young Audh (not the Audh with whom we are concerned, Audh the Deep-Minded, wife and mother of chieftains Gaelic and Scandinavian, who went at last via the Faroes, where she landed to see some of her grandchildren, to Iceland, where she died and lies buried in one of its cold jokulls) in the following poem :

> Upon that morning following the night
> Which anxiously had passed with calls, unrest
> And tumult, all the sea broke up once more
> And cried. And when the crying slowly closed
> Again and from the pallid day and heaven's
> Beginning fell within the chasm of mute fish :
> The sea brought forth.
>
> And with the earliest sun the hairfoam
> Of the waves' broad vulva shimmered, on whose rim
> The girl stood upright, white, confused, and wet.
> Just as a young green leaf bestirs itself
> And stretches forth and slow unfurls its inrolled
> Whorlings, so her body's form unfolded into coolness,
> And into the untouched early wind.

---

[1] It is supremely necessary in Scotland never to forget the appropriate stanza in ' John Brown's Body ' ;—

> ' They tried to fit you with an English song
> And clip your speech into the English tale,
> But even from the first the words went wrong.
> The catbird pecked away the nightingale.'

And where we were concerned as here with the intimate linkage of land and people, the further we penetrate into either the dark backward and abysm of time or into the vast cave of the future, the keener need will we realize for that illumination and guidance which can be had only through the Gaelic speech,

> . . . the mystery of our Gaelic speech
> In which *rughadh* was at once a blush,
> A promontory, a headland, a cape ;
> *Leadan*, musical notes, litany, hair of the head,
> And *fonn*, land, earth, delight, and a time in music.

As moons the knees rose upwards clear and dived
Within the cloudy outlines of the thighs.
The narrow shadow of the legs retreated
And the feet grew tightened and became as light
As silence and the joints lived like the throats
Of drinking ones.

And in the hollow of the hip's deep bowl
The belly lay and seemed a fresh young fruit
Within a child's hand.   In its navel's narrow
Cup was all the darkness of this brilliant life.
A little wave below it lightly raised
Itself and ever sped across towards the loins,
Whereon from time to time a silent rippling was.
But all translumined and already without shadow,
Like a copse of silver birches pale in April,
Warm and empty and unhidden lay the sex.

Now stood the shoulders' poised and mobile scales
In perfect balance on the upright body,
Which from the bowl of hips arose as though
It were a fountain, downward falling,
Hesitating in the long and slender arms,
And faster in the fullest fall of hair.

Then went the face quite slowly past ;
From out the deep foreshortened darkness of
Its inclination into clear and horizontal
High-upliftedness.   And 'neath it was the chin closed steeply
And when the throat was now forthstretched and seemed
A water-ray or flowerstem in which sap rose,
The arms stretched also forth like necks of swans
Who seek the shore.

Then came into this body's darkened earliness
Like morning wind the first indrawal of breath.
Within the tender branching of the veintrees
There arose a whispering and the blood began
To purl and murmur o'er its deepest places.
And this wind increased : it threw itself
With every breath into the newborn breasts
And filled them full and pressed far into them—
So that like sails, full of the distances,
They urged the windlight maiden t'wards the shore.

So landed the goddess.

Behind her,
Quickly stepping through the young green shores,
The flowers and flower-stalks raised themselves
All morning long, confused and warm, as though
From deep embraces.   And she went, and ran.

But at the noon of day, all in the heaviest hour,
The ocean once more roused itself and threw
Upon the self-same spot a dolphin.
Dead, red and open.

The Enemy is Anglo-Scotland, the *droit administratif*, the pluto-
bureaucracy, the mindless mob, the chaos of our great cities, the
megalopolitan madness, European civilization's ruthless and relentless depreciation and denial and destruction of the Gaelic Genius,
worse than Nazi anti-semiticism at its worst, and for a portrait of her
to serve as a companion piece to the foregoing, recourse may be had
to Spenser, who not only limns her in all her horror, but in the
phrases in his poem which are italicized here issues the warning and
the advice in regard to the spirit and means required if she is to be
overcome which it has been one of the main purposes of this book to
amplify and insist upon with every art in my power. Here, then, is
Audh's Enemy, the Duessa :

BOOK I, CANTO VIII

(Prologue)   Faire virgin, to redeeme her deare,
        Bringe Arthure to the fight :
    Who slays the Gyaunt, wounds the beast,
        And strips Duessa quight.

Which when that Champion heard, with percing point
. . . he rent that yron dore
With furious force and indignation fell ;
Where entred in his foot could find no flore,
But all a deepe descent, as darke as hell,
That breathed ever forth a filthie banefull smell.

But neither darknesse fowle, nor filthy bands,
Nor noyous smell, his purpose could withhold,
(*Entire affection hateth nicer hands*)
But that with constant zele and corage bold,
After long paines and labors manifold,
He found the meanes that Prisoner to up reare . . .

But fie on Fortune, our avowed foe,
Whose wrathful wreakes them selves doe now alay,
And for these wronges shall treble penaunce pay
Of treble good : *good grows of evil's priefe* . . .

' Henceforth, Sir Knight, take to you wonted strength,
And maister these mishaps with patient might.
Loe ! where your foe lies stretcht in monstrous length

' To doe her die (quoth Una) were despight,
And shame t'avenge so weake an enimy ;
But spoile her of her scarlet robe, and let her fly.'

So as she bad that witch they disaraid, . . .
Ne spared they to strip her naked all.

Her crafty head was altogether bald,
And, as in hate of honorable eld,
Was overgrowne with scurfe and filthy scald ;
Her teeth out of her rotten gummes were feld,

And her sowre breath abhominably smeld ;
Her dried dugs, lyke bladders lacking wind,
Hong downe, and filthy matter from them weld ;
Her wrizled skin, as rough as maple rind,
So scabby was as would have loathed all womankind.

Her neather parts, the shame of all her kind,
My chaster Muse for shame doth blush to write ;
But at her rompe she growing had behind
A foxe's taile, with dong all fowly dight . . .

Which when the knights beheld amazd they were,
And wondred at so fowle deformed wight.
' Such then ' (said Una) ' as she seemeth here,
Such is the face of falsehood : such the sight
Of fowle Duessa, when her borrowed light
Is laid away, and counterfesaunce knowne.'

Another way of expressing the opposition is to say that it is between those cities in which, in the course of a recent inquiry, the educational authorities found that a considerable percentage of the children had never so much as seen a live cow or sheep, or indeed had any relationships with any of the animal world except dogs and cats and a few pigeons, sparrows, and canaries, and that vast unknown world of Scotland at their very doors where a happy naturalist can cry :

> ' The great seals of Rona accept me as those of the Treshnish Isles never did. It has been grand and inspiring to go down to the sea's edge and see two or three hundred seals come racing through the water in joyful movement towards me. I have found the way to speak to them so that they are not afraid but pleased. These old bulls of the great dignity remain on the outer ring of the group of faces, though one of the biggest of them will come close in. The cows are nearer to me, their expressions soft and inquisitive, but the yearling seals have the wondering faces of little children, and in their confidence they have come out of the water to my feet as I sat there on the rock, using my voice in the way I have learned. . . . One day I called a blind cow seal out of the sea, and she came near until her muzzle was but a few inches from my face. She was unafraid and returned quietly to the sea. And now the mother seals are high on Rona near the door of our hut and our own child plays among them.'

That happy land the peace and serenity of one of the little islands of which a recent writer attributes to the fact that the islanders have individual names for, and as they go about are in the habit of talking to, every bird and beast and insect in the place, just as on the little island of Eynhallow in the Orkneys, which is a sanctuary of sea-birds, the keeper knows, and has a pet name for, every one of the nesting birds, while in the Shetlands and the Orkneys the older people at any rate have similar names for every movement of the wind and sea. A magnificent land, the most glorious in Europe, where you may see an eagle stooping over a conical mountain to the edge of a plantation two miles away—an incomparably majestic stoop, for the bird's speed increases on its downward plane and the *finale* is a perpendicular drop on a luckless rabbit. The land, too, of the mountain hares—homeless, if not landless, creatures. They have no sheltering burrows, like the rabbits, but creep for shelter into their ' form ' among the grass or heather tufts. There they make the best of things, squatting closely, and so far protected against the underground damp and cold by the thick fur that encases their hind legs. When hunted they will run uphill and squeeze between boulders or the splintered fragments of an outcrop of rocks, but this is only a temporary haven. And the discomforts of their life are, in a manner of speaking, of their own choosing. The mountain hare has maintained its identity and a stubborn independence, letting the chances of adaptation go by. It has remained true to its original type of habitat and proof against the attractions of the easier life. Or look at the birds here. The tide is at the full, and the wading birds are resting on a low skerry, awaiting the coming of the ebb. Out to sea a handsome golden eye drake is diving, and a red-throated diver in winter plumage swimming low through the small waves. The low golden rays of the sun shine upon the crowded ranks of the waders, so that they stand out with great beauty against the dark rock on which they rest. Dunlin predominate in this alert assembly, but there are scarlet-legged turnstones, and handsome ringed dotterel among them, and other rarer and more wary birds besides. Look, for instance, at that small family party of godwits—long-legged birds of curlew-like build, but smaller than curlew, and with the tail slightly upturned at the tip. The godwit shares the curlew's wariness ; if a passer-by walks near them along the shore, the dunlin are unperturbed, but the godwits fly away low over the sea. . . . The winter sun sinks and disappears ; the warm glow leaves the shore, and a damp, frosty air lies above the wet sands. In a sheltered nook, a cowslip flowers shyly, protected from the winds by the strong bents. From the deep purple glow of the eastern horizon climbs the full moon, throwing a golden track upon the sea. The dark forms of birds fly along the shore. The wailing cry of curlew, the shrill whistle of redshank, the twittering of many turnstones, all mingle with the movement of the sea. . . . One species of whale, the ' bottle-nosed ', is named by fishermen the ' herring whale ' because of its partiality for herrings, but all kinds of ' killers ', and there are several sub-species, prefer a salmon diet to any other. The sight of salmon leaping in air to escape a grampus is not uncommon. The grampus with its Pelorous Jack-like habit of racing boats and steamers, and its innate destructiveness ! Our observations of the grampus in salt water in these parts show it as a ' monster ' of comparatively small size, from a dozen to eighteen feet in length, of a uniform brown colour (showing lead colour at a distance), built on mackerel-like lines and with five great canine teeth in its lower jaw. There

are several varieties of the grampus species, but not one of the many
we see round these coasts is ' snow-white ', the nearest to that in
colouring being a few (probably aged ones) which have light-coloured
heads and shoulders.   Wild geese to the number of many hundreds
passed over in the shape of a great horizon-filling ' V ' in the early
morning yesterday.   The ' V ' had successive expansive and re-
tractive movement, and at each contraction of the line individual
geese were forced out of it, flying in the blank space of the ' V ' until
the next undulatory expansion afforded them room to get into
formation again.   The geese were heading almost due north, and
their clamour as they disappeared over the Ross-shire hills was
loudly audible.   They were pink-footed geese, for that species has a
distinctive light tenor call.   There is an old Highland saying to the
effect that we cannot have summer weather until the wild geese have
left us for their northern breeding-grounds, but the birds fly north
at the end of April pretty regularly each year.   The white-fronted
geese remain here until the middle of May on some occasions,
however, and the date of the departure of the Bernicle geese from the
Treshnish Islands, Mull, is May 4th.   Wounded wild geese sometimes elect to remain in these parts all summer, and one such bird,
a gander with two consorts, got his hurt when on the oat-braird in
April.   The bird was not injured vitally by the long-range charge of
small-shot aimed at him, but he did not risk the overseas journey,
and his two mates kept him company in his wounded exile.   He had
quite recovered by the shooting season, and at the first shots fired
at duck at the lake which he frequented in August, he and his convoy
ringed up into the air, and were gone for good from the district.   A
Greenland falcon came aboard a vessel 600 miles south of the country
of its birth.   It is a young ' falcon ' (female), and its legs and feet are
grey, not yellow.   The Greenland falcon seems to resemble the
Iceland variety very closely when in immature plumage.   This one
seemed identical with one shot in Argyll and named as *Falco ger-falco
Icelandis* by a competent authority.   It, too, had flesh-coloured feet,
but was rather spoiled as a specimen by the bird-stuffer, who painted
them yellow.   This Icelander used to attack and kill large seagulls
in a method of its own, quite unlike that of its cousin the peregrine.
Attacking the gull in short stoops, it gripped, dragged it through the
air, and let it go time and again, until the exhausted bird came to
earth, when the hawk continued to stoop at it on the ground until all
resistance ceased, when it alighted on it and killed it by twisting its
neck.   Other immature Iceland (or Greenland) falcons have been
seen on several occasions.   An adult (almost white) specimen was
seen in Mull (a half larger than the largest peregrine), and a very fine
stuffed couple (shot in the Isle of Skye) make up the tale of the great
' Gers ' of the Arctic, which as the result of excessive breeding
multiply, and so seek a southern outlet for the surplus.

It has been said that a fish after Louis Agassiz had explained it, drawn it, or supervised its drawing was not just any fish; it was unmistakably that fish. And so every bird and beast is in the observation of the people of these islands (the older people, at any rate), if not in what they can communicate about them to others—to outsiders, that is, for among themselves there is a common consciousness that conveys complete understanding not only by the movement of an eyebrow, the moue of a mouth, a gesture of the hands, but just by the way a speaker holds his body as he speaks. A great deal has been lost, of course—and much that is probably irrecoverable. A single osprey—' an t-Iasgair ', the Fisherman, as the Gaelic speakers called it—may still be seen, at intervals of several years, passing high over Loch Arkaig, where formerly there was an eyrie. But otherwise that fine bird has gone. So has the white-tailed or sea eagle, the erne, while the golden eagle, a comparatively rare bird when the sea eagle was numerous, is holding its own in certain parts of our area. The golden eagle takes at least four years to reach maturity and probably lives to a great age. It is seldom that any proof is forthcoming as to the age of an eagle, but a golden eagle shot in France in 1845 had round its neck a collar of gold with the inscription : ' Caucasus patria Fulgor nomen Badinski dominus, mihi est 1750 ' (Caucasus is my native country, Lightning is my name, Badinski is my master, 1750). The eagle was shot ninety-five years after the inscription on the gold collar was engraved.

The kite, now holding its own in Wales, is lost to us. The kite was formerly abundant in the Highlands. An old Glengarry record shows that in that district over a period of years 275 kites and eighteen ospreys were killed. In Gaelic the kite is ' Clabhan gobhlach nan cearc ', the fork-tailed hawk of the hens, so called because of the number of poultry it killed. Among our rarer birds to-day, and in danger of extinction, are greenshank, crested tit, whooper swan, and, most in danger, the dotterel, that attractive wader, so tame and so much sought after because of the beauty and rarity of the three richly marked eggs the female lays.

> A sad story, bens of the shapely summits.
> Ere the English were here 'twas good to roam your hillsides.
> Many hounds and gillies were on your slopes, many a stalwart hero, many a sharp, bright bugle.
> Beagles called in your valleys, when wild boars were hunted ; every huntsman had lovely, leashed greyhounds.
> Your heron's call at night-time, the heather hen on your uplands, together made kind music—right sweet it was to listen.
> 'Twould lift the heart within me, to hear the voice of your eagles, the sweet noise of your otters, and the calling of your foxes.
> Your blackbirds and your thrushes, 'tis I am lonely for them ; the doves in your thick tree-tops would lift their grief from women.
> And often-time were gathered, by the shining women, fragrant and tasty berries among your tangled brambles.

> Bogberries, brightly scarlet ; cuckoo-flower and cresses ; brook-lime, strawberries, raspberries, sloes, and honeysuckle—
> These we gathered often . . . to-night I am old and withered ; I lived of yore right gaily.

We have only touched as yet on the richness and beauty of nature in these areas—that nature which in all its fullness is the nature of Audh. But

> This stag eastward sleepeth not, ceaseth not from bellowing. . . . The hornless doe sleepeth not. . . . The lively linnet sleepeth not ; even the thrush does not sleep. . . .
> To-night the grouse sleepeth not up in the stormy heaths of the height : sweet is the sound of her clear cry : between the streamlets she does not sleep.

Once again we raise the immemorial cry :

> Hail to her level places, and a thousand times to her hill-sides (O lucky he that dwells there !)—hail to her lochs and waters !
> Hail to her heavy forests ; hail, likewise, to her fish-weirs ; hail to her moors and meadows ; hail to her raths and marshes !
> Hail from my heart to her harbours ; hail, too, to her fruitful drylands ; luck to her hill-top hostings ; hail to her bending branches !

But a great deal more than that is needed. Audh gives us to drink a mead not unlike that the young woman gave in a *cuach* of white silver to Fionn, that straightway compelled him to turn his face upon the host of the Fianna, and antagonize all its chieftains, since ' every harm and flaw and mishap of battle that he knew against any man of them, he, by operation of the frenzy that the young woman had worked in him, threw in their teeth '.

That is one side of it. The other is the fact that in Scotland *An Claidheamb Soluis* (The Sword of Light) that hand after devoted hand has grasped and fought with against impossible odds in Ireland and that, finally carried to victory, flashes more magically to-day than for many centuries, has found no one to grip it in right earnest in Scotland yet, though Scotland's need is no less to-day than Ireland's ever was, and the championship and re-enthronement of Audh in her proper place can be accomplished by only such devoted labours as those of John O'Donovan in Ireland.

Young Scots must be conjured to like tasks in the name of Audh [1]—

[1] She runs through the whole of Scottish history pretty much as in the history of Hungary, with dynasties, boundaries, religion, and alien immigration all so fluid, there is only a shrinking or expanding core of Magyar race and custom to hold the story together—as, while Arpads gives place to Angevins, Angevins to Hapsburgs, Constantinople cedes to Rome, Huns, Turks, and Germans filter in as unwanted guests or sweep the country as invaders, yet there is always, from Andrew II to Kossuth, that zeal for social perfection which first expressed itself in *The Golden Bull*, a greater and almost contemporary Magna Carta. Her name is variously spelt Audh (the form the present writer prefers), Unn, Uthar, Aud, &c. She married

> O servant of the high God, Galahad!
> Rise and be arm'd, the Sangreal is gone forth
> Through the great forest and you must be had
> Unto the sea that lieth on the north.

Only so can it be said of any one of them :

> And his own mind did like a tempest strong
> Come to him thus.

And to that end the charge must be laid upon them in these terms :

' The history of our own country and its language has especial claims on our consideration unless we choose to renounce the name of Scotsmen. It is not morbid feeling which leads us to turn with longing and affectionate interest to the ancient history and literature. It is no fond national conceit which inspires us with the desire to gather and preserve those of its scattered records which have escaped the tooth of Time, the ravages of barbarism, and the persecuting vigour of a miscalculating policy. It is indeed wise in us to soar as high as we may, seeking wide and clear views of the entire horizons of human knowledge and science ; but even to those elevated regions let us carry with us a loving remembrance of the spot of earth from which we took our flight—of our birthplace, and the home which is the sanctuary of the purest and strongest of our earthly affections.'

Olaf the White, King of Dublin. Mr. W. G. Collingwood, like Dasent, Munch, and Vigfusson, assumes that Olaf's marriage to Kenneth Mac Alpin's daughter preceded his marriage to Audh, and inclines to the view that his first wife had died before he married Audh. ' It may have been a case of polygamy . . . but from what we know of Audh (Unn) this is doubtful.' As Mr. Robert Locke Bremner, in *The Norsemen in Alban*, shows, however, Olaf must have married Audh not later than 845, and probably not later than 840. Kenneth Mac Alpin did not ascend the throne of the Picts until 844, and it seems likely that the noteworthy matrimonial alliances of his daughters were effected after that date, when for one thing their dowries would be more substantial than at an earlier date. Mr. Collingwood (in his *Scandinavian Britain*), moreover, ignores the fact that Olaf had a third wife, the daughter of Aedh Finnliath, one of the Northern Hy Neill and King of Erin 863 to 879, and his niece by marriage (since her mother was Maelmaire, one of the daughters of Kenneth Mac Alpin). Of Olaf's sons, Thorstein the Red, by far the most famous, was the son of Audh. ' Neither the Irish annalists nor the Scotic chronicles ', says Mr. Bremner, ' make any reference to Unn. We may infer that the latter, whom we know from *Laxdaela* to have been a lady of proud and imperious temper, did not accompany her husband to Dublin, or if she did, left him and returned to her father's protection at an early stage of her married life. Landnama 1, 15, however, gives the impression that she was in Erin when Olaf was slain in battle (perhaps in 871). How Audh the Deep-minded acted after the death of her husband Olaf the White ; how she cared for her grandchildren and finally settled and died in Iceland, is told in the opening chapters of the saga of the Laxdalers (see *The Laxdale-Saga*, translated by Mrs. Muriel Press, 1899). In the Sagas her name is variously given as Unnr, Uor, and Auor, Djupuoga, or Djupauoga. The latter epithet may mean ' deeply-wealthy ' and is so translated by Morris and Magnusson. The reading djupuoga, however, occurs in *Laxdaela* and *Eyrbyggia* and in all the Heimskringla MSS. save one ; and this means ' deep-minded ' (see Magnusson's Index to *Heimskringla*, Saga Library, vol. 6, p. 15, *sub voce* ' Aud ').

The Scots have always had the reputation of being hard workers. So they have been. But almost always at the wrong job. They must turn to the right task now. It is very late, but not too late. There is perhaps little that can be said to the credit of the late J. M. Barrie, but (though he probably had no conception of the infinitely hard work the championship of Audh must involve) he spoke truly when he said :

> ' As for myself, I leave to the Authors' Club the most precious possession I ever had—my joy in hard work. . . . She is not at all heavy jowled and weary. She is young and gay and lively. . . . She is the prettiest thing in literature.'

And her name in Scotland—most intensely hard and long sustained work devoted to the highest proper end—is Audh. Scotland's writers henceforth will of a surety need to avail themselves of all they can procure from Barrie's bequest. A young Scottish essayist has said :

> ' Scotland, that strange, infuriating, enchanting country that has almost ceased to be a country, has, with its ingrained Puritanism of the last three hundred years, proved to be an easy prey for the levelling and dulling tendency of modern pleasure. Our Americanism is peculiarly unpleasant Americanism, our middle class is peculiarly middle, our dancing peculiarly dull, our civic nosy parkerism peculiarly nosy . . . and so it could go on. But, at the same time, one of the most tantalizing things about this most lovable ghost of a country is that it has a habit of justifying itself just when you least expect it. There are in Scotland remains of the old life which are so vivid that for a moment the observer is tricked or charmed into forgetting the slow death all around him, and sees in the vigour on which he has stumbled signs of a vitality which may reanimate Scotland once again.'

That vigour is Audh.

Another glimpse of her is afforded by my friend, F. G. Scott, the composer, concerned with the great pipe music, the Piobaireachd, who writes :

> ' The important point to remember is not that one notation differs from another, but that no piper plays *according to the book*. That was *my* discovery—a most valuable one, proving the existence to-day in Scotland of a kind of art, like all real traditional art going back beyond the invention of notation, and, therefore, free, spontaneous, unfettered melody. And, mark, it is to this kind of uncompartmented music that all kinds of modernism are again tending. We are sick of the tyranny of the bar-line, sick of the equality of bars, sick of melodies in symmetrical and conventional forms, and even in the highest issue of all, sick of FORM in its accepted sense.'

But ah, if one denounces the fake-glamour which distorts the spectacle of the Hebrides, and declares that ' a sense of actuality will stand us in better stead than any artificial allure ', what a miserably wrong impression the word ' actuality ' conveys to almost everybody, how few have any conception of ' all the changes of approach and mood ' a sense of actuality demands—and Audh is the sum of all these changes, actuality rendered completely and not excluding the least graduation.

Audh is far more than that ; no one can catch the most fleeting glimpse of her who cannot cry with John Cowper Powys :

> ' When I think of the subtle and tremulous intensity of our Celtic legends, all this Nietzschean laudation of hot, violent, Southern Toreador-passion rouses me to a tense pitch of contrariety. . . . What I like about the Germans is that they *take ideas seriously*, and regard the conflict of ideas as the most deeply stirring drama upon this planet, as in my opinion it most certainly is ; and though the aesthetic type of traveller who takes nothing seriously but certain recondite ' auras ' and ' atmospheres ', and who hates everything that belongs to the mental drama of the human spirit, looks upon these *romanticists of ideas* with weary disdain, it seems to me that the pleasure of indulging in half-poetic, half-philosophic generalizations about the history of human ideas is one of the most entrancing delights there is, and one that carries with it an intoxication second only to the intoxication of erotic ecstasy. . . . Most people are not sceptical enough. If you are sceptical enough about all human hypotheses, clear down to the very bottom of the abyss, then, and then only, and not till then, are you in a position to enjoy the significance, not merely of the spiritual atmosphere of the countries through which you travel, but of the great romantic drama of races, cults, religions, and philosophies concerning which almost every stone in these historic places has its own particular palimpsest. . . . To believe in nothing, to be a Pyrrhonian sceptic down to the very bottom of your nature, and yet to put into practice—if not actually to feel—many of the most subtle emotions which have been from time immemorial linked up with the idea of a saint, does not that strike your mind, reader, as having in it not only something for which irony, with all its nuances, is only a rough-and-tumble synonym, but something which marks a real step forward in that planetary *casuistry* with the difficulties of which all higher intelligences are forever struggling ? '

And against that you have to set, as the Enemy of Audh, ' the mysterious *meaninglessness*, the absence of all that in human life is reassuring, satisfying, symbolic ' that our great industrial centres present.

In such a world, in such a Scotland, all the more must we cling, in the words of a great soldier, to Audh—

> ' to that highest which need not and must not be resigned while strength is left to perceive it—to that particular manifestation of immortal power by which each individual spirit is most deeply moved. I believe and proclaim my faith, that this solace will proceed increasingly from the glories of Gaelic literature ; both from their own splendour and from their contrast with the limitations of modern life. True, we may rise from Mr. Wells' enchanting *Autobiography* convinced for the moment that the paramount of life is physical science. Yet throughout the War, and after, I never saw one tired man refreshing his soul with a scientific treatise or a mathematical problem ; whereas there were many transported far from their fatigues and anxieties by following those of Patroclus or Odysseus. But these enchantments of delight are strong

not only in the stress of a campaign. There are troubles deeper than those of War ; reversals of fortune perhaps no better deserved than previous unexpected felicities ; tragic personal surprises from which, as we have recently seen, nations and Empires are no more immune than individuals ; " situations and events so monstrously unjust that the mind can hardly register a protest—no man can complain when he is struck by lightning ". These are indefinable periods of time when a blind-working universe lies cold beneath the grin of a skull hung in an astral vacuum : *hypochondrie, maladie qui consiste a voir les choses telles qu'elles sont.* Some happy there are, for whose vision in such dread hours Faith shines through the darkness with the steady radiance of an altar lamp. For others, it flares and flickers fitfully as a torch in the wind and the rain. Yet even for these less happy, consolations are near ; and, to such as worship them from the heart, in spirit and in truth, easier of access and more prodigal of their effulgence with the gradually unveiling years. For me they have been and will always be the glories of Gaelic literature and the *piobaireachd*—the great music of the pipes. Before such Epiphanies of the God in Man I can but repeat the prayer of a Moslem, uttered in Basra more than a thousand years ago : "O my Lord ! If I worship Thee from fear of Hell, burn me in Hell ; and if I worship Thee from hope of Paradise, exclude me thence ; but if I worship Thee for Thine own sake, then withhold not from me Thine Eternal Beauty." '

Helgi, husband of Audh's sister, Thorun, went finally from the Hebrides to Iceland.

' He is described as a Christian settler in Iceland, but his creed was a mixed one ; nominally a believer in the Founder of Christianity, he nevertheless invoked Thor for aid in sea voyages and difficulties : a hybrid creed which was very common among the Norwegians in the early days of their Christianity.'

But in these late days the descendants and protagonists of Audh must at least disavow and rid themselves of Christianity altogether for reasons which, if not immediately apparent, must become abundantly clear as this story proceeds ; they, of all people, must remember with Leon Bloy in *Belluaires et Porchers* :

' Art is an aboriginal parasite of the skin of the first serpent. Hence derive its overweening pride and power of suggestion. It is self-sufficient like a god, and the flowered crowns of princes, compared with its head-dress of lightning, are like necklaces of paste. It will no more submit to worship than to obedience and no man's will can make it bow before any altar. It may consent, out of the superfluity of its riches, to give alms to temples and palaces, when it finds there what it wants, but you must not ask it for a thimbleful over and above. . . . There may be exceptionally unhappy souls to be encountered who are at once artists and Christians, but there cannot possibly be a Christian art.'

Why, why must one go and take thus on oneself
strange things, just as, perhaps, the carrier
from stall to stall lifts up the market-basket
more and more filled full by strangers, and
thus loaded follows on and cannot say :
Lord, wherefore the banquet ?

Why, why must one stand there like a shepherd
so exposed to all excess of influence
and so assigned to spaces full of swift
event, that, leaning up against a landscape-tree,
he would possess his fate with no more action
yet has not in the much too great beholding
the quiet solace of the herd.   Has naught
but world, has world in every looking up,
in every bending downwards world.   What fain
belongs to others blindly penetrates
into his blood, as hostilely as music,
changing on its way.

There rises he at night and has the call
of birds outside already in his being and
feels bold because he takes with difficulty all
the stars into his vision—not, O not as one
who now prepares the night for the beloved
and indulges her with all the felt heavens.[1]

---

[1] After the German of Stefan George.

CHAPTER IX

VALEDICTORY

' Fantasies by which I endeavour not to make things known, but my selfe.'—MONTAIGNE.

' Es handelt sich hier also nicht um ein mythisches, vorgeschichtliches Werden, sondern die gegenwärtige Natur selbst *ist* der Mythus.'—K. J. OBENAUER : *Hölderlin-Novalis* (Jena, 1925).

I AM coming near to the end of my book. As I have shown, I have often been in a position similar to that Father Gilbert Blackhall dreamed of (and describes in his *A Brieffe Narration of the Services done to Three Noble Ladyes*, by Gilbert Blackhall, *Priest of the Scots Mission, in France, in the Low Countries, and in Scotland*) :

> ' I thought that I was going to Scotland, and in my way I thought that I did find myself suddenly upon a mervelous great precipice, a whole liggue of lenth, having at my left hand an rock of that lenth, and as heigh as the steeples or toures of Notre Dame at Paris, and as straight up ; and at my right hand a precipice along the rock, and deip as the rock was heigh ; and the way betwixt the rock and the precipice no broader than the breadth of my foot . . . which affrighted me most, because, standing on my left foot, and my right foot in the aire, above the precipice, for want of place to sette it on, which I could not find unles I would sette the inner side of it closse to the rock, which, if I should doe, I could not move any more, for my left foot could never passe between the rock and my legge unthrowing me downe in the precipice. . . . Then I thought that I said, Jesus, How am I come thus in the middle of this precipice or how shal I winne out of it ? And looking downe into the deipth, I (did) sie many bones of men and horses who had fallen downe in it and so perished ; and looking upon theis terrible things I beganne to faunte, and said to myself, heir I sie I must end my lyffe, for my hart did never give over until now in any danger that ever did befal me. And . . . bowing to fall downe I heard a voice calling and saying, Feare not, feare not : I am come to sauve you. . . . I looked to sie who it was that called so, and I perceived that it was my Lady Aboyne . . . coming very nimbly along the side of the rock, notwithstanding the narrownes of the way. . . . I thought I did sie her juste as she used to go when she was liveing, with a great mourning vale of black taffetas."

Lady Aboyne took his hand in hers and led him to the end of the precipice. So I have been extricated again and again from like difficulties, not by Lady Aboyne, but by Audh, or the Scottish Muse, by beloved Hodegetria, Chrysopantanasa (Golden-universal-Queen), or Brigit the goddess whom poets adored, because very great, very famous was her protecting care—Carlyle's ' actual Air-Maiden, incorporated tangibility and reality ', whose electric glance has fascinated the Gaelic world—often in the form of friends like my wife Valda, or Helen Cruickshank, or Mary Ramsay, or some other friend. Her-Audh's-comings to me remind me of Van Gogh's declaration :

> ' Pour travailler ainsi il faut aussi être un peu magicien, ce qui coute cher a apprendre.—Poser son sujet nettement en premier coup, mais avec un effort absolument complet de tout son esprit et de tout son attention—Une technique étonnante, *mais avec rien*, et comme spontanée.'

Her comings always sound the *fead chruim chruaidh Chaoilte*—Caoilte's shrill round whistle over the brae, betokening the breaking of another winter's frost ; the springing of another flower ; another rig turned over, *dearg-lasrach bho'n talamh dubh na h-Alba* ; another voice stirring, rippling, throbbing into life. And if I have not escaped without a few bruises I have never yet lacked some ' oile of hypericon, or mille pertuis ', wherewith to rub them to their advantage.

My life has been like the place in Venezuela where Mother Earth drops sheer into a gulf whose distant, further side is formed from the massive shoulders of the famous ' Silla de Avila ', or Eagle's Seat. Down the nearer face of this stupendous rent in the globe's crust creeps a narrow mountain-road bounded on one side by the cliff-face and on the other by the sickening depths.

' Yes, there's our way home all right ', my Muse has told me, regarding me with a sympathetic grin. ' Don't you like its appearance ? Then look, instead, straight between the ears of Jenny, your mule. If you leave your beast alone, she'll bring you down quite safely, even though she does happen to prefer walking on the track's extremest outside edge. On no account must you ever argue with the madam here. All mules shun the wall, you know, and a struggle to compel yours to hug it might easily put both of you over the precipice. . . . You'll never heed this road after traversing it a few times.'

I have followed that advice and it has never failed me. And even now I am often up in the boughs, and seldom have any want of power to flash.

My experience has been only a special case of a predicament general to modern poets, for as Delmore Schwartz says :

> ' The increasing inadequacy of Christianity, at least in a definite period of history, to provide that map of life for Europe is only part of the condition which inspired Rimbaud and then defeated him. An equally important part is the social order which in its whole development was in conflict even with the new and diluted versions of Christianity which weakly attempted to come to terms with it. The whole condition became a problem for every serious poet. The poet above all is the one who feels the central lack in what men do, know, and believe, because he works in terms of consciousness as in terms of words. We ought to remember that perhaps the greatest evil of capitalism is its oppression or perversion of *all* values and thus of *all* lives, not only

the lives of the working class (although one does not wish to under-estimate *that* oppression for a moment). And it is in the lives of the most intelligent and the most sensitive that the greatest harm is done, at least to the intelligence and the sensibility. The history of poetry since Blake, from this important perspective, is the history of men who found the social order into which they were born increasingly inade-quate in every *human* respect and wholly deficient in satisfying the inevitable human need for a whole view of life.'

I have named Leo Chestov as my master (he is little known in Britain—yet he was mentioned in, of all places, an issue of *Punch*, not at first hand but quoting a reference of Katherine Mansfield's to his saying that ' any kind of artificial completion is absolutely superfluous '), and it can, I think, be said of my position in its degree as another writer has said of Chestov's, which is mine :

> ' Chestov sounds that note of approval of Tertullian's famous " *credo quia impossibile* " and of Pascal's " *enchantement et assoupissement surnaturel* ", which echoes and re-echoes through his pages, and of that passionate repudiation of Spinoza's " *Non ridere non lugere non detestari* " which is repeated for the last time in his final counter-blast against Hering and Husserl. It is only when these two terminal points of Chestov's thought are viewed synoptically that it is possible to enter into full possession of all that lies between ; and almost all that can here be said of the great central portion of Chestov's book (*Job's Balances*) is that it begins with " Revelations of Death " conjured up by the nethermost abysses of the thought of Dostoevsky and Tolstoy, con-tinues with a somewhat desultory sequence of thoughts on " revolt and submission " (particularly revolt), and concludes with four essays on the philosophy of history which complete the rout of Descartes and Spinoza and extol the unique atmosphere of Pascal's *Pensées* and of the most mystical pole of the thought of Plotinus, and which lead up to the final contention that the most baneful of all the works of rationalization lies in the resolution of ontology into ethics. All this tends to strike the mind as the extreme of pessimism ; and indeed it is hard to extract either positive doctrine or consolation for philosophy from Chestov, who proclaims and almost seems to glory in the attitude that " victrix causa deis placuit " and that the cause in question involves the death of the soul. Nevertheless, by a strange paradox, Chestov remains anything but a pessimist, and it is the atomistic hopelessness which holds " omnia paulatim tabescere et re ad capulum " which is his real foe. His philosophy is—a vital expression of the faith that the weak things of the world must and will eventually confound the strong (traditional philoso-phy being one of the strongest) when the age of iron comes to its appointed close.'

George Bernard Shaw once said : ' When domestic servants are treated as human beings, it is not worth while to keep them '. I feel that if they ever became human beings—were treated as such, or realized themselves as such—the huge numbers of parasites on the workers, the bankers, lawyers, teachers, gentry, nobility, and all the rest of it, would not think it worth while to continue to be these things at all. I have, in short, no use for anything between genius and the working man.

Most people are bogged in needless drudgery and plume themselves on virtues that (applied as they apply them at any rate) are utter anachronisms. As Gunnar Seidenfaden says, in his book on *Modern Arctic Exploration*, the traditional hardships and endurances and excitements of polar adventure are, or should be, largely things of the past. The greatest glories of arctic exploration have flowered because men have been willing to die to get a map ; Seidenfaden demonstrates how a map of merciless country may be made simply and accurately by flying an aeroplane over it in a certain way and dissecting the photographic results by means of a certain technique.

Something of the same sort is true in every department of human affairs to-day. And yet we are still expected for the most part to admire—or regard as desirable or necessary—exertions which are as hopelessly out of date as would be an obstinate refusal of a polar cartographer to avail himself of these new methods instead of clinging to the old way and perishing as a consequence.

I am therefore wholly at one with Dr. Ananda Coomaraswamy when he says :

> ' The fact is that those who aspire to " empire " (in the modern connotation of the term) cannot also afford a culture, or even an agriculture ; we do not sufficiently realize that the " civilization " that men are supposed to be fighting for is already a museum piece. If at the present day we are not shocked by this last consequence of individualism and *laissez faire*, a consequence that violates the nature of every man who is not a soldier born and bred, it is because we are inured to membership in industrial societies that are not organic structures but atomic aggregates of servile units that can be put to any task that may be required of them by a deified " nation " : the individual, who was not " free " before the war, but already part of a " system ", is not now " free " to stand aloof from it.'

What of the present war and the outlook after it ? I have quoted elsewhere in this book what Lenin says of Communism and the heritage of human culture. A vast extension and intensification of education is, indeed, the only hope. Since knowledge can be acquired there is no excuse for ignorance. What Lenin preached in this connexion the Soviet Union has practised. ' The Soviet authorities consider that a high degree of accurate knowledge of one's history and literature, geography, and economics, as well as that of other countries and other epochs, is essential for citizens of a planned socialist society. Only on the basis of this knowledge is it possible to build communism," Beatrice King wrote in 1941, in a survey of ' Recent Developments in Soviet Education '. She also pointed out that ' the danger of cramming is eliminated by the Soviet type of examination. . . . The questions are so searching, there is no hurry about the examination, that no one can get away with a superficial knowledge. It is this very system of examinations which has uncovered so many failures, failures which under another system would often be successes.'

The very opposite, of course, is true of Scottish education in both these respects. There is no thoroughness, the whole thing is a ghastly farce, the knowledge acquired is for the most part incredibly superficial, and the 'art of seeming to know it when you don't' almost all that is sought or secured.

Anglo-Scottish education to-day is such that few Scots ever enter into their national (let alone their international) heritage or glimpse the shining vision of Alba at all; the few who do win to it very slowly, by long and painful indirections finding directions out, and if they ever attain to anything like a full view of it, have occasion to exclaim, as Busoni did in 1910 : 'At last I have learnt how to get hold of (*anpacken*) the first movement of the Waldstein Sonata, which would never unfold its full beauty just as it should (*so rechte blüten wollte*) and I have been playing it for nearly thirty years ! '

Reverting to what I have said about the East–West synthesis, for Aldous Huxley's synthetic Yogo–Buddhic–Christian religion, and that new faith which requires from the believer the abandonment of all desires likely to lead to striving and rivalry, a complete control of the bodily functions, a concentration leading to St. Teresa's 'seventh mansion', in which one can be conscious of the mystical light while buying puppy-biscuit, and for Gerald Heard's Neo-Brahminism, I am not without a certain sympathy, but regard them merely as signs that these authors realize to a large extent what is wrong, and the general direction in which the cure may be found—and are to that extent in alignment with myself—but do not go about the business with anything like the necessary thoroughness. While I am generally in alignment with Huxley and Heard in their recourse to the wisdom of the East, however, I am in much closer and more specific agreement with the latter in the contention he advances in *Pain, Sex, and Time* (1939), i.e. a new mutation is occurring in the 'soul' of man, as a result of which his consciousness will be so enlarged as to be capable of conceiving and pursuing new ends commensurate with his technical mastery of means ; 'man's own self-consciousness decides and can alone decide whether he will mutate and the mutation is instantaneous ; as a result of this mutation the barrier between consciousness and the unconscious will disappear, we shall consciously realize our oneness with life as a whole with which the unconscious is already continuous, though the fact is at present withheld from us, and our enlarged consciousness will give us direct insight into the nature of reality.'

And I am not in the least perturbed by Professor Joad's criticism that ' Consciousness is always of something, and an enlarged consciousness is only meaningful in terms of what the enlarged consciousness knows. Thus the enlarged consciousness of Plato's

Guardians contemplated the Forms; of Shaw's Ancients, mathematical and metaphysical entities. But the extended consciousness
of Mr. Heard's mutated man appears to operate in a vacuum.'

Hard-headed practical people may feel that my insistence on the
necessity of such a mutation as the only hope for human life is
intolerably far-fetched, but they must be sharply reminded that it is
the plain man innocent of philosophy and not Hegel that lives in an
unreal world of abstraction, and however far-fetched and fantastic
some of my ideas may seem, while conscious that they, like those of
Yeats and others, have an appearance of ' silliness ' at times, I never
forget that, as Engels said in his *Dialektik und Natur* (in *Marx-Engels
Archiv*, edited by D. Riazanov, Bd. II, pp. 207–16) :

> ' It is an ancient saying incorporated in the dialectic of popular
> consciousness that extremes meet. We are therefore hardly likely to
> err if we look for the extremest degree of fantasy, credulity, and super-
> stition not in that scientific tendency which, like the German *Natur-
> philosophie*, seeks to force the objective world into the framework of its
> subjective thought, but rather in the opposite tendency which boasts of
> its dependence upon pure experience, treats thought with sovereign
> contempt, and in fact has carried matters to the furthest point of
> thoughtlessness. This school rules in England.'

It may be asked what earthly hope there is of such a mutation—
such a tremendous mental development—in Scotland of all places.
When I have been reproached at times for a propaganda that could
succeed only if there were a sudden and profound change in the
psychology of the majority of my compatriots, I have replied that it
would be by no means the first time to conspire together for its
advancement. An unidentified pamphleteer, writing in 1696,
comments on this change in the Scottish attitude : ' For,' he says,
' the bias of their people seems generally to be another way . . . yet
that is merely the effect of custom and not of nature, and as it would
not have been difficult at any time heretofore to have diverted and
turned their inclinations and humours from soldiering to commerce,
so it is not to be doubted but that upon their being once brought to
apply unto it, they would be found as ingenious and brilliant in Trade
as they have had the character to be helpful and brave in War.'

I have therefore ample grounds for believing it to be far from
impossible that the Scottish national genius may yet be turned to
Literature and the Arts, and certainly it is urgently in need to-day of
such an application to adult education and to scientific thought and
research as have been brought about in a single generation both in
Russia and in Turkey, and I still hope and believe that I may see such
a concentration of Scottish national purpose as is long overdue and
most desperately needed in these neglected fields. Scotland's sudden
switchover to Trade has in the intervening centuries more than
abundantly justified the unknown pamphleteer's prophecy. I have

no doubt whatever that if a like switch-over could be effected, it would
justify itself as completely in its revelation of the national aptitude in
departments in which it has hitherto been content to play second
fiddle to many other European countries really incapable of competing
with it at all were it once effectively roused to apply itself in these
connexions.

> And art is still a pinnacle, a sword,
> Giving no respite, offering no reward,
> Man's last clear hope.

As matters stand, we are living in a world of which Dr. Virgil
Jordan, President of the National Industrial Conference Board, in
his address to the annual convention of the Investment Bankers'
Association of America, at Hollywood, Florida, in December, 1940,
can smoothly say : ' In peace time it is the accepted custom and
normal manners of modern government to conceal all important
facts from the public, or to lie about them ; in war it is a political
vice which becomes a public necessity. People in every country,
including our own, have more or less reconciled themselves to being
pushed around by their public employees and treated as though they
were helpless wards or incompetent inmates of some vast institution
for the indigent and feeble-minded.'

And a writer much of whose other work I greatly admire, Mr.
F. D. Ommanney, can write, apparently with approval :

> ' In the wardroom was another young officer who spoke with equal
> pride and affection about his job, but from a rather more egotistical
> angle than the other boy. It was his glorious and newly-attained status
> as naval officer that he was enjoying, a position of importance and some
> power, the object of flattering and often feminine attention. Now these
> two young men before the war had been " in business ". They were
> salesmen. One sold chemicals for a chemical combine and the other
> furniture for a furniture firm. No doubt I was wrong, but that sounded
> to me like spiritual if not bodily slavery. And I believe it was, too,
> though I doubt if they realized it consciously. But as I sipped my gin
> out of smeared glasses in that little cubby-hole, inhaling smoke-laden
> air and listening to those boys talking joyfully about their war-job, I
> was aware suddenly that something had happened to them. Life for
> both of them had achieved a significance. It meant something. They
> had been set free. They were no longer cogs in a great soulless
> machine, grinding out money for other people, but living, thinking
> human beings with a purpose and a mission in life.'

I have no doubt hundreds of thousands of war-workers feel like
that—but ' living, thinking human beings ' is just what they do *not*
become, and it would be better they had never been born than
mistake such war-time titillations of their vacuous lives for real life,
a purpose and a mission. There can be no end to war, to mutual
mass-extermination, so long as most people remain such morons.
Their condition—their attitude to life—is in fact a species of cancer,
entirely similar to the way in which cancer cells develop in the body

of the host, by the failure of his own tissues to abandon their embryonic form and assume adult status and responsibility. That exactly describes the content of the lives of all but an infinitesimal minority of mankind—that infinitesimal minority, constant through all history, who have built up our entire human heritage of arts and sciences, not only without any help or understanding but in the teeth of extreme indifference and often active opposition from the vast majority who, if that minority were killed out, would speedily lose and be utterly helpless to do anything to replace all the gains of civilization. That is the truth, and, in face of it, it is useless to prate of saving or advancing civilization by national service, democratic war effort, or anything of the sort. From this point of view Scotland to-day (like every other country) is a land of yahoos, and a convincing illustration of the fact that 'lacking truth, justice, freedom, a community may have the courage of lions, the infernal resourcefulness of rats, and the perfect social organization of ants; but the members of it will still not be human. . . . Divorced from a system of moral and aesthetic values the most powerful individual, organization, or political state lacks human validity.'

So far as the war which has been going on while I have been writing this book is concerned, therefore, I have no apology to make for my attitude, which has resulted in a book similar to the pages of Hugo von Hofmannsthal's diary from the year 1915 to 1921, in which there is nothing about the war or the misery that followed it; the poet is absorbed in his reflections, his reading, his creation.

I have held myself like Dr. William Harvey at the Battle of Edgehill, ' who was so much interested in a new theory of his that he continued to work it out on paper instead of watching the course of the battle '. And if I had to defend my book, I would say : ' I used words which were strange to them to express ideas unimagined by them, while their half-developed minds were more than half-occupied, not in listening to me but in contemplating me, and in trying to form their particular idea of me by the aid of the " *Vulgi sensus imperiti* ", the imperfection of undisciplined senses, at their disposal.'

My war-work, as I have shown, has been to dream of creating a poetry which will operate on mankind as one obituarist of James Joyce said of Joyce's novels—that ' even the strongest of his characters seems dwarfed by the great apparatus of learning that he brings to bear on them. They are almost like atoms being smashed by a 250-ton cyclotron.' This, indeed, is what I would like to see people, not characters in books but all their readers, subjected to ; I dream of a literary equipment which may bring immense erudition to bear on the general unsanity of mankind, on the appalling mindlessness of almost everybody, like the insulin and metrazol ' shock ' treatments, or Dr. Lother Kalinowsky's later utilization of electricity, for dementia præcox. The recent powerful Russian cyclotron, capable of imparting energies up to 50 million electron volts to deutons (heavy hydrogen ions), would, of course, be nothing to what is needed to overcome the *vis inertiae* and stimulate most people to begin to realize those unused potentialities of theirs which, biologists assure us, are so great that the mental and spiritual level of the greatest thinkers and artists in human history should be the general level to-day instead of Everest-high beyond the reach of all but a handful of individuals. I am not an optimist; I realize only too well that bombarding bismuth with alpha particles from a cyclotron, moving at speeds near that of light, and so producing a new radio-active element which is almost certainly the missing epaiodine, is a small matter compared with bombarding most people with knowledge and evoking any mental development in them.

But certainly nothing else is worth doing or trying to do.

It is for this reason that I not only claim to be an Advaitin, holding Sankara's Vedanta philosophy, which, as Dr. P. T. Raju of Andhra University, in his admirable exposition, *Thought and Reality: Hegelianism and Advaita* (1937), overcomes the problems left unsolved by Hegel at the highest point of his philosophy, but vindicates ' the supremacy of spirit and its freedom ', since ' according to Sankara the spirit is non-difference and there are no eternal ideas. Hence the spirit can find itself intact in any change of content, choosing some and rejecting the others. . . . The same idea of freedom is expressed when it is said that creation is due to the spirit overflowing itself. It means that the phenomenal world is what has overflowed, while the spirit does not spend itself in creation. It remains a whole, free and intact, and is not affected by the phenomenal world '.

I also agree with M. Rene Guenon, in his *East and West* (English translation, 1941), that ' the West has nothing to teach the East, except in the purely material domain ', and that we owe nothing to the sciences and philosophies of the West : ' What we are intellectually we owe to the East alone '. M. Guenon emphasizes the value of ' metaphysical knowledge,' meaning by it something ' super-individual and super-rational, knowledge that is intuitive, beyond all analysis and independent of what is relative ', and strongly deprecates the predominance of feeling over intelligence. There are no limits, he says, ' to the blindness that is caused by the intrusion of sentiment into domains that should be reserved for the intelligence '. The West is ceaselessly exploring ' sentimental roads which lead always further and further from intellectuality. . . . The one true remedy (for the disorder in the West) lies in the restoration of pure intellectuality.' And as a first step we must detach ourselves from ' rationalism and intuitionism, positivism and pragmatism, materialism and spiritualism, " scientism " and " moralism " '. Then only can we reach ' the transcendent domain of metaphysic '. ' The ultimate outcome of western science and philosophy is the suicide of intelligence.' Therefore ' only let pure intellectual knowledge be restored, and all the rest will grow normal again '. I agree entirely with this, and have no sympathy whatever with those who object to putting knowledge above love in this way, who deprecate banking all upon the intellect and putting knowledge, however high, in the supreme position, and would instead put the religious sentiment in the chief place (e.g. the German philosopher, Rudolf Otto, who also propounded a scheme for bringing the East and West together).

(I owe a great deal to Dr. Raju's book in particular, and to Professor K. C. Bhattacharya's small but difficult work, *The Subject as Freedom*, in which he formulates a view akin to Advaita; and am convinced that the West must accept Dr. Raju's contention that one of its greatest speculative traditions is little but a not too consistent approximation to Sankara, falling into more or less fatal errors when and in so far as it deviates from this archetype. Those who would fain combine the necessary recognition of Sankara's lofty genius with a measure of hesitation concerning his ultimacy must make the best use they can of hints such as that which Dr. Raju gives when he remarks that Sankara's ' lower Brahman ' is asserted by him to exist ' only as a compromise to some people's demand that philosophy should satisfy our religious instinct '. It may seem to those who, unlike the present writer, are zealous for the fair fame of the West that this looks less satisfactory than Bradley's vindication of the utter reality (for us) of religious experience; but even this line of thought must not be pressed too far, for it is essential to Dr. Raju's argument (if not to Sankara's) that the mystical experience may be veridical and may represent the direct intuition of Reality. How far I am personally from any such hesitation may be gauged by my delight in such a ' find ' as the fact that Ludwig Feuerbach, translated by George Eliot under the title of *The Essence of Christianity*, but remaining little understood and receiving no adequate treatment in the English language, has just had a book on his teaching published under the most amusingly different title, *Heaven Wasn't His Destination !*)

All this is only one of many reasons why (recognizing with Nietzsche, whose educational ideas have far greater significance than the more sensational ideas by which he is best known, that—and nowhere more so than in Scotland !—' Education ' is making the common people not more but less cultured, the chaotic public education of the day making increasingly impossible that ' unity or artistic style in all the expressions of a people's life ' which constitutes Culture) I advocate ' speech-culture ' in Scotland—i.e. that the spoken (Scots) language should be given pride of place in the curriculum. Scottish education has been ruined by ignoring an all-important principle : the cross-fertilization of theory and experience. Little wonder, then, that it has failed in all its major tasks, which are, in the words of T. S. Eliot, ' to unify the active and the contemplative life, action and speculation, politics and the arts '. As Professor Joad says : ' Do our governors want an educated democracy of adult persons? No, many of them do not. They prefer sheep who are easier to govern. Do we want to be full men and women whose lives can be made lovely and agreeable by the riches of the mind and the spirit that are brought to their enjoyment? No, most of us do not, for having never possessed the riches we do not know that they are enjoyable, and instead of loving the highest when we see it, we have been taught by our schools, the pulpit and the press to heave a brick at it.'

These are the thoughts with which I sit by my Shetland window completing the writing of this book, about which (finding it far too much of a lulu for their liking) I know many will feel and say as was said about Mayakowsky's autobiography—and I must reply in the same way—' Many people have said : " Your autobiography is not seriously written ". Right ! I am not yet academized and am not in the habit of fussing about myself, and what's more, I am interested in myself only when things hum. The rise and fall of many literatures, of symbolists, realists, and so on, as well as our struggle with them—all of which has taken place before my eyes—constitutes part of the most momentous period of history. It needs to be written about, and write about it I will ! ' In any case, in writing this book, I have borne in mind the excellent counsel of a man who, taking a lady out to lunch, landed her in a place that didn't look at all what she expected. 'Are you sure this is a restaurant? ' she asked. ' Looks like a bar. . . .' He pouted. ' Of course,' he told her, ' you can eat here if you insist. But I don't advise it. Always bad to eat on an empty stomach.' He waved at the waiter, who ushered them into a red-coloured booth. ' *Dos* champagne cocktails.' He gave her a long and interesting black cigarette. Then he leaned upon his elbows, studying her white skin as if he wished to commit every soft brown freckle to memory. . . .

So now I can say with William Morris :

> ' What other blessings in life are there save these, fearless rest and hopeful work ? Troublous as life is, it has surely given to each one of us here some times and seasons when, surrounded by simple and beautiful things, we have felt really at rest ; when the earth and all its plenteous growth, and the token of the varied life of men, and the very sky and waste of air above us, have seemed all to conspire together to make us calm and happy, not slothful but restful. Still oftener belike it has given us those other times, when at last, after many a struggle with incongruous hindrances, our own chosen work has lain before us disentangled from all encumbrances and unrealities, and we have felt that nothing could withhold us, not even ourselves, from doing the

work we were born to do, and that we were men and worthy of life. Such rest and such work, I earnestly wish for myself and for you and for all men : to have space and freedom to gain such rest and such work is the end of politics : to learn how best to gain it is the end of education ; to learn its inmost meaning is the end of religion.'

I foresaw this years ago and became a communist. In the same way Kierkegaard too considered communism as a final and probably necessary stage in saving the individual—and losing the masses, and justifies the ' levelling process ' in order ' to bring the highest into relation with the individual '. Kierkegaard, with whom I have shared ' the martyrdom of being a genius in a provincial town ', the prolonged agony of ' being trampled to death by geese '.

' Where is God ', asks Van Gogh in a letter, ' if not among the artists?' I share to the full at any rate Rimbaud's detestation of the whole of *bourgeois* culture—even his preliminary thought that Europe and even Christianity are identical with the systematic abomination of *bourgeois* society. I have been intensively engaged in recent years in surveying the whole field of Scottish national biography, and while it is true that I have achieved a certain reputation and remember with Gerard Manley Hopkins that ' fame, the being known, though in itself one of the most dangerous things to man, is nevertheless the true and appointed air, element, and setting of genius and its works . . .', it is impossible to read as I have done and remember carefully the lives of many thousands of one's compatriots in all ages without realizing that—to look at the Armed Forces first—' harvests of military glory have been reaped—and spilt and lost—and famous names proclaimed the world over. Yet the glory of it has proved doubtful in colour and strangely transient, truly " a bubble reputation at the cannon's mouth " ; and, to judge from the volumes written by some of them, he is a rare general whose record is found to be impressive after a time. With all the publicity of wireless, biographies, autobiographies, and that of the Press with its laudatory obituaries, the sum-total of glory amounts to little more than that of the village Hampdens and mute inglorious Miltons who sleep in the churchyard of Gray's *Elegy* '.

This is equally true of every other sphere (except Arts and Letters —and Science, which last has not perhaps for the most part even yet got its relative due)—true of the Law, of Politics, of the Peerage, of Royalty, of Business, and of the Church. The Church has occupied a big place in Scottish biography, yet in all the hosts of our dead divines there are exceedingly few of any permanent value—the interest of almost all of them died with them ; and the general epitaph on the whole of our ecclesiastics might well be that on the tomb of an Italian cardinal, once abbot, bishop, and prince of the Church

Abbas, Episcopus, Princeps,
Pulvis, Umbra, Nikil.

It is no wonder then that I have no use for any between highbrow artists at the one end of the scale and the working class at the other—sailors, fishermen, agricultural labourers, rural workers of all kinds, buck navvies, and other non-bogus people. As a writer on the last-named says :

> ' Loyalty, I think, was their most well-developed trait. They might cheerfully put their foot through each of the ten commandments one after the other, but they wouldn't let a pal down. . . . This splendid camaraderie permeated everybody on the job. From the humblest " nipper " looking after a set of railway points to the engineer at the head of the whole huge undertaking everybody went out of their way to help the " under dog ". And help generously and practically, too. A hungry man wants food, not words of advice. At times, of course, really good men, men known as such to all the gangers on the job, rolled up in search of a start. Perhaps, owing to weather or other contingencies, he could not be given one. He might have tramped all the way from Newcastle or Hull or any other place for that matter, and would now have to tramp back. A quick whip-round would be organized at once, and the coins given would not be coppers or threepenny-bits : everyone gave royally—" it might be my turn next "—and the old fellow, the mud of his last wayfaring not yet dry upon his boots, would set off on the weary search once more, but with ten or twelve pounds, perhaps more, in his purse to help him on his way. Any man off work six weeks got a collection. It made up what he had lost in wages. We weren't quite masters of our fate, but, collectively, we came very near to it. Nobody was going to lose by hard luck if we could help it.—It was really splendid, this generous, unquestioning comradeship. I never came across it elsewhere, save in the war. There were no unctuous, hypo-critical words of advice as to how he should spend the money. What matter if the whole lot *was* blued in at the next pub ? " The poor devil will have a good drink, anyway." Sentimentalists ? Perhaps. But do not forget that these were men with a contemptuous familiarity with the world, the flesh, and the devil ; men who knew toil as few men know it, privation, violence, and debauchery, famine and thirst, and all the rest of the miseries ; hard-bitten toughs who had no fear of anything or anyone on earth, and who would have smashed the tablets of the law into smithereens with one deft crack of their twenty-eight pound hammers. Sentimentalists they might be ; cynicism and meanness were the things they most despised.'

I would not exchange one of them for all the nobility and landed gentry and naval and military officers and plutocrats and M.P.s and ministers and lawyers and bankers and teachers in Great Britain.

The writer I have quoted ends :

> ' I have known one after the other of these restless old fellows call at the pay-window for his " time ". " What's wrong, Snowy ? Got across with the ganger ? " Snowy would smile. Then with an express-ive sweep of his arm towards the sun-bathed world around him, " My feet itch ", he would explain simply, " I'm going for a walk ! " He might have half-a-crown to draw. Half-a-crown with which to face the world again ! With no definite idea, even, where he intended making for. Yes, I think they feel the call all right.'

That is the stuff—a million times better than all the safe jobs in creation ; these are men of the world—not of this place or that ; not stuck in any rut ; no ' servile units ' in any system—and if that sort of life is not literally possible for all of us, I would at any rate have everybody fully human as these men are, and, in their mental if not in their physical life, owners of the whole wide world, wafted from one remembered place to another like Clare Leighton in her latest book, passing without a moment's pause from Pyrenees to Greenland's icy peaks, or Shenandoan valleys, where negroes grow, then away to Algiers, the Balkans, Brittany, Canada, or the juicy vintage of Burgundy, where she stamps the purple grapes with the peasants and drinks with them, into still more rapid adventures. Wherever she flies she is quite at home, and, to her, mankind, like the seven seas, are all one. The miracle of fertility and reproduction runs like a radiant thread throughout the whole book. She feels its pulsation in everything that has life—grasses and flowers, insects, birds, beasts, and mankind. At first she is ashamed to look at a hen-blackbird brooding on her young, but on discovering herself with child she can look the blackbird full in her shining eye.

That most people cannot share this full life, becoming Dryden's

> A man so various that he seemed to be
> Not one, but all mankind's epitome,

is just for the opposite reason—because they have death inside themselves, they are not completely alive, let alone pregnant with new life.

If I cannot acquiesce in the sentimental

> Praise to the lowly and the little-known
> Who never saw Earth's banners raised on high
> As they went by,
> Yet kept great store
> Of faith, of love, of gladness,

I do share the vision of which James Stephens sings :

> She brings her timid one
> To bravery :
> Her knave and fool
> Into her honesty :
> Her brute
> To friendship,
> And her wise
> To jollity.

> Like and unlike,
> When to her grace they bow,
> The moon doth rise in them,
> And spring allow
> Green leaves
> In every heart :
> Laurels
> On every brow.

I stand side by side with one of the very few intelligent occupants
of any Scottish professorial chair to-day, one of the very few really
of the present time, Professor Lancelot Hogben of Aberdeen—
smiling a little wryly to myself when he says :

> ' The history of Marxism is a record of repeated mistakes which could
> have been avoided if Marxists relied more on research which would
> reveal a number of possible contingencies and less on reasoning from
> insufficient data to seemingly inevitable conclusions '—

thoroughly approving and enjoying his attack on Oxford and
Cambridge, where dwell the high priests of humane studies and pure,
knowledge, the censors, through Civil Service and Scholarship
Examinations, of what is taught in the schools and what is done in
Whitehall—philosophic kings in true Platonic style, by their cult of
the elegantly useless and their preference for verbal clarity over
obscure discovery, ensuring that Britain shall remain the static home
of social anachronisms—and entirely, entirely with the reviewer of
Hogben's latest book, who says :

> ' Professor Hogben deliberately returns to the tradition of Robert
> Owen. He is the first of the scientific Utopians, convinced that we can,
> if we really will it and scientifically plan it, create a new social order, in
> which we exploit the unexplored potentialities of nature in the service
> of the unexplored potentialities of man. But this is impossible unless
> we can develop a new philosophy of education, freed from the dogmas
> both of scientific materialism and of classical humanism, new politicians
> who really believe in the possibility of a new order and understand the
> forces which are preventing its development, a new sort of teacher who
> wants his pupils not to imitate the correct procedure and appreciate
> the right things, but to understand the world around them and change
> it for the better, and, lastly, a salariat, technicians, civil servants, and
> scientists, conscious of the social responsibility which expert knowledge
> brings and willing to lead the democratic movement in its struggle
> against the vested interests of capital and labour.—I find in it what I
> have long been searching for, a philosophy true to the tradition of
> British radicalism, which strengthens that tradition with the power of
> systematic knowledge.'

I object to the adjective *British* radicalism, however. Scottish
radicalism I know. I have no faith in England whatever. I agree
with the second of Odette Keun's adjectives when she says :

> ' Often I ask myself whether there exists, in the world to-day, a people
> as naturally good as the English, and as immeasurably stupid. I
> honestly believe there isn't—and I also believe that this same calamitous
> combination of goodness and stupidity is principally responsible for the
> mistakes committed since 1936 (the fatal year of the German reoccupation
> of the Rhineland, a move that England persuaded France to accept,
> and that made this war unavoidable) and of which we are now reaping
> the deadly harvest.'

And I believe with that brilliant writer Gens, in the *New English*

Weekly—discussing the cause of the world revolt, i.e. Money— that this is a world revolt ' against which England is leading the reaction. . . . Nothing can remove the ever-recurring cause, except such a revaluation of Western values as none of the nations concerned appears to have in mind. It is also true that England is the most responsible—which does not necessarily mean most to blame—for what is wrong.'

But Scotland can re-establish her Independence and should be one of the leaders in this world revolt, and, incidentally, in the break-up of the Empire and England's relegation to relative insignificance. I believe because it can it must, and to that I have devoted—and will continue to devote—my life. And certainly these scientific Utopians will need to be real intellectual toughs with all the buck-navvy's devil-may-care spirit and expertise with twenty-eight-pound hammers !

And that is the sort of poet I have tried to be—and am.

I read a short story the other day in which it was said of a character that ' life had given him far too much, and taken too much away, for the future to have any significance '. That may apply to me too— without the last clause. I can say as another writer has said :

> ' It is evident that from the very first the fates planned for me to walk alone and to possess nothing that I have not earned ; and once in possession they snatch what I have away from me as quickly as possible. Yet I am content enough. I have lived fully and travelled widely. I have fought poverty and ill-health. What success I have had has been due to my own energy and courage, since for the most part my life has been a lonely one. Whatever life may bring in the end, it has carried an infinite variety upon its stream.'

And like that ' old man mad about writing ', Ford Madox Ford, as he called himself in a phrase that I too (albeit not yet old in years) might well adopt for myself, I claim a place among the ' writers who had lived ', agreeing entirely that (destructive as such a conclusion is in particular of the claims of the majority of English authors of ' established reputation ') it is evident by the example of great writers that a man must have lived a full life of action, danger, and even despair before he could render the life that surrounded him. For how can you estimate the real values of life unless you have fought to preserve your-own with rapier and dagger, unless you have faced, like Villon, starvation, or unless you have at the very least learned the value of mere money, like Richardson, who supported himself as a printer before he even thought of feeding the presses. (I have even at times felt like Kierkegaard—that I must confine my reading to the writings of men who have been executed.)

I read with complete approval then of a young author, Pietro Di Donato, in his book *Christ in Concrete*, that ' the business of being a labourer is so stringent that he doesn't get around to a discussion of

labour movements '; and, with reference to the present war, note a
Canadian comment :

> ' Does not Herr Rauschning in his book, *The Revolution of Nihilism*,
> which has now become the bible of our right-thinking people, tell us
> that a revived German conservatism would necessarily be international
> because the civilization that has to be saved from the nihilists of the
> Nazi movement is European and not merely German ?   So what our
> allied leadership may seek in Germany is a little revolution from above
> which would upset Hitler and also would forestall the big revolution from
> below.   And what will the British Labour Party or the French socialists
> be able to do when they discover that the cause for which they are really
> fighting is the restoration in Europe of government by gentlemen ? '

There can be no outcome I at least would not prefer to *that*, and
my life will continue to the end to fight with all the weapons at its
command against anything of the sort, wholly concerned as I am
with a revolutionary force of which the dynamism is automatically
provided by the very struggle for life ; the elemental struggle for a
decent livelihood in and by itself a dynamic force of primary
importance, upon which, alone, any movement that seeks a more
equitable system can be built and live.

I will always be a ' leasing-maker ' (Scots word for rebel or
sedition-monger) against ' government by gentlemen', whether in
the State or in any department of human arts and affairs.   I have no
use at all for any of the freemasonries of mediocrity, knowing, as my
friend Guy Aldred says, that

> ' few great doctors have held degrees or have been honoured or recog-
> nized by the medical profession.   Many have been outcast.   The
> corner stones of the temple are rejected.   Few men of vision have been
> divines.   The greatest of English Jurists was not entitled to practise
> law.   Jesus typifies the same truth.   He was without scholarship and
> had no legal status of divinity.   He scorned professional learning.   The
> adjective applied and not the noun.   The latter was deleted that the
> shadow might become the substance.   Did not Hans Andersen im-
> mortalize this truth in a fairy tale ? '

I would allow no man who has undertaken to render unquestioning
obedience to any authority—that is to say, no soldier, no sailor, no
policeman—to cross my threshold or give him any friendship or
recognition.   I regard all such as outside the pale of humanity and
would fain join others in ostracizing them completely and denying
them all social intercourse, and taking such other steps as might
render the continuance of their kind in the world impossible as
speedily as possible.   I have no use whatever for the mystical
fervour of the Germans, for whom not any manifestation of indi-
vidualism but ' the perfect unity of marching men is the highest
expression of Freiheit ', nor, by the side of her consummate ' civilized '
appeal, for the pettiness and gracelessness of lower middle class life
in France, which is a devastating and unanswerable criticism of any

claims that may be made for the former, and if the essential difference
between culture and civilization is, as I think it is, that, as Bernard
Wall has pithily put it, ' civilization pays sixpence and goes to look at
culture in the National Gallery ', I have no use for civilization, and
least of all for that form of it whereby, thanks to the radio, people
can have the music and other arts of every other age and country on
tap, and none of their own at all.

I certainly have no objection to being subjected constantly to the
most diverse emotional and intellectual stimuli in order to discover
whether I would behave like those poor rats who after months of
finding their food behind a red light find it no longer there but
behind a green one.

Their intelligences disintegrate.

Mine doesn't.

I take my stand side by side then with Robert Burns (I have
shown scant respect to English literature in these pages, believing
it has been enormously over-boosted in keeping with the growth of
the British Empire—with the break-up of which it will shrink in
world esteem again to its proper very modest proportions ; it will be
time enough for me to look on English literature with a kindlier eye
when the English reading public ceases to pay a little lip-service to
Burns, leaving him unread, and begins to realize that he is a truer man
and better poet than almost all the English poets put together !) and
cry with him again :

> A fig for those by law protected !
> Liberty's a glorious feast !
> Courts for cowards were erected,
> Churches built to please the priest.

For

' in these lines began the Revolution of Revolutions, compared with
which the French Revolution is but a ripple on the sea of change.   The
Revolution of Burns is an insurrection of the naked spirit of man.   It
goes deeper than the pimples and blotches of wars and legislations,
those cutaneous abrasions on the skin of society produced by kings and
soldiers, priests and politicians ; for it transforms the inner soul of
humanity.   It affects not merely the physical arrangement of units,
but the unit itself. . . . The new revolution seeks to free the personality of the separate man from spiritual and intellectual oppressions.
Burns foresaw the future revolt against all the external compulsions of
collective opinion.   He descried the dawn of law that is lawless and
lawlessness that is law.   He grasped the great principle that each man
ought to be law unto himself, and out to do that which is right in his
own eyes, regulating his conduct by no outer criterion of corporate
conventions, but solely by the statutes of his own conscience.   He
realized that the only moral law is that which is enacted in the parliament of the spirit and that the highest standard is set up not outside
but inside the soul.   He perceived that there is only one person who can
never forgive sin, namely, the sinner.   He knew that the virtue that is
rooted in conformity to external menace is an immoral cowardice and

P

that the free play of the free mind in the free body is the ideal goal
towards which man is marching over the ruins of philosophies and
civilizations, moralities and creeds. . . . He challenged everything
that speaks with authority, reverencing nothing save irreverence and
fearing nothing save fear.'

Vive l'anarchie !

Two of the great images that have always played a dominant part
in my poetic life have been the horse and the ship, which is not
surprising, since I come of a race of horse-lovers on the one hand and
on the other have spent so much time at sea in all manner of craft
and know of no boast I would be more proud to be able to make than
that of the piper MacPhie in one of John Ferguson's novels : ' My
family have taken good care ever since the Flood never to be without
a boat of their own ! ' And in one of my notebooks I find on
consecutive pages snatches of poems I have written and prose
passages in which I express my attitude to life in terms of these two
great symbols, and I cannot close this book better than just by
reproducing these here. The pages in question run as follows :

> Every inch of canvas must catch and pull,
> Every line, brace, and clew hold,
> The running rigging render
> And the standing rigging stand.

' It always seemed incredible that a ship, any man's ship, even one
of the monstrous screw-driven ironclads, could live through a real
storm. The old ocean is big : its depth would engulf the highest
mountain range nor leave a peak to mark the spot : all the dry land of
earth could be shovelled into the seven seas, eaten, absorbed, vanished.
And men treat that old ocean with insolent familiarity ; pit their wood
and will against it—and win ! The Skipper was out there perfectly
aware that he could do nothing, except by the luckiest of chances.
Even so he went through his days and nights, seemingly without fear
and with no hope. He had something in him that answered every
challenge, even that of such a night as this. He would not quit, he
would not shirk, he would not lash the helm and go below. . . . The
deck rose and fell, down, down, with the low slow drop of a pitching
ship, then up as if being raised to the clouds. From time to time the
water came over with a hoarse, engulfing rush and buried him to the
waist, to his neck, occasionally it seemed covering him from sight. It
was a distinct surprise to see him emerge each time, though I knew very
well he could not be swept away. There was, however, a good deal of
that strange quality of his which seemed to seize on the hardest, most
grinding strain, and meet it. Being covered and lost under water
meant nothing to him. But the blow of the water—that was something ! The deck had been boarded by a moving mountain—

> " He'll be drowned ! "
> " No more than a fish."

—The mountain had slid off. The deck was clear of water. In a
flare of lightning he was still there as if he had passed through nothing
more than a wisp of fog. He was leaning slightly forward, eyes set to

pierce the darkness, or rather to catch the farthest distance in the quick thrusts of lightning.'

Then on the next page :

> When I see a possible poem, I work
> With the utmost economy of effort.
> The old scarred Visalia kak is stripped
> To fundamentals—the skirts trimmed down
> Till they barely cover the tree—the stirrups
> Cut off close to the rosettes.   No stirrup fenders,
> And the doubled stirrup straps wrapped
> With rawhide to keep the stirrups in position.
> A lass-rope and hackamore
> Complete my equipment
> —And you can bet your boots I'm going to take
> A good whirl at breaking it !

> And ever and again it shall be with me
> As when on the night called *lailat ul mi'raj*
> Muhammad ascended to Heaven from Jerusalem
> On the fabulous mule named Burak.

Post-Union Scottish history reminds me of a poor man with a pot-bellied grey mare, foaled by a famous dam and with a still more famous sire.   A man living on next to nothing, sacrificing everything for that grey mare, from which he gets at last a runty little filly no better than her ma ! . . . Then he spends patient years while *she* grows up, and he breeds her to a namely stallion. . . . Yet that foal was no good either.   It was another filly.   Runty like the rest. Couldn't raise a gallop.   You couldn't discourage the man, though. When this one grew up, he took all his savings again—mind you, he lived worse than a squatter—and away he takes her again.   The father is another famous steed.   And he gets another filly, the worst of the whole string.   Broke down in front when it was two, and not so good behind either.

' What a grand middle piece though ! ' says the poor man.

We all figured he was a crazy man by this time though.

Then comes the time he takes this one away to a stallion—a stallion of the same line this time.   And, by the jumping Jiminy, he gets the first colt he's had, and the name of that colt is a name all the world knows now.

Not that we believed in him.   The poor man had failed so often that we couldn't believe.   But a couple of the boys offered a good price for the foal, and the poor man, he just laughed at them.

' You can't buy history that cheap ', he said.   And that horse made history all right.   I remember his first great victory.   The longer that race went, the harder he fought for his head, the more the fool lump of a jockey held back, and the wider that horse split himself.   And he came up on the outside faster than fire in dry stubble. And he left those three doggone high-priced thorough-breds to study the look of his tail, and he opened up a couple of lengths of daylight and made it three for luck as he went under the wire with fifteen pound overweight. And he ran another half-mile past the finish and then bucked his jockey off to show that he was only beginning. . . .

Turf memories are short. Racehorses themselves are brittle stuff. The two-year-old of one season becomes the broken-down cripple of the next. The three-year-old champion retires with a bowed tendon. And the handicapper, as he studies form, realizes that the horse that did a mile in one thirty-six on Monday may work hard to do one-forty on the Sunday following. Only now and then some great Eclipse, Colon, Simon, or Man-o'-War proves to be made of iron and defies defeat. The public comes to love such horses, for they are ' honest ' in an almost spiritual sense. Flesh and bone in them will not fail, and their hearts will not fail either. No matter what weight is heaped above their withers, or how gruelling the drive down the stretch, though they are challenged, they never stagger but stretch out straight and true ; they work unfaltering to the end, nostrils flaring red, eyes glaring with pride and disdain of defeat. They are world champions and they know it.

We who love her know that Scotland will cast such a foal again—next time—or the next time. Like a king in stable, in paddock, or ready at the start—noble in beauty, noble in soul, disdaining flightinesses, tricks, or trouble of any kind. His heart as great as his speed, and the world will know it. Therefore it will love him, rejoice in his victories, shake its head in disbelief of two or three unimportant failures when weight anchored him on muddy tracks, and swarm to the track to see him triumph again. And put Scotland on the map again.

And my notes end :

> ' The words of an old song : " He who gallops too early will walk very late ! " . . . Then he knew that he was not riding a mere creature of flesh and blood, but that he was mounted upon an idea, to the forging of which one old man had contributed his money, his time, his thought, his prayers, the happiness of his children, the whole of his energy, love, and ambition during a long life. The horse does not fail, because the first sire of its line had enough bottom to carry a mountain. The horse is not slow, because, with delicate and prayerful care, the old man had added to that original stock of endurance the fine flight of speed which is in this horse like wings. And it seems to the rider that mere horse-flesh does not account for the composition of this horse's mind. That cheerful and undaunted air with which he carries his head, and some-times, turning it a little, looks back at his rider with a bright content with life, reminds him of the old man. As though something of the old man has passed into the line of his horses ! '

What more can a man desire ? As the Egyptian proverb says :

' *Kulla haraka fi-ha baruka* ' (All agitation brings some compensation).   I have always believed—and lived by—Matthew Arnold's dictum that ' ideas cannot be too much prized in and for themselves —cannot be too much lived with '.   The other great thing is the *animus manendi*—the intention of permanence ; but I cannot deal with that here—I would require to write another book to show the way in which this informs me.

Finally, I would say of Scotland what Michael Drayton, in a foreword to his *Poly-olbion* says, speaking of Wales : ' If I have not done her right, the want is in my ability, not in my love '—that Scotland the condition of which to-day is perhaps best described in Malory, Book IV, chapter 15—a landscape that speaks ' with a grimly voice '.

In these circumstances—' pressed on every side, yet not straitened ; perplexed, yet not unto despair ; pursued, yet not forsaken ; smitten down, yet not destroyed '—I sing not only for Ireland—but for Scotland and Wales and Cornwall—

> ' For now the morn is breakin', me boys,
> The pirate ship is lakin', me boys,
> Our villainous foes to the bottom they goes,
> For their cursed ould impire is shakin', me boys ',

and instead of any feeling of despair, I feel in the lines of another song,

> Well, well, some say her voice is gone
> Though loud and hoarse she tries to roar it.
> They hint her tyrant race is run
> And I'd be sorry to ignore it.
> I think, as sets her blood-red sun,
> One emerald star may glitter o'er it.
> What do you think, Paddy Cooney,
> Tim O'Farrell, Teddy Mooney,
> Angus Mackay, Donald MacDonald,
> Peter Fraser, Hugh Ronald,
> David Davies, Richard Lloyd, Tom Hughes
> —Come all you Celts and give me your views.
> I think, as sets England's blood-red sun,
> Gaeldom's emerald star may glitter o'er it.
> Do you take my sense, Mulrooney ?

Yet in all this, while seeming to wander here, there, and everywhere perhaps, I have kept my course, always determined to be *there* all right, remembering Bromley-Davenport's lines :

> . . . The bitches are racing before us.
> Not a nose to the earth—not a stern in the air ;
> And we know from the notes of that modified chorus
> How straight we must ride if we wish to be there.

People who are not concerned to deny that Scotland has little or no head are usually quick to assert that she is at least big-hearted. I am reminded of what Johnny Best, the boxing promoter, whom I knew in Liverpool, said once about Henry (' Homicide ') Armstrong. Twenty minutes before an important fight was due to start, Mr. Best walked into Armstrong's dressing-room to see if there was anything he might need. ' To my amazement ', said Mr. Best, ' I found him indulging in a spell of hectic shadow boxing. " I'm fine, Mr. Best ", was all he said as he continued weaving and bobbing round the room slinging punches with both hands at an imaginary opponent. It all seemed very strange to me, for though most boxers " limber up " before going into the ring, they are careful to do so for only a minute or two, so that their physical resources should be husbanded for the fight itself. Eddie Mead (Armstrong's manager) let me into Armstrong's secret. The champion possesses an extraordinarily large heart, and in order to make his leg and arm muscles resilient he has to force the heart to pump blood quicker than it normally does. This he can achieve only by warming up for at least half an hour. Mead told me that in many of his earlier fights he had failed to show any sort of form in the first four or five rounds. It was not till a leading American doctor ran the rule over him that the cause and remedy were discovered. Nor does the added work seem to have any effect on Armstrong's powers of endurance, which are apparently illimitable. I doubt whether Armstrong's like has or will ever be produced. He is a fighting phenomenon, who neither abides by the teachings of any text-book nor imitates the methods of any of his predecessors.'

I feel sure something similar will be said about Scotland, if and when it ever learns to properly work up that big heart first. The trouble is that, unlike Homicide Armstrong, Scotland has been under rank bad management since the Union, compelled to follow the teachings of the English text-book, and never taught how long its abnormal constitution requires it to ' limber up ' to bring anything like its full powers into play. What would I not give or do to see Scotland really ' het up ' ? The heather on fire at last !

Now that in addition to my home on Whalsay here I have (at a fair distance from the other) a separate cottage which I use as an office—an indescribable chaos stuffed with hundreds of thousands of newspaper cuttings (for all my work needs a lot of ' hot information ' not yet congealed into books), and letters, files of periodicals as various as the *Scots Independent*, the *Irish Nationalist*, the *Welsh Review*, *Europaische Revue*, the New York *Nation*, *International Literature* (Moscow), *Crois Tara*, *Breiz Atao*, *Tir Newydd* and countless others, and decorated in addition to mural paintings of my ' Curly Snake ', the Green Spot-bellied Cencrastus, and a Cavorting

Cow (developed from a doodle of my little boy's), with portraits of friends as diverse as Ezra Pound, Philip O'Connor, Mary Rhys (authoress of a book on the Scilly Islands), Ruth Pitter, T. S. Eliot, James Joyce, and Nazim Khikmet, the poet of Turkish liberation, it is not surprising that I have hung up by way of my professional motto a printed card bearing this passage from Marcus Aurelius : ' How all things upon Earth are pesle mesle ; and how miraculously things contrary one to another, concurre to the beautie and perfection of this Universe ' !

It is, no doubt, a very strange and utterly unexpectable cottage—incredibly unlike any of its neighbours (internally—outwardly it is identical with these)—to find on a little Shetland island ; the very kind of thing, indeed, a patriotic populace would be apt to burn out like a wasps' nest in a war. Yet while I have an insatiable liking for many things which are—most of them permanently—caviare to the general, I have also a keen appetite for the staples of human life in general. And I am in the habit of indulging both to the full ; just as I like low pubs and ' tough joints ' of all kinds and the company of quite illiterate people (but never half-educated mediocrities !) simultaneously with difficult high-brow literature and the friendship in many countries and several continents of many of the keenest intellects of my time—men like T. S. Eliot, Oliver Gogarty, Ezra Pound, C. H. Douglas.

And—to most minds perhaps the most extreme of all these straddling disparities—the fact that with such interests and such friendships, and a score of books to my name, and a measure of international reputation, I am perhaps the poorest, and certainly the most precariously situated on this poor little island, where there is no one else who comes within a million miles of conceiving, let alone sharing or comprehending in any degree, any of my major interests. And here I will remain, contented enough, so long as I can continue to keep my head above water at all—and certainly with a very minimum of effort to ' better myself ' in the conventional sense of that extremely questionable phrase.

So long, I say, in these times when, as the Chinese Ambassador says, the air is black with the hosts of chickens coming home to roost, as I can continue to keep my head above water, and go on with my work. And that work ? To serve Scotland—to develop an Audhology comparable in spiritual reach and intellectual elaboration to the Sophiology that has been developed elsewhere ; and, first and foremost all the time, to write (alternately, and happily now and again—and perhaps, with increasing frequency, simultaneously) a poetry of strange architecture, sometimes learnt from such masters as Hermesianax, Alexander of Etolia, Lycophron, and above all, Simmias of Rhodes—' Itineraire '—*poems* ' *avec parenthese* '—musical and sober, and warm, pure, like the classical chorus, graven as

though in marble—and, again, poems that exemplify *more boreali*
the declaration of Francis Jammes : ' What strength there is in verses
when feeling is put into them ! Poetry ought not to be formal. As
to those moderns who introduce cubism into poetry, it is the negation
of all, the desolation of desolations ! ' And, above all, what I want
is a poetry

> ' Full of august reverberations of world-literature and world-history,
>   Like the analogies between the Axiochus and the poet's argument
> In the splendours of the close of the Third Book of Lucretius,'

a poetry also in which, as in Arno Holz's *Phantasus*, ' rhyme and
stanza vanish ; the " natural and necessary " rhythm constitutes the
poem, which turns on an invisible central pivot (*Mittelachse*) '.
   While I can declare like Henri Beraud, ' Je ne depends de personne ',
and the portraits I have named look down upon me as Talleyrand,
Boileau, Regnard, Racine, and Gluck are set on pedestals round him,
I have no need of the valuable books he has lying about, nor of his
fifteen hundred phonograph records. Nor does my Shetland
cottage require like Francis Carco's flat in the rue de Douai, climbing
up the side of the Butte, a gunshot away from the Moulin Rouge, a
few yards away from the Place Blanche and the Place Pigalle, pictures
signed by Utrillo, a spongy production of de Segonzac's, Derain,
Duragnes, Suzanne Valadou, some crayon sketches by Luc Albert
Moreau, a nude figure of a girl by Modigliani. Nor the portrait of
Aristide Briand by Toulouse Lautrec that hangs above Roland
Dorgeles's writing-table, the lion's skin *a la Tartarin* on the divan, the
glass globe with a map of the world, a head of Angkor in stone
wearing an unchanging smile, a silver-handled Bedouin knife
stained with the blood of captives, an Indian idol preaching serenity.
Nor the Chinese ruler, the mah-jong set in mother-of-pearl, and other
quaint objects on Jean Girandoux's smooth and shining writing-table
in the venerable house in the rue du Pre-aux-Clercs. Still less have
I any need of the yellow silk hangings embroidered in gold, the
imposing chandelier, the dignified, impressive furniture, consoles and
tables of marble, tapestry-covered armchairs, sumptuous church
candlesticks, the screen made of mirrors, the fans, snuff-boxes,
porcelain flowers, ivory knick-knacks, Spanish figures of the Madonna
of Paul Souday's salon in the rue Guegnegaud. Or the fantasy by
Touchagues, the study by Delaunay, the wax design by Vidal-
Salisch, the imprint of the palm and fingers of the writer's hand read
by the clever Maryse Choisy on the walls of Joseph Delteil's study
on the Boulevard de la Chapelle ; or the Crooks Tube, the Chagall
water-colours, the Tahitian necklace made of shells in Philippe
Soupault's ground-floor flat at Auteuil ; or Jean Cocteau's studio,
full of bric-à-brac, cartoons, plasters, figurines in straw or wire,

devinettes, paper cocottes, Greek heads, locks of hair, ships. Or Fernand Divoire's walls plastered with queer paintings and inscriptions ; a proclamation about fishing, a prayer ' From hideousness and heaviness, good Saint Louis, deliver us ! ', and, on another wall, these words : ' Les biophages sont des gens qui viennent inutilement manger la vie des autres '. Nor do I accumulate or covet such things as the crab from the cocoa-trees of Oceania, the wooden bowl from the Marquesas, birds made out of horn from Madagascar, the jaw of a sacred pig of the New Hebrides, a weird dagger, a fan signed by members of the Imperial Family of Japan, an ikon, the horns of a stag shot in New Caledonia, Chrysanthemums, a panel of a Breton bed, a portrait of herself by Faoryi (' People think I am a Hindoo. I am a Parisienne ! '), to be found in Titayna's rooms. Or Maurice Dekobra's accompaniments when he writes—a Babenké fetish, an Egyptian scarabaeus, and a Kakris dagger. Or. the head of a Bacchante in red clay against the veined marble of Gerard Bauer's mantelpiece. Or Francis de Miomandre musing in the company of his chameleon, perched on the branch of a plum-tree ; a creature of the moon, fragile and majestic, whom he adores ; and whose greyish-green turns in the sun to white. No ; I do not need these things, for I have them all (it is indeed only amongst such things and such people that one can realize what La Bruyere meant by work ' made by the hand of the workers '), and thousands more, in my memory. But if there were to be one sentence from any of these writers I might still paint on the walls of my Shetland cotttage I think it would be Cocteau's : ' I do not like scandal, but it is necessary to shake up the mutts '.

I sit here then, in my incredible *plerophoria* (full assurance, cf. 1 Thess. 1 : 5), remote from the so-called ' centres of civilization ' yet confident that it is impossible for anything to happen to me now like what happened to Kierkegaard in Berlin when he was so bitterly disappointed by Schelling's lectures—yet never heard Trendelenburg because he too readily trusted the report of a Danish compatriot that he was not worth listening to. ' It is like ships that pass in the night ', says Dr. Lowrie, in his biography of Kierkegaard. ' But it seems to be even sadder that he came near knowing Gustav Theodor Fechner, the greatest philosopher that lived in his day, and one who, like him, has been ignored by the English-speaking world, in spite of the effort of William James to make him known. There would have been much in Fechner's philosophy distasteful to Kierkegaard—and yet there was so much he might have learnt from him, and he came so near it. And certainly Fechner was dealing with reality.' (Incidentally I may explain in view of my many references to Kierkegaard that it is with me as with Martin Heidegger and Karl Jaspers, of whom it has been said : ' They may be pagan philosophers for anything that appears to the contrary. It is evident that it is not a religous interest which attracts them to Kierkegaard '. No, I do not miss much, if anything.)

And my last word here is that, if I had to choose a motto to be engraved under my name and the dates of my birth and death on my tombstone, it would be :

'A disgrace to the community.'—Mr. Justice Mugge.

INDEX